THE COMMON CORE OF EUROPEAN ADMINISTRATIVE LAWS

General Editors

GIACINTO DELLA CANANEA

MAURO BUSSANI

Tort Liability of Public Authorities in European Laws

THE COMMON CORE OF EUROPEAN ADMINISTRATIVE LAWS

General Editors

Giacinto della Cananea, Professor of Administrative Law at Bocconi University; and Mauro Bussani, Professor of Comparative Law at the University of Trieste and Adjunct Professor of Comparative Law at the University of Macao (People's Republic of China).

Tort Liability of Public Authorities in European Laws

Edited by

GIACINTO DELLA CANANEA

and

ROBERTO CARANTA

OXFORD
UNIVERSITY PRESS

OXFORD
UNIVERSITY PRESS

Great Clarendon Street, Oxford, OX2 6DP,
United Kingdom

Oxford University Press is a department of the University of Oxford.
It furthers the University's objective of excellence in research, scholarship,
and education by publishing worldwide. Oxford is a registered trade mark of
Oxford University Press in the UK and in certain other countries

First Edition published in 2020

Impression: 1

Published in the United States of America by Oxford University Press
198 Madison Avenue, New York, NY 10016, United States of America

British Library Cataloguing in Publication Data

Data available

Library of Congress Control Number: 2020942237

ISBN 978–0–19–886755–5

DOI: 10.1093/oso/9780198867555.001.0001

Printed and bound by
CPI Group (UK) Ltd, Croydon, CR0 4YY

General Editors' Preface

This is the first book of a new series, 'The Common Core of European Administrative Laws' (CoCEAL), based on a comparative research for which the European Research Council has awarded us an advanced grant. From the outset, it was decided that this research would have two major themes. The first concerns the methodology of comparative analysis. Our intent is to confront a plurality of legal systems, going beyond the mainstream scrutiny of the most influential ones, and seeking to understand the role of various legal formants therein. Second, and more importantly, this comparison has a particular end in view. The aim of our analysis is to open a large-scale debate not only on commonalities and differences within the European legal space, but also—and more importantly—on how commonality and diversity reach out and interact with one another, within and across legal systems, both diachronically and synchronically, over time and today.

From the first point of view, the methodology that is tested in this book and in the ones that follow owes much to the pioneer seminars convened at Cornell Law School during the 1960s and to the 'Common Core of European Private Law' project that was launched in 1993 at the University of Trento. This methodology is based on a 'factual analysis' in the sense that it is based on hypothetical cases that are previously subject to scrutiny during workshops with the experts of the legal systems selected for comparison, in order to ascertain whether those cases are plausible and meaningful. Only at a later stage are those cases sent to the experts, who elaborate their answers on the basis of all relevant legal formants. A further step consists in comparing those answers, with a view to understanding the relevance and significance of both commonality and diversity.

From the second point of view, unlike less recent comparative studies on administrative law, which focused mainly on judicial review of individual decisions, the new research has a strong focus on administrative procedure, and thus considers various types of administrative action, including both adjudication and rule-making, without neglecting the importance of traditional sets of issues, such as those relating to judicial review and government liability in tort. The last one is precisely that which we have chosen for opening this new series, because it is at the same time 'classic' and innovative. It allows us to take into due account the works of those who have gone before, using legal comparison for various purposes. It permits us to call for heightened attention on what is new and original in the European legal space, where national legal systems interact one with each other and with the two supranational organizations, the EU and the Council of Europe. The research's website, <www.coceal.it>, provides information on the other lines of research that are being developed and on the next steps.

We express our gratitude to those who contributed, in various ways, to this first volume, as well as to all those who were involved in the drafting of the research project;

that is, Mads Andenas, Jean-Bernard Auby, and one of the editors of this book, Roberto Caranta. We are grateful also to other colleagues who, in a number of conferences, seminars, and workshops held in various corners of Europe, gave advice and feedback, not without critical remarks on some aspects, thus helping us to adjust and broaden our initial views, including Stanislaw Biernat, Sabino Cassese, Marcello Clarich, Victor Comelles, Delphine Costa, Luca De Lucia, Bruno De Witte, Luis Maria Diez-Picazo, Mariolina Eliantonio, Leonardo Ferrara, Claudio Franchini, Michel Fromont, Diana-Urania Galetta, Michele Graziadei, Jeffrey Jowell, Marco Mazzamuto, Oriol Mir Puigpelat, Mauro Renna, Aldo Sandulli, Alec Stone Sweet, Stefan Storr, Robert Thomas, Simone Torricelli, Aldo Travi, Takis Tridimas, Andràs Varga, Ellen Vos, and Jacques Ziller. The support of the Universities of Rome 'Tor Vergata', Bocconi, and Trieste is gratefully acknowledged, as well as that of the Centro Studi di Diritto Comparato of Trieste and of the Fondazione Manes of Rome.

Giacinto della Cananea
Mauro Bussani
Rome and Trieste, 31 March 2020

Editors' Preface

Every legal system has to make choices on various aspects of government tortious liability and such aspects evolve rapidly, in response to the impulse of social, economic, and political factors. This makes legal comparison both interesting and important.

This book seeks to contribute to comparative legal analysis in two ways that are related but distinct. First, it examines government liability in tort in an attempt to take into account the realities of governmental action and to make sense of both commonality and diversity between European legal systems. Second, it tests the validity of the methodology of legal comparison, which is based on a 'factual analysis' and thus requires to consider how a series of hypothetical cases would be solved on the basis of a plurality of legal formants. The latter purpose is important in itself and in view of a broader comparative enterprise concerning the common core of European administrative laws (CoCEAL). For this purpose, a questionnaire including various hypothetical cases has been elaborated by the research team, subjected to scrutiny in an international workshop convened in Trieste (in May 2017) by professor Mauro Bussani, and sent to the national experts who participated to the workshop. The answers given by national experts have subsequently been compared, with a view to throwing light on both commonalities and diversities.

The structure of the book is, therefore, as follows. Part I presents an overview of the framework for analysis which lies at the basis of our comparative enquiry and explains its roots. Part II illustrates the context in which the hypothetical cases are examined, from both a historic and a constitutional perspective. Part III, which is the heart of the 'Common Core' method, contains the solutions that, according to experts, can reasonably be expected to be given within the legal systems selected for our comparison, including that of the EU, for which sometimes it is more difficult to provide answers than it is for national systems. Part IV serves to examine comparatively those answers with a particular need in view; that is, not so much to ascertain whether a 'common core' exists, but how it is shaped and evolves, also in response to the influence exerted by the EU and the European Convention on Human Rights.

It goes without saying that there is more material on government tortious liability, from the viewpoint of the control of the powers exercised by public authorities within administrative procedures and outside them, than we could possibly include in this book, and so we had to be selective. We are aware of the importance of other issues concerning liability, which require autonomous treatment. However, our hope is that the cases we have elaborated, often on the basis of precedent administrative and judicial decisions, will allow the conjecture concerning the 'common core' to be adequately tested, even though those cases do not exhaust the multiplicity of issues that all legal systems face.

We owe considerable debts of gratitude to many people. CoCEAL's research team (including Martina Conticelli, Angela Ferrari Zumbini, Marta Infantino, and Laura

Muzi) has contributed to the elaboration and refinement of the questionnaire. Several national experts have been willing to engage in this experiment in legal research, which has few precedents—or none—in the field of public law. Finally, Adrian Bedford and Paola Monaco have reviewed all chapters linguistically and on the basis of Oxford University Press's guidelines, respectively.

Precisely because it is an experiment in a highly complex legal field, we are aware that there will be many failings in this final product, and we take full responsibility for them. This book is the first of a new series concerning an important comparative project, which will be improved also on the basis of the feedback received in the course of the years.

Giacinto della Cananea, Bocconi University
Roberto Caranta, University of Turin
Rome and Turin, 31 March 2020

Contents

III. CASES

IV. COMPARATIVE ANALYSES

Detailed Contents

II. THE LEGAL SYSTEMS SELECTED FOR COMPARISON: PRINCIPLES AND REMEDIES

III. CASES

The authors of the respective country reports in Cases 2-11 are the same as in Case 1 unless otherwise noted.

List of Abbreviations

ABAJ	American Bar Association Journal
ABGB	*Allgemeines bürgerliches Gesetzbuch* (Civil Law Code)(Austria)
AC	Law Reports, Appeal Cases (Third Series)
AG	Advocate General
AGAP	Act of General Administrative Procedure (Hungary)
AHG	*Amtshaftungsgesetz* (Federal Act on the Liability of Territorial Authorities and other Bodies and Institutions of Public Law for Damage caused when Implementing the Law) (Austria)
AJCL	American Journal of Comparative Law
AJDA	*Actualité juridique, droit administratif*
ALI	American Law Institute
AJFP	*Actualité juridique,. Fonctions publiques*
Am U Int'l L Rev	American University International Law Review
AMF	*Autorité des marchés financiers* (France)
AMG	*Arzneimittelgesetz* (Law on Medicinal Products) (Austria)
APA	Administrative Procedure Act (Switzerland)
APC	Administrative Procedure Code (Poland)
ArbGG	*Arbeitsgerichtsgesetz* (Labour Courts Act) (Germany)
ARCEP	*Autorité de régulation de communications électroniques et des postes* (France)
Art/Arts	Article/s
AVG	*Allgemeines Verwaltungsverfahrensgesetz* (General Administrative Procedure Act) (Austria)
BAGE	*Entscheidungen des Bundesarbeitsgerichts* (Decisions oft he Federal Labour Court) (Germany)
BASG	*Bundesamt für Sicherheit im Gesundheitswesen* (drug authority) (Austria)
BayBesG	*Bayerisches Besoldungsgesetz* (Bavarian Remuneration Act) (Germany)
BayDG	*Bayerisches Disziplinargesetz* (Germany)
BayVBl	*Bayerische Verwaltungsblätter* (Germany)
BB	*Betriebs-Berater* (Germany)
BBesG	*Bundesbesoldungsgesetz* (Germany)
BBG	*Bundesbeamtengesetz* (Federal Civil Service Act) (Germany)
BDG	*Bundesdisziplinargesetz* (Germany)
BDG	*Bundesgesetz über das Dienstrecht der Beamten* (Federal Civil Servants Employment Act) (Austria)
BeamtStG	*Beamtenstatusgesetz* (Federal Civil Service Status Act) (Germany)
BeckOGK	*Beck'scher Online-Großkommentar*

BeckOK	*Beck'scher Online-Kommentar*
BeckRS	*Beck Online Rechtsprechung*
BGB	*Bürgerliches Gesetzbuch* (Civil Code) (Germany)
BGBl	*Bundesgesetzblatt* (Basic Law, Constitutional Statute on the Austrian Republic's Membership of the European Union) (Austria)
BGHZ	*Entscheidungen des Bundesgerichtshofs in Zivilsachen* (Compilation of Decisions of the Federal Supreme Court in civil matters) (Germany)
BMVIT	*Bundesministerium für Verkehr, Innovation und Technologie* (Federal Ministry of Transport, Innovation and Technology) (Austria)
BVerfG	*Bundesverfassungsgericht* (Federal Constitutional Court) (Germany)
BVerfGE	*Entscheidungen des Bundesverfassungsgerichts* (Official Gazette of Decisions of the Federal Constitutional Court) (Germany)
BVerfGG	*Bundesverfassungsgerichtsgesetz* (Act on the Federal Constitutional Court) (Germany)
BVerfK	*Kammerentscheidungen des Bundesverfassungsgerichts* (Chamber Decisions of Federal Constitutional Court) (Germany)
BVergG	Bundesver*gabegesetz* (Federal Public Procurement Law) (Austria)
BVerwGE	*Entscheidungen des Bundesverwaltungsgerichts* (Decisions of the Federal Administrative Court) (Germany)
B-VG	Bundes-V*erfassungsgesetz* (Federal Constitutional Law) (Austria)
BVwG	*Bundesverwaltungsgericht* (Federal Administrative Court) (Austria)
c	contre
C Pu P	Code of Public Procurement (Italy)
CAP	Code of Administrative Procedure (Poland)
Cardozo J Int'l & Comp L	Cardozo Journal of International and Comparative Law
CAT	Code of Administrative Trial (Italy)
CC	Civil Code
CCP	Code of Civil Procedure (Poland)
CCt	Constitutional Court
CE	*Conseil d'État*
CFR	Charter of Fundamental Rights of the EU
ChemA	Federal Chemical Act 2000 (Switzerland)
CJA	*Code de la justice administrative* (France)
CJEL	Columbia Journal of European Law
CJEU	Court of Justice of the European Union
CLJ	Cambridge Law Journal
CLR	Commonwealth Law Reports
CMLR	Common Market Law Review

CoCEAL	The Common Core of European Administrative Laws
Colum L Rev	Columbia Law Review
concl	conclusions
Cons Const	*Conseil Constitutionnel*
Consob	*Commissione nazionale per le società e la Borsa* (National Commission for Companies and the Stock Exchange) (Italy)
Const	Constitution
CRPA	*Code des relations entre le public et l'administration* (France)
crim	*criminelle*
CRPA	*Code des relations entre le public et l'administration* (France)
D	Dalloz
DC	*décision de conformité*
Dir amm	*Diritto Amministrativo*
Dir proc amm	Diritto Processuale Amministrativo
DL	Decree Law (Italy)
DÖV	*Die Öffentliche Verwaltung*
DPR	Decree of the President of the Republic of Italy
DSS	Department of Social Security
DVBl	*Deutsches Verwaltungsblatt*
ECC	Electronic Communications Committee
ECHR	European Convention on Human Rights
ECJ	European Court of Justice
ECLI	European Case Law Identifier
ECR	European Courts Reports
ECtHR	European Court of Human Rights
ECTIL	European Centre of Tort and Insurance Law
ed(s)	editor(s)
edn	edition
EEA	European Economic Area
EEC	European Economic Community
eg	exampli gratia
EGGVG	*Einführungsgesetz zu den Verwaltungsverfahrensgesetzen* (Introductory Act to the Courts Constitution Act) (Austria)
ELRev	European Law Review
EMA	European Medicines Agency
EPL	European Public Law
EPPPL	European Procurement and Public Private Partnership Law Review
ERPL	European Review of Public Law
EU	European Union
Eur L J	European Law Journal
Eur Lawyer J	European Lawyer Journal
Eur Legal F	European Legal Forum
EuZW	*Europäische Zeitschrift für Wirtschaftsrecht* (European Journal of Business Law) (Germany)
EWCA	England and Wales Court of Appeal

FAT	Federal Administrative Tribunal (Switzerland)
FCSA	Federal Civil Service Act (Switzerland)
ff	following
FinDAG	*Finanzdienstleistungsaufsichtsgesetz* (Financial Supervisory Authority Act) (Germany)
FINMA	Financial Market Supervisory Authority (Switzerland)
FINMASA	Financial Markets Supervision Act (Switzerland)
FMABG	*Finanzmarktaufsichtsbehördengesetz* (Federal Act on the Institution and Organisation of the Financial Market) (Austria)
FMSA	Financial Market Supervision Act (Poland)
FSA	Foodstuffs Act 2014
FTA	Federal Tribunal Act (Switzerland)
FZV	*Verordnung über die Zulassung von Fahrzeugen zum Straßenverkehr* (Ordinance on Vehicle Registration) (Germany)
GAJA	*Grands arrêts de la Jurisprudence Administrative*
GBl	*Gesetzblatt* (Official Gazette) (Austria)
GCJA	*Grandes conclusions de la jurisprudence administrative*
GewO	*Gewerbeordnung* (Commercial Code) (Germany)
GG	*Grundgesetz* (German Constitution) (Germany)
GLA	Government Liability Act 1958 (Switzerland)
GmbHG	*Gesetz betreffend die Gesellschaften mit beschränkter Haftung* (Limited Liability Companies Act) (Germany)
GWB	*Gesetz gegen Wettbewerbsbeschränkungen* (Act against Restraints of Competition) (Germany)
HA	health authority
Harv L Rev	Harvard Law Review
HICLR	Hastings International and Comparative Law Review
ibid	ibidem
ICLQ	International and Comparative Law Quarterly
ICON	International Journal of Constitutional Law
ICR	Industrial Cases Reports
ie	that is
IETL	Institute for European Tort Law
Ind L J	Indiana Law Journal
IPSR	International Political Science Review
It J Publ L	Italian Journal of Public Law
J Comp Leg & Int'l Law	Journal of Comparative Legislation and International Law
J Tort Law	Journal of Tort Law
JCP	*Semaine juridique (JurisClasseur Périodique)*
JETL	Journal of European Tort Law
JL & Soc'y	Journal of Law & Society
KB	Law Reports, King's Bench Division
King's L J	King's Law Journal
KNF	*Komisja Nadzoru Finansowego* (Financial Supervision Authority) (Poland)
KSchG	Kündigungsschutzgesetz (Germany)

KWG	*Gesetz über das Kreditwesen* (Banking Act) (Germany)
L	Law
L	Loi
Law & Soc'y Rev	Law and Society Review
LCP	Law and Contemporary Problems
LD	Legislative Decree (Italy)
Leg Econ Rev	Legal and Economic Review
LFGB	*Lebensmittel-, Bedarfsgegenstände- und Futtermittelgesetzbuch* (Food, Consumer Goods and Feed Act) (Germany)
LKV	*Landes- und Kommunalverwaltung*
LMSVG	*Lebensmittelsicherheits- und Verbraucherschutzgesetz* (Food Safety and Consumer Protection Act) (Austria)
LQR	Law Quarterly Review
LVwG	*Landesverwaltungsgericht* (provincial administrative courts) (Austria)
Maastricht J Eur & Comp L	Maastricht Journal of European and Comparative Law
MABl	*Ministerialamtsblatt*
Mcgill L J	McGill Law Journal
Mich L Rev	Michigan Law Review
Minn L Rev	Minnesota Law Review
MLR	Modern Law Review
NBR	national banking regulator
NGO	non-governmental organization
NHA	National Health Authority
NICA	Northern Ireland Court of Appeal
NIQB	Northern Ireland, High Court, Queen's Bench division
NJW	*Neue Juristische Wochenschrift*
NLCC	*Nuove leggi civili commentate*
no(s)	number(s)
NVwZ	*Neue Zeitschrift für Verwaltungsrecht*
NVwZ-RR	*Neue Zeitschrift für Verwaltungsrecht Rechtsprechungs*-Report
NZA	*Neue Zeitschrift für Arbeitsrecht*
NZBau	Neue Zeitschrift für Baurecht und Vergaberecht
OFII	*Office Français de l'Immigration et de l'Intégration* (France)
OGH	*Oberste Gerichtshof* (Supreme Court on Civil (and Criminal) Matters) (Austria)
OJLS	Oxford Journal of Legal Studies
Otago L R	Otago Law Review
OWiG	*Gesetz über Ordnungswidrigkeiten* (Act on Regulatory Offences) (Germany)
PA	Public Administration
PAG	*Gesetz über die Aufgaben und Befugnisse der Bayerischen Staatlichen Polizei* (Bavarian Police Duties Act) (Germany)
para(s)	paragraph(s)
PEL	*Principles of European Law*
PETL	*Principles of European Tort Law*

PEOPIL	Pan-European Organisation of Personal Injury Lawyers
PL	public law
PPA	Public Procurement Act (Poland)
PPLR	Public Procurement Law Review
Pub Admin	Public Administration
QB	Law Reports, Queen's Bench
QPC	*question prioritaire de constitutionnalité*
R	*Règlement*
RD publ	*Revue de droit public*
Rec	*Recueil des décisions du Conseil d'Etat*
Rev adm	*Revue administrative*
Rev Eur Adm L	Review of European Administrative Law
Rev fr adm publ	*Revue Française d'Administration Publique*
RFDA	*Revue française de droit administratif*
RIDC	*Revue Internationale de Droit Comparé*
RIS-Justiz	*RIS-Justiz Rechtssache*
Riv It Dir Pubbl Comun	*Rivista italiana di diritto pubblico comunitario* (Italian Review of Communitarian Public Law) (Italy)
RMCUE	Revue du Marché Commun et de l'Union Européenne
SGB V	*Sozialgesetzbuch fünftes Buch* (Social Security Code V) (Germany)
SGB X	*Sozialgesetzbuch zehntes Buch* (Social Security Code X) (Germany)
SPG	*Sicherheitspolizeigesetz* (Security Act) (Austria)
Stan L Rev	Stanford Law Review
STC	*Tribunal Constitucional de España*
Stmk FischereiG	*Steiermärkisches Fischereigesetz* (Styrian Fishing Act) (Austria)
Stmk L-DBR	*Dienst- und Besoldungsrecht der Bediensteten des Landes Steiermark* (Styrian Civil Servants and Salaries Act) (Austria)
StPO	*Strafprozessordnung* (Code of Criminal Procedure) (Austria)
StrEG	*Gesetz über die Entschädigung für Strafverfolgungsmaßnahmen* (Prosecution Compensation Act) (Germany)
StVG	*Straßenverkehrsgesetz* (German Road Traffic Act) (Germany)
StVO	*Straßenverkehrsordnung* (German Road Traffic Rules) (Germany)
suppl	*Supplément*
T	Tables
T confl	*Tribunal des conflits*
TEC	Treaty Establishing the Economic Community
TFEU	Treaty on the Functioning of the European Union
TKG	Telecommunications Act 2003 (Austria)
TPA	Therapeutic Products Act (Switzerland)
transl	translation
Tul L Rev	Tulane Law Review
UKEAT	UK Employment Appeal Tribunal
UKHL	UK House of Lords

UKSC	UK Supreme Court
Univ Chicago L Rev	University of Chicago Law Review
US	United States
UTLJ	University of Toronto Law Journal
Va L Rev	Virginia Law Review
VerwArch	*Verwaltungsarchiv*
VfGH	*Verfassungsgerichtshof* (Constitutional Court) (Austria)
VG	*Verantwortlichkeitsgesetz* (Germany)
vol	volume
VStG	*Verwaltungsstrasfesetz* (Administrative Penal Act) (Austria)
VVDStRL	*Veröffentlichungen der Deutschen Staatsrechtslehrer* (Germany)
VVG	*Versicherungsvertragsgesetz* (Insurance Contract Act) (Germany)
VwG	*Verwaltungsgericht* (Supreme Administrative Court) (Austria)
VwGG	*Verwaltungsgerichtshofgesetz* (Supreme Administrative Court Act) (Austria)
VwGH	*Verwaltungsgerichtshof* (Supreme Administrative Court) (Austria)
VwGO	*Verwaltungsgerichtsordnung* (German Code of Administrative Court Procedure) (Germany)
VwGVG	*Verwaltungsgerichtsverfahrensgesetz* (Proceedings of Administrative Courts Act) (Austria)
VwVfG	*Verwaltungsverfahrensgesetz* (Administrative Procedures Act) (Germany)
VwV-StVO	*Allgemeine Verwaltungsvorschrift zur Straßenverkehrs-Ordnung* (General Administrative Instructions on the Road Traffic Rules) (Germany)
Wash U L R	Washington University Law Review
WLR	Weekly Law Reports
WRP	*Wettbewerb in Recht und Praxis* (Economic Competition in Law and Practice Journal) (Germany)
ZfBR	*Zeitschrift für deutsches und internationales Bau- und Vergaberecht* (German and International Construction and Procurement Law Journal) (Germany)
ZPO	*Zivilprozessordnung* (Code of Civil Procedure)(Germany)
ZRP	*Zeitschrift für Rechtspolitik*

List of Contributors

Gordon Anthony, Professor of Public Law, Queen's University Belfast (UK)

Jean-Bernard Auby, Emeritus Public Law Professor of Sciences Po Paris (France)

Zbigniew Banaszczyk, Professor of Civil Law, Warsaw University (Poland)

Kathrin Bayer, Attorney of Eisenberger Rechtsanwälte GmbH, Graz (Austria)

Daniela Bereiter, Austrian Constitutional Court, Vienna (Austria)

Lilla Berkes, Assistant Professor, Pázmány Péter Catholic University (Hungary)

Mauro Bussani, Professor of Comparative Law, University of Trieste (Italy), and Adjunct Professor of Law at the University of Macao (P.R. of China)

Roberto Caranta, Professor of Administrative Law, University of Turin (Italy)

Katarzyna Chojecka, PhD candidate, Warsaw University (Poland)

Fulvio Cortese, Professor of Administrative Law, University of Trento (Italy)

Paul Craig, Emeritus Professor of English Law, St John's College, University of Oxford (UK)

Joanna Róg Dyrda, Associate Professor of Administrative Law, Warsaw University (Poland)

Łukasz Dziamski, PhD candidate, Warsaw University (Poland)

Giacinto della Cananea, Professor of Administrative Law, Bocconi University (Italy); Principal Investigator CoCEAL

Angela Ferrari Zumbini, Associate Professor of Administrative Law, University of Naples Federico II

Marek Grzywacz, Assistant Professor of Administrative Law, Warsaw University (Poland)

Carol Harlow, Emeritus Professor of Law, London School of Economics and Political Science (UK)

Aleksander Jakubowski, Associate Professor of Administrative Law, Warsaw University (Poland)

Barbara Marchetti, Professor of Administrative Law, University of Trento (Italy)

Eva Maria Nieto Garrido, Professor of Administrative Law, Universidad de Castilla-La Mancha (Spain)

Luca Mischensky, Freshfields Bruckhaus Deringer LLP, Vienna (Austria)

Thomas Perroud, Professor of Public Law, Université Paris 2 Panthéon-Assas (France)

Otto Pfersmann, Professor of Law, École des hautes études en sciences sociales - EHESS (France)

Zofia Roguska, PhD candidate, Warsaw University (Poland)

Johannes Stapf, Research Assistant, Augsburg University (Germany)

Stefan Storr, Professor of Law, Vienna University of Economics and Business (Austria)

Thierry Tanquerel, Emeritus Professor of Law, Université de Genève (Switzerland)

Roxana Vornicu, Research Associate, Centre of Construction Law and Dispute Resolution, King's College London (UK); Managing Partner at SIRBU & VORNICU in Bucharest (Romania)

Marek Wierzbowski, Professor of Law, Warsaw University (Poland)

Sebastian Wijas, PhD candidate, Warsaw University (Poland)

Ferdinand Wollenschläger, Professor of Public Law, European Law and Public Economic Law, Augsburg University (Germany)

Katarzyna Ziółkowska, PhD candidate, Warsaw University (Poland)

Dawid Ziółkowski, PhD candidate, Warsaw University (Poland)

PART I
THE 'COMMON CORE' OF EUROPEAN ADMINISTRATIVE LAWS
An Introduction

1

A 'Common Core' Research on Government Liability in Tort

A Comparative Introduction

Giacinto della Cananea

I. The nature and structure of the study

This book examines various issues concerning what is traditionally called the non-contractual liability of the State. It does so within the framework of a broader research project concerning European administrative laws.

The project, which has been launched with the scientific support of some distinguished experts, has two main themes: the first concerns administrative laws in Europe, and the second the methodology of this comparative analysis. At the heart of the new research there is a conjecture. The conjecture is not so much that, to borrow the words of Rudolf Schlesinger, 'behind and beyond [the differences between legal systems described in countless comparative studies] there are shared and connecting elements', that is to say a 'common core';[1] it is, rather, that such a common core exists and is particularly relevant and significant. Arguably, not only can administrative law be better understood in comparative terms,[2] but there is a peculiar interplay between the common and distinctive traits of European legal systems. The second theme is how to promote the advancement of knowledge in the area. The new research includes both a diachronic and a synchronic comparison and the latter is based on a 'factual analysis'.

The goal of this chapter is neither to discuss the difficulties that beset the traditional approaches to the comparative study of administrative law nor to indicate the arguments in favour of the use of history and comparison. My views on these matters have been set out on an earlier occasion.[3] Just a few words may suffice to explain the main choices concerning this comparative research; namely its purpose, nature, and object (section II). For our purposes here, it is important to address two sets of related, but distinct, issues. They concern the choice of the topic (section III) and the methodology

[1] R Schlesinger, 'The Common Core of Legal Systems: An Emerging Subject of Study' in K Nadelmann, AT von Mehren, and JN Hazard (eds), *XXth Comparative and Conflict of Law. Legal Essays in Honour of Hessel E. Yntema* (Sijthoff 1961) 65; R Schlesinger, 'Introduction' in R Schlesinger (ed), *Formation of Contracts. A Study of the Common Core of Legal Systems* I (Oceana Publications 1968) 1.

[2] For this thesis, see J Rivero, *Cours de droit administratif comparé* (Les cours de droit 1956–57) 5; E Schmidt-Aßmann and S Dagron, 'Les fondements comparés des systèmes de droit administratif français et allemand' (2008) 127 Rev fr adm publ 525.

[3] See G della Cananea and M Bussani, 'The Common Core of European Administrative Laws: A Framework for Analysis' (2019) 26 Maastricht J Eur & Comp L 217.

Giacinto della Cananea, *A 'Common Core' Research on Government Liability in Tort* In: *Tort Liability of Public Authorities in European Laws.* Edited by: Giacinto della Cananea and Roberto Caranta, Oxford University Press (2020). © The Contributors.
DOI: 10.1093/oso/9780198867555.003.0001.

for its study (section IV). It is important to explain why, in a research concerning administrative law, it is interesting and useful to consider government liability in tort. The initial focus is on the history of ideas, in order to show the importance of government liability in the context of comparative studies. This is followed in section V by an examination of the legal realities that justify comparative inquiry in this field. The discussion thus shifts from 'why' government liability in tort is important for a comparative research in this field to 'how' such research is shaped with regard to the various roles played by government. Two further issues concern the choice of the legal systems selected for our comparative analysis and the drawing up of the questionnaire. Finally, the discussion in section VI of the chapter is more theoretical insofar as the focus is on the implications of the existence of common and distinctive traits between European administrative laws.

II. A new comparative research

A. A research for the advancement of knowledge

For some, the comparative study of public administrations and the law that applies to them is quite recent.[4] Others affirm that it has a long tradition, spanning almost two centuries.[5] Interestingly, in his essay on *Democracy in America*, Tocqueville compared the regime of government liability in tort that existed in France with that of the US and argued that the latter was based on equality, while in the former respect for the law was overcome by the *raison d'Etat*.[6] In a later work, however, he held that what was called the French model of administrative law would sooner or later become that of all civilized nations.[7] At the end of the nineteenth century, Albert Venn Dicey expressed his dislike for administrative law. This view has shaped legal scholarship for a long period of time. We will thus return to it in section III.

Meanwhile, it is important to clarify the nature of this comparative research. In the past, many studies concerning public administrations and administrative law have been of a practical nature. Government liability is no exception. Also a recent and interesting volume sets out the goal of addressing 'the possibility for harmonization in the area'.[8] This is in itself a legitimate purpose.

We should, however, be mindful of the distinction between description and prescription. At one extreme is the view that a comparative research can be instrumental to defining or refining legal rules. At the opposite extreme is the view that a comparison

[4] J Boughey, 'Administrative Law: The Next Frontier for Comparative Law' (2013) 62 ICLQ 55.

[5] J Bell, 'Comparative Administrative Law' in M Reimann and R Zimmermann (eds), *The Oxford Handbook of Comparative Law* (OUP 2006) 1260 (for whom 'comparative administrative law is a long-standing discipline'); S Rose-Ackermann and P Lindseth (eds), *Comparative Administrative Law* (2nd edn, Elgar 2016).

[6] A de Tocqueville, *De la démocratie en Amérique* I (Saunders and Otley 1831) ch 6, 172.

[7] A de Tocqueville, 'Rapport fait à l'Académie des sciences morales et politiques sur le livre de M Macarel, intitulé Cours de droit administratif' in *Œuvres complètes d'Alexis de Tocqueville. Etudes économiques, politiques et littéraires par Alexis de Tocqueville* (Lévy 1866) 63.

[8] K Oliphant, 'Introduction' in K Oliphant (ed), *The Liability of Public Authorities in Comparative Perspective* (Intersentia 2016) 3.

serves to gather and check data in order to ensure the validity of legal analysis, as in other social sciences. Delineating a continuum, instead of clear-cut boundaries, helps us to clarify that the goal of our research is to have greater and better knowledge than is presently available, though such research is susceptible to a number of practical implications, for example for purposes of teaching and training.

B. Administrative law: a focus on process

A second choice concerns the scope of the comparative research. It is always useful for a discipline to reflect on its areas of interest and to take stock of more or less recent developments, as well as to gauge future directions. This is no easy task, from the twofold perspective of inclusiveness and topical development.

The opposite risks of over- and under-inclusiveness must be avoided. Over-inclusiveness may give rise to a work that is too broad to be meaningful. The importance of this general assumption becomes evident when considering the increasing scope and complexity of administrative law. At the same time, the topic chosen for comparative exploration must not be too narrow, because this would not lead to the discovery of the connections between a large number of precepts and concepts.[9]

The evolution of legal institutions is equally important. Some prefer to focus on 'classic' or 'timeless' concepts. Others propose to devote attention to the more innovative part of public law. The choice that has been made is to focus on administrative procedures, for three reasons. First, in the field of public law, processes are legally more relevant than in private law. Public authorities are subject to standards of fairness and transparency that are more intense than those applied to private bodies if not actually different in nature,[10] as a result of the public interests that must be protected and promoted.[11] Second, while legislative and judicial powers are exercised through a limited set of processes, administrative action must face 'through its varied and commodious channels, the torrents of demand pressing against the dam of the State'.[12] Accordingly, administrative procedure has been gaining in importance. Third, especially after 1989, administrative procedures have been more intensively governed by political institutions either through the legislative regulation of procedures[13] or through political guidance to administrators.[14] For all these reasons, it is increasingly accepted that administrative procedure is 'a concept at the heart of administrative law'.[15]

[9] Schlesinger, 'Introduction' (n 1) 3.

[10] D Oliver, *Common Values and the Public–Private Divide* (CUP 1999) 7.

[11] For this characterization of the public interest, see G Vedel, *Essai sur la notion de cause en droit administratif français* (Sirey 1934); AH Feller, 'Administrative Procedure and the Public Interest—the Results of Due Process' (1940) 25 Wash U L R 308.

[12] LJ Jaffe, 'Administrative Procedure Re-Examined: The Benjamin Report' (1943) 5 Harv L Rev 704. See also RB Stewart, 'The Reformation of American Administrative Law' (1974–75) 88 Harv L Rev 1667, 1669.

[13] See S Cassese, 'Legislative Regulation of Adjudicative Procedures: An Introduction' (1993) 5 ERPL 15; J-B Auby (ed), *Codification of Administrative Procedure* (Bruylant 2014).

[14] See P Craig, 'Perspectives on Process: Common Law, Statutory and Political' [2010] PL 275.

[15] N Walker, 'Review of Dennis J Galligan, Due Process and Fair Procedures: A Study of Administrative Procedures' (1999) 62 MLR 962.

C. A diachronic and synchronic comparison

Two other features of the new research are the ideas that an adequate comparison cannot focus on either common or distinctive features alone and that, constructively, a comparison must be both diachronic and synchronic.

The traditional approaches that focus mainly, if not solely, on either similarities or differences, are questionable both descriptively and prescriptively. Descriptively, focusing either on the analogies between the legal systems selected for analysis or on their differences fails to consider an important part of the 'real'. Prescriptively, such focus is incoherent with the particular features of the European legal area,[16] which is characterized by the existence of both common and national constitutional traditions. These are referred to by two provisions laid down by the treaties constituting the EU: Article 6 (which refers to common constitutional traditions) and Article 67 of the Treaty on the Functioning of the European Union (TFEU), according to which EU institutions must respect national laws and traditions in the areas of freedom, security, and justice.

Constructively, our method is historical and comparative. It is historical, not only because the conjecture of the existence of a common core derives plausibility from historical studies,[17] though further verification is required, but also because it is important to have an idea of the evolving realities of government,[18] as well as exchanges between legal cultures. Together with the diachronic comparison, there is a synchronic appraisal, which serves to confront problems and solutions in a variety of European jurisdictions, in order to discern both common and distinctive aspects. The goal is to ascertain not so much whether a common core exists, but rather its relevance and significance.

III. Comparing government liability in tort

After explaining the main choices on which our comparative research is based, it is important to illustrate the reasons supporting the view that government liability is a fertile topic for comparison. It is widely accepted that the term 'liability' refers to a principle of general application, but its applicability to administrations has been regarded as one of the main variables among the European systems of public law. However, every system of law must face and solve certain problems. Moreover, the autonomy of the States in facing such problems is variously limited by the obligations stemming from their membership of European organizations.

[16] On this concept, see MP Chiti, 'Lo spazio giuridico europeo' in MP Chiti (ed), *Mutazioni del diritto pubblico nello spazio giuridico europeo* (Clueb 2003) 321; A von Bogdandy, 'National Legal Scholarship in the European Legal Area—a Manifesto' (2012) 10 ICON 614, 618; E Chévalier, 'L'espace administratif européen' in J-B Auby and J Dutheil de la Rochére (eds), *Traité de droit administratif européen* (2nd edn, Bruylant 2015) 451.

[17] See Schlesinger, 'The Common Core of Legal Systems' (n 1) 65 and G Gorla, *Diritto comparato e diritto comune europeo* (Giuffrè 1981) 24; R Sacco, 'Legal Formants: A Dynamic Approach to Comparative Law' (1991) 39(I) AJCL 1.

[18] B Schwartz, 'The Administrative Agency in Historical Perspective' (1961) 36 Ind L J 263.

A. Background: the importance of government liability in comparative studies

Government liability has always been regarded as one of the main variables even within the legal systems that belong to the Western legal tradition. One reason was emphasized by Dicey in his famous attack on French administrative courts, viewed as an instrument of despotism. Another one was the traditional principle, shared by UK and US public law, that the State was not liable for the wrongdoing of its servants. In this latter respect, Dicey criticized the

> opposition specially apparent in the protection given in foreign countries to servants of the State or ... of the Crown, who, whilst acting in pursuance of official orders, or in the bona fide attempt to discharge official duties, are guilty of acts which in themselves are wrongful or unlawful.

He added that 'with us every official, from the Prime Minister down to a constable or collector of taxes, is under the same responsibility for every act done without legal justification as any other citizen'.[19] For Dicey, any special protection accorded to government officers would infringe the principle of equality before the law, which was guaranteed by the ordinary courts of the land.

However, the main idea in the UK was that, like a corporation, government departments were not liable for the wrongdoings of their officers, whereas in continental legal systems liability had to be borne by the State,[20] at the expense of all. More generally, as observed by Dicey's critics, not only did he consider just 'one small part of French administrative law and ignored the rest',[21] but he also focused on less recent rules, essentially as they were before 1848, while much had been done through the jurisprudence of the *Conseil d'Etat* concerning liability, as Maurice Hauriou and others had observed.[22] Dicey's account of English law also failed to acknowledge the limits of judicial review. More importantly for our purposes here, he disregarded the fact that at that time English law accorded extensive immunities from being sued in tort to the Crown.

In a similar vein, as early as in the 1950s, an expert of US administrative law such as Kenneth Culp Davis argued that 'one may have difficulty understanding why the doctrine that the king can do no wrong ever found any acceptance in the American democracy', given that such an immunity was not endorsed by the drafters of the Constitution and that the Supreme Court had observed that governmental immunity

[19] AV Dicey, *Introduction to the Study of the Law of the Constitution*, (10th edn, under the supervision of ECS Wade, MacMillan 1959 [1885]) 328–29.

[20] See JW Garner, 'La conception anglo-américaine du droit administratif' in M Hauriou (ed), *Mélanges Hauriou* (Sirey 1929) 362 and R Bonnard, 'Civil Responsibility towards Private Persons in French Administrative Law' (1932) 36 Economica 141, 143.

[21] WI Jennings, 'Administrative Law and Administrative Jurisdiction' (1938) 20 J Comp Leg & Int'l Law 99.

[22] See Bonnard (n 20) 143.

from suit had fallen into disfavour.[23] Some years later, Davis extended his analysis to UK law. He cast into doubt 'whether English courts at any time would have held the Prime Minister liable personally on account of exercise of discretionary powers'.[24] In the following decades, several English public lawyers observed that things had become increasingly different from Dicey's account. As observed by one of the contributors of this book, 'in practice ... state officials are often acting under statutory powers which set them apart from private citizens, and when these statutory powers are invoked the courts hesitate to impose civil liability'.[25] Another one added that the courts were showing an increasing willingness to 'articulate and assess what the justifiable, distinct needs of the public body might ... be'.[26]

B. A worst-case scenario?

The remarks just made raise the question of whether government liability in tort is a sort of worst-case scenario, in the sense illustrated by Martin Shapiro; that is, as the 'body of known legal phenomena most likely to falsify' a conjecture or position.[27] In this sense, it has been noted that government liability is dominated by differences,[28] both substantively and procedurally. Substantively, unlike other European legal systems, in the UK there is no general principle of liability. Procedurally, even a cursive glance at national systems shows that government liability in tort is considered within some of them by the same courts that judge on the legitimacy of administrative action, while in other legal systems the former issues are adjudicated by ordinary courts after the latter have been dealt with by administrative courts.

However, this is not an impediment to a comparative inquiry. There are two types of argument supporting the view that government liability is both an important and a fertile field for comparative analysis. First, the existence of several and significant distinctive traits is not a problem in itself. Second, even though the connotation of 'tortious' liability is not staked out in the same manner in the various legal systems, they are confronted with similar problems, if not the same. It is therefore interesting to understand whether they opt for either similar or different solutions and why.

The existence of several and significant distinctive traits between European legal systems is not an impediment to a comparative inquiry for two reasons. On the one hand, it is always interesting to challenge certain commonly accepted propositions concerning a given field of study, in order to ascertain whether they are (still) sufficiently founded, as well as to see if there can be an exchange of ideas between legal systems.[29] On the other hand, this new comparative research does not aim to

[23] KC Davis, 'Tort Liability of Governmental Units' (1956) 40 Minn L Rev 751, 752. See also GA Bermann, 'Integrating Government and Officer Tort Liability' (1977) 77 Colum L Rev 1175 (noting that the coexistence of governmental and officer liability created a new problem of coordination).

[24] KC Davis, 'Administrative Officers' Tort Liability' (1956) 55 Mich L Rev 201, 202.

[25] C Harlow, *Understanding Tort Law* (Fontana 1987) 128.

[26] P Craig, *Administrative Law* (5th edn, Sweet & Maxwell 2005) 11.

[27] M Shapiro, *Courts. A Comparative and Political Analysis* (University of Chicago Press 1981) vii.

[28] P Gonod, 'Les tendances contemporaines de la responsabilité administrative en France et à l'étranger: quelle convergences?' (2013) 147 Rev fr adm publ 720 ('la disparité ... domine').

[29] In a similar vein, see D Fairgrieve, *State Liability in Tort: A Comparative Law Study* (OUP 2003) 269.

emphasize only distinctive or common traits, but to examine and seek to explain both. Consequently, if the outcome of this line of research is that there are no common and connecting elements between those legal systems, this is not a problem. Indeed, the purpose of the research as a whole is to move towards a more general analysis of the common core.

Despite the different constructions of government liability, the idea of a distinction between the liability arising from a contract and the liability arising from administrative action is similar, if not the same, everywhere, because all legal systems have to decide on the conceptual and institutional foundations of liability.[30] Several decisions must be taken, and they involve a number of issues with ramifications for the structure of government in a given society. What is at issue is, first, whether 'the law under which government officials operate permits them to inflict injury on others, under prescribed circumstances, in established ways, and in carefully (and sometimes not so carefully) calibrated amounts'.[31] That being the case, insofar as there is no unlimited and unchecked power to inflict injury on others, as might be the case in a country that is not 'well-ordered', there are several basic options available. The law under which government officials operate can be viewed as part of the legal framework that governs liability or as a distinct, if not wholly separate, body of law. There may be a variety of relationships between unlawfulness and liability, in the sense that the former can be viewed either as the necessary and sufficient pre-condition for the existence of the latter or as one important element, but not the only one; for example, if some sort of liability is recognized for lawful conduct, too. This is the case in EU law for acts or measures that must be taken in order to enforce a requirement stemming from the international legal order in the context of either a war or an embargo. There can be an additional requirement insofar as liability arises only if the conduct of government officials is connoted either by a fault or by intentional wrongdoing. Moreover, compensation can be based on different criteria, with the purpose of ensuring a full recovery of damages or only a part of them. Finally, a choice has to be made with regard to the allocation of two logically distinct functions; that is, reviewing the legality of administrative action and judging on the actions for damages deriving from such action.

Despite the scope for differentiation, comparative studies have identified some common features or trends. Some years ago, a comparative survey found that in no legal system was the liability of the State the same as that of corporations, in part for reasons of a historical nature, relating to the doctrine of sovereign immunity, and in part for practical reasons that have variable importance in modern systems of government.[32] Among these reasons are the differing roles of private and public officials, the latter working for the benefit of society as a whole, the resulting necessity not to discourage them from the discharge of functions and powers, and concern for the State's financial resources. A decade later, another comparative research found that, outside the areas covered by European Community (EC)/EU law, there were significant

[30] Craig, *Administrative Law* (n 26) 881.

[31] J Mashaw, 'Civil Liability of Government Officers: Property Rights and Official Accountability' (1978) 42 LCP 8.

[32] AW Bradley and J Bell, 'Governmental Liability: A Preliminary Assessment' in AW Bradley and J Bell (eds), *Governmental Liability: A Comparative Study* (BIICL 1991) 2.

spillover effects into purely national laws,[33] an aspect that will be examined in greater detail in section IV.

C. The European dimension of government liability

The European dimension of government liability is increasingly important, insofar as the solution of these problems is no longer entirely left to each individual State. A distinction needs to be made between the two supranational organizations: the Council of Europe and the EC/EU.

After issuing various acts concerning the exercise of administrative powers,[34] the Council of Europe's Committee of Ministers adopted a recommendation relating to public liability.[35] Though the recommendation was not binding on the Member States, it was interesting because it highlighted a dualism that was inherent in most legal systems. It recognized fault as a basis of government liability. This was evident in the first principle laid down by the Recommendation; that is, reparation should be ensured 'for damage caused by an act due to a failure of a public authority to conduct itself in a way that can be reasonably expected from it in law', with the presumption that a failure occurred 'in case of transgression of an established legal rule'. There was, thus, the desire to foster the liability of public authorities. However, not all legal systems impose liability for fault in itself, but only for serious fault. Moreover, limitations are provided for the exercise of discretionary powers, as observed by Davis.[36] In this respect, the aim of the Recommendation was to ensure better judicial protection for the injured party. It is for this purpose that the right to bring an action was not to be subject to the obligation to act against the responsible agent or official and had not to be jeopardized by institutional and procedural rules. Again, this was not the case in more than one Member State. Suffice it to recall the consequences flowing from the division of competence from the courts that could annul the contested measures and those that could accord damages. However, it may be said that the Recommendation reflected current thinking about government liability.[37]

The EU has also taken some measures that have had an impact on national systems of liability. Some of these measures are sector-specific, as they concern a given field, for example that of public procurement. EU directives require the Member States to ensure that if those who participate in government procurement suffer unjust damage arising from the conduct of public authorities, they can seek financial compensation. A more general limitation to the autonomy of the Member States derives from the

[33] D Fairgrieve, M Andenas, and J Bell, *Tort Liability of Public Authorities in Comparative Perspective* (BIICL 2002).

[34] See Committee of Ministers, Resolution (77) 31 on the protection of the individual in relation to the acts of administrative authorities and Recommendation No R (80) 2, concerning the exercise of discretionary powers by administrative authorities.

[35] Committee of Ministers, Recommendation No R (84) 15, of 18 September 1984, relating to public liability.

[36] See Davis (n 23) 793.

[37] Bradley and Bell (n 32) 7. See also J Bell, 'Mechanisms for the Cross-Fertilisation of Administrative Law in Europe' in J Beatson and T Tridimas (eds), *New Directions in European Public Law* (Hart Publishing 1998) 147.

Court of Justice's assertion of the general rule, 'inherent in the system laid down by the treaties', whereby a State that fails to respect the rights stemming from EC legislation is financially liable for the damage caused to those rights and cannot claim the sovereign immunity.[38] More recently, the Court has ruled that the criteria governing State liability can be applied to judicial decisions, too, in the case of a sufficiently serious breach of EU law, though in a more restricted manner.[39]

Finally, the legal system of the EC/EU is interesting for its own regime of liability. While the first Treaty, that of Paris (1952) followed the French model of liability for *faute de service*, the Treaty of Rome made the European Economic Community (EEC) liable for all the torts committed by themselves or by their agents and rested liability on the 'general principles common to the laws of the Member States'.[40] Literally, such provision referred to the Community. However, it could be interpreted as implying that the six founding States shared a general principle of tort liability. The existence of such a principle was implicit in the substantive decision that not only ruled out immunity, but also clarified that the Community, not the employee, should bear the burden for the normal consequences of administrative action. It was implicit, too, in the *renvoi* to the 'general principles common to the laws of the Member States'. For some decades, the Court defined and refined those principles, sometimes going well beyond the limits attained by national legal systems, for example when it endorsed action brought by individuals against measures that had a legislative character.

IV. Issues in methodology

After explaining why a comparative research in this field is both important and interesting, it is useful to discuss the main choices that have been made concerning the types of government activity under examination, the legal systems selected for comparison, and the construction of the questionnaire.

A. A focus on administrative action: an evolutionary view

The limitations of the comparative inquiry follow on from the remarks made in section II earlier with regard to the concern to avoid both over-inclusiveness and under-inclusiveness.[41] The research team decided to focus on government liability in tort, excluding issues concerning contracts. A second delimitation concerns the nature of

[38] Case C-6/90 *Francovich, Bonifaci ea v Italy* [1991] ECR I-5357 and Joined Cases C-178/94, C-179/94, C-188/94, C-189/94, and C-190/94 *Dillenkofer and others* [1996] ECR I-4845. For further analysis, see R Caranta, 'Governmental Liability after Francovich' (1993) 52 CLJ 272; C Harlow, 'Francovich and the Problem of the Disobedient State' (1996) 2 Eur L J 199.

[39] Case C-224/01 *Köbler v Republik Österreich* [2003] ECR I-10239. For further details, see A Davies, 'State Liability for Judicial Decisions in European Union and International Law' (2012) 61 ICLQ 585.

[40] Article 215 EEC Treaty, now Article 340 TFEU. See W Lorenz, 'General Principles of Law: Their Elaboration in the Court of Justice of the European Communities' (1964) 13 AJCL 1, 24.

[41] See P Mathijsen, 'Review of V. Mosler (ed.), Liability of the State for Illegal Conduct of its Organs' (1968) 66 Mich L Rev 823, 825 (for the remark that the scope of the research was overambitious).

the action examined. Given the research's focus on administrative procedure, the issues considered here deal with the exercise of administrative powers, as distinct from legislative and judicial powers, which require separate treatment.

This raises some intriguing questions concerning government functions and powers, which require a little digression. At the end of the nineteenth century, the literature on administrative law was dominated by the prevalent paradigm of the 'negative' State. In particular, Dicey strongly advocated the tradition of limited government, that of the 'night-watchman state'.[42] But the limited size and scope of central government that had characterized the first three or four decades of the nineteenth century had undergone important changes during the first part of the Victorian period, due to economic and social legislation.[43] At the end of the century, an expansion of government was evident also on the other side of the Atlantic Ocean.[44] It was perhaps even more evident in Continental Europe, particularly in France, where doctrines of *service public* were developed by scholars such as Leon Duguit,[45] on the basis of the case law of the *Conseil d'Etat*. In Germany, too, Otto Mayer observed that the State had the authority to tax and also had vast police powers, but it could—and did—expropriate private rights of ownership, and limit the action of market forces for fear of monopoly or for concern for health and safety, as happened for railways.[46] There was a much greater involvement of government in economic and social life than there had been before, and this supported new theories of the State.[47] At a more practical level, the importance of judicial review grew, and administrative law was mainly procedural in character, because—for example, in France, Germany, and Italy—the courts preferred to engage in a review of the ways in which powers were exercised than to discuss the merits of discretionary choices made by administrators.[48]

The economic crisis of the 1930s and the measures taken by political institutions to contrast its consequences marked a further step. In the US, the New Deal increased the powers of administrative authorities.[49] Several countries of Continental Europe concentrated huge powers within public bodies. Even in the UK, according to a leading expert, 'if the common law were codified, it would probably be found that two-thirds of English law—in bulk and not necessarily in importance—was administrative law'.[50]

[42] AV Dicey, *Lectures on the Relation between Law and Public Opinion in England during the Nineteenth Century* (Macmillan 1905).

[43] Craig, *Administrative Law* (n 26) 48.

[44] See E Freund, 'The Law of the Administration in America' (1894) 9 Pol Sci Q 403, AA Berle, 'The Expansion of American Administrative Law' (1916) 30 Harv L Rev 430 and, for a critique of 'administrative absolutism', R Pound, 'The Challenge of the Administrative Process' (1944) 30 ABAJ 121. For a retrospective, see JL Mashaw, *Creating the Administrative Constitution. The Lost One Hundred Years of American Administrative Law* (Yale UP 2012).

[45] L Duguit, *Les transformations du droit public* (Armand Colin 1913) 32–33.

[46] O Mayer, *Deutsches Verwaltungsrecht* (1894), French transl by the author, *Droit administratif allemand* (Giard et Brière 1905).

[47] Duguit (n 45) XVI.

[48] See MJ Remington, 'The Tribunaux Administratifs: Protectors of the French Citizens' (1976) 51 Tul L Rev 59, 87 (noting the latitude with which administrative judges formulated equitable remedies); and G della Cananea and S Mannoni (eds), *Administrative Justice Fin-de-siècle. Judicial Standards of Administrative Conduct 1890–1910* (OUP 2021).

[49] Stewart (n 12) 1669; M Shapiro, 'On Predicting the Future of Administrative Law' (1982) 6 Regulation 19.

[50] Jennings (n 21) 99.

There has not been simply an increase in the interests that are affected by administrative action. Indeed, all interests are potentially affected by it, and not only by way of 'interference'. Many individual and collective interests—for example, those of beneficiaries of government largesse—depend on the action of government bodies, in the logic of the 'positive State'. As a result, administrative law has no longer the sole aim of ensuring that agencies do not make errors or abuse their powers. It also concerns the efficacious achievement of public policies.[51] It is for this reason that, administrative procedures have become the place where a variety of interests are confronted and weighed. This explains the greater political importance of the regulation of administrative procedures, either in the form of legislative or regulatory schemes or that of guidance to government officials.

There is yet another consequence of the growth of government, because a great part of the population works for the administration in one way or another. That the State is viewed as an employer is not of interest only to political scientists and sociologists who study bureaucracies. It is of interest to lawyers, too. From this viewpoint, what matters is not so much which rights of employees should fall within the protected legal sphere. It is, rather, which vision of the employment relationship should be adopted, in order to ensure that at least some minimum guarantees of autonomy (or independence) for civil servants are respected, for example in the context of disciplinary procedures.

This brief survey did not set out to trace the changes undergone by the structures of administrative law, but, more simply, to suggest that it must be considered in an evolutionary manner. All the aspects of modern government just mentioned—the 'negative State, the 'positive' State, and the State as employer[52]—deserve attention and will thus be considered in our comparative analysis. Moreover, in accordance with the Council of Europe's Recommendation on liability, our analysis considers both administrative acts and 'physical acts' or measures. It also considers issues concerning the inaction of public authorities in line with the case law of the European Court of Human Rights (ECtHR).[53]

B. The choice of legal systems

Another set of decisions concerns the choice of the legal systems to be considered. In this respect, it was necessary to steer a course between two opposite approaches. The first limits comparison to two or three legal systems, on the assumption that they are the 'major legal systems' of the world or of a specific area; in our case, Europe. This approach is immune to weaknesses, not only because of its limited basis, but also because identifying the 'major legal systems' is questionable for the simple reason that, for certain subject matters, the most interesting and innovative solutions may be provided by a legal system that is not one of those traditionally studied.[54] The other approach

[51] See C Harlow and R Rawlings, *Law and Administration* (3rd edn, CUP 2009).

[52] See S Cassese, 'The Rise and Decline of the Notion of State' (1986) 7 IPSR 120 (for the observation that the notion of State is not a good analytical tool, in view of the diversity of governmental functions).

[53] Case 38433/09 *Centro Europa 7 v Italy* [2012] ECHR 974 (failure to issue a licence), ECtHR judgment of 7 June 2012.

[54] Schlesinger, 'Introduction' (n 1) 2–3.

covers a higher number of legal systems, with the practical problems that this inevitably raises and without the assurance that such legal systems are the only ones to be significant from the viewpoint of the research questions being examined.

Another option is suggested by Michel Fromont, according to whom three main models emerge in the field of administrative law: first, there are France, Italy, Portugal, Greece, and in some respects, Spain; second, there is England, with Ireland and Norway; third, there is a group including Germany, Austria, Switzerland, and in some respects Poland.[55] This typology is questionable, as is always the case, but has some advantages. It goes beyond the traditional dualism between civil law and common law countries. Moreover, it is based on criteria that are related to the principles and structures of public law. Following this typology, an attempt has been made to include at least one system of administrative law for each of those models, though a more inclusive approach may be desirable.

Two further issues must be considered. First, our comparative research concerns the European legal space, but is not limited to the EU. Accordingly, we decided to include not only a certain number of EU Member States, but also Switzerland, which has entered into a complex web of arrangements with the EU. Second, we thought that it could be interesting to compare national legal systems with that of a non-State entity, such as the EU. It is clear that many public law cases will be concerned with the application of EU law principles at national level, when the Member States implement EU law. National departments and agencies are thus under a duty to apply general principles of EU law, including the respect for fundamental rights,[56] as well as its rules. Moreover, those principles and rules often have a sort of 'spillover' effect for the solution of similar problems of a purely domestic character.[57] For example, the fact that the 'interests' of those who participate in public procurement were to be protected by virtue of EC law operated as a factor that favoured rethinking this issue within Italian administrative law at the end of the twentieth century, because it looked odd and unacceptable from the viewpoint of equality that those interests would receive full legal protection, including damages, while others would not. The legal system of the EU is also relevant in itself because of the existence of a European administration entrusted with the discharge of functions and powers, sometimes in a direct relationship with individuals and business, and has to respect standards of legality and due process. It acts, moreover, under a general principle of liability. It is interesting, therefore, to see whether the particularities of its organization and functioning have repercussions on the ways in which the principle is developed and applied by EU courts.

Within this general framework, some further remarks may be helpful to emphasize the choice we made to deal with some legal experiences that are regrettably too often taken out of the radar screen of mainstream comparative literature. The reference is, in particular, to the choice of Spain, Hungary, Romania, and Switzerland. The Spanish legal system is important both in itself—for example, for its choice not of an administrative court, but of a specialized panel within the highest judicial institution—and for

[55] M Fromont, *Droit administratif des Etats membres de l'Union européenne* (PUF 2006) 15.

[56] This concerns fundamental rights, as indicated by Article 51 of the Charter of Fundamental Rights of the EU.

[57] Craig, *Administrative Law* (n 26) 324.

its varying influence on Latin American legal systems, which will be considered at a later stage of this comparative research.[58] As regards Hungary, for a part of its history it shared in the same legal regime that governed Austria. For another period, like Poland and Romania, it was subject to radically different ideas, beliefs, and values about public law from those typical of liberal democracies. It may be interesting to see how lawyers and judges make sense of the principle of liability, which is broadly laid down by the Constitution but which can be shaped by Parliament in the exercise of its legislative power. Romania, too, was initially subject to the influence of a foreign legal culture, in this case that of France, and subsequently 'socialism', and it is precisely for this reason that it is important to see whether the legacy of that period has consequences with regard to government liability. The Swiss legal order has variously been influenced by those of France and Germany, which differ remarkably with regard to government liability in tort. An additional element of interest regards the structure of the Swiss internal legal order, with federal, cantonal, and local levels. Both these elements are relevant for our purposes here. As observed by Thierry Tanquerel (one of the contributors to this volume), as in French law, Swiss law states that the liability of public authorities is not subject to the rules of federal private law when they act outside their boundaries; moreover, while federal legislation provides a derogation, due to the exclusive competence granted by the Constitution, cantonal rules can only derogate to the rules of the Civil Code with specific federal authorization.[59] There is also discussion as to whether, even in the absence of particular rules requesting it, a body entrusted with the discharge of public functions and powers would be subject to liability by virtue of general principles of justice and equality of treatment and, as a consequence of this, the rules of the Civil code may be applicable, albeit in a subsidiary manner.[60]

Finally, something needs to be said about the exclusions. As observed earlier in this section, the exclusion of some legal systems depended on the necessity to make a selection within the main administrative models that exist in Europe. In other cases, as sometimes happens in this type of project,[61] the completeness of the comparative analysis was affected by unforeseen events that prevented some invitees taking part in the workshop where the questionnaire was debated in order to see whether its cases made sense within all the legal systems selected for comparison. The fact remains that broader coverage is desirable and it has been secured for the following line of research, which concerns judicial review of administration with special regard to formal or procedural flaws.

C. The questionnaire and levels of analysis

Two further sets of issues in methodology must be considered. They concern the construction of the questionnaire and the levels of analysis.

58 See della Cananea and Bussani (n 3).
59 T Tanquerel, *Manuel de droit administratif* (2nd edn, Schulthess 2018) 545–46.
60 ibid 547.
61 Schlesinger, 'Introduction' (n 1) 21 (referring to 'human and accidental factors').

Unlike in previous attempts to examine government liability in a comparative perspective,[62] for which the questionnaire was formulated by the conveners alone, in our case after a draft was prepared, it was discussed with national experts during a workshop. This was because it was necessary to ascertain whether the questions it included make sense within all the legal systems selected for comparison. It can therefore be said that the design of the questionnaire is a collective enterprise. Moreover, although the questionnaire focuses strongly on factual analysis,[63] the research team felt that it might be useful to begin with some general questions concerning the general criteria regarding the non-contractual liability of government and the remedies available against public authorities. There is, instead, an analogy with long-standing research on the common core of European private law with regard to the elaboration of the cases. As a starting point, we focused on reported cases, but we sought only to draw inspiration from them.[64] The logic was that it is both interesting and important to ascertain whether certain facts relating to the exercise of power produces litigation in some legal systems more than in others and what the underlying factors might be. For example, there are disputes concerning the use of government largesse everywhere, whether in the form of concessions, licences, or the like, but there are important differences concerning the (more or less) discretionary nature of the powers exercised by public authorities.

During the workshop, where the questionnaire was debated with national experts and other discussants, the question arose as to whether our hypothetical cases had to be written in a very concise manner, without giving too many elements of fact and law. This option has more than one advantage, including simplicity and comprehensibility, and, perhaps more importantly, a greater adaptability to a variety of national legal contexts. There is, however, another side of the coin. It is precisely because a concise formulation of the case makes it easier to compare solutions that some important aspects of how legal institutions work may not come to the surface or lose all their weight, while ours is an interpretative exercise. This explains why some cases are longer and more complex than others. Of course, those that include more elements of fact are more likely to bring out the existence of differences, but this is not a problem, for two reasons. First, unlike previous comparative approaches in this field, the purpose of this comparative research is not to focus only, or mainly, on either the common or distinctive traits between the legal systems considered, but to include both and seek to make sense of them. Second, from the viewpoint of relevance and significance, not all the differences concerning the functioning of legal institutions can be included in the same class. Some of them may simply show the varying weight—across time and nations—that is given to the same legal institution (eg the dismissal of a civil servant without prior hearing), while others may show the existence of such a profound divergence between legal systems that it prevents the discovery of a common core.

[62] See A von Bogdandy, 'The Transformation of European Law: The Reformed Concept and its Quest for Comparison' (2016), Max Planck Institute for Comparative Public Law & International Law (MPIL) Research Paper No 2016-14 <https://papers.ssrn.com/sol3/papers.cfm?abstract_id=2783702> accessed 4 July 2020>.

[63] A partially similar approach has been used within the 'European Group on Tort Law': see Oliphant (ed), *The Liability of Public Authorities* (n 8).

[64] On this distinction, see Gorla (n 17) 26.

There is an important consequence that follows from the choice to consider the administrative systems of the EU, in order not give a misleading picture of administrative institutions. Indeed, not only are many important rules and decisions made by the EU, but it also has its own administration, which takes some decisions (authorizations, orders, and sanctions) that are very similar to those that are taken by national authorities and are subject to the rules governing agency liability in damages.[65] For them, the hypothetical cases do not raise particular problems. This is not the case for other administrative measures, such as concessions and licenses. For them, the cases are examined on the assumption that, should such a case arise, the European administration would handle it similarly to how it does in other cases and EU courts would apply both the general principles governing administrative procedure and the law applicable to the non-contractual liability of the EU.

The final issue concerns the level of analysis. Our choice of a factual analysis raises the question whether the conclusions can be generalized outside the specific cases that are examined. This is a challenging question that requires treatment on its own. There are nonetheless certain factors that may enhance the added value of a factual analysis. As explained in della Cananea and Bussani's previous article, as well as in Bussani's chapter in this volume,[66] we do not ask our national experts only to indicate the solution that is more likely to be provided by jurists in their respective legal orders, but we also encourage them to reflect on the underlying institutional and cultural reasons, including the role played by legal formants. Consistently with the critical remarks made with regard to the traditional attitude consisting in juxtaposing the reports concerning national administrative laws, instead of comparing them, from a constructive point of view, we thought that it could be interesting and useful to provide two types of comparison: between a limited group of national legal systems and between all the systems selected for comparison. The last two parts of this volume are devoted to these distinct levels of analysis.

V. Implications for the study of the 'common core' of European administrative laws

The discussion thus far has focused upon the main choices made initially. It is, of course, important to assess the research outcome; that is, the end result of conducting research on a particular topic, in this case government liability in tort. This deserves autonomous treatment, in the final chapter of this book.[67] To stop here would, however, be to leave out of consideration the impact of this particular line of research on the general conjectures that were set out initially: the shift from mere juxtaposition to comparison, in the form of a 'common core' research, and the interplay of common

[65] P Craig, *EU Administrative Law* (CUP 2006) 40.

[66] See Cananea and Bussani (n 3) and M Bussani, 'On the "Common Core of European Administrative Laws" Methodology (and European Tort Laws)', Chapter 2 in this volume.

[67] See R Caranta, 'Concluding Remarks: Towards Convergence? The Road beyond Institutional and Doctrinal Path-Dependence', Chapter 20 in this volume.

and distinctive traits in Europe. This section therefore briefly examines the implications concerning each of them.

A. A factual analysis

While the necessity of comparative studies is widely felt in contemporary public law scholarship,[68] there is a variety of opinion about the approaches or perspectives that can be followed for this goal. To use again the metaphor of a continuum, it may be said that at the two extremes lie the micro- and macro-perspectives. The former focuses primarily on the functioning of a certain principle or legal institution, such as the position of the specific individual who seeks redress for maladministration in a case concerning the withdrawal of a concession or licence. The macro-perspective looks to more systemic concerns and seeks to address them, including the respect for the rule of law and the role of judicial review of administrative action. This is by all means a helpful approach, which can shed light on similarities and differences from a very high level of abstraction. However, at such a high level of abstraction, some differences and similarities may appear more evident than they are in the real world. It was precisely for this purpose that Schlesinger promoted the use of a factual approach as early as the 1960s. In his words, when

> attention is directed . . . to details of what the French call *le fond du droit*, then similarities and dissimilarities between legal systems are . . . complex and intertwined; thus, [. . .] their comparison [. . .] involves at the very least the identification and formulation of elements of similarity as well as dissimilarity.[69]

It remains to be seen whether this method can be used in the field of public law. The question may be considered both *ex ante* and *ex post*. *Ex ante*, it was found that looking at administrative law from a comparative perspective was an important contribution to the academic literature, so much of which is written from the angle of only one legal system. Moreover, it was held that a factual analysis could be justified on three grounds. First, although administrative law is distinct from private law, at least some of the general principles of law which are imposed on public authorities, such as fairness, are not intrinsically different from those that are applied to the conduct of individuals and firms, though they can be, and often are, applied in a more intense manner.[70] Second, in the field of administrative law, due to the greater scarcity of general rules established by legislation, an analysis of sector-specific legislation, as well as of the ways in which the courts interpret it in the light of general principles, is even more necessary. Third, the statement of problems in factual terms is increasingly used in some academic and non-academic circles where scholars and judges—respectively—regularly meet to

[68] See R Caranta, 'Learning from our Neighbours: Public Law Remedies Homogenization from Bottom Up' (1997) 4 Maastricht J Eur & Comp L 220–48 and von Bogdandy, 'The Transformation of European Law' (n 62).

[69] Schlesinger, 'Introduction' (n 1) 2–3.

[70] Oliver (n 10) 27.

discuss administrative law.[71] This is in itself an innovative and interesting aspect. It is innovative, because nothing of the kind existed only two or three decades ago. It is interesting because it confirms that not only the necessity of a comparative analysis is widely felt among judges and practitioners, but also the use of a factual analysis receives their consent.

Ex post, applying factual analysis to a set of issues concerning government liability in tort has made a positive contribution to understanding the points of contact and the differences that exist in the field of administrative law. Similarly to what was observed in the course of the Cornell seminars, framing questions in factual terms allowed participants to avoid the risk of unduly emphasizing similarities that existed only on the surface of the legal institutions examined. While in some legal systems there is a general principle of liability, in others nothing similar exists, and there are persistent differences concerning the remedies available to those who intend to sue the State. The factual analysis conducted on government liability has also allowed us to positively test the importance of our focus on administrative procedure. Although the distinction between process and substance is conventional and evolves, it makes sense and is legally relevant within all the legal systems concerned. In particular, if a certain pattern of action has been previously established, public authorities are expected to follow such patterns of action and, if they do not do so, must provide a justification for this, either in the sense that more particular canons of conduct apply or in terms of an exception made necessary by some event. Moreover, public authorities are obliged to respect standards of legality and fairness that are either more intense or distinct in nature from those that apply to private bodies and, in particular, they are requested to open up their procedures and to give reasons for their choices. Finally, the claims brought by individuals against public authorities increasingly concern rights. This is interesting in itself and for its ramifications for the interplay between common and distinctive traits.

B. Commonality and difference

In a previous article, where the theoretical framework for this comparative research was illustrated,[72] certain commonly accepted propositions about the comparative study of administrative law were challenged. One of the contested assumptions is that each system of administrative law is shaped by history and culture and thus reflects national ideas and beliefs about public law and is inevitably different from others. This argument is taken to extremes by those who argue that national legal systems are incommensurable.[73] Another challenged assumption is that 'in the field of administrative law all civilized countries have much the same problems and much the same desire for their proper solution'.[74] My intent is not to discuss these propositions in an

[71] It's the Association of the Councils of State and Supreme Administrative Jurisdictions of the EU: see its <www.aca-europe.eu> accessed 18 February 2020.

[72] See della Cananea and Bussani (n 3).

[73] P Legrand, 'European Legal Systems Are Not Converging' (1996) 45 ICLQ 52.

[74] F Lawson, 'Review of C.H. Hamson, Executive Discretion and Judicial Control and B. Schwartz, French Administrative Law in the Common-Law World' (1955) 7 Stan L Rev 159.

abstract manner. It is rather to seek to disprove them in the light of the studies collected in this volume and thus to move towards an alternative theory of legal comparison in the European administrative space.

Certain deficiencies in the traditional approach, emphasizing the differences between the administrative law operating in the European countries, viewed as a province of the State, have been touched upon in the preceding discussion. At the most basic level, the traditional approach was based upon distrust of the administrative State. But the twentieth century was characterized by the growth of administrative law. It was no longer taken for granted that traditional remedies against public authorities sufficed to ensure justice. It became simply impossible to draw a divide between legal systems with and without administrative law. Such a divide became even less conceivable due to the influence of supranational legal orders, particularly the EC–EU, with its emphasis on the distinction between public and private law. Moreover, both the EU and the Council of Europe defined and refined general standards which all the Member States must respect, even in the field of government liability. The differences between legal systems are thus 'less unbridgeable than before'.[75]

These changes explain the growing favour with which the theory of the gradual convergence between European administrative laws was met, at least until some years ago. The basis of this theory was of a functional nature. There is surely some truth in the proposition that national legal systems face similar problems and are subject to common principles of law. However, at least three problems can be identified, all of which undermine the prophecy of a steady convergence. First, comparative analysis confirms the existence of several significant distinctive traits. Some of them are the product of history and culture. Others depend on political preferences. All these factors explain the varying importance of both the justice dispensed by the ordinary courts and the role of administrative appeals. Second, these factors reflect distinct ways to consider and concretize values such the rule of law, which are common to European legal systems. For example, the reasoning of the courts variably combines considerations about the distinctive nature of the interests at stake and the financial repercussions of liability. Finally, on a more theoretical level, for all the importance of common standards regulating government liability in tort, they are largely variable, as distinct from the invariable standards.[76] In brief, domestic variables are both relevant and significant, because context matters, including our vision of legal realities. It is for these reasons that convergence and divergence must be viewed together[77] and must be regarded in a dynamic (as opposed to static) manner.

[75] W Van Gerwen, 'Bridging the Unbridgeable: Community and National Tort Laws after Francovich and Brasserie' (1996) 45 ICLQ 597.

[76] This distinction is borrowed from HLA Hart, *The Concept of Law* (Clarendon 1961) 133.

[77] P Craig, 'Comparative Administrative Law and Political Structure' (2017) 37 OJLS 947 (according to whom the 'study of comparative administrative law reveals commonality and difference between the systems studies. That is axiomatic and self-evident').

C. Divergences within convergence

It is precisely because the respective relevance of common and distinctive traits differs from the past that an attempt is made in this section to outline three themes that are related but distinct, and which have been emphasized by diverse strands of legal theory. It can be helpful to summarize them briefly here, while a more structured analysis will be possible after all the parts of our comparative research have been carried out. The three themes are 'the nature of things', prestige, and the influence of supranational organizations.

There is, first, an important strand in public law, which in effect reflects a broader vision of law in itself. In former times, until the mid-eighteenth century, for example in Vattel, this strand found expression in an identification between 'the nature of things' and human nature. Unlike Vattel, Montesquieu did not hesitate to acknowledge the existence of an endless diversity of laws and customs.[78] However, he did not stop looking for invariable laws,[79] which gained increasing support simply because they were better than others. Following this strand, it may be argued that certain developments, such as the repudiation of old doctrines whereby sovereignty excluded liability (doctrines still accepted in Russia and to some extent in other socialist regimes), are but a natural consequence of certain fundamental assumptions about the nature of the polities we live in, which place limits on the possibility of arguing that government powers are non-justiciable.

In parallel to this traditional theory runs a second strand, which focuses on the diffusion of certain legal principles and institutions based on their prestige. In particular, the prestige in which the French administrative judge is held was demonstrated by the creation of special courts in Austria and in Germany between 1862 and 1870, in Italy in 1890, and even in Belgium in 1946.[80] The French framework governing judicial review of administrative action has also influenced supranational and international institutions, such as the Court of Justice and the Administrative Tribunal of the United Nations, respectively.[81] In our case, it is the Austrian and German model of regulating government liability in tort that has exerted a strong influence on other legal systems of Central and Eastern Europe. This influence emerges when the courts of these legal systems take government liability both to exclude immunity and to justify the imposition of duties, in the broader sense, procedural fairness, and rationality in the exercise of discretionary powers.

Whatever the explanation, whether functional or based on diffusion, one thing is clear; some general principles of law shared by all European legal systems within the first European Communities exist. This was acknowledged by the Treaty of Rome as early as 1957 and later in the case law of the European Court of Justice (ECJ). The

[78] Montesquieu, *De l'esprit des lois*, ed V Goldscmidt (Flammarion 1979 [1748]) 115 and 123. For Vattel's view, see his *Le droit des gens ou principes de la loi naturelle, appliqués à la conduite et aux affaires des Nations et des Souverains* (1758).

[79] ibid 125.

[80] See W Friedmann, 'Review of C.J. Hamson, Executive Discretion and Judicial Control: An Aspect of the French Conseil d'Etat' (1955) 21 UTLJ 140, 141. On administrative courts, see Fromont (n 55) 111–40.

[81] On the Court of Justice, see E Stein and P Hay, 'Legal Remedies of Enterprises in the European Economic Community' (1960) 9 AJCL 381, 383.

question that thus arises is whether an obstacle to commonality was created with the accession of the UK. Some years ago, Duncan Fairgrieve observed that, despite some major differences between French and English law, on deeper study, they were quite similar.[82] This is confirmed by Gordon Anthony's analysis in Chapter 13 of this book. More generally, Paul Craig and Sabino Cassese have observed that the Council of Europe and the EC/EU have had the effect of 'bringing the public law systems of the differing European countries closer together'.[83] Carol Harlow and Richard Rawlings, too, have noticed that a gradual convergence is emerging.[84] Within this strand, further distinctions emerge. On the one hand, 'natural' convergence, especially in the area of the EU shared administration, is opposed to 'imposed uniformity'.[85] On the other hand, there are diverse foundations for the procedural duties imposed on public authorities. Some opine that these duties flow from shared general principles and values. For others, it is because individuals are regarded as holders of rights, not as passive receptors of decisions taken by public decision-makers, and that the latter are obliged to respect those duties and to give reasons for their choices.

VI. The next steps

It would be hazardous to draw conclusions too firmly from the findings on government liability set out in this volume. They should rather be viewed as partial, requiring further verification, also using other research methods. As a first step, an analysis of the judicial definition of early standards of administrative conduct (1890–1910) has been completed and will soon be published.[86] Moreover, the relevance and significance of the findings discussed here will be compared with findings concerning other specific issues within administrative law, including a synchronic comparison of judicial review of procedural infringements and the relationship between general principles of administrative procedure and sector-specific norms. A better insight may also be provided by comparisons with the legal principles and institutions of other regions of the world.

[82] Faigrieve (n 29) 261.

[83] S Cassese, *La construction du droit administratif: France et Royaume-Uni* (Montchrestien 2000) 147; Craig, *Administrative Law* (n 26) 324.

[84] C Harlow and R Rawlings, 'National Administrative Procedures in a European Perspective: Pathways to a Slow Convergence' (2010) 2 It J Publ L 259.

[85] RJ Widdershoven, 'Developing Administrative Law in Europe: Natural Convergence or Imposed Uniformity?' (2014) 7 Rev Eur Adm L 5.

[86] See G della Cananea and S Mannoni (eds), *Administrative Justice Fin-de-Siècle. Early Judicial Standards of Administrative Conduct in Europe (1890–1910)* (OUP 2021, forthcoming).

2
On the 'Common Core of European Administrative Laws' Methodology (and European Tort Laws)

Mauro Bussani

I. Introduction

The general purpose of this volume is to inquire to what extent, if any, there exists a common core of non-contractual State liability across European administrative and tort laws. The analysis aims to identify the rules in place and enforced in each of the jurisdictions under review, seeking to verify whether the results that these rules help secure are mutually coherent, and to understand how the overall architecture of the legal systems impacts on the role that public liability is called upon to play.

This volume takes its basic methodology from the 'Common Core of European Administrative Laws' project, of which it constitutes a branch of research. It is a methodology worth some explanation, along with the potential contribution that this volume may bring to the debates on comparative tort law and, more specifically, on the the European law(s) of public liability. From this perspective, I first introduce the current state of European tort law (section II) and the scholarly initiatives focusing on it (section III).[1] I then present the basic outlines of the 'Common Core' methodology (sections IV and V) and the rationale behind the three-level responses, which is one of the distinctive features of the whole project (section VI). The concluding remarks address the caveats that must accompany any assessment of the results and the promises that this book is expected to fulfil (section VII).

II. European tort law

European tort laws are notoriously far from harmonized. At first sight (but only at first sight), the great variety of European tort laws may resemble the scenario in the US, where increasing divergence between the federal and state laws (also in tort

[1] Mostly from the private law perspective, deferring for an analysis of the public law side of the scenario to G della Cananea, 'A "Common Core" Research on Government Liability in Tort: A Comparative Approach'Chapter 1 in this volume, B Marchetti, 'The EU Institutions Liability between the Member States Principles and the Causality Standards of the EU Court of Justice', Chapter 4 in this volume, and R Caranta, 'Concluding Remarks: Towards Convergence? The Road beyond Institutional and Dotrinal Path-Dependence', Chapter 20 in this volume.

Mauro Bussani, *On the 'Common Core of European Administrative Laws' Methodology (and European Tort Laws)* In: *Tort Liability of Public Authorities in European Laws*. Edited by: Giacinto della Cananea and Roberto Caranta, Oxford University Press (2020).
 DOI: 10.1093/oso/9780198867555.003.0002.

law matters) inspired the American Law Institute (ALI) to launch the idea of the Restatements of the Law in the 1920s.[2] This first impression created by the analogy would, however, be wrong. There are considerable differences between the European case and that of the US. It is clear that punitive damages, jury trials, aggregation of claims, and contingency fee agreements are largely unknown to European tort laws, while they shape the basic vocabulary of tort law in the US.[3] Yet there is so much more to it than this. Although the US has fifty-one tort law jurisdictions, including federal jurisdiction, these regimes largely share a common language and employ the same reservoir of notions and technicalities. Most US legislatures are affected by the same pressures coming from power groups acting across state boundaries, such as the insurance industry and the American Trial Lawyers Association. Moreover, the US Supreme Court, in matters where it can intervene, operates as a driving force for uniform outcomes.[4] Europe, by contrast, lacks one Supreme Court whose task and scope of intervention are comparable to those of the US Supreme Court. The insurance market is still not homogeneous, and lawyers are associated only at national level. There is not one common language, but twenty-four distinct ones, and each legal system relies upon its own set of notions and technicalities—a set that may significantly overlap, but may also diverge enormously among different jurisdictions.

That being said, just as in US federal law-making, it is true that, according to the EU treaties the Union does not have the general and comprehensive power to intervene in the field of tort law. The only competence assigned to the EU by the treaties with regard to tort law concerns the responsibility of Member States and the EU itself in cases where they breach their obligations under the treaties themselves (see Arts 260(1)–(3) and Art 340(2) of the Treaty on the Functioning of the European Union, TFEU).[5]

Equally true is the fact that the EU has tried, over time, to carve out new competencies in the realm of tort law.[6] It has done so through the adoption of statutory laws—mostly directives—aiming to harmonize the segments of tort law deemed to most

[2] The ALI was established in 1923 to promote the clarification and simplification of US common law and its adaptation to changing social needs. Members of ALI basically include law professors, attorneys, and judges. ALI drafts, approves, and publishes Restatements of the Law (besides Principles of the Law, model codes, and other proposals for law reform). Individual Restatement volumes are essentially compilations of case law, which are common law judge-made doctrines. Although Restatements of the Law are not binding authorities in and of themselves, they are highly persuasive because they are formulated over several years, with extensive input from the above legal actors. They are meant to reflect the consensus of the US legal community as to what the law is, and, in some cases, what it should become.

[3] U Magnus, 'Why is US Tort Law So Different?' (2010) 1 JETL 102, 102–24.

[4] J Stapleton, 'Benefits of Comparative Tort Reasoning: Lost in Translation' (2007) 1 J Tort Law 1, 25; VV Palmer and M Bussani, *Pure Economic Loss: New Horizons in Comparative Law* (Routledge-Cavendish 2008) 52–53.

[5] The task of judging the compliance of Member States and the EU institutions with the treaties is entrusted to the Court of Justice of the European Union (CJEU), whose case law on this point has played an important role in shaping the States' liability across Europe. See, eg, W van Gerven, 'Judicial Convergence of Laws and Minds in European Tort Law and Related Matters' in A Colombi Ciacchi and others (eds), *Haftungsrecht im dritten Millennium* (*Liability in the Third Millennium*) (Nomos 2009); see also B Marchetti, 'The EU Institutions liability between the Member States Principles and the Causality Standards of the EU Court of Justice', Chapter 4 in this volume.

[6] G Brüggemeier, *Tort Law in the European Union* (Kluwer 2015); P Giliker (ed), *Research Handbook on EU Tort Law* (Elgar 2017).

often cross national boundaries and/or have the greatest impact on the development of the internal market.[7]

The trend started in the 1970s, with the directive on liability insurance aiming to establish a harmonized insurance system to facilitate people's free movement and guarantee compensation to persons injured in a Member State other than their own (Council Directive 73/239/EEC of 24 July 1973 on the coordination of laws, regulations, and administrative provisions relating to the taking-up and pursuit of the business of direct insurance other than life assurance, now replaced by the Commission Directive 2009/138/EU of 25 November 2009 on the taking-up and pursuit of the business of insurance and reinsurance). In 1985, a directive on product liability pursued consumer safety through the adoption of a strict-liability regime for producers of defective products (Council Directive 85/374/EEC of 25 July 1985 on the approximation of the laws, regulations, and administrative provisions of Member States concerning liability for defective products, currently under revision). In 1995, a directive on data protection made 'controllers' of personal data liable for unlawful data collection and treatment (European Parliament and Council Directive 95/46/EEC of 24 October 1995 on the protection of individuals with regard to the processing of personal data and the free movement of such data, now replaced by Regulation 2016/679/EU of 27 April 2016 on the protection of natural persons with regard to the processing of personal data and their free movement, which extended the liability rule to 'controllers' and 'processors' of data). In 2001, rules on jurisdiction in transnational tort law claims were harmonized by Regulation (Regulation 44/2001/EC of 22 December 2000 on jurisdiction and the recognition and enforcement of judgments in civil and commercial matters, now replaced by Regulation 1215/2012/EU of 12 December 2012 on jurisdiction and the recognition and enforcement of judgments in civil and commercial matters).

In 2004, two other directives introduced a common framework, one for compensating crime victims (Council Directive 2004/80/EC of 29 April 2004 relating to compensation to crime victims) and the other for protecting the environment on the basis of the 'polluter pays' principle (European Parliament and Council Directive 2004/35/CE of 21 April 2004 on environmental liability with regard to the prevention and remedying of environmental damage). On the assumption that cross-border externalities may be countered by harmonized rules of private international law, the EU enacted a regulation in 2007 enabling conflict-of-law rules to designate the law applicable to transnational tort claims (Regulation 864/2007/EC of 11 July 2007 on the law applicable to non-contractual obligations). In 2013, the European Commission issued a recommendation on a set of common, non-binding principles for collective redress mechanisms (Commission Recommendation of 11 June 2013 on common principles for injunctive and compensatory collective redress mechanisms in Member States concerning the infringement of rights granted under Union Law), followed in 2014 by the adoption of a Directive aimed at removing practical obstacles to compensation for victims of infringement of EU antitrust law (European Parliament and Council Directive 2014/104/EU on certain rules governing actions for damages under

[7] C von Bar, *The Common European Law of Torts*, vol 1 (OUP 1998) 401–07.

national law for infringements of the competition law provisions of Member States and the EU).

Some of the above-mentioned reforms have apparently enjoyed remarkable success, both within and outside the EU's borders. Compulsory vehicle insurance, for instance, is now a reality throughout the EU. The directive on products liability has inspired many legislators around the world, who preferred to follow the newly established EU model rather than the US model.[8]

Yet the actual effectiveness of the above-mentioned EU laws is overall much debated. To illustrate, studies carried out on the insurance sector have pointed out that the liability regimes underlying compulsory insurance for traffic accidents are still remarkably divergent among European jurisdictions.[9] In a similar vein, it has been noted that, despite the external success of the products liability directive, the convergence created by the act has been minimal, and the rate of litigation grounded on the EU-branded products liability regime has remained incredibly low.[10]

Many reasons have been put forward to explain the limited effect of the EU's harmonizing strategy in the field of tort law.

A first explanation points to the piecemeal approach taken by the EU. The EU institutions have up to now kept themselves far from any intervention in the general architecture of substantive tort law. They implicitly assume that tort law can be divided into a core of general rules to be left to national jurisdictions and 'special' rules where the EU legislation can effectively intervene.[11] Yet the 'special' rules can only be applied within, and through, the framework of the general rules. This is why planting the seeds of a special EU discipline in national tort law frameworks risks being a bad strategy for achieving the goal of minimizing the differences between national tort laws.[12]

Such a risk is increased by both the contradictory character of the EU's patchwork of statutory tort law provisions and the absence of a court entrusted with general competence over the interpretation of the provisions.[13]

All the above flaws are said to be worsened by the very use of the directives as the EU's main legislative tool.[14] Directives have the virtue of flexibility, ie of guaranteeing that each State can adapt the EU acts in its national categories, but the flip side is that the outcomes of the process of implementation are frequently divergent due to the tendency of Member States to replicate the traditional features of their legal system in

[8] M Reimann, 'Product Liability in a Global Context: The Hollow Victory of the European Model' (2003) 2 ERPL 128.

[9] C van Dam, *European Tort Law* (2nd edn, OUP 2013) 459.

[10] G Howells, 'Is European Product Liability Harmonised?' in H Koziol and R Schulze (eds), *Tort Law of the European Community* (Springer 2008); M Reimann, 'Products Liability', in M Bussani and AJ Sebok (eds), *Comparative Tort Law. Global Perspectives* (Elgar 2015).

[11] von Bar, *The Common European Law of Torts* (n 7) 408.

[12] von Bar, *The Common European Law of Torts* (n 7) 408; W van Gerven, J Lever, and P Larouche, *Tort Law* (Hart 2000) 10; H Koziol, 'Harmonising Tort Law in the European Union: Advantages and Difficulties' (2013) 1 ELTE L J 73, 74–78.

[13] M Faure, 'How Law and Economics May Contribute to the Harmonisation of Tort Law in Europe' in R Zimmermann (ed), *Grundstrukturen des Europäischen Deliktsrecths* (Nomos 2003); R van den Bergh and L Visscher, 'The Principles of European Tort Law: The Right Path to Harmonization?' (2006) 14 ERPL 511; H Koziol, 'Comparative Law—a Must in the European Union: Demonstrated by Tort Law as an Example' (2007) 1 J Tort L 1, 5–6.

[14] von Bar, *The Common European Law of Torts* (n 7) 410; Koziol, 'Comparative Law' (n 13) 5–6.

the implemented rules. Thus, directives may result in intensifying legal differences as opposed to supporting uniformity.[15]

Resorting to regulations rather than directives is only a limited cure. With regard to the only regulation so far adopted in the field of tort law (Regulation No 864/2007 on the law applicable to non-contractual obligations), it has been noted that many factors may hinder uniform application. Divergence, for instance, may stem from the lack of agreement on the meaning of notions, such as 'tort claim', 'injury', 'direct', and 'indirect' consequences.[16] Differences may also arise from the well-known tendency of national jurists to interpret foreign law in the light of their national notions, categories, and rules of law, or to even apply their own national law to transnational cases, irrespective of what the conflict-of-law criteria say.[17]

The above observations also apply to the harmonization results achieved so far by the other supranational organization at work in the European region: the Council of Europe. The enforcement of the European Convention on Human Rights (ECHR) by the European Court of Human Rights (ECtHR) under the Council of Europe has empowered victims of a breach of the Convention to bring a compensation claim against the State before national courts, thus transforming the violation of an international human rights treaty into an actionable domestic tort.[18] Yet, the requirements and technicalities of ECHR-based torts are governed by the law of each national legal system and are thus subject to a variety of regimes and interpretations that follow divergent paths.[19]

III. . . . and its scholars

The foregoing considerations have led many scholars to pave their own way forward to a truly common European tort law.

The aims and methods of all these endeavours are very dissimilar. There are groups, such as the European Group on Tort Law[20] and the Study Group on a European Civil

[15] W van Gerven and others, *Tort Law* (n 12), 9–10; for some concrete examples, see M Infantino, 'Making European Tort Law: The Game and Its Players' (2010) 18 Cardozo J Int'l & Comp L 45, 58.

[16] P Hay, 'Contemporary Approaches to Non-Contractual Obligations in Private International Law (Conflict of Laws) and the European Community's "Rome II" Regulation' (2007) 7 Eur Legal F 137, 139–40, 144, 149.

[17] B Fauvarque-Cosson, 'Comparative Law and Conflict of Laws: Allies or Enemies? New Perspectives on an Old Couple' (2001) 49 AJCL 407, 412.

[18] A Fenyves, E Karner, H Koziol, and E Steiner (eds), *Tort Law in the Jurisprudence of the European Court of Human Rights* (De Gruyter 2011).

[19] K Oliphant, 'The Liability of Public Authorities in Comparative Perspective' in K Oliphant (ed), *The Liability of Public Authorities in Comparative Perspective* (Intersentia 2016) 850–54.

[20] The European Group on Tort Law was established in 1992 within the Viennese European Centre of Tort and Insurance Law, whose main sponsor is the German reinsurance company Munich Re (for more information, see <http://egtl.org> accessed 18 June and <http://ectil.org> accessed 18 June 2020). From 1992 to 2005, the group accomplished many studies, the results of which have been collected in a series called *Principles of European Tort Law* (*PETL*), published by Kluwer Law International: H Koziol (ed), *Unification of Tort Law: Wrongfulness* (Kluwer Law International 1998); J Spier (ed), *The Limits of Expanding Liability: Eight Fundamental Cases in a Comparative Perspective* (Kluwer Law International 1998); J Spier, *The Limits of Liability: Keeping the Floodgates Shut* (2000); J Spier (ed), *Unification of Tort Law: Causation* (2000); U Magnus (ed), *Unification of Tort Law: Damages* (Kluwer Law International 2001); BA Koch and H Koziol (eds), *Unification of Tort Law: Strict Liability* (Kluwer Law International 2002);

Code,[21] which have engaged in assessing solutions that may best regulate certain legal problems and in codifying those solutions in the text of a would-be European code.

Other associations pursue the aim of supporting victims and courts in transnational law claims. For instance, the Pan-European Organisation of Personal Injury Lawyers (PEOPIL), promotes judicial cooperation between the European jurisdictions in personal injury litigation.[22] The Foreign Law Translations project, led by professor Markesinis, collects, translates, and makes tort law decisions from different European jurisdictions available online in order to ease judicial use of comparative law.[23]

J Spier (ed), *Unification of Tort Law: Liability for Damage Caused by Others* (2003); U Magnus and M Martín Casals (eds), *Unification of Tort Law: Contributory Negligence* (Kluwer Law International 2004); HWW Rogers (ed), *Unification of Tort Law: Multiple Tortfeasors* (Kluwer Law International 2004); P Widmer (ed), *Unification of Tort Law: Fault* (Kluwer Law International 2005). Each volume gathered national reports and comparative results of an inquiry carried out on a specific tort law topic (eg causation, fault, wrongfulness, strict liability, etc). Contributors were asked to describe the legal treatment of the assigned topic in their country by responding to some theoretical issues and solving concrete cases; the editors then summarized the results (European Group of Tort Law, *Principles of European Tort Law* (Springer 2005) 14–16). The outcomes of the research were used as a starting point for drafting the *PETL*, which were published in 2005. The *PETL* are divided into ten chapters: Basic Norm, Damage, Causation, Liability Based on Fault, Strict Liability, Liability for Others, Defences in General, Contributory Conduct or Activity, Multiple Tortfeasors, and Damages (for a general overview of the contents of the *PETL*, see van den Bergh and Visscher (n 13); Koziol, 'Comparative Law' (n 13); WH van Boom and A Pinna, 'Le droit de la responsabilité civil de demain en Europe: questions choisies' in B Winiger (ed), *La responsabilité civile européenne de demain—projets de révision nationaux et principes européens* (Bruylant 2008); BA Koch, 'Principles of European Tort Law' (2009) 20 King's L J 203; K Oliphant, 'Introduction: European Tort Law' (2009) 20 King's LJ 189; M Martín-Casals, 'The Principles of European Tort Law (PETL) at the Beginning of a Second Decade' in Giliker (n 6) 361–413). The group is currently working on a new edition, which will cover also prescription, relationship with contractual liability, and state and products liability: see P Machnikowski (ed), *European Product Liability* (Intersentia 2016); Oliphant, *The Liability of Public Authorities in Comparative Perspective* (n 19); M Martín-Casals (ed), *The Borderlines of Tort Law: Interactions with Contract Law* (Intersentia 2019); I Gilead and B Askeland (eds), *Prescription in Tort Law: Analytical and Comparative Perspectives* (Intersentia 2020).

[21] The Study Group on a European Civil Code was founded in 1998 by Professor Christian von Bar. The Study Group had the more general purpose of drafting a European code on the whole of private economic law (C von Bar, 'Le groupe d'études sur un code civil européen' (2001) 53 RIDC 127). In the Study Group's view, the preparatory work on a European code had to be performed by scholars, who are the only ones endowed with the necessary expertise to conduct the essential basic research and to set up rules unaffected by the particularities of national interests; the legislator's role could begin only once the academic work of selecting the *Principles of European Law* (*PEL*) was completed (C von Bar, 'A European Civil Code, International Agreements and European Directives' (1999) European parliament, directorate general for research, working paper No JURI 103 EN, 1999) <http://europarl.europa.eu/workingpapers/juri/pdf/103_en.pdf> accessed 18 June 2020). In 2006, the drafting of the tort law book for the would-be European code was completed. The *Principles of European Law on Non-Contractual Liability Arising Out of Damage Caused to Another* were included, with minimal modifications, in the *Draft Common Frame of Reference* prepared by the Study Group for the European Commission in 2008 and officially published by Sellier in 2009. The *PEL* are composed of seven chapters: Fundamental Provisions, Particular Instances of Legally Relevant Damage, Accountability, Causation, Defences, Remedies, and Ancillary Rules (C von Bar (ed), *Non-Contractual Liability Arising Out of Damage Caused to Another* (Sellier 2009); for a general overview of the *PEL* contents, see J Blackie, 'The Torts Provisions of the Study Group on a European Civil Code' in M Bussani (ed), *European Tort Law: Eastern and Western Perspectives* (Stämpfli 2007); J Blackie, 'The Provisions for "Non-Contractual Liability Arising Out of Damage Caused to Another" in the Draft Common Frame of Reference' (2009) 20 King's LJ 215; Oliphant, 'Introduction' (n 20); J Blackie, 'The Tort Provisions of the Study Group on a European Civil Code and Their Uses' in Giliker (n 6)).

[22] See <http://peopil.com> accessed 18 June 2020.

[23] See <http://law.utexas.edu/transnational/foreign-law-translations/> accessed 18 June 2020. A similar enterprise is carried out by the Institute for European Tort Law (on which see below in the text) with its EUROTORT database, at <http://ectil.org/ectil/Eurotort.aspx> accessed 18 June 2020.

Some other groups are more inclined towards comparative research *per se*. This is the main objective of enterprises exclusively centred on tort law. The France-based and French-speaking *Groupe de recherche européen sur la responsabilité civile et l'assurance* fosters yearly thematic comparisons whose results are collected in a series published by Larcier and Bruylant.[24] Two closely connected Austrian-based institutions, the European Centre of Tort and Insurance Law (ECTIL) and the Institute for European Tort Law (IETL), besides supporting the European Group on Tort Law, provide a forum for research on comparative tort law and a venue for publication of up-to-date information and commentary about European tort law. Every year, ECTIL and IETL organize an Annual Conference on European Tort Law, maintain a database of European case law on tort,[25] coordinate a peer-reviewed dedicated tort law journal (the *Journal of European Tort Law*) and publish many series on tort law (such as the *Digest of European Tort Law*, the *European Tort Law Yearbook* and the *Tort Law and Insurance Series*).[26]

Regardless of the uses to which knowledge may be applied, which may or may not include the pursuit of legal harmonization, knowledge-building is both the starting point and the final aim of the *Ius Commune Casebooks for the Common Law of Europe* project, whose scope is broader than those we have just mentioned, insofar as its focus goes beyond tort law alone. The *Ius Commune Casebooks* initiative was launched in 1994 by Professor Walter van Gerven with the aim of producing a collection of casebooks covering each of the main fields of European law.[27] The long-term purpose of the *Ius Commune* project is to 'uncover common general principles which are already present in the living law of the European countries' for the benefit of European students.[28] In this view, the casebooks are primarily conceived as teaching materials to be used in the curricula of law schools in order to promote a common European education.[29]

[24] See <http://iode.univ-rennes1.fr/grerca> accessed 18 June 2020.

[25] See the EUROTORT database mentioned above (n 23).

[26] For more information, see <http://ectil.org> and <http://etl.oeaw.ac.at> accessed 18 June 2020.

[27] On the aims and methods of such a project, see W van Gerven, 'Casebooks for the Common Law of Europe: Presentation of the Project' (1996) 4 ERPL 67;P Larouche, 'Ius Commune Casebooks for the Common Law of Europe: Presentation, Progress, Rationale' (2000) 8 ERPL 101; P Larouche, 'L'intégration, les systèmes juridiques et la formation juridique' (2001) 46 Mcgill L J 1011; W van Gerven, 'Comparative Law in a Regionally Integrated Europe' in A Harding and E Örücü (eds), *Comparative Law in the Twenty-First Century* (Kluwer 2002); W van Gerven, 'A Common Framework of Reference and Teaching' in Bussani, *European Tort Law* (n 21).

[28] van Gerven and others, *Tort Law* (n 12) 68.

[29] As of now, eight volumes have been published by Hart, and many are forthcoming, on issues as diverse as employment law, law and art, constitutional law, conflicts of law, and legal history (see <http://casebooks.eu> accessed 18 June 2020). Two volumes concerning tort law have already been published (van Gerven and others, *Tort Law—Scope of Protection* (Hart Publishing 1998), van Gerven and others, *Tort Law* (n 12); one of them (van Gerven and others, *Tort Law*) is under review for the second edition (see <http://www.casebooks.eu/project/approach> Accessed 26 August 2020). Every casebook, whose table of contents and materials are partly accessible on the project's website, collates legislation, excerpts from books, articles, and, above all, cases from various jurisdictions—mostly from France, England, and Germany, which are considered representative of the main European legal families. Materials from other legal systems are included in the casebooks only if they present an original solution compared with the above legal systems. These materials are accompanied by introductory and explicatory notes, stressing the similarities among European legal systems, and the impact of the EU law 'as a driving force towards the emergence of a new *ius commune*' (see <http://casebooks.eu/research.php> accessed 18 June 2020). The casebooks are written by a task force composed of academics representing what are deemed to be the 'main' European legal families (van Gerven

IV. The distinctiveness of the 'Common Core' approach

The Common Core of European Private Law project, the antecedent and the methodological parent of the current scholarly endeavour, has been running since 1994, when it was launched by Ugo Mattei and the author of this chapter.

The research carried out under The Common Core of European Private Law initiative was published as volumes in a dedicated series by Cambridge University Press until 2018 (although some books were also published by Stämpfli and Carolina Academic Press); after that date, the series passed into the hands of Intersentia. Of the seventeen volumes published so far, six deal with civil liability issues, such as causation,[30] recoverability of pure economic losses,[31] the protection of personality rights,[32] the boundaries of strict liability,[33] ecological damage,[34] and pre-contractual liability.[35] Two other volumes on tort law, dealing respectively with standards of care in negligence and with products liability, are under preparation.[36]

The Common Core of European Private Law has a different target audience, methodology, and primary goals from any other project mentioned above. The research aims to unearth what is common, and what is not, between the EU Member States' private laws, in order to provide a reliable description of the actual state of the art of the European multi-legal framework.[37] In particular, unlike the *Ius Commune Casebook* project, which emphasizes the solutions given by the legal systems considered to be leading or paradigmatic, the 'Common Core' project focuses equally on all the EU national legal systems.

Moreover, with the aim of unearthing what, if anything, is already common to European private law, and drawing the main outlines of a reliable 'map' of the European multi-legal framework,[38] the project has never taken a preservationist approach, nor—in spite of its name—has it ever pushed in the direction of uniformity.

and others, *Tort Law* (n 12) vi–vii). A distinctive feature of the project is that each task force member, rather than dealing solely with his/her national legal system, is tasked with writing an entire thematic chapter, even if it refers to legal systems different from his/her country of origin or education. This distribution of work guarantees that the final outcome is not a patchwork of national reports, but rather the genuine result of a truly comparative effort.

[30] M Infantino and E Zervogianni (eds), *Causation in European Tort Law* (CUP 2017).

[31] M Bussani and VV Palmer, *Pure Economic Loss in Europe* (CUP 2003).

[32] G Brüggemeier, A Colombi Ciacchi, and P O'Callaghan (eds), *Personality Rights in European Tort Law* (CUP 2010).

[33] F Werro and VV Palmer (eds), *The Boundaries of Strict Liability in European Tort Law* (Carolina Academic Press 2004).

[34] M Hinteregger (ed), *Environmental Liability and Ecological Damage in European Law* (CUP 2008).

[35] J Cartwright and M Hesselink (eds), *Precontractual Liability in European Private Law* (CUP 2008).

[36] See <http://common-core.org> accessed 18 June 2020.

[37] For a general overview of the project, see M Bussani, 'Current Trends in European Comparative Law: The Common Core Approach' (1998) 21 HICLR 785;M Bussani and U Mattei, 'The Common Core Approach to European Private Law' (1998) 3 CJEL 339; M Bussani and U Mattei, 'Le fonds commun du droit privé europeén' (2000) 52 RIDC 29; M Bussani and U Mattei (eds) *The Common Core of European Private Law. Essays on the Project* (Kluwer 2003); M Bussani and U Mattei (eds), *Opening Up European Law* (Staempfli—Bruylant—Ant N Sakkoulas 2007); M Bussani, 'The "Common Core of European Private Law" Project Two Decades After: A New Beginning' (2015) 15 Eur Lawyer J 9.

[38] For a more extensive presentation of the project, with specific regard to tort law, see M Bussani, M Infantino, and F Werro, 'The Common Core Sound: Short Notes on Themes, Harmonies and Disharmonies in European Tort Law' (2009) 20 King's L J 239–55.

This is possibly the most important cultural difference between the 'Common Core' project and the other Restatement-like enterprises—such as, in the tort law field, those carried out by the European Group on Tort Law[39] and by the Study Group on a European Civil Code.[40] Both of these initiatives pursued 'integrative'[41] enterprises, embracing ideals of harmonization/unification, and implying a selection of the legal rules that would be best suited to them. In their attempt to draft a common European tort law, both the European Group on Tort Law and the Study Group on a European Civil Code decided not to look for the rules most widely accepted across European countries. They instead chose to seek the 'best' solution to every tort law problem, whether or not this 'best solution' reflected rules already established within any European jurisdiction.[42]

It is true that through the use of the comparative method, many common features that remained obscure in traditional legal analysis of the field may be unearthed. But this is because the instruments and techniques provide more accurate and correct analysis, not because they force convergence where none exists. It is also true that a 'Common Core' research may be a useful instrument for legal harmonization, insofar as it provides reliable data to be used in devising new common solutions that may prove workable in practice. But this has nothing to do with the 'Common Core' research in itself, which is simply devoted to producing accurate and reliable information.

V. At the core of the 'Common Core' method

The first problem the editors of this book (as of any other 'Common Core' book) had to resolve was how to obtain comparable answers to the questions that are to be posed about different legal systems. The answers had to refer to identical questions interpreted as identically as possible by all the respondents. Besides, the answers had to be self-sufficient in two ways. First, they had to be complete answers: additional explanations should not be required. The level of specificity to be expected, therefore, was to be on a par with the most detailed rules. Second, they had to be authoritative answers which could be accepted at 'face value'. The editors would therefore refrain from superimposing their own views upon the scenario depicted by the national contributors.

[39] In 2005, the European Group on Tort Law published the *Principles of European Tort Law (PETL)*: see above (n 20).

[40] The 'Study Group on a European Civil Code', led by Christian von Bar, published its *Principles of European Law on Non-Contractual Liability Arising out of Damage Caused to Another (PEL)* in 2006. See above (n 21).

[41] To use Schlesinger's terminology: see RB Schlesinger, 'The Past and Future of Comparative Law' (1995) 43 AJCL 477, 479; see also M Bussani, "Integrative' Comparative Law Enterprises and the Inner Stratification of Legal Systems' (2000) 8 ERPL 85.

[42] As for the European Group on Tort Law, see J Spier, 'General Introduction' in European Group on Tort Law, *Principles of European Tort Law* (Springer 2005) 12, 15; for the Study Group, see C von Bar, 'The Study Group on a European Civil Code' in European Parliament, *The Study of the Systems of Private Law in the EU with Regard to Discrimination and the Creation of a European Civil Code* (1999) Working Paper, Legal Affairs Series No JURI 103 EN, 130, 133–35, <europarl.europa.eu/RegData/etudes/etudes/join/1999/168511/IPOL-JURI_ET(1999)168511_EN.pdf> accessed 26 August 2020.

To obtain consistency, after lengthy discussions within the work group, each hypothetical case was formulated with a view to taking account of any relevant circumstance occurring in any of the legal systems under consideration, so that these circumstances would be considered in—and therefore become comparable with—the analysis of all the other systems. In this way, another important objective was achieved. Often, the circumstances that operate explicitly and officially in one system are officially ignored and considered to be irrelevant in another system and yet, in that other system, they operate secretly, slipping in silently between the formulation of the rule and its application by the courts. Thus, one of the special features of this work is that it has made jurists think explicitly about the circumstances that matter, forcing them to answer identically formulated questions, and asking them about the results that would be reached in particular cases, and not about a doctrinal system.

As a result, the responses may have given a picture of the law which is substantially different from the one usually found in the monographs, handbooks, or casebooks circulating in the individual countries. This comes as no surprise. What we learned from the methodology of Rudolf Schlesinger and Rodolfo Sacco is that, in order to have a complete knowledge of a country's law, we cannot entirely trust what the jurists say, for there may be wide gaps between operative rules and what is commonly stated. Needless to say, a list of all the reasons given for the decisions made by the courts is not the entire law, the statutes are not the entire law, neither are the definitions given by scholarly writings. In order to know what the law is, it is necessary to analyse the entire complex relationship between the so-called 'legal formants' of a system, ie all those formative elements that make any given rule of law amidst statutes, general propositions, particular definitions, reasons, holdings, and so forth.[43] None of these formative elements are necessarily coherent with each other within each system, even though domestic jurists usually assume such coherence exists. On the contrary, legal formants may be in conflict and can be pictured in a competitive relationship with one another.

A full understanding of what the legal formants are and how they relate to each other allows us to ascertain the factors that affect solutions, making clear the weight that interpretative practices (grounded on scholarly writings, on legal debate aroused by previous judicial decision, etc) have in moulding the actual outcomes. Hence, the notion of legal formant is far more than an esoteric neologism for the traditional distinction between *loi*, *jurisprudence*, and *doctrine*, ie between enacted law, case law, and scholarly writings. Within a given legal system, the legal rule is not uniform, and not only because one rule may be given by case law, one by scholars, and one by statutes. Within each of these sources, as I said, one may find formants competing with one another. For example, the rule described in the headnotes of a case can be inconsistent with the actual rationale of the decision, or the definition in a statute can be inconsistent with the detailed rules contained in the same statute.[44] This complex dynamic may change considerably from one legal system to another, as well as from one area of the law to another. In particular, in a given legal system, certain legal formants are clearly leading in a different direction: the differences in

[43] See R Sacco, 'Legal Formants: A Dynamic Approach to Comparative Law' (1991) 39 AJCL 1.
[44] See ibid 21–27.

formants' leadership are particularly clear in the (traditional) distinction between common law and civil law.

VI. The three-level responses

The questionnaire which is the backbone of this volume was drafted with a sufficient degree of specificity as to require the rapporteurs' answers to address all the factors in their system that have a practical impact on the operative rules. This is the best guarantee that rules formulated in an identical way (by an identical statutory provision, for example), but which may produce different applications, or even different doctrinal rhetoric, will not be regarded as identical.

As mentioned in section V above, these considerations are particularly important because the systems within this study belong to the common law as well as to the civil law tradition. The structure of the judicial process and the 'style' of the legal system (in the broad sense described by Zweigert and Kötz and John Merryman),[45] could not be neglected if we were to obtain correct results. It is indeed in the structure of the legal process, which municipal lawyers take as given, that most of the differences can be detected, understood, and possibly explained.

All this hopefully leads to an understanding of why one of the distinctive features of the project is the requirement that every contributor set her or his answers up on three levels, labelled I. 'Operative Rules', II. 'Descriptive Formants', and III. 'Metalegal Formants'. In the interest of readability, we have taken these working titles out of the responses; nevertheless, we have left intact the inner structure of each response. Thus, the three levels are maintained and are now simply indicated by the division of the responses into paragraphs marked I, II, and III.

The level dealing with 'Operative Rules' is designed to be a concise summary. The reporters are asked to summarize the basic applicable rules and to state the outcome of the case that would be reached under national law. Reporters are also asked to indicate whether the reasoning and outcome would be considered clear and undisputed, or only doubtful and problematic.

The aim of the level called 'Descriptive Formants' is to reveal the reasons jurists feel obliged to give in support of the 'operative rules', and the extent to which the various solutions are consistent either with specific and general legislative provisions, or with general principles (traditional as well as emerging ones). The rapporteur is therefore obliged to investigate how the hypothetical case has been solved by the case law of the given legal system; whether this is the solution given by the other legal formants or not; whether all these formants are concordant, both from an internal point of view (the source of disaccord may be minority doctrines, including dissenting opinions in leading cases, opposite opinions in scholarly writings, etc), and from a diachronic point of view (whether the various solutions are recent achievements or were identical in the past), as well as whether the solution is considered to be a question of fact

[45] JH Merryman, *The Civil Law Tradition: An Introduction to the Legal Systems of Western Europe and Latin America* (2nd edn, Stanford UP 1985); K Zweigert and H Kötz, *Introduction to Comparative Law*, transl T Weir (3rd edn, OUP 1998) 63.

or a question of law. The latter factor may, of course, determine not only the degree to which the solution can be enforced by supreme courts on lower courts, but also the impact of judicial precedents on the solution.

Finally, the 'Metalegal Formants' level asks for a clear picture of the other elements affecting the operative and descriptive levels, such as policy considerations, economic factors, and social context and values, as well as the structure of the legal process (the organization of courts, constitutional architecture, etc): the kind of data no researcher can ever leave out whenever the aim is to understand what the law is.

VII. Caveats and promises

The analysis conducted in any book cannot be dissociated from the techniques through which the information and insights have been produced, and the present volume was largely carried out according to the methodology just described. However, to fully appreciate the strength and the limits of our survey, a few caveats need to be borne in mind.

First of all, at the core of the study are the responses given to the questionnaire by the rapporteurs. Responses inevitably express rapporteurs' subjective views on how their legal system would handle the claims envisaged by the questionnaire. Commitments to a school of thought, methodological and writing styles, deeply embedded beliefs, and self-narratives are likely to have affected our rapporteurs' answers to some extent.

Second, under many legal systems certain cases have received divergent interpretations, or have not yet been adjudicated by courts, regulated by statute, or discussed by scholars. When more than one interpretation was available, the rapporteurs were asked to present all the possible interpretations of the case, and to explain which one courts would be more likely to endorse (and possibly why). When no answer was easily available, the rapporteurs were asked not only to state overtly that the case had not yet been dealt with within their legal system, possibly explaining why, but also to analyse the position the courts could take when facing the problem in question. Although rapporteurs were called upon to base their interpretations and predictions on the state-of-the-art of their systems' legal formants, it is fairly clear that interpretation and prediction involve a great deal of discretion that cannot be eliminated.

Third, a further layer of complexity comes from the fact that European legal systems sometimes differ not only in their rules but also in the vocabulary, technicalities, and general frameworks they draw upon to solve tort law cases. Rules, vocabulary, technicalities, and frameworks have often led rapporteurs to read the cases in the light of their own understanding, thus affecting the tenor and breadth of the answers. While this understanding conveyed to us the 'spirit' of the legal culture it stemmed from, it also affected the comparability of the ensuing results. For instance, it is clear that, faced with similar facts, rapporteurs often focused their attention on different issues, depending on the cultural lens through which they understood the case.

Additional problems concern the language of the answers. It should be recalled that the language of the majority of the legal systems involved in this study is not English. Rapporteurs were thus obliged to translate concepts, notions, and rules from their own language to English—a process that often implies a good deal of simplification and (sometimes) distortion of national public tort law discourses.[46]

All the above are common features of all collective enterprises (whether acknowledged or not by their editors), as is the fact that not each and every national rapporteur has abided in full by the guidelines that were established at the outset of the project. Nevertheless, in most cases there is, I believe, broad enough compliance to produce the high-quality scientific output that the series editors hoped for.

[46] Contradictions often arise within the EU legal framework itself, because the EU institutions lack, among other features, a common vocabulary and a standard terminology capable of summarizing the different notions arising from the European linguistic and legal plurality. Contradictions may also appear within national legal contexts where the EU rules are to be implemented, due to the lack of homogeneity between the EU and national languages, concepts, and rules (von Bar, *The Common European Law of Torts* (n 7) 387–89; Koziol, 'Harmonising Tort Law' (n 12) 74–78).

PART II
THE LEGAL SYSTEMS SELECTED FOR COMPARISON
Principles and Remedies

3

Constitutional Foundations and the Design of the Austrian Liability of Public Bodies Act

Stefan Storr, Kathrin Bayer, Daniela Bereiter, and Luca Mischensky

I. Is there any formal constitutional provision concerning public authority liability?

Under Austrian law, public bodies may be liable under both public and private law. The formal constitutional provision concerning the liability under public law is Article 23 of the Federal Constitutional Law (hereinafter B-VG).[1]

Article 23 B-VG regulates the liability of the Federation, the Provinces, the municipalities and the other bodies and institutions (legal entities) established under public law. They are liable for the injury that persons (eg public officials) acting on their behalf in the execution of the laws have, through their unlawful behaviour, culpably inflicted on someone (Article 23(1) B-VG). The term 'in execution of the law' includes acts of jurisdiction and sovereign administration, meaning that a person must have caused damage while acting under public law. The Federal Act on the Liability of Territorial Authorities and other Bodies and Institutions of Public Law for Damage caused when Implementing the Law (hereinafter AHG)[2] regulates public authority liability in greater detail.

The AHG is not a strict public liability law; it refers rather to the civil law: According to § 1(1) AHG, the State entity is liable under the provisions of civil law for any damage to any person or any property caused by unlawful acts of persons at fault when implementing the law. In fact, the question of whether the claim for damages against a State entity exists is examined by the general rules of civil tort law.

A claim for damages is always brought against the State entity, and never against the unlawful and culpable acting organs implementing the law.

The conditions for a public liability claim are as follows:

(1) a sovereign action of a natural or legal person (organ) implementing the law on behalf of a State entity;
(2) damage (*Schaden*) caused by the person implementing the law;
(3) causality (*Kausalität*) between the damage and the implementation of the law;
(4) the unlawfulness (*Rechtswidrigkeit*) of the implementation; and
(5) fault (*Verschulden*).

[1] *Bundes-Verfassungsgesetz*, Federal Law Gazette No 1/1930 as amended.
[2] Abbreviated form: Liability of Public Bodies Act, Federal Law Gazette No 20/1949 as amended.

Stefan Storr, Kathrin Bayer, Daniela Bereiter, and Luca Mischensky, *Constitutional Foundations and the Design of the Austrian Liability of Public Bodies Act* In: *Tort Liability of Public Authorities in European Laws*. Edited by: Giacinto della Cananea and Roberto Caranta, Oxford University Press (2020). © The Contributors. DOI: 10.1093/oso/9780198867555.003.0003.

A natural or legal person acts unlawfully if it acts against legal provisions aiming to prevent damage.

According to § 1(1) AHG, public liability requires a culpable action or omission by a person implementing the law on behalf of a State entity. The State is liable for every degree of fault: for intent, gross negligence, and slight negligence. The degree of fault is important for two reasons. First, it determines the extent of public authority liability. If the organ acts in a way that is slightly negligent, the State is liable for the positive damage (financial loss); in the case of gross negligence or intent, the State is additionally liable for lost profit § 1324 Civil Law Code, hereinafter: ABGB[3]).[4] Further, the State entity has a right of recourse against its organs acting with intent or gross negligence (§ 3(1) AHG).

State organs are liable as experts under the provison of § 1299 ABGB, meaning that the Supreme Court on Civil (and Criminal) Matters (hereinafter OGH)[5] measures fault objectively. Hence, fault does not depend on the skills and abilities of the individual person in charge. The decisive factor is the behaviour that could be expected from a person entrusted with certain competences.[6] In fact, it needs to be examined whether the actions of the civil servant amount—taking into account the expectations of the legislator—to a gross breach of diligence,[7] especially if the civil servant has neglected obvious deliberations or actions in order to prevent the damage.[8] However, not every instance of incorrect behaviour justifies the assumption of fault from an objective perspective. Fault is to be denied if the application of the law, the legal opinion, or the interpretation of the law was still justifiable.[9]

II. Is there any general requirement to bring an administrative appeal or a complaint before an ombudsman or other public agency before bringing an action for damages against public authorities?

The procedure for a claim against a State entity is regulated in §§ 8 et seq AHG. Before taking legal action against the respective legal entity, the injured party is not required to consult an ombudsman or another public body.

However, before the injured party files a lawsuit, it must request a statement from the defendant State entity within a period of three months, declaring whether it wholly or partially accepts or totally rejects the claim for damages. The request to accept the compensation claim against the Federal Government has to be addressed to the *Finanzprokuratur* (finance procuration). If the injured party fails to issue such a request for compensation and the State entity thus acknowledges the claim in the legal

[3] *Allgemeines Bürgerliches Gesetzbuch*, JGS 946/1811 as amended.
[4] RIS-Justiz RS0030552.
[5] Pursuant to Article 92(1) B-VG, the OGH is the court of final instance in civil and criminal suits.
[6] RIS-Justiz RS0026381; OGH 4 April 2006, 1 Ob 51/06s.
[7] W Schragel, *Kommentar zum Amtshaftungsgesetz* (3rd edn, Manz 2003) para 168.
[8] OGH 17 October 1995, 1 Ob 20/94 = ecolex 1996, 168 (Graf) = ÖBA 1996, 549 (Rebhahn).
[9] RIS-Justiz RS0049951; RS0049955; RS0050216; eg OGH 28 July 2017, 1 Ob 105/17y.

dispute, the State entity may demand reimbursement of costs for the legal action (§ 8(2) AHG).

Further, the injured party has the obligation to minimize damages. According to § 2(2) AHG, an action for damages is not admissible if the injured person would have been able to avoid damages by pursuing any legal remedy or by an appeal to an administrative court and a final appeal to the Supreme Administrative Court (*Verwaltungsgerichtshof*, hereinafter VwGH).

III. Are there different courts or other public agencies for the annulment of unlawful administrative decisions and for the award of damages?

In Austria, there is a strict separation of jurisdiction between claims against administrative actions and claims concerning public liability.

The administrative legal protection system focuses on an appeal to an Administrative Court (*Verwaltungsgericht*, hereinafter VwG). Appeals brought before the VwG may regard unlawful rulings by administrative authorities, the unlawful exercise of direct administrative power, and compulsion, as well as those on the ground of breach of the duty to reach a decision by an administrative authority (Article 130(1) B-VG). The VwG's decision may be subject to an appeal, addressed to the VwGH or to the Constitutional Court (*Verfassungsgerichtshof*, hereinafter VfGH) if constitutional issues are involved (Article 144(1) B-VG).

The jurisdiction for a decision regarding a claim in first instance against the State entity rests exclusively with the regional court in charge of civil matters (*Landesgericht*) in whose jurisdiction the infringement of the law occurred (§ 9(1) AHG). This jurisdiction is exclusive; the VwGs are not competent to decide on public liability claims. An appeal has to be addressed to the Higher Regional Court (*Oberlandesgericht*) and then to the OGH.

If the decision concerning public liability depends on whether the decision of an administrative authority or a VwG is unlawful, and if there is no relevant finding by the VwGH or the VfGH, the civil court suspends its proceeding and files a request to the VwGH for a ruling (§ 11 AHG). This does not apply in legal matters falling under the jurisdiction of the VfGH.

4

The EU Institutions Liability between the Member States Principles and the Causality Standards of the EU Court of Justice

Barbara Marchetti

The analysis of the EU administration from the viewpoint of tort liability is both interesting and important, but raises some particular issues. Two preliminary remarks are thus necessary. First, both the quick introduction that follows and the answers given to the hypothetical cases refer exclusively to the liability of the institutions and agencies of the EU. Any issue concerning Member States' liability for EU law infringement is excluded. Second, as observed in Chapter 1, some of the cases covered by the questionnaire are difficult to replicate in the context of the EU, either because of the difficulty of identifying similar functions (eg the case concerning police officers' liability), or because of certain peculiarities of the administrative procedures through which the EU exercises its administrative functions.

I. Is there any formal constitutional provision concerning public authority liability?

The EU liability system is regulated by Article 340 paragraph II of the Treaty on the Functioning of the EU (TFEU):

> [T]he Union shall, in accordance with the general principles common to the laws of the Member States, make good any damage caused by its institutions or its servants in the performance of their duties.

This provision does not contain any substantial rule or principle itself, but entrusts the Court with developing and creating these principles in the light of the common principles of the Member States.

According to the case law, the tort liability of the Union is established when the injured party succeeds in proving three conditions: (i) the institution's unlawful conduct; (ii) the causal link between the unlawful conduct and the damage; and (iii) the existence of certain and current damage.

A conduct is unlawful not only when the act of the institution is illegal, but if it is demonstrated that the rule breached is intended to protect the individual and that its infringement is sufficiently qualified because the authority seriously and manifestly

Barbara Marchetti, *The EU Institutions Liability between the Member States Principles and the Causality Standards of the EU Court of Justice* In: *Tort Liability of Public Authorities in European Laws.* Edited by: Giacinto della Cananea and Roberto Caranta, Oxford University Press (2020). © The Contributors. DOI: 10.1093/oso/9780198867555.003.0004.

violated the limits of its discretionary power.[1] Consequently, the mere fact that a decision of the Commission holding that a concentration is incompatible with the common market has been quashed by the Court is not sufficient to prove the serious character of the breach. Mere errors of assessment would not suffice for the purposes of liability in tort, since this could inhibit the Commission as a regulator of competition.[2]

On the contrary, in the event that the institution has a considerably reduced—or even non-existent—margin of discretion, the mere infringement of EU law may be sufficient to establish the existence of a serious and manifest infringement.[3]

The injured party must also prove the causal link between the unlawful conduct and the damage. According to the case law, there is a causal link when there is a sufficiently direct relationship between the unlawful conduct and the alleged damage. The contested conduct must, specifically, be the determining cause of the damage.[4]

It may be noted that the EU Court does not always consider the general principles of administrative law as higher law intended to protect individuals. While this is the case with the right to be heard,[5] legitimate expectations,[6] non-discrimination,[7] and proportionality recognized as conferring rights on individuals, major doubts exist regarding the principle of good administration, which confers rights only when it is an expression of specific rights, including the right to have one's affairs handled impartially and fairly.[8]

II. Is there any general requirement to bring an administrative appeal or a complaint before an ombudsman or other public agency before bringing an action for damages against public authorities?

In EU law, a private party is not required to apply for an administrative remedy before bringing an action for compensation before the Court. The injured person can also sue

[1] It should be noted that not every judgment by the Court contains an assessment of each of the conditions for liability, as the Court readily stops examining the case if it finds that one of the conditions for liability is not fulfilled. See P Aalto, *Public Liability in EU Law* (Hart Publishing 2011) 110.

[2] On the relationship between discretion and sufficiently serious breach, after *Bergaderm*, see Case T-155/99 *Dieckmann & Hansen v Commission* [2001] ECR II-3143, judgment of the Court of First Instance 23 October 2001; Case T-196/99 *Area Cova and others v Commission and Council* [2001] ECR II-3597, judgment of the Court of First Instance 6 December 2001, but also Case T-285/03 *Agraz and others v Commission* [2005] ECR II-1063, judgment of the Court of First Instance 17 March 2005.

[3] See, also for references to the case law, C Hilson 'The Role of Discretion in EC Law on Non-Contractual Liability' (2005) 42 CMLR 677; Aalto (n 1) 134.

[4] Joined cases T-440/03, T-121/04, T-208/04, T-365/04, and T-484/04 *Arizmendi and others v Council and Commission* [2009] ECR II-04883, judgment of the Court 18 December 2009, and the cited case law; Case T-217/11 *Claire Staelen v European Ombudsman* [2017] ECLI:EU:C:2017:256, judgment of the Court 29 April 2015.

[5] Joined cases T-481/93 and 484/93 *Vereniging van Exporteurs in Levende Varkens v Commissio* [1995] ECR II-02941, judgment of the Court of First Instance 13 December 1995.

[6] Case 74/74 *CNTA v Commission* [1975] ECR 533, judgment of the Court 15 June 1976.

[7] Case T-57/00 *Banan-Kompaniet v Conseil and Commission* [2003] ECR II-00607, judgment of the Court of First Instance 6 March 2003.

[8] Case T-193/04 *Tillack v Commission* [2006] ECR II-3995, judgment of the Court of First Instance 4 October 2006.

the EU for damages without challenging the unlawful act before the Court through Article 263 TFEU.[9]

Recently, the Court held that the action for damages is 'an autonomous form of action, with a particular purpose to fulfil within the system of legal remedies and subject to conditions of use dictated by its specific purpose'.[10] However, an action for damages cannot seek to obtain the same effects that could have been achieved by promptly proposing annulment.[11]

It should also be noted that if the claim for damages concerns damages deriving from the unlawfulness of the contested administrative decision, the Court rejects the claim for compensation when it has a close link with the application for annulment which has itself been rejected.[12] A particular problem arises when the damage is produced by a national measure implementing an EU act: in this case, the action for damages before the EU courts is conditioned by the fact that the party has obtained effective protection before the national court, including with regard to the compensation for the prejudice to its own interests through the national measure.[13]

III. Are there different courts or other public agencies for the annulment of unlawful administrative decisions and for the award of damages?

According to the provisions of Article 268 TFEU, actions for damages are brought before the Court of Justice of the European Union (General Court and Court of Justice), which is also the court for bringing an action for annulment (Art 263 TFEU).

With regard to acts adopted by some European administrative agencies, however, the founding regulations may provide that the challenge of the decision must first be made before specific Boards of Appeal instituted within the agencies. In this case, an application for review has to be brought before the administrative Board of Appeal, while an action for damages should be brought before the EU courts pursuant to Article 340 TFEU. However, if the administrative appeal is not satisfactory to the

[9] Case 4/69 *Lütticke v Commission* [1971] ECR 325, judgment of the Court 28 April 1971; Case 5/71 *Aktien-Zuckerfabrik Schöppensstedt v Council* [1971] ECR 975, judgment of the Court 2 December 1971; see also E Cujo, 'L'autonomie du recourse en indemnité par rapport au recourse en annulation—évolutions jurisprudentielles' [1999] RMCUE 414; F Cortese, *La questione della pregiudizialità amministrativa. Il risarcimento del danno da provvedimento illegittimo tra diritto sostanziale e diritto processuale* (Cedam 2007).

[10] Case 234/02 *Mediator v Lamberts* [2004] ECR I-02803, judgment of the Court 23 March 2004.

[11] Case 25/62 *Plaumann & Co v Commission* [1963] ECR 95, judgment of the Court 15 July 1963; Case T-514/93 *Cobrecaf v Commission* [1995] ECR II-00621, judgment of the Court 15 March 1995; see also K Gutman, 'The Evolution of the Action for Damages against the European Union and Its Place in the System of Judicial Protection' (2011) 48 CMLR 704: '[T]he development of this line of case law indicates that the Union courts strictly patrol the boundaries of this exception, so as to preserve as far as possible the autonomous nature of the action for damages.' See also Case T-166/98 *Dolianova and others* [2004] ECR II-3991, judgment of the Court of First Instance 23 November 2004.

[12] Case C-274/99 *Connolly v Commission* [2001] ECR I-1611 para 129, judgment of the Court 6 March 2001; Case C-417/05 *Commission v Fernández Gómez* [2006] ECR I-8481, judgment of the Court 14 September 2006; Case T-584/16 *HF v Parliament* [2017] OJ C187/14, judgment of the General Court 24 April 2017.

[13] Case 281/82 *Uniflex v Commission and Council* [1983] ECR 4063, judgment of the Court 12 April 1984; Case 175/84 *Krohn v Commission* [1986] ECR 753, judgment of the Court 26 February 1986.

appellant, they could bring an action for annulment before the Court of Justice and, at the same time, bring the action for damages before it.

Until 1 September 2016, a Civil Service Tribunal, created on 2 November 2004, had a specialized jurisdiction for civil service disputes alongside the Court of Justice and the General Court.

5

Government Liability in France

A Special Regime under General Principles

Thomas Perroud

I. Is there any formal constitutional provision concerning public authority liability?

There is no formal provision in the French Constitution of 1958 (*Cinquième République*) concerning public authority liability. This is due, in part, to the fact that French administrative law has been developed principally by the *Conseil d'Etat* (Council of State). However, the *Conseil Constitutionnel* ('Constitutional Council') has established some principles regarding compensation.

First, concerning private persons, the *Conseil Constitutionnel* established that the right to claim for damages is a requirement derived from Article 4 of the Declaration of the Rights of Man and of the Citizen (1789),[1] and that any person whose negligent or voluntary act (*faute*) causes an injury to another is obliged to pay compensation for damage.[2] Therefore, the legislator cannot exclude any type of reparation, even when it is competent to limit it or to create a special regime. This conclusion was recognized for the first time in decision 82-144 DC,[3] when the *Conseil Constitutionnel* declared Article 8 of a legislative project unconstitutional for eliminating any possibility of reparation in cases of prejudices caused by negligent or voluntary acts of workers in the context of a labour conflict.

Second, there is no 'constitutionalization of public authorities' liability',[4] and the *Conseil Constitutionnel* has not established any principle regarding their liability. Nevertheless, the *Conseil* has limited the legislator's power when it disproportionately restrains the right to compensation when public authorities' acts infringe the equality principle:

> 16. Considering that paragraph 3 of Article 3-II, conceived in restrictive terms, necessarily limits the compensation for 'damage resulting only from the installation, maintenance of the means of diffusion by radio or the equipment necessary for their operation'; that this wording dismisses the reparation of all losses other than those

[1] Article 4—'Liberty consists of doing anything *which does not harm others*: thus, the exercise of the natural rights of each man has only those borders which assure other members of the society the fruition of these same rights. These borders can be determined only by the law.'

[2] Cons Const 9 November 1999 No 99-419 DC (concerning civil solidarity pacts).

[3] Cons Const 22 October 1982 No 82-144 DC (concerning staff representatives).

[4] J Moreau, 'La responsabilité administrative' in P Gonod, F Melleray, and P Yolka (eds), *Traité de droit administratif*, vol 2 (Dalloz 2011) 636.

Thomas Perroud, *Government Liability in France* In: *Tort Liability of Public Authorities in European Laws*.
Edited by: Giacinto della Cananea and Roberto Caranta, Oxford University Press (2020). © The Contributors.
DOI: 10.1093/oso/9780198867555.003.0005.

> strictly specified; that, however, the principle of equality of public burdens would not allow exclusion from the right to compensation of an element of compensable damage resulting from the public work [. . .].[5]

According to this decision, Article 13 of the Declaration[6] can be understood as the constitutional foundation of one of the legal regimes of liability without misconduct—the breach of the equality of public burdens.[7] *The Conseil Constitutionnel* also explained that the Law's silence does not obstruct the right to claim for reparation when the legal provisions create special and abnormal damage, repaired in the case of a breach of equality of public burdens.[8] In another decision, the *Conseil Constitutionnel* declared the exclusion of moral suffering constitutional as a recoverable loss in the event of expropriation.[9]

In conclusion, there is no general constitutional principle regarding the liability of the public authorities, but this does not prevent the *Conseil Constitutionnel* from controlling laws passed in this domain using other principles. However, the heart of the French public authorities' liability is defined by the *Conseil d'Etat*.

II. Is there any general requirement to bring an administrative appeal or a complaint before an ombudsman or other public agency before bringing an action for damages against public authorities?

The French tradition, now codified in Article R421-3 of the Administrative justice code (*Code de la Justice Administrative*, CJA) is that the existence of an administrative act is a prior requirement for any action before the administrative court (*decision préalable*). If the Administration has not issued any act, the person must make a request and wait for an explicit or implicit answer before bringing any action. Since 1864, no answer from the authority after two months has been considered a refusal, and it allows the party to bring an action before the administrative court. However, Law 2013/1005 of 12 November 2013 establishes the general rule that administrative silence means acceptance.[10]

In cases of government liability under Article R- 421- 1 of the CJA, 'any claim concerning the payment of an amount of money (which includes any claim of liability) will be heard only if the party has made a formal request to the Administration first'. Therefore, the aggrieved person must first make a request to the Administration.

[5] Cons Const 13 December 1985 No 85-198 DC (concerning television broadcasting).

[6] Article 13—'For the maintenance of the public force and for the expenditures of administration, a common contribution is indispensable; *it must be equally distributed to all the citizens*, according to their ability to pay.'

[7] However, some scholars disagree: see Moreau (n 4) 636.

[8] Cons Const 27 November 2001 No 2001-451 DC (concerning work accidents).

[9] Cons Const 11 June 2011 No 2010-87 DC (concerning *expropriation*).

[10] Though the general rule is: silence means acceptance, there are 2,400 exceptions and 1,200 cases of positive administrative silence. See the Senate report: <www.senat.fr/rap/r14-629/r14-6293.html> accessed 18 June 2020.

After two months, the lack of an answer is considered a refusal of the payment requested under Article L 231-4 of CRPA (Code of the relations between the public and the administration—*Code des relations entre le public et l'administration*) and the aggrieved person is entitled to bring an action before the courts.

In the case of damage caused by an explicit administrative act, it is important to verify on a case-by-case basis whether an administrative appeal is a prior requirement for the action (*recours administratif préalable*). For example, in the case of decisions concerning the military, including sanctions, it is mandatory to appeal to a special commission before bringing the action to the court.

III. Are there different courts or other public agencies for the annulment of unlawful administrative decisions and for the award of damages?

One of the main characteristics of French law is the existence of two separate jurisdictions: ordinary courts and administrative courts. This duality officially came into being in 1790, when Law 16-24 provided that 'judicial functions are and should remain separated from administrative ones. Ordinary courts *should not interfere* in any way whatsoever with the activities of public authorities, *nor hear a claim brought against a public authority* in relation to the performance of their official duty.' Both the administration and the *Conseil d'Etat* were in charge of hearing such claims until Law 24 May of 1872 transformed the *Conseil d'Etat* into an independent entity from the administration.[11]

When a statute does not determine the competent jurisdiction, the general principles established by the Law of 1790 and the *Tribunal des conflits* case law must be followed. That is first, the organic criteria: is there any public entity involved in the case, including the State, a local authority, or another agency or a public enterprise? Second, does this entity act as a 'public authority' *(puissance publique)*? Third, does the activity aim to provide a public service (*service public*)?

The importance of these factors varies. If the State acts as an authority to guarantee a public service, then the administrative court will hear the claim. However, the administrative court will also be competent to judge the acts of private entities in charge of a public service when they use public privileges. In other cases, ordinary courts will judge the questions related to the economic and industrial services of public enterprises and ordinary acts of public entities.

In other circumstances, including some regarding public authority liability, the legislator identified the relevant jurisdiction:

1. The Education code establishes that any prejudice caused by a student or to any student concerning the school activities should be raised before the ordinary court of the place where the damage was caused.[12]

[11] S Braconnier, 'France' in J-B Auby (ed), *Codification of Administrative Procedure* (Bruylant 2014) 188.
[12] Article L911-4, 5 April 1937.

2. Law 31 December of 1957 determines that ordinary courts are competent in any claim in tort seeking the reparation of damage caused by any vehicle.
3. According to the Public Health Code, ordinary courts are competent to establish liability and reparation in cases of unlawful hospitalization ordered by the departmental authority (*le préfet*) or the mayor.[13]
4. In the event of damage caused by crimes during gatherings and manifestations, the State is liable and the administrative court is competent.[14]
5. The 'adjudicatory acts' (*décisions individuelles*) of the Financial Markets Authority (*Autorité des marchés financiers*—AMF),[15] including sanctions, will be judged by the ordinary courts.
6. The annulment of some decisions of the *Autorité de régulation de communications électroniques et des postes (ARCEP—Regulatory Authority for Electronic Communications and Postal Services)* regarding the interconnection obligations and access to infrastructure will be raised before the Court of Appeal of Paris.[16] However, the *Conseil d'Etat* is the competent forum regarding the sanctions ordered by the ARCEP.[17]

There is no substantial difference in terms of public liability between national and local authorities. Liability depends on their functions. For example, Article L211-10 of the homeland security code (*Code de la sécurité intérieure*) establishes that the State is liable in cases of crimes and offences committed during gatherings (strict liability),[18] but the State may bring an action against the local authorities if the damage was a consequence of their misconduct because local authorities oversee public order.[19]

In general, the *Tribunal des conflits* determined that: 'administrative courts are competent for the litigation of acts and operations of public authorities'[20] following the three criteria, unless statutory legislation defines otherwise.

[13] Article L3216-1 *Code de la santé publique*.
[14] Article L2216-3 *Code de collectivités territoriales*.
[15] Article L621-30 *Code monétaire et financier*.
[16] Article L36-8 *Code des postes et des communications électroniques*.
[17] Article L311-4 *Code de la justice administrative*.
[18] In France, the State will be liable in case of *attroupements ou rassemblements*, and it is the *Conseil d'Etat* that defines what is considered a spontaneous gathering. If the damage is not the consequence of a crime during a gathering, the victim can claim damages, but he or she must prove the fault.
[19] Article L211-10 *Code de la sécurité intérieure*.
[20] T confl, 10 July 1956, *Soc Bourgogne-Bois*, R 586 No 1565.

6
The System of Public Authority Liability in Germany

Ferdinand Wollenschläger and Johannes Stapf

I. Is there any formal constitutional provision concerning public authority liability?

From a general constitutional law perspective, public authority liability constitutes one form of legal protection of the individual and may thus be rooted in the *Rechtsstaatsprinzip* (rule of law), the individual (fundamental) right interfered with, and the guarantee to effective legal protection (Art 19 para 4 *Grundgesetz*, GG).[1] In terms of legal protection, primary legal protection, ie the possibility to challenge unlawful State action, and secondary legal protection, ie the award of compensation for damage resulting from such action, must be distinguished (cf on their relationship section II below).

More specifically, the German constitution (Grundgesetz; GG) contains a provision concerning public authority liability, namely Article 34 GG[2]. It stipulates:

> [1]If any person, in the exercise of a public office entrusted to him, violates his official duty to a third party, liability shall rest principally with the state or public body that employs him.[2] In the event of intentional wrongdoing or gross negligence, the right of recourse against the individual officer shall be preserved.[3] The ordinary courts shall not be closed to claims for compensation or indemnity.

This provision can only be fully understood by considering first the various models of liability for wrongful State action, namely (i) the personal liability of an official acting for the State; (ii) a direct liability of the State for wrongful action of its officials (*Staatshaftung*); (iii) derived liability of the State, ie a shift of the official's liability to the State (*Amtshaftung*); and (iv) cumulative liability of the State and the official acting on its behalf.[3] Second, it has to be noted that § 839 of the German Civil Code (BGB)[4], which entered into force on 1 January 1900 and thus before the Basic Law, stipulates the liability of the official in case of breach of official duty. Paragraph 1 sentence 1 of

[1] J Wieland, 'Art 34' in H Dreier (ed), *Grundgesetz Kommentar*, vol 2 (3rd edn, Mohr Siebeck 2015) para 30.

[2] *Grundgesetz* (German Basic Law), English version <www.gesetze-im-internet.de/englisch_gg/englisch_gg.html> accessed 19 June 2020.

[3] H Maurer and C Waldhoff, *Allgemeines Verwaltungsrecht* (19th edn, CH Beck 2017) § 26 para 1.

[4] *Bürgerliches Gesetzbuch* (German Civil Code), English version <www.gesetze-im-internet.de/englisch_bgb/englisch_bgb.html#p3524> accessed 19 June 2020.

Ferdinand Wollenschläger and Johannes Stapf, *The System of Public Authority Liability in Germany* In: *Tort Liability of Public Authorities in European Laws.* Edited by: Giacinto della Cananea and Roberto Caranta, Oxford University Press (2020).
 DOI: 10.1093/oso/9780198867555.003.0006.

this provision reads: 'If an official intentionally or negligently breaches the official duty incumbent upon him in relation to a third party, then he must compensate the third party for damage arising from this.'

Against this background, Article 34 GG is widely and notably (in view of the historical development)[5] understood as a provision ordering the assumption of the liability of the official stipulated for in § 839 BGB by the State (*Amtshaftung*), but not as a basis for claims itself.[6] Other views in the literature read Article 34 GG as the legal basis for claims which is concretized by § 839 BGB.[7] At any rate, it must be noted that both provisions have a partially diverging scope of application. Whereas Article 34 GG is limited to public law action of officials, but extends to civil servants and other employees of the State, § 839 BGB covers public and private law actions of the State, but is limited to civil servants as far as private law action of the State is concerned.[8]

Article 34 sentence 2 GG provides for 'recourse against the individual officer' in cases of intent or gross negligence, whereas sentence 3 establishes the jurisdiction of the ordinary courts for claims for compensation (see in this regard section III below).[9]

With regard to the intra-State distribution of liability for breaches of supra- and international obligations, Article 104a para 6 sentence 1 GG stipulates: 'In accord with the internal allocation of competencies and responsibilities, the Federation and the *Länder* shall bear the costs entailed by a violation of obligations incumbent on Germany under supranational or international law.'

Finally, it should be noted that, in addition to the aforementioned constitutional provisions, German law comprises further claims resulting from State interference with individual rights: written and unwritten, established for centuries and comparatively new, widely accepted and controversial, general and sector-specific, general and rights-specific, directed specifically against the State and of general application, reacting to unlawful and—exceptionally—also to lawful actions, aiming at financial and further forms of compensation. Moreover, the EU law requirement of State liability for breaches of EU law had to be accommodated within the national system, which has entailed some modifications (eg liability for wrongful acts of the judiciary and the legislature). This background and variety explains the constant calls for consolidation, reform, and codification. Yet, a codification of the year 1981 was annulled by the *Bundesverfassungsgericht* because of the lack of specific competence of the Federal State.[10] Such competence was created in 1994,[11] but has not yet been implemented.[12]

[5] On the historical background, see Maurer and Waldhoff (n 3) § 26 paras 2ff.

[6] BVerfG 19 October 1982—2 BvF 1/81, BVerfGE 61, 149 (198); H-J Papier, 'Art 34' in T Maunz and G Dürig (eds), *Grundgesetz Kommentar* (54th edn, CH Beck January 2009) para 11; Wieland (n 1) paras 10, 33.

[7] Maurer and Waldhoff (n 3) § 26 para 8; similar H Jarass and B Pieroth, *Grundgesetz für die Bundesrepublik Deutschland* (16th edn, CH Beck 2020) Art 34 para 1. Diverging SU Pieper, 'Art 34' in B Schmidt-Bleibtreu, H Hofmann, and H-G Henneke (eds), *Kommentar zum Grundgesetz* (14th edn, CH Beck 2017) para 3.

[8] See Maurer and Waldhoff (n 3) § 26 para 9.

[9] For a detailed discussion of Art 34 sentences 2 and 3 GG, see eg Wieland (n 1) paras 61ff.

[10] BVerfG 19 October 1982—2 BvF 1/81, BVerfGE 61, 149.

[11] See Art 74 para 1 no 25 GG, introduced by the *Gesetz zur Änderung des Grundgesetzes (Artikel 3, 20a, 28, 29, 72, 74, 75, 76, 77, 80, 87, 93, 118a, and 125a)* of 27 October 1994, BGBl I 3146ff.

[12] On the design of a future implementation, namely the assumption of a violation of subjective rights as a basis for liability, see B Grzeszick, *Rechte und Ansprüche* (Mohr Siebeck 2002) 169 ff; B Grzeszick, 'Notwendigkeit und Grundzüge eines Staatshaftungsgesetzes' [2015] ZRP 162.

A peculiarity of State liability law resulted from German reunification in 1990: unlike in West Germany, a State liability code[13] had existed in former East Germany.[14] Its provisions were incorporated into the law of the new eastern *Länder*.[15] Nowadays, traces of this can still be found in the law of Brandenburg, Saxony-Anhalt, and Thuringia, although it should be highlighted that its overall meaning is limited[16]: in Saxony-Anhalt, the provisions have been restricted to claims brought for an infringement of the right to property, and only 'appropriate compensation' may be obtained;[17] in Brandenburg and Thuringia, procedural and substantive amendments[18] were made and the courts construe the (otherwise wide[19]) provisions narrowly.[20]

II. Is there any general requirement to bring an administrative appeal or a complaint before an ombudsman or other public agency before bringing an action for damages against public authorities?

As constitutional background, it should be noted that the guarantee to effective legal protection (Art 19 para 4 GG) implies the primacy of primary legal protection, ie the primacy of quashing unlawful decisions over awarding damages for having to tolerate them, since the former has to be considered more effective than the latter.[21]

[13] *Gesetz zur Regelung der Staatshaftung in der Deutschen Demokratischen Republik* (East German Public Authority Liability Act) of 12 May 1969, GBl I 34.

[14] Elaborately, F Ossenbühl and M Cornils, *Staatshaftungsrecht* (6th edn, CH Beck 2013) 554 ff, also addressing its legal deficiencies (565).

[15] Anlage II (chapter III, topic B: Bürgerliches Recht, section III) of the unification treaty; see *Gesetz zu dem Vertrag vom 31. August 1990 zwischen der Bundesrepublik Deutschland und der Deutschen Demokratischen Republik über die Herstellung der Einheit Deutschlands—Einigungsvertragsgesetz—und der Vereinbarung vom 18. September 1990* of 23 September 1990, BGBl II 885, 1168.

[16] T von Danwitz, 'Art 34' in H von Mangoldt and others (eds), *Grundgesetz*, vol 2 (7th edn, CH Beck 2018) paras 135f.

[17] See § 1 para 1 of the *Gesetz zur Regelung von Entschädigungsansprüchen im Lande Sachsen-Anhalt in der Fassung der Bekanntmachung vom 1. Januar 1997*, GVBl II 17; cf Ossenbühl and Cornils (n 14) 572. The provisions can, therefore, be regarded as more restrictive than the conditions of an 'enteignungsgleicher Eingriff', cf von Danwitz (n 16) para 137.

[18] C Dörr, '§ 839' in B Gsell and others (eds), *BeckOGK BGB* (CH Beck 1 July 2020) paras 951f.

[19] The East German State Liability Code, representing a concept of direct liability (see text above), does not, for instance, stipulate intent or negligence as a requirement for liability; see von Danwitz (n 16) para 136.

[20] See Grzeszick, 'Notwendigkeit und Grundzüge eines Staatshaftungsgesetzes' (n 12) 162, 163; P Reinert, '§ 839' in G Bamberger and others (eds), *BeckOK BGB* (54th edn, CH Beck 1 May 2020) para 159 with further references. As to further differences compared with the old western *Länder*, see T Gelen, 'Staatshaftungsgesetz in Brandenburg und Änderungen des Anwendungsbereichs' [2009] LKV 15.

[21] F Wollenschläger, 'The Allocation of Limited Rights by the Administration: Challenges of Legal Protection' in P Adriaanse and others (eds), *Scarcity and the State*, vol 1: *The Allocation of Limited Rights by the Administration* (Intersentia 2016) 93ff, 96ff, 119; cf F Wollenschläger, *Verteilungsverfahren* (Mohr Siebeck 2010) 89, 634; see ibid 131ff and F Wollenschläger, 'EU Law Principles for Allocating Scarce Goods and the Emergence of an Allocation Procedure. Identifying Substantive and Procedural Standards and Developing a New Type of Administrative Procedure' (2015–16) 8 REALaw 205, 226ff for the corresponding EU law principle.

Turning to the specific question, § 839 para 3 BGB stipulates an exclusion of damages if the claimant has not brought an administrative appeal or a complaint before another public agency prior to bringing an action for damages against public authorities. It reads: 'Liability for damage does not arise if the injured person has intentionally or negligently failed to avert the damage by having recourse to appeal.' This provision reflects the general principle of contributory negligence.[22] Consequently, damages are excluded if the claimant failed to appeal against the administrative decision itself.[23]

III. Are there different courts or other public agencies for the annulment of unlawful administrative decisions and for the award of damages?

Article 34 sentence 3 GG provides that '[t]he ordinary courts shall not be closed to claims for compensation or indemnity'. This provision establishes the jurisdiction of ordinary (ie private law) courts for claims resulting from public authority liability,[24] a choice which may be explained by the history of public authority liability in Germany: With § 839 BGB as a pre-constitutional basis for claims (see section I above), liability of the official had been established; thus, both claimant and respondent had been private parties in those days. Notwithstanding the later introduction of Article 34 sentence 1 GG, which orders the assumption of liability by the state (see section I above), jurisdiction rested with the ordinary courts.[25] Furthermore, administrative courts had been introduced only from the middle of the nineteenth century in Germany and, thus, significantly later than the ordinary courts.[26] For this reason, their independence was doubted in earlier days and, consequently, jurisdiction in cases dealing with public authority liability was vested in the ordinary courts;[27] however, this argument no longer applies.[28] Additionally, ordinary courts are more often concerned with questions of liability, which is regarded as an argument in favour of their competence to hear cases of public authority liability.[29] In contrast, jurisdiction for the annulment of unlawful administrative decisions lies with the administrative courts, whose jurisdiction extends to 'all public-law disputes of a non-constitutional nature

[22] M Morlok, '§ 52' in W Hoffmann-Riem, E Schmidt-Aßmann, and A Voßkuhle (eds), *Grundlagen des Verwaltungsrechts*, vol 3 (2nd edn, CH Beck 2013) para 116; Wollenschläger, 'The Allocation of Limited Rights by the Administration' (n 21) 93ff, 119; H-J Papier and F Shirvani, '§ 839' in FJ Säcker and others (eds), *Münchener Kommentar zum Bürgerlichen Gesetzbuch*, vol 6 (7th edn, CH Beck 2017) para 329.

[23] Morlok (n 22) para 116.

[24] Wieland (n 1) para 63.

[25] Ossenbühl and Cornils (n 14) 122; von Danwitz (n 16) 130.

[26] cf C Waldhoff, 'Einführung' in KF Gärditz (ed), VwGO (2nd edn, Carl Heymanns 2018) paras 8ff.

[27] Papier and Shirvani (n 22) para 377.

[28] See P Dagtoglou, 'Art 34' in W Kahl, C Waldhof, and C Walter (eds), *Bonner Kommentar zum Grundgesetz* (2nd rev, 25th edn, CF Müller September 1970) para 365.

[29] Maurer and Waldhoff (n 3) § 26 para 50. Doubting, von Danwitz (n 16) para 130.

insofar as the disputes are not explicitly allocated to another court by a federal statute' (§ 40 para 1 sentence 1 VwGO[30]). Thus, jurisdiction is split,[31] a situation which has been criticized.[32] It has to be added, though, that in cases of the administration acting in the forms of private law (eg conclusion of a private law contract), civil courts have jurisdiction.

[30] *Verwaltungsgerichtsordnung* (German Code of Administrative Court Procedure), English version <www.gesetze-im-internet.de/englisch_vwgo/englisch_vwgo.html> accessed 19 June 2020.

[31] Ossenbühl and Cornils (n 14) 121f; cf K Stern, *Das Staatsrecht der Bundesrepublik Deutschland*, vol IV/ 2 (CH Beck 2011) 2097; Wieland (n 1) para 63.

[32] Elaborately, Stern (n 31) 2096ff.

7
Public Authority Liability in Hungary
Constitutional Principles and Judicial Remedies

Lilla Berkes

I. Is there any formal constitutional provision concerning public authority liability?

Government liability is regulated by the Hungarian Constitution.[1] Before 2012, the old constitution only contained a very general provision, Article 70/K,[2] supplemented by another concerning unlawful arrest or detainment (Art 55(3)), but none was taken into account in civil procedures. Within the new Constitution (2011), which entered into force in 2012, two provisions regulate government liability. First, Article XXIV (2) explicitly states the liability of public authorities. It states that 'Everyone shall have the right to compensation for any damage unlawfully caused to him or her by the authorities in the performance of their duties, as provided for by an Act.' Second, Article IV (4) includes compensation for restrictions implemented by administrative bodies.[3] It provides that '[e]veryone shall have the right to compensation, whose liberty has been restricted without a well-founded reason or unlawfully'.[4] Though there are some minor decisions of the Constitutional Court regarding Article XXIV (2), according to

[1] Over the past eight years, all the important acts and regulations (decrees) have been changed in Hungary, some of them recently, so the numbers of available judicial cases are limited. Also, in Hungary, not all the decisions are available to the public. According to Act CLXI of 2011—on the Organization and Administration of the Courts s 163:

> (1) The Kúria (Curia) shall publish uniformity decisions, Curia decisions on principle, court decisions on principle and its decisions adopted on the substance of a matter; the Court of Appeal shall publish its decisions adopted on the substance of a matter, the Administrative and Labour court shall publish its decisions adopted in administrative actions on the substance of a matter if the reviewed administrative decision was adopted in a single instance proceeding, and no ordinary appeal may be lodged against the court decision in the *Bírósági Határozatok Gyűjteménye* (Register of Court Decisions) in digital form.

Other decisions are only published if the president of the court orders it.

Regarding the translations used: in the first version of this chatper, there were no translations for the latest acts available, so I used mine. This changed later: currently <www.njt.hu> accessed 19 June 2020 (the official collection of national laws) has some unofficial translations available for public use. However, I used other, not publicly available unofficial translations published by Wolters Kluwer as part of their collection of national laws in a database widely used in Hungary, but it is only for individual and institutional subscription holders. The advantage of this database is that the repealed acts and regulations are also available. For the translations, a higher subscription price is required.

[2] Article 70/K stated that 'Claims arising from infringement on fundamental rights, and objections to the decisions of public authorities regarding the fulfilment of duties may be brought before a court of law.'

[3] eg custody, confinement, detention.

[4] Decision 3105/2018, only available in Hungarian.

Lilla Berkes, *Public Authority Liability in Hungary* In: *Tort Liability of Public Authorities in European Laws.* Edited by: Giacinto della Cananea and Roberto Caranta, Oxford University Press (2020). © The Contributors.
DOI: 10.1093/oso/9780198867555.003.0007.

the Civil Code (CC), such provision recognizes and protects a fundamental right, and is implemented by the detailed rules of the CC governing public authority liability.

II. Is there any general requirement to bring an administrative appeal or a complaint before an ombudsman or other public agency before bringing an action for damages against public authorities?

In Hungary, there was always a need to exhaust the possible remedies before bringing an action for damages against a public authority, but there was uncertainty whether this included only the administrative appeal or the review by the administrative court as well. The previous CC required only the ordinary remedy—the administrative appeal—to be exhausted. Judicial review of the administrative decision was an extraordinary remedy. However, according to judicial practice, if there was a theoretical possibility of repairing the damage through the administrative court procedure, this remedy had to be exhausted, too.[5] If the ordinary remedy was unable to repair the damage, there was no need to exhaust it.[6]

With the entry into force of the new CC (15 March 2014), judicial review of the administrative decision also became a requisite.[7] However, to award compensation it is enough that the administrative court has previously found unlawfulness: there is no need to annul the decision itself.

It is also necessary to emphasize changes in the procedural rules. With the entry into force of the new Act on the Code of Civil Procedure (1 January 2018), the final decision of the administrative court concerning the lawfulness of an administrative decision binds the general court in the civil procedures for damages.[8] Previously, the claimant needed to exhaust the remedies, but the court did not need to take the reasoning of the administrative courts into consideration. Therefore the content of unlawfulness in civil law was not necessarily the same as the content of unlawfulness in administrative law[9] (there had been criticisms that the civil courts tended to

[5] Act IV of 1959—on the Civil Code of the Republic of Hungary s 349 '(1) Liability for damages caused within the jurisdiction of government administration shall be established only if the damage cannot be abated by common legal remedies or the aggrieved person resorts to ordinary legal remedies for the abatement of damage.' PK (Civil Collegium of the Supreme Court) Resolution 43: Regarding s 349(1), the judicial review of the administrative decision is not an ordinary remedy. EBH2004.1121 (decision by the Supreme Court on principle): even when there is no legal possibility for an appeal against the administrative decision, judicial review of the administrative decision is still not an ordinary remedy. (These decisions are only available in Hungarian.)

[6] See eg EBH2004.12 (decision by the Supreme Court): a person's failure to lodge an administrative appeal cannot be considered as their fault if the appeal cannot repair the damage.

[7] Act V of 2013—on the Civil Code of Hungary s 6:548 [Liability for the actions of administrative authorities]: '(1) Liability for damages caused within the scope of administrative jurisdiction shall be established only if the damage results from actions or omissions in the exercise of public authority, and if the damage cannot be abated by common remedies or by way of administrative actions.'

[8] Act CXXX of 2016—on the Code of Civil Procedure s 24(3): 'Liability for damages caused within the scope of administrative jurisdiction shall be enforceable on condition that the court of competence for administrative actions—if administrative judicial process is available—established the infringement by final decision.'

[9] See eg EBH2013.44.

misinterpret the administrative law and therefore legally unfounded decisions had been made). The requirement of the judicial practice is that the court needs to find not just an infringement, but a very serious and obvious one to award the damages remaining the same (see the general remarks in section III).

Administrative appeals have undergone some changes, too, due to the entry into force of the new Act of General Administrative Procedure (1 January 2018). The cases where an appeal can be lodged became limited. There is a possibility for appeal only when the decision was made by the head of the district authority or by a body of a municipal government (except for the council of representatives) or by a local branch of a law enforcement agency. Even this has changed from 1 January 2020: it is now not possible to appeal against the decision of the head of district anymore. In all other cases, only a judicial remedy is open.[10]

III. Are there different courts or other public agencies for the annulment of unlawful administrative decisions and for the award of damages?

In Hungary, there are no independent administrative courts; the general court system has specialized jurisdiction for administrative cases. Before 1 April 2020, the so-called administrative and labour courts (as part of the general court system) were the first instance in most of the cases, but these courts ceased to exist on 1 April. From that day on, the regional courts with administrative colleges have proceeded in the first instance in administrative cases.

Claims for damages—including those against public authorities—are judged by the civil court on the basis of the rules of civil procedure. With the entry into force of the new Act on the Code of Administrative Court Procedure, claims for damages caused by the administrative contractual relationship or public service relationship are judged by the administrative and labour courts on the basis of the rules of administrative court procedure.[11] But this only considers the damage arising within these legal relationships; the damage caused to persons outside of this relationship is judged by the general court. The administrative court can annul unlawful administrative decisions. Most of the cases are ruled by the general court, so there are different courts for the annulment of unlawful administrative decisions and for the award of damages.

It can be helpful to add some general remarks about government liability in Hungarian civil and administrative law.

[10] Act CL of 2016—on General Public Administration Procedures s 116:
(1) The client or a party in respect of whom the decision contains provisions may appeal the decision of first instance only if expressly authorized by an act.
(2) A resolution may be appealed against if it was brought:
a) by the head of a district (Budapest district) office, or a body of a municipal government, other than the council of representatives; or
b) by the local branch of a law enforcement agency.

[11] Act I of 2017—on the Code of Administrative Litigation s 38(1): 'In the claim, the plaintiff may request
e) obligation to compensate the damage caused in relation to an legal administrative contract relation or civil service legal relation.'

First, during the socialist era, after a Supreme Court decision on principle in 1955, compensation for damage caused by a public authority was only possible if the employee of the authority was found guilty at a criminal or disciplinary proceeding. From 1960[12] onwards, the CC followed this principle. In 1978, the latter requirement was cancelled, and only the requirement to exhaust the possible remedies remained. However, the limitation period remained one year until 1992, when the Constitutional Court found this restriction unconstitutional. The burden of proof was on the claimant. Also, the remedies needed to be exhausted beforehand. Before the transition, it was practically impossible to successfully bring a claim for damages to the court, not only because of these legal restrictions but also because of judicial practice, which treated the possibility of liability of administrative authorities with reservation.[13] Currently, the conditions for awarding damage for public authority liability are the following: the existence of damage, unlawful conduct, civil law culpability, causal link between the action and the damage and its predictability, and the loss was not (cannot be) averted (repaired) by legal remedies.

Second, there was also a dispute about the subjective basis of liability. From 1978 onwards, a factor deemed reasonable under the given circumstances was the given level of responsibility, but practically it was mostly inapplicable. Consequently, judicial practice developed the doctrine of particularly serious error in the application and interpretation of law. Errors in the findings of facts and errors in the decisions if they were a result of discretion were not considered such a serious error. According to more recent judicial practice, the fact that public authorities misapply, or may not apply, the law is not enough to justify the claim for damages. Government liability can only be based on a very serious infringement of the law. The misinterpretation of the law itself, the erroneous assessment of the evidence, the different assessment of the probative value of the evidence, and the fact that the decision of the authority was later held unlawful cannot lead to its liability.[14] The rare exceptions are the ones when the provisions of the law were completely and manifestly clear, the finding of fact and the decision were not discretionary, the authority ignored the administrative court's clear instructions, or the authority gave false information to the claimant. Failure to take a necessary measure and failure to comply with the deadline for action can be a basis for liability only if the authority cannot prove that it has acted as it was expected to.

Third, to award damages on account of legislative acts was impossible until the new CC slightly changed the legal environment in this area. There is now a possibility of awarding damage arising from legislative acts, but there are yet only a few cases. As of 2018, the civil courts are bound to follow the interpretation of the administrative courts; this was not a requirement before.[15] Also, as mentioned in section II, administrative court procedure as a remedy must be exhausted.

[12] When the (Socialist) Civil Code entered into force.

[13] A Varga Zs, *Ombudsman, ügyész, magánjogi felelősség. Alternatív közigazgatási kontroll Magyarországon* (Pázmány Press 2012) 217–18.

[14] L Vékás and P Gárdos (eds), *Kommentár a Polgári Törvénykönyvről szóló 2013. évi V törvényhez* (*Commentary of the Civil Code*) Ptk 6:548. §-ához (Wolters Kluwer 2018).

[15] Act CXXX of 2016—on the Code of Civil Procedure s 264(2): 'The final decision of the court of competence for administrative actions concerning the legality of public administration activities shall be binding upon the court hearing a case governed under this Act.'

Fourth, there are cases when some or all of the rules of the public administration are used only because an act (sectoral law) requires these rules to be applied.[16] Which procedural guarantees are available depends on the act that refers to the Act of General Administrative Procedures (AGAP). The special regulations about the liability of public authorities can be used only in cases when the public authority has acted in the possession of the State power, which means that in cases when the public authority has acted as a private entity (depending on the nature of the legal relationship), the injured party probably needs to sue according to the general rules.

Fifth, general rules of determination of the amount: the total loss (*damnum emergens* and *lucrum cessans* as well) must be reimbursed.[17] The claimant must prove the infringement, the exact amount of the loss (eg based on regular sales), and the causal link between the infringement and the damage. Determining the loss of profit is normally based on an expert opinion: there is no formula or minimal–maximal amount specified in law. Two main problems emerge from judicial decisions. The first one is to prove that the infringement is very serious. The second is to prove the causal link between the infringement and the alleged damage, especially the loss of profit. This problem also emerges if the general rules of liability are used (eg the legal relationship is not a public legal one, as in public procurement procedures, when contracting authorities are sued). It is hard to prove the causal link in cases when, as a result of an infringement, a person loses the possibility to conclude a contract

[16] Act CL of 2016—on General Public Administration Procedures s 8(1):

This Act shall not apply to:
a) misdemeanour proceedings;
b) election procedures, referendum initiatives and referendum procedures;
c) taxation and customs procedures;
d) asylum and immigration procedures, and—with the exception of the issue of certificates of citizenship—to citizenship proceedings;
e) competition control proceedings; and
f) administrative proceedings of the Magyar Nemzeti Bank (National Bank of Hungary) carried out within the scope of its duties delegated in Subsections (2) and (5)–(9) of Section 4 of Act CXXXIX of 2013 on the National Bank of Hungary, and in Act XV of 2014 on Fiduciaries and on the Regulations Governing Their Activities.
   (2) The legislation pertaining to administrative proceedings other than those mentioned in Subsection (1) may derogate from this Act only if expressly permitted in this Act.
   (3) Supplementary procedural provisions which are in harmony with the provisions of this Act may be prescribed by law.

The commentary also mentions tendering procedures that do not fall within the scope of the AGAP because here the applicant applies for a subsequent establishment of a legal relationship.

[17] Act V of 2013—on the Civil Code s 6:522:

[Extent of liability]
(1) The tortfeasor shall compensate the aggrieved party for all losses in full.
(2) Under the principle of the right to full compensation the tortfeasor shall cover:
   a) any depreciation in value of the property of the aggrieved party;
   b) any pecuniary advantage lost; and
   c) the costs necessary for the mitigation or elimination of the financial losses sustained by the aggrieved party.
(3) The amount of compensation shall be reduced by any financial advantage of the aggrieved party resulting from the tort, unless this is deemed redundant having regard to the circumstances of the case.
(4) In cases of exceptional circumstances, the court may award compensation in an amount lower than the amount of the total loss.

(eg public procurement procedures and tenders) because it is necessary to prove what would have happened without the infringement, and, the more complicated the conditions to win the tender or public procurement procedure are, the lesser the chances to prove this alternative ending, especially when the tender notice did not contain an obligation to conclude the contract. In public procurement procedures, neither the Public Procurement Arbitration Board, nor the administrative court has the right to decide on the admissibility of the tender, so in the renewed proceedings, new disqualification criteria could be found too.[18]

Last but not least, as far as the right to be heard is concerned, although the European Court of Justice considers this right as part of the rights of the defence and the requirement that the authority shall give an opportunity to an affected individual to express their point of view before the decision is taken as a core element in a procedure, this standpoint is not widespread in the Hungarian administrative procedural practice, nor in the academic sphere. The previous Code of Administrative Procedures and the new one both contain principles, and ensuring the rights of the client (applicant) is part of these principles; however, it is a rare occurrence that the central element of the decision is about one of these principles. It is a regular course of the procedure, however, that the client is informed by the authority of the initiation of the procedure, about the procedural acts in which they can actively participate, or that they receive the documents to which they can react and have a right to make a motion. The procedure usually takes place on the basis of documents, and the authority and the client communicate in writing. The client will only be heard if it is necessary to clarify the facts on the basis of the already available evidence, including when the nature of the case allows it and at an on-site inspection. The legal practice (especially in the administrative law) is quite positivist, which leads to the conclusion that the application of legal principles requires a positive legal basis: principles that are not included in the applicable legislation cannot be used. The judicial practice sometimes uses analogy, but there is no consistent pattern or method concerning when to do so. Also, judicial decisions refer to judicial practice (Curia or Supreme Court decisions, decisions on principle, etc), commentaries, or academic papers.[19] In the academic sphere, there are not many studies about the application and interpretation of principles in judicial practice, or even simply in general.

[18] EBH2005.1220 (decision of the Supreme Court on principle), Curia decisions Gfv VII.30.220/2013/4, Gfv VII.30.459/2017/18.

[19] Based mainly on personal experience. I also carried out a piece of research using the Register of Court Decisions (<https://birosag.hu/birosagi-hatarozatok-gyujtemenye> accessed 19 June 2020, which does not contain all decisions), searching for the name of the leading legal journals in Hungary and also for the words 'publisher' and 'study', focused on administrative and civil cases. Decisions referring to books other than commentaries are quite rare, and I could not find a reference to any studies. This may also be a problem of the site. On the other hand, the textbooks used in legal education do not refer to court judgments much either.

8

The Liability of Public Administration

A Special Regime between Formal Requirements and Substantial Goals

Fulvio Cortese

I. Is there any formal constitutional provision concerning public authority liability?

From a formal point of view, Article 28 Constitution deals with the subject of public authority liability.

This provision states that '[o]fficials and employees of the State and of public bodies are directly responsible, according to the criminal, civil, and administrative laws, for acts committed in violation of rights' and that '[i]n such cases, civil responsibility extends to the State and to public bodies'.

The sense of this provision, however, lies essentially in the establishment of two principles: one according to which those who act in the name and on behalf of a public authority do not enjoy, generally speaking, exemption from *any form of liability*; and one according to which public authorities are *always and in any case guarantors* of payment of damages that are caused by their employees.

It has been stated that, in general and with respect to the previous discipline, such principles are particularly innovative: they tend to exclude that exceptional and different rules apply to public employees.[1]

From a realistic point of view, the standards usually governing the civil liability of public authorities have always had a practical basis in Article 2043 of the Civil Code (CC)—in other words, in the provision that establishes the fundamental criteria of non-contractual civil liability in Italian law—according to which '[a]ny intentional or negligent act that causes an unjustified injury to another obliges the person who has committed the act to pay damages'.

In the traditional interpretation of this provision, a distinction has always been drawn between cases where the public administration acts through an *administrative order*—which means that it shows its authority—and cases in which it acts through *material behaviour* similar to that of other private parties.

[1] See, in particular, C Esposito, 'La responsabilità dei funzionari e dipendenti pubblici secondo la Costituzione (1951)' in C Esposito (ed), *La Costituzione italiana. Saggi* (Cedam 1954) 104. In general, about Art 28 Const, see F Merusi and M Clarich, 'Art 28' in G Branca (ed), *Commentario della Costituzione, Rapporti civili (artt. 27–28)* (Zanichelli 1991) 356; M Benvenuti, 'Art 28' in R Bifulco, A Celotto, and M Olivetti (eds), *Commentario alla Costituzione*, vol I (Utet 2006) 580.

Fulvio Cortese, *The Liability of Public Administration* In: *Tort Liability of Public Authorities in European Laws*. Edited by: Giacinto della Cananea and Roberto Caranta, Oxford University Press (2020). © The Contributors.
DOI: 10.1093/oso/9780198867555.003.0008.

In the second case, there have never been particular issues: the administration has always been considered potentially liable, just like other parties.

In the first case, however, it was long ruled out that not all damages caused by the administration should be compensated; this was because the notion of 'unjustified injury' tended to be understood as referring exclusively to cases in which the *diritti soggettivi* (subjective rights) of citizens were undermined.

It was indeed denied that, with regard to formal expressions of administrative authority (administrative orders), citizens were holders of *diritti soggettivi*, in the belief that they were the holders of other 'interests', defined as *interessi legittimi* (legitimate interests).

This kind of interest can usually be defined as *oppositivo* or *pretensivo* ('opposing' or 'potential'); in fact, an administrative decision either has the effect of downgrading (reducing) a pre-existing enforceable right (eg a property right that has been undermined by an order for expropriation becomes an *interesse legittimo oppositivo*) or that of identifying as important a substantive interest that was not classifiable as a true right (for instance, the interest possessed by someone who wishes to obtain an authorization is taken to be an *interesse legittimo pretensivo*).

With the important ruling No 500/1999, however, the Joint Sessions of the Court of Cassation partially changed the traditional interpretation and admitted that, generally speaking, even the violation of *interessi legittimi* can be considered as 'unjustified injury'. This new direction was strongly influenced by EU law, in particular by guidelines around the need for, in the public procurement sector, Member States of the Union to guarantee full and effective protection, including compensation for any kind of damage (this legislation was implemented in Italy for the first time with Art 35 LD No 80/1998).[2]

In any case, since leading case No 500/1999, there has been a general trend to distinguish between two different types of cases.

The first type is represented by damages arising from an unlawful decision harming *interessi legittimi oppositivi* (eg a loss arising from unlawful appropriation; damage caused by an unlawful annulment carried out ex officio or the unlawful revocation of an authorization/permit or, in any case, of a favourable decision; however, more generally, damage occurring to someone as a result of a decision in favour of another person can also be included: such a case may arise, for instance, in the case of buildings erected in the absence of planning permission being unlawfully approved).

In this case, the majority opinion holds that establishing damages to a legally protected interest is automatic in itself, and that therefore, the element of 'unjustified injury' always exists.

The second type, on the other hand, is represented by a loss arising from an unlawful decision that hurts *interessi legittimi pretensivi* (eg damages arising from the unlawful denial of an authorization/permit or other favourable decision; or, further, the loss arising from unlawful exclusion from bidding for a tender).

[2] A Travi, G Avanzini, and L Bertonazzi, 'La nuova giurisdizione esclusiva del giudice amministrativo' (1998) 21 NLCC 207.

In cases like this, legal scholars frequently invoke the theory of 'entitlement to the ultimate benefit' (*spettanza del bene della vita*):[3] the 'injury' can be said to be 'unjustified' only where the court finds, by way of a preliminary ruling, that if the administration had respected the law, the interest of the citizen would have been satisfied (that is, the hoped-for benefit would have accrued).

Clearly, in most instances, this theory is bound to exclude compensation in cases where the court finds, in the specific case, that the administration has discretionary power: given such power, in fact, it is not easy to understand whether, in the individual case, the citizen's interest could ever have been credibly satisfied.[4]

As far as the liability of public employees and civil servants is concerned, Article 2049 CC has always applied, according to which '[m]asters and employers are liable for the damage caused by an unlawful act of their servants and employees in the exercise of the functions to which they are assigned', as well as Article 22 of the Decree of the President of the Republic of Italy (DPR) No 3/1957, which establishes a limitation of liability of public employees to damages incurred 'due to malice or gross negligence' alone.

This means that a party injured by the action of the administration can request compensation directly, and at the same time both from the administration to which the official or employee who actually committed the action belongs and from the individual official or employee. If the requirements laid out in Article 2043 CC are met, the administration will always be liable, even for simple negligence (unless it is proven that the official or employee acted for strictly personal reasons or outside their assigned tasks); vice versa, an individual official or employee will be liable only if found guilty of particularly gross negligence.

Usually—and therefore contrary to what seems to be generally and expressly provided for in Article 28 Const, according to which, as mentioned at the beginning of the section, liability lies first and foremost with public officials and civil servants[5]—the aggrieved parties litigate directly and exclusively against the authority (moreover, the administration is usually the only subject that is certainly solvent).

With all the damage that the authority might thus have to compensate due to the inappropriate actions of its own employees, it is still possible that the employees who are found guilty of serious offences might be asked to refund the authority whatever it has paid. To this end, the authority can act directly by offering compensation for damages before a civil law court; but the individual public official may also be asked to refund what the administration has paid in a special trial before the *Corte dei conti* (Court of Auditors), initiated by a public prosecutor.

[3] G Falcon, 'Il giudice amministrativo tra giurisdizione di legittimità e giurisdizione di spettanza' [2001] Dir proc amm 287.

[4] This is one of reasons because a minority (but clever) interpretation holds that, in reality (despite the majority opinion), the liability of the public administration must be considered special: see L Garofalo, 'La responsabilità dell'amministrazione: per l'autonomia degli schemi ricostruttivi' [2005] Dir amm 1.

[5] The author, who strongly affirmed the need to observe this textual approach, is E Casetta, *L'illecito degli enti pubblici* (Giappichelli 1953). This is a minority interpretation.

II. Is there any general requirement to bring an administrative appeal or a complaint before an ombudsman or other public agency before bringing an action for damages against public authorities?

With regard to damages caused by the public administration through acts that are an expression of its authority, it has long been held that it is necessary, before claiming compensation, to challenge the legitimacy of the actions through recourse to a specific remedy seeking their annulment.

For example, before ruling No 500/1999 of the Court of Cassation (mentioned in section I), this remedy was considered necessary when annulling the acts of the administration and 'reviving' any of the 'subjective rights' that they had violated (eg to remove an illegitimate expropriation decree and re-establish the 'property right' it violated). Only this way could compensation for 'unjustified injury' as defined by Article 2043 CC (see section I) be awarded.

After ruling No 500, this belief has lost ground, although administrative courts (the Regional Administrative Courts and Council of State) would continue to accept it as valid. Indeed, with Article 7 L No 205/2000, these courts had gained jurisdiction over all material damages resulting from illegitimate administrative orders and had, therefore, adopted the traditional interpretation, rather than the one followed by the Court of Cassation. In particular, the main theory regarding the administrative courts stated that, in order to claim compensation for damages from unlawful administrative orders, it is necessary to obtain prior annulment of the harmful and unlawful administrative decision (theory of *pregiudizialità amministrativa*).[6]

Today, Article 30 of the Code of Administrative Trial (CAT) expressly provides that it is no longer necessary to implement prior remediation to annul the order, and that it is sufficient to provide compensation within 120 days from when the damaging act was issued or from when the damage was acknowledged.

However, the very same Article 30, in paragraph 3, establishes that, in these cases, the administrative court can also reject an action for damages or reduce the compensation when they assess that the aggrieved party could have reduced the damages if they had diligently and promptly exercised all the remedies available by law.[7]

Among the remedies under particular consideration are the courses of legal action that the aggrieved party could have brought the administrative court (and therefore also the remedy for the annulment of the unlawful order) and the other forms of

[6] See eg Council of State, Plenary Session Nos 4/2003, 2/2006, 12/2007; the Court of Cassation decidedly followed the opposing interpretation: Joint Session Nos 13659 and 13660/2006, 35/2008. In general, on this topic see F Cortese, *La questione della pregiudizialità amministrativa: il risarcimento del danno da provvedimento illegittimo tra diritto sostanziale e diritto processuale* (Cedam 2007).

[7] This solution is similar to that followed before the CAT—which has been approved by LD No 104/2010—by a minority interpretation: see eg C Consolo, 'Il processo amministrativo tra snellezza e "civilizzazione"' [2000] Corr giur 1265; F Trimarchi Banfi, *Tutela specifica e tutela risarcitoria degli interessi legittimi* (Giappichelli 2000) 47; A Romano Tassone, 'Sul problema della "pregiudiziale amministrativa"' in G Falcon (ed), *La tutela dell'interesse al provvedimento* (University of Trent 2001) 285–86; S Valaguzza, 'Riflessioni sull'onere di impugnativa del provvedimento illegittimo in un *petitum* risarcitorio' [2001] Dir proc amm 1117–18. According to this interpretation, Art 1227 para 2 CC would have been applicable ('Compensation is not due for damages that the creditor could have avoided by using ordinary diligence').

protection that are available before the administration (such as administrative proceedings or different appeals to the administration to repeal the order itself).

This solution has been interpreted as the expression of a general ban on abuse of process, based on the fundamental principle of solidarity as expressed in Article 2 Const[8] (on this interpretation, see the important ruling by the Plenary Session of the Council of State No 3/2011).

III. Are there different courts or other public agencies for the annulment of unlawful administrative decisions and for the award of damages?

In Italy, remedies to annul unlawful administrative orders are sought before administrative courts (regional administrative courts, at first instance; Council of State, on appeal). In particular, administrative orders can be contested within sixty days and ultimately annulled when considered vitiated by violation of law, incompetence, or abuse of power (see Art 21-*octies* L No 241/1990; Art 29 CAT).

For all harm caused by these orders, administrative courts that have the jurisdiction to annul them can also establish compensation to the aggrieved party.

However, as mentioned in section II, the injured party can also seek compensation independently, but within a deadline (120 days; the fact that lawmakers established such a short and different term to the one—of 5 years—laid down for general remediation regulated by Art 2043 CC was considered legitimate by the Constitutional Court in ruling No 97/2017).

Normally, however, the injured party requests compensation together with the one provided for annulment (also in consideration of Art 30 para 3 CAT: see section II).

The compensation can also be initiated within the deadline of 120 days from when the ruling that annulled the unlawful administrative order became binding.

Exceptions to this general framework are a few particular situations, such as, for example, when the lawfulness of an order by which the administration has dismissed an employee, is contested (in this scenario, the civil court has jurisdiction and rules according to a special procedure: the employee will have access to this protection only if they contest the dismissal promptly within a specific deadline by means of an act addressed to the administration); or when orders that impose administrative sanctions are contested (also in this scenario, it is nearly always the civil court that has specific jurisdiction).

[8] 'The Republic recognizes and guarantees inviolable rights of man, for the individual, and for social groups where personality is expressed, and demands the fulfilment of the fundamental duties of political, economic, and social solidarity.'

9

The Principles Governing Public Authority Liability in Poland

Marek Wierzbowski, Marek Grzywacz, Joanna Róg Dyrda, and Katarzyna Ziółkowska

I. Is there any formal constitutional provision concerning public authority liability?

According to Article 77, section 1 of the Constitution of the Republic of Poland, everyone shall have the right to be awarded damages for any harm done to him by an action of an organ of public authority contrary to law.[1] The more detailed provisions of the Civil Code supplement this general rule.[2]

[1] Article 77 of the Constitution states that: '1 Everyone shall have the right to compensation for any harm done to him by any action of an organ of public authority contrary to law. 2. Statutes shall not bar the recourse by any person to the courts in pursuit of claims alleging infringement of freedoms or rights.'

[2] Article 417 CC provides that:

1. The State Treasury or a local government unit or another person exercising public authority by force of law is liable for any damage caused by an unlawful action or omission while exercising public authority.
2. If performance of public authority tasks is contracted under an agreement to a local government unit or another legal person, joint and several liability for any damage caused is borne by the contractor and the local government unit contracting the tasks or the State Treasury.

Article 417(1) states that:

1. If damage is caused by a legislative act, remedy thereof may be demanded once it has been declared incompliant with the Constitution, a ratified international treaty or the law in the course of appropriate proceedings.
2. If damage is caused by a final and non-revisable court decision or other final decision, remedy thereof may be demanded once such decision has been declared incompliant with the law in the course of appropriate proceedings, unless separate regulations provide otherwise. This also applies to cases where a final and non-revisable court decision or other final decision has been issued based on a legislative act that is incompliant with the Constitution, a ratified international treaty or the law.
3. If damage is caused through failure for a court decision or other decision to be issued and the obligation to issue the same is provided for by a legal regulation, remedy of damage may be demanded once the failure to issue the court decision or other decision is declared incompliant with the law in the course of appropriate proceedings unless separate regulations provide otherwise.
4. If damage is caused by failure for a legislative act to be issued and the obligation to issue the same is provided for by a legal regulation, the failure to issue the act is declared incompliant with the law by the court hearing the case for remedy of damage.

Article 417(2) states that:

If personal injury is caused through the lawful exercise of public authority, the aggrieved party may demand full or partial remedy of and monetary recompense for the harm caused if the

Marek Wierzbowski, Marek Grzywacz, Joanna Róg Dyrda, and Katarzyna Ziółkowska, *The Principles Governing Public Authority Liability in Poland* In: *Tort Liability of Public Authorities in European Laws.* Edited by: Giacinto della Cananea and Roberto Caranta, Oxford University Press (2020). © The Contributors. DOI: 10.1093/oso/9780198867555.003.0009.

Before illustrating the relevant provisions of the Civil Code (CC), it is helpful to make some general remarks. The Polish legal system belongs to the tradition of the European continent, with a clear distinction between private and public law. However, the boundary between private and public law was moved towards subjecting several governmental activities to private law. This relates to the area of obligations—both contractual and in tort. Each contract entered into by the government is subject to the CC, and disputes arising from such a contract belong to the jurisdiction of ordinary courts. Government as a party to such a contract is not called the 'government' but is a separate type of legal entity, known as the State Treasury.[3]

Concerning tort cases, the government of Poland, and local authorities are again subject to civil law, under the jurisdiction of ordinary courts. State (again, 'State Treasury') liability creates no doubts in the case, for example, of a car accident caused by a car belonging to the government. The case becomes more difficult when harm was done through other government actions, including an administrative decision later declared unlawful and annulled. The CC provisions concerning situations like this can be found in the new wording of Article 417, Articles 417(1), 417(2), and the new wording of Article 421.[4]

As a result of such a broad understanding of private law liability in Poland, first, administrative courts do not decide on contracts entered by the government, nor on damages to be awarded against governmental entities; second, there is no category of public law contracts. A part of administrative law scholarship mentions the category of public law contracts, but without giving any example under Polish law; third, regulation of damages to be awarded to private parties at the expense of the government is considered regulated by private, not by public, law; finally, the system of awarding damages against governmental authorities is the same as against private parties. Accordingly, in the cases that follow, reference will be made to Article 417 or 417(1) CC. The damages granted under the provisions of Article 417 CC are calculated according to general principles pertaining to the estimate of damage and include actual losses (*damnum emergens*) and loss of profit (*lucrum cessans*). Attempts to limit the amount of damages to the compensation of actual losses were declared unconstitutional by the Constitutional Tribunal in the decision of 23 September 2003.[5]

There are very few separate regulations concerning seeking damages from government. Article 421 CC refers to such exceptions. One of these exceptions can be found, for instance, in the Code of Criminal Procedure: its chapter 58 is devoted to compensation for wrongful conviction and provisional arrest or detention. There is also a separate regulation concerning compensation for legal acts of the government: there exists, in fact, government compensation for expropriation. The Code of

circumstances, and especially the aggrieved party's inability to work or his difficult financial situation, indicate that the remedy is required under the equitable principle.

Article 421 states that 'The provisions of Articles 417, 417(1) and 417(2) do not apply if the liability for damage caused through the exercise of public authority is regulated by specific provision.'

[3] K Poludniak, 'Civil Liability of Public Administration for Unlawful Conduct or Omission or Causing Personal Injury in Polish Law' (2015) 31 Leg Econ Rev 66.

[4] See n 2.

[5] K 20/02, OTK-A 2003 No 7 Item 76.

Administrative Procedure (CAP) gives grounds for some exceptional circumstances (danger to human life, great loses for national economy, or grave interests of the State) to set aside or amend any final administrative decision. The party who suffered loss due to such a decision is given compensation equivalent to the amount of actual losses (*damnum emergens*). The decision on compensation is made by the authority setting aside the decision; however, the party may bring the case to court to decide about compensation.

II. Is there any general requirement to bring an administrative appeal or a complaint before an ombudsman or other public agency before bringing an action for damages against public authorities?

As noted in section I, litigation against government (State Treasury) is subject to the same regulation as litigation against private parties. Therefore, there is no statutory requirement for any introductory procedure; a private party may bring the statement of claim against government directly to the court. However, to prove the unlawfulness of the action taken by administrative authorities, it is necessary to obtain a decision or judgment from the administrative court declaring the unlawfulness of the action under Article 417(1) CC.

III. Are there different courts or other public agencies for the annulment of unlawful administrative decisions and for the award of damages?

Awarding damages rests within the jurisdiction of the ordinary courts. Setting aside an administrative decision or declaring it to be invalid rests within the jurisdiction of two-tier administrative courts. A person who wants to claim compensation must therefore first obtain, as a prerequisite, a ruling from an administrative court stating that the administrative decision in question was deemed unlawful. Such a ruling later makes it possible to claim damages before an ordinary court on the basis of Article 417(1) § 2 CC.

10
Public Authority Liability in Romania

Roxana Vornicu

I. Is there any formal constitutional provision concerning public authority liability?

Yes: under the Romanian Constitution there is a formal provision regarding public liability. Article 52 paragraph (1) reads:

> Persons whose rights or legitimate interests have been breached by a public authority, whether through an administrative act or by not issuing the act within the legal time limit, are entitled to have their right or legitimate interest acknowledged, to have the act annulled and receive compensation for their loss.

Paragraph (2) states that limits to this right are established through organic law, whilst paragraph (3) provides that the State is liable for judicial errors, that the State's liability for judicial acts is established though organic law, and that magistrates will be held liable in cases of negligence or misfeasance. In addition, under the Constitution, Article 126 paragraph (3) provides that:

> The judicial review of administrative acts is guaranteed, except for the acts that concern relations with the Parliament or the military acts. The specialized administrative courts have jurisdiction to rule on claims for damage caused through Government Ordinances or legal provisions that have been declared unconstitutional.

These provisions represent the constitutional framework for public liability in the Romanian legal system. Law 554/2004 on judicial review of administrative action (Romanian: *Legea contenciosului administrativ*) establishes the detailed conditions and general legal framework for review of illegal administrative actions. Law 554/2004 includes procedural law and substantive administrative law provisions and, although it is not a true administrative code, it is the general legislation applicable to the functioning of the Romanian administration. Unlike French administrative law, in the Romanian legal system, judicial review of administrative action entails the possibility of bringing a claim for annulment of the illegal administrative act as well as a claim for damages through the same procedure. Special provisions on compensation for illegal administrative action in various fields of law are also found in other statutory instruments (for instance, the law on remedies for illegal acts in public procurement).

Roxana Vornicu, *Public Authority Liability in Romania* In: *Tort Liability of Public Authorities in European Laws*. Edited by: Giacinto della Cananea and Roberto Caranta, Oxford University Press (2020). © The Contributors.
DOI: 10.1093/oso/9780198867555.003.0010.

Law 554/2004 (Art 8) sets the framework for appeals for judicial review of administrative actions and establishes that a person whose rights or legitimate interests[1] were breached through a unilateral administrative act is entitled to go before the judicial review court to ask for partial or total annulment of the administrative act, compensation for damage, and moral damages. The claim can be brought only if the claimant followed the preliminary administrative procedure and if the claimant was not satisfied with the answer received during this procedure, or did not receive any answer at all. Therefore, under Romanian administrative law, the preliminary administrative appeal before the public body (or before the superior hierarchical body) is a mandatory prerequisite for the admissibility of the claim for judicial review.

Article 18(3) under Law 554/2004 on judicial review establishes that 'the court, when ruling on the annulment claim shall also decide on the damages for illegal administrative action if a claim for damages have been lodged'. A claim for harm caused through illegal administrative action can only be brought if a simultaneous (or previous) claim for annulment is lodged. Therefore, the claim for damages cannot be independent of the appeal for annulment. The claim for damages may be brought in the same proceedings as the request for annulment or in separate proceedings, but no later than a year from the day when the claimant became aware of the loss.

Furthermore, a petition for annulment can be brought only if the claimant justifies a personal interest when lodging the claim. For a claim for damages to be successful, the following conditions must be met:

(1) there must be an illegal administrative act (or an action subject to review, such as the refusal to issue an act);
(2) the claimant must have suffered harm;
(3) there must be a causal link between the act and the harm; this is a condition that applies to all forms of liability and is assessed by the courts on a case by case basis. The general principles on exonerating causes apply (such as *force majeure* or the fortuitous event).[2]

As far as fault is concerned, there are two main positions in Romanian legal literature. The first stance sees Romanian administrative liability as an objective liability, and the argument lies in the fact that neither the first post-communist general act on administrative action (Law 29/1990 on judicial review of the administration), nor the law currently in force (Law 554/2004) made or make any express mention of the administration's fault as a condition for liability, and that this should be viewed

[1] The notion of legitimate interest is defined by Law 554/2004. It can be either private or public. A private legitimate interest is defined as the possibility to expect a certain conduct in consideration of a future subjective, prefigured, and predictable right, whereas the public legitimate interest is the interest connected to the rule of law and constitutional democracy, rights, liberties and public duties, community needs, and the realization of the functions of public bodies (Art 2 para I (p)–(r) of Law 554/2004). It should be noted here that in the Romanian legal system, a private party does not have *locus standi* to lodge a claim for annulment if it can only justify a public legitimate interest, and not a private one.

[2] Scholarly works on the topic in Romanian include RN Petrescu, *Drept Administrativ* (Editura Hamangiu 2009) 620–31; DA Tofan, *Drept Administrativ*, vol II (2nd edn, CH Beck 2009); G Bogasiu, 'Angajarea răspunderii patrimoniale a autorităţilor publice în cadrul contenciosului administrativ' (2011) 6 Revista Romana de Jurisprudenţa.

as the legislator's intention to shape administrative liability as an objective one.[3] The other stance takes inspiration from the French adage, '*toute illégalité commise par l'administration est fautive*' and considers the illegality of the act (or conduct consisting in the refusal to issue the act or the lack of answer to a citizen's request) as culpable.[4]

The latter seems to have also been the Supreme Court's approach in a 2016 taxation case decision where, through a simplistic legal reasoning, the court reiterated that an action for damages cannot be brought without a prior claim for annulment of the illegal administrative act because the fault of the administration is encompassed in the unlawfulness of the act:

> The fault of the public authority, as a condition for triggering administrative liability can only be assessed through the action for annulment of the illegal administrative act.[5]

Under Article 16 of Law 554/2004 (the law on judicial review), a claim for damages can be brought against the public body that issued the act (or refused to issue it, as the case may be), as well as against the civil servant who contributed to the act being issued/the refusal to issue an act (the public body and the public servant will therefore both be respondents in the same proceedings).

II. Is there any general requirement to carry out an administrative appeal or to bring a complaint before an ombudsman or another public agency before bringing an action for damages against public authorities?

Yes, there is a general requirement to carry out an administrative appeal before bringing an action for damages. This preliminary administrative appeal should be brought before the body that issued the administrative act (or acted unlawfully by refusing to issue and act or to respond to a request for an act to be issued). The preliminary administrative appeal can also be brought before the hierarchical superior body where such a superior public body exists.

III. Are there different courts or other public agencies for the annulment of unlawful administrative decisions and for the award of damages?

Yes, there are. The administrative jurisdiction in Romania is a specialized jurisdiction, and petitions for annulment of administrative acts and award of damages caused through illegal administrative action should be brought before specialized

[3] L Pop, *Contributii la studiul obligatiilor civile* (Universul Juridic 2010) 56.
[4] A Iorgovan, *Tratat Elementar*, vol III (Lumina Lex 1998) 303.
[5] Decision 2132/2016 of the Supreme Court, available on the Supreme Court's website in Romanian <www.scj.ro/> accessed 19 June 2020.

administrative courts. However, the judges ruling on these cases belong to the same body of magistrates as the ones that rule on civil or criminal matters. They do not have specialist training prior to starting their activity as administrative judges but undergo what could be called a de facto specialization. When administrative judges are promoted from the Tribunal to the Court of Appeal, they tend to keep this de facto specialization, although sometimes, in practice, in small towns throughout the country, a judge might go from ruling in the administrative court to holding office in civil courts due to lack of personnel or because of docket management choices. In practice, these administrative courts are in fact specialized units/departments of the Tribunals, Courts of Appeal, and the Supreme Court (in Romanian, the 'High Court of Cassation and Justice', referred to as the Supreme Court) and function on the same premises as other courts.

11
Constitutional Foundations of Government Liability in Spain

Eva Maria Nieto Garrido

I. Is there any formal constitutional provision concerning public authority liability?

The Spanish Constitution (1978) regulates both administrative procedure and government liability in tort. Before examining the more detailed rules and case law in this area, it may be helpful to consider their constitutional foundations. With regard to administrative procedures, Article 105 of the Constitutions recognizes citizens' right to participate in the drafting of administrative provisions, their right to have access to files, and their right to be heard in administrative procedures that may affect them.[1] Article 106 lays down the foundations of both judicial review and government liability in tort. While its first paragraph entrusts the courts with the power to ensure that the rule of law is respected in administrative action and that the latter is subordinated to the ends that justify it, the second paragraph concerns liability and, for its importance, deserves full quotation: 'Private individuals, according to the terms established by the law, have the right to be compensated for any harm to their goods and rights, except in cases of *force majeure*, whenever the harm is a consequence of actions by the public services.'[2]

This provision, which reflects the national legal tradition, derives from two previous Acts, the *Ley de Expropiación Forzosa* of 1954 and the *Ley de Régimen Jurídico de la Administración del Estado* of 1957. The constitutional provisions, however, include a call for regulation by the national legislator. Currently, public authority liability for damages caused by actions by the public services is regulated by Articles 32–37 of *Ley 40/2015, de 1 de octubre, de Régimen Jurídico del Sector Público*, Chapter IV, called

[1] Article 105 of the Spanish Constitution provides that:

> The law shall make provision for: a) The hearing of citizens, directly, or through the organizations and associations recognised by the law, in the process of drawing up the administrative provisions which affect them. b) The access of citizens to administrative files and records, except to the extent that they may concern the security and defence of the State, the investigation of crimes and the privacy of persons. c) The procedures for the taking of administrative action, with due safeguards for the hearing of interested parties when appropriate.'

Source: <www.boe.es/buscar/act.php?id=BOE-A-1978-31229#a105> accessed 19 June 2020.

[2] The original text in Spanish is as follows: 'Los particulares, en los términos establecidos por la ley, tendrán derecho a ser indemnizados por toda lesión que sufran en cualquiera de sus bienes y derechos, salvo en los casos de fuerza mayor, siempre que la lesión sea consecuencia del funcionamiento de los servicios públicos.'

Eva Maria Nieto Garrido, *Constitutional Foundations of Government Liability in Spain* In: *Tort Liability of Public Authorities in European Laws*. Edited by: Giacinto della Cananea and Roberto Caranta, Oxford University Press (2020). © The Contributors.
DOI: 10.1093/oso/9780198867555.003.0011.

'*De la responsabilidad patrimonial de las Administraciones Públicas*'. Paragraphs 3, 4, and 5 of Article 32 focus on liability for legislative acts, whereas paragraphs 7 and 8 of the same Article 32 regulate liability for judicial acts, which are excluded from the goal of the project.

In spite of Article 106 Spanish Constitution (1978) is the constitutional base of government liability in tort regulation, there are laws on that topic no founded on such Article. For instance, Article 3.2 of the law of State alarm, declared in Spain recentcly due to the Covid-19 pandemic, regulates a compensation for damages caused by acts or norms adopted by public authorities for State alarm.[3]

For a better understanding of the Spanish legal system, it is important to bear in mind a twofold feature. First, there has been not simply a development of regional and local authorities in the twentieth century, but Autonomous Communities also have legislative powers and municipalities have regulatory powers concerning the organization and functioning of public authorities in their territories. Second, however, the State—that is, the institutions of central government—has exclusive legislative competence on some sectors or matters. An understanding of this is essential, since some of such matters are amongst the most important ones in the public law sphere.

According to Article 149(1) of the Constitution, 'the State shall have exclusive competence over the following matters', including the

> basic rules of the legal system of Public Administrations and the status of their officials which shall, in any case, guarantee that all persons under said administrations will receive equal treatment; the common administrative procedure, without prejudice to the special features of the Self-governing Communities' own organizations; legislation on compulsory expropriation; basic legislation on contracts and administrative concessions and *the system of liability of all Public Administrations* [paragraph 18].

This constitutional provision thus establishes that public authority liability in the Spanish legal system is the exclusive competence of the State. It guarantees the unity of the Spanish regulation of public authority liability, as the Autonomous Communities have no competence with regard to this topic.

II. Is there any general requirement to bring an administrative appeal or a complaint before an ombudsman or other public agency before bringing an action for damages against public authorities?

A body may review the rejection of a case in tort, within the '*juridición contencioso-administrativa*'. This was created in 1845 as a specialized administrative body to monitor administrative decisions, with a similar role to the *Conseil d'Etat*, but it has constituted a specialized section of the Spanish Supreme Court since 1904. Other

[3] E Nieto Garrido 'La indemnización de daños o perjuicios causados por las medidas adoptadas durante el estado de alarma'(2020) Diario La Ley, 15.09.2020, Wolters Kluwer Publisher.

important legislative changes occurred in 1956 and in 1998. Judicial review of administrative action is carried out by specialized panels within the judiciary, including a chamber of the highest court ('*Sala Tercera, de lo Contencioso-Administrativo*').

Before considering judicial remedies, it is important to give a quick glance over how public administrations handle claims for damages, in order to consider both existing rules and administrative practices. The Spanish legal order provides an administrative procedure to seek damages, which is called '*reclamación de responsabilidad patrimonial*'. Such administrative procedure is regulated by the Act of 1 October 2015, n 39 (*Ley de Procedimiento Administrativo Común*, Arts 65, 67, 81, 91, 92, and 96.4), which provide various main steps. First, there is a deadline of one year for claiming compensation, for example after a doctor in a public hospital declares that a certain damage may not be recovered or a judicial decision annuls either a license or a contract. Second, before taking a decision, each public authority must ask the opinion of the Council of State or, where there is one, of the autonomic consultant organ, for compensations up to 50.000 €. The report is compulsory, though it has no binding effects. Third, the administrative unit that is responsible for the harm caused must produce a report. Finally, the procedure ends with a decision taken by central or local political authorities, which either declares that public liability exists or denies its existence.

When considering administrative practices, however, it soon becomes evident that public administrations refuse to recognize their liability, unless in clear cases and where the amount of compensation is low. This explains why most of the cases in which issues concerning government liability arise end with a judicial decision. Such decision will not only declare that the contested administrative act, in which the competent public authority denied its liability, is void, but it will also determine the amount of the compensation that is due to the private individual who was damaged.

III. Are there different courts or other public agencies for the annulment of unlawful administrative decisions and for the award of damages?

No. The main features of Spanish public authority liability can be summarized as follows:[4]

(1) It is tortious liability borne by a public authority causing harm as a consequence of action by the public services. The last concept is used in broad terms, in a 'superduguitiana' concept. (A Guaita 'Veinticinco años de la Administración y jurisdicción: 1939-1964' (1964) 78-79 Documentación Administrativa 22).

[4] L Medina Alcoz, *La teoría de la pérdida de oportunidad: estudio doctrinal y jurisprudencial de derecho de daños público y privado* (Thomson Reuters Aranzadi 2007); J González Pérez, *Responsabilidad patrimonial de las administraciones públicas* (Civitas 2015); L Martín Rebollo, *Leyes Administrativas* (24th edn, Aranzadi 2018) chs 5 and 13; L Martín Rebollo 'Responsabilidad de los poderes públicos: Administración, Poder Judicial, Estado Legislador' in *España constitucional (1978–2018): trayectorias y perspectivas*, vol 5, Tomo 5, (Centro de Estudios Políticos y Constitucionales 2018) 3757–72; JC Laguna de Paz 'La responsabilidad patrimonial de los poderes públicos' (2019) 196 *Revista española de derecho administrativo* 31–68.

(2) There is a sole discipline: State Regulation relating to Public Authority Liability due to the Constitutional Order of the Distribution of Competences between the State and the Autonomous Communities, pursuant to Article 149(1) paragraph 18, mentioned in section I.
(3) Public authority liability can arise from administrative or material acts (action without procedure) and also the lack of activity by a public authority when it is required.
(4) In general, it is defined as a direct, rather than a subsidiary liability. The latter only operates in the case of a criminal offence.
(5) It is defined an objective system because it is not only based on misconduct.[5] There is an academic debate on this feature, which can be appreciated in recents judgements of Spanish Constitutional Court.[6]
(6) The aim is to offer complete reparation for damages (*reparación integral*).
(7) A time limitation of one year after the harm was suffered precludes resort to this legal remedy, and recourse must be sought before the public administration that caused the damage.
(8) Only one body may review the rejection of a case in tort, that which is entrusted with the jurisdiction '*contencioso-administrativa*'.
(9) Compensation may only be awarded on the basis of the following criteria: damage is produced by administrative action (in broad term); the damage is real and not hypothetical; it can be assessed in economic terms; and it concerns an individual or group of individuals; the damages is not due to undiligent conduct of the individual.

[5] Nonetheless, some authors point out that it is not only formally based on misconduct but on other doctrines, such as loss of chance and *lex artis*, such as when harm is caused by the national health system. See F Pantaleón Prieto, 'Los anteojos del civilista: hacia una revisión del régimen de la responsabilidad de las Administraciones públicas' (1994) 237–38 *Documentación administrativa* 239–52; L Medina Alcoz, 'Mitos y ficciones en la responsabilidad patrimonial de las Administraciones Públicas' (2012) 153 *Revista Española de derecho administrativo* 152–81.

[6] STC 112/2018 17 October 2018. JM Alegre Ávila, '¿La legislación preconstitucional, parámetro de integración de las prescripciones constitucionales?: Acerca del carácter "objetivo" de la responsabilidad patrimonial o civil extracontractual de las Administraciones Públicas en la Sentencia del Tribunal Constitucional 112/2018, de 17 de octubre de 2018' (2019) 196 *Revista española de derecho administrativo* 307–36. See also, Sentencia del Tribunal Constitucional 85/2019, de 19 de junio, on compensation for damages suffered by whom was in jail (temporary prison) for a criminal investigation, but later was realesed free from punishment. Compensation is based on special sacrifice of those indiviuals, a necessity for peaceful and secure living of society.

12
Constitutional Principles and Judicial Remedies in Switzerland

Thierry Tanquerel

I. Is there any formal constitutional provision concerning public authority liability?

Article 146 of the Federal Constitution of the Swiss Confederation of 18 April 1999 states that 'The Confederation shall be liable for damage or loss unlawfully caused by its organs in the exercise of official activities.'

'Organs' of the Swiss Confederation, within the meaning of Article 146, are not only elected officials but also individuals acting for and on behalf of the Swiss Confederation. It doesn't matter whether those persons perform a legal action (such as enacting a regulation or issuing a ruling) or simply carry out a material task (such as giving information or conducting scientific research). The legal nature of the link between those persons and the Confederation doesn't matter either.

For liability to apply, the unlawfulness of the act causing the damage is sufficient. A fault of the author of the act is in principle not required. However, we shall see in section II that, in some instances (see case 1 in Chapter 14), the way unlawfulness is constructed actually implies the existence of a fault.

Before 2000, when the 1999 Federal Constitution entered into force, there was no constitutional provision on the federal level regarding State liability. Such liability was, however, governed by the Government Liability Act 1958 (GLA), which is still in force and follows the same principles as Article 146. The latter thus simply solidifies the liability of the Confederation in the Constitution.

It should be stressed that both Article 146 and the GLA apply only to the Confederation (ie the Federal Government and its agents). As Switzerland is a federal State, the issue of the liability of cantons and municipalities pertains to cantonal law. It has long been asserted that, based on the principle of the legality of the administration, in the absence of a constitutional or statutory provision to that effect, there could be no State liability for unlawful official actions. Nowadays, the prevailing view in public law literature is that such a liability could be derived from the equality clause of the Federal Constitution (Art 8). The question is anyway moot, since all cantons now have a constitutional[1] or statutory basis providing for State liability along the lines of Article 146.

One important feature of Swiss law pertaining to State liability is that only the State is liable towards the injured person. The latter may not ask for damages directly from

[1] See eg Art 12 of the Constitution of the canton of Geneva.

Thierry Tanquerel, *Constitutional Principles and Judicial Remedies in Switzerland* In: *Tort Liability of Public Authorities in European Laws.* Edited by: Giacinto della Cananea and Roberto Caranta, Oxford University Press (2020).
DOI: 10.1093/oso/9780198867555.003.0012.

the agents of the State (members of an authority, elected officials, civil servants) (Art 3 III GLA and the relevant cantonal provisions). The State can eventually turn to the guilty agent, provided the fault is not minor.

II. Is there any general requirement to carry out an administrative appeal or to bring a complaint before an ombudsman or another public agency before bringing an action for damages against public authorities?

To answer this question, one has to clearly distinguish between two different situations.

When the action unlawfully causing alleged harm is material, for example spreading harmful information or destroying a property, a claim for damages can be brought before the appropriate venue—which, depending on the jurisdiction, can be an administrative authority or a court (see section III below)—without any preliminary proceedings. It is, of course, always possible to enter into discussion with the authority allegedly liable in view of a settlement.

When the action is of a legal nature (most frequently an administrative ruling),[2] it is no longer possible to ask for damages on the ground that the said action was unlawful if one has not challenged the action in time through the avenues provided by law. With very few exceptions, in Swiss law, administrative decisions (or rulings) can be appealed before a court (sometimes after an administrative appeal) within the appeal deadline (usually thirty days). Article 12 GLA provides that 'the legality of a ruling entered into force cannot be challenged in proceedings for liability'. A ruling enters into force when it is not, or is no longer, possible to lodge an ordinary appeal against it. The same principle applies at the cantonal level. It must be stressed that the claimant for liability must have challenged the ruling himself: it is not possible to take advantage of the fact that a third party might have successfully challenged the ruling. Of course, if an appeal is rejected and the ruling is upheld, the same principle applies, and it will not be possible to claim damages.

III. Are there different courts or other public agencies for the annulment of unlawful administrative decisions and for the award of damages?

On the federal level, the person claiming for damages under the GLA has to file a claim with the Federal Ministry of Finances, which will adjudicate the claim through a ruling. This ruling can be appealed before the Federal Administrative Tribunal (FAT). The decision of the FAT can in turn be appealed before the Federal Tribunal (which is the highest court of Switzerland), provided, pursuant to Article 85 I of the Federal

[2] In Switzerland, an administrative 'ruling' is an individual decision, not a regulation whose scope is general and covers an indefinite number of situations. The substantive and procedural requirements are quite different for the process of adjudication by way of a 'decision' or 'ruling' and for the enactment of a regulation through rule-making.

Tribunal Act 2009 (FTA), that the amount in dispute is higher than 30,000 Swiss francs or that a (legal) question of principle is at stake. Since both the FAT and the Federal Tribunal may also be called upon to decide on the lawfulness of an administrative decision, one cannot say that there are different courts for the annulment of unlawful administrative decisions and for the award of damages, but these questions are dealt with in completely different proceedings.

In many cantons, the system is the same as on the federal level. In some cantons, there is no ruling by an administrative authority on the claim for damages: the claimant has to file suit directly with the cantonal administrative court.

In other cantons, for example in Geneva, the claim for damages has to be brought before a civil court. In that case, different courts will decide on the lawfulness of the administrative decision and the award of damages (bearing in mind that the civil court will be bound by the judgment of the administrative court on the lawfulness of the litigated decision).

The judgment of the higher cantonal court (administrative or civil) on the award of damages can be challenged by an 'appeal in public law matters' (Art 82 FTA) to the Federal Tribunal, provided that the amount in dispute is higher than 30,000 Swiss francs or that a question of principle is at stake (Art 85 I FTA).

13

Public Authority Liability in the United Kingdom

A Common Law Perspective

Gordon Anthony

Before turning to the questionnaire in Chapter 14, the following, overarching points about administrative procedure and public authority liability in UK law might be made:[1]

(1) Administrative procedure

(a) The rules of administrative procedure are found in three main sources: (i) statute law; (ii) the common law; and (iii) the European Convention on Human Rights (ECHR) (as has effect under the Human Rights Act 1998). Prior to 'Brexit', EU law provided a fourth source under the terms of the European Communities Act 1972, but that Act has now been repealed. Some such rules of procedure can, however, still be found in 'retained EU law' within the meaning of the European Union (Withdrawal) Act 2018.[2]

(b) Statute law may, or may not, impose procedural requirements on decision-makers—all will depend upon the statute in question and whether the legislature has chosen to impose such requirements. Where procedural requirements are included, they should ordinarily be observed, as a decision will otherwise be ultra vires and/or vitiated by 'procedural impropriety'. Examples of procedural requirements in statute include consultation duties and the duty to give reasons for decisions.

[1] Two caveats are helpful. First, this report has been written in the light of discussions held at the University of Trieste on 18–19 May 2017 and the resulting questionnaire of the Common Core of European Administrative Laws (COCEAL) project dated 30 July 2017. It follows the structure of that questionnaire and, consistent with the guidance note from the organizers, tries 'not only to provide answers to the questions raised ... but also to shed light on the doctrines and broader sets of beliefs and ideas about the law that the courts or other public agencies would use when dealing with those cases'. Second, the term 'UK law' is used here for ease of reference. However, it is to be noted that the majority of the principles, etc that are discussed are synonymous with the law of England and Wales and, in many instances, the law of Northern Ireland. Scottish law, in particular where the questionnaire raises issues about private law principles, has different historical reference points, which are not explored here. On Scottish law see, *The Laws of Scotland: Stairs Memorial Encyclopaedia* (LexisNexis 2000 and re-issues).

[2] There are many accounts on the rules of procedure and their origins: see eg P Craig, *Administrative Law* (8th edn, Sweet and Maxwell 2016) chs 12–14. Note that there is not, at the time of writing, a comprehensive commentary on the European Union (Withdrawal) Act 2018.

Gordon Anthony, *Public Authority Liability in the United Kingdom* In: *Tort Liability of Public Authorities in European Laws.*
Edited by: Giacinto della Cananea and Roberto Caranta, Oxford University Press (2020). © The Contributors.
DOI: 10.1093/oso/9780198867555.003.0013.

(c) The common law is famously associated with the rules of natural justice, or 'fairness', namely the 'right to a fair hearing' and 'the rule against bias'. These rules are 'context sensitive', which means that the requirements of fairness vary according to: (i) the nature of the decision-maker; (ii) the nature of the decision-maker's power; (iii) the implications that a decision may have for an individual; and (iv) the 'public interests' that may be engaged by a decision.[3] The rules co-exist with statutory requirements, and they can fill gaps in statutory schemes where this is needed in the interests of 'fairness'. A failure to give effect to the common law rules will usually mean that a decision is unlawful.

(d) Article 6 ECHR is the provision of the ECHR that is most immediately relevant to administrative procedure, albeit the UK courts can adopt a narrow approach to the meaning of 'civil rights' in this context.[4] Procedural requirements can, however, also arise from other Articles, for example Article 2 ECHR (the right to life) and Article 8 ECHR (the right to private and family life, home and correspondence).

(e) 'Retained EU law' can impose procedural requirements either through Directives that had been transposed into national law pre-Brexit or through pre-Brexit Regulations that required no such transposition. The general principles of EU law—for instance, as relate to the giving of reasons—can also have effects where they relate to retained EU law.[5]

(2) Public authority liability

(f) The law on public authority liability is complex insofar as it straddles the public–private divide in UK law, where there are particular statutory and common law requirements that govern damages claims.[6] In contrast to continental legal systems, UK law has not developed with reference to a conception of 'the State', but rather in a piecemeal manner that has reflected the general evolution of administrative law. Historically speaking, the primary reference point in UK law has been the Crown and the administration of justice through its courts, where the Diceyan idea of the 'rule of law' emphasized that all persons, whether public or private, were equally subject to the law of the land. That conception of the rule of law has, however, long since been overtaken by procedural and substantive rules that in effect recognize the existence of a public–private divide.[7]

(g) The starting point in the modern era is that public authorities will be subject to many of the same legal rules as private individuals and that their liability will be determined accordingly (the position in respect of the Crown was different, but was aligned in large part by the Crown

[3] See further Lord Bridge's comments in *Lloyd v McMahon* [1987] 1 AC 625, 702.

[4] See, most recently, *Poshteh v Kensington LBC* [2017] UKSC 36, [2017] AC 624.

[5] European Union (Withdrawal) Act 2018 ss 2–7.

[6] Leading accounts include D Fairgrieve, *State Liability in Tort: A Comparative Law Study* (OUP 2003); C Harlow, *State Liability: Tort Law and Beyond* (OUP 2004); and T Cornford, *Towards a Public Law of Tort* (Routledge 2008). See also P Leyland and G Anthony, *Textbook on Administrative Law* (8th edn, OUP 2016) ch 20.

[7] For a critical account, see JWF Allison, *A Continental Distinction in the Common Law: A Historical and Comparative Perspective on English Public Law* (OUP 2000).

Proceedings Act 1947).[8] However, the nature of the public–private divide is such that the courts accept that there may be sound reasons of principle for treating public authorities as distinct from private individuals in certain cases. An example is in the context of negligence actions against the police, where the courts have sometimes held that 'public policy' militates against liability in cases arising from the investigation and suppression of crime.[9] The rules of contract law can also reflect the unique position of public bodies, whether as a result of common law rules or statutory intervention (where EU rules on procurement have previously provided an example).

(h) Where an individual is suing a public body, an important distinction is to be drawn between (i) cases where an individual seeks *damages alone*; and (ii) cases where an individual contends that *a public authority has acted unlawfully in a public law sense and that he or she is entitled to damages* as a result of that act. In the first scenario, the individual will sue the public authority in a private law action, most obviously under the law of tort or for breach of contract. However, if the individual wishes to challenge the (public law) legality of a public authority's decision as well as to claim damages, he or she should ordinarily bring an application for judicial review. In that alternative scenario, damages would be available, but only if the court were satisfied that the facts of the case would also be actionable in private law (eg in negligence, breach of statutory duty, trespass to the person, etc). In some instances, the court may, on having heard part of an application for judicial review, direct that the matter should continue as a private law action (eg where the facts in dispute are more suited to resolution by way of such an action).

(i) There are four further points that should be made about public authority liability.

(j) The first is that there is no separate, or dedicated, court that deals with liability, as all public law and private law proceedings will be brought in the High Court (or, depending on quantum of damages, the County Court). Within the High Court, there are, however, different divisions that deal with cases, depending on whether they are 'public law' or 'private law' in nature, and transfer of cases between divisions is possible (as *per* point (h) above). This possibility is subject to one important qualification arising from time limits: applications for judicial review must typically be brought within three months of the relevant act or decision being taken, and transfer to the public law divisions may not be possible where that period of time has lapsed. (To continue with that example, tort actions have a three-year time limit.)

[8] For recent judicial consideration of the relevant principles, see *N v Poole Borough Council* [2019] UKSC 25, [2019] 2 WLR 1478.

[9] See eg *Michael v Chief Constable South Wales Police* [2015] 1 AC 1732. But compare *Robinson v Chief Constable of West Yorkshire* [2018] AC 736.

(k) The second point is that claims for damages are possible under the Human Rights Act 1998, where the High Court will follow the general principles on liability that are applied by the European Court of Human Rights (ECtHR). Procedurally, such a claim may be brought either as a private law action for breach of statutory duty (the duty arising from the Human Rights Act itself), or within an application for judicial review. In the latter instance, the violation of a right under the ECHR would constitute both a public law wrong and a breach of statutory duty under the Human Rights Act 1998.

(l) The third point is that there is one cause of action in tort law that is available only against public bodies, ie misfeasance in public office. This tort provides a remedy to individuals who have suffered loss as a result of the 'abuse of power' by a public officer, where it centres upon the concept of 'bad faith'. While claims for misfeasance in public office are rare in the case law, it provides an important outer marker for the protection of individual rights and interests.

(m) The fourth point concerns the quantum of damages. While awards of damages are typically meant to put the individual back in the position that he or she would have been in had he or she not suffered loss (damages actions may, of course, also be brought by companies), awards of 'exemplary' damages can be made where the courts are particularly disapproving of the actions or inactions of public bodies. Statutory schemes can also include requirements for compensation (for instance, in the area of planning law), while the government may, in other instances, make awards of compensation on an *ex gratia* basis. Ombudsmen can also make recommendations for awards of compensation in cases of 'maladministration', albeit such recommendations are not binding on the authorities to whom they are made.[10]

I. Is there any formal constitutional provision concerning public authority liability?

The short answer, here, is 'no'. The UK does not have a codified constitution, and all damages claims are brought as in the introductory section above. However, it is sometimes said that the Human Rights Act 1998 has a constitutional quality (it has been described as a common law 'constitutional statute') so, insofar as damages claims may be brought under that Act, there may be a constitutional element involved. The same was previously true of damages claims brought under EU law—the European Communities Act 1972 had also been described as 'a constitutional statute'.[11]

[10] On the ombudsman principle, see further G Anthony, 'Administrative Justice in the United Kingdom' (2015) 7 It J Publ L 9 <www.ijpl.eu/assets/files/pdf/2015_volume_1/3.Anthony.pdf> accessed 20 June 2020.

[11] For the origins of the term see *Thoburn v Sunderland CC* [2003] QB 151.

II. Is there any general requirement to carry an administrative appeal or to bring a complaint before an ombudsman or another public agency before bringing an action for damages against public authorities?

The answer to this question depends on whether an individual is bringing a private law claim seeking damages alone, or whether he or she is bringing an application for judicial review that includes a damages claim.

In the first scenario, that of a private law claim, there is no formal need to consider an administrative appeal or a complaint to an ombudsman before initiating proceedings. The private law action will stand on its own and, so long as the claimant has observed any pre-action requirements that have been specified by the courts, the action can proceed. That said, an individual may, depending on the nature of his or her dispute with a public authority, wish to make a complaint of 'maladministration' to the parliamentary ombudsman or the local government ombudsman. In the event that a complaint is upheld, the relevant ombudsman may make a non-binding recommendation in favour of compensation—see comment (m) above.

Where an individual wishes to bring an application for judicial review, he or she can do so only where he or she does not have an effective alternative remedy in the form of, for instance, a right of administrative appeal. The High Court has enforced this rule strictly over the years, for a number of reasons: (i) constitutional propriety—appeals will be statutory in form and have been created by the legislature; (ii) effectiveness—appeals often offer an individual fuller scope for challenging decisions; and (iii) limited resources—the High Court would otherwise face a very large and potentially unmanageable number of cases. However, there is one interesting footnote to all of this: ombudsmen deal with questions of 'maladministration' rather than 'legality' and so, on one reading, they can never provide an effective alternative remedy if there is a query about the lawfulness of government action.

It should also be noted that, before an application for judicial review can be commenced, the individual should first engage with what is known as the 'pre-action protocol'. This is a judge-imposed requirement that is intended to encourage individuals and public bodies to try to resolve a grievance informally before legal proceedings are initiated. A failure fully to engage with the protocol can later have implications in costs for the relevant party during the hearing of an application for judicial review.

III. Are there different courts or other public agencies for the annulment of unlawful administrative decisions and for the award of damages?

This is a complex matter that raises questions about the role of tribunals in the UK and their relationship to the High Court as the forum for bringing applications for judicial review. As per the answer to the question posed in section II, the starting point here is that individuals would be expected to bring challenges to a range of administrative decisions within tribunals where those have been established by the legislature (for instance, in the areas of immigration, freedom of information, social security, etc). The relevant rules of procedure for a tribunal will specify what remedies it can grant, and may include a power to annul a decision and/or to require it be retaken by the original decision-maker. A power to make an award of damages would be rarer, albeit that, for instance, employment tribunals may have such a power in discrimination cases (where statutory intervention would arguably give a claim a public law quality).[12]

Outside of the tribunal system, the forum for seeking the annulment of an unlawful administrative decision is the High Court. Again, the rules of on effective alternative remedies, noted under section II, will apply.

[12] On tribunals and appeal structures see further Anthony (n 10).

PART III
CASES

14
Cases

I. *Questionnaire*

1. The dismissal of a civil servant for improper conduct
2. An unjustified denial of licences for electronic communications
3. Sanctions against a bank
4. The exclusion of a tenderer by the contracting authority
5. A delay in issuing a concession for the use of the waterfront
6. Prohibiting fruit imports
7. A licence withdrawal *inaudita altera parte*
8. A licensed fisherman
9. Suspending the sale of beauty creams
10. A negligent drug authority
11. A violent police officer

A. Case 1—the dismissal of a civil servant for improper conduct

Under the Department of Public Administration's (PA's) 'Alcohol and Drugs Misuse Policy' (hereinafter PA's policy guidelines), civil servants must refrain from drinking any kind of alcoholic beverage in the workplace. But Maurice, a civil servant, is accused by some colleagues of having drunk a bottle of wine and of having thrown some glasses out of the window of the third floor of his place of work. The head of the unit where Maurice works thus begins a disciplinary procedure against him. After a quick investigation of the facts, but without giving Maurice any possibility of being heard on the matter, the head of the unit deems that the truth of the alleged facts is sufficiently established, and concludes that such facts reveal an attitude incompatible with the proper functioning of a public administration. He thus dismisses Maurice, who contests the decision before a court for lack of due care during the investigation and infringement of his right to be heard under national law. Meanwhile, he must look for another job.

Would the national court endorse Maurice's argument only if the PA's policy guidelines set out a specific duty of care during the investigation, as well as the civil servant's right to be heard before an unfavourable decision is taken? Or would the court consider those arguments in the light of general principles of law, including Article 6 of the European Convention on Human Rights (ECHR)? Is Maurice's action likely to be successful? If so, could he obtain: (i) the salary that he would have received if he had not been unlawfully dismissed; (ii) interests; (iii) damages for the dismissal's negative consequences on his reputation and for having been obliged to look for a new job?

Giacinto della Cananea and Roberto Caranta, *Cases* In: *Tort Liability of Public Authorities in European Laws*.
Edited by: Giacinto della Cananea and Roberto Caranta, Oxford University Press (2020). © The Contributors.
DOI: 10.1093/oso/9780198867555.003.0014.

B. Case 2—an unjustified denial of licences for electronic communications

The Ministry for Telecommunications of Terranova, a new member of the European Economic Area (EEA), must assign licences for 100 frequencies. Under national legislation, before taking its decision, the Ministry must consult the Electronic Communications Committee (ECC), whose opinion is of a technical nature and has no binding effects. Many operators apply for a licence, including New Tv, a legal entity constituted under Terranova law. Unexpectedly, the Ministry does not follow the procedure previously established, in that it does not consult the ECC before taking its decision. It simply asserts that there were so many applications that the administrative process had to be simplified in order to be concluded on time and give a new shape to such an important market. But New Tv, which has not been awarded a licence, brings an action before a Terranova court, claiming that the denial of frequencies was unlawful. It also alleges that, as a consequence of the Ministry's wrongful action, it lost the significant investments it had made for developing its business in Terranova, as well as the profits it could have gained by becoming a national broadcaster, including the money it could have obtained from advertisers.

Would New Tv's action be successful? Would damages, if any, be limited to the actual loss or extend to cover lost profit?

C. Case 3—sanctions against a bank

'Totally Unnecessary Investments' (TUI) is an investment company whose business consists of receiving and executing orders for third parties and trading on its own behalf. After some years of activity, TUI is subject to an inspection by the national banking regulator (NBR). A few weeks later, the NBR issues a pecuniary sanction against TUI for its alleged negligent behaviour in keeping its documentation. TUI therefore brings an action before the national court competent for reviewing the NBR's acts, claiming that the disciplinary measure is unjustified because the inspection was irregular and the sanction was based on a gross misunderstanding of the facts, because some important documents were not taken into account. TUI asks the court, first to quash the sanction, and second to award damages for harm to its commercial reputation.

Would TUI's action be successful? And if damages are awarded, how would their amount be assessed?

D. Case 4—the exclusion of a tenderer by the contracting authority

Under national public procurement law, contracting authorities can exclude participants from an administrative procedure if they are considered unreliable and therefore unsuitable to be awarded the contract. In particular, contracting authorities can exclude from a procurement procedure an operator who has been convicted for systematic failure to pay social security contributions. During the procurement procedure initiated by the municipality of Mandeville, it receives information from the Department of Social Security (DSS) showing that a bidder, Alphagroup, has systematically failed to pay social security contributions. Mandevilles' officers use the information received by DSS, which is not informed about it, and drops its offer. It is only after the conclusion of the tendering procedure, when Alphagroup has access to the documentation held by the municipality, that it discovers that its offer had been dropped because of its alleged systematic failure to pay social security contributions. It then brings an action before the national court arguing that: (i) the municipality could not use information against it without giving it a real opportunity to contest it; (ii) factually, the DSS had made a mistake, insofar as the economic operator that failed to respect the obligations stemming from social security legislation was not Alphagroup but another one named 'Alpha Group Ltd'.

Alphagroup brings an action for damages against the Mandeville municipality before a national court. The municipality objects that liability, if any, should be imposed upon the DSS. Would Alphagroup's action be successful? If so, what damages could Alphagroup recover? And if the municipality of Mandeville is held liable, could they turn to the DSS in order to place the burden on them, or at least to share it?

E. Case 5—a delay in issuing a concession for the use of the waterfront

The waterfront of the City of Sanibel, in front of a famous lake, is traditionally used to provide services, including restaurants and cafés, for both residents and visitors. Each provider must have a concession, and, in order to make concessions available for a plurality of operators, the City of Sanibel has established that, as a rule, concessions can be operated for a maximum of three years, after which they are re-issued on the basis of an open procedure. The rules procedure provides that interested parties can apply within thirty days, and the City will then have sixty days to compare the offers and choose the next concessionaire. North Lake, a newcomer, applies for a concession for a specific site on the waterfront. Despite the fact that North Lake is the sole applicant, the City of Sanibel does not conclude the procedure within the deadline. In an attempt to justify its delay, the City of Sanibel asserts that the available documentation is incomplete, but it is unable to indicate any defect in the application. As a result, North Lake does not obtain the concession in time for the summer season and sues the City of Sanibel before the court.

Would its action be successful? Would damages, if any, be limited to actual loss or extend to cover lost profit? How would they be determined?

F. Case 6—prohibiting fruit imports

'Forest's Jewels' (FJ) is registered in Terranova, an Eastern European country that is member of the EEA. FJ is a company specializing in the import of 'fruits of the forest' (eg cranberries and blueberries) from Blefuscu Island in the Black Sea. After an alleged incident in a nuclear power plant in Russia, under the Feed and Food Regulation, the government of Terranova restricts the importation of 'fruits of the forest' in two ways: (i) a generalized block of all imports for all importers for one month; (ii) a set of new rules for testing imports to make sure that they are not radioactive. FJ challenges the block and the new rules before a Terranova court on two grounds: first, because they are—especially the block—individual measures under the guise of general measures, since FJ is the only importer from Blefuscu Island; second, and consequently, because the ban is based on limited information, rather than on an accurate analysis of all the relevant facts before individual measures adversely affecting an undertaking are taken by a public authority. FJ also asks the court to award damages.

Is the action for damages brought by FJ admissible only if the court annuls the block and the new rules? Or is it admissible independently of any annulment? In any case, would damages, if any, cover lost profit and, if so, how would be the amount of the compensation be determined?

G. Case 7—a licence withdrawal *inaudita altera parte*

Ms Tramp has a licence to sell newspapers and maps in a kiosk. The licensing authority decides to withdraw her licence because it intends to renew the offer of such services, but gives her no opportunity to be heard. Ms Tramp challenges the withdrawal before a court, arguing that the decision was taken in breach of duties of fairness and rationality in decision-making, and asks for damages.

Would the national court endorse Ms Tramp's argument only if a specific requirement to hear affected parties has been laid down by legislation for this type of administrative procedure, or would it use general principles of law such as fairness or due process? And would the court be satisfied to ascertain the existence of a procedural wrong, or would it also consider whether the licensing authority was in breach of rationality? In either case, would Ms Tramp's action be successful? Is annulment a precondition for awarding damages? And would damages cover lost profit?

H. Case 8—a licensed fisherman

Santiago is a licensed fisherman. Licensing is the prerogative of a local authority, namely the Fisheries Commission ('the Commission'), which reviews existing licences and renews an unlimited number every four years. Under existing rules, the Commission may, at its discretion, refuse to renew any licence upon conviction within national territory of any person for breach of any of the commercial fishing laws or rules. When Santiago applies for renewal of the licence, the Commission refuses to grant it, claiming that he had loaned his licence to another person. Santiago challenges this decision before the competent court on two grounds. He argues, first, that no existing rule explicitly prohibited anyone to borrow from or loan to any other person any licence or permit issued by the Commission and, second, that no evidence was brought against him.

Is Santiago's argumentation likely to be endorsed by the court? If so, can he claim damages against the Commission and, that being the case, would damages, if any, be limited to actual loss or extend to cover lost profit?

I. Case 9—suspending the sale of beauty creams

Beauty Box has been authorized by the National Health Authority (NHA) to produce and sell a new set of beauty creams. Following a press campaign sponsored by activists who claim that Beauty Box used certain undisclosed ingredients in its new creams, which might be hazardous for human health, the NHA decides to temporarily suspend the sale of Beauty Box's new set of creams. Beauty Box then challenges the NHA's suspension order before a national court, and claims damages on the ground that the order was not preceded and justified by an adequate fact-finding scientific procedure.

Would Beauty Box's action be successful? If so, how would the amount of any damage be determined?

J. Case 10—a negligent drug authority

Peter's young son, Luka, is harmed by a defective pharmaceutical product. The product entered the market with the approval of the national drug authority a month before Luka's accident. Subsequently, due to the high number of adverse drug reactions, the company producing the product withdraws it from the market and goes bankrupt. Peter, on behalf of his child and himself, sues the national drug authority for damages on two grounds: (i) the authority had received scientific evidence from a non-governmental organization (NGO) contrary to issuing the authorization, but this evidence was not taken into account; (ii) under national legislation, when private parties provide different or contrary scientific evidence, the national drug authority is obliged to consult a technical body, but in this case it failed to do so.

Would the national drug authority be held liable, and if so, under what conditions?

K. Case 11—a violent police officer

Two police officers stop a driver, Agatha, and ask her quite ruthlessly to get out of the vehicle and show her documents to the officers. Agatha vehemently protests and resists the officers' request, stating that she is being treated unfairly. One of the two officers, without warning Agatha, as required by Police Department rules, moves towards her, grabs her left arm, and twists it into an armlock. The torsion causes Agatha's elbow to crack, and permanent injury ensues. She refuses any assistance from police officers and is brought to the hospital by some witnesses. Subsequently, Agatha sues the two police officers and the State for damages.

Under what conditions would her action be successful, and to what extent? Would it be relevant that the two policemen infringed the guidelines set out by the Police Department?

II. Case 1—the dismissal of a civil servant for improper conduct

Under the Department of Public Administration's 'Alcohol and Drugs Misuse Policy' ('PA's policy guidelines'), civil servants must refrain from drinking any kind of alcoholic beverage in the workplace. But Maurice, a civil servant, is accused by some colleagues of having drunk a bottle of wine and of having thrown some glasses out of the window of the third floor of his place of work. The head of the unit where Maurice works thus begins a disciplinary procedure against him. After a quick investigation of the facts, but without giving Maurice any possibility to be heard on the matter, the head of the unit deems that the truth of the alleged facts is sufficiently established, and concludes that such facts reveal an attitude incompatible with the proper functioning of a public administration. He thus dismisses Maurice, who contests the decision before a court for lack of due care during the investigation and infringement of his right to be heard under national law. Meanwhile, he must look for another job.

Would the national court endorse Maurice's argument only if the PA's policy guidelines set out a specific duty of care during the investigation, as well as the civil servant's right to be heard before an unfavourable decision is taken? Or would the court consider those arguments in the light of general principles of law, including Article 6 ECHR? Is Maurice's action likely to be successful? If so, could he obtain: (i) the salary that he would have received if he had not been unlawfully dismissed; (ii) interests; (iii) damages for the dismissal's negative consequences on his reputation and for having been obliged to look for a new job?

A. Austria

Stefan Storr, Kathrin Bayer, Daniela Bereiter, and Luca Mischensky

The dismissal of a civil servant is a disciplinary sanction imposed by a disciplinary commission. The disciplinary proceedings for the dismissal of a federal civil servant are regulated in § 105 et seq of the Federal Civil Servants Employment Act (BDG).[1] The different provincial laws—eg § 117 et seq of the Civil Service and Salary law of Styria[2]—regulate the proceeding for the dismissal of a provincial civil servant in Styria. The following overview of the procedural law only refers to the disciplinary proceedings regulated in the BDG, because the Styrian Civil Servants and Salaries Act (Stmk L-DBR) contains the same procedural rights for civil servants as the BDG. In general, according to § 105 BDG, the General Administrative Procedure Act (AVG)[3] is subsidiarily applicable in disciplinary proceedings. In Austrian law, mere guidelines are never a court's standard of review.

[1] *Bundesgesetz über das Dienstrecht der Beamten*, Federal Law Gazette No 333/1979 as amended.

[2] *Dienst- und Besoldungsrecht der Bediensteten des Landes Steiermark*, Provincial Law Gazette No 29/2003 as amended.

[3] *Allgemeines Verwaltungsverfahrensgesetz* 1991, Federal Law Gazette No 51/1991 as amended.

Before initiating a disciplinary proceeding, the administrative authority to which the civil servant concerned belongs has to carry out necessary investigations. If the disciplinary commission has decided to conduct disciplinary proceedings, it has to serve the opening decision on the accused (§ 123(1) and (2) BDG). The disciplinary commission has to conduct an oral proceeding, take the relevant evidence, and summon witnesses as well as the accused for the hearing. The accused has the right to be heard in the proceeding (§ 124 BDG). The disciplinary commission may conduct a hearing in the absence of the accused, if he or she has been properly summoned and demonstrably informed of the consequences of this default. Before the written version of the finding, the disciplinary commission has to give the accused the opportunity to take note of the results from the evidence and comment on it (§ 125a BDG).

Assuming the BDG does not provide that the accused has the right to be heard in the investigation and in the disciplinary proceeding, § 8 AVG contains a general right of a person who has an interest in an administrative proceedings to participate in the proceeding as a party. Special laws can exclude the application of certain paragraphs of the AVG. However, § 105 BDG does not exclude the application of § 8 AVG in the disciplinary proceeding. As far as Maurice is concerned, he has an interest in the outcome of the disciplinary proceeding and therefore has to be a party to this proceeding. One of the crucial rights that parties in administrative proceedings have is the right to be heard.[4] Pursuant to § 37 AVG, '[i]t is the purpose of the investigation procedure to ascertain the state of the facts relevant for processing an administrative matter and to enable the parties to claim their rights and legal interests'. The public authority competent for the prohibition is thus, *ex officio*, obliged to allow an inspection of the files, to confront the affected party with the facts of the proceedings and the results of the authority's investigation, and to issue a statement.[5]

As a result, the authority carrying out the necessary investigations—before initiating disciplinary proceedings—should have confronted Maurice with the accusations of his colleagues and would have been obliged to give him the opportunity to comment on them. Further, in the disciplinary proceedings, the disciplinary commission should also have given Maurice the opportunity to comment (orally) on the allegations. Hence, Maurice's procedural right to be heard has been infringed.

The Federal Administrative Court (BVwG), in its constitution as senate is competent to hear appeals against the decision of the disciplinary commission (§ 135a(3) No 1 BDG). The Proceedings of Administrative Courts Act (VwGVG)[6] is a specific procedural law concerning proceedings before the BVwG that also applies to provincial administrative courts (LVwG). Unless the appeal has to be dismissed for formal reasons or the proceedings have to be discontinued, an administrative court shall terminate a legal matter by means of a ruling (§ 28(1) VwGVG). The BVwG decides on the merits of a case if the relevant facts are clear. The BVwG may further determine the relevant facts by itself in the interest of speed or the substantial saving of costs (§ 28(2)

[4] §§ 37, 43(2) and (3), 45(3), and 65 AVG; for further information, see, for instance, J Hengstschläger and D Leeb, '§ 37' in J Hengstschläger and D Leeb, *[Commentary on the] AVG* (Manz 2005) para 11-14.

[5] § 45(3) AVG; Hengstschläger and Leeb (n 4) para 24ff.

[6] *Verwaltungsgerichtsverfahrensgesetz*, Federal Law Gazette I No 122/2013 as amended.

VwGVG). According to § 17 VwGVG, § 8 AVG and the general principles of § 37 et seq AVG are also applicable in the proceeding before the BVwG.[7] If the administrative authority—here the disciplinary commission—has completely failed to investigate the relevant facts, the BVwG may annul the contested decision and refer it back to renew the decision. In doing so, the authority is bound by the legal assessment of the BVwG (§ 28(3) VwGVG). However, according to the VwGH, annulling and referring back to the authority has to be the exception. The administrative courts may only consider annulling a decision and referring it back if the authority has omitted any investigative activity or has taken completely inappropriate investigative steps. In general, the BVwG has to decide on the case itself.[8]

In this case, the BVwG will therefore decide on the merits of the case. Prior to that, it will establish the relevant facts on its own. The court will hold a public oral hearing if it is requested by a party, or if the court deems it necessary (§ 24(1) VwGVG). It can refrain from scheduling a hearing irrespective of a party's request if the files reveal that an oral discussion is not expected to further clarify the legal matter and if dispensing with the hearing is neither in conflict with Article 6(1) ECHR nor with Article 47 of the Charter of Fundamental Rights of the EU (CFR) (§ 24(4) VwGVG). Due to a ruling of the Austrian Constitutional Court (VfGH),[9] disciplinary measures against civil servants are within the scope of Article 6 ECHR. As for disputes concerning the individual rights or obligations of civil servants, Article 6 ECHR applies in its civil law part. Hence, if Maurice requests a public oral hearing, the court will hold this hearing. If Maurice was not granted a hearing in the first instance, regardless of whether or not this was required by procedural law, the BVwG would call for an *ex officio* hearing. The BVwG will review the facts and give Maurice the opportunity to comment on the allegations against him.[10]

Giving him the right to be heard, the procedural error before the disciplinary commission will be remedied. Maurice's action will be successful if the complaint proceeding reveals that the allegations against him are unfounded.

The disciplinary commission is an organ acting to implement laws on behalf of the Federation. Hence, Maurice has to bring a claim for damages against the federal government (§ 1(1) of the Federal Act on the Liability of Territorial Authorities and other Bodies and Institutions of Public Law for Damage caused when Implementing the Law, AHG). The disciplinary commission acted unlawfully if it did not grant Maurice a hearing, as required by law. The disciplinary commission has disregarded the purpose of the procedural regulation, since the purpose of granting a legal hearing is to prevent unlawful disciplinary measures and to avoid resulting claims for damages. The infringement is also substantial, because by granting the accused the right to be heard, he or she gets an opportunity to comment on the accusations. It is the authority's duty to ensure a fair trial and a balanced investigation.

[7] D Kolonovits, G Muzak, and K Stöger, *Verwaltungsverfahrensrecht* (11th edn, Manz 2019) para 797.

[8] This is established case law of the VwGH; see, for instance, VwGH 26 June 2014 Ro 2014/03/0063; 24 June 2015 Ra 2015/04/0019.

[9] VfGH 3 December 2009 B 1008/07.

[10] With regard to the legal situation before the introduction of the VwG in 2014, see VwGH 5 September 2013, 2013/09/0053.

The authority is at fault for the infringement if it can be accused of unlawful omission. The staff members of the disciplinary commission can be expected to conduct a disciplinary proceeding within the legal procedural rules. Hence, they can be subjectively accused of non-compliance with the procedural rules. Random actions or actions without a legal basis may even constitute gross negligence. If the staff acted with gross negligence or intent, Maurice would be compensated for positive damage and loss of profit. However, this only applies to damages that cannot be averted by legal remedies and that have not yet become time-barred.

§ 1293 of the Civil Law Code (ABGB) defines 'positive damage' as a disadvantage to property, rights, or to a person (interests). The salaries that Maurice would have received if he had not been unlawfully dismissed are compensable positive damages.[11] The loss of an earning opportunity is not to be considered positive damage but as lost profit if no legal position had been secured at the time of damage.[12] Compensation for positive damages also includes expenses for the restitution of damage.[13] The rescue effort to prevent an increase in damage is also considered positive damage.[14] Time and costs actually spent looking for a job can also be regarded as compensable positive damages.

Damage to a person's reputation caused by the enforcement of the law is not compensable in public liability law.[15] Compensation for damage to reputation can only be considered if the organ acted as a private individual under private law; for example, if a member of the authority damaged Maurice's reputation during an interview. This person is then privately liable according to § 1330 ABGB. If the BVwG amends the decision of the disciplinary commission, its procedural infringement would also by causal to the damages.

B. European Union

Barbara Marchetti

A dismissal decision based on disciplinary reasons requires that the employee be represented during the hearing before the Disciplinary Board as provided for by Articles 16 par, 1 and 4 of Annex IX of the EU Staff Regulations (Regulation 1023/2013) and the Charter of Fundamental Rights of the EU.[16]

The dismissal decision is therefore unlawful because of the infringement of the principle of the right to be heard, and will be annulled by the court.

The action for damages proposed by the official can compensate the injured party, awarding the salaries not received because of the unlawful dismissal, the interest accrued since the decision was adopted, and the possible moral damage to the official's

[11] OGH 30 September 2008 1 Ob 225/07ff; 3 April 2008 1 Ob 44/08i.

[12] G Kodek, '§ 1293' in A Kletečka and M Schauer (eds), *ABGB-ON*[1.03] (version of 1 Janaury 2018, rdb.at) (Manz 2018) para 16.

[13] ibid para 10.

[14] RIS-Justiz RS0030558.

[15] OGH 14 October 1997 1 Ob 303/97h; 19 May 1998 1 Ob 140/98i; 31 March 2009 1 Ob 190/08k.

[16] Case F-107/13 *De Brito Sequeira Carvalho v Commission* [2009] ECR II-551, judgment of the Civil Service Tribunal 15 October 2014; Case F-26/10 *Az v Commission* [2011] OJ C362/23, judgment of the Civil Service Tribunal 28 September 2011.

reputation arising from the loss if he or she can demonstrate the unlawfulness of the act, as well as the causal link, and the damage. The employee does not have to prove that the rule breached is intended to protect them, nor that the administration has violated it in a serious and manifest manner. In public employment disputes, the EU acts as an employer, in a legal relationship with rights and obligations proper to both parties, and is subject to a greater responsibility, which obliges it to compensate the harm caused to its staff by any unlawful act committed in its capacity as employer.[17]

C. France

Thomas Perroud

Maurice's case would be considered as an unlawful dismissal and his claim would be successful concerning the sanction's annulment. However, this does not mean that he would automatically have the right to compensation, which depends on the misconduct and the well-founded nature of the sanction.

The right of defence (*les droits de la defense*) has been a well-established general principle of French administrative law since 1944. In *Dame Veuve Trompier-Gravier*,[18] the *Conseil d'Etat* considered that public bodies must guarantee the right to be heard when an administrative sanction is imposed, an individual decision is taken regarding the person,[19] or a decision has negative effects upon that person. In 1976, the *Conseil Constitutionnel* ruled that the right to a defence is a constitutional provision belonging to the 'fundamental principles recognized by the Laws of the Republic' (*principes fondamentaux reconnus par les lois de la République*),[20] and in 2006, the *Conseil Constitutionnel* established that the constitutional authority for the right to a defence was reinforced by its direct derivation from Article 16 of the Declaration of the Rights of Man and the Citizen.[21]

According to *Conseil d'Etat* case law, defence rights include: the possibility of knowing the charges and the documents of the file,[22] the right to present a written or oral[23] defence, and the right to have legal assistance if necessary. Currently, the obligation of a prior procedure including the right to a defence is codified in Articles L 122-1 and L 122-2 of the Code of relations between the public and the administration (CRPA), and it should be guaranteed before any individual decision which would adversely affect a person.[24]

[17] Case C-298/93 *Kinkle v Court of Justice* [1994] ECR I-03009, judgment of the Court 29 June 1994; Case C-274/99 *Connolly v Commission* [2001] ECR I-01611, judgment of the Court 6 March 2001; Case T-143/09 *Commission v Petrilli* [2010] ECR II-0000, judgment of the General Court 16 December 2010 (https://eur-lex.europa.eu/legal-context/IT/TXT/?uri=CELEX:62009TJo143> accessed 8 July 2020).

[18] CE 5 May 1944 *Dame Veuve Trompier-Gravier* No 69751 Rec 133.

[19] CE 26 October 1984 *Centre Hospitalier général de Firminy c Mme Chapuis* No 54263 Rec 342.

[20] Cons Const 17 January 1989 No 88-248 DC.

[21] Cons Const 30 March 2006 No 2006-535 DC. Article XVI—'Any society in which the guarantee of rights is not assured, nor the separation of powers determined, has no Constitution.'

[22] CE *avis* 22 November 1995 *C* No 171045 Rec.

[23] CE 26 March 1982 *C-P* No 20569 T.

[24] Article L211-2 CRPA.

Article 6 ECHR may be considered if the case is 'a civil obligation or a criminal charge' for the purposes of the Convention, because the meaning of these terms in the Convention may be different from their use in France, and it includes some administrative law situations. The *Conseil d'Etat*, following the criteria of the ECtHR, established that Article 6 must be applied in the case of economic sanctions ordered by the Financial Markets Authority (FMA)[25] and the *Office des migrations internationales*[26] (currently OFII—*Office Français de l'Immigration et de l'Intégration*). However, arguments from Article 6 § 1 regarding criminal charges in the administrative procedure will be endorsed only if the absence of guarantees in this first part has irreversible consequences impeding due process before the courts.[27]

In the case of civil servants, there are three rights that must be respected before a disciplinary sanction is imposed: the right to present a defence;[28] the right to review the complete case file on time (Art 65 of Law 22 April 1905); and the right to have a consultation procedure before a *Conseil de discipline* (discipline council).[29] This procedure includes a hearing where the agent, as well as the witnesses appointed by the agent and the administration, should be heard. The opinion of the *Conseil* is not binding on the disciplinary authority, but the latter must explain why it did not follow the sanction proposed. Nevertheless, the absence of consultation or its irregularity will lead to an unlawful sanction. In our case, therefore, if the *Conseil* had been consulted, Maurice would have had the opportunity to be heard. If not, the sanction would have been unlawful because the French authority did not guarantee either Maurice's right to defence or his right to due process. In conclusion, Maurice's case is an unlawful dismissal of a civil servant, and his claim would be successful before the courts.

After demonstrating that the decision in Maurice's case was unlawful and that, if challenged before an administrative jurisdiction, it would be annulled, it must be said that this does not necessarily imply that the administration would be liable and would be obligated to pay a compensation.

Government liability in France has two general dimensions: with or without misconduct.[30] In the first case, liability rests on three elements, simplified as follows: (1) the administration's misconduct (decision, operation, or omission) that (2—the causal link) had caused (3) damage to a person. Any unlawful decision of the administration is misconduct in French administrative law, and condition (1) is satisfied here; still it will be necessary to prove the damage (3) and the direct connection between this damage and the administration's misconduct (2).[31] We will analyse elements (2) and (3) regarding the awarding of damages.

If liability is established because of an unlawful dismissal, the act is annulled, and the judge may order:

[25] CE 24 February 2005 *Société GSD Gestions et MYX* No 269001 Rec.
[26] CE 28 July 1999 *GIE Mumm-Perriet-Jouet* No 188973 Rec.
[27] CE 26 May 2008 *Société Norélec* No 288583 Rec.
[28] CE 5 July 2000 *Mermet* No 200622 203356 Rec 292 D 2000 687, note Prélot.
[29] The *Conseil* has representatives of the administration and civil servants. See O Dord, *Droit de la fonction publique* (3rd edn, Themos Droit 2017).
[30] We will see some aspects of strict liability in case 6.
[31] CE 18 June 1986 *Krier* No 49813 Rec 166.

(1) the re-instatement of the civil servant in the same or an equivalent position as a primary remedy if practicable;
(2) a 'reconstruction' of his or her career[32] as if the unlawful decision had not been made;
(3) the award of compensation.

The amount of compensation is not established simply as the net wages and other benefits the agent would have earned during the period between the dismissal and re-instatement, for the following two reasons. First, there is a public financial principle that prohibits paying for a service that was not 'in fact' rendered (*service fait*). Second, it is important to consider the civil agent's misconduct too. The *Conseil d'Etat* stated the rule for reparation in *Deberles*:[33] the administration will compensate the damages really caused. The assessment of compensation ponders three factors:

(1) The damage actually suffered. It is necessary to deduct from the net wages any unemployment payment, new salaries, or any compensation that the agent had earned during the period he or she was not working due to the dismissal. In general, it should be considered as a base of calculation: (i) the salary and (ii) the loss of chance of other benefits that he or she could have usually earned; but that does not only depend on the agent's effective work.[34] The second part of the rule has been recently stated by the *Conseil d'Etat* in *Commune d'Ajaccio*,[35] which distinguished between these two types of benefits: one may be compensated as a loss of chance, another will not. The former concerns the annual performance bonus, earned over the past five years, the latter an additional allocation because he was working in a foreign country.[36] The court will consider the salary and the loss of chance of the annual bonus he usually earned, but it will not order the award of any amount of money for the additional allocation because, in fact, the agent was not working in a foreign country at that time. French legal scholarship considers that including the loss of chance of one type of benefit as a recoverable loss derives from the equity principle and it increases compensation in cases of unlawful dismissal.[37]
(2) The administration's misconduct: the court will consider the nature of the unlawfulness. If it is only an external or procedural irregularity regarding the administrative act, but the purpose of the decision is justified, the agent may not receive any compensation.[38] However, if the decision is substantially unlawful, the reparation may be total, as explained earlier in the section.

[32] It shows all the situations that may arise during the career and the rights related to each civil servant or employee.
[33] CE 7 April 1933 *Deberles* No 4711 GAJA.
[34] CE 6 December 2013 *Commune d'Ajaccio* No 365155.
[35] ibid.
[36] ibid.
[37] M Odile Diemer, 'L'indemnisation de l'agent public illégalement évincé: la nouvelle jeunesse de la jurisprudence Deberle' [2014] AJFP 326.
[38] In this case, the agent will not receive any compensation, even if the sanction has violated his right to present a defence. *Krier* (n 31); CE 9 February 2011 *D* No 332627 Rec; CE 5 October 2016 *L* No 380783 T.

(3) The agent's misconduct: compensation can be reduced, even to nil, where the employee has caused or contributed to his own dismissal. If his misconduct could justify the dismissal, reparation may be excluded. If the misconduct would not have led to dismissal because it was not serious enough, the reparation could be reduced proportionately, for example, by excluding the loss of chance concerning the annual performance bonus.

In conclusion, to determine the lawfulness of the decision and the administration's liability, the court will examine the reality of the alleged facts (*exactitude materielle des faits*),[39] their qualification as disciplinary misconduct (*qualification juridique des faits*),[40] the lawfulness of the decision, and the proportionality between the misconduct and the sanction.[41]

To sum up, in this case there has been an unlawful dismissal because Maurice has not been heard, and the court would thus annul the decision.[42] But compensation depends on the gravity of the misconduct and the well-foundedness of the sanction.

If the misconduct is not established during the process, full compensation would be paid, and the court would only deduct the sums that Maurice actually earned during that period as unemployment benefit. The compensation would include the loss of chance of any regular benefits. If Maurice were to prove the reputational damage or any direct loss caused by the dismissal, he could be compensated for this as well.

If Maurice drank wine[43] in the office and threw glasses outside, the court would consider the proportionality of the sanction, especially considering how the action would affect the public function and whether he caused any harm to third persons. In the light of the alleged facts, the court would probably conclude that dismissal was a disproportionate punishment for Maurice, who would receive a loss in salary. For example, it would not include the loss of opportunity of receiving the annual performance bonus.[44]

D. Germany

Ferdinand Wollenschläger and Johannes Stapf

Public employees can be employed under two different legal regimes in Germany, as *Beamte* (civil servants) or *Angestellte im öffentlichen Dienst* (contractual employees in the public service). The former fall under a specific public law regime characterized by a relationship of service and loyalty (cf s 4 BBG[45] and s 3 BeamtStG[46]), whereas

[39] CE 16 June 1965 *Morin* No 62105 Rec.

[40] CE 27 February 2015 *La Poste* No 376598 Rec.

[41] CE 13 November 2013 *M D* No 347704.

[42] *D* (n 38); *L* (n 38).

[43] Cour Administrative d'Appel de Bordeaux 30 June 2008 No 06BX00646. In fact, in France wine is one of the alcoholic beverages that may be authorized in the office in some situations.

[44] Conclusions of M Bertrand Dacosta, *rapporteur public* in the CE case *Commune d'Ajaccio* (n 34).

[45] *Bundesbeamtengesetz* (German Federal Civil Service Act), German version <www.gesetze-im-internet.de/bbg_2009/__4.html> accessed 20 June 2020.

[46] *Beamtenstatusgesetz* (German Federal Civil Servant Status Act), German version <www.gesetze-im-internet.de/beamtstg/__3.html> accessed 20 June 2020.

the latter are subject to the rules of labour law (with some peculiarities). According to Article 33 paragraph 4 GG (*Grundgesetz*, German Constitution), '[t]he exercise of sovereign authority on a regular basis shall, as a rule, be entrusted to members of the public service who stand in a relationship of service and loyalty defined by public law'. The distinction between civil servants and employees is relevant for jurisdiction: administrative courts are competent to review cases regarding civil servants (s 54 para 1 BeamtStG), whereas labour courts sit on cases involving employees (ss 2ff ArbGG[47]).

Under German law, Maurice's action would be primarily dealt with under the rules of employment and civil service law; the general provisions on public authority liability play only a limited role.

If Maurice were employed as *Beamter*, his dismissal would follow the rules laid down in either the federal disciplinary law[48] or the *Länder* disciplinary law[49], depending on the employing entity. These statutes stipulate a duty to hear civil servants subject to disciplinary proceedings prior to their dismissal (cf s 20 para 2, s 30 BDG and the corresponding *Länder* law)[50] and establish a specific standard of care (conducting all relevant inquiries, also with regard to exonerating evidence; cf s 21 para 1 sentences 1 and 2 BDG and the corresponding *Länder* law). Due to these express procedural guidelines, the courts do not need to refer to general principles of law or to Article 6 ECHR. The merits of the case depend on whether or not Maurice's dismissal was justified.

With regard to the omitted hearing, the rules of general administrative law apply (s 3 BDG).[51] The employing entity could, therefore, remedy this procedural error by hearing Maurice and reconsidering the decision taken (irrespective of the result) before the end of the court proceedings (the last instance competent to review the facts of the case and not only legal issues counts; see s 45 para 1 No 3 para 2 VwVfG[52] and the corresponding *Länder* legislation). If the authority fails to do so, the omitted hearing alone would not justify an annulment if it is evident that the procedural error did not influence the outcome of the decision (s 46 VwVfG). This requires that no different outcome would have been conceivable, even if the authority had heard Maurice.[53] Taking into account the fact that the head of Maurice's unit relied exclusively on accusations by his colleagues, and that Maurice might have produced arguments in favour of the continuation of his occupation, an alternative decision on his dismissal in

[47] *Arbeitsgerichtsgesetz* (German Labour Courts Act), German version <www.gesetze-im-internet.de/arbgg/BJNR012670953.html> accessed 20 June 2020.

[48] *Bundesdisziplinargesetz* (German Federal Disciplinary Act), German version <www.gesetze-im-internet.de/bdg/BJNR151010001.html> accessed 20 June 2020.

[49] See eg in Bavaria: *Bayerisches Disziplinargesetz* (Bavarian Disciplinary Act), German version <www.gesetze-bayern.de/Content/Document/BayDG?AspxAutoDetectCookieSupport=1> accessed 20 June 2020.

[50] Regarding corresponding *Länder* law, see B Wittkowski, '§ 20' in R Urban and B Wittkowski (eds), *Bundesdisziplinargesetz Kommentar* (2nd edn, CH Beck 2017) paras 16ff: *Länder* law rules differ at the outside with regard to the terms of the right to be heard.

[51] Wittkowski (n 50) para 14; cf BVerwG 1 November 1985—1 DB 45.85, BVerwGE 83, 77 (78f).

[52] *Verwaltungsverfahrensgesetz* (German Administrative Procedures Act), German version <www.gesetze-im-internet.de/vwvfg/BJNR012530976.html> accessed 20 June 2020.

[53] BVerwG 20 December 2013—7 B 18/13, [2014] DVBl 303 (306); cf K-A Schwarz, '§ 46 VwVfG' in M Fehling, B Kastner, and R Störmer (eds), *Verwaltungsrecht Handkommentar* (4th edn, Nomos 2016) para 24; U Ramsauer, '§ 46' in FO Kopp and U Ramsauer (eds), *Verwaltungsverfahrensgesetz Kommentar* ((21st edn, CH Beck 2020) para 25.

the case of his being heard seems possible. Thus, if the procedural error (no hearing) is not remedied, Maurice's dismissal is (formally) unlawful and may successfully be challenged.

The same finding applies to Maurice's second allegation: a lack of accuracy during the investigation might give rise to a claim based on a breach of § 21 paragraph 1 sentence 2 BDG, since this statute requires the employing entity to also inquire into exonerating evidence. § 4 BDG urges an expeditious disciplinary investigation and may allow the employing entity to skip the inquiry of certain exonerating evidence in cases where the evidence would be objectively irrelevant to the case or subjectively lead to no other assessment of the facts.[54] This is not the case here, since Maurice's dismissal seems to be based exclusively on rather vague evidence, which may easily be refuted. Unlike the omitted hearing, the scenario of an inaccurate investigation is not explicitly listed in § 45 paragraph 1 VwVfG and the corresponding *Länder* law. However, this provision can be applied analogously in cases where an agency failed to investigate all relevant facts.[55] Hence, the authority could remedy the procedural error before the end of the court proceedings, as set forth earlier in the section. If it fails to do so, § 46 VwVfG would not apply here either, since the investigation of facts in favour of Maurice could at least influence the decision. Thus, if the procedural error (no sufficient investigation) is not remedied, Maurice's dismissal is (formally) unlawful and may be challenged successfully.

Before initiating procedures in court, Maurice must file an objection with the Department of Public Administration as the employing entity (s 41 para 1 sentence 1 BDG, ss 72f of the German Code of Administrative Court Procedure, VwGO). The decision is taken by the supreme authority of the employing entity (s 42 para 2 BDG). If his objection were rejected, Maurice would have to initiate court proceedings (ss 52ff VwGO) before a chamber for disciplinary matters within the administrative court (ss 45 sentences 1f, 46 BDG). Maurice's rescissory action would have suspensive effect (§ 80 para 1 VwGO) if the authority had not ordered immediate execution for urgent reasons of public interest (s 80 para 2 No 4 VwGO).[56]

Thus, if according to the foregoing considerations a relevant procedural error can be established, Maurice may successfully challenge his dismissal and bring financial claims resulting from it before the administrative courts (s 45 sentence 1 BDG, s 40 para 2 sentence 2 alternative 1 VwGO). Since a rescinded dismissal does not terminate Maurice's employment, he is entitled to be paid under the rules on civil servant salaries (s 3 BBesG[57] and the corresponding *Länder* laws) although he has not worked.[58] However, § 3 para 5 BBesG, as well as the law of some German *Länder* (eg Art 4 para 4

[54] cf VG Münster 10 October 2014—20 K 18/14.BDG juris, para 21.

[55] U Ramsauer, '§ 45' in Kopp and Ramsauer (n 53) para 8; M Sachs, '§ 45' in P Stelkens, HJ Bonk, and M Sachs (eds), *Verwaltungsverfahrensgesetz* (9th edn, CH Beck 2018) para 145. More restrictive, K-A Schwarz, '§ 45 VwVfG' in Fehling and others (n 53) para 3.

[56] See (with regard to the objection) K Herrmann, '§ 7' in K Herrmann and H Sandkuhl (eds), *Beamtendisziplinarrecht—Beamtenstrafrecht* (CH Beck 2014) para 746; Wittkowski '§ 41' (n 50) para 4.

[57] *Bundesbesoldungsgesetz* (German Public Service Emoluments Act), German version <www.gesetze-im-internet.de/bbesg/BJNR011740975.html> accessed 20 June 2020.

[58] § 40 para 2 sentence 1 BDG provides for the payment of arrears in cases where a temporary suspension of a Beamter from office has been reversed.

BayBesG[59]) expressly rule out the granting of interests for delayed public service salaries, which is held justified in view of the special relationship between a civil servant and the State.[60] With regard to damages for the dismissal's negative consequences on his reputation and for having been obliged to look for a new job, Maurice might invoke § 280 para 1 sentence 1 BGB read in conjunction with the special duty of care which the employing agency owes to civil servants (s 78 BBG).[61] Hence, Maurice would have to prove that there was a 'breach of duty'. The head of Maurice's unit has clearly breached the fair trial obligations set out above. This applies even if he was not aware of these obligations: an official is obliged to analyse a matter in depth, which also implies the duty to ask for support if necessary.[62] With regard to the negative consequences on Maurice's reputation, § 253 BGB establishes a strict standard: § 253 paragraph 1 BGB requires an explicit provision for the award of damages for non-financial loss. § 253 para 2 BGB, which grants damages for 'injury to body, health, freedom or sexual self-determination', constitutes an example of such a provision. Even though there is no written provision regarding damages for an impaired reputation, the Federal Court of Justice understands Article 2 paragraph 1 read in conjunction with Article 1 paragraph 1 GG as the legal basis for such claims if the loss amounts to an infringement of the general right to free development of one's personality.[63] This may be the case whenever the infringement is particularly intense.[64] However, monetary compensation is subsidiary, ie limited to cases where no other form of restitution exists.[65] With regard to Maurice's impaired reputation, a public counter-statement seems more appropriate.[66]

He also claims compensation for damages arising from 'having been obliged to look for a new job'. As far as expenses for applications, interviews etc are concerned, these expenses may be claimed as damages (s 249 para 1 BGB); any non-financial losses may only be recovered according to the aforementioned conditions laid down in s 253 BGB.

The general provisions on public authority liability (Art 34 sentence 1 GG read in conjunction with s 839 para 1 sentence 1 BGB) are applicable.[67] These provisions grant

[59] *Bayerisches Besoldungsgesetz* (Bavarian Public Service Emoluments Act), German version <www.gesetze-bayern.de/Content/Document/BayBesG-4> accessed 20 June 2020. See BayVGH 27 June 2013—16 a DZ 12.558, [2013] NVwZ-RR 973.

[60] cf BVerwG 8 June 1966—VIII C 153/63, BVerwGE 24, 186 (190); 28 April 1994—2 WDB 1/94, BVerwGE 103, 111 (115f); BayVGH 27 June 2013—16 a DZ 12.558, [2013] NVwZ-RR 973 (973); A Reich and U Preißler, *Bundesbesoldungsgesetz Kommentar* (CH Beck 2014) s 3 para 11.

[61] H-W Laubinger, 'Höchstrichterliche Rechtsprechung zum Verwaltungsrecht: Der beamtenrechtliche Schadensersatzanspruch' (2008) 99 VerwArch 291ff; E Badenhausen-Fähnle, '§ 78 BBG' in R Brinktrine and K Schollendorf (eds), *BeckOK Beamtenrecht* (9th edn, CH Beck 1 April 2020) para 45; KJ Grigoleit, '§ 78 BBG' in U Battis (ed), *Bundesbeamtengesetz Kommentar* (5th edn, CH Beck 2017) para 21.

[62] H Wöstmann, '§ 839' in J von Staudinger and others (eds), *Kommentar zum Bürgerlichen Gesetzbuch mit Einführungsgesetz und Nebengesetzen* (14th edn, Sellier de Gruyter 2013) para 129.

[63] BGH 19 September 1961—VI ZR 259/60, BGHZ 35, 363 (366ff); G Spindler, '§ 253' in G Bamberger and others (eds), *BeckOK BGB* (54th edn, CH Beck 1 May 2020) para 24 with further references; cf BGH 14 February 1958—I ZR 151/56, BGHZ 26, 349 (354ff).

[64] BGH 17 December 2013—VI ZR 211/12, BGHZ 199, 237 (256f para 38).

[65] BGH 19 September 1961—VI ZR 259/60, BGHZ 35, 363 (369); G Schiemann, '§ 253' in von Staudinger and others (n 62, revised edn 2017) para 59.

[66] cf Schiemann, '§ 253' (n 65) para 59.

[67] Grigoleit (n 61) para 21; cf BGH 9 March 1965—VI ZR 218/63, BGHZ 43, 178 (183f); BayVGH 19 June 2012—6 C 12.857 juris para 9.

the award of damages in cases where (1) an official (2) intentionally or negligently (3) breached an official duty incumbent upon him or her (4) in relation to a third party, thereby (5) causing (6) the claimant harm.

With regard to (3) and (4), the official duties incumbent on the official having dismissed Maurice comprise the duty to hear civil servants subject to disciplinary proceedings prior to their dismissal (cf s 20 para 2, s 30 BDG, and the corresponding *Länder* law), the duty to also inquire into exonerating evidence (s 21 para 1 sentence 2 BDG), and the special duty of care which the employing agency owes to civil servants, as outlined earlier in the section.

With regard to the positions Maurice is entitled to claim ((5) and (6)), it has to be noted first that a claim with regard to his salary is unfounded. For, if Maurice's action before the administrative court is successful because the unlawfulness of his dismissal can be established, his salary will be paid retrospectively so that there is no damage. With regard to interest on the repayments, the rules on public authority liability, unlike those of civil servant law (s 3 para 5 BBesG), allow an award.[68] With regard to negative consequences for Maurice's reputation, § 253 para 1 BGB applies (see above).

Finally, it should be highlighted that in view of the primacy of primary legal protection, Maurice has to challenge his (unlawful) dismissal, but is not entitled to accept his (unlawful) dismissal and claim damages (s 839 para 3 BGB).

If Maurice is an *Angestellter im öffentlichen Dienst* (contractual employee in the public service), his dismissal would follow the general rules of employment law laid down in §§ 611a ff BGB. A dismissal on grounds of conduct[69] generally requires the issuing of a notice of warning[70] unless 'it is discernible *ex ante* that there is no change in behaviour to be expected or that the breach of a duty is particularly severe so that even its first-time toleration is unacceptable for the employer and thereby obviously—also discernible for the employee—impossible'[71]. Nonetheless, 'if the breach of a contractual duty arises from controllable behaviour by the employee, it is generally to be assumed that his or her future behaviour can be positively influenced by threatening with consequences for the continuance of the employment relationship'.[72] Even if the allegations by Maurice's colleagues were true, the issuance of a notice of warning by his employer would most likely have been necessary, since Maurice is to be assumed to abide by the PA's policy guidelines in future. Furthermore, his breach of duty, though potentially dangerous, does not amount to the degree of intensity which would allow the employer to refrain from issuing a notice of warning. The consumption of alcohol at the workplace generally does not render a notice of warning unnecessary, even if there is an explicit ban on alcohol (as stipulated in the PA's policy guidelines).[73]

68 Reich and Preißler (n 60) s 3 para 11.

69 There are no indications that Maurice suffers from alcoholism. If this were the case, it might justify a dismissal on personal grounds (*personenbedingte Kündigung*); cf M Henssler, '§ 626' in FJ Säcker and others (eds), *Münchener Kommentar zum Bürgerlichen Gesetzbuch*, vol 4 (8th edn, CH Beck 2020) paras 222ff; J Günther, '§ 626' in B Gsell and others (eds), *BeckOGK BGB* (CH Beck 1 August 2020) paras 311ff.

70 W Dütz and G Thüsing, *Arbeitsrecht* (24th edn, CH Beck 2019) para 406.

71 Own translation of BAG 20 November 2014—2 AZR 651/13, BAGE 150, 109 (113). See also R Vossen, '§ 1 KSchG' in R Ascheid, U Preis, and I Schmidt (eds), *Kündigungsrecht* (5th edn, CH Beck 2017) paras 368ff.

72 Own translation of BAG 23 January 2014—2 AZR 638/13, [2014] NZA 965 (966).

73 Günther (n 69) para 309, also mentioning exceptions.

Even if a notice of warning was regarded as unnecessary, additional requirements would arise from the fact that the head of Maurice's department relied exclusively on the allegations by Maurice's colleagues. The dismissal would be possible only if Maurice's employer had carried out all reasonable efforts to investigate the case[74] and if he had heard him before.[75]

Since these requirements were not observed, Maurice may (and also must) challenge his dismissal before the labour courts according to the rules of the *Kündigun gsschutzgesetz*[76] (ss 4f) within a three-week period. Otherwise, his dismissal will be deemed lawful.

In the event of a successful court action, his employment would not have been terminated. Thus, Maurice may claim his regular salary also for the periods in which he did not work following the dismissal since (and if) his employer failed to accept his performance (s 615 BGB).[77] Furthermore, he may also claim default interest (s 288 BGB) without having to issue a prior warning notice, since the salaries were due on a predetermined date (s 286 para 2 No 1 BGB).[78] That an employee on a contract may, unlike a civil servant, claim default interest results from the fact that a special relationship with specific duties is only assumed for the latter category of public employees.

Moreover, a claim for damages with regard to the damage to Maurice's reputation and the expenses for looking for a new job may be based on § 280 paragraph 1 BGB if this damage results from an at least negligent (§ 280 para 1 sentence 2 BGB read in conjunction with § 276 para 1 sentence 1 BGB) breach of a contractual duty, ie his employment agreement. A breach of duty might be seen in Maurice's dismissal which was unlawful, as seen above, since it came without a notice of warning and without a hearing.[79] However, according to the jurisprudence of the Federal Labour Court, an unlawful dismissal gives rise to a claim for damages only 'if it took place under undue circumstances, for example by harming, denouncing, and dishonouring the claimant more than required by the purpose of the dismissal'[80], which is presumably not the case here. Even if a breach of a contractual duty may be found, responsibility for the breach must also be established. This requires that the employer knew or should have known both about the nullity of the dismissal and about its undue circumstances.[81] The Federal Labour Court expressly declined responsibility for breach of a contractual duty in a case where a dismissal was based merely on allegations by a third party, since this indicated that the dismissing entity is convinced of the validity of the dismissal.[82]

[74] BAG 4 June 1964—2 AZR 310/63, BAGE 16, 72 (83); 26 March 1992—2 AZR 519/91, [1992] NZA 1121 (1122 with further references); see also J-M Niemann, '§ 626 BGB' in R Müller-Glöge, U Preis, and I Schmidt (eds), *Erfurter Kommentar zum Arbeitsrecht* (17th edn, CH Beck 2017) paras 216ff.

[75] Dütz and Thüsing (n 70) para 405; P Conze, 'Kündigung, allgemein' in P Conze, S Karb, and W Wölk (eds), *Personalbuch Arbeits- und Tarifrecht öffentlicher Dienst* (6th edn, CH Beck 2020) para 2021.

[76] *Kündigungsschutzgesetz* (Employment Protection Act), German version <www.gesetze-im-internet.de/kschg/BJNR004990951.html> accessed 20 June 2020.

[77] cf Günther (n 69) paras 678, 681.

[78] BAG 13 June 2002—2 AZR 391/01, BAGE 101, 328 (338), on the old version (s 284 BGB), and for the conditions under which an employer can exculpate an omitted payment.

[79] cf Günther (n 69) para 682.

[80] BAG 24 October 1974—3 AZR 488/73, [1974] BB 1640 (1640).

[81] ibid. See also Henssler (n 69) para 374; Günther (n 69) para 682.

[82] BAG 24 October 1974—3 AZR 488/73, [1974] BB 1640 (1640); Günther (n 69) para 682.1. Note: this is to be distinguished from the finding of unlawfulness of the act itself.

Thus, damages can be awarded neither for Maurice's impaired reputation nor for having been obliged to look for a new job.

The general rules on public liability (Art 34 sentence 1 GG read in conjunction with s 839 para 1 sentence 1 BGB) only apply to relationships governed by public law[83] and therefore do not apply here, since Maurice is employed under the rules of civil law.

In summary, the adjudication of damages depends on whether Maurice is a *Beamter* or an *Angestellter im öffentlichen Dienst*. If Maurice has successfully challenged his dismissal, his salaries will be paid, although he did not work. As an *Angestellter*, he may also claim interest. However, Maurice will not be compensated (in money) for his sullied reputation. Damages 'for having been obliged to look for a new job', at least the actual loss, may be claimed if he is a *Beamter*.

E. Hungary

Lilla Berkes

In Hungary, using such guidelines is not so common in the public administration: normally there are only ethical rules, for which the most serious consequence is a reprimand. However, the right to be heard and the main procedural rules have such importance and a close connection to constitutional rights that they are regulated by an Act. According to Article I (3) of the Constitution, 'The rules relating to fundamental rights and obligations shall be laid down in Acts.' It is, therefore, common for these rights to be stated in the relevant act and decree.

The previous act on civil servants (before 1 March 2012) saw a period when it had no regulation about the right to be heard in case of unworthiness. According to judicial practice, the decisive factor before the court was whether the hearing of the person concerned and other actions were necessary to establish the facts or not, so the court would find an infringement in connection with probative proceedings without mentioning general rules of law or constitutional rights. Also, even if there were no legal provisions in an act or decree, a direct reference to the constitution in a judicial decision has never been the practice.[84]

[83] J Wieland, 'Art 34' in H Dreier (ed), *Grundgesetz Kommentar*, vol 2 (3rd edn, Mohr Siebeck 2015) para 38.

[84] In both judicial practice and theory, there was a debate on whether judges could interpret the provisions of the Constitution or base their decisions on it. Before the transition, the Constitution was more a political document than a legal norm, so the judges did not refer to it in the decisions, and after the transition this practice remained. After the transition, there were cases when the decisions referred to the constitution, or to the ECHR, but not to fulfil the lack of a normative provision, but rather to help to decide the case, eg in criminal cases or personality rights cases. The application of the Constitution rather than the acts and regulations would have meant that the courts would be judging the constitutionality of the law.

According to Art 28 of the Constitution, the courts need to interpret the laws according to the Constitution. This is one of the provisions that was not part of the previous Constitution and which is slowly changing judicial practice. Article 28 states that:

> In the course of the application of law, the courts shall, in principle, interpret the laws in accordance with their objective and with the Fundamental Law. The objectives of a law shall in principle be determined relying on its preamble, and/or on the explanatory memorandums of the relevant legislative or amendment proposal. When interpreting the Fundamental Law or any

According to the current Act on Civil Servants,[85] there are two options for the case in the example: one is the procedure to determine unworthiness, and the other is disciplinary. If the civil servant is unworthy of his or her position, he or she must be dismissed. The public employer must give reasons for the dismissal. These reasons must be clearly stated, and the employer must demonstrate that the reason for the exemption is real and reasonable. Before the dismissal, the civil servant should be given the opportunity to know the grounds for the dismissal and to defend themselves, unless this is not to be expected from the employer due to all the circumstances of the case. So there is a legal option to dismiss the civil servant without hearing, which could probably be used in a case similar to Maurice's. Also, the dismissed civil servant may file a complaint with the Civil Service Arbitration Committee, which conducts probative proceedings and also holds a hearing, with sixty days for a reasoned decision. If the dismissal was unlawful, the civil servant could obtain the lost salary and compensation (two–twenty-four months' liquidated damages) too. The decision of the Civil Service Arbitration Committee can be reviewed by the labour court, which may also apply the same legal consequences. In the case of violation of the civil servant's personality rights, the civil servant must bring the action for damages to the general court.

In the case of a wrongful breach of obligations, a disciplinary procedure can be conducted. The civil servant committed a disciplinary offence through the behaviour mentioned in our case. Deprivation of office as a disciplinary sanction automatically means dismissal without further decision. However, the rules of the disciplinary procedure are stricter and more detailed than those of the determination-of-unworthiness procedure. The civil servant must be notified of the initiation of the disciplinary proceedings in writing. The written notification must contain the alleged infringement. The investigating officer will conduct the investigation, during which there is a duty to hear the civil servant. After the investigation, a Disciplinary Board will be selected, and will hold a hearing. In the case of an unlawful decision, the legal consequences are the same as those mentioned before, but the civil servant cannot file a complaint with the Civil Service Arbitration Committee. There is an opinion of the administrative and labour college of the Curia about the questions of the review of the Civil Service Arbitration Committee,[86] according to which, in the case of a wrongful breach of

other law, it shall be presumed that they are reasonable and of benefit to the public, serving virtuous and economical ends.

In 2016–17, one of the jurisprudence analysis groups of the Curia prepared a summary opinion about the implementation of the Fundamental Law in judicial practice. They examined 500 decisions, and the conclusion was that around 43 per cent of the decisions referred to the Fundamental Law at a certain point, but among these decisions there were ones with only a formal reference or that only referred to Art 28, and the substantive references were mostly in personality rights cases (A Kúria, 'Az Alaptörvény követelményeinek érvényesülése a bírósági ítélkezésben. Összefoglaló vélemény' (2016) 38 <www.lb.hu/sites/default/files/joggyak/alaptorveny_osszefoglalo_velemeny.pdf> accessed 20 June 2020).

[85] Act CXCIX of 2011—there is no available English translation. There is a new act (Act CXXV of 2018—on the government administration, with no available English translation; promulgated on 21 December 2018); it has regulations on government administration personnel, but the regulations are similar regarding the dismissal of the personnel, and Act CXCIX of 2011 is also applicable as underlying legislation.

[86] 3/2016 (III. 21) *KMK vélemény* (opinion of the Administrative and Labour Collegium of the Curia).

obligations ruled under the regulations of disciplinary proceedings, the civil servant cannot be dismissed on grounds of unworthiness.

The Act regarding Civil Servants took effect in March 2012, but there are not many available cases, so it is not possible to answer with any certainty that the lack of a hearing in the disciplinary procedure by itself could cause the unlawfulness of the decision. Together with lack of accuracy, the civil servant has better chances. But it is much easier to dismiss the public servant because of unworthiness.

F. Italy

Fulvio Cortese

In Italy, the case in which Maurice is involved is considered to be a case of disciplinary dismissal.

Most certainly, if Maurice was not heard before the sanction was imposed, he could obtain from the court an assessment of the invalidity of the sanction as well as compensation for all the harm mentioned in section C above at points (1), (2), and (3).

First of all, it should be noted that the employment of civil servants in Italy is usually governed by the same rules as private-sector employees. However, there are exceptions for specific categories of civil servants; for example judges, policemen, the military, university professors: the employment of these civil servants is regulated by public law.[87] This special system also applies to disciplinary sanctions.

In the context of the general and common rules, the court to which the dismissed employee can appeal is the civil court in its specific role as a labour court.

The verdict will not only consider whether or not the employee committed certain actions that are prohibited by law, according to the collective contract signed with trade union representatives or the code of conduct that employees are supposed to observe when performing their work. The court must also assess whether the administration respected the strict procedural rules established by the law, with no exception, for cases where the employer intends to take punitive measures.[88]

These rules specifically guarantee that the employee is notified promptly and in writing of the charges they have incurred, so that they can defend themselves during the procedure, during which the employee also has the right to be heard in person and to request assistance, for example from the trade unions.

In the event that the administration adopts the disciplinary sanction (in this case, dismissal) without having guaranteed the employee's right to defence, the dismissal is not valid.[89]

[87] Article 3 LD No 165/2001.

[88] Article 7 L No 300/1970; Art 55-*bis* LD No 165/2001.

[89] Violation of the strict procedure laid down by law does not normally determine the invalidity of the acts of the procedure itself or the sanctions imposed: this only occurs if the right of defence of the employee is recognized as irrecoverably compromised, and if the forms of the procedure are recognized as incompatible with the principle of timeliness regarding the procedure itself (Art 55-*bis* para 9-*ter*, LD No 165/2001).

G. Poland

Aleksander Jakubowski

Under Polish law, Maurice's appeal would probably be successful. The procedural irregularities described below constitute grounds for the invalidity of the disciplinary decisions. Therefore, the appellate court would overrule them, annul proceedings insofar as such proceedings are invalid, and refer the case to a disciplinary committee for re-examination. Nevertheless, the appellate court will not decide on any damages to be awarded to Maurice.

Damages can be sought in separate proceedings before an ordinary court. In Maurice's case, damages can only be considered if, during the re-examination of the case under appropriate procedure and by proper authorities, denial of the allegations regarding Maurice's improper conduct emerge, which seems to be unlikely.

On the basis of the provisions described below, the actions of the head of the unit concerning Maurice should be deemed procedurally improper. The head of the unit should have asked a disciplinary officer to carry out disciplinary proceedings, and if, following exploratory proceedings, it was ascertained that there are grounds for Maurice's disciplinary liability, he or she would have requested a disciplinary commission to institute disciplinary proceedings against Maurice. It is for a disciplinary commission, as a collegial body, and not the head of the unit, to expel Maurice from public service. Maurice could appeal against the decision to the Higher Disciplinary Commission of the Civil Service,[90] and subsequently to the appeal court, ie the ordinary court, against the decision of the Higher Disciplinary Commission. It should be noted that the decision was made by the wrong authority.

Further, in the course of disciplinary proceedings, the defendant (*obwiniony*) should be entitled to actively participate in the proceedings, and especially to be able to make their case in a hearing. This stems from statutory legal provisions and ordinances of the President of the Council of Ministers, which are generally applicable, regardless of the internal rules and regulations of the civil service. Additionally, disciplinary authorities or courts may invoke legal provisions providing for the right of a person to be heard pursuant to the fair trial principle, including Article 2 of the Polish Constitution or Article 6 ECHR. The facts of Maurice's case show beyond doubt that he was expelled from civil service without being given an opportunity to be heard: he was deprived of the right to actively participate in the proceedings.

These observations support the invalidity of the disciplinary proceedings; hence, the appellate court would overrule the appealed disciplinary decision, annulling the proceedings as invalid and referring the case to disciplinary committee for re-examination.

A civil servant may be expelled from service in the event of any breach of internal rules prohibiting drinking alcohol during working hours, all the more so for being inebriated at work and throwing wine glasses out of a window. Such behaviour on the

[90] Higher Disciplinary Commission; see The Chancellery of the Prime Minister, 'Two Decades of the Polish Civil Service—Achievements and Challenges' 8–9 <https://dsc.kprm.gov.pl/sites/default/files/pliki/two_decades_of_the_polish_civil_service.pdf> accessed 20 June 2020.

part of a public employee violates the legal obligation of a public employee to behave respectfully both during working hours and after work.[91] Consequently, during the re-examination of the case under appropriate procedure and by proper authorities, the same decision on expelling him from the civil service would be issued, should allegations be confirmed.[92]

Maurice may seek damages against the State Treasury before an ordinary court. In any such action he will have to prove that he sustained damage due to an unlawful decision regarding his dismissal, which is causally linked to defective proceedings as such. This concerns both real losses (*damnum emergens*) and loss of profit, which the injured party might have gained had it not been for the damage (*lucrum cessans*). However, since the decision is not final and will be re-examined by the disciplinary commission, the unlawfulness of the decision can only be established if the allegations of Maurice's improper conduct are not confirmed. In the case at hand, it seems to be unlikely. Despite the fact that the decision was not final, Maurice was prevented from performing his duties and was in fact forced to look for another job. In this situation, he may demand to be paid also the remuneration for 'readiness to work' provided for in labour law.

A distinct issue is whether Maurice can seek damages for damage to his reputation. It seems that there are no grounds to seek such damages, because even if a personal good such as his honour was violated, there was nothing unlawful provided that the allegations against him are subsequently confirmed. Moreover Maurice, as a public employee, is treated as a public official, and information about his dismissal is related to his duties as a public official and deemed public information. It should be pointed out here that if the allegations are found groundless, Maurice could seek damages for the fact that his honour was tarnished only if this personal good was damaged unlawfully (ie it was not a result of legal disciplinary proceedings).

The disciplinary liability of members of the civil service corps is regulated by Chapter 9 of the Act of 21 November 2008 on Civil Service (the Civil Service Act). Pursuant to the provisions of Article 113 section 1 of the Civil Service Act, a civil service corps member shall be disciplinarily liable for violating the responsibilities of a civil service corps member. The civil servant shall, in particular, be obliged to behave in a dignified manner inside and outside the service (Art 76 s 1 item 7 of the Civil Service Act). In accordance with Article 114 section 1 item 6 of the Civil Service Act, one of the disciplinary penalties applicable to civil servants is expulsion from the civil service.[93] The disciplinary commission shall, in general, conduct disciplinary proceedings involving civil service corps members in the first instance, and the Higher

[91] See J-C Garcia-Zamor, 'Pathologies in Public Administration: How Critical is the Concept of Administrative Ethics?' in D Kijowski and P Suwaj (eds), *Patologie w administracji publicznej* (Wolters Kluwer 2009) 54; M Elliott and R Thomas, *Public Law* (OUP 2017) 384.

[92] See T Barankiewicz, 'Civil Service—Poland's Experience in the Development of Its Ethics and Ethos' in J Itrich-Drabarek, S Mazur, and J Wiśniewska-Grzelak (eds), *The Transformations of the Civil Service in Poland in Comparison with International Experience* (Peter Lang 2008) 151–52; J Itrich-Drabarek and K Mroczka, 'Ethical by Choice or Obligation? Ethical Management in the Civil Service in the Light of the Results of Empirical Research' in Itrich-Drabarek and others (ibid) 172, 175, 190 172, 175, 190.

[93] See also K Mroczka, 'Human Resource Management in Civil Service – Selected Aspects' in J Itrich-Drabarek, K Mroczka, and Ł Świetlikowski, *Civil Service in Poland* (Oficyna Wydawnicza ASPRA-JR 2012) 69–70.

Disciplinary Commission, in the event of appeal (Art 116 s 1 and Art 121 of the Civil Service Act). If the disciplinary ombudsman requests the application of the penalty of expulsion from civil service, the disciplinary commission adjudicates in a panel comprising five members, including a chairperson with a legal background. The Higher Disciplinary Commission shall also adjudicate in a panel composed of the same number of members, including two with a legal background (Art 123 s 1 of the Civil Service Act).

Pursuant to the provisions of Article 125 sections 1 and 2 of the Civil Service Act, the disciplinary officer initiates explanatory proceedings upon the order of the head of the unit and requests the disciplinary commission to initiate disciplinary proceedings. Pursuant to the provisions of § 8 section 1 of the Ordinance of the President of the Council of Ministers of 9 April 2009 on explanatory proceedings and disciplinary proceedings in the civil service (hereinafter the Ordinance), through a notice of initiation of the proceedings, the disciplinary ombudsman informs the defendant of the allegations against him or her and the rights he or she enjoys. Section 4 of the Article provides that if a person concerned is absent, the exploratory proceeding is suspended until a person concerned may testify. In turn, § 9 of the Ordinance specifies that in the course of the exploratory proceedings, the person concerned may submit evidence and provide explanation, examine files, and appoint a defence attorney of choice. After completion of the proceedings, the disciplinary ombudsman immediately notifies the person concerned of the completion of the proceedings, provides them with the gathered evidence, and allows them to furnish additional explanations (§ 10 s 1 of the Ordinance). If, in the course of the exploratory proceedings, the allegations against the person concerned are confirmed, the disciplinary officer draws up a request to initiate disciplinary proceedings and sends it immediately, in duplicate, to the disciplinary commission (§ 11 s 1 of the Ordinance). The disciplinary commission issues a decision after the hearing, during which both the disciplinary ombudsman, the accused, and his or her defence attorney, if appointed, testify, and having considered other evidence material to the case (Art 126 s 3 of the Civil Service Act). According to § 24 section 1 item 3 of the Ordinance, the disciplinary commission adjourns the hearing if the accused, having been duly served the summons, fails to appear. The hearing ends with closing speeches of the parties and the defence attorney, with the defendant having the final word (§ 27 of the Ordinance).

Pursuant to the provisions of Article 126 section 7 of the Civil Service Act, the parties may appeal against the adjudication of the disciplinary commission to the Higher Disciplinary Commission within fourteen days from the delivery of the adjudication. According to § 35 of the Ordinance, after the Higher Disciplinary Commission receives an appeal, the chairperson of the Higher Disciplinary Commission appoints the adjudication panel and refers the case to them to be heard, also determining the date of the hearing. After the hearing, the Higher Disciplinary Commission awards a decision (§ 36 s 1 of the Ordinance). The parties and the Head of Civil Service may appeal against the adjudications of the Higher Disciplinary Commission to the court of appeal—the labour and social insurance court having jurisdiction over the defendant's place of residence. The appeal is lodged via the Higher Disciplinary Commission. This means that the appeal against the disciplinary decision concerning the expulsion of a person from the civil service is examined by an ordinary court based on the merits (the decision may be revoked and amended by a new decision, or '*reformatoryjny*') and not by an administrative court, which may dismiss the decision, but cannot amend it ('*kasatoryjny*'). Hence, pursuant to the provisions of Article 127 section 3 of the Civil Service Act, the examination of the appeal is executed according to the provisions of the Code of Civil Procedure. The decision of the appellate court cannot be appealed against to the Supreme Court. Disciplinary decisions shall become final and non-revisable if they may no longer be appealed against or otherwise challenged (see Art 363 § 1 in conjunction with Art 777 § 1 item 1 of the Code of Civil Procedure).

Pursuant to Article 378 § 1 of the Code, the court of appeal hears cases within the limits of the appeal; however, the court shall *ex officio*, take into account the invalidity of proceedings. The proceedings will be ruled invalid according to the provisions of Article 379 section 5 of the Code of Civil Procedure if the party was deprived of the right to defend his or her case. This provision makes the rule of law (stemming from Art 2 of the Constitution) more specific.[94] Additionally, the court adjudicating within the boundaries of systemic argument (*wykładnia systemowa*) may take into account that the provision quoted includes the disposition provided for in Article 6 ECHR, which under certain circumstances may also refer to a public employee, because he or she was deprived of the right to be heard with respect to the facts of the case otherwise than due to the interest of the State.[95] In the light of the established case law, the lack of notification served on the accused with respect to disciplinary proceedings, which makes it impossible for him or her to participate and voice his or her opinion concerning the case, means that he or she is deprived of their right to participate and voice an opinion in the course of the proceedings, thus being unable to protect their rights within the meaning of the quoted provision.[96] However, the proceedings are not invalid if a party failed to exercise its procedural rights at its own discretion.[97] It is worth stressing that pursuant to Article 381 of the Code of Civil Procedure (CCP), the court of appeal may disregard new facts and evidence if the party could have adduced them at trial before the court of first instance, unless the need to adduce the same arose at a later date. If the appeal is found groundless, then the court of appeal under the provisions of Article 385 CCP will dismiss it. If the appeal is taken into account, then the court of appeal, under the provisions of Article 386 § 1 CCP will change the appealed judgment and rule on the merits of the case. Pursuant to the provisions of Article 386 § 2 of the Civil Code (CC), if the proceedings are declared invalid, the court of second instance will set aside the appealed judgment and cancel the proceedings insofar as they have been declared invalid, and remand the case to the Higher Disciplinary Commission for re-examination. Additionally, except for the

[94] See D Pożaroszczyk, 'Disciplinary Procedure in Polish Special Services in the Light of the Concept of a Fair Trial Exemplified by the Disciplinary Procedure of the Internal Security Agency' (2017) 22 Bialostockie Studia Prawnicze 44–45, 48–49.

[95] *Vilho Eskelinen and others v Finland* App No 63235/00, ECR II-2007 1, ECtHR judgment 19 April 2007, ss 43–62; *Wallishauser v Austria* App No 156/04, ECtHR judgment 17 July 2012.

[96] See, respectively, II CSK 325/12, judgment of the Supreme Court 7 February 2013; II PK 260/15; III AUa 1908/15, judgment of the Appellate Court in Łódź 23 November 2016; VI ACa 1624/13, judgment of the Appellate Court in Warsaw 17 July 2014; III AUa 1190/15, judgment of the Appellate Court in Gdańsk 28 October 2015.

[97] V CSK 526/15, judgment of the Supreme Court 20 April 2016.

case discussed here, the court of appeal may overrule the appealed judgment and refer the case for re-examination only if the Higher Disciplinary Commission failed to discuss the case on its merits (eg if the decision was made by the head of unit and not by the Commission) or when the judgment may only be pronounced as a result of the rules of evidence being carried out in full.

The case law provides that in the event of a disciplinary issue, the case cannot be based on probability, but must stem from clear and unquestionable facts, which prove that a member of the civil service corps violated his or her duties.[98]

Regardless of the above, it is worth adding that according to Article 71 section 1 item 7 of the Civil Service Act, the termination of employment of a public employee without notice due to the misconduct of the civil servant can result from a serious infringement of the fundamental duties of a civil servant when the misconduct is obvious. This premise is independent of any disciplinary proceedings.[99] However, this does not concern the case in question, because the accused was expelled in the course of disciplinary proceedings.

Pursuant to the provisions of Article 417 § CC, the State Treasury, the local government unit, or any other legal person exercising power under the rule of law may be liable for damages inflicted by unlawful action and/or omission during the exercise of public authority under the law in force. Liability for damages under Article 417 CC may, within the meaning of 361 § 2 CC, encompass real damage (*damnum emergens*), and loss of profit that the aggrieved party might have gained if it were not for the damage (*lucrum cessans*) caused. This view is well established in case law.[100] It should be added here that pursuant to the first sentence of Article 417^1 CC, if damage is caused by a final decision or a final judgment, a remedy may be sought once it has been declared non-compliant with the law, unless otherwise provided for by separate legal provisions.

It is worth noting that under Article 9 section 1 of the Civil Service Act, the provisions of the Labour Code and other provisions of the labour law shall apply to all issues not regulated in this Act and concerning public sector employment. Pursuant to the provisions of Article 81 § 1 of the Labour Code, if an employee is willing to work but is unable to do so due to reasons concerning the employer, the employee is entitled to remuneration for the fallow time based on his or her personal pay scale according to an hourly or monthly rate, and if this aspect of remuneration was not established when the pay conditions were set, then he or she will receive 60 per cent of the employee's remuneration. In any case, this remuneration may not be lower than the amount of the minimum wage, as set out in separate provisions.

According to the provisions of Article 23 CC, the personal interests of a human being—in particular, health; freedom; dignity; freedom of conscience; name or pseudonym; image; privacy of correspondence; inviolability of the home; and scientific, artistic, inventive, or improvement achievements—are protected by civil law, independently of protection under other regulations. Article 24 § 1 and 2 of the Code

[98] See III APo 5/12, judgment of the Appellate Court in Szczecin 11 December 2012.

[99] See II PK 259/14, judgment of the Supreme Court 7 October 2015.

[100] K 20/02, judgment of the Constitutional Tribunal 23 September 2003; I ACa 222/10, judgment of the Appellate Court in Poznań 7 April 2010.

provide that any person whose personal interests are threatened by another person's actions may demand that the actions be ceased unless they are not unlawful. In the case of infringement, he or she may also demand that the person committing the infringement perform the actions necessary to remove its effects, in particular that the person make a declaration of the appropriate form and substance. On the terms provided for in this Code, he or she may also demand monetary recompense or that an appropriate amount of money be paid to a specific public cause. Article 448 § 1 CC establishes that in the event of infringement of one's personal interests the court may award the person whose interests have been infringed an appropriate amount as monetary recompense for the harm suffered or may, upon request, award an appropriate amount of money to be paid for a social cause of their choice, irrespective of other means necessary to remove the effects of the infringement. If the re-examination of Maurice's case under appropriate procedure and by proper authorities results in allegations regarding his improper conduct, it could be considered that his honour was tarnished by the actions of the head of the unit.

It should be borne in mind that a disciplinary decision constitutes public information within the meaning of Article 6 section 1 item 4 letter a) of the Act of 6 September 2001 on access to public information, being an official document under section 2 of said Article, so it is subject to publication in the Public Information Bulletin (*Biuletyn Informacji Publicznej*) of the authority under Article 7 section 1 item 1 of the said act, albeit respecting, pursuant to Article 5 sections 1 and 2, any restrictions relating to privacy. Such restrictions do not, however, concern persons holding public office or holding positions related to public office. As explained by the Supreme Administrative Court,[101] the term 'person holding public office' used in Article 5 section 2 of the Act on access to public information included any person who may have an impact on public matters within the meaning of Article 1 section 1, ie on the 'public sphere'. Therefore, it would be legal to publish information about penalizing Maurice, a public official.

H. Romania

Roxana Vornicu

In the Romanian legal system, case 1 would be assessed by looking at the rules applicable regarding the disciplinary liability of public servants. The disciplinary liability of public servants is one of three types of administrative liability and is also sometimes referred to by scholars as administrative disciplinary liability.[102] The disciplinary liability of public servants is triggered pursuant to a procedure regulated under Law 188/1990 on the status of public servants.[103] The legal procedure describes the

[101] I OSK 1530/14, judgment 8 July 2015.

[102] Legal scholars include here: (i) administrative disciplinary liability; (ii) liability for contraventions; and (iii) patrimonial liability of the administration (contractual or extra-contractual). See, for instance, in Romanian DA Tofan, *Drept Administrativ*, vol II (2nd edn, CH Beck 2009).

[103] Law 188/1990 on the statute of public servants, republished in the Official Gazette No 365 of 29 May 2007.

grounds for triggering the disciplinary liability of civil servants, the phases and the principles of the disciplinary investigation procedure, and its possible outcomes (the disciplinary sanctions). The disciplinary investigation procedure is finalized through the issuance of an administrative act. If a civil servant is not satisfied with the outcome of the disciplinary investigation, he or she can seek annulment of the act before the administrative courts. This claim is regulated under Article 80 of Law 188/1999, stating that: 'The public servant unsatisfied with the sanction applied can bring a claim before the administrative court asking for the modification or the annulment of the sanctioning act.' This provision does not specifically mention the civil servant's option of lodging a claim for damages, but the law on civil servants does state under Article 117 that the provisions in this act should be read in conjunction with administrative, civil, and labour law rules and principles. In practice, Article 80 of Law 188/1999 has been read in conjunction with the general provisions under Law 554/2004 on judicial review and Article 52 of the Constitution guaranteeing the right to compensation for illegal administrative action. Under Romanian law, Maurice could therefore in principle bring a claim for annulment of the dismissal act and seek both material and moral damages.

In Romania, the fact that Maurice had been dismissed without being heard during the investigation and that he had been investigated by the head of the unit would be considered unlawful. Administrative disciplinary liability is triggered based on the provisions under Article 77 of Law 188/1990 stating that whenever public servants culpably breach their public duties or the regulations applicable to their professional or civic conduct, their demeanour will qualify as disciplinary misconduct and their disciplinary liability will be triggered. For reasons of clarity, in this section I will go through (i) the forms of conduct that could lead to disciplinary liability being triggered under Romanian law; (ii) the sanctions that can be applied for disciplinary misconduct of a public servant; (iii) the bodies that can apply the disciplinary sanctions; and (iv) the procedure that should be followed for a public servant to be held liable for disciplinary misconduct.

The actions triggering disciplinary liability under Law 188/1999 (Art 77 para 2) regarding the status of public servants include '(g) Attitudes or behaviour that affect the service's or the public body's prestige' that might be relevant here.

The disciplinary sanctions for misconduct by civil servants under Romanian law are: (i) written notice; (ii) a 5–30 per cent reduction in salary for up to 3 months; (iii) suspending their right to promotion for a period from one to three years; (iv) demotion for a period of up to one year; (v) dismissal from public service.

It is important to note that in order for these sanctions to be applied, the investigation must be conducted by the disciplinary commission, with one exception. The head of the unit can conduct the investigation him- or herself and apply the sanction if the latter consists in written notice. Should any of the other sanctions be applied (therefore, including Maurice's *dismissal*), the investigation must be conducted by the disciplinary commission (Art 78 of Law 188/1999.

However, irrespective of the sanction applied and whether the investigation is conducted by the head of unit alone, or by the commission, Article 78(3) of Law 188/1990 reads that:

> disciplinary sanctions can only be applied after a prior investigation of the misconduct and after the public servant is heard. There shall be a written record of the public servant's hearing, under pain of nullity.

The Government Decision No 1344/2007 on the organization and functioning of disciplinary commissions establishes that all public authorities should organize a disciplinary commission functioning on a permanent basis within the public body and that all disciplinary investigations should be conducted in respect of a number of principles, including presumption of innocence, right to defence and to be heard, and proportionality.

The principle of proportionality springs from Article 77(4) under Law 188/1999 on the status of public servants[104] and is also listed as one of the principles applicable to administrative disciplinary investigations under Government Decision N 1344/2007 on the organization and functioning of disciplinary commissions.[105] It should be mentioned that Romanian courts have often used the proportionality principle enshrined in Article 77(4) of Law 188/1990 when ruling on the illegality of disciplinary sanctioning decision, and have even replaced the sanction with a lighter one based on the same principle.[106]

Maurice's dismissal therefore breaches the provisions of Law 188/1999 on the status of public servants, and Government Decision No 1344/2007 in that: (i) the investigation procedure was not conducted by the disciplinary commission;[107] (ii) Maurice's right to be heard and to be presumed innocent was breached; and, arguably, (iii) the sanction was disproportionate, given the conduct of the public servant.

It therefore follows that, irrespective of the administration's policy guidelines and whether they mention a specific duty of care during the investigation, and the civil servant's right to be heard before an unfavourable decision is taken, there are several statutory acts in force that regulate these duties of care during the investigation and the civil servant's right to be heard.

But even if these statutory acts had not been enacted, the Romanian courts of justice would have interpreted the rights of civil servants during disciplinary investigations in the light of Article 6 ECHR and would have included the right to be heard within the safeguards of both the ECHR right to a fair trial and the constitutional principle of the rule of law.[108]

104

> When identifying the disciplinary sanction, the causes and gravity of the misconduct must be considered as well as the circumstances in which it was committed, the degree of fault and the consequences of the misconduct as well as the general behaviour of the public servant or his/her previous history of misconduct that has not been discharged according to the law.

(All translations of legal provisions, case law excerpts, and scholarly contributions are the those of the author.)

105 Published in the Official Gazette No 768 of 13 November 2007.

106 See Decision No 1059 of 15 June 2010, issued by the Ploiesti Court of Appeal.

107 See a decision of the Supreme Court in which it annulled the dismissal order and decided that the public servant (in this case, an employee of the National Pension Fund) should be reintegrated in his public function and paid damages due to the illegal composition of the disciplinary commission—Decision No 3787 of 15 November 2012, Supreme Court in Romanian on the Supreme Court's website <www.scj.ro/> accessed 20 June 2020.

108 See, for instance, a decision of the Bacau Court of Appeal regarding a disciplinary investigation on the conduct of an employee of the National Forests Agency, who could not justify a certain amount of wood. The court reopened the case by applying Art 6 ECHR directly because the civil servant's right to be heard was

As for damages, Maurice would be entitled to obtain the salary that he would have received had he not been unlawfully dismissed, as well as interests, which would qualify as material damages. In the Romanian legal system, the consequences of the facts set out above would be (i) the annulment of the act; (ii) the reintegration of Maurice in his position; and (iii) the compensation of loss suffered as a result of illegal dismissal. For the compensation of loss, the applicable principle is that of integral reparation. Integral reparation entails that both material and moral damages should be compensated for.

The damages for the negative effects on Maurice's reputation would qualify as moral damages. As a principle, moral damages caused through illegal administrative action can be repaired and the loss compensated, and this rule is affirmed under Article 8(1) of Law 554/2004 on the judicial review of administrative action, which states:

> A person whose rights or legitimate interests have been breached through a unilateral administrative act, who is not satisfied with the answer to the preliminary administrative claim or who did not receive any answer at all during the preliminary procedure within the timeframe established under article 2 para.1 h), can bring a claim before the judicial review court seeking the total or partial annulment of the act, the recovery of the loss, and for moral damages.

When ruling on moral damages for illegal dismissal of a public servant, a court will apply Article 8 of Law 554/2004 on administrative liability in conjunction with Article 1357 CC on the general conditions for liability, and both provisions will be interpreted in the light of the ECHR case law on moral damages.

On a similar set of facts, the Romanian Supreme Court of Justice ruled that:

> The grounds for granting moral damages lie in the civil law on liability and in the principle of integral repair of loss, which entails that the damaged person should be compensated for all the consequences of the illegal act, whether material or moral. As far as civil servants are concerned, the applicable statutory act (Law 188/1999) does not expressly mention the possibility of the recovery of moral damages (article 106 para. 1 of Law 188/1999 states that damages consist of the indexed salaries as well as other rights and entitlements). However, considering articles 8 (1) and 18 (3) of Law 554/2004, moral damages can be granted if requested by the claimant.

The claimant asked the court of first instance to order compensation or moral damages to the value of 278,400 Romanian lei, and this amount was also subject to appeal.

Legal scholars have often commented that moral damages are a category of damages concerning the physical integrity of a person, but also his or her health, honour, dignity, reputation, or professional prestige. According to Article 1169 CC, the burden of proof for these damages belongs to the claimant, following the *actor incumbit probatio* principle. In other words, according to the generally applicable law, the claimant bears

breached during the investigation and throughout the judicial proceedings, due to the fact that the appeal court did not address all the criticisms/grounds for appeal formulated by the civil servant. Court of Appeal Bacau Decision No 126/2010 with commentary in Romanian <www.juridice.ro/223328/articolul-6-cedo-si-dreptul-intimatului-la-introducerea-contestatiei-in-anulare-speciala.html≥ accessed 20 June 2020.

the burden of proof regarding the moral damages, meaning that he or she must bring evidence of the moral damage, the illegal damaging act, and the fact that the act was committed culpably, as well as the causal link between the prejudice and the illicit act. As such, moral damages shall not be automatically granted as a mere effect of the fact that the claim for annulment was successful, but evidence should be brought in order to justify the moral damage suffered as a result of the act.[109]

Therefore, the general rule is that, in order for moral damages to be granted, the claimant must show the direct link between the harm suffered and the unlawful dismissal; the loss must be proven and not merely affirmed.[110] However, this is to be assessed on a case-by-case basis, and the courts have sufficient discretion when ruling on moral damages. This is clear from a recent Supreme Court decision on the right of a person to be awarded moral damages for a public body's illegal conduct consisting in prolonging legal uncertainty on a person's right to property (the administration had legally begun an expropriation procedure that was not finalized for several years). On the claim for moral damages, the court ruled that:

> As far as moral damages are concerned, the court rules that the amount of 20,000 euros is appropriate to cover the damages suffered by the claimant. To reach this conclusion the court has taken into consideration all the details of the case as well as the claimant's attitude from 2009 up to the present time, the fact that the claimant had to abandon his intention to build a small church on his property and that this intention was related to the claimant's grief for having lost a loved one as well as the importance that this building would have had for the claimant resulting from the obstinacy with which he followed this objective. The court also considered the fact that due to the legal uncertainty around his property right and the fact that compensation for expropriation wasn't granted within the timeframe agreed, the claimant had lost his sources of funding. The Court also considered the fact that the compensation of the aggrieved party must not be speculative but rather, it must represent an adequate reparation for his or her rights having been breached, and thus the *quantum* of the reparation must also consider the attitudes shown by the defendant regarding this circumstance. Furthermore, given that liability not only has a compensatory function but also a punitive one, the Court's intention is to prevent and not only repair, by endorsing conduct that would prevent such reactions in future and help identify the best solutions for whenever a private party's interests collide with public authority.[111]

[109] Supreme Court Decision 4094/2012 in Romanian <https://legeaz.net/spete-contencios-inalta-curte-iccj-2012/decizia-4094-2012≥ accessed 20 June 2020.

[110] See also Decision No 4583 of 4 October 2013, issued by the Bucharest Court of Appeal:

> [...] Breaches that are brought to non-patrimonial values or attributes, as a consequence of culpable and unlawful conduct must be proven, and in this case, the claimant has not proven such prejudice. The existence of moral damage cannot be ascertained without sufficient evidence. (...) In order for liability to be triggered, whether for moral or material damage, all the liability conditions need to be met, ie the unlawfulness, the harm, the causal link between the employer's conduct and the harm, and the employer's fault. The onus probandi in this case lies with the claimant.

[111] Decision No 1 of 9 January 2014, Supreme Court of Justice. All the translations of case law or legal provisions are the author's.

I. Spain

Eva Maria Nieto Garrido

The Spanish courts would endorse Maurice's argument because the head of the unit infringed disciplinary procedure in reaching this decision, namely the duty of care during the investigation and the right to be heard before any unfavourable decision is taken, which are fundamental rights in a criminal or administrative proceeding under Article 24.2 of the Spanish Constitution.[112] Maurice has the right to obtain not only material damages (salary plus interests), but also compensation for moral or psychological damage (negative consequences for his reputation, psychological harm). Nonetheless, to obtain compensation, Maurice should have been diligent in his conduct and claim; additionally, damage must be real and quantifiable in economic terms—that is, salaries plus interest and psychological damage that, for instance, has caused some kind of illness.

J. Switzerland

Thierry Tanquerel

This case will be answered within the framework of Swiss federal law. There are too many different legal frameworks for the civil service on the cantonal and municipal levels to give a comprehensive answer for these.

The right to be heard is a general principle of Swiss administrative law enshrined in the Federal Constitution (Art 29 II)[113] and in the Administrative Procedure Act 1968 (APA) (Art 29[114] and 30 I[115]). It is thus clear that, in this case, the proceedings leading to the dismissal of Maurice were irregular, irrespective of any specific duty of care during the investigation or the right to be heard set out by the PA guidelines. In addition, it appears that the dismissal is based on facts that have not been proven.

In such a case, Maurice can appeal the dismissal to the Federal Administrative Tribunal (FAT). He can ask for a stay of the dismissal during the appeal. If a stay is granted, he will receive his salary during the proceedings. If the dismissal is deemed unlawful, the FAT can send the case back to the PA for a new decision.

If the new decision rescinds the dismissal, Maurice will not lose any salary. He might, however, ask for damages, under the Government Liability Act (GLA) 1958, for the harm to his professional reputation and, provided he can demonstrate an actual injury, for the fact that he had, for a while, to look for another job. He will have to demonstrate that the head of his unit violated a 'fundamental duty of office'. The Swiss courts consider that the mere illegality of a decision causing harm does not suffice. It is fair to say that, with the requirement of the breach of a fundamental duty,

[112] Article 24(1) states that: 'All persons have the right to obtain effective protection from the judges and the courts in the exercise of their rights and legitimate interests, and in no case may there be a lack of defense.'

[113] 'Each party to a case has the right to be heard.'

[114] 'The parties shall have the right to be heard.'

[115] 'The authority shall hear the parties before issuing a ruling.'

the courts reinstated the fault—namely intentional misconduct or negligence—of the perpetrator of the harmful legal act as a condition of State liability. To the extent that Maurice claims compensation for a moral wrong (in the sense of the harm to his reputation), the fault of the perpetrator of the act is anyway a statutory requirement (Art 6 II GLA).

If the FAT does not stay the dismissal, and then, in its decision on the merits, exceptionally does not send the case back to the PA, or if the PA, on remand, after, duly hearing Maurice, dismisses him again, and, on appeal, the FAT finds the dismissal unjustified, the FAT can, based on Article 34*b* I of the Federal Civil Service Act 2000 (FCSA), award Maurice damages of an amount set 'in general' between six months and one year of salary. The FAT will determine the amount of the award taking into account the 'circumstances' of the case (Art 34*b* II FCSA). In this case, the harm to the reputation of Maurice and the difficulty of finding another job will be amongst the circumstances to be taken into account.

K. United Kingdom

Gordon Anthony

The first point that should be made in relation to this problem scenario is that civil servants in the UK are known as 'Crown servants'. While it has long been established that civil servants have enforceable contracts of employment,[116] there are some differences in how employment matters are addressed within the Civil Service. One of these is the existence of the Civil Service's own disciplinary structures and procedures, which include internal rights of appeal to, in some cases, the Civil Service Appeals Commission. The basic rule in relation to such appeal rights is that they should be exhausted before a civil servant has recourse to an employment tribunal or the High Court (whether on an application for judicial review or in a damages claim for breach of contract).

Turning to Maurice's circumstances, the following points can be made:

(1) The decision-making process in this case apparently includes many manifest breaches of the common law's rules of fairness. While the application of those rules always depends on context—see comment (c) at the beginning of Chapter 13—the fact that any investigation into the allegations could result in Maurice's dismissal would mean that the full range of common law requirements may well be engaged. On the facts as described, there would thus be (minimum) concerns about: (i) the nature of the evidence that was being used against Maurice (how it was gathered; whether he had a chance to see it in advance of the decision being taken; whether he was able to submit his own evidence by way of rebuttal, etc); (ii) the absence of a hearing, including the chance to question those who gave evidence against him (hearings are required where the implications for an individual are more severe); (iii) whether

[116] See eg *R v Lord Chancellor's Department, ex parte Nangle* [1991] ICR 743.

Maurice was given sufficient reasons for his dismissal (the common law does not impose a general duty to give reasons, but would require 'adequate and intelligible' reasons in a case of this kind); and (iv) the apparent absence of any internal right of appeal to a person who would be notionally independent from the complainants and the head of Maurice's unit. (It might be noted, again, that the absence of an appeal right would not comport with existing practice within the UK's Civil Service.)

(2) Provisions within the PA's policy guidelines would potentially be relevant to the issues before any judicial body, at least by way of adding detail about the context to the dispute. However, they would not be determinative of any question of fairness—such questions are solely questions of law for the courts, and departmental policies can never override common law requirements.

(3) An interesting feature of the common law's approach to procedural fairness is its use of what is sometimes called the 'curative principle'. At its most basic, this principle means that the requirements of fairness will not be violated if an individual has a right of redress before an independent judicial body that can 'cure' unfairness through its (usually) appellate procedures. Would the curative principle work here given the obvious unfairness to Maurice during the decision-making process? On the one hand, it might be said that, if Maurice could bring proceedings before (for instance) an employment tribunal, that body's procedures should allow him to question witnesses, adduce evidence, query the Civil Service's disciplinary procedures, and so on. However, it is also the case that the common law prefers fairness at all stages in a decision-making process, not just on appeal, and it may be that the failings here would be regarded as so egregious as to offend the common law's basic notions of fairness. A finding of that kind would be more likely to made by the High Court, viz if Maurice were to proceed by way of an application for judicial review (it being assumed for present purposes that that remedy would be open to him).[117]

(4) A similar point might be made about Article 6 ECHR (it is generally accepted that civil servants can rely upon the Article in employment disputes).[118] Article 6 ECHR, as applied by the UK courts, is sometimes linked to a concept of 'composite compliance', meaning that the courts will not regard the Article as having been violated where initial procedural breaches can be remedied by a subsequent right of appeal. However, the very concerns that could be raised with reference to the common law might also be raised here—the procedural failings within the civil service are so pronounced that they may run contrary to the essential logic of Article 6 ECHR. A court may therefore state that internal procedures should be addressed notwithstanding the notional possibility of 'composite compliance'.

(5) In terms of the remedies that might be available to Maurice, three points can be made (the first two of these would be relevant if he were to seek relief in an

[117] On the applicable principles, see *McClaren v Home Office* [1990] ICR 824.
[118] See eg *Brown v Department of Regional Development* [2013] NICA 17.

employment tribunal; the third if he were to proceed by way of an application for judicial review).

(a) The first point is that a tribunal may order that Maurice be reinstated to his former position (if Maurice has requested that outcome and it is a realistic option) and also that he receive damages for lost earnings (which would include any amount of interest determined in accordance with tribunal rules). In the event that reinstatement would not be an option, the tribunal would consider solely a remedy in damages where, once again, interest would be payable in accordance with the rules of the tribunal. In the event that Maurice had not sought reinstatement, the fact that he had had to look for alternative employment would be unremarkable: there is a general rule whereby litigants are expected to mitigate their loss, and seeking alternative employment would be consistent with that principle (indeed, manifest failure to seek to mitigate loss could count against Maurice in terms of quantum).

(b) The second point concerns the negative implications that the affair would have had for Maurice's reputation. This is probably a matter that moves towards the law on defamation, where defendants in the UK can rely upon the defence of 'privilege' when being sued. That defence will be defeated where the plaintiff can show that the defendant acted with 'malice', but it can be factually challenging to establish that state of mind. Moreover, in this case, it is unclear whether the egregious procedural failings were a result of simply the Civil Service's rules, or whether they were largely a result of discretion exercised by Maurice's head of unit. If they were a result of the application of the rules, a damages claim for loss of reputation would face significant difficulties, while loss caused by an exercise of discretion *might* (though no means *would*) be actionable. On balance, it is unlikely that Maurice would be unable to succeed in defamation (which would require a separate procedure from a tribunal action).

(c) The third point concerns the remedies that would be available if Maurice were to challenge his dismissal by way an application for judicial review. In theory, it is possible that the High Court would quash the original decision to dismiss him, something that would render the decision *void ab initio* and without any legal effects. However, it is to be emphasized that the High Court has a discretion in relation to remedies, and it may not wish to grant a remedy that would create real practical difficulties (a quashing order could amount to reinstatement by proxy, and that may not be a workable solution). In reality, the High Court may therefore make a declaration that the public authority has acted unlawfully and suggest that a damages claim be brought in a tribunal or, depending on quantum, by way of a High Court action for breach of contract. It is also possible that a public body that has been found to have acted unlawfully would give an undertaking to the court that it would pay an appropriate amount of compensation to Maurice.

To recap: (i) Maurice has clearly been treated unfairly in this case, whether viewed from the perspective of the common law or Article 6 ECHR; (ii) interesting questions about the 'curative principle' and/or 'composite compliance' might be raised in any proceedings; (iii) damages plus interest would be payable in tribunal proceedings, subject to Maurice's obligation to mitigate his loss; and (iv) it is unlikely that Maurice would succeed in a claim for loss of reputation—the defence of privilege would be available to the public authority.

III. Case 2—an unjustified denial of licences for electronic communications

The Ministry for Telecommunications of Terranova, a new member of the EEA, must assign licences for 100 frequencies. Under national legislation, before taking its decision, the Ministry must consult the Electronic Communications Committee (ECC), whose opinion is of a technical nature and has no binding effects. Many operators apply for a licence, including New Tv, a legal entity constituted under Terranova law. Unexpectedly, the Ministry does not follow the procedure previously established in that it does not consult the ECC before taking its decision. It simply asserts that there were so many applications that the administrative process had to be simplified in order to be concluded on time and give a new shape to such an important market. But New Tv, which has not been awarded a licence, brings an action before a Terranova court, claiming that the denial of frequencies was unlawful. It also alleges that, as a consequence of the Ministry's wrongful action, it lost the significant investments it had made for developing its business in Terranova, as well as the profits it could have gained by becoming a national broadcaster, including the money it could have obtained from advertisers.

Would New Tv's action be successful? Would damages, if any, be limited to the actual loss or extend to cover lost profit?

A. Austria

SS, KB, DB, and LM

Under § 51 of the 2003 Telecommunications Act (TKG),[119] the Federal Ministry of Transport, Innovation and Technology (BMVIT) awards licences for frequencies. New Tv may appeal against this decision before the BVwG (§ 121a TKG). The BVwG itself decides whether the award of licences was unlawful and can therefore conduct additional investigations (§ 28 VwGVG). In the course of supplementary investigations on the facts of the case, the BVwG may consult the ECC. If the BVwG adopts a deviating decision based on the ECC's statement, it has to annul the decision and refer it back to the BMVIT for a new decision (§ 28(5) VwGVG). However, the BMVIT is bound by the legal assessment of the BVwG (§ 28(3) VwGVG).

If, nevertheless, damage has occurred which cannot be remedied through the appeal granted, New Tv may bring an action for damages against the federal government under § 1(1) AHG. The BMVIT is an organ acting on behalf of the Federation. Not consulting the ECC, although mandatory, is a procedural error and was objectively unlawful. The BMVIT must further be culpable with regard to the unlawfulness. This means that the action of the BMVIT was unjustifiable. If the BMVIT acted with slight negligence, New Tv could claim positive damage caused by the delay.[120] New Tv can

[119] *Telekommunikationsgesetz*, Federal Law Gazette I No 70/2003 as amended.
[120] OGH 1 July 2004 1 Ob 173, 03 b = RdW 2004, 726 = JBl 2004, 793.

only claim lost profits if the BMVIT has acted with gross negligence (or with intent). However, gross negligence can only be assumed if the BMVIT acted randomly and completely ignored the principles of an open, fair, and non-discriminatory procedure as stated in § 55(2) TKG. In general, under § 1293 ABGB, lost profit is compensable if the profit can be expected after the usual course of events. Whether or not the authority has acted culpably, the BVwG's decision in favour of New Tv protected the company from certain positive damages, such as losing its investments or objective profit opportunities.

B. European Union

BM

The EU administrative decision is unlawful due to a procedural irregularity consisting in the failure to request a mandatory (although non-binding) opinion on the matter. Procedural invalidity may certainly give rise to an annulment judgment by the court for infringement of an essential procedural requirement or infringement of EU law (Art 263 para II Treaty on the Functioning of the European Union, TFEU).

The competent EU body will therefore adopt a new decision in the light of the ECC's opinion, which could be favourable (or unfavourable) to the applicant.

For the purpose of supporting its claim for compensation, New Tv should prove, in addition to the damage, three conditions that are not easy to demonstrate: the causal link between the initial denial of the licence and the damage suffered; the circumstance that the infringed rule was intended to protect its rights, and the clear and serious nature of the infringement. These requirements are not easy to prove: the Court of Justice has stated that the rules on division of powers between the various EU institutions do not generally aim to protect individuals, but rather the institutional balance alone.[121] More recently, the General Court held that the rules on the division of competences between EU institutions and Member States do not confer rights on individuals for the purposes of non-contractual liability.[122] The injured party also has to prove that the rule has been violated in a serious and manifest manner, which is hard to do in the case of activity characterized by discretion. Also the causal link between the unlawful conduct and the damage is not easy to demonstrate, because it has to be proved that, without the unlawful action, the licence would have been granted.[123]

[121] Case C-282/90 *Vrengdenhil v Commission* [1992] ECR I-01937, judgment of the Court 13 March 1992.

[122] K Gutman, 'The Evolution of the Action for Damages against the European Union and Its place in the System of Judicial Protection' (2011) 48 CMLR 713. In the case law, Case T-429/05 *Artegodan v Commission* [2010] ECR II-00491, judgment of the General Court 3 March 2010.

[123] A Toth, 'The Concepts of Damage and Causality as Elements of Non-Contractual Liability' in T Heukels and AM McDonnell, *The Action for Damages in Community Law* (Kluwer Law International 1997) 192; P Craig, *EU Administrative Law* (OUP 2012) 691.

C. France

TP

New Tv's action would be successful considering the procedural irregularity, but this would not necessarily lead to compensation, which depends on the real chance of being awarded a licence.

The lawfulness of administrative decisions may be challenged on two grounds: form and procedure. Public bodies must respect pre-established procedures as an essential part of the legality principle. However, only irregularities that have 'real' consequences will be considered, in order to avoid administrative paralysis. In 2011, legislation aiming to simplify rules[124] determined which phases, in connection with consultations, can be endorsed for annulment:

> Where the administrative authority, before taking a decision, consults a body, only irregularities that may have influenced the sense of the decision taken, considering the opinion given may, where appropriate, be invoked against the decision.

The same year, a claimant challenged the merger of two universities because neither of them consulted its joint committee before the decision, and the two councils voted for the merger together. The *Conseil d'Etat* used this *Danthony* case to complete the new Law.[125] First, the irregularity could be an omission of a procedure or its defective execution; for example, if the answers were provided by the commission, but more than one-half of the members were not present. Second, the irregularity will lead to annulment only if this defect (i) deprives the interested parties of a guarantee or a right; or (ii) will influence the outcome of the decision. The former defect concerns the right to present a defence, the employees' right to participate in an enterprise, and the right to participate in some public decision-making concerning the city or the environment. In these cases, courts check on a case-by-case basis the intended purpose of the specific consultation or procedure omitted (or wrongly executed), and its connection with a procedural guarantee or a right. For example, in *Danthony*, the court found that consultation of the joint committee is a guarantee derived from the participation principle of employees in their working conditions according to the Preamble of Constitution of 1946 (under the doctrine of *Bloc de constitutionnalité*) and annulled the administrative act, even if effective participation could not influence the outcome of the decision.[126] As regards the latter defect, the court will consider the effects of the irregularity, on a case-by-case basis, as to whether consultation would have given different or contrasting information, as well as the conditions that have affected the decision's outcome. In *Danthony*, the court established that, as the two councils had decided together about their merger, this might have influenced the decision because

[124] Article 70 L No 2011-525, 17 May 2011.

[125] CE 23 December 2011 *Danthony et autres* Rec 649, RFDA 2012.284, concl Dumontier 296.

[126] In other cases, the *Conseil d'Etat* considered that giving notice of the consequences of paying a transit fine is related to the right to present a defence because once the person has paid, they have admitted the traffic violation; thus, a procedural irregularity regarding information may lead to annulment. CE 9 *Mme C* December 2016 No 395893, AJDA 2017.575.

members vote in the presence of the other university, so this irregular procedure led to the annulment. In another case, the *Conseil d'Etat* established that an obligatory opinion rendered one day after the relevant decision could not have influenced the outcome because the unanimous opinion had the same outcome as the decision, and the working group of the consulted body had proposed the favourable opinion one month before.[127]

Since 2011, courts have considered these two factors before annulling any decision procedural irregularities. In New Tv's case, it is necessary to determine whether the ECC's opinion could have influenced the decision. The conclusion does not depend on the binding nature of the opinion, but on the possible effects of the opinion. The court must consider the type of question, the object and the nature of the consultation, and the decision on a case-by-case basis. It is not possible for us to reach a conclusion because the only information available is the 'technical nature' of this opinion. However, we can infer that this technical opinion includes some references regarding the operators' technical abilities, and in this way, it could influence the assignment of licences. This being the case, the decision would be annulled, and the Ministry would have to begin the assignment procedure again lawfully. In any case, this does not mean that New Tv would be awarded a licence, because the public authority may be able to issue the same substantive decision even after this successful action.

Compensation for the loss of opportunity suffered by excluded operators is moot in France[128] because administrative case law is not uniform with regard to how to calculate and compensate the loss of opportunity in different fields. For example, public medical liability has a rule of percentage, considering the probability of the patient's recovery; but for contracts and licences, the case law distinguishes between 'no chance', 'simple chance', and a 'serious chance' to apply an overarching rule.[129]

If New Tv had no chance of being awarded a licence, it would not receive any compensation. If the company has proved a 'simple' chance of being awarded, having, for example, all the requirements and a reasonable offer, the court would order only the reimbursement of the expenses related to the procedure. However, if New Tv proved that it was the best candidate and should have been awarded some of the licences, the court would order compensation for the total loss of profit,[130] including the amount of money it could have obtained for advertising.

The latter solution has been criticized because there is no compensation for a 'loss of chance'. The chance is considered as an element in establishing the causal link between the unlawful procedure and the damage but is not, in itself, the damage to be repaired. If there is just a chance, the compensation will not correspond to the loss of

[127] CE 17 February 2012 *Société Chiesi SA* No 332509. Another recent example is CE 27 October 2015 *Société CFA Méditerranée* No 369113.

[128] A Minet, *La perte de chance en droit administratif* (LGDJ 2014).

[129] CE 7 June 2010 *Cristophe* No 312909; CE 10 July 2013 *Compagnie martiniquaise de transports* No 362777, AJDA 2013.1482.

[130] In public procurement cases, courts usually protect the stability of contract and only order compensation for the excluded company; in this case, loss of profit will take into account the full period of the contract. In other cases, if the authority has to go through assignment again, the period for calculation will be between the unlawful decision and the new procedure.

the chance of securing the contract but to the expenses; and if the chance is a 'serious' one, the compensation will be for the lost profits and not for the loss of chance.[131] Nevertheless, for some, this solution avoids the situation in which every excluded candidate in an irregular procedure asks for proportional compensation in connection with his chance.[132]

There are further complex aspects. The first is how the court distinguishes between a 'chance' and 'a serious chance' and whether, in different cases, it is possible for different courts to consider that two candidates have serious chances. The second is how to calculate the loss of profits and, during which period, whether it is possible to consider the renewal period[133] or the probability of the renewal.

In the event of the unlawful denial of a licence, the *Conseil d'Etat* has confirmed the analysis of the appeal court when it applies the explained rule. First, after comparing the situation of the company that was awarded the licence with that of the company that was unlawfully excluded,[134] the court determines whether the excluded company had a serious chance. Second, damages are determined as the loss of profit of the licences between the date of the assignment until a new assignment procedure. To calculate the net income, the court considers the target population and the time, deducting the costs, expenses (including publicity), and taxes, including copyright.[135]

We cannot assert whether New Tv would receive compensation for an actual loss and/or a loss of profit because it depends on the evaluation of the facts and the competitor companies regarding the legal criteria. However, if the application was lawful and reasonable, New Tv would receive at least the reimbursement of its expenses.

D. Germany

FW and JS

In view of the primacy of primary legal protection, New Tv must challenge the allocation decision to avoid an exclusion of its claim to damages.[136]

However, it is questionable whether New Tv has standing. Under the German administrative law system, with regard to access to administrative courts focussing primarily on the defence of subjective rights but not on securing the lawfulness of

[131] E Lambert, 'La perte de chance de remporter un contrat en matière de commande publique' [2015] AJDA 289.

[132] Minet (n 128).

[133] Lambert (n 131).

[134] CE 24 January 2014 *Vortex* No 351274.

[135] ibid.

[136] See F Wollenschläger and J Stapf, 'The System of Public Authority Liability in Germany' Chapter 6 in this volume, section III. Under the German Telecommunications Act, New Tv would have to challenge decisions regarding the allocation procedure, such as the choice of an auction immediately; it is not permissible to challenge the final allocation decision claiming such procedural defects: BVerwG 1 September 2009—6 C 4/09, BVerwGE 134, 368. See also F Wollenschläger, 'The Allocation of Limited Rights by the Administration: Challenges of Legal Protection' in P Adriaanse and others (eds), *Scarcity and the State, Vol 1: The Allocation of Limited Rights by the Administration* (Intersentia 2016) 93ff, 118.

administrative action, this requires New Tv to be able to claim that its rights have been violated by the administrative act or its refusal (according to § 42 para 2 VwGO). This is the case if the rule not respected by the administrative authority aims not only to serve the public interest but—at least also—the interests of a delimitable group of individuals.[137] In the event of a violation of procedural requirements like the obligation to consult the Electronic Communications Committee (ECC) at issue here, the violation must, moreover, have had an effect on the applicant's position.[138] Since, according to the questionnaire, the ECC's 'opinion is of a technical nature' and 'has no binding effects', it is questionable whether these requirements (protection of specific individual interests and relevance of the omission for the content of the decision) are met. If this is not the case, a violation of the consultation obligation cannot be challenged by New Tv or other stakeholders who share the same position. Furthermore, § 46 VwVfG expressly rules out the annulment of administrative acts merely for procedural errors if it is evident that the procedural error did not influence the outcome of the decision (see case 1).[139] Ultimately, the intention of the obligation to consult the ECC is decisive.

New Tv might claim damages under the general state liability provisions.[140] It must prove that (1) an official (2) intentionally or negligently (3) breached the official duty incumbent upon him (4) in relation to a third party, and that this (5) caused (6) the claimant damage.

At the outset, it shall be recalled that New Tv is obliged to challenge the allocation decision in order not to be precluded from obtaining damages.

Somebody who had been entrusted with carrying out official tasks, thus an official within the meaning of § 839 paragraph 1 sentence 1 BGB,[141] failed to ensure the correct consultation prior to the assignment of licences for the 100 frequencies. New Tv would, furthermore, have to prove the official's intent or negligence. Even though the Ministry for Telecommunications of Terranova was aware of the obligation to consult the ECC, it did not comply, thereby acting knowingly and willingly,[142] ie with intent. The omission of consultations also constitutes a breach of an official duty by the Ministry. The fact that there were allegedly too many applications does not exempt from the duty to consult, since it is stipulated by law without exceptions (principle of legality, Art 20 para 3 GG[143]). The core issue is the fourth prerequisite, ie whether the duty to consult ECC constitutes a duty owed to New Tv.

With regard to the standing discussed above, this requirement is fulfilled if the duty aims to protect the interests of a delimitable group of individuals, and not just the

[137] BVerwG 15 November 1985—8 C 43/83, BVerwGE 72, 226 (229ff). This effect is referred to as *Drittschutz*; see R Wahl and P Schütz '§ 42 Abs 2' in F Schoch, J-P Schneider, and W Bier (eds), *Verwaltungsgerichtsordnung* (effective of the first publication, CH Beck) paras 2, 110ff.

[138] Wollenschläger, 'The Allocation of Limited Rights by the Administration' (n 136) 93ff, 115. See for more details F Wollenschläger, *Verteilungsverfahren* (Mohr Siebeck 2010) 603 ff.

[139] The provision also applies in the context of enforcement actions, see Ramsauer, '§ 46' (n 53) para 40.

[140] cf the relief sought by the claimant at the VG Köln 3 September 2014—21 K 4413/11 juris, para 137.

[141] BGH 9 December 2008—VI ZR 277/07, BGHZ 179, 115 (119); H-J Papier and F Shirvani, '§ 839' in FJ Säcker and others (eds), *Münchener Kommentar zum Bürgerlichen Gesetzbuch*, vol 6 (7th edn, CH Beck 2017) para 130 with further references.

[142] cf Papier and Shirvani (n 141) para 285 with further references.

[143] Art 20 para 3 GG stipulates: 'The legislature shall be bound by the constitutional order, the executive and the judiciary by law and justice.'

general interest.[144] If standing to challenge the allocation decision is affirmed, this may indicate an official duty in relation to a third party.[145]

With regard to lost profits, these are recoverable under German law. On this, § 252 BGB states that 'the damage to be compensated for also comprises the lost profits. Those profits are considered lost that in the normal course of events or in the special circumstances, particularly due to the measures and precautions taken, could probably be expected.'

However, causation is difficult to prove if the administration enjoys discretion, which is very likely the case for the allocation decision of the Ministry for Telecommunications of Terranova and for the opinion of the ECC. Generally speaking, causation of damage is to be assessed by considering 'the course of events if the official had acted according to the law and what the financial situation of the aggrieved party would look like in this case'[146].

In the event of administrative discretion, the outcome of a procedure with proper consultation of the ECC cannot be established. This is a general problem in allocation procedures, which has been explained in more detail by the author in his book *Verteilungsverfahren*[147] and his article 'The Allocation of Limited Rights by the Administration: Challenges of Legal Protection':[148]

> If the unsuccessful applicant seeks damages for the economic loss resulting from the non-allocation of the desired asset, such as income as a public servant that is not received, or the loss of profit from a public contract, it is incumbent on him/her to particularly explain and prove that he/she did indeed suffer damage as a result of the violation of the right; this is conditional on whether he/she would indeed have received the allocation had the selection been carried out properly. This proof of causality triggering liability is very difficult to furnish where a margin of appreciation exists for administrative decisions, as well as in constellations in which the causality of the error committed in awarding the contract can be neither confirmed nor ruled out (e.g. alleged lack of suitability leading to the consequence of non-admission to the drawing or auction).[149]
>
> This is the dilemma of secondary legal protection. Unlike in primary legal protection, there is no possibility—as would do justice to remedying such rights violations—to repeal the awarding decision and order it to be repeated; this procedure would then reveal the prospects of success of the applicant who was (initially)

[144] cf BGH 6 July 1989—III ZR 251/87, BGHZ 108, 224 (227f); 1 February 2001—III ZR 193/99, BGHZ 146, 365 (368f); 6 June 2013—III ZR 196/12, [2013] NJW 3370 (3371); Papier and Shirvani (n 141) para 227 with further references.

[145] F Ossenbühl and M Cornils, *Staatshaftungsrecht* (6th edn, CH Beck 2013) 61; Papier and Shirvani (n 141) para 234.

[146] Own translation of BGH 6 April 1995—III ZR 183/94, BGHZ 129, 226 (232f).

[147] Wollenschläger, *Verteilungsverfahren* (n 138) 658ff.

[148] See the following quote from Wollenschläger, 'The Allocation of Limited Rights by the Administration' (n 136) 93ff, 121ff.

[149] BGH 6 April 1995—III ZR 183/94, [1995] NJW 2344 (2345); BVerwG 21 August 2003—2 C 14/02, BVerwGE 118, 370 (378ff); 17 August 2005—2 C 37/04, BVerwGE 124, 99 (108); 11 February 2009—2 A 7/06, [2009] NVwZ 787 (789).

unsuccessful.[150] In secondary legal protection, by contrast, it is only possible to award or deny compensation claims, frustration however being the potential result of its too restrictive treatment, but excessive liability arising if this treatment is overgenerous. The dilemma is exacerbated by the fact that, in some allocation procedures, exclusively secondary legal protection is available, and this must therefore—also for constitutional reasons[151]—compensate for the refused primary legal protection. The question thus arises of how to deal adequately with such frustrated opportunities.

Where proof of the causality of the infringement of rights is demanded in order to receive damages, and causality is then negated where a margin of appreciation exists for administrative decisions, and no decision could have been reached in favour of the claimant, claims for damages are ruled out from the outset.[152] This view however appears to be too restrictive in terms of the interest of effective legal protection. Rather, in the view of the Bundesverfassungsgericht, in any case where primary legal protection is not available, this guarantee certainly impacts 'the interpretation and application of the provisions of private and civil procedure law which an unsuccessful bidder can invoke in order to obtain legal protection against being unlawfully disregarded. The factual preconditions and legal consequences of the provisions from which the unsuccessful bidder can derive a claim to damages must be determined in a manner which adequately does justice to their interest in legal protection aiming to comply with Article 3 paragraph 1 GG.'[153] On the other hand, it also does not appear reasonable to permit the mere possibility of being taken into account as a sufficient basis for total compensation as this would lead to limitless liability.[154]

As is recognised in the law on public service, it is however possible to do justice to legitimate legal protection interests by reversing the burden of providing evidence and the burden of proof, assuming that a breach of the law and damage have been established.[155] True, 'the party who has been injured by a breach of official duty must as a matter of principle also provide proof of having suffered damage as a result. If

[150] The BVerfG (3rd chamber) 13 January 2010—2 BvR 811/09, juris para 8, rightly states as follows:

> In regard to the promotion decision which—in accordance with the principle of the stability of offices—is irreversible as a matter of principle, the primary claim which applies regardless of fault aims—prior to this decision—to halt application procedures in which procedural violations have occurred and where the respective claimant is one of the candidates to be considered. Primary legal protection as manifested in conflict between rivals permits, in this regard, damage to be limited at an early stage, or rather the risk originating from a basis for decision-making which may still be unsure to be minimised.

[151] BVerfG 13 June 2006—1 BvR 1160/03, BVerfGE 116, 135 (159); in addition, BVerfG 23 May 2006—1 BvR 2530/04, BVerfGE 116, 1 (22). The fact that this is not true whether or not adequate primary legal protection is available is underlined by BVerfG (3rd chamber) 13 January 2010—2 BvR 811/09, juris paras 6ff.

[152] See LG Berlin 27 June 1995—9 O 722/94, [1997] NVwZ-RR 35 (36).

[153] BVerfG 13 June 2006—1 BvR 1160/03, BVerfGE 116, 135 (159).

[154] Also cf BVerfG (3rd chamber) 13 January 2010—2 BVR 811/09, juris paras 6ff.

[155] BGH 3 March 1983—III ZR 34/82, [1983] NJW 2241 (2242); 6 April 1995—III ZR 183/94, [1995] NJW 2344 (2345); BVerwG 17 August 2005—2 C 37/04, BVerwGE 124, 99 (108f); W Spoerr, *Treuhandanstalt und Treuhandunternehmen zwischen Verfassungs-, Verwaltungs- und Gesellschaftsrecht* (Verlag Kommunikationsforum 1993), 187. Facilitating the review of the handling of frustrated chances in the law of evidence, G Mäsch, *Chance und Schaden, Zur Dienstleisterhaftung bei unaufklärbaren Kausalverläufen* (Mohr Siebeck 2004), 127ff.

however the breach of official duty and the damage which subsequently resulted from it have been established, the injured party may leave it up to the public body to prove that the damage was not caused by the breach of official duty; this however only applies if experience shows that a *de facto* presumption or an actual probability of the causative connection exists, otherwise the burden of proof continues to be incumbent on the injured party.'[156] The relaxation of the burden of proof under § 287 ZPO [Code of Civil Procedure] also applies if difficulties in investigation result from a breach of official duty.[157] The objection can be put forward against this solution in terms of the law on evidence—apart from the vagaries which it entails—that it is based merely on the alternative between full and denied liability, thus it constitutes an 'all-or-nothing' approach.[158] This gives rise to reservations not only in terms of the lack of legal protection if the compensation claim is turned down; it is rather also particularly questionable in multipolar allocation conflicts in terms of the threat of overcompensation in the event of there being more than one applicant with chances of success, to whom compensation must hence be awarded although there is no doubt that only one applicant may be successful.

Against this background, the question arises of whether the missed opportunity itself is not to be regarded as damage amenable to compensation.[159] A measure that appears to go in this direction is contained in a provision of the public procurement law covered by the EU directives, namely § 126 sentence 1 GWB [= § 181 sentence 1 GWB new version], which hence resolves the dilemma of furnishing proof by granting a right to compensation for expenditure incurred through participation in the procedure unless the bid had no reasonable chance from the outset. § 126 sentence 1 GWB [= § 181 sentence 1 GWB new version] reads as follows: 'If the contracting entity violates a provision intended to protect undertakings, and if the undertaking would have had a real chance without this violation of being granted the award upon an assessment of the tenders, which, as a consequence of that infringement, was adversely affected, the undertaking may demand compensation for the costs of preparing the tender or of participating in an award procedure.' A bid had a 'real' chance, and this is the crux of the issue, if 'the contracting entity would have been entitled to award the contract within its margin of appreciation.'[160] However, this specific provision, which ultimately provides for a compensation entitlement with a relaxed burden of proof in comparison to general law on compensation, does not establish a right to compensation for missed opportunities, as it does not compensate for these because of its being limited to the negative interest.[161]

Such a right however appears to be justified in view of the fact that it is incumbent on the public authority, stemming from the constitutional right to participation, to refrain from frustrating the opportunities of the applicants participating in

[156] BGH 3 March 1983—III ZR 34/82, [1983] NJW 2241 (2242).

[157] BGH 6 April 1995—III ZR 183/94, [1995] NJW 2344 (2345); in addition, BGH 22 May 1986—III ZR 237/84, [1986] NJW 2829 (2832).

[158] Mäsch (n 155) 143ff.

[159] Comprehensively, Mäsch (n 155). Also cf T Pollmann, *Der verfassungsrechtliche Gleichbehandlungsgrundsatz im öffentlichen Vergaberecht* (Duncker and Humblot 2009), 165.

[160] BGH 16 July 2009—I ZR 50/07, [2008] WRP 370 (373).

[161] Also Mäsch (n 155) 153ff.

> the procedure.[162] When it comes to liability for missed opportunities, the problem of causality becomes the problem of determining the damage incurred. In this regard, the damage incurred is calculated by multiplying the anticipated profit by the chances of acquiring that profit.[163] This also ensures that there is no overcompensation; what is more, the prospects for success of an opportunity are to be valued at 0 % if consideration of the bid is ruled out for instance because there are grounds for its exclusion.

The answer to the question whether New Tv is entitled to claim damages for lost profits thus depends on the standards applied to prove causation as set out before.

The amount that can be adjudicated as lost profits may be assessed under § 287 paragraph 1 sentence 1 ZPO[164]. This provision applies to the benefit of the claimant and simplifies proving the lost profit.[165] Under a relaxed burden of proof, it is sufficient for the judge to be convinced of a preponderant probability based on established facts. Consequently, it is sufficient for the claimant 'to present and prove facts which provide sufficient evidence for an assessment according to § 287 ZPO. The requirements for demonstrating hypothetical events must not be exaggerated'[166]. This leads to a hypothetic assessment of the obtainable amount.[167]

One might argue that the course of events would not have changed if the Ministry for Telecommunications had consulted the ECC, which excludes the award of damages;[168] the mere possibility of causing a similar effect is not sufficient, though[169]. Even though the ECC's opinion is 'of a technical nature', the absence of a binding effect does not rule out from the outset that a different course of events would have occurred if the ECC had been consulted.

In summary, New Tv may be awarded damages under the general provisions on public authority liability only if causation can be established in accordance with the standards put forth above.

The actual loss, ie the investments New Tv has made in view of the allocation procedure, do not, as such, constitute recoverable damage. For, considering—as explained above—'the course of events if the official had acted according to the law and what the

[162] cf Mäsch (n 155) 145f, 240ff, 266ff also regarding objections. In light of the constitutional entitlement, in this context liability for lost opportunities is governed by Art 823 para 2 BGB (for the contrary opinion, see Mäsch (n 155, 302f), rejecting it for systematic reasons). Outside the scope of such provision, liability cannot be supported in this context; besides there is a quasi-contractual relationship—also in the opinion of Mäsch (n 155) 312ff—legitimating liability.

[163] In detail, Mäsch (n 155) 320ff; regarding procedural implications ibid 317ff.

[164] *Zivilprozessordnung* (German Code of Civil Procedure), English version <www.gesetze-im-internet.de/englisch_zpo/englisch_zpo.html#p1070> accessed 20 June 2020.

[165] U Foerste, '§ 287 ZPO' in H-J Musielak and W Voit (eds), *Zivilprozessordnung* (17th edn, Vahlen 2020) para 3.

[166] BGH 23 November 2006—IX ZR 21/03, [2007] NJW-RR 569 (571); cf H Prütting, '§ 287' in T Rauscher and W Krüger (eds), *Münchener Kommentar zur Zivilprozessordnung*, vol 1 (6th edn, CH Beck 2020) para 17; Foerste (n 165) para 7.

[167] I Saenger, '§ 287' in I Saenger (ed), ZPO (8th edn, Nomos 2019) paras 8, 14.

[168] This, strictly speaking, refers to the question whether the administration can be held accountable for the damage it caused; cf BGH 24 October 1985—IX ZR 91/84, BGHZ 96, 157 (172f); Wollenschläger, *Verteilungsverfahren* (n 138) 271; Ossenbühl and Cornils (n 145) 74. See also case 4 (section V), case 8 (section IX), case 10 (section XI), and case 11 (section XII).

[169] BGH 9 March 2012—V ZR 156/11, [2012] NJW 2022 (2023).

financial situation of the aggrieved party would look like in this case',[170] New Tv would have incurred these expenses even if it had won the competition. Thus, investments—or more precisely, the profits resulting from them—may only be claimed as lost profits under the conditions set out above.[171] Moreover, there is no general rule in German law stipulating that expenses incurred by the applicant in view of administrative procedures are to be compensated for.[172] The positions mentioned might also amount to damage under the provisions on precontractual liability.

It should be added that a similar problem also arises in public procurement law. In this context (see case 4, a specific claim has been introduced and, moreover, the general civil law provisions governing a breach of pre-contractual obligations (§ 280 para 1 read in conjunction with §§ 241 para 2 and 311 para 2 BGB) apply. A claim for damages based on such a breach requires (1) a precontractual relationship; (2) the breach of a duty arising from this relationship; (3) the causation of (4) a damage; and (5) the defendant's responsibility, ie intent or negligence (§ 276 para 2 BGB). Whether the allocation of frequencies may be considered to create such a precontractual relationship has not been discussed yet; it is acknowledged, though, that precontractual liability may also arise in a public law context. However, even if this is answered in the affirmative, only the participant with the best bid would be entitled to damages (see again case 4).

In summary, whether New Tv may challenge the allocation decision and claim damages depends first of all on the qualification of the obligation to consult the ECC as protecting individual interests of the applicants or not. In the affirmative, New Tv may be awarded compensation for lost profits provided that these positions can be proven according to the outlined standards. Damages with regard to New Tv's investments as such may only be claimed if a precontractual relationship may be assumed and New Tv submitted the best bid.

E. Hungary

LB

Administrative courts distinguish the infringements that affect the merits of the case from those that do not. Because the ECC's opinion has no binding effect, there is a

[170] Own translation of BGH 6 April 1995—III ZR 183/94, BGHZ 129, 226 (232f).

[171] The fact that the investment might have amortized by running the broadcasting business can lead to a different finding in contract law, where business-related expenses can be regarded as compensable damage if the expenses had been profitable under regular circumstances (*Rentabilitätsvermutung* = presumption of profitability); cf BGH 21 April 1978—V ZR 235/77, BGHZ 71, 234 (238f); 26 March 1999—V ZR 364–97, [1999] NJW 2269 (2269 with further references); V Emmerich, 'Vorb § 281' in FJ Säcker and others (eds), *Münchener Kommentar zum Bürgerlichen Gesetzbuch*, vol 2 (8th edn, CH Beck 2019) paras 19, 21. See also AG Bremen 19 September 2013—9 C 167/13, juris para 27, explicitly ruling out this presumption in the context of tort law. Furthermore, s 284 read in conjunction with s 281 para 1 sentence 1 BGB provides for compensation for expenses; it comes with more stringent requirements, but also covers expenses which are not business-related, cf W Ernst, '§ 284' in Säcker and others, ibid paras 5, 14.

[172] BVerwG 20 May 1987—7 C 83/84, BVerwGE 77, 268 (275f); 17 February 2005—7 C 14/04, BVerwGE 123, 7 (17); U Ramsauer, '§ 80' in Kopp and Ramsauer (n 53) para 15; cf D Kallerhoff and K Keller, '§ 80' in Stelkens and others (n 55) para 10; where they also discuss s 80 VwVfG, which stipulates the compensation of expenditures made for preliminary proceedings.

high chance that even if the consultation itself is obligatory, the infringement would be considered as one that does not affect the merits of the case. As a result, the administrative court would not annul or change the decision of the public authority.

There are some procedures in Hungarian administrative law where the authority must obtain an opinion from other administrative bodies or NGOs, but the consequences differ each time.

If the law requires the authority to obtain—in connection with certain questions that require expertise that the authority lacks—an assessment by another authority (a 'specialist authority'), without which a decision cannot be made, even if the former authority does not obtain this assessment, the decision must be declared null by the second instance or the court. This is considered one of the most serious infringements.[173]

If it is the law that requires other type of opinions to be obtained, there are two options. First, the law itself can declare that a decision cannot be made without the opinion. In this case, this infringement also leads the administrative court to annul or change the decision (this is a different kind of annulment than the previously mentioned one: here the decision has an effect, and the court annuls this effect, while in the previous option the infringement is so serious that the decision is unable to have an effect). Second, the law may contain no provision concerning the consequences of infringement. The court then decides on the scope of its appreciation whether the infringement can be considered so significant that it reaches the level of affecting the merits of the case.

In civil procedure, to award the damages a very serious infringement must be stated, and a causal link between the damage and the infringement must also be proven. The burden of proof is on the claimant. Because the infringement in this case is not a particularly serious one, and in addition, the Ministry needed to deal with a lot of applications, and there is no evidence that New TV would have been awarded a licence if the Ministry had obtained the opinion, the court would not award damages.

There is a slightly similar case in Hungary, which can show how the civil procedure of damages works. In 2010, Klubrádió ('Club Radio') won a free frequency for five years but the authority did not reach the quorum, so they could not contract. Later, a legal succession occurred on the authority's side, and the successor authority did not contract with Klubrádió because the applicable law itself had changed too. After a few

[173] Act CL of 2016—on General Public Administration Procedures.

Section 55
[Specialist authority proceedings]
(1) An act or a government decree on the delegation of specialist authorities may – on the basis of overriding reasons relating to the public interest – require the competent authority to adopt a decision on the merits of the case to obtain the binding assessment decision of another authority (hereinafter referred to as 'specialist authority') concerning the specific issue, and within the time-limit defined therein.

Section 123
[General rules on nullity]
(1) In the proceedings governed under this Chapter, the decision shall be annulled or withdrawn, and if necessary new proceedings shall be opened if:
b) it was adopted without having consulted the specialist authority as required, or without taking into consideration the assessment of the specialist authority;

years, the radio finally won the lawsuit (the administrative court established the contract) so they could broadcast at the given frequency. In the meantime, they had had to pay for another frequency. After that, they brought an action for damages against the public authority. According to the radio's claim, they had suffered the following damage: a broadcast service fee for the other frequency that they needed to use in the meantime (103 million forints = € 345,000); loss of sales and violation of personality rights (1 billion 212 million forints = € 4,040,000) in pecuniary damages; and non-pecuniary damages for violation of personality rights (30 million forints = € 100,000). However, the court of first instance did not examine the claim for pecuniary damages because the claimant could not prove the serious infringement (eg they did not attach the decisions of the administrative court) of the authority and the causal link between the damage and the infringement of the authority. The radio only obtained 17 million forints (€ 57,000) in non-pecuniary damages. At second instance, the claimant could prove the infringement which was considered serious (in all of the administrative court procedures the courts found an infringement), so the court awarded the 103 million forints for the frequency fee. However, regarding the loss of sales, a new proceeding began in 2016, and there is no decision yet.

F. Italy

FC

In Italian law, New Tv would be able to challenge the lawfulness of the rejection by the Ministry, proposing, within sixty days, a remediation to have it quashed before an administrative court. Together with the motion to quash, New Tv could also claim compensation for damages before the same court. This compensation claim could also be made independently, as long as it is within 120 days from the enforcement of the damaging order.[174]

In the motion to quash, New Tv could claim that there are two instances of misconduct: a breach of the law (because the Ministry did not observe the law that requires it to uphold the opinion of the technical body) and, in any case, an abuse of power (because the Ministry deviated from its previous procedure, bringing a not entirely convincing or logical argument; on the other hand, the fact that the deadline for concluding the procedure must be respected in an efficient manner does not mean *per se* that the procedural steps required by law and potentially significant for the decision-making process can be omitted). The move to quash, therefore, would most probably be accepted.

A slightly different situation applies to the claim for compensation.

Since New Tv's position relates to the desire to obtain a good that it is within the power of the administration to make available, the court, after assessing the unlawful nature of the denial, should also verify whether New Tv would have presumably obtained the licence if the Ministry had correctly observed the procedural rules.[175]

[174] See F Cortese, 'The Liability of Public Administration: A Special Regime between Formal Requirements and Substantial Goals', Chapter 8 in this volume, section III.

[175] This type of assessment was required by the Cour de Cassation, in ruling No 500/1999, mentioned in Cortese, Chapter 8 in this volume (n 174), section I.

According to the prevailing interpretation, this might happen only if the court assessed that—based on the effectively applicable regulations—the power to issue the licence in question is actually 'bound': in other words, only if the administration had the task of verifying the assessment of whether New Tv met clear and predefined prerequisites and conditions, without performing a discretionary evaluation.[176]

In that case, the damages for which New Tv could obtain compensation would be both those relating to expenses and costs borne in the meantime in order to make the claim and prepare for broadcasting activities, and those regarding the loss of profits that in the meantime it would have gained if it had obtained the licence.

Otherwise, the only benefit that New Tv could obtain relates to the result of the quashing of the denial; in other words, the possibility that the administration, starting the procedure all over again in the proper way, could reach a favourable conclusion.

G. Poland

Sebastian Wijas

An unjustified denial of licences for electronic communications specified in this case must be regarded as being unlawful pursuant to both domestic and EU law. Thus, damages would be awarded under the principles of both domestic and EU law.

In the case in question, the facts are based on refusal to award a licence to a TV broadcasting company for frequencies, where the broadcasting company is subjected to domestic law, despite not being a Polish company, having been registered in Terranova. New Tv brought an action before a domestic court, arguing that a public administrative body, in this case the Ministry of Telecommunications, had made an unlawful decision. Additionally, New Tv demonstrated loss of benefits and profit of a commercial nature ensuing from the said unlawful decision.

First of all, it is important to note that the problem manifested in this case refers to liability for damages on the part of the public authorities. This issue is regulated in Polish law by the provisions of Article 417 and Article 417(1) CC. Moreover, both legal commentaries and case law interpret the damage provided for in Article 361 § 2 in a broad sense, comprising two elements: *damnum emergens*, ie actual loss, meaning a loss in the value of the assets or an increase in the value of the liabilities of the injured

[176] In the absence of discretionary power, a private applicant could also use another remedy: (they could, within sixty days, ask the court to order the administration to issue the licence (Art 34 para 1.c), Code of Administrative Trial, CAT). In any case, where discretionary power is concerned, the court could find the 'harm' sustained by the private applicant to be 'unjustified eg in the event of delayed recognition by the administration of such a benefit (eg following a ruling that resulted in the quashing of an unlawful rejection) (see Council of State No 1945/2003; Council of State Plenary Session No 10/2004). This does not mean that the private applicant cannot seek a different form of compensation. In particular, the following interpretations have been advanced: (i) the theory of pre-contractual liability (Art 1337 CC); (ii) the theory of 'contractual', 'paracontractual', or 'quasicontractual' liability (Cour de Cassation No 157/2003; Council of State No 4239/2001; Council of State No 3796/2002; Council of State No 240/2003). The main consequences of adhesion to these theories are as follows: it is always possible to claim for compensation of *interessi legittimi pretensivi* ('potential' interests), even in cases where no 'entitlement' or 'chance' can be verified; however, the compensation is limited only to the equivalent of the economic loss that the private applicant has incurred for having in any case entered into a 'relationship' with the administration.

party; and *lucrum cessans*, ie the loss of profit understood as the inability to gain any benefits in future. This was further confirmed by a decision of the Constitutional Tribunal of 2003, Case Reference No K 20/02. Liability for damages exists if: (i) the damage exists; (ii) the damage is inflicted due to the unlawful fulfilment of duties by a public authority; and (iii) there is a causal link between these two events.

From the perspective of Polish law, New Tv could seek damages for loss of profit, provided that the liability for damages of the State has been asserted. The following elements should be considered. First, Terranova, as a member of the EEA, has a specific legal status: on the base on Article 1 of the Agreement on the European Economic Area, it is committed to protecting legitimate economic interests within the free movement of the EU internal market (ie goods, persons, services, and capital). Second, there is liability for damages of an individual State for breaching EU law. According to the case law of the Court of Justice of the European Union (CJEU), there are two areas of such liability: for failure to transpose an EU directive into national law;[177] and for legislative actions or omissions.[178]

If the refusal to award a licence to New Tv stems from an improper transposition of EU law into Terranova law, the TV station is entitled to invoke liability for damages in respect of the EU Member State. Additionally, in this situation, New Tv may also invoke a general principle of EU and anti-discrimination legislation pertaining to freedoms of the EU internal market.

H. Romania

RV

In order for New Tv to bring a claim for judicial review before the Romanian administrative courts, it would first need to make an administrative appeal before the Ministry of Telecommunication asking for the revocation/reconsideration of the Ministry's decision. This administrative appeal shall be brought under Article 7 of Law 554/2005 on the judicial review of administrative decisions, and the authority has a thirty-day time limit to formulate a reply. If New Tv is not satisfied with the reply or if the Ministry does not formulate a reply at all, New Tv can bring a petition before the court of appeal no later than six months from the date when it received the authority's reply.

For its application to be successful under Romanian law, New Tv would have to prove that (i) the refusal to issue the licence breached the legislation on telecommunication licences; (ii) that New Tv complied with all the legal requirements for the license to be granted; and (iii) that the damage for lost profit can be assessed with certainty.

[177] Joint cases C-6/90 and C-9/90; *Andrea Francovich and Danila Bonifaci and others v Italian Republic* [1991] ECR I-5357, judgment of the Court 19 November 1991.

[178] Joint cases C-46/93 and C-48/93; *Brasserie du pêcheur SA v Bundesrepublik Deutschland (beer purity) and The Queen and Secretary of State for Transport ex parte: Factortame Ltd and others* [1996] ECR I-01029, judgement of 5 March 1996.

Damages for *lucrum cessans* can be awarded under Romanian general law on extra-contractual liability as long as the conditions for liability are met: (i) there is an unlawful act or conduct causing harm; (ii) the harm exists; and (iii) there is a causal link between the illegal act/conduct and the harm suffered. When assessing a claim for damages for *lucrum cessans*, the Romanian Supreme Court ruled, for instance, that:

> (…) loss of profit is therefore hypothetical, and it represents the profit lost by the claimant, had the defendant fulfilled its legal obligations. It is therefore situated at the level of a probability but not that of an undoubtable outcome. However, the probability indeed means that the claimant must be rigorous in its assertions and the evidence he brings, and it does not suffice to show that there was merely a possibility of that profit being obtained, but it must be in fact proven that the realization of this future profit was the most probable outcome. This is why it was necessary and useful for the outcome of the case for the claimant to show exactly what the lost profit consisted of and if there are contracts that were not signed because of the defendant's conduct, to bring evidence that these contracts would have been concluded as per article 1169 C. civ.[179]

Given the lack of special provisions in the field of administrative liability, damages for *lucrum cessans* will be awarded based on the provisions of Article 1385 of the Romanian CC[180] on the principle of integral reparation of damage, which reads:

> (1) The damage will be compensated for in full if special legal provisions do not establish the contrary.
> (2) Damages for future harm are also allowed if their existence is undoubted.
> (3) The compensation should include the actual loss, the advantage/gain that he would normally have obtained and that he will no longer obtain as well as the expenses for the avoidance of the harm.
>
> If the unlawful act also determined the loss of a chance to obtain an advantage or to avoid a loss, the reparation will be proportional to the probability of obtaining the advantage or avoiding the loss, according to the details of the case and the specific situation of the injured party.

Also relevant is Article 1532 paragraph (2) CC:

> The damage consisting in the loss of a chance to obtain an advantage will be repaired proportionally to the probability of obtaining that chance and according to the details of the case and the specific situation of the injured party.

In addition, paragraph (3) reads that 'the damage that cannot be assessed with certainty will be determined by the court'.

[179] See Decision of the Supreme Court of Justice No 3970 of 11 December 2014.

[180] The new Romanian Civil Code was adopted through Law No 287/2009, which was published on 15 July 2011 and has been in force since 1 October 2011.

I. Spain

EMNG

A public decision taken without observing the prescribed procedure, including the request for a mandatory report despite having binding effects, is void. In the same action, in which New Tv challenges the unlawful decision, it must ask for compensation for damages including the investments made, actual loss, and lost profit. The latter would be assessed by taking into account the annual profit of companies with a licence for the same frequency as Terranova.

The court would declare the Ministry's decision void but would not uphold New Tv's claim for compensation, mainly because the Ministry could start a new procedure, consulting the ECC, so there is no real damage to the investment as yet. Regarding New Tv's claim for lost profit, the court would consider it to be the simple expectation of benefits.

J. Switzerland

TT

In this case, New Tv has first to appeal the decision of the Ministry before the FAT. If it fails to appeal within the appeal deadline or if the appeal is finally rejected, notwithstanding the lack of consultation of the ECC, New Tv has no chance of obtaining any damages under GLA, since, as stated before when the Swiss institutional framework was delineated in Part II, the lawfulness of the decision of the Ministry can no longer be challenged.

An appeal against the decision of the Ministry will normally have suspensive effect (Art. 55 I APA). Thus if New Tv prevails, and the Ministry is ordered to start again the process of granting licences, it will suffer no harm outside the costs of litigation which are not a question of State liability.

A claim for damages could thus arise only if, pursuant to Article 55 II APA, the Ministry revokes the suspensive effect, and the FAT denies a motion to reinstate it, or if, on request of the Ministry, the FAT revokes the suspensive effect, and the decision of the Ministry is fully implemented making it impossible for New Tv to receive a license even if it prevails on the merits. Such a hypothesis is highly unlikely, as the FAT has to take into account the odds of the appeal being successful in reaching its decision on whether to revoke (or reinstate) the suspensive effect of the said appeal.

If this were nevertheless the case, New Tv could ask for damages under the GLA. As already noted, New Tv would have to demonstrate that the lack of consultation of the ECC by the officials of the Ministry in charge of granting the licences amounted to a breach of a fundamental duty of their office. In addition, New Tv would have to demonstrate that, if the procedure had been conducted lawfully, it would have received a licence. Normally, damages under the GLA would cover not only the actual loss but also the lost profit. Whether the court would actually go that far remains, however, to be seen.

If New Tv, after successfully appealing the Ministry's decision, is finally granted a licence, it could theoretically be granted damages for the delay in obtaining it, provided it demonstrates, as noted above, that the initial decision of the Ministry amounted to a breach of a fundamental duty by the officials in charge of the case. In addition, New Tv would have to prove the amount of its actual loss and lost profit stemming from the delay. On both counts, it might be a tall order.

K. United Kingdom

GA

The facts presented here would give rise to (related) issues about: (i) illegality (in the sense that the Ministry has misunderstood the nature of its legal powers and duties); (ii) breach of a procedural requirement (which might here be described in terms of 'procedural impropriety'); (iii) substantive legitimate expectations; and (iv) damages. The first three issues—illegality, procedural impropriety, and substantive legitimate expectations—would all be dealt with by way of an application for judicial review in the High Court. The damages claim (which would be likely to face very real difficulties) might also be heard in that forum, viz as a claim for breach of statutory duty. Alternatively, it could be brought by way of a free-standing private law claim, again for breach of statutory duty.

In terms of how arguments in the case might be developed, the following points can be noted:

(1) Illegality and procedural impropriety would be regarded as two sides of the same coin. The relevant legislation specifies that the Ministry should consult the ECC and it has failed to do so—any pleaded 'illegality' could therefore be defined as a failure to follow a statutorily prescribed rule.

(2) There are various arguments that could be advanced about why the Ministry has acted illegally/in a procedurally improper manner:

  (a) One is that the procedural requirement at hand is mandatory, viz 'before taking its decision, the Ministry *must* consult' the ECC. While the courts will not automatically hold that a breach of a mandatory procedural requirement has rendered a decision unlawful (they will try to ascertain the purpose of the rule), they will often do so given the apparent legislative intent that underlies the rule. Any other approach would risk undermining the principle of legislative supremacy.

  (b) A second argument is that, by failing to consult with the ECC, the Ministry might be said not to have taken all relevant considerations into account when making its decision. The requirement that decision-makers should take all relevant considerations into account is one that is of fundamental importance, particularly where, as here, the requirement has a statutory basis. By failing to consult, the Ministry might therefore be said to have breached this first principle of public law.

(c) A further argument that might be made is that the Ministry has exercised its power for a 'collateral', 'extraneous', or 'ulterior' purpose. This argument—which would be closely related to those directly above—would centre upon the point that the statutory purpose(s) of consulting with the ECC will inevitably have been defeated by the failure to consult. While it is not immediately clear quite what is the purpose of the duty to consult, it can be presumed that it relates to gathering expert evidence in advance of all licensing decisions (the expert evidence constituting a 'relevant consideration'). By failing to consult, the Ministry has closed off that possibility and, depending on its motivation for doing so, it might even be said to have used its power for an improper purpose (the term 'improper' sometimes connoting an intention to misuse a power).

(3) Some of the counter-arguments that might be made on behalf of the Ministry include:

(a) The statutory requirement to consult, whilst couched in mandatory language, must always be read in context and in a way as avoids absurdities. In the circumstances, where there were far more applicants for licences than there were licences available for distribution, the Ministry might argue that an enforceable duty to consult would only further complicate an already complicated state of affairs. (This is an argument that might have some merit if the Ministry first reduced the numbers to a manageable proportion and then consulted before deciding on the allocation of licences; it might have less merit were it to be used an excuse to avoid the consultation process altogether.)

(b) Depending on the evidence that is before the court, the Ministry might argue that it has never before failed to consult the ECC and that it has done so in this instance simply because of the administrative pressures generated by the high number of applications. It can be surmised that, for any argument of this kind to succeed, there would need to be compelling evidence before the court of prior adherence to the statutory scheme.

(c) A related argument—which is already touched upon in the scenario—is that the 'public interest' demanded some flexibility on the facts of the case. Here, the nature of the pleaded public interest would perhaps be self-evident—licences for frequencies play an important role in facilitating the flow of information and the Ministry acted appropriately, *in extremis*, to ensure that such a flow was protected.

(d) The Ministry might further argue that New Tv's interest in the case is so remote that, even if consultation had been carried out, it would not have resulted in any different outcome in relation to New Tv. An argument of this kind would depend very much on the evidence before the court, and the Ministry would have to be able to show that there was some feature of New Tv's application that rendered it hopeless. Even then, the court may consider that the rule of law that has been breached was of such importance that a finding of illegality should be made.

(4) In terms of New Tv bringing proceedings, there are three points to note.

(a) The first is that New Tv would be free to raise arguments about the more general nature of the illegality/procedural impropriety at hand, as UK law adopts a very generous approach to standing. While the law on standing was previously restrictive, the courts have, since the 1990s in particular, adopted a very liberal approach so that genuine questions about the legality of government action can be heard in court. It might therefore be expected that New Tv could bring a broadly drawn challenge to the Ministry's actions.

(b) The second point concerns substantive legitimate expectations, noted above, where there is some factual cross-over with any potential damages claim. While it could be expected that New Tv would first argue that the failure to consult had denied it the chance to obtain a licence, it appears from the scenario that New Tv had some reason to believe that it would be awarded a licence and that it had made significant investments on foot of that belief. This is the realm of substantive legitimate expectations in UK law, where, to be successful, New Tv would have to be able to demonstrate that there had been a clear and unambiguous Ministerial statement to the effect that it would receive a licence and that it had relied upon that statement. From the limited facts available, it appears not only that no such statement was ever made but, moreover, that any such statement would have been *ultra vires*—the Ministry would, in essence, have been pre-empting the outcome of a consultative process that it was required to carry out by statute.

(c) The third point concerns damages, where any claim would likely be brought as an action for breach of statutory duty (whether within the application for judicial review or as a related, private law action). As indicated above, any such claim would be likely to face formidable difficulties. For instance, one difficulty lies in the fact that is unclear whether the statutory duty in question was owed to New Tv or whether it was a duty that was imposed for the public good—if it can it is assumed that it was a duty of the latter kind, New Tv would be unable to sue in its own name. Another difficulty is even more fundamental: even it a duty were owed to New Tv, the losses it has incurred are speculative and have resulted from what would appear to have been its own assumption about the likelihood that a licence would have been granted.

(5) One final point concerns the remedy that the court might grant in the event that it finds that the Ministry acted unlawfully by failing to carry out the consultation exercise. While the court could quash the Ministry's decision to allocate licences without completing the consultation, it could alternatively grant a declaration that the Ministry acted unlawfully or, indeed, make no order at all (the remedies on an application for judicial review are at the discretion of the court). An approach of this latter kind is sometimes taken where the court considers that a quashing order may cause undue administrative inconvenience or where it is of the view that there would be little to be gained from requiring the procedure to be followed (a point that might be notably true if it is of the view

> that New Tv would not in all likelihood have received a licence). As against that, the court will jealously guard the rule of the law and it could, for that very reason, require that a consultation exercise should now be conducted in accordance with the strict letter of the statute.

To recap: (i) this is a complex matter that raises difficult questions about the tension between the rule of law and administrative efficiency; (ii) New Tv would be able to challenge the Ministry's actions in the High Court, where it may well succeed with an argument about breach of a mandatory procedural requirement; (iii) New Tv's related arguments about substantive legitimate expectations and damages would be extremely difficult—if not impossible—to sustain; and (iv) the court may adopt a flexible approach towards remedies for breach of the procedural requirement if it considers that such an approach would be merited on the facts of the case.

IV. Case 3—sanctions against a bank

'Totally Unnecessary Investments' (TUI) is an investment company whose business consists of receiving and executing orders for third parties and trading on its own behalf. After some years of activity, TUI is subject to an inspection by the national banking regulator (NBR). A few weeks later, the NBR issues a pecuniary sanction against TUI for its alleged negligent behaviour in keeping its documentation. TUI therefore brings an action before the national court competent for reviewing the NBR's acts, claiming that the disciplinary measure is unjustified because the inspection was irregular and the sanction was based on a gross misunderstanding of the facts, because some important documents were not taken into account. TUI asks the court, first, to quash the sanction and, second, to award damages for harm to its commercial reputation.

Would TUI's action be successful? And if damages are awarded, how would their amount be assessed?

A. Austria

SS, KB, DB, and LM

Banking supervision is a sovereign task. This is also true of imposing sanctions in this context. According to Article 10(1) No 5 B-VG, the federal government has legislative and executive powers in the banking sector. Hence, the competent court for an appeal against a sanction is the BVwG (Art 130(1) No 1 and Art 131(2) B-VG). According to § 28 VwGVG, the BVwG itself decides whether the sanction was unlawful and can therefore conduct additional investigations. If the BVwG concludes that there was no legal basis for the inspection and the sanction, it has to annul the contested decision and quash the sanction.

If the unlawfully imposed penalty has caused damage that remains in existence even after the court has repealed it, TUI may claim damages under public liability law and bring an action against the Federation. According to § 3(2) of the Federal Act on the Institution and Organisation of the Financial Market (FMABG),[181] the federal government is liable (pursuant to the provisions of the AHG) for damages caused by the financial market authority (*Finanzmarktaufsicht*), their bodies, and employees in the execution of the federal laws listed in § 2 FMABG. The federal government is only liable for damages directly caused to the supervised legal entity.

Damage to TUI's commercial reputation could occur, for example, if the NBR publishes its decision. Publication of the NBR's decision would also be part of its sovereign area.[182] This means damage caused by the publication occurring directly in the execution of the laws and within the framework of supervisory activities. However, damage to one's reputation caused by the execution of the law can also be compensated under

[181] *Bundesgesetz über die Errichtung und Organisation der Finanzmarktaufsichtsbehörde* (*Finanzmarktauf sichtsbehördengesetz*), Federal Law Gazette I No 97/2001 as amended.
[182] OGH 27 May 2015 6 Ob 38/15d.

the AHG. Therefore, TUI's claim for damages against the federal government will not be successful.

B. European Union

BM

In the EU judicial system, the investment company TUI could challenge the sanction before the Court of Justice. With regard to decisions imposing fines, the court can review fully the facts of the dispute and can exercise a review of the merits.

If the measure was actually based on inaccurate and incomplete information, the decision will also be annulled (or reduced) in the light of the applicant's conduct during the inspection.

Once the decision has been quashed (or the unsuitability of the measure has been established), in order to maintain compensation the investment company would have to demonstrate the unlawful conduct of the authority.

In particular, in this case, given the limited degree of discretion of the Authority, the injured party has to prove that the irregularities carried out by the Authority are such that no diligent administration would have committed them.[183]

If the sanction were only reduced, however, it is unlikely that compensation would be awarded for damage to TUI's reputation.

In the EU case law, the annulment of the decision is at times considered a sufficient measure to repair non-material damage.[184]

C. France

TP

TUI's action could be successful if the company proves that the irregularity during the inspection affected its right to present a defence and, this being the case, the direct damage caused by the unlawful decision in order to be entitled to compensation. We will explain the suspension procedure to avoid damage in these cases, then the effects of an irregularity in an inspection before the administrative sanction procedure, and finally some remarks about the compensation.

According to Article L521-1 of the Administrative Justice Code, the affected person can claim the suspension of the effects or some effects of an administrative act before the court's final decision. Two elements must be proved: a serious doubt regarding the lawfulness of the contested act and the urgency of the suspension.[185]

[183] Case T-178/98 *Fresh Marine v Commission* [2000] ECR II-3331, judgment of the Court 24 October 2000; Case C-47/07 *P Masdar UK v Commission* [2008] ECR I-9761, judgment of the Court 16 December 2008.

[184] Case T-89/01 *Willeme v Commission* [2002] ECR-SC I-A-153, judgment of the Court of First Instance 11 September 2002.

[185] Article L521-1 CJA.

In the case of pecuniary sanctions against financial institutions, the *Conseil d'Etat* holds that urgency may be established if the amount of the sanction causes immediate problems of solvency ratio or capital adequacy required by law or if the sanction's publicity results in a loss of clients that affects the company's stability. If the company itself is in danger, the condition of urgency could be recognized for a suspension claim.[186] The company should also prove, using the general grounds against administrative acts,[187] that there is a serious doubt about lawfulness, for example, if there is evidence that the procedure did not respect the right of defence, that the company was informed of the charges too late to present observations, or that the sanction may be disproportionate. It is important to refer to all possible grounds to point out the seriousness of the infringement.

In TUI's case, the company should contest the validity of the sanction and claim the suspension while the main judicial procedure is decided. It may have enough elements to prove the two conditions. However, the commercial reputation itself will not demonstrate the urgency requirement if it does not go hand in hand with other immediate and serious damage.

The regulatory authorities' privileges of inspection ('*contrôles et enquêtes*') and their competence to sanction the institutions based on the information collected before the administrative procedure for the sanction is a key question regarding process rights.

The inspection's requirements regarding the FMA are set out by the Monetary and Financial Code. The officer in charge of an inspection is authorized to visit financial institutions, to ask for any document, and interview any person[188] regarding the purpose of the inspection established in the inspection order. The financial institution's employees have the right to legal assistance of their choice to answer the officer' questions.[189] More stringent requirements apply to administrative sanctions, for which the guarantees of Article 6 § 1 ECHR must be respected.[190] Procedural requirements differ,[191] for example, if the person questioned does not have the right to remain silent during an inspection.[192] The question that thus arises is which failure in the inspection procedure may cause the 'unlawfulness' of the sanction.

The *Conseil d'Etat* established that inspections 'must be conducted under conditions that ensure that the right to present a defence of the person to whom charges are subsequently notified is not irreparably affected'. In other words, they cannot prevent the company from exercising its right to present a defence in a future procedure. In fact, the inspection ends with a '*rapport de contrôle*' (control report) that is sent to the company which, in turn, has at least ten days to answer before the FMA makes any recommendation.[193] The *Conseil d'Etat* also considered that

[186] CE *Ordonnance du 17 avril 2015. Société Bernheim Dreyfus et autres* No 389093.

[187] The external formal and procedural grounds, and the internal related to the substantial unlawfulness.

[188] Article L621-9-1 and Art L621-10 *Code monétaire et financier.*

[189] Article L621-11 *Code monétaire et financier.*

[190] The *Conseil d'Etat* will have full jurisdiction to review the sanction, and this is why the administrative authority does not have to respect all guarantees like a 'tribunal' within the meaning of Art 6 s 1 ECHR, but it must assure some aspects of the right to due process, such as impartiality. CE *Société GSD Gestions et MYX* (n 25).

[191] CE 15 May 2013 *Société Alternative Leaders France* No 356054.

[192] CE 12 June 2013 *Société Natixis* No 349185.

[193] Article 143-5 of the *Autorité des marches financiers* (AMF) regulation.

the possibility to have access to and review the entire file and present observations during the sanction procedure assures the right to present a defence.[194] In another case, it examined the complexity of the questions and the interrogation conditions during inspections to determine whether they seriously affected the right to present a defence in the future sanction procedure.[195] On this basis, TUI may assert that the inspection was irregular, for example, if the officer did not explain to the employees that they could have legal assistance during the interview, or the FMA did not send the report for the company's observations. If the unlawfulness of the inspection procedure prevents TUI from exercising its right to present a defence, the claim could be successful.

In cases of pecuniary sanctions, the *Conseil d'Etat* carefully considers the reasons for the decision, the material accuracy of the facts (*inexactitude matérielle*), and the Authority's interpretation (*erreur de qualification juridique*). In these cases, it examines all questions of fact and law. TUI's second argument may therefore be endorsed if the company proves that the alleged facts did not really happen as the FMA established, ie TUI has all the required documents.

The misconduct of the FMA evidenced in the unlawfulness of the sanction would not automatically imply compensation for TUI because it must prove the direct damage and the causal link between this and the administrative sanction.

Three options must be considered. The first concerns the '*référé suspension*' (petition for suspension). If the court finds that the suspension is not possible, but the final decision is the annulment of the sanction, TUI can bring a claim for damages, proving the damage by showing the company's turnover before and after the publication of the penalty, or some other information that establishes the causal link between the sanction and the damage. Second, the harm to the company's reputation may be awarded on a case-by-case basis considering the publicity of the sanction and the impact on the company, shown, for example by a reduction on investments and/or particular conditions such as press news regarding the case.[196] Finally, TUI can claim interests and capitalization of interests.[197] The court must explicitly address the interest[198] and capitalization questions from the date of the reparation claim.[199] The interest rate is the legal one,[200] defined every six months

[194] CE *Société Alternative Leaders France* (n 191).

[195] CE *Société Natixis* (n 192).

[196] Cour Administrative d'Appel de Paris 25 March 1993 No 90PA00839, Lebon T.

[197] E Picard, *Répertoire de responsabilité de la puissance publique* (Dalloz 2015) No 256.

[198] 'L'arrêt de la cour administrative d'appel de Paris du 6 mai 2008 est annulé en tant qu'il limite à 18 872 € la somme que le département de Seine-et-Marne est condamné à payer à la Société Pradeau et Morin et qu'il n'assortit pas la deparation di des intérêts moratoires.' CE 27 October 2010 *Société Pradeau et Morin* No 318023.

[199] On interest and its capitalization: 15.

> Considérant que Mme B...a droit aux intérêts au taux légal sur la somme qui lui est due à compter du 9 mai 1996, date de réception de sa réclamation préalable; qu'elle a demandé la capitalisation des intérêts à cette date; qu'il y a lieu d'ordonner cette capitalisation au 9 mai 1997, date à laquelle a été due une année d'intérêts, puis à chaque échéance annuelle ultérieure (CE *Mme Moraes* 16 December 2013 No 346575).

[200] This rate is defined on the basis of financial and monetary conditions, and the methodology for its calculation is established in a Decree; Art L313-2 *Code monétaire et financier*.

by an order (*'arrêté'*) of the Ministry of the Economy, and interests can be capitalized after a delay of more than one year for payment according to Article 1343-2 CC.[201]

D. Germany

FW and JS

The *Bundesanstalt für Finanzdienstleistungsaufsicht* (the *Bundesanstalt*) acts as the supervisor of banking activities in Germany unless the supervisory task has been transferred to the European Central Bank (§ 1 para 5 No 2 and No 1 KWG[202]). Based on the information provided, the European Central Bank does not seem to be involved here. Therefore, the *Bundesanstalt* is formally charged with imposing the fine (§ 60 KWG read in conjunction with § 36 para 1 No 1 OWiG[203]) and can be regarded as the equivalent of the NBR. TUI would have to file an objection to the fining with the NBR first (§ 67 para 1 OWiG). If the NBR does not revoke the fine, the prosecutor of the Frankfurt am Main[204] local court would be charged with the case and could submit the files to the judge (§ 69 paras 3 and 4 OWiG). The judge would then decide on the case (§ 68 para 1 OWiG). The procedural rules on administrative offences thus stipulate that after an objection both the agency and the judge reassess the case.[205] If the fine is 'based on a gross misunderstanding of the facts' and thus not justified in substance, the action would be successful, since no regulatory offence may be established; the relevance of the irregularity of the inspection cannot be decided conclusively based upon the information provided.

The court does not review the fining notice which was issued by the agency, but decides on the matter itself.[206] Hence, errors made by the agency generally do not impede the court from upholding a fining notice.[207] As a result, it may be said that if the court finds after a comprehensive assessment of the documents that the inspection was unlawful (and the disciplinary measure unjustified), it would quash the sanction.

§ 110 paragraph 1 OWiG read in conjunction with § 8 StrEG[208] provides for damages caused by the investigation into and fining of regulatory offences. However,

201 'Les intérêts échus, dus au moins pour une année depara, produisent intérêt si le contrat l'a prévu ou si une deparati de justice le precise.'

202 *Gesetz über das Kreditwesen* (German Banking Act), German version <www.gesetze-im-internet.de/kredwg/BJNR008810961.html> accessed 21 June 2020.

203 *Gesetz über Ordnungswidrigkeiten* (German Act on Regulatory Offences), English version <www.gesetze-im-internet.de/englisch_owig/englisch_owig.html#p0214> accessed 21 June 2020.

204 Frankfurt is the forum for legal action against the Bundesanstalt, s 1 para 3 sentence 2 of the *Finanzdienstleistungsaufsichtsgesetz* (German Financial Supervisory Authority Act), German version <www.gesetze-im-internet.de/findag/BJNR131010002.html> accessed 21 June 2020.

205 J Bohnert and J Bülte, *Ordnungswidrigkeitenrecht* (5th edn, CH Beck 2016) § 3 paras 223ff, 239.

206 K-H Kurz, '§ 65' in L Senge (ed), *Karlsruher Kommentar zum OWiG* (5th edn, CH Beck 2018) para 28.

207 K Sackreuther, '§ 65' in J-P Graf (ed), *BeckOK OWiG* (27th edn, CH Beck 1 July 2020) para 15.

208 *Gesetz über die Entschädigung für Strafverfolgungsmaßnahmen* (Prosecution Compensation Act), German version <www.gesetze-im-internet.de/streg/BJNR001570971.html> accessed 22 June 2020.

compensation is expressly limited to actual loss and does not comprise damages for harm to business reputation.[209]

The aforementioned provisions do not rule out the applicability of the general provisions on public authority liability, ie Article 34 sentence 1 GG read in conjunction with § 839 paragraph 1 sentence 1 BGB.[210] The conditions for liability have been set out above (see case 1), requiring that (1) an official (2) intentionally or negligently (3) breached the official duty incumbent upon him or her (4) in relation to a third party, and that this (5) caused (6) the claimant harm.

Officers with the NBR are officials within the meaning of § 839 paragraph 1 sentence 1 BGB. They would also have acted negligently, ie they did not exercise reasonable care (§ 276 para 2 BGB), if TUI's allegations were true. With regard to requirement (3), specific duties in the context of prosecuting regulatory offences exist. They correspond to the official duties applying in criminal procedural law, including that the decision to investigate must be reasonable and sufficiently substantiated[211,212]. Provided that TUI's claim that 'the inspection was irregular and the sanction was based on a gross misunderstanding of the facts, because some documents were not taken into account' is true, both official duties would have been breached. These duties exist in relation to the suspect, thus a third party whose interests these duties aim to protect[213]. However, it must also be established whether the reputation of those affected is included as a protected interest.[214] This is not the case here, given that the investigation into regulatory offences does not follow other rules than the prosecution of criminal offences;[215] even in this context, a breach of official duties gives rise to damages for non-financial loss only if a deprivation of liberty is involved (cf § 7 para 1 StrEG), which is not a sanction in the context of regulatory offences.[216] The breached duties therefore do not extend to covering the kind of damage TUI has suffered.

Causation is—moreover—assessed by considering 'the course of events if the official had acted according to the law and what the (financial) situation of the aggrieved party would look like in this case'.[217] *In casu*, the harm to TUI's reputation does not primarily result from the prosecution, but from the publicity. Hence, causation can only be established if NBR may also be held responsible for this, which cannot be assessed on the basis of the information given in the questionnaire.

Even if one finds that the prerequisites of Article 34 sentence 1 GG read in conjunction with § 839 paragraph 1 BGB are fulfilled, assessment of the compensable damages

[209] cf OLG Köln 14 March 1985—7 W 14/84, [1986] Das juristische Büro 247 (247).

[210] ibid.

[211] Concerning reasonability cf BGH 29 April 1993—III ZR 3/92, BGHZ 122, 268 (271 with further references). Concerning substantiation cf BGH 18 May 2000—III ZR 180/99, [2000] NJW 2672 (2673).

[212] A-C Brodöfel, 'Die Haftung für Amtspflichtverletzungen' in K Haag (ed), *Geigel. Der Haftpflichtprozess* (28th edn, CH Beck 2020) ch 20 paras 92, 118; cf BGH 24 February 1994—III ZR 76/92, [1994] NJW 3162 (3162).

[213] See case 2 in section III.

[214] M Baldus, B Grzeszick, and S Wienhues, *Staatshaftungsrecht* (5th edn, CF Müller 2018) para 153.

[215] See n 212.

[216] Ossenbühl and Cornils (n 145) 460; K Cornelius, '§ 7 StrEG' in J-P Graf (ed), *BeckOK I* (37th edn, CH Beck 1 July 2020) para 15; S Grommes, '§ 7 StrEG' in Graf, *BeckOK OWiG* (n 207) para 3.

[217] Own translation of BGH 6 April 1995—III ZR 183/94, BGHZ 129, 226 (232f); see previous case 2 in section III.

would prove difficult. With regard to damages for harm to TUI's commercial reputation, as in case 1, § 253 BGB would apply. TUI might invoke § 253 paragraph 2 BGB, which reads: 'If damages are to be paid for an injury to body, health, freedom or sexual self-determination, reasonable compensation in money may also be demanded for any damage that is not pecuniary loss.' This provision also covers damages for unjustified interferences with the 'general right to free development of one's personality'. If this is affirmed, the further question would arise as to whether TUI, a company, is able to rely on the general right to free development of one's personality as a basis for damages. Civil courts tend to extend this right to legal persons.[218] However, they do not award damages but envisage, for example, injunctive relief[219] or a *dementi*. This is justified by the fact that the satisfactory effect of monetary compensation for infringements of personality rights does not apply to legal persons.[220] It should be noted, though, that such claims (*dementi*, injunctive relief) are not encompassed by the general provisions on public liability limited to financial compensation;[221] different actions apply in this regard.[222]

TUI is not entitled to claim damages for the harm to its commercial reputation since the duty breached does not aim to protect TUI's commercial interests.

E. Hungary

LB

In Hungary, the National Bank has exclusive supervisory power over the whole financial intermediary system.[223] For its procedures, the Act of General Administrative Procedure (AGAP) is not applicable, although its own procedural rules are quite similar and the Act of 2013 on the National Bank of Hungary also requires the application of some rules of the AGAP.

In general, it is legal and quite normal to make unscheduled inspections, so this would not be a problem. Although the previous AGAP required the publication of an inspection plan, this did not mean that the authority was obliged only to follow the plan and could not make an unscheduled inspection. The new AGAP no longer requires such publication, precisely because the authority can make an inspection any time. Also, after an inspection, an administrative procedure will be initiated by the authority because the inspection itself is not considered to be an

[218] H Dreier, 'Art 2 I' in H Dreier (ed), *Grundgesetz Kommentar*, vol 1 (3rd edn, Mohr Siebeck 2013) para 86 with further references.

[219] BGH 8 July 1980—VI ZR 177/78, BGHZ 78, 24 (25ff). BGH 25 September 1980—III ZR 74/78, BGHZ 78, 274 (280), might be seen as an exception, but it dealt with a religious denomination. See H Merkt, '§ 13' in H Fleischer and W Goette (eds), *Münchener Kommentar zum GmbHG* (3rd edn, CH Beck 2018) para 32 with fn 92.

[220] cf BGH 8 July 1980—VI ZR 177/78, BGHZ 78, 24 (27f).

[221] cf BGH 19 December 1960—GSZ 1/60, BGHZ 34, 99 (106f); Papier and Shirvani (n 141) para 295.

[222] For action for injunctive relief/for remedy of effects of an unlawful act (*Folgenbeseitigungsanspruch*), see H-J Papier, 'Art. 34' in T Maunz and G Dürig (eds), *Grundgesetz Kommentar* (54th edn, CH Beck January 2009) paras 62ff; cf H Maurer and C Waldhoff, *Allgemeines Verwaltungsrecht* (19th edn, CH Beck 2017) § 30.

[223] Slovakia and the Czech Republic have a similar system.

administrative procedure (but the rules of the administrative procedure need to be used).[224]

As regards evidence, there is a possibility in the administrative court procedure to carry out probative proceedings, so TUI can prove its allegations. If it can prove that it did not commit any infringement at all and the decision was unfounded, the administrative court would annul the decision. If there were some infringements on TUI's side, the court can change the decision, mitigating the fine.

Concerning damages, if the facts are deemed unfounded, the harm done to a company's business reputation is part of the personality rights. Infringement of a personality right, such as good reputation, gives rise to objective liability, which is based on three elements: the information that was communicated to another person was untrue; it was directed against a personality; and it was offensive. The information communicated must be objectively capable of inducing a negative social judgement of the person concerned. To prove that the damage actually occurred is no longer a precondition because the CC presumes the occurrence of the damage from the infringement itself. If the infringement is proven, the claimant has a right to restitution.[225] One can be exempt from liability if he or she proves that the damage occurred through no fault of his or her own (eg compliant with the requirements of the profession). The amount of damages is determined by the court, taking into consideration all the circumstances of the case, including the gravity of the infringement, its recurrence, the extent of the accusation, and the impact of the infringement on the victim and his environment.

So, for TUI to award damages for the harm to its commercial reputation, positive and negative conditions must be fulfilled: it must prove that the decision contained untrue facts, that these facts were about them and were objectively capable of inducing the disadvantaged social judgement, and that the authority cannot exempt itself (eg they knew the real facts).

It can be interesting to consider a recent judicial decision regarding a violation of personality rights. The administrative authority stated that criminal proceedings were being conducted against the claimant because he or she has endangered his or her child, a minor. This fact was based on information from another authority, but it

[224] Act CL of 2016—on General Public Administration Procedures s 101 states that:

> (1) Where the regulatory inspection finds any infringement: a) the authority shall open proceedings, or b) if the infringement that comes to light falls within the jurisdiction of another body, the authority shall initiate the proceedings of that body. (2) Where the authority finds no infringement during the regulatory inspection conducted at the client's request, it shall make out an official instrument to that effect. In the own-motion regulatory inspections, the authority shall issue an official instrument on its findings at the client's request.

[225] Section 2:52 CC concerning restitution provides that '(1) Any person whose rights relating to personality have been violated shall be entitled to restitution for any non-material violation suffered.'

The new Civil Code separates the rules of restitution (book 2) from the rules of compensation in cases of liability (book 6). Previously, non-pecuniary (non-material) damage was awarded, and the damage had to be proven (this was one branch of the judicial practice; another one did not ask to prove the damages in some cases, eg cases concerning the right of personal portrayal, and the third branch only investigated the damage to decide the amount of compensation), but now the rules of liability are not applied here and the damage need not be proven. The name has changed, too, from 'compensation for non-pecuniary damage' to 'restitution'.

was untrue. The courts of first and second instance rejected the claim. According to these decisions, the reasoning in an administrative or judicial decision does not in itself give rise to a violation of personality rights because it is not directed against the personality, but it is an expression of a decision that was made according to the applicable rules. So the reasoning does not constitute a violation of personality rights, even if it proves to be untrue in whole or in part. To remedy this, administrative remedies must be exhausted, which happened in this case, so the administrative court annulled this part of the decision. The Curia (Supreme Court), however, did not accept this argument. According to the Curia, the untrue fact was (grammatically and logically) clearly directed against the claimant, and the decision of the authority regarded both the parents, so the court ruled that there was an infringement, but the authority could exempt itself of liability because it was proven that it got the information from another authority.

F. Italy

FC

In Italy, TUI would certainly be able to challenge the validity of the sanction issued by NBR, in particular by turning to an ordinary court (more specifically, to the court of appeal of the city where NBR has its headquarters: this is the solution that applies to challenges to sanctions issued by the Bank of Italy, as well as sanctions issued by Consob (Italy's Securities and Exchange Commission); this solution is strongly contested by interpreters of the law, since it does not apply to challenges to many other administrative orders issued by other independent authorities, for which the jurisdiction of the administrative court is binding).[226]

The solution to this case depends on a number of variables.

In general, the fact that an administrative authority issues an unfavourable order without considering all the relevant documentation can be deemed enough to render the order unlawful (specifically, the misconduct may lie with the preliminary investigation, which can exert an abuse of power).

However, Italian courts—also influenced by similar guidelines from the CJEU,[227] from the EU law,[228] and from national law[229]—deem that the right to a defence cannot be invoked when the sanctioned party has intentionally concealed important documents. In these cases, a principle of rightful procedural collaboration applies,

[226] Article 113 para 1.l), CAT; Constitutional Court No 162/2012; Constitutional Court No 94/2014.

[227] See eg European Court of Justice Case 374/87 *Orkem v Commission* [1989] ECR 3283; Court of First Instance T-112/98 *Mannesmannröhren-Werke AG* [2001] ECR II-729.

[228] See Directive 2003/6/EC of the European Parliament and of the Council of 28 January 2003 on insider dealing and market manipulation (market abuse) [2003] OJ L96/16, in part. Article 14 para 3 and Regulation (EU) No 596/2014 of the European Parliament and of the Council of 16 April 2014 on market abuse (market abuse regulation) and repealing Directive 2003/6/EC of the European Parliament and of the Council and Commission Directives 2003/124/EC, 2003/125/EC and 2004/72/EC [2014] OJ L173/1, in part. Article 30 para 1.b.

[229] See Article 187-*quinquiesdecies* LD No 58/1998 para 1 concerning sanctions ruled by finance and banking law.

also involving private individuals and tasking them with a very broad burden of discovery.[230]

However, if procedural negligence is prevalently attributable only to the administration, then TUI's appeal would have a good chance of being accepted, in accordance with the general principles of proper procedure and impartiality.

Similarly, the compensation claim could be accepted, particularly in terms of compensation for damages to the image of the business and the reputation of the unlawfully sanctioned party.

G. Poland

Dawid Ziółkowski

The analysis of the data contained in the case does not allow for an unequivocal thesis as to the legitimacy of imposing a pecuniary penalty on the TUI company for violation of the law related to improper storage of documents. Hypothetically, however, it can be assumed that if the administrative court repeals the decision on the basis of which the sanction was imposed, the company will be able to bring a civil action and claim compensation for the damage suffered as a result of the unlawful actions of the public authority. The company should be compensated, but it has to take into account the fact that it will face many years of proceedings, first before the administrative courts and then before the civil courts.

The regulations relevant to the case are provided first of all in the Financial Market Supervision Act of 21 July 2006.[231] The entity referred to in the case as the '*National Banking Regulator*' is the Polish Financial Supervision Authority (Komisja Nadzoru Finansowego—the 'KNF') which is the body competent for regulating the financial market pursuant to the FMSA. Moreover, TUI is an investment firm and, as such, it is governed by Regulation (EU) No 1286/2014 of the European Parliament and of the Council of 26 November 2014, which casuistically mandate certain procedures with regard to investment documents.

In the light of Article 3b of the FMSA, a provision which, together with Article 3c of the FMSA, came into force as of 1 January 2018, the KNF is the body competent for ensuring compliance with Regulation No 1286/2014. Any breach of this regulation exposes the violator (whether a natural or legal person) to a pecuniary penalty referred to in Article 3c section 1 item 5 of the FMSA.

In this case, the KNF officials 'accuse' investment firm TUI of negligence in keeping documents. Admittedly, pursuant to the FMSA, the KNF is authorized to levy a pecuniary penalty on investment firms.

[230] Recently, however, the constitutional legitimacy of this interpretation has been questioned by the Cour de Cassation No 3831/2018. In particular, the court doubts a conflict not only between this interpretation and the general principle *nemo tenetur se detegere*, but also between this interpretation and Art 117 para 1 Const, which provides for compliance of Italian law with EU law and international obligations (in particular, with Art 47 Charter of Fundamental Rights of the European Union, concerning 'Right to an effective remedy and to a fair trial', and with the ECHR).

[231] Consolidated text in *Dziennik Ustaw* of 2019 item 298 (the Financial Market Supervision Act, FMSA).

Essentially, the dispute boils down to the question whether the investment firm TUI, which lodged a complaint may appeal to a court to have the pecuniary penalty lifted and seek damages for any losses incurred as a result of the activities of the KNF agencies. In short, there is the issue of state liability for illegal activities of public authorities.[232]

The pecuniary sanction will be imposed on TUI in the form of an administrative decision. Importantly, such a decision will be immediately enforceable by operation of law (see Art 3c s 2 of the FMSA). The 'unusual' position of the KNF within the structures of the governmental administration precludes any possibility to appeal against its decision to an authority of higher instance.[233] In this situation, a substitute for such an appeal is a motion to reconsider the case by the KNF, because KNF's decision comes within the scope of application of Article 127 § 3 of the APC (see Art 11 s 6 of the FMSA).

If the KNF reconsiders the case and upholds its previous position imposing the pecuniary penalty on TUI, the company will have a right to lodge a complaint with an administrative court.

However, damages for any losses incurred by TUI as a result of a temporary deterioration of its financial condition, interest paid, or damage to its market reputation may only be sought on civil law grounds. Pursuant to Article 417 § 1 CC, liability for damage caused by an unlawful action or omission in the exercise of public authority lies with the State Treasury or the relevant local government's body, or another legal person exercising such authority by operation of law. A decision of the administrative court will also constitute an important argument based on *praeiudicium*.

The prejudication in question will be of key importance for the compensation case examined by the civil court. It should be emphasized that it is the claimant (in this case TUI) who will have to prove the unlawfulness of proceedings of the public authority (KNF), the damage suffered, and the causal link between the infringement of the law by the public authorities and the resulting damage. This is a result of the fact that in Polish law there is a general rule of evidence according to which the burden of proof lies with the person who derives legal effects from the fact (Art 6 CC). It is settled case law that the parties are obliged to provide evidence to confirm the facts from which they derive legal effects, and the court may only in exceptional cases admit evidence not indicated by the plaintiff or the defendant.[234] An earlier administrative court ruling repealing the KNF's decision will be of significant importance in determining the unlawfulness of public authority action.

In conclusion, if TUI successfully proves in an administrative court that the KNF unlawfully imposed the pecuniary penalty, the administrative court will have the authority to repeal the KNF's decision. However, any claims for damages will need to be sought in civil court acting upon a company's action. This court will also consider the question of the scope of damages.

232 For more information, see D Fairgrieve, *State Liability in Tort. A Comparative Law Study* (OUP 2003).

233 A Nadolska, 'Status prawny Komisji Nadzoru Finansowego (Legal Status of the Financial Supervision Authority)' (2011) 2 Annales Universitatis Mariae Curie-Skłodowska 129.

234 Decision of the Supreme Court of 24 April 2019 No V CSK 486/18, similarly to the judgment of the Court of Appeal in Szczecin 25 October 2018 No IiI AUa 183/18.

H. Romania

RV

The body competent to apply such sanctions in Romania is the Financial Supervising Authority. The statutory instrument regulating its powers and activity is Government Emergency Ordinance No 93/2012.[235] According to Article 3 of this Ordinance, the Financial Supervising Authority is competent to:

(1) grant, suspend, withdraw or refuse to grant authorizations, licences, endorsements, permits and derogations;
(2) issue regulations that will be published in the Official Gazette;
(3) control the activity of entities mentioned under Article 2paragraph 1, based on reports and through verifications at their headquarters;
(4) take measures and apply sanctions.

The entities mentioned under Article 2 paragraph 1 are: financial instruments operations, intermediaries, investment companies, collective placing bodies, companies that manage investments, investment finance consultants, market and system operators, central depositaries, market operations, companies that issue movable assets, the investment compensation fund, and other companies that carry out activities pursuant to Law 297/2004 on capital markets.

Therefore, in the case under analysis, TUI would qualify as an intermediary of financial instrument operations and would be subject to supervising, control, and sanctioning measures taken by the Financial Supervising Authority under Article 3 of Government Emergency Ordinance No 93/2012.

The measures taken by the Financial Supervising Authority can be challenged according to the general provisions on judicial review, Law 554/2004. This is stipulated under Government Emergency Ordinance No 93/2012, which establishes (Art 21^3) that: 'The acts issued by the Financial Supervising Authority are subject to judicial review and will be challenged as per the procedure established under Law 554/2004 on judicial review.'

In the case analysed here, TUI should first lodge a preliminary administrative appeal before the Financial Supervising Authority under Article 7 of Law 554/2004 and, if unsatisfied with the answer to the preliminary appeal, lodge a claim for annulment before the Bucharest Court of Appeal (which is the court that would have jurisdiction in this case), together with a claim for moral damages for the compensation for harm done to its reputation.

There was discussion in Romania on whether moral damages might be granted to legal persons. This controversy concerns the status quo prior to the judicial reform in Romania and the entry into force of the new CC. Lacking an express provision on the issue, the courts' practice was quite inconsistent, as some recognized the legal person's

[235] Published in the Official Gazette No 874 of 21 December 2012. The control procedure should be conducted as established under Regulation No 1 of 17 January 2014 on the Financial Supervising Authority's control activity, published in the Official Gazette No 61 of 24 January 2014.

right to moral damages and others did not.[236] A 2016 decision by the Supreme Court applying the old rules based on the *tempus regit actum* principle holds that:

> Under the civil code previously in force, which is applicable to the facts of this dispute, the issue of granting moral damage to a legal person was a controversial one. It was often mentioned in case law that article 54 of Decree 31/1954 regarding natural and legal persons does not set out differences in treatment and neither does it limit the non-patrimonial rights it protected, and to be granted moral damages for the breach of any such rights is guaranteed.
>
> Although in this given case, the Court of Appeal had given the above an entirely different interpretation by granting the claimant moral damages for the breaches brought by the defendant to its non-patrimonial rights, the Supreme Court considers that we should give credit to the fact that the legal protection of non-patrimonial rights belonging to legal persons is limited to those specific rights that can be attributed to legal persons. We cannot completely ignore that the very existence of moral damage was initially recognized out of need to grant reparation for the physical and moral suffering of natural persons. Moral damage touches the values that define the human person and refer to the person's existence, corporal integrity and feelings of affection, honesty, dignity, professional prestige and similar values. It is true that some of these values can also been attributed to legal persons, but in these cases, the legislator expressly recognized the possibility of granting moral damages to legal persons—for example, for unfair competition (art. 9 under Law 11/1991). Furthermore, legal persons can ask for compensation for breaches of their rights regarding names, trademarks, and headquarters. Therefore, the possibility of granting moral damages cannot artificially be extended because when the claimant is a legal person it cannot claim for psychological or physical suffering.[237]

This decision is highly questionable, as it is both incompatible with the ECHR and the Romanian Constitution and inconsistent with the court's previous case law. For instance, in a 2015 decision, the Supreme Court had accepted the possibility for courts to decide that compensation should be granted for moral damage caused to a legal person, provided that the conditions for triggering liability are met:

> The Supreme Court with Decision 900/2015 reiterates that, as far as liability is concerned, prejudice should not be presumed either by the law or by the judge. It should be proven with evidence brought in the case as well as the causal link with the culpable act. Even for granting moral damages, it is necessary that arguments and evidence be brought, evidence that clearly shows how the non-patrimonial rights have been breached. Moreover, this is so in the present case, given that the person claiming for moral damage is a legal person, whose entire economic activity is registered and is

[236] See on the topic A Ionaşcu, 'La reparation des dommages moraux dans le droit socialiste roumain' (1966) 2 Revue roumaine des sciences sociales 207.

[237] Romanian Supreme Court Decision No 373 of 24 February 2016 in Romanian on the Supreme Court's website <www.scj.ro/1093/Detalii-jurisprudenta?customQuery[0].Key=id&customQuery[0].Value=128553≥ accessed 22 June 2020.

> held accountable. The purpose behind the activity of any company is to obtain profit, finis mercatorum est lucrum, and consequently, any moral prejudice to a commercial company can be quantified through a judicial accountancy expert opinion. In any case, the compensation must be proportional to the loss and must consider the social values that are protected as well as the intensity with which the breach was caused.

The new CC in force since 1 October 2011 replaced the previous one, in force since 1864 and strongly influenced by the Napoleonic Civil Code. The new CC clearly establishes under Article 257 that legal persons enjoy the same non-patrimonial rights as natural persons and that these rights are protected by law. At the time of writing, there is no case law from the Supreme Court on damages granted to legal persons in the new normative context, but TUI's claim should be considered admissible, and moral damages could be granted if the causal link between the prejudice and the harm to its reputation were to be confirmed.

No consistent methodology can be seen to be applied by Romanian courts (civil or administrative) when assessing claims for moral damage, but the general approach is that the claimant should produce some evidence regarding the harm suffered; in our case, TUI would have to show that the illegal sanctioning act issued by the Financial Supervising Authority had a negative impact on its income and profit. Pursuant to proving the existence of the prejudice, TUI should also prove the causal link between this prejudice and the annulled administrative act.

I. Spain

EMNG

TUI's action would be successful whether or not it can be proved that the inspection was irregular and the sanction was based on a gross misunderstanding of the facts, in this case due to some important documents not being taken into consideration. Hidden documents in a judicial or administrative process can open up extraordinary ways of challenging the administrative or judicial decision.

The compensation must be real and adequate, and the award can be assessed by taking into account the usual income for that time of year, the loss since the sanction was imposed, and the cost of the measures that must be taken to recover TUI's commercial reputation.

J. Switzerland

TT

It must be stressed at the outset that TUI could not bring just one action before a court to ask simultaneously for the sanction to be quashed and for damages.

The sanction issued by NBR, which in Switzerland is the Swiss Financial Market Supervisory Authority (FINMA), should be appealed within thirty days of its notification before the FAT. The decision of the FAT will in turn be subject to appeal before the Federal Tribunal. The FAT and the Federal Tribunal could dismiss the appeal, modify the sanction, or quash it altogether. If TUI fails to lodge an appeal or its appeal is dismissed, the lawfulness of the sanction could not be questioned in eventual liability proceedings. Whether an appeal by TUI would be successful depends, of course, on whether it is true that the inspection was irregular, that some important documents were not taken into account, and that the facts were grossly misunderstood.

If the sanction is quashed by the FAT or the Federal Tribunal, then the question of damages for the harm to TUI commercial reputation arises.

According to Article 19 of the Financial Markets Supervision Act 2007 (FINMASA), the liability of FINMA and its agents is governed by the GLA. However, FINMA and its agents are liable only if (i) they have committed a breach of fundamental duties; and (ii) loss or damage is not due to a breach of duty by a supervised person or entity (Art 19 II FINMASA). Since FINMA is an independent federal agency with financial autonomy, it is directly liable, the liability of the Swiss Confederation being only subsidiary (Art 19 I GLA).

TUI should thus claim for damages directly before FINMA, which will issue a ruling on the claim. This ruling can be appealed before the FAT, and eventually, if the conditions of Article 85 I FTA are met (as explained earlier in section II), before the Federal Tribunal.

TUI will have to demonstrate that the sanction was issued in breach of a fundamental duty of FINMA. In addition, it will have to prove the existence of an actual economic loss due to actual harm to its commercial reputation. There are no punitive damages in Switzerland. TUI could also claim that it has suffered a moral wrong through the harm to its reputation. Of course, the commercial reputation of TUI could only be harmed if the sanction were made public, by FINMA or one of its agents, before all appeals were exhausted, which normally would not occur, because Article 34 FINMASA provides for the publication of supervisory rulings only when such rulings take full legal effect, which would not be the case until all appeals were exhausted. Premature disclosure of the sanction would thus probably be deemed a breach of a fundamental duty and also a fault within the meaning of Article 6 II GLA.[238]

If there had been premature disclosure of the sanction, it would be very difficult to guess how the courts would assess the amount of the damages due to the lack of court decisions pertaining to this precise matter and due to the vast discretion enjoyed by the courts in awarding damages for moral wrong. Whereas it is not possible to point out meaningful standards used by the courts in awarding damages for wrongful harm to a commercial reputation, it can, however, be stressed that, as a general rule, damages awarded by Swiss courts for moral wrong are notoriously meagre.

K. United Kingdom

GA

It is possible to answer the questions that have been posed here in relatively short form.

Taking first the question whether TUI would be able to obtain a quashing order, there would appear to be strong grounds for it to do so. As has already been outlined

[238] Switzerland, case 1.

above in relation to case 2, public decision-makers are expected to take all relevant considerations into account when making decisions. If, as is suggested here, a regulatory authority were to omit to consider key documents that were plainly relevant to its recommendation, that would be an elementary error that might be expected to draw censure from a court. Indeed, if the error was as rudimentary as the given scenario suggests, this is something that might even be resolved without the need for legal proceedings. The procedure governing judicial review in the UK now includes a pre-action protocol whereby individuals must write to a public authority and ask it to retake a decision in the light of (in this instance) an identifiable error. If the NBR were to accept that it had omitted to consider key documents, it might be expected to—and certainly should be advised to—rescind it decision.

The question of damages is less straightforward. For instance, if TUI's concern is damage to its commercial reputation, this would take the matter towards the law of defamation, where the NBR's actions could be expected to attract privilege. While the privilege in question would be qualified and could be defeated by 'bad faith' (or 'malice', in the language of the common law), the problem does not suggest that the NBR had intentionally and/or unlawfully sought to prejudice TUI when making its determination. As against that, were the NBR to fail to engage with a pre-action request to revisit its decision, this might be something that would assist TUI in seeking to question NBR's motives (though the threshold for 'bad faith' remains a very high one indeed).

Another option would be an action in negligence, where TUI would argue: (i) that the NBR owed it a common law duty of care; (ii) that the NBR breached that duty of care by failing to consider all plainly relevant documents; and (iii) that the NBR's breach of its duty caused TUI to suffer loss. While it would appear that element (ii) would be satisfied on the facts, it is much less clear that elements (i) and (iii) could be established. For instance, in respect of element (i), the common law often identifies public policy reasons for limiting the negligence liability of bodies with the power to inspect and impose sanctions, viz it is thought that the ready imposition of duties might complicate the work of such bodies to the detriment of the wider public interest in, for instance, combatting fraud or corruption (see further comment (g) at the beginning of Chapter 13). Moreover, even if there were a duty in this case, it is not clear that the claimed loss would be such as would be actionable in the law of negligence. The point here is that TUI is arguing that it has suffered reputational loss, which, as noted above, comes within the realm of the law of defamation, rather than negligence. It might be doubted whether an action in negligence could be sustained, notably if the court was to think that that cause of action was being used as a proxy means of avoiding a defence of privilege in the law of defamation.

TUI might also try to claim damages for breach of statutory duty, although it is unlikely that the statutory scheme under which the NBR was operating would be read as imposing a statutory duty towards TUI. Duties under such statutes that are typically said to be owed to the public at large—there is an overlap here with the public policy reasoning in the law of negligence—and TUI may therefore have difficulty in convincing the court that a duty was also owed to it.

A further option would be an action for misfeasance in public office. As outlined above comment (l) at the beginning of Chapter 13), this is a tort that provides a means of redress to individuals who have suffered loss as a result of the 'abuse of power' by a public officer, where it centres upon the concept of 'bad faith'. Would TUI succeed under this tort? Probably not, at least by an extension of the above analysis of the law of defamation. To put the point bluntly: if a defence of privilege could not be defeated on grounds of malice, it is difficult to see how the same facts could sustain a claim for misfeasance under which TUI would be required to establish bad faith on the part of the NBR.

To recap: (i) TUI would have strong grounds for asking a court to quash the NBR's sanction; but (ii) it would have difficulty in seeking a related remedy in damages.

V. Case 4—the exclusion of a tenderer by the contracting authority

Under national public procurement law, contracting authorities can exclude participants from an administrative procedure if they are considered unreliable and therefore unsuitable to be awarded the contract. In particular, contracting authorities can exclude from a procurement procedure an operator who has been convicted for systematic failure to pay social security contributions. During the procurement procedure initiated by the municipality of Mandeville, it receives information from the Department of Social Security (DSS) showing that a bidder, Alphagroup, has systematically failed to pay social security contributions. Mandevilles' officers use the information received by DSS, which is not informed about it, and drop its offer. It is only after the conclusion of the tendering procedure, when Alphagroup has access to the documentation held by the municipality, that it discovers that its offer had been dropped because of its alleged systematic failure to pay social security contributions. It then brings an action before the national court, arguing that: (i) the municipality could not use information against it without giving it a real opportunity to contest it; and (ii) factually, thc DSS had made a mistake, insofar as the economic operator that failed to respect the obligations stemming from social security legislation was not Alphagroup but another one named 'Alpha Group Ltd'.

Alphagroup brings an action for damages against the Mandeville municipality before a national court. The municipality objects that liability, if any, should be imposed upon the DSS. Would Alphagroup's action be successful? If so, what damages could Alphagroup recover? And if the municipality of Mandeville is held liable, could they turn to the DSS in order to place the burden on them, or at least to share it?

A. Austria

SS, KB, DB, and LM

The following reflections will focus on the legal situation above the threshold of public contracts and within the scope of Federal Public Procurement Law (BVergG).[239]

There are two alternative options. First, § 141(3) BVergG provides that the contracting authority has to verifiably notify the tenderer of the withdrawal of his or her tender, stating the reason.

The client must have come to the full conviction—in a comprehensible manner—of the unlawfulness of the procedure of the company which he or she accuses of misconduct. With regard to objectivity, strict criteria must apply. In this process of objectification, the discussion of any explanations and counterarguments by the tenderer concerned plays an essential role.[240] The precondition for this is that the tenderer has been informed in detail of the allegations raised against him or her. Moreover, an action by the contracting authority that does not give the tenderer the opportunity to

[239] *Bundesgesetz über die Vergabe von Aufträgen* (Bundesvergabegesetz 2018—BVergG 2018) Federal Law Gazette I No 65/2018 as amended.

[240] See VfGH 24 June 1998 G 462/97.

comment on specific allegations infringes the principle of equal treatment, its pre-contractual duty of care and, more generally, the fundamental requirements of a legal system based on the rule of law. If the requirement of consultation of the tenderer concerned is not met by the contracting authority, its exclusion is unlawful. This is the case if the tenderer was only informed of the exclusion after the decision of the contracting authority without specifying the reasons for the decision and without giving the tenderer the opportunity to make a timely statement.[241]

§ 2 No 15 BVergG provides that specific decisions of the contracting authority may be contested separately, ie in open procedure for the withdrawal of a tender. It is also possible to challenge the award decision itself. Hence, Alphagroup may apply for the review of a separate contestable decision by the contracting authority in the award procedure for unlawfulness until the award of the contract. It must claim an interest in concluding the contract and that he or she has suffered or may suffer damage because of the alleged unlawfulness (§ 342(1) BVergG).

The VwG (Administrative Court) is competent to determine whether, contrary to the provisions of the BVergG, the contract was not awarded to the tenderer offering the lowest price or the most technically and economically advantageous offer as stated in the invitation to tender (§ 334(1) BVergG). According to § 333 BVergG, both the VwGVG and the AVG are applicable in this proceeding. The BVwG will decide whether exclusion from the procurement procedure was unlawful (§ 28 VwGVG) and will establish the relevant facts. Therefore, the BVwG may hold a public oral hearing if this is requested by one of the parties, or if the court deems it necessary (§ 24(1) VwGVG). Due to a ruling of the VfGH,[242] review of the lawfulness of an award procedure falls under Article 6 ECHR. The BVwG will grant Alphagroup a right to contest these allegations. If the proceeding reveals that the allegations against the entity were incorrect, the appeal will be successful.

The second alternative is similar to the one in (i). In the course of supplementary investigations on the facts of the case, the VwG may give Alphagroup a right to contest these allegations and consult the DSS. If the BVwG comes to a different decision from the contracting authority, it has to annul the decision and refer it back for a new decision (§ 28(5) VwGVG). The contracting authority is bound by the legal assessment of the BVwG (§ 28(3) VwGVG).

Awarding damages to unsuccessful tenderers falls within the jurisdiction of the civil courts. § 369 (1) BVergG provides that an unsuccessful tenderer may claim damages against the contracting authority if there is a sufficiently qualified violation of public procurement laws. However, a claim for damages may only apply if the unsuccessful tenderer would have had a real chance of being awarded the contract. A claim may be rejected if the injured party could have averted the damage by applying for interim relief or by submitting a remedy (§ 369(2) BVergG). The claim for compensation includes the costs of preparing the offer and the costs of participation in the award procedure (§ 369(1) BVergG). In this case, it is not possible to determine whether Alphagroup had a real chance of winning the award.

[241] See, for instance, BVA 7 August 2007 N/0065-BVA/15/2007-75.
[242] VfGH 28 February 2000 B 420/97.

If there is a sufficiently clear breach of public procurement laws, and if the unsuccessful tenderer should have been awarded the contract, the claim may include compensation for interest in the performance ('*Erfüllungsinteresse*', § 369(3) BVergG); lost profit will be compensated for.

B. European Union
BM

The EU has its own rules on public procurement (Regulation (EU, Euratom) 2018/1046 on the financial rules applicable to the general budget of the Union, specifically Arts 160 et seq). These rules are inspired by the directives issued by the EU for awarding public contracts in the Member States, but the directives do not bind the EU. An exception is the Remedies Directive 89/665, which the court considers applicable to disputes between the EU administration and economic operators.[243]

Article 136(1)(b) of the Financial regulation provides that failure to comply with obligations relating to the payment of welfare and social security contributions may lead to exclusion from the tender. The tenderers have to prove the fulfilment of these obligations.

The Regulation does not provide specific rules for cases when an incorrect certificate leads to a competitor's exclusion.

However, it can be assumed that the administration has an obligation to invite bidders to provide proof to the contrary before excluding them. The decision to exclude will therefore be unlawful due to infringement of the principle of the right to be heard, and could be annulled by the court pursuant to Article 263 TFEU.

An action for damages may be proposed under Article 340 TFEU, even without bringing an annulment action, but there needs to be proof of the infringement of a rule intended to protect individuals and the serious and manifest character of its violation. The court might consider that in the event of an action with a low discretionary content, any infringement of EU law could be a serious and manifest violation.

However, it has to be considered that the court does not compensate the loss of profit when the interested party cannot prove that, in the event of participation, it would have been awarded the contract.[244] In *Agriconsulting Europe*, the court held that even if the error of assessment had not been made, Agriconsulting would have not been ranked in first position.[245] If no causal link between the irregularity and the loss of profit is demonstrated, the European administration cannot be ordered to pay damages.[246]

[243] Case C-35/15 *European Commission v Vanbreda Risk and Benefits* [2015] ECLI:EU:C:2015:275, Order of the Vice-President of the Court 23 April 2015.

[244] See Case T-217/11 *Claire Staelen v European Ombudsman* [2017] ECLI:EU:C:2017:256, judgment of the General Court 29 April 2015: 'however the applicant's claim for compensation for the loss of opportunity of recruitment must be rejected because there is not a sufficiently direct link between that damage and the unlawful acts committed by the Authority'.

[245] Case C-198/16P *Agriconsulting Europe v Commission*, judgment of the Court 19 October 2017 (CJEU 19 October 2017); Case C-677/15P [2017] ECLI:EU:C:2017:363, concl AGH Saugmandsgaard Øe.

[246] 'I conclude from this, given the cumulative nature of the conditions to be satisfied in order for the European Union to incur non-contractual liability, that the claim for damages brought by European Dynamics Luxembourg and Others must be rejected' (Opinion of AG Saugmandsgaard ØE para 128).

C. France

TP

Alphagroup's action would be successful against the municipality of Mandeville because the latter omitted to notify the refusal in a timely manner, and this prevented the former from being considered for the tender. Nevertheless, we cannot assess precisely which damages Alphagroup could recover because this depends on the quality of the offers. As Mandeville's misconduct bears a direct relation to the damage caused, it cannot put the burden on DSS. Although it is unlikely, Mandeville could try to share liability if it can prove DSS's misconduct.

In France, there are different types of administrative contracts. Procedures, conditions, and delays may vary, depending on the type of services and the value of the contract. In this case, we consider that it would be a formalized public procurement procedure to purchase services, works, and supplies, and it would be worth more than the threshold established in line with EU directives. In this case, we consider that the procedure would be an '*appel d'offres*' because there is no particular condition to justify a special negotiation procedure.[247]

In Alphagroup's case, the first option would be a claim using the '*référé précontractuel*' (precontractual petition), an urgency motion before an administrative court to avoid the signing and execution of a contract awarded in breach of publicity and competition rules.

Once the tendering procedure is concluded, the authority must notify the candidates of their rejection, after which there is a standstill period of eleven or sixteen days[248] between the notification and the contract signature, during which Alphagroup could refer the matter to a court. This claim would not be admissible once the contract has been signed.[249]

Alphagroup's claim would suspend signing[250] until the court's decision, which must take place within the following twenty days. Under existing rules (Art L551-1)[251] the *référé précontractuel* may only be used in case of a breach of competition and publicity rules affecting or that may affect the claimant,[252] and it would not be useful to look for the fulfilment of any other obligations regarding the tendering procedure. In this case, the candidate should have been informed of the exclusion before the end of the procedure, including the reasons for exclusion. In fact, the breach of this publicity duty directly affected Alphagroup because the company was excluded and its offer was not considered.

The court has ample powers to assess the conditions and order the Authority to respect publicity and competition obligations. It could issue an order to start the procedure all over again, or, from the date of the breach, the inclusion of the candidate, the annulment of any intermediate decision, or the cancellation of discriminatory

[247] Decree No 2016-360 of 25 March modified by decree No 2017-516 of 10 April.
[248] The standstill would be of eleven days if the notification was electronic.
[249] CE 3 November 1995 *CCI Tarbes et des Hautes Pyrénées* No 157304.
[250] Article L551-4.
[251] There might be an order of the court's chair.
[252] CE 3 October 2008 SMIRGEOMES Req No 305420.

clauses. It must consider the public interest and avoid orders that could seriously affect it.[253]

If the contract had already been signed, and Alphagroup did not refer the matter to the court via *référé précontractuel*, the company would not be able to claim a *référé contractuel* (contractual procedure petition),[254] which is a subsidiary action for candidates[255] when they could not bring a claim before signing because the authority did not disclose the decision, or did not respect the time between notification and signing.[256] In this context, the court may annul the contract on very limited grounds[257] regarding serious breaches of publicity and competition obligations and/or the violation of the standstill period. The latter would be an option for Alphagroup only if Mandeville signs the contract before the end of the standstill period. That not being the case, if the contract is signed without any *référé* procedure, there are still two options for Alphagroup: a claim against the contract (*recours en pleine juridiction*) and for damages, or a claim for damages only.

After 2014, in *Département de Tarn-et-Garonne,* the *Conseil d'Etat* changed the rules regarding third-party claims against an administrative contract. Currently, unsuccessful candidates may challenge the validity of the contract itself or some of its clauses on two grounds: serious breaches of legality that the court is obliged to consider without petition, and/or the breach of obligations that have had a direct effect on the claimant's exclusion or refusal. However, even if the court finds that the claim is admissible and that there was a breach of procedure, the result for Alphagroup is uncertain. Depending on the importance of the public interest and the stability of contracts, the court may order to continue with the execution of the contract plus a fine, the possible regularization of the contract, the termination of the contract, or its annulment. In any case, Alphagroup should, in addition to challenging the contract, expressly claim for damages.[258] As challenging the whole contract due to misconduct with regard to notification of its exclusion would probably not lead to its annulment, it would be simpler for Alphagroup to claim only for damages.

After considering procedural aspects, we must examine those of substance. General rules require a misconduct, damage, and a direct causal link between them to engage public liability. In the field of administrative contracts, case law is very strict regarding the existence of the causal link. Even if there are irregularities in the procedure, the action would not be successful if the damage is not a *direct* consequence of the irregularity.[259]

In our case, Alphagroup's offer was not assessed, because the company was excluded from the tendering procedure[260] considering its alleged fault to pay social security contributions codified in Article 45 of the Public Procurement Code.

[253] Article L551-7.
[254] Article L551-13 of the Administrative Code.
[255] This action is open to the departmental authorities regarding municipalities without restrictions.
[256] CE 19 January 2011 *Grand Port Maritime du Havre* No 343435.
[257] ibid.
[258] CE 11 May 2011 *Avis* No 347002.
[259] CE *Compagnie martiniquaise de transports* (n 129).
[260] *Ordonnance* No 2015-899, modified by Law 2016-1691 Art 39.

According to Article 99 the Code,[261] in the event of formalized procedures, the city has the obligation to notify the tenderer that is has been excluded as soon as the authority decides it, indicating the reasons for the exclusion. Timely notification could have given the tenderer the opportunity to present evidence and show that the certification concerned Alpha Group Ltd, and not Alphagroup. Mandeville's disregard of Article 99 is thus misconduct, and Alphagroup lost its chance to be awarded with the contract because it was not notified. If this had been done, as legally required, Alphagroup could have challenged its exclusion on time and participated in the tendering. There is thus a causal link between the irregularity and the damage caused to Alphagroup. However, the exclusion of a tendering procedure has particular rules regarding damages.

Compensation for loss of opportunity on the part of an excluded tenderer is moot in France[262] because administrative case law is not uniform with regard to how to calculate and compensate the loss of chance in different fields. It distinguishes between 'no' chance, 'simple chance', and a 'serious chance' to apply an overarching rule.[263]

If Alphagroup had no chance to be awarded the contract, it would not receive any pecuniary compensation; for example, if its offer was not valid for any reason other than the one wrongfully sustained by Mandeville.[264]

If Alphagroup proved it had a 'simple' chance to be awarded the contract, possessing, for example, the requirements and making a reasonable offer, the court would only order reimbursement of the expenses relating to the procedure, but if the tenderer had a 'serious chance', as its offer was more advantageous than the selected candidate, the court would order compensation for the total loss of profit expected from the contract.[265]

In this case, we cannot assess what chances Alphagroup had of getting compensation, because this would require knowing the contract award criteria, the final award of the contract, and the successful offer conditions in order to measure its chance. However, if the offer was lawful and reasonable, Alphagroup would receive at least the reimbursement of its expenses for the tendering procedure.

We explained above why Mandeville city would be liable towards Alphagroup. It is now necessary to address the question of whether it is fully liable, or whether it can share the burden with the DSS, as a third-party claim regarding Alphagroup.

In the case of two instances of misconduct by different entities causing damage, courts seldom consider the solution of joint liability, especially with regard to a private body. If they accepted joint liability as a general principle, the victim could be compensated by the State for the total amount, and would probably find the private

[261] Decree 2016-360 of 25 March 2016.

[262] Minet (n 128).

[263] CE *Christophe* (n 129); CE *Compagnie martiniquaise de transports* (n 129).

[264] See CE 4 June 1976 *Desforets* No 96356, Lebon 301; Cour Administrative d'Appel de Bordeaux 1 December 2016 No 14BX01718.

[265] In public procurements, the courts usually protect the stability of the contract and only order compensation for the excluded company. In this case, the loss of profit will take into account the full period of the contract. In other cases, if the Authority must do the assignment again, the period for the calculation will be between the unlawful decision and the new procedure.

individual insolvent.[266] Thus, to avoid the State becoming a form of insurance in the event of third-party misconduct, administrative case law only provides for compensation in relation to the part involving State responsibility, ie proportionate liability. For example, if the damage was caused by the misconduct of a public agent and someone else, the State will be ordered to pay only 60 per cent, and the victim must seek compensation for the rest before the ordinary courts.[267] Some criticize this solution because the victim must bring two legal actions if he or she wants full compensation, and as the ordinary court is not bound by the administrative court's decision, it may consider the State fully liable.[268]

In application of this doctrine, if the judge considers that a part of the fault lies with DSS, Mandeville will only pay its proportionate part (70 per cent) and Alphagroup has to claim again against the DSS for its respective part of the damages (30 per cent).[269]

Considering the problems that this solution can cause for a victim, the *Conseil d'Etat* has facilitated some conditions, especially when it comes to two public entities acting together. In some cases, the *Conseil d'Etat* has established that the public misconduct is so serious that it is the only one to take into account.[270] There is joint liability when the two instances are independent, but both suffice to cause the damage,[271] and when there is a close collaboration for public services between two public bodies. The last option is particularly common in such fields as health,[272] public transportation,[273] security, and firefighting services.[274] In this case, Alphagroup would be entitled to receive full compensation from Mandeville, depending on its chance, because the lack of notification was the determining factor in the damage.[275] The claim is only for damages because Mandeville did not notify and respect the standstill period necessary for the *référé précontractuel*, which could have avoided the damage. These are two serious infringements that would justify the city paying the whole compensation.

If Mandeville paid all the damages, the municipality could bring an '*action récursoire*' against the DSS to obtain partial reimbursement by alleging the misconduct of the latter: for example, gross negligence regarding the recordings and/or not

[266] One important exception to the general principle of proportionate liability was the case of T Confl 14 February 2000 Req No 02929, when joint liability was ordered in relation to the public hospital which sent the wrong blood type and the private doctor that did not make the prior test before a transfusion.

[267] CE 7 July 1976 *Cne de Villiers-Semeuse c Bihay et autre*, Lebon T 110.

[268] See M Fornacciari, 'Exonérations ou atténuations de responsabilité' [2011] Répertoire de la responsabilité de la puissance publique (updated: Dec 2017) (for whom, this solution is based on practical considerations).

[269] CE 31 December 1976 *Hôpital psychiatrique de Saint-Egrève*, Lebon 584; CE 26 November 2008 *Parc National de Cevennes* No 274061.

[270] CE 19 March 1976 *Min Intérieur c Cts Danel* No 97599. Recently, Cour Administrative d'Appel de Bordeaux 7 February 1994 *Baudette* No 92BX01142.

[271] CE 2 July 2010 *Madranges* No 323890.

[272] CE 9 April 1993 *M D* No 138653.

[273] CE 30 May 1986 *Épx Faix*, Lebon 710.

[274] Cour Administrative d'Appel de Bordeaux 18 June 2002 *SARL Portex* No 98BX01728.

[275] In this case, the first misconduct was by the taxi driver who did not have the required insurance coverage. However, it was the authority's duty to verify this in order to grant the taxi licence, therefore the misconduct of the administration covers the taxi, and the authority will pay full compensation. CE 29 November 1961 *Goarin*, Lebon 671.

verifying the name of Alphagroup. However, there are only a few examples of this type of cases because the general rule is the proportionate liability in this field.[276]

D. Germany

FW and JS

Apart from the issue of damages, Alphagroup may challenge the award of the contract. Jurisdiction and available remedies depend on whether the contract falls under the harmonized EU regime, applicable if certain thresholds have been reached (§ 106 paras 1 and 2 GWB—Competition Act[277]).[278] If this is the case, which cannot be fully determined based on the information provided, the award may be challenged before public procurement tribunals (§§ 155ff GWB).[279] Other award procedures fall within the jurisdiction of the courts competent to review the subject matter of the contract, notably civil courts for procurement contracts.[280] At any rate, a preventive remedy has to be sought, since stability (excluding an ex-post repeal) is accorded to awards;[281] § 168 paragraph 2 sentence 1 GWB stipulates in this respect: 'Once an award has been made, it cannot be revoked.'

§ 181 GWB stipulates that:

> [i]f the contracting entity has violated a provision intended to protect undertakings, the undertaking may claim damages for the costs incurred in connection with the preparation of the tender or the participation in a procurement procedure if, without the breach, the undertaking would have had a real chance of being awarded the contract after assessment of the tenders, and provided that such a chance was impaired as a consequence of the breach. Further claims for damages shall remain unaffected.

Hence, Alphagroup has to prove that (1) the contracting authority breached a duty aiming to protect the undertaking, (2) that the undertaking would have had a real chance to succeed, and that the breach (3) caused (4) damage.[282]

The first prerequisite is fulfilled if dropping Alphagroup's offer breached a provision of procurement law. *In casu*, § 122 paragraph 1 GWB may be infringed: It requires

[276] One exceptional case of *action récursoire* by a private person against a public body: CE 12 June 2006 *Mme Goetz* Req No 228841. *L'action récursoire* is more common in cases of public services and public works; see C Moniolle, 'Actions en garantie: actions récursoires et actions subrogatoires' [2014] Répertoire de la responsabilité de la puissance publique (updated: June 2018).

[277] *Gesetz gegen Wettbewerbsbeschränkungen* (Act against Restraints of Competition), English version <www.gesetze-im-internet.de/englisch_gwb/englisch_gwb.html> accessed 22 June 2020.

[278] See Wollenschläger, 'The Allocation of Limited Rights by the Administration' (n 136) 93ff, 109ff, referring to the former version of the GWB.

[279] See M Burgi, *Vergaberecht* (2nd edn, CH Beck 2018) § 20 paras 219ff, and the explications of ss 155ff in M Burgi and M Dreher (eds), *Beck'scher Vergaberechtskommentar*, vol 1 (3rd edn, CH Beck 2017).

[280] Wollenschläger, *Verteilungsverfahren* (n 138) 207, 230ff; Burgi (n 279) § 26 paras 12ff; L Horn and H Hofmann, '§ 155 GWB' in Burgi and Dreher, *Beck'scher Vergaberechtskommentar* (n 279) paras 44ff.

[281] Wollenschläger, 'The Allocation of Limited Rights by the Administration' (n 136) 93ff, 111f.

[282] cf C Antweiler, '§ 181 GWB' in Burgi and Dreher, *Beck'scher Vergaberechtskommentar* (n 279) paras 10ff. See also Burgi (n 279) § 21 para 7 (three-step test).

public contracts to 'be awarded to skilled, efficient (eligible) undertakings that have not been excluded under §§ 123 or 124'. Thus, only if Alphagroup was excluded by the municipality of Mandeville in accordance with §§ 123f GWB, would § 122 paragraph 1 GWB, a provision aiming to protect undertakings,[283] have been respected. § 123 paragraph 4 sentence 1 No 1 GWB obliges the contracting authority to:

> exclude an undertaking from participating in the procurement procedure if […] the undertaking has not fulfilled its obligations relating to the payment of taxes, charges or social security contributions and this has been established by a judicial or administrative decision having final and binding effect […].

It is unclear here whether or not there has already been a (final) administrative decision. Prior to a final decision,[284] the municipality of Mandeville may also invoke § 124 paragraph 1 No 3 GWB. This provision allows for the exclusion of an undertaking 'if […] the undertaking has demonstrably committed grave professional misconduct which renders its integrity questionable'. This rule does not require a final court or administrative decision, but a well-founded assessment of the contracting entity.[285] Consequently, the latter must investigate the facts that might give rise to an exclusion.[286]

Against this background, it is questionable whether the municipality of Mandeville may exonerate itself by referring to the responsibility of the DSS which provided false information. Relying on information obtained from another agency does not automatically amount to a breach of the duty to properly investigate the facts,[287] but neither does it allow the contracting authority acting in relation to the undertaking to exonerate itself.[288] *In casu*, to fulfil its duty, the municipality of Mandeville should have at least heard Alphagroup before its exclusion,[289] even though there is no express requirement to do so. Thus, it seems tenable to assume that the municipality of Mandeville, as the contracting entity, committed a breach of duty.

[283] M Opitz, '§ 122 GWB' in Burgi and Dreher, *Beck'scher Vergaberechtskommentar* (n 279) para 14 with further references.

[284] Directive 2014/24/EU of 26 February 2014 on public procurement and repealing Directive 2004/18/EC [2014] OJ L94/65, the basis for the relevant provisions of the GWB, predetermines the application of s 124 GWB 'before a final and binding decision on the presence of mandatory exclusion grounds has been rendered' (recital 101), ie before the prerequisites of s 123 GWB are fulfilled, see P Braun, '§ 16' in M Gabriel, W Krohn, and A Neun (eds), *Handbuch Vergaberecht* (2nd edn, CH Beck 2017) para 30; M Opitz, '§ 123 GWB' in Burgi and Dreher, *Beck'scher Vergaberechtskommentar* (n 279) para 28 with further references.

[285] cf BGH 26 October 1999—X ZR 30/98, [2000] NJW 661 (662): '[…] schließt die Berücksichtigung von Umständen aus, die nicht auf einer gesicherten eigenen Erkenntnis des Ausschreibenden beruhen'.

[286] T Kirch, B Haverland and J Mieruszewski, 'Die Vergabe von Lieferungen, Leistungen und Dienstleistungen nach VgV' in R Leinemann, E-D Leinemann, and T Kirch (ed), *Die Vergabe öffentlicher Aufträge* (6th edn, Bundesanzeiger Verlag 2016) para 531; cf M Opitz, '§ 124 GWB' in Burgi and Dreher, *Beck'scher Vergaberechtskommentar* (n 279) para 43.

[287] cf Opitz, '§ 123 GWB' (n 284) paras 50f, and Opitz, '§ 124 GWB' (n 286) para 44, also stating that 'it is not easy for the contracting authority to gain knowledge about the court or administrative decisions'.

[288] cf Ossenbühl and Cornils (n 145) 115ff.

[289] Based on the former version of the GWB VK Sachsen 25 June 2003—1-SVK/51/03, [2004] BeckRS 439 (headnotes 2 and 4); consenting: N Ohrtmann, 'Korruption im Vergaberecht. Konsequenzen und Prävention—Teil 1: Ausschlussgründe' [2007] NZBau 201 (204f).

The second prerequisite of having had a real chance to succeed implies a relaxed burden of proof in comparison to general law on compensation requiring the most acceptable offer to have been submitted.[290] A bid would have a 'real' chance if 'the contracting entity, taking account of its margin of appreciation, had been entitled to award the contract to the claimant'.[291] The civil courts have been rather strict in assessing this prerequisite, considering, for example, the preciseness of the tender when deciding on the chance of success.[292] Whether or not a 'real' chance existed thus depends on the merits of Alphagroup's tender in relation to the award criteria, which cannot be assessed without further information.

The same is true for the third prerequisite (causation), which is fulfilled if the breach of the duty cannot be assumed to be non-existent without causing the impairment—ie the failure of the tender—not to occur.[293] It has to be noted that the contracting authority:

> is obliged to submit the applied award criteria, unless they were communicated in the contract notice or the procurement documents, as well as their weighting and, as the case may be, to substantiate why it would not have been able to award the tender to the claimant's undertaking.[294]

Generally speaking, damages may be claimed 'for the costs incurred in connection with the preparation of the tender or the participation in a procurement procedure' as laid down in § 181 sentence 1 GWB. This claim is limited to negative interest and does not allow for the compensation of lost profits.

§ 839 paragraph 3 BGB, excluding damages if primary legal protection has not been sought, does not apply directly, since it is a rule related to the general liability of public authorities. However, it reflects a general principle of law (contributory negligence).[295] A legal basis for this is § 254 BGB, the general rule on contributory negligence.[296] Thus, Alphagroup's claim may be reduced, or even excluded, if it did not try to avert the damage by having recourse to primary legal protection. However, the applicant's duties in this respect are controversial: some argue that the applicant must initiate proceedings under §§ 160ff GWB, or at least complain to the contracting authority,[297] while other commentators deny an obligation to avert damage in the context of the

[290] Wollenschläger, 'The Allocation of Limited Rights by the Administration' (n 136) 93ff, 123.

[291] BGH 27 November 2007—X ZR 18/07, [2008] ZfBR 299 (302). See also C Freytag, '§ 38' in Gabriel and others (n 284) paras 66ff.

[292] See Antweiler (n 282) paras 12ff, referring to BGH 1 August 2006—X ZR 146/03, [2007] NZBau 58 (58); ibid (Antweiler para 14) also criticism with regard to the EU law foundation of s 181 GWB.

[293] BGH 27 November 2007—X ZR 18/07, [2008] ZfBR 299 (300).

[294] Own translation of BGH 27 November 2007—X ZR 18/07, [2008] ZfBR 299 (304). See also O Homann and R Leinemann, in Leinemann and others (n 286) para 2362; Freytag (n 291) para 90.

[295] Wollenschläger, 'The Allocation of Limited Rights by the Administration' (n 136) 93ff, 119.

[296] Freytag (n 291) paras 81ff.

[297] Favouring a duty to initiate proceedings L Horn, 'Neues zum Schadensersatz bei Vergabe öffentlicher Aufträge' [2000] NZBau 63 (64). For a duty to complain see Antweiler (n 282) para 22. Cf also C Alexander, '§ 181' in H Pünder and M Schellenberg (eds), *Vergaberecht* (3rd edn, Nomos 2019) para 47.

procurement procedure, since it is not explicitly stipulated for in § 181 GWB[298,299] Depending on one's position with regard to this legal debate and—moreover, on whether Alphagroup has challenged its exclusion, which is not clear from the case—a claim for damages may be excluded.

Alphagroup may also invoke the general civil law provisions governing a breach of pre-contractual obligations (§ 280 para 1 read in conjunction with §§ 241 para 2 and 311 para 2 BGB) which apply alongside the specific claim for frustration of chances under public procurement law (see § 181 sentence 2 GWB).[300] Unlike § 181 sentence 1 GWB, the rules on precontractual liability also apply to cases not falling under the harmonized EU regime; moreover, the claimant may also claim positive interest as damage under certain conditions.[301] A claim for damages based on a breach of precontractual duties requires (1) a precontractual relationship; (2) the breach of a duty arising from this relationship; (3) the causation of (4) damage; and (5) the defendant's responsibility, ie intent or negligence (§ 276 para 2 BGB). Whether the latter requirement of acting at least negligently applies to public procurement cases falling under the EU regime is questioned by some commentators in view of the ECJ's *Strabag* ruling.[302]

Participation in a tender creates a precontractual relationship obliging the contracting authority to respect the procurement rules.[303] A specific confidence in the regularity of the procedure[304] is no longer required, since public procurement law comprehensively regulates the procurement procedure and the contracting authority's duties, and since the wording of the provisions on precontractual liability does not expressly require confidence.[305] By not respecting procurement rules, the municipality of Mandeville has—as seen before—breached a duty,[306] thereby acting at least negligently, since its officials did not exercise reasonable care (§ 276 para 2 BGB).

In view of the competitive nature of the procurement procedure, entitlement to a claim to damages is limited to the bidder who has submitted the 'most acceptable'

[298] A Losch, '§ 181 GWB' in J Ziekow and U-C Völlink (eds), *Vergaberecht* (4nd edn, CH Beck 2020) paras 37ff; Homann and Leinemann (n 294) para 2359.

[299] 302 cf Freytag (n 291) para 83.

[300] See Burgi (n 279) § 21 para 9; Antweiler (n 282) paras 30ff. Concerning the prerequisites of this claim, see case 2 in section III.

[301] Homann and Leinemann (n 294) paras 2364, 2383ff.

[302] See Antweiler (n 282) para 38; Freytag (n 291) para 107. In the *Strabag* ruling—Case C-314/09 *Stadt Graz v Strabag AG and others* [2010] ECR I-08769—the ECJ held (para 39):

> Against that background, the remedy of damages provided for in Art 2(1)(c) of Directive 89/665 can constitute, where appropriate, a procedural alternative which is compatible with the principle of effectiveness underlying the objective pursued by that directive of ensuring effective review procedures [...] only where the possibility of damages being awarded in the event of infringement of the public procurement rules is no more dependent than the other legal remedies provided for in Art 2(1) of Directive 89/665 on a finding that the contracting authority is at fault.

Whether or not this finding can be transferred to the German law of damages has not yet been decided; cf BGH 9 June 2011—X ZR 143/10, BGHZ 190, 89 (93f); Homann and Leinemann (n 294) para 2380.

[303] cf for a general view, C Herresthal, '§ 311' in Gsell and others (n 69) para 358.

[304] See eg BGH 8 September 1998—X ZR 48/97, BGHZ 139, 259 (261).

[305] BGH 9 June 2011—X ZR 143/10, BGHZ 190, 89 (94f); cf Freytag (n 291) para 100.

[306] This could be the breach of s 122 para 1 GWB or, in cases not falling under the harmonized EU regime, the general duty to take account of the interests of bidders; cf Freytag (n 291) paras 101f.

offer.[307] This standard is stricter than the 'real chance' that applies under § 181 GWB.[308] An exception is made, though, if the bidder proves that it would not have participated in the procurement procedure if it had known about the fact that provisions of procurement law were not respected.[309]

The recoverable damage extends to the costs of participating in the tender, notably the costs of preparing the bid.[310] Moreover, under certain conditions, lost profits may be recovered.[311] This requires the contract to have actually been awarded and that Alphagroup succeeds in proving that it—and not the successful undertaking—would have been awarded the contract if the municipality of Mandeville had not breached its duty.[312] Again, this is difficult to prove, in particular if discretion is involved; this issue has been discussed in detail in case 2 above.

The municipality of Mandeville cannot argue that the damage would even have occurred had it not breached its duty.[313] In fact, the mere possibility of causing such an effect is not sufficient.[314] If the municipality of Mandeville had acted as required by the law, it would have heard Alphagroup, and thus not excluded it based on wrong data. A different course of events would then seem likely.

If Alphagroup succeeds in proving causation, its burden of proof with regard to the actual amount of the damage is relaxed under § 287 paragraph 1 sentence 1 ZPO, as presented in case 2.

The general rule of contributory negligence (§ 254 BGB) also applies here,[315] leading to the question of the claimant's duties discussed above.[316]

The general rules on public authority liability are held not applicable in the context of public procurement law[317] since the contracting authority does not act under a public, but a civil law regime.[318]

Hence, the general rules of tort law apply. In this regard, Alphagroup may invoke § 823 paragraph 2 BGB read in conjunction with § 97 paragraph 6 GWB, which stipulates that '[u]ndertakings shall have a right to have the provisions concerning the procurement procedure complied with'. The latter rule only applies to contracts falling under the

[307] BGH 8 September 1998—X ZR 48/97 BGHZ 139, 259 (264); cf Wollenschläger, *Verteilungsverfahren* (n 138) 270.

[308] cf n 290.

[309] cf BGH 27 November 2007—X ZR 18/07, [2008] ZfBR 299 (302); Wollenschläger, *Verteilungsverfahren* (n 138) 270. See also BGH, 27 June 2007—X ZR 34/04, BGHZ 173, 33 (39f).

[310] BGH 8 September 1998—X ZR 48/97, BGHZ 139, 259 (261, 268); moreover 26 October 1999—X ZR 30/98, [2000] NJW 661 (663).

[311] Herresthal (n 303) paras 338ff.

[312] BGH 18 September 2007—X ZR 89/04, [2008] NZBau 137 (137ff with further references); cf Wollenschläger, *Verteilungsverfahren* (n 138) 271.

[313] See case 2 with n 168; see also case 8, case 10, and case 11.

[314] BGH 9 March 2012—V ZR 156/11, [2012] NJW 2022 (2023).

[315] Freytag (n 291) para 115.

[316] Losch (n 299) para 37ff. Denying any duty G Franßen, '§ 181' in J Byok and W Jäger (eds), *Kommentar zum Vergaberecht* (4th edn, Deutscher Fachverlag GmbH 2018) para 55. For cases falling under the harmonized EU regime, the duties presented in nn 297ff can be discussed.

[317] Losch (n 299) para 74; Burgi (n 279) § 21 para 8; Freytag (n 291) para 121.

[318] BVerfG 13 June 2006—1 BvR 1160/03, BVerfGE 116, 135 (149f). Some regard the procurement procedure as governed by public law, cf Maurer and Waldhoff (n 222) § 3 para 23. This would allow for a claim brought under Art 34 sentence 1 GG in conjunction with s 839 para 1 sentence 1 BGB; cf Wollenschläger, *Verteilungsverfahren* (n 138) 228 (with fn 151), 269 (with fn 322).

harmonized EU regime;[319] in other award procedures, one has to rely primarily on fundamental rights and fundamental freedoms that cannot be discussed here[320]. The problems with regard to causation are, however, similar to what has been outlined above.[321]

Support by sharing information between agencies (so called *Informationshilfe*) constitutes a special matter of administrative cooperation (§§ 4ff of the Administrative Procedures Act (VwVfG)).[322] Externally, ie in relation to third parties such as Alphagroup, the acting authority is liable.[323] *In casu*, this is the municipality of Mandeville, which is a legal person.

However, the municipality of Mandeville may claim reimbursement from the DSS for its external liability. The relationship between the agencies is disciplined by § 7 paragraph 2 VwVfG which stipulates that the agency that provided support is internally liable for its performance. Hence, the DSS is liable for the wrong information it provided, and the municipality of Mandeville may claim reimbursement. As the legal basis for the claim to reimbursement, the municipality may rely on the private law rules on mandates (§§ 662ff BGB); a breach of obligations gives rise to contractual liability (§ 280 para 1 BGB), also in cases of negligence by the supporting agency.[324]

In summary, Alphagroup may bring claims against the municipality of Mandeville under § 181 GWB if it proves that its offer had a real chance to succeed. The obtainable compensation is limited to 'the costs incurred in connection with the preparation of the tender or the participation in a procurement procedure'. If Alphagroup successfully proves that it submitted the most acceptable offer, it might also claim its positive interest under the rules on precontractual liability; the general provisions of tort law also apply, with similar consequences. The municipality of Mandeville can claim reimbursement from the DSS. If the applicability of the rules on contributory negligence is affirmed (which is controversial), Alphagroup may only claim damages if it has challenged the award of the contract.

E. Hungary

LB

The principle of company exclusivity essentially means that the names of companies must be so different that they exclude the likelihood of confusion. The name of the

[319] Freytag (n 291) para 119.

[320] See on the obligations of the contracting authorities in this respect Wollenschläger, *Verteilungsverfahren* (n 138) 102ff; F Wollenschläger, 'EU Law Principles for Allocating Scarce Goods and the Emergence of an Allocation Procedure. Identifying Substantive and Procedural Standards and Developing a New Type of Administrative Procedure' (2015–16) 8 REALaw 205, 209ff.

[321] See case 2 (section III).

[322] B Kastner, '§ 4 VwVfG' in Fehling and others (n 53) paras 35ff; differentiating U Ramsauer, '§ 4' in Kopp and Ramsauer (n 53) paras 13, 18. The case facts do not provide any information concerning the initiative for the information exchange process.

[323] F Shirvani, '§ 7 VwVfG' in T Mann, C Sennekamp, and M Uechtritz (eds), *Verwaltungsverfahrensgesetz* (2nd edn, Nomos 2019) para 20; U Ramsauer, '§ 7' in Kopp and Ramsauer (n 53) paras 12ff. Exceptions could apply only in cases where the legal person which provided support directly caused the damage, see H Schmitz, '§ 7' in Stelkens and others (n 55) para 10.

[324] U Schliesky, '§ 7' in H Knack and H-G Henneke (eds), *Verwaltungsverfahrensgesetz* (11th edn, Heymanns 2020) para 25.

company must clearly differ from the name of the other company that represents the same activity in the company's name in the same country. If Alphagroup and Alpha Group Ltd. are the same, there is no infringement. The municipality also did not have to question whether information from another authority was in line with reality, especially when that information was about Alphagroup and not about the other company with a similar name, so even if there was an infringement, it is not culpable. The two authorities can be sued jointly, according to the rules of joint liability.[325] Also, the other authority can be drawn into the procedure too, and the claimant can bring an action for damages against the DSS later. Theoretically, the municipality may sue the DSS too, but this is unprecedented in Hungary.

Because exhausting the remedies is a prerequisite, Alphagroup can submit a claim to the Public Procurement Arbitration Board, which conducts proceedings initiated against any infringement of the legislative provisions applicable to public procurement or contract award procedures, including the proceeding initiated against the rejection of the request for prequalification specified in a separate act of legislation, and deletion from the prequalification list. There is also an opportunity for preliminary dispute settlement. The Board declares void any decision made by the contracting authority either during the contract award procedure or as a decision closing that procedure, provided that no contract has yet been concluded. The Board's decision can be reviewed by the administrative court. To successfully sue the authorities, these instances first need to find an infringement. Because the contracting authority has to explicitly exclude the operator from the proceedings rather than keep quiet, the Board would probably annul the decision. This implies that Alphagroup would not yet receive damages.

F. Italy

FC

In Italy, this kind of dispute can be brought before the administrative court, following a specific trial procedure, expressly provided for for the subject of public procurement.[326]

First of all, it is important to note that in this procedure a party that is excluded from a tender must immediately challenge the exclusion order, challenging it within thirty days from the communication of the exclusion.[327] The term of thirty days does not expire until the excluded party is able to access all the documentation and discover the reason for the exclusion.

Therefore, in Italy, Alphagroup would certainly have to challenge the exclusion, without having to wait until the end of the tendering procedure.

[325] Act V of 2013—on the CC:

Section 6:524

[Joint tortfeasors]

(1) If the damage is caused jointly by two or more persons, their liability shall be joint and several towards the aggrieved person.

[326] Articles 119–125 CAT.

[327] See Art 120 CAT para 5.

In that forum, however, it would not be easy for Alphagroup to argue that the authority that excluded it—in this case the municipality—made a mistake in identifying the party at fault (and that the mistake could easily have been avoided if the right to adversarial proceedings had been guaranteed in the exclusion procedure), since the law requires the tendering authority to consider the certifications issued by the competent national body binding.[328] Alphagroup, therefore, would also have to challenge the incorrect certification: faced with this challenge, the municipality would have to review its decision to exclude the party, and the administrative court, in any case, would have to suspend its enforceability as a precautionary measure.

As far as the compensation claim is concerned, it could still be presented before an administrative court, first of all against the national authority that issued the incorrect certification.

In particular, if, in the meantime, the result of the tender was that the contract was awarded to another company, and if it is impossible to declare the contract ineffective,[329] the court might only award Alphagroup (should it be able to prove that if it had taken part in the tender, it would have had a good chance of winning) compensation for damages in equivalent measure,[330] relating to unnecessary expenses incurred to present its offer and the so-called loss of a chance for not being able to compete effectively.

The prevalent opinion for calculating this specific damage is that it can vary according to the concrete loss of profit by the private applicant[331] (in particular, (he or she has to provide evidence about the specific level of lost profit; this calculation, however, includes additional, more complicated, parameters that take into account, for the purposes of any reduction of the amount to be paid, any other gainful activities carried out by the injured party in the same period, in other words the so-called *aliunde perceptum*). To this amount might be added other damages, which the court will evaluate on an equitable basis[332] (eg so-called 'curricular damage', which is the damage arising from not being able to attach to future tenders proof of winning the tender from which one was unlawfully excluded).

G. Poland

Dawid Ziółkowski

The analysis of the presented facts allows a thesis to be put forward that the exclusion of the Alphagroup company from the tender was in fact the result of a mistake, for which the State Department of Social Security is responsible. It has to be recognized that this exclusion was caused by State authorities (unlawful), which opens the debate on the possibility of the company obtaining compensation. Compensation for

[328] See Art 80 C Pub P para 4. See also Council of State Plenary Session No 15/2013.

[329] See Art 122 CAT: if it were still possible to declare the contract ineffective, the applicant could get the tender.

[330] See Art 124 CAT.

[331] See the guidelines provided by Council of State Plenary Session No 2/2017.

[332] See Art 1226 CC.

damages should be awarded, albeit to a fairly limited extent. Anyway, Alphagroup is likely to face complex and lengthy legal proceedings.

In the case of exclusion of Alphagroup from the procurement procedure due to its alleged arrears in payments of social insurance premiums, the company may appeal to the President of the National Board of Appeal (*Krajowa Izba Odwoławcza*) (Art 180 of the Public Procurement Act, PPA), and then lodge a complaint with an ordinary court (Art 198a PPA). In such proceedings, Alphagroup will be able to argue that it was not permitted to respond to the information delivered to the commune by the social insurance body.

What will happen if Alphagroup does not file such an appeal (and the subsequent complaint), and several months later it turns out that the arrears never existed (the social insurance office made a mistake, as in this case)? *De lege lata*, Alphagroup may seek remedies based on Article 417 § 1 CC, which stipulates that liability for unlawful actions or omissions in the exercise of public authority rests with the State Treasury or a local government's body, or another legal person having such authority by operation of law.

The key issue in this case is whether the authority here was exercised by the commune of Mandeville or by the social insurance office. The key to resolving this case is to impose the burden of liability under Article 417 CC on the social insurance office that informed the Mandeville commune of the company's arrears with social insurance premiums. This action had far-fetched ramifications and in fact precluded the company's further participation in the tender proceedings.

In its judgment of 18 October 2005 (case ref SK 48/03) the Constitutional Tribunal stated that 'exercising public authority means any functions of the state, local governments and other public institutions, which may take on very different forms. In principle, although not every time, exercising such functions involves an authority to shape the situation of an entity.' I believe that in the light of Article 24 PPA the information offered by the social insurance office was decisively important in the context of excluding the company from the tender proceedings and, consequently, the social insurance office exposed itself to the liability based on Article 417 CC.

The importance of the social insurance office's mistake must be emphasized. The office confused the company Alphagroup with Alpha Group Ltd, even though they are two completely separate entities. The company with arrears in payment of public levies was Alpha Group Ltd, rather than the contemplated company Alphagroup. Legal scholarship highlights the importance of modern concepts of State liability for damage caused by its authorities and officers, which increasingly stress the need for real (factual) protection of the rights of the individual who suffered damage.[333] This makes it possible to put forward a thesis that even in such a complicated scenario as the one presented in this case, Alphagroup can achieve success and obtain money compensation.

As far as the other questions are concerned, Alphagroup may only count on damages limited to so-called *negative contractual interests*. These damages will cover

[333] See C Harlow, *State Liability. Tort Law and Beyond* (OUP 2004);G Dari-Mattiacci, N Garoupa, and F Gómez-Pomar, 'State Liability' (2010) 18 ERPL 773.

the costs of participation in the tender proceedings, such as the costs of preparation of the bid, legal services, or negotiations with potential subcontractors. Moreover, in relation to holding the Mandeville municipality liable, the municipality will be able to take action against the social insurance office. A legal basis for this liability can be found in the CC. Pursuant to Article 441 § 3 CC, whoever redresses damage for which it has been liable without fault may bring a claim to the party responsible for damage. In such an event, the Mandeville commune will face significant procedural problems. It will have to prove the misconduct of the social insurance office in delivering the incorrect information regarding Alphagroup, and also a causal link between that fault and the occurring damage in the form of damages paid by the municipality.

In conclusion, Alphagroup may challenge the decisions made in the tender proceeding decisions using the process based on provisions of the PPA and, ultimately, seek damages in a civil court pursuant to Article 417 CC. However, in such an eventuality, the social insurance office's liability will be limited to the negative contractual interests. The municipality will be able to raise recourse claims against the social insurance office (Art 441 § 3 CC).

H. Romania

RV

In the Romanian legal system, Alphagroup would bring a claim for damages under Article 53 of Law 101/2016 on remedies and review procedures regarding the concession of public contracts, public contracts in the utilities sector, works, and services.[334] This statutory act is part of a group of Romanian legislative acts meant to implement the European reform package in the field of public procurement.[335] Article 53 of Law 101/2016 reads thus:

> Claims for damages caused during tendering procedures as well as those on the performance, annulment, nullity and termination of public contracts are brought before the administrative tribunal in the jurisdiction where the contracting authority has its headquarters. They are all urgent matters.
>
> (...)
>
> Damages caused by an unlawful act performed by the contracting authority or through refusal to issue an act during the tendering procedure or by omitting to address a motion during such a procedure, can only be granted after the act is annulled or after remedial measures are taken by the contracting authority.
>
> If the claimant asks for compensation for loss representing the costs of preparing the bid or participating in the award procedure, the claimant must prove the loss, the

[334] Published in the Official Gazette No 393 of 23 May 2016.

[335] Directive 2014/23/EU of 26 February 2014 on the award of concession contracts [2014] OJ L94/1; Directive 2014/24/EU of 26 February 2014 on public procurement and repealing Directive 2004/18/EC on public works [2014] OJ L94/65; Directive 2014/25/EU of 26 February 2014 on procurement by entities operating in the water, energy, transport and postal services sector and repealing Directive 2004/17/EC, [2014] OJ L94/243.

> illegal application of public procurement legal provisions, and the fact that he or she would have had a real chance of winning the contract, which was compromised as a result of that breach.

When ruling on Alphagroup's claim for damages, the national court would also consider the provisions of Directive 89/665/EEC on the coordination of the laws, regulations and administrative provisions relating to the application of review procedures to the award of public supply and public works contracts.[336] Article 2 thereof provides that the Member States shall ensure that the measures taken concerning the review procedures include provision *inter alia* for powers to '(c) award damages to persons harmed by an infringement'. Moreover,

> 6. Member States may provide that where damages are claimed on the grounds that a decision was taken unlawfully, the contested decision must first be set aside by a body having the necessary powers.

The first question is whether the municipality could be exonerated of liability by invoking that liability should be imposed on the DSS, since they are the ones at fault for the material mistake?

Under the EU public procurement rules, the liability of contracting authorities for breach of public procurement regulations should not be made dependent on the element of fault. The standard of liability when awarding damages for breach of public procurement regulations is strict, irrespective of the national rules applicable to administrative liability, and this was established through the CJEU decisions in the *Commission v Portugal*[337] and the *Strabag*[338] cases.[339] In *Commission v Portugal*, the Court found that Portugal had breached Directive 89/665/EC by failing to repeal a domestic legal provision that made liability for breach of procurement rules conditional on proof of fault. In *Strabag*, the main question referred to the CJEU was whether the national legislation contravened the Remedies Directive if it made the right to damages for a breach of the procurement rules conditional on the contracting authority being at fault for the breach, in circumstances where the national legislation presumed that the contracting authority was at fault and the contracting authority was not permitted to rely on the defence that the breach arose as a result of its own lack of skills. The court answered the question above by recalling its ruling in the *Commission v Portugal* decision. It established that the remedy of damages can only constitute a procedural alternative compatible with the principle of effectiveness when the possibility of being awarded damages is no more dependent than the other legal remedies

[336] As modified by Directive 2007/66/EC of the European Parliament and of the Council of 11 December 2007 [2007] OJ L335/31.

[337] Case C-275/03 *Commission of the European Communities v Portuguese Republic* [2008] ECR I-1.

[338] Case *Strabag* (n 302).

[339] See on the topic R Vornicu, 'Procurement Damages in the UK and France—Why So Different? Special Issue on the Legal Remedies and Implications from the Fosen-Linjen Case' (2019) 14 EPPPL 222–29; and R Vornicu, 'The Sufficiently Serious Breach Test in Action. Damages in Procurement Law and a Tale of Three Courts: the CJEU, the UK Supreme Court and the EFTA Court' (2019) 25 EPL 587–614.

provided for in Article 2(1) of Directive 89/665 on a finding that the contracting authority is at fault, including where the application of that legislation rests on a presumption that the contracting authority is at fault and on the fact that the latter cannot rely on a lack of individual abilities, and therefore on the defence that it cannot be held accountable for the alleged infringement.

As we have seen above, Romanian administrative liability draws inspiration from the French adage '*toute illégalité commise par l'administration est fautive*',[340] but there is little Romanian scholarship or case law on the requirements of liability for breach of procurement legislation.

There is no legal provision in the public procurement legislation making liability dependent on proof of fault, and we have identified no judicial decisions contrary to the *Strabag* ruling. The most likely situation is that, when ruling on Alphagroup's claim or similar ones, Romanian courts will comply with the principles of effective judicial protection and procedural equivalence and apply Article 53 of Law 101/2016 in the light of the CJEU case law, thus not making liability dependent on fault, but rather conceptualizing it as a *lex specialis* derogating with regard to the conditions for fault (although claimants could also bring the argument that liability for illegal award procedures should follow the *Francovich* State liability doctrine and that, in fact, it should be considered as a *lex specialis* by reference to the doctrine of State liability, rather than national rules on administrative liability[341]).

Irrespective of the debate on the nature of the remedy of damages for breach of public procurement rules, in the case at hand, the municipality's liability would be triggered under Article 53 of Law 101/2016 and, in accordance with EU law and CJEU case law, it would not be made dependent on whether the administration was at fault when rejecting Alphagroup's offer or whether it had taken its decision based on the wrong information that DSS had culpably sent to the municipality. At the time of writing, we have not identified any Romanian case law that tackles or clarifies the matter of the element of fault when triggering a contracting authority's liability.

The second question to be address refers to what type of damages Alphagroup could recover. There are no specific provisions under Law 101/2016 on the type of damage

[340] Chapus states that whenever an administrative decision is unlawful, the administrative body that issued it committed a fault. All illegality therefore entails a fault. Historically, the illegality–fault parity is said to have started with the *Driancourt* decision, although the judge in Driancourt did not use the expression *toute illégalité est fautive*, but the scholarship observed that after this decision, it became a general rule that all illegality comprises fault (*désormais toute illégalité est fautive*, and *toute llegal administrative llegal constitue ipso facto une faute susceptible d'engager une responsabilité*). See CE 26 January 1973 *Ville de Paris c Driancourt*, Lebon 78, AJDA 1973, 245 chron P Cabanes and D Leger; see S Galand-Carval, 'Fault under French Law. The Unification of Tort' in P Widmer (ed), *Principles, Unification of Tort Law: Fault* (Kluwer Law International 2005) 89.

[341] See K Kruger, 'Action for Damages Due to Bad Procurement: On the Intersection between EU/EEA Law and National Law, with Special Reference to the Norwegian Experience' [2006] PPLR (2006) 211; a similar view is suggested in D Fairgrieve and F Lichère, 'Procedure and Access to Justice in Damages Claims for Public Procurement Breaches' in D Fairgrieve and F Lichère (eds), *Public Procurement Law: Damages as an Effective Remedy* (Hart Publishing 2011) 149. See also, in Romanian, DC Dragos and R Vornicu, 'Sinteza teoretica de practica judecatoreasca a Curtii de Justitie a Uniunii Europene in legatura cu daunele-interese pentru repararea prejudiciilor cauzate in cadrul procedurilor de atribuire a contractelor de achizitii publice' (2015) 10 Revista Dreptul, 25-39, 28.

that an aggrieved bidder can recover and neither did the statutory act previously in force (ie Government Emergency Ordinance No 34/2006 on public contracts, on procurement by entities operating in the water, energy, transport and postal services sectors and repealing and concession contracts) mention further details on the remedy of damages. The provision currently in force on damages is in fact almost a replica of the provision previously in force under Article 286(1) of the Government Emergency Ordinance No 34/2006. As a consequence, *as far as the type of damages available* is concerned, the case will be decided according to general rules applicable to damages caused by illegal administrative action, which, in turn, follow the general rules established under Articles 1382 and 1385 CC.

The Romanian legal concept of administrative liability has not evolved into a concept entirely distinct from civil liability, as is the case in French law. Nonetheless, there are some recognizable features of administrative liability in Romanian law, and these lie in: (i) the jurisdiction of administrative courts; (ii) dependency on the prior annulment of the administrative act; (iii) the different statute of limitation applicable to claims for damages; and (iv) the fault implicit in the unlawful act.

However, there are no special rules on grounds for relief from liability or the type of damages available, nor on how damages should be calculated. Since the Romanian civil law rules on liability allow compensation for loss of profit and loss of opportunity to be granted, and administrative liability rules to the contrary do not exist, it follows that Alphagroup is able to receive compensation for the loss representing the costs of preparing the bid or of participating in the award procedure, as well as compensation for loss of the profit it would have made had the contract been awarded to it.

However, the aggrieved bidder should be able to prove that he would have won the contract had the illegality not been committed, since, in order to be compensated for the cost of the bid, he needs to show that he had a real chance of winning the contract.

The third question refers to the possibility for the municipality of Mandeville to turn to the DSS in order to place the burden on them, or at least to share it. This possibility is recognized by Law 554/2004 on judicial review of administrative action, and can even take place during the same proceedings. Article 16 of Law 554/2004 reads that: 'The administrative court can introduce in proceedings, ex officio or pursuant to a party's request, any third person which has an interest or should be a party in the proceedings.' Furthermore, there is no reason why the municipality cannot bring a general claim for damages in separate proceedings should it be forced to pay compensation, provided, of course, that the general conditions for liability be met (for DSS to be held liable for the loss suffered by the municipality).

I. Spain

EMNG

A decision by a public authority to drop a bidder's offer for tender is void if it is taken without respecting their right to be heard or if it was based on error, as in the Alphagroup case. In both circumstances, the public authority must compensate the bidder. The aggrieved party can claim compensation from the municipality for the whole sum, regardless of who was responsible for the final decision.

Liability among public authorities is joint and several, so individuals can bring a claim against one for the whole of the compensation.

In my opinion, the DSS would share liability with the municipality because it sent the wrong information concerning the individuals to other public authorities, which is not compliant with public law, nor does it respect the rights of the individual.

Loss of chances would not be taken into account because the mere fact that Alphagroup would have participated in other procurement procedures does not mean it would have obtained any public contract, and also because Alphagroup could participate in other procurement procedures at the same time. In this case, therefore, loss of chance would not be taken into account. However, the loss-of-chance doctrine is taken into account in cases related to damages caused by the National Health System, such as delays or incorrect diagnosis, and in cases where doctors respected the *lex artis*, but their interventions led to injury.[342]

J. Switzerland

TT

It is assumed here that Alphagroup discovered both that its offers had been dropped and the reason for that exclusion before the appeal deadline against the decision concluding the tendering procedure had expired. It is further assumed that Alphagroup brought an appeal against the decision awarding the contract to another bidder within the appeal deadline. If it failed to do so, the lawfulness of the decision concluding the tendering procedure can no longer be challenged. Any claim for damages would then fail. It is also assumed that the decision of the municipality of Mandeville had been implemented immediately, ie that the contract had been concluded with the successful bidder. It is finally assumed that DSS is a federal agency.

If the court deciding on the appeal finds that Alphagroup should not have been excluded from the procedure, it will issue a declaratory judgment on the unlawfulness of the procedure.

What could follow depends on the law of the canton in which Mandeville is located.

Some cantons do not have special provisions governing the liability of contracting authorities in the field of public procurement. The general rules of State liability—which are basically the same as those of the GLA—apply. In that case, to successfully claim for damages from the municipality of Mandeville, Alphagroup would have to show that in dropping its offer, the municipality of Mandeville was in breach of a fundamental duty. Since the municipality had no reason to doubt the information given by DSS, it is hard to see how such a showing could be made. Alphagroup could then turn to the Swiss Confederation and claim damages under the GLA. It would probably be relatively easy to show that giving an erroneous information to the municipality of Mandeville was unlawful (there would be no need to demonstrate a breach of a

342 For all, STS 20 March 2018 Rec 2820/2016. This decision summarizes the Supreme Court's case law on compensation for damage caused by the public authorities for loss of chances. On this topic, see L Medina Alcoz, *La teoría de la pérdida de oportunidad: estudio doctrinal y jurisprudencial de derecho de daños público y privado* (Thomson Reuters Aranzadi 2007).

fundamental duty). Then Alphagroup could be awarded damages for the actual loss linked to its unsuccessful participation in the tendering procedure. To obtain more, namely compensation for loss of profit, it would have to prove that, barring the information given to the municipality by DSS, it would have been awarded the contract (natural causation), and that this information 'under the usual course of events and experience of life' was able to produce, or at least facilitate, the exclusion of Alphagroup (adequate causation).

In other cantons, which follow the model of federal law in the matter, public procurement law provides that the mere unlawfulness of the award of the contract allows for compensation by the contracting authority of the costs arising from participation in the tendering procedure. In some cantons (as on the federal level), compensation for lost profit is always excluded; in others it can be awarded, provided the claimant can prove that without the unlawfulness it would have been awarded the contract.

K. United Kingdom

GA

There are three main issues that arise from this scenario: (i) procedural fairness; (ii) Alphagroup's 'loss of chance' to win a contract; and (iii) liability as between Mandeville and DSS. The nature of the case—primarily a dispute about a contract—means that it would probably be heard in the Chancery Division in the High Court.

In terms of procedural fairness, the question is whether Mandeville's officers should have disclosed the damaging information to Alphagroup in advance of making the decision to drop its tender, so that Alphagroup might have made representations about the information. It is suggested that, on the given facts, Mandeville should have done so. Fairness, while context sensitive (see comment (c) at the beginning of Chapter 13), is intended to provide procedural safeguards for individuals unless, for instance, there is some reason of public interest which means that disclosure need not be made. While advance disclosure may not need to be given where, for instance, documents relate to a criminal investigation (disclosure would happen at trial, subject to any argument about public interest immunity), there does not appear to be any interest of that kind involved here. Given the serious implications for Alphagroup's commercial interests, it is difficult to conceive of why advance disclosure was not made.

In terms of the damages that would be payable, this is the realm of 'loss of chance' under the law of contract.[343] This is a notoriously complex area of the law of damages, as the courts here try to assess the value of the opportunity that has been denied to the plaintiff. In a case such as this, that exercise is further complicated by the fact that it cannot be assumed that Alphagroup would definitely have been awarded the contract—there would have been other applicants for contracts and factors to be considered. It can therefore be expected that the court would try to assess damages on a basis that is fair and proportionate given the context of the case. It is impossible to guess what those damages would be on the given facts.

[343] See, most famously, *Chaplin v Hicks* [1911] 2 KB 786.

The remaining matter is that of who would be liable to pay damages—Mandeville or DSS. Ordinarily, where Mandeville considers that the error at hand was caused by DSS, it would apply to the court to have DSS joined as a co-defendant or as a defendant in its own right. On the given facts, there is no reason to believe that the court would do anything other than join DSS, so the issue would be whether DSS was responsible, in law, for any of the loss suffered by Alphagroup. Factually, all would seem to depend on how the mistake in relation to Alphagroup's name came to be made in the documentation: if, as is suggested in the scenario, it was contained in the original document sent by DSS, that may assist Mandeville in its argument that liability should be shared. As against that, there is also the argument that the real source of Alphagroup's loss in this case was Mandeville's failure to disclose the documents in advance of terminating its application for a contract. Had it done so, it may well have been that the error would have been identified before any loss of chance had occurred.

To recap: Alphagroup would have a strong case that there had been a procedural unfairness that resulted in a 'loss of chance' to obtain the contract. The primary defendant would be Mandeville, though it could be expected that DSS would be joined as a defendant.

VI. Case 5—a delay in issuing a concession for the use of the waterfront

The waterfront of the City of Sanibel, in front of a famous lake, is traditionally used to provide services, including restaurants and cafés, for both residents and visitors. Each provider must have a concession, and, in order to make concessions available for a plurality of operators, the City of Sanibel has established that, as a rule, concessions can be operated for a maximum of three years, after which they are re-issued on the basis of an open procedure. The rules procedure provides that interested parties can apply within thirty days and the City will then have sixty days to compare the offers and choose the next concessionaire. North Lake, a newcomer, applies for a concession for a specific site on the waterfront. Despite the fact that North Lake is the sole applicant, the City of Sanibel does not conclude the procedure within the deadline. In an attempt to justify its delay, the City of Sanibel asserts that the available documentation is incomplete, but it is unable to indicate any defect in the application. As a result, North Lake does not obtain the concession in time for the summer season and sues the City of Sanibel before the court.

Would its action be successful? Would damages, if any, be limited to actual loss or extend to cover lost profit? How would they be determined?

A. Austria

SS, KB, DB, and LM

Pursuant to § 2(2) AHG, damages under a public liability claim are not admissible if the injured person would have been able to avoid the damage by means of a legal remedy or a complaint to an administrative court and a final appeal to the Supreme Administrative Court. Therefore, North Lake must first pursue the relevant administrative legal remedies in order to be able to successfully assert a public liability claim. Public liability is only subsidiary.[344]

In the event of delayed rulings by an authority (as in this case), Austrian law provides for an appeal after the decision period prescribed by law expires. In principle, due to § 73(1) AVG and § 8 VwGVG, this decision period is six months; unless established differently (longer or shorter) by special administrative rules and regulations.

In this case, a shorter decision period is applicable—namely sixty days. At the end of this period, North Lake may bring a complaint for the breach of the duty to reach a timely decision ('*Säumnisbeschwerde*') against the City of Sansibel as the defaulting authority. It must be argued that the decision period has expired and that this delay predominantly results from a fault on the part of the competent authority (City of Sansibel). Pursuant to § 16 VwGVG, the City of Sansibel can (again, within a shorter period of sixty days—in principle, if no procedural provision specifies a shorter deadline, within three months) issue an administrative decision; or the City of Sansibel

[344] See also, S Storr, K Bayer, D Bereiter, and L Mischensky, 'Constitutional Foundations and the Design of the Austrian Liability of Public Bodies Act', Chapter 3 in this volume, section II.

must submit the complaint, together with the files of the administrative proceedings, to the competent administrative court. In this case, regarding trade-related matters (Art 10(1) No 8 B-VG), the VwG of the Austrian province (LVwG) where the City of Sansibel is situated, would be competent. This LVwG then decides whether there had been a breach of the duty to reach a decision; if so, the administrative court has to decide about the initially filed issue.

According to the case law of the VwGH, an objective standard must be applied when assessing a breach of the duty to reach a decision.[345] Since, according to the facts in this case, there were no transparent reasons for the delay outside the authority's sphere of influence (but merely the claim that the documents were incomplete), it is to be assumed that the City of Sansibel was at fault for the delayed decision. If, in fact, documents were missing, the City of Sansibel would have been obliged under § 13(3) AVG to request that North Lake remedy the application within an adequate time limit, with the proviso that the submission would be rejected after expiry. In addition, an alleged overloading of the authority, according to the rulings of the VwGH, does not justify the delay.[346] And no such overload can be assumed in this case, as there was only one candidate.

As granting licences is to be considered to be 'implementing the law', a public liability claim is possible if the delay was found to be predominantly due to the fault of the City of Sansibel. As for § 1(1) AHG, only the Federation, the provinces, municipalities, other bodies of public law, and social insurance institutions—all as legal entities—can be sued; therefore, the claim would have to be filed against the City of Sansibel (as a municipality, and not, for instance, against the physical person acting in implementation of the laws).

In civil liability proceedings, North Lake would have to demonstrate:

(1) damage (*Schaden*) caused by the delay;
(2) causality (*Kausalität*) of damage and delay;
(3) unlawfulness (*Rechtswidrigkeit*) of the delay; and
(4) fault (*Verschulden*) in the delay.

'Fault' in civil liability proceedings is not to be equated with fault in administrative proceedings—even if civil liability proceedings also require fault to be measured objectively and does not therefore depend on the ability of the physical person acting in implementation of the laws.[347] The unlawful delay must be condemnable—in particular, it must be based on an unjustifiable legal view. As the case law is very strict when ruling on delays, this will be difficult to prove.

If North Lake succeeds, both financial loss and (in the event of gross negligence) lost profits can be claimed. Procedural costs could also be claimed. The financial loss would have to be proven objectively. If a claim is also made for lost profit, the same applies here—North Lake would have to objectively explain how expected profit (on

[345] VwGH 14 September 2016 Ra 2016/18/0127; for the objective parameter, see also Storr and others, Chapter 3 in this volume (n 344), section I.
[346] See eg VwGH 20 March 2018 Ro 2017/03/0033.
[347] RIS-Justiz RS0026381.

the basis of past figures and prospective orders, for example wedding parties in the summer) would have been excluded if the licence had been granted in time.

B. European Union

BM

Article 265 TFEU provides a judicial remedy for reviewing the EU administration's failure to act.[348] More specifically, non-privileged applicants[349] can bring proceedings under Article 265 TFEU when the institutions fail to adopt an act having binding legal effects[350] which concerns them directly and individually.[351] This condition is met in our case, since the administration has a precise duty to respond to North Lake's application within sixty days.

The Treaty provides for a special procedure that has to be completed before bringing the dispute before the court. The applicant has first to call on the institution to act (formal notice). If the administration does not define its position within two months of the request, the applicant can bring the action before the court within a further period of two months.

If the action is well founded, the institution has to take the necessary steps to comply with the judgment, even if it retains the power regarding how to act.[352]

The claim for damages due to inaction can only be successful when the usual three conditions laid down by the court's case law on liability are satisfied.[353]

In particular, the party is required to demonstrate not only that the inaction constitutes a sufficiently demonstrable breach of a rule aimed at protecting the individual,[354]

[348] See G Bebr, *Development of Judicial Control of the European Communities* (Nijhoff 1981) 158.

[349] See A Türk, *Judicial Review in EU Law* (Edward Elgar 2009) 177.

[350] The requirement of legal effects is a precondition for the admissibility of the action under Art 265 TFUE: the remedy cannot be used to complain that the EU institutions failed to adopt an opinion or recommendation (see Case 15/70, *Chevalley v Commission* [1970] ECR 975, judgment of Court 18 November 1970; Case T-103/99 *ACSV v European Ombudsman and European Parliament* [2000] ECR II-4165, judgment of the Court of First Instance.

[351] According to the Court's case law, an individual can bring an action for failure to act only when the EU Institution or body has failed to take a decision on it. The individual cannot bring an action for failure to act with respect to an act that is addressed to a Member State or with respect to normative acts. The action of Art 265 TFEU, from this perspective, mirrors the action for annulment, in the sense that the individual can complain about the failure to adopt a decision under the same conditions (to be individually concerned) in which he could challenge an act under Art 263 TFEU. However, the remedy has very limited use: competition and state aid are the areas in which recourse to this action is most frequent. In EUCJ case law see eg Case T-95/96, *Telecinco v Commission* [1998] ECR II-3407, judgment of the Court of First Instance 15 September 1998; Case T-127/98 *UPS Europe v Commission* [1999] ECR II-2633, judgment of the Court of First Instance 9 September 1999; Case T-79/96, T-260/97, and T-117/98 *Camar and Tico v Commission and Council* [2000] ECR 2193, judgment of the Court of First Instance 8 June 2000.

[352] See Türk (n 349) 171: 'after the request has been made, the Institution has two months within which it has to define its position positively or negatively'.

[353] See Case 377/87 *Parliament v Council* [1988] ECR 4017, judgment of the Court 12 July 1988; Case T-28/90 *Asia Motor France v Commission* [1992] ECR II-2285, judgment of the Court of First Instance 18 September 1992; Case T-276/03 *Azienda Agricola Le Canne v Commission* [2006] ECR II-10, judgment of the Court of First Instance 25 January 2006.

[354] Case T-196/99 *Area Cova v Conseil and Commission* [2001] ECR II-3597, judgment of the Court of First Instance 6 December 2001.

but also the causal link between the administration's failure to act and the damage suffered, having to prove that, if the administration had acted promptly, it would have issued the requested concession.

With regard to the first condition, the applicant can claim that the City of Sanibel violated the principle of care and sound administration. This principle can be considered a rule of law granting rights to individuals, even if the case law concerning its relevance in liability actions does not always seem coherent.[355]

The causal link could be demonstrated only if the administration decided in favour of the applicant as a consequence of the action brought under Article 265 TFEU.

In this case, compensation will cover the damages deriving from the delay with which the administration has adopted the favourable act.

Conversely, the court will dismiss the action in the event that, with delay, the authority should deny the requested concession to the applicant.

C. France

TP

We may suppose that North Lake has (i) obtained the concession for three years, but too late for summer; or (ii) it has not obtained the concession yet. In the former case, North Lake's action would be successful regarding the lost profits; in the latter, the damage would not be considered certain.

We must first determine whether the City of Sanibel's delay would be a misconduct or not, and then whether it is possible to establish the three elements of public liability. When the law does not establish a deadline for an administrative procedure, unlike in the case of the rules for individual requests,[356] courts consider that the delay should be reasonable with respect to the complexity of the case, its technical aspects, and related legal issues.[357] However, in this case, the open procedure should have been concluded within sixty days, and the city did not comply with this term. Usually, this delay would automatically imply a fault, unless the court finds good reasons to justify the additional time taken by the City of Sanibel.[358]

Administrative courts usually recognize three types of grounds to justify additional delays to make or execute decisions: (i) the public interest;[359] (ii) the complexity of the cases;[360] and (iii) the cases' technical or practical problems.[361] Given that North Lake is the sole applicant and the city is unable to indicate any defect in the application that may justify the extra time taken by the City of Sanibel, this delay would be considered

[355] See P Aalto, *Public Liability in EU Law* (Hart Publishing 2011) 121.

[356] This is an open procedure initiated by the city and not a request regulated by the rules of administrative silence, explained earlier in case 2, as in these cases the misconduct is not the delay but the decision of refusal according to the meaning of 'silence'.

[357] CE 4 July 2001 *Société d' aménagement du Bois de Bouis* No 219658.

[358] Cour Administrative d'Appel de Paris 27 June 1995 No 94PA00554.

[359] In this case, the delay is not misconduct; but strict liability may be considered. See eg CE 20 January 1989 *Ministre de la Culture c SCI Villa Jacob* No 79367 90410.

[360] CE 10 December1975 *Soriano*, Lebon 1242.

[361] CE 11 June 2014 *Ministre de l'Économie et des Finances* No 368314.

as a misconduct that may engage public liability if the damage and the causal link are established.

If the concession was awarded too late, and North Lake lost the summer season's profits of the first year, the compensation would consider the profits that North Lake did not earn during the first summer, rather than for the whole concession. As the concession has a period of three years, North Lake would be able to have this site for the following two years, and it could only ask for the lost profits caused directly by the delay during the first summer.

There are two main options to establish the lost profits: sometimes, the *Conseil d'Etat* refers to the average income of such companies based on tax administration reports, rather than the income that the aggrieved party made afterwards.[362] In other cases, it takes as reference the profits that the company obtained afterwards, when the business started, with the respective adjustments, as it did in the case of a delay for the authorization of a pharmacy.[363]

Since North Lake is a newcomer, there is no information about its turnover with which to assess the damage, or for verifying that the number of clients in the autumn season is not comparable with summertime. The court would then consider the average income to calculate the lost profits. An opinion from an expert would be necessary[364] to establish the margin of gain by searching for information from competitors with a similar location in the lake. But if North Lake has not yet signed the concession or Sanibel City have decided to refuse its application, it would not be entitled to any compensation.

If the final decision of the City of Sanibel is the rejection of North Lake's application, the delay itself has not caused any loss of profits. North Lake must challenge the refusal if it has grounds to claim.

If North Lake looks only for damages, the court would consider that the damage is not certain, and it would not establish Sanibel City's liability on this ground.[365] Even if North Lake is the sole applicant, Sanibel City has power of appraisal for choosing the concessionaires and it may, lawfully, reject an application based on the public interest.

As damage must be a direct and certain consequence of misconduct, and in this last scenario, there would be no certitude regarding the outcome of the City's decision that ought to have been made on time, North Lake would not be awarded damages.

D. Germany

FW and JS

Again, this case raises the issue of the primacy of primary legal protection (§ 839 para 3 BGB): North Lake was obliged to lodge an action against failure to act (§ 42 para 1 variant 3 VwGO) in the main proceedings before the administrative courts.

[362] CE 10 November 1976 *Conseil national de l'ordre des médecins* No 98628.

[363] CE 25 July1975 *Ministre de la Santé publique et de la Sécurité sociale c Union des sociétés de secours mutualiste de la région de Dieppe* No 92616.

[364] CE 26 March 1976 *Sieur Colboc* No 88811.

[365] CE 5 March 2008 *Société d'aménagement du Bois de Bouis* No 255266.

Moreover, in view of the imminent summer season, North Lake was also obliged to ask for an interim order (§ 123 para 1 VwGO). If North Lake failed to do so, a claim for damages was excluded insofar as the damage could have been averted by asking for an interim order.

Given the primacy of primary legal protection, damage to North Lake can be caused only in two situations: first, if North Lake asked for an interim order but did not succeed, although the claim was well founded; second, if damage incurred before the successful interim decision was handed down. However, liability for judicial acts is restricted by § 839 para 2 sentence 1 BGB, and comes with multiple implications, which cannot be assessed here.[366] Therefore, the focus is on the delayed decision by the City of Sanibel: The claimant must prove that (1) an official (2) intentionally or negligently (3) breached the official duty incumbent upon him (4) in relation to a third party, and that this (5) caused (6) the claimant damage.

An official of the City of Sanibel breached her or his duty to act in accordance with the law (*gesetzmäßiges Verhalten*)[367] by failing to issue the concession within the time period stipulated in the rules of procedure (sixty days)[368] against the backdrop of clear circumstances (North Lake as the sole applicant). In addition, there is an official duty to act without undue delay.[369] These duties may be regarded as being designed to protect the interests of the persons participating in an administrative procedure, since their purpose[370] is to guarantee a prompt decision. With at least negligence being established, the court may award damages covering both the actual loss and lost profit according to the legal principles put forth in case 2 (§§ 249 para 1, 252 BGB). The burden of proof with regard to the actual amount of the damage is relaxed under § 287 paragraph 1 sentence 1 ZPO, as put forth in case 2.

In view of the exclusion contained in § 839 paragraph 3 BGB, a claim to damages is only possible with regard to damages not avertable by a remedy, notably because they occurred before an order for interim relief was available, and/or in the case of an unsuccessful court action, ie if the administrative court rejects the injunction or holds North Lake's action in the main proceedings unfounded. In the latter situation, the issue arises whether the civil court hearing the subsequent liability case is bound by the administrative judiciary's decisions.[371] In cases where primary legal protection confirms the legality of the challenged administrative action, the civil court is held bound by this prevenient finding of the administrative court as *res judicata* (§ 121 VwGO).[372]

366 See Papier and Shirvani (n 141) para 323ff. As to the inclusion of interim orders under s 839 para 2 sentence 1 BGB, see BGH 9 December 2004—III ZR 200/04, BGHZ 161, 298 (301ff). See also Wöstmann (n 62) paras 325, 328. As to the diverging standard in case of a breach of EU law, see ECJ Case C-224/01 *Köbler* [2003] ECR I-10239 para 53.

367 See n 143. See also Papier and Shirvani (n 141) paras 193ff.

368 Official duties can arise from all kinds of sources of law (Ossenbühl and Cornils (n 145) 44), which also comprises the rules of procedure.

369 BGH 11 January 2007—III ZR 302/05, BGHZ 170, 260 (266); Papier and Shirvani (n 141) para 217.

370 Papier and Shirvani (n 141) para 229.

371 cf Maurer and Waldhoff (n 222) § 26 para 51. See also BGH 15 November 1990—III ZR 302/89, BGHZ 113, 17 (20), explicitly denying a binding effect in these cases. Sceptical, CM Jeromin, 'Die Bestandskraft von Verwaltungsakten im Amtshaftungsprozeß' [1991] NVwZ 543.

372 BGH 15 November 1990—III ZR 302/89, BGHZ 113, 17 (20); BGH 7 February 2008—III ZR 76/07, BGHZ 175, 221 (225 with further references); B Grzeszick, 'Art 34' in V Epping and C Hillgruber (eds),

Opposed to that, preliminary orders do not have the effect of *res judicata* and do not bind the civil court.[373] Thus, the civil court hearing North Lake's case would be bound by a judgment delivered in the main proceedings, but not by an interim order.

In addition, a prevenient court decision can also rule out the finding that an agency acted with intent or negligence in the context of § 839 paragraph 1 sentence 1 BGB: Based on the assumption that an officer who has to decide on his or her own and in limited time cannot act more appropriately than a court, intent and negligence have been denied in cases where courts upheld administrative decisions after an in-depth analysis of the facts and the law (*Kollegialgerichts-Richtlinie*).[374] However, this does not apply to interim orders according to § 123 VwGO, since they imply only a summary assessment.[375] Moreover, as the term *Kollegialgericht* implies, more than one judge must have decided on the matter.[376] This is often not the case under § 123 VwGO, since an interim order may also be handed down by a single judge.[377] In addition, the assumption does not apply if certain grave errors occurred in the court's assessment of the case,[378] which might have happened in North Lake's case.

In summary, North Lake may only claim damages for harm that could not have been averted by challenging the authority's failure to act. This comprises damage incurred before the successful interim decision was handed down or because of an unjustified rejection of an interim order. However, the civil court hearing the liability matter would be bound by a final court decision. Thus, only very limited space remains for a claim for damages.

E. Hungary

LB

In this case, the municipality's delay would infringe the rules of administrative law and may give rise to government liability. It is helpful to say at the outset that Act CXCVI of

BeckOK GG (43rd edn, CH Beck 15 May 2020) para 35; J F Lindner, '§ 121' in H Posser and HA Wolff (eds), *BeckOK VwGO* (54th edn, CH Beck 1 January 2020) para 22; cf also para 23.1; cf Maurer and Waldhoff (n 222) § 26 para 51.

373 With regard to s 80 para 5 V VwGO BGH 16 November 2000—III ZR 265/99, [2001] NVwZ 352 (353f); Grzeszick, 'Art 34' (n 372) para 35.1. The effect of *res judicata* in the context of interim orders is, however, disputed; cf B Clausing, '§ 121' in F Schoch, J-P Schneider, and W Bier (eds), *Verwaltungsgerichtsordnung* (23rd edn, CH Beck January 2012) para 16.

374 BGH 2 April 1998—III ZR 111/97, [1998] NVwZ 878 (878); 13 July 2000—III ZR 131/99, [2000] NVwZ-RR 744 (744); Wöstmann (n 62) paras 211ff. This effect is rendered not only on administrative decisions made after the issuing of a court decision, but also on the assessment of the prerequisite of intent or negligence in the context of state liability claims, see Baldus and others (n 214) para 179. See also Papier and Shirvani (n 141) para 290, pointing out that this measure has only guiding effect and that recent decisions have often deviated.

375 BGH 22 April 1986—III ZR 104/85 juris para 5; Wöstmann (n 62) para 216; BGH 7 September 2017—III ZR 618/16, [2018] ZfBR 43 (46).

376 See BGH 2 April 1998—III ZR 111/97, [1998] NVwZ 878 (878); 13 July 2000—III ZR 131/99, [2000] NVwZ-RR 744 (744).

377 See F Wollenschläger, '§ 123' in KF Gärditz (ed), *VwGO* (2nd edn, Carl Heymanns 2018) paras 146f.

378 Wöstmann (n 62) para 213, referring among others to BGH 29 May 1957—III ZR 38/57, BGHZ 27, 338 (343), where the Federal High Court declined to accept the binding effect in a case where the lower court showed 'a palpable misconstruction of an unambiguous decision'.

2011—on the national property—establishes a list of the exclusive state-controlled or municipal government-controlled economic activities. Using waters is not part of this list. These activities can be carried out by the successful bidder through a concession. The basic substantive rules for concessions were set out by legislation in 1991. The detailed procedural rules are set out either by the Act governing public procurement or by sector-specific legislation. These activities are not necessarily administrative, because the legal relationship is considered rather to be of a civil nature. However, an act can impose the application of (all or some of the) administrative rules, too.

In most administrative procedures, since 2015 there has been an opportunity to issue a so-called conditional decision; that is, if the authority misses the deadline, the conditional decision becomes the decision of the case, so there will be no damages. In cases where issuing a conditional decision is not possible, a failure to meet the deadline is an infringement, but it is not usually considered as a serious and culpable infringement in a civil procedure. Breaching the requirement of a reasonable time limit is a serious infringement, however. To determine what delay is not reasonable, the overall circumstances of the proceedings must be taken into consideration. For (civil law) culpability, if the authority cannot prove the cause for its delay at all and cannot make reasonable arguments for the cause, it can be held culpable.

In our case, the general rules of liability should be used. There are no signs that the municipality had any reasons to miss the deadline, so there is an infringement. North Lake also needs to prove its damage and the causal link between the damage and the infringement. However, there is still a question related to proving the damage and the causal link that even North Lake is the only interested party: would the municipality announce it to be the winner of the procedure? This depends on the breadth of discretion of the authority provided by the law and the tender document (there is not necessarily an obligation to contract).

F. Italy

FC

In Italy, an administrative court would have jurisdiction over the appeal filed by North Lake. Italian law in fact also provides for compensation for damages resulting from delay in exercising administrative authority.[379]

According to the most widespread interpretation,[380] compensation for such damage can be obtained only if the damaged party can prove that, regardless of the delay, the authority would have granted them the concession requested. Basically, North Lake could obtain compensation for the damage incurred due to being unable to set up its business right from the start of the season if it can prove that it should have been awarded the concession (the court, in this case, should carry out the same assessment as mentioned above for case 2).[381]

[379] See Art 2-*bis* L No 241/1990; see also Art 30 CAT.
[380] See eg Council of State No 818/2017.
[381] See also the remarks illustrated in n 177.

It is therefore a minority opinion[382] that North Lake could obtain compensation for damages in any case, namely compensation for damages due to a 'mere delay', on the basis that it did not receive a reply from the authority that would have given it enough time to refocus business efforts elsewhere.[383]

Beyond this, according to the majority opinion, in order to actually obtain compensation, the aggrieved party would also need to promptly initiate the legally established procedures to obtain a remedy in the event of 'silence' from the administrative authority (Art 31 CAT regulates *ad hoc* actions, and many judgments of administrative courts apply to such cases the limitations provided for in Art 30 para 3, CAT, mentioned earlier: therefore, in the absence of a claim against 'silence', the damaged party may well hear the counterargument that their negligent behaviour aggravated the damage incurred).

G. Poland

Sebastian Wijas and Marek Wierzbowski

A delay in issuing the concession can be regarded as being unlawful in the light of the specific provisions (requirements). Thus damages would be awarded within the framework of Article 417(1) CC and the relevant case law. However, legislation sets out time limits for issuing administrative acts, including a concession. If the procedure lasts longer, the administrative authority shall inform the party about reasons for such delay, indicate the new date of issuing the decision, and provide information about the right to make a special 'hurry-up' motion. In reality, such expansion of the time limit may take place legally several times. There are several cases of procedures lasting three years instead of the statutory limit of two months, while there is no known case damages granted for a delay, though it might be possible.

More specifically, opening a restaurant does not require concession. There may be a civil case of renting space in the building own by the municipality, but this is then a pure civil case, in which liability of the municipality arises for not keeping to what they promised. In some cases, a concession is issued after special tender procedure, a special sort of administrative procedure, not a private law matter subject to scrutiny of common courts.

In the case of North Lake, it would be much simpler to claim damages. Although a concession, unlike a regular permit, is regarded as a discretionary act, if there is any obstruction in the course of the administrative decision-making process, the effect of a decision which has not been made may also constitute damage under the provisions of Article 417(1) CC. As usual, liability for damages arises if: (i) the damage exists; (ii)

382 See eg Council of State No 875/2005; Council of Administrative Justice for the Region of Sicily No 1368/2010; Council of State No 1271/2011; Council of State No 1739/2011; Council of State No 468/2014.

383 This interpretation considers interest in temporal certainty as a legally relevant interest in itself. Those who support this thesis also usually support the position that in these cases the nature of liability of the public administration is not 'non-contractual', but 'paracontractual' or 'quasi-contractual' (see also n 177). It should be noted that Art 28 DL No 98/2013 provided a sort of penalty for any day of 'mere delay' on the part of a public authority. But it is a measure restricted to a very limited category of procedures.

the damage is inflicted due to the unlawful fulfilment of duties by a public authority; and (iii) there is a causal link between these two events.

Hence, the complaint of North Lake, which did not receive a concession to manage a specific site on the waterfront prior to the opening of the season, should be taken into account when damages, understood in a broad sense (*damnum emergens* and *lucrum cessans*), are awarded. It ought to be added that a concession is a declaratory decision, ie the specific criteria enshrined in the relevant legal conditions should be reflected by the content of the concession. The role of the authority is to verify the application in terms of compliance with the mentioned legal requirements. The value of damages for loss of profit should be assessed according to variable criteria, ie from the angle of seasonality of profits in tourism and leisure industry, its characteristics, and weather conditions in the period in which the loss occurred.

H. Romania

RV

From the description of the site situated at the waterfront of the City of Sanibel, I will assume that the site belongs to the public property of the municipality (Romanian law distinguishes between public property of the State, whose main characteristics are a public function and public utility, as well as the fact that it is inalienable, and private property of the State that follows the general regime of private property). If this is the case, in the Romanian legal system, the applicable legislative act would be the Government Emergency Ordinance No 54/2006 on the concession of assets that are public property of the State.[384]

Article 1 thereof provides that the concession of an asset belonging to the State is a written contract concluded between a public authority and a concessionaire, pursuant to which the public authority transfers the right to exploit the asset to the concessionaire for a specific period and provided that the concessionaire acts on its own risk and pays the royalty fee. Article 2 reads that the Ordinance shall not be applicable to contracts concluded under Law 100/2016 on the concession of services and works.[385] The latter implemented Directive 23/2004/EU into Romanian legislation concerning the award of concession contracts.

Government Emergency Ordinance No 54/2006 establishes a competitive procedure for the award of concessions, and the principles applicable are somewhat similar to the principles applicable in the European law of public contracting (ie transparency, fairness, equal treatment, and non-discrimination). As far as signing the contract and the refusal of the authority to sign a concession contract is concerned, this legislative act stipulates under Article 50 paragraph (1) that 'The refusal to sign the concession agreement within 20 days of the timeline stipulated under article 42 can lead to damages being granted to the aggrieved party.'

[384] Published in the Official Gazette No 569 of 30 June 2006.

[385] Directive 2014/23/EU of the European Parliament and of the Council of 26 February 2014 on the award of concession contracts [2014] OJ L94/1 (the 'Concessions Directive').

Methodological provisions for the application of the Government Emergency Ordinance were also enacted on 17 February 2006.[386] Article 45 of the provisions establishes that, whenever the concession contract is not concluded, the claim for damages regulated under Article 50 of the Government Emergency Ordinance should be lodged before the tribunal competent where the public authority has its headquarters.

The compensation that the court could order would cover the costs incurred for participating in the competitive selection procedure as well as loss of profit. However, the concessionaire will have to prove that the authority was at fault, as Article 50 of Government Emergency Ordinance No 50/2006 specifically mentions this requirement.

The claim that North Lake could typically bring under Romanian law would include the following: (i) annulment of an unlawful (assimilated administrative act in Romanian law[387]) administrative act consisting in the refusal to sign the contract; (ii) a request for the City of Sanibel to be forced to sign the concession contract (if North Lake still has an interest in being a party to such an agreement); and (iii) compensation for loss resulting from the fact that the contract was not concluded within twenty days of the moment when the results of the competitive procedure had been communicated to North Lake (as per Art 42 of Government Emergency Ordinance No 54/2006).

North Lake should provide documents that would prove and indicate to the court the estimated profit for the summer months. This would, for example, consist in accounting documents for similar activities (if North Lake had carried out similar activities in other areas with the same potential for tourism as the waterfront of the Sanibel Lake), or the estimates it used when preparing the offer. However, should North Lake not be able to produce such documents, it should be mentioned that Article 1532 of the Civil Code reads that, 'The damage consisting in the loss of a chance to obtain an advantage will be repaired proportionally to the probability of obtaining that chance and according to the details of the case and the *specific* situation of the injured party.' Furthermore, paragraph 3 reads that 'damage that cannot be assessed with certainty will be determined by the court'. Since there are no special provisions applicable in the field of administrative liability, the administrative court should apply the general civil law on the concept of loss of profit or compensation for loss of chance stipulated under the CC.

I. Spain

EMNG

In the Spanish public authorities liability system, North Lake would not obtain compensation for damages because the Spanish system requires real damage, insofar as

[386] Published in the Official Gazette No 146 of 28 February 2007.

[387] According to Art 2 of Law 554/2004: 'The unjustified refusal to respond to a person's petition or request regarding his or her rights or legitimate interests, as well as the fact of not answering a person's request within the legal timeframe, are assimilated as administrative acts.'

no hypothetical damage can be considered. The City of Sanibel could conclude the procedure without granting the concession to North Lake, even though it was the only company to apply.

A hypothetical claim for compensation, including for loss of chances, would have to prove real damages, which is very difficult under these circumstances. Ultimately, the Spanish courts would not accept a claim for damages on these terms.

J. Switzerland

TT

To answer the questions concerning this case, two assumptions, which are rather unusual in the Swiss legal context, must be made: first, that the City ordinance creates a legal right for applicants to obtain a concession on public property if they meet some basic requirements and if the number of applicants is not higher than the number of concessions; second, that the deadline set by the municipal rule is strictly binding.

Upon these two assumptions, if North Lake's application actually met all the legal requirements, the failure of the City to issue a decision in time would be an unlawful action. Since this failure to act would be, in its result, the equivalent of a denial of the concession, ie the equivalent of an administrative decision, the liability of the City would only apply if the delay could be deemed a breach of a fundamental duty.[388] If it were the case, compensation for the actual loss would be awarded. Since, in principle, full compensation would be due, lost profit would also be considered. But in assessing lost profit, the possibility for North Lake to devolve its resources to another profitable activity during the summer season should be taken into account.

K. United Kingdom

GA

It is possible to approach this scenario in one of two ways. The first is to regard it as *a problem of law* that engages property rights, commercial interests, and matters of public interest, where North Lake may ultimately have a remedy only through an application for judicial review. The second is to regard it as *a problem of maladministration*, where the failings on the part of the City of Sanibel may not attract legal sanction, but might be a matter for complaint to the ombudsman. (The term 'ombudsman' is used loosely here—in England and Wales, such a complaint would be made to the local government ombudsman.)

In terms of approaching the scenario as *a problem of law*, the following points are to be noted:

(1) It first has to be assumed that the City of Sanibel is the legal owner of the area of land that surrounds the lake. In the context of the UK, this is not a

[388] For the judicial doctrine of 'breach of fundamental duty', see Switzerland, case 1.

straightforward assumption, as beaches (if those surround the lake) can either be owned by the Crown, by public authorities, or by private parties. Should ownership not lie with the City of Sanibel, concessions, or licences, to operate on the land would be a matter for the rightful owner, subject to any overarching regulatory framework that might be imposed by legislation.

(2) Second, it might also be assumed that the City of Sanibel, in providing for concessions, has voluntarily adopted a non-statutory scheme that is intended to work to the benefit of the City of Sanibel itself, its inhabitants, and the private actors who obtain licences. In the alternative scenario, where the scheme was mandated by statute, any dispute with North Lake would plainly be a matter of public law, as the delay in this case would have frustrated the operation of the underlying statute. However, to the extent that the absence of a statutory framework might be taken to mean that this would not be a matter of public law, North Lake may still be able to obtain a remedy by way of an application for judicial review. This is because it is well established that the High Court will sometimes hear disputes about non-statutory powers where the disputes in question give rise to matters of 'public interest'. In this case, North Lake would argue that the concessions are at least partly matters of 'public interest'—they are intended to benefit the City and its inhabitants, and the delay in question means that that potential benefit is being lost (North Lake's own interest would be primarily commercial).[389]

(3) The non-statutory nature of the powers at issue would probably mean that any challenge to the delay would centre upon unreasonableness. The challenge here might have four, related limbs: (i) the delay in question was unreasonable given the rules of the scheme; (ii) the failure to make due enquiry into the documentation meant that there had been a failure to take relevant considerations into account; (iii) the reasons that were given (incomplete documentation) were based upon the failure to have due regard for all relevant facts; and (iv) there has been a breach of common law's conception of equality. According to that conception, decision-makers must treat like situations alike and different situations differently, unless there is good reason not to do so, and that. principle *prima facie* has been offended on the given facts: there is a scheme that states that applications will be processed within a set period of time, and it can be assumed that previous applications under the scheme have been treated on the terms specified. (This might also be pleaded as a procedural failing, albeit the non-statutory nature of the scheme may complicate such arguments.)

(4) The issue of damages is more difficult. As noted in comment (h) at the beginning of Chapter 13, North Lake could bring a damages claim as part of its application for judicial review only if the facts would lend themselves to a private law cause of action (it may alternatively bring a separate private law action, though that would increase its potential costs exposure). However, on the facts as outlined, it is not readily apparent that there would be any such action open to North Lake. For instance, there does not appear to be any contractual

[389] For an example of the 'public interest' being used where a commercial interest has been at stake, see *Re City Hotel (Derry) Ltd's Application* [2004] NIQB 38.

relationship between North Lake and the City of Sanibel, and nor do the facts seem to disclose any cause of action in tort (there is no statute for the purposes of breach of statutory duty; it might be doubted whether there would be a duty of care for the purposes of the law of negligence). At most, North Lake might therefore be left with only a claim for misfeasance in public office—though the given facts may not sit easily with the 'abuse-of-power' model that underlies that (rarely litigated) tort (see point (l) of the listed comments at the beginning of Chapter 13).

In terms of approaching the scenario as *a problem of maladministration*, the following points might be made:

(1) The nub of the problem is delay, and an apparent failure properly to process documentation.
(2) 'Maladministration' does not have a settled definition in UK law, but it is generally said to encompass 'bias, neglect, inattention, delay, incompetence, ineptitude, arbitrariness and so on' (these are the so-called 'Crossman catalogue').[390]
(3) Where the ombudsman investigates a public body and makes a finding of maladministration, it will publish a report that recommends that the investigated department should take one or several courses of action. While the ombudsman does not have power to force a body to quash a decision, or change its practices and/or pay compensation, the investigated body will often act on the recommendation. Moreover, where the investigated body is minded to reject a finding of fact on the part of the ombudsman, case law has established that it may only do so for 'cogent reasons'. Where no such reasons exist, it may be that the public body will have acted in a manner that is irrational in public law terms and that its decision may be quashed by way of an application for judicial review.
(4) On the facts of this case, it is plain that there has been delay, and perhaps also neglect and incompetence. The question for North Lake would therefore be whether any such findings by the Ombudsman would result in a recommendation of compensation.

To recap: North Lake could conceivably bring an application for judicial review on the facts of this case, but doing so may not enable it to claim compensation from the City of Sanibel (there does not appear to be any related, recognized cause of action open to North Lake). On the assumption that its primary objective is to obtain compensation, it may be that a complaint about maladministration would offer a more realistic option.

[390] See further eg *R v Local Commissioner for Administration, ex p Bradford MCC* [1979] QB 287.

VII. Case 6—prohibiting fruit imports

'Forest's Jewels' (FJ) is registered in Terranova, an Eastern European country that is a member of the EEA. FJ is a company specializing in the import of 'fruits of the forest' (eg cranberries and blueberries) from Blefuscu Island in the Black Sea. After an alleged incident in a nuclear power plant in Russia, under the Feed and Food Regulation, the government of Terranova restricts the importation of 'fruits of the forest' in two ways: (i) a generalized block of all imports for all importers for one month; (ii) a set of new rules for testing imports to make sure that they are not radioactive. FJ challenges the block and the new rules before a Terranova court on two grounds: first, because they are—especially the block—individual measures under the guise of general measures, since FJ is the only importer from Blefuscu Island; second, and consequently, because the ban is based on limited information, rather than on an accurate analysis of all the relevant facts before individual measures adversely affecting an undertaking are taken by a public authority. FJ also asks the court to award damages.

Is the action for damages brought by FJ admissible only if the court annuls the block and the new rules? Or is it admissible independently of any annulment? In any case, would damages, if any, cover lost profit and, if so, how would be the amount of the compensation be determined?

A. Austria

SS, KB, DB, and LM

In cases like the one described here (danger ahead), §§ 39 et seq and §§ 48 et seq of the Food Safety and Consumer Protection Act (LMSVG)[391] contain measures for actions by an authority, such as the import blocks mentioned here. As for § 39(1) LMSVG, such measures should always be carried out taking into account the principle of proportionality. Authorities therefore have discretion, but they must always bear in mind the proportionality principle.

In principle, the VfGH does not consider individual measures that, in fact, only affect one addressee, to be unconstitutional.[392] However, according to the facts, FJ is burdened with measures against an objective future danger; the measures are only directed exclusively to FJ because only FJ imports the potentially contaminated food. The trade block generally refers to 'fruits of the forest', and does not exclusively refer to the Blefuscu Islands. For these reasons, it is therefore unlikely that FJ can penetrate and successfully combat the trade block or the mentioned set of new rules by means of an administrative procedure.

However, a successful liability claim usually depends on the trade block or the new regulations being considered unlawful during the administrative procedure (and therefore repealed). Even though the official liability procedure can be initiated in parallel with administrative proceedings, a civil court will always wait for the

[391] Food Safety and Consumer Protection Act (*Lebensmittelsicherheits- und Verbraucherschutzgesetz—* LMSVG), Federal Law Gazette No I 13/2006 as amended.

[392] VfGH 30 June 2017 G 53/2017 with further evidence.

administrative proceedings to end. Without the measure being declared unlawful, a liability claim will rarely succeed.

Fault is assessed very carefully in civil proceedings. As long as there are sufficient public interests for the trade block/new set of rules, and the proportionality of the measures has been examined (and explained), the liability claim usually fails.

If FJ succeeds nonetheless, both financial loss and (in the event of gross negligence) lost profits can be claimed for. Procedural costs could also be claimed. Only the Federation could be sued, not Terranova itself (as Terranova's legal entity responsible for food law, according to Article 10(1) No 12 of the Federal Constitutional Law (B-VG), is the Federation). The financial loss would have to be proven objectively. If the lost profit is also claimed, the same applies here—FJ would have to objectively explain how expected profit (on the basis of past figures and prospective orders, for instance, future acceptances for major customers) would have been excluded if there had been no trade blocks/new set of rules.

B. European Union

BM

The annulment action brought by FJ could be declared inadmissible because of the company's lack of *locus standi* in challenging general acts. As the court stated in the well-known *Plaumann* case in 1963, the circumstance that FJ was the unique importer of these fruits does not imply that the act concerns it individually.[393]

This does not mean, however, that FJ cannot bring an action for damages. However, it will have to show that the act of general application violates in a serious and manifest manner a superior law for the protection of individuals.[394]

This condition is not easy to demonstrate, considering both the normative nature of the relevant act and the discretion granted to the authority, which is wide also because of the power to adopt precautionary measures to protect public health.

If the infringement of the principle of proportionality is proven, so that a violation of law aimed at protecting individuals is demonstrated, it would also be necessary to prove a sufficiently explicit violation, a condition which is quite often excluded by the court if the decision is discretionary and founded on objectively complex and uncertain assessments.[395] Furthermore, even if the principle of proportionality can be

[393] On the Plaumann doctrine and the standing issue of private parties, see P Craig, 'Legality, Standing and Substantial Review in Community Law' [1994] OJLS 507; A Ward, *Judicial Review and the Rights of Private Parties in EC Law* (OUP 2000) ch 6; A Arnull, 'Private Applicants and the Action for Annulment since Codorniu' (2001) 38 CMLR 7; A Albors-Llorens, 'The Standing of Private Parties in Challenge Community Measures: Has the European Court Missed the Boat?' [2003] CLJ 72; B Marchetti, 'L'impugnazione degli atti normative da parte dei privati nell'art 263 TFUE' (2010) 6 Riv It Dir Pubbl Comun 1471; A Albors-Llorens, 'Remedies against the EU Institutions after Lisbon: An Era of Opportunity?' (2012) 71 CLJ 507; R Matsroianni and A Pezza, 'Striking the Right Balance: Limits on the Right to Bring an Action under Art 263(4) of the Treaty on the Functioning of the European Union' [2015] Am U Int'l L Rev 744.

[394] Recently, see Case C-350/16 *Aniello Pappalardo and others v Commission* [2017] OJ C382/24, judgment of the Court 13 September 2017.

[395] Case C-221/10 *Artegodan v Commission* [2010] ECR II-00491, judgment of the Court 19 April 2012.

considered a rule of law for the protection of the individual, it has not been very successfully invoked in damages cases.[396]

Considering the normative nature of the act and the difficulty of proving the gravity of the violation, the court will probably dismiss the damage action.

C. France

TP

Although FJ's action for damages is admissible without the measures being annulled, the company would probably not be awarded any compensation because the damage would not be considered 'abnormal' in its field of business, and therefore, strict public liability would not be established.

If Terrranova is part of the EEA, the State is entitled to take the first action; but the European Commission supervises import restrictions in the European market. For example, in March 2011, when a nuclear accident happened in Fukushima, it reacted quickly and adopted new regulations with restrictions to imports from some regions of Japan, including declaration of origin, certificates of levels of radionuclides, and random tests in EU entry.[397]

For our purposes here, only national measures will be considered. Article 24 of the French Custom Code entrusts the Minister of economy and finances with the power to set out rules concerning goods[398] in addition to phytosanitary regulations.[399] According to the Code of public health, governmental authorities are empowered to take measures to protect people from radioactive contamination risk of the environment or from products coming from affected zones, always considering advantages and disadvantages of taking such action.[400] They may also take the urgent measures that are considered necessary to protect human life or health within the national territory.

In our case, the fact that the decision affects only one importer, FJ, does not mean that the decision is individual, because the new set of regulations would apply to any future importer, and this is not a ground to challenge a general import restriction based on a human health risk. However, as only FJ is affected, it may argue that it suffered 'special' damage, as we will see later. An option for challenging the decisions' lawfulness is to prove that the facts—the nuclear incident—did not happen or that the radioactive materials did not reach Blefuscu Island. FJ, though, argues that the decision was made with limited information. Even so, reinforced import controls can be based on the precautionary principle, which in France is laid down by the

[396] Case T-489/93 *Unifruit Hellas v Commission* [1994] ECR II-01201, judgment of the Court of First Instance 15 December 199) and Case T-16/04 *Arcelor v Parliament and Council* [2010] ECR II-00211, judgment of the General Court 2 March 2010; see Aalto (n 355) 119.

[397] Commission Implementing Regulation (EU) No 297/2011 of 25 March 2011. In November 2017, the EU announced a partial lifting of restrictions.

[398] Section 6 of the Code, in particular Art 24, concerns measures limiting the import of products.

[399] *Arrêté du 24 May 2006 concerning vegetal products.*

[400] See Art L 1333-3.

'*Charte de l'environnement*' (included within the *bloc de constitutionnalité*). Article 5 provides that:

> Where the occurrence of damage, although uncertain in the state of scientific knowledge, could seriously and irreversibly affect the environment, the public authorities shall ensure, by applying the precautionary principle and in their fields of competence, the implementation of risk assessment procedures and the adoption of provisional and proportionate measures to avoid the damage.[401]

In 2013, the *Conseil d'Etat* determined that the precautionary principle should also be considered where there are risks to human health related to the environment,[402] and not only when there could be direct damage to the environment.

In cases of scientific uncertainty, it first ascertains whether the precautionary principle is applicable, then if risk evaluations have been carried out, and finally, if there has been a manifest error of assessment regarding the choice of measures. Although we do not know precisely what happened, if the nuclear incident occurred and Blefuscu island is in the affected zone, a high level of radiation is not uncertain, and the measure would be established, in view of real and present risk and not the precautionary principle.

In conclusion, either because the risk is clearly determined or because the precautionary principle applies, the import restrictions seem lawful. However, in France there is public liability without misconduct for legal administrative decisions; therefore, it is possible for FJ to claim damages even if the measures are not annulled.

In France, government liability may arise regardless of misconduct in situations of exceptional risk (such as the use of weapons),[403] and in cases of breach of equality before public burdens.[404] Since 1923, the *Conseil d'Etat* accepts the possibility of strict public liability when an administration acts lawfully, but its decision imposes burdens that an individual usually does not have to endure.[405] In *M Couitéas*, the police refused to execute a judicial order for restitution on grounds of public order, but this implied that the plaintiff could not use his lands, occupied by 8,000 indigenous people. Subsequently, in 1963, the *Conseil d'Etat* decided the first case of liability due to a general administrative decision. In *Commune de Gavarnie*, the city restricted transport on foot or using animals along some pathways so as to avoid accidents. This was a lawful decision, but on one of those pathways there was a souvenir shop that was left

401

> Lorsque la réalisation d'un dommage, bien qu'incertaine en l'état des connaissances scientifiques, pourrait affecter de manière grave et irréversible l'environnement, les autorités publiques veillent, par application du principe de précaution et dans leurs domaines d'attributions, à la mise-en-oeuvre de procédures d'évaluation des risques et à l'adoption de mesures provisoires et proportionnées afin de parer à la réalisation du dommage.

402 CE 12 April 2013 *Association coordination interrégationale THT* No 342409.

403 CE 24 June 1949 *Consorts Lecomte* No 87335 Rec 307.

404 For a discussion, see S Hennette-Vauchez, 'Responsabilité sans faute' in *Répertoire de la Responsabilité Publique* (Dalloz 2010) ss 11, 12, and 13.

405 CE 30 November 1923 *Couitéas* Rec 789; D1923.3.59 concl Rivet; RD publ 1924.75 and 208 concl, note Jeze.

without clients after the decision. Since only that shop suffered an exceptional burden, it had to be compensated.[406]

French legal scholarship discusses the basis for strict liability, namely whether it is the breach of equality or rather the type of damage caused. For some, the court would have to order compensation of the exceptional damage impacting one individual.[407] Strict liability in the event of legal administrative decisions has two necessary conditions: (i) the damage must be special, meaning that it affects only one person or a limited number of people in a singular way; and (ii) the damage should be 'abnormal', ie it must be of a certain gravity (not just a small nuisance) and be exceptional (unpredictable). In the case of the souvenir shop, all the street residents and passers-by were affected by the measure, but only one store (special) had a serious drop of clients caused by a new traffic rule, which was not a usual business risk.

Liability for breaching equality before the public burden is a '*moyen d'ordre public*' (ground of public order); thus, the court must examine it, even though the claimant lamented government misconduct.[408] If the court finds that this regime is applicable, it must inform the parties to guarantee equality between them before its decision.[409] It must determine whether FJ has a right to a compensation regardless of the State's misconduct.

Initially, the *Conseil d'Etat* established that lawful administrative measures issued according to powers conferred by the law were not subject to claims for damages, especially in the economic area, including international commerce. For example, in the *Martin et Sté Michel Martin* case, the complainant lost his business because the government changed the rules concerning French investment in foreign countries. The court held that '[i]n view of the purpose for which the legislation has been established, the regulations lawfully issued pursuant to this legislation *shall not imply the liability of the administration*'.[410]

More recently, the *Conseil d'Etat* did not automatically exclude the claim and considered whether the damage was special and abnormal. It held that even a legal measure may imply government liability. In one case, though, the claimants did not prove that the prejudice was 'certain',[411] and in another the court affirmed that changes in food regulation were one of the normal risks for any slaughterhouse business;[412] thus, even when the damage existed, it was not abnormal.

In the case of FJ, the company faces a lawful administrative measure that causes certain damage: the loss of profits during the block. Moreover, we can reasonably suppose that the new set of rules seriously increases import costs. As FJ is the only importer from Blefuscu Island, the damage is special. It remains to be seen whether it is abnormal. In French case law, damage is 'abnormal' if it is serious and exceptional,

406 CE 22 February 1963 *Commune de Gavarnie* No 50438, Rec 113.

407 Hennette-Vauchez (n 404) s 13.

408 CE 30 June 1999 *Foucher* No 190038, Lebon 232; RFDA 1999 1210, concl Bergeal.

409 See Art R 611-7 of the Code of Administrative Justice.

410 CE 8 January 1960 *Laiterie Saint-Cyprien* No 39760, Lebon 10; CE 16 November 1960 *Secr d'État aux Affaires économiques c Sté d'exploitation des chantiers d'Ajaccio* No 09688, Lebon 621; CE 24 October 1984 *Société Claude Publicité* No 40204; CE 23 December 1988 *Martin et Sté Michel Martin*, Lebon 470.

411 CE 28 July 1995 *Société des Etablissements 'Lefebvre' Frère Soeur and others* No 126728.

412 CE 22 February 2002 *M Ml* No 224809.

beyond the normal risks of a business. In the case of the block, the measure is temporally limited to one month, which is the reason why it would not be considered serious damage unless additional special circumstances existed (ie this is the only month of the cranberry season). The courts should also consider whether the damage is the consequence of a normal risk related to the business model[413] or if it was a risk acknowledged by the company when it started the activity.[414] In our case, FJ knew that the fruit grows near a nuclear power plant and was aware of the risks associated with radiation. FJ also knows that conditions and restrictions to import are government prerogatives, especially when related to phytosanitary measures and human health. Therefore, a regulatory change that increases the business costs would probably be considered a normal risk for FJ. FJ would not thus have much chance of receiving any compensation.

D. Germany

FW and JS

Again, this case raises the issue of the primacy of primary legal protection. Here, FJ must challenge two measures, the block and the new testing rules.

If these measures were taken as regulations on the federal level, they could be subject to legal review under § 43 VwGO, which stipulates that '[t]he establishment of the […] non-existence of a legal relationship […] may be requested by means of an action if the claimant has a justified interest in the establishment being made soon (action for a declaratory judgment)'[415]. FJ would thus have to bring an action to have the legal relationship between it and the public authorities declared as not being governed by the regulations.[416] However, this would be possible only if the regulation directly creates duties for FJ,[417] thereby constituting a self-executing provision.[418] If an administrative act or decision enforcing these measures were necessary,[419] one could argue that FJ would have to wait for an implementation of the measures, which could then be challenged.[420] However, with regard to the general block of all imports for one month, a direct duty for FJ (not to import the fruit) is established. With regard to the testing rules, there is no information about who is obliged

[413] CE 19 February 1988 *Société Robatel* No 51456 concerning the international commerce of nuclear material.

[414] CE 16 June 1997 *Société arboricole et fruitière de l'Agenais* No 161900.

[415] See the English version <www.gesetze-im-internet.de/englisch_vwgo/englisch_vwgo.html> accessed 22 June 2020. A constitutional complaint (Art 93 para 1 number 4a GG) is possible only if all legal remedies have been exhausted, see Art 94 para 2 sentence 2 GG, s 90 para 2 BVerfGG (*Bundesverfassungsgerichtsg esetz* (Act on the Federal Constitutional Court), English version <www.gesetze-im-internet.de/englisch_bverfgg/englisch_bverfgg.html#p0399> accessed 22 June 2020). This also extends to the declaratory action under s 43 VwGO, BVerfG (1st chamber) 18 October 2004—1 BvR 2057/02, BVerfGK 4, 113 (114).

[416] cf BVerfG (1st chamber) 18 October 2004—1 BvR 2057/02, BVerfGK 4, 113 (114); cf in general JP Terhechte, '§ 43 VwGO' in Fehling and others (n 53) para 18.

[417] BVerwG 28 January 2010—8 C 19/09, BVerwGE 136, 54 (60).

[418] Terhechte (n 416) para 18; cf JF Lindner, *Öffentliches Recht in Bayern* (2nd edn, Boorberg 2017) para 1230.

[419] cf Terhechte (n 416) para 18.

[420] cf ibid; Lindner, *Öffentliches Recht* (n 418) paras 815, 1229.

to implement these. If they address the companies directly, a direct duty would be established. If this was not the case, FJ would have to wait for the administrative implementation and could then try to challenge the individual measures. Since the questionnaire explicitly states that FJ 'challenges the block and the new rules', this will be assumed for the subsequent considerations. FJ should also ask for an interim order (§ 123 para 1 sentence 1 VwGO).[421]

Legal standing (§ 42 para 2 VwGO by analogy)[422] requires that an infringement of a subjective right may not be ruled out.[423] FJ may invoke its occupational freedom (Art 12 para 1 GG), which also applies to legal persons (§ 19 para 3 GG),[424] and which might be impaired. Moreover, an equality issue may arise (Art 3 para 1 GG). Furthermore, an interest in the declaratory judgment is necessary (§ 43 para 1 VwGO);[425] *in casu*, this follows from FJ's economic interest in not being subject to the block and the new rules for testing.

With regard to standing, it has to be highlighted that—unlike under EU law, for instance (see Art 263 para 4 TFEU and the Plaumann formula)—challenging legislative acts such as a regulation by an individual does not depend on a specific individualization of the claimant; (potential) interference with subjective rights of the claimant is sufficient, even if the claimant is affected in the same way as all the other addressees of the legislative act.

Regarding the merits, it has to be established that the legal relationship between FJ and the public authorities is not governed by the regulations.[426] This would be the case if the measures either lacked a legal basis or if they were formally or substantively unlawful and infringed on of the claimant's individual rights.[427] Legal bases could be found in § 56 paras 1 and 2 LFGB[428]. which authorize certain measures by the Ministry of Food and Agriculture to guarantee food safety.

With regard to the substantive prerequisites, the legal bases stipulate among other things that the measures must be necessary to prevent or to defend against a hazard to human health. This can be seen in radiation originating from a nuclear power plant. However, the measure must be necessary to prevent or defend against the hazard. Defending against a hazard is permissible even before the actual existence of a danger.[429] Even in situations where scientific evidence of a hazard does not exist, preventing measures may be taken under the precautionary principle.[430]

421 See Wollenschläger '§ 123' (n 377) paras 15, 78f.

422 The necessity of an analogous application of 42 para 2 VwGO is disputed, but the courts uphold this requirement; cf BVerwG 29 June 1995—2 C 32/94, BVerwGE 99, 64 (66). See H Gersdorf, *Verwaltungsprozessrecht* (6th edn, CF Müller 2019) para 120.

423 RP Schenke, '§ 42' in FO Kopp and WR Schenke (eds), *Verwaltungsgerichtsordnung* (26th edn, CH Beck 2020) para 78.

424 J Wieland, 'Art 12' in Dreier, *Grundgesetz Kommentar*, vol 1 (n 218) para 56 with further references.

425 BVerwG 26 January 1996—8 C 19/94, BVerwGE 100, 262 (271).

426 cf BVerfG (1st chamber) 18 October 2004—1 BvR 2057/02, BVerfGK 4, 113 (114).

427 cf Terhechte (n 416) para 37.

428 Under German law, the case would be governed by s 56 of the *Lebensmittel-, Bedarfsgegenstände- und Futtermittelgesetzbuch* (Food, Consumer Goods and Feed Act), German version <www.gesetze-im-internet.de/lfgb/BJNR261810005.html> accessed 22 June 2020.

429 K-D Rathke, '§ 1' in W Zipfel and K-D Rathke (eds), Lebensmittelrecht (175th edn, CH Beck November 2019) para 14.

430 ibid para 15, pointing out Art 7 of Regulation (EC) 178/2002 of the European Parliament and of the Council of 28 January 2002 laying down the general principles and requirements of food law, establishing

Regarding fundamental rights, FJ's freedom of occupation (Art 12 para 1 GG) might be impaired by the measures, at least by the block of imports.[431] The reason for this is that FJ is the only importer and its imports are thus easy to supervise. As long as it is justified to address the measures to the actual addressees of the regulation (ie because a risk results from these products), no equality issue arises. Thus, the right to equality (Art 3 para 1 GG) is not violated.[432]

While the individualization of FJ is immaterial to standing (see above), it raises a substantive issue, as the regulations might breach Article 19 paragraph 1 sentence 1 GG, which stipulates: 'Insofar as, under this Basic Law, a basic right may be restricted by or pursuant to a law, such law must apply generally and not merely to a single case.'[433] The term 'law' is construed narrowly, thereby covering only a formal (ie parliamentary) law.[434] Hence, it does not apply to a regulation. Moreover, even if applied, the regulation does not explicitly name FJ, but is only *de facto* limited to it in its effects. Situations where a 'provision is [...] abstractly worded and referenced to a number of enterprises that cannot be conclusively fixed when the provision is issued'[435] do not violate Article 19 paragraph 1 sentence 1 GG in the context of formal law, and a 'disguised' individual measure can only be assumed where 'future cases of application can be ruled out from the outset'[436].

Depending on the assessment in terms of substance, the court may find that the legal relationship between FJ and the public authorities of Terranova is or is not governed by the regulation with regard to the block of imports.

With regard to damages under the general rules on public authority liability, the situation of FJ corresponds to the situation of North Lake in case 5. If only the block of imports is regarded as not governing the legal relationship between FJ and the public authorities of Terranova, FJ could claim damages only for the effects arising from the block, but not from the new set of testing rules. Moreover, in view of the exclusion contained in § 839 paragraph 3 BGB (see above), a claim for damages is only possible with regard to damages not avertable by a remedy, notably because they occurred

the European Food Safety Authority and laying down procedures in matters of food safety, [2002] OJ L31/9, which says in number 1:

> In specific circumstances where, following an assessment of available information, the possibility of harmful effects on health is identified but scientific uncertainty persists, provisional risk management measures necessary to ensure the high level of health protection chosen in the Community may be adopted, pending further scientific information for a more comprehensive risk assessment.

Cf also T Boch, *Lebensmittel- und Futtermittelgesetzbuch* (8th online edn, Nomos 2019) s 1 para 2.

[431] As to the applicable standard for a justification, see BVerfG 9 June 2004—1 BvR 636/02, BVerfGE 111, 10 (32); cf Wieland 'Art 12' (n 424) para 99.

[432] As to the relation between Art 3 para 1 and Art 19 GG para 1 sentence 1, see F Wollenschläger, 'Art 3' in H von Mangoldt and others (eds), *Grundgesetz*, vol 1 (7th edn, CH Beck 2018) para 166.

[433] See the English version <www.gesetze-im-internet.de/englisch_gg/englisch_gg.html#p0112> accessed 22 June 2020.

[434] B Remmert, 'Art 19 Abs 1' in T Maunz and G Dürig (eds), *Grundgesetz Kommentar* (52nd edn, CH Beck May 2008) para 26; M Sachs, 'Art 19' in M Sachs (ed), *Grundgesetz Kommentar* (8th edn, CH Beck 2018) para 14.

[435] BVerfG 2 March 1999—1 BvL 2/91, BVerfGE 99, 367 (400).

[436] BVerfG 2 March 1999—1 BvL 2/91, BVerfGE 99, 367 (400); cf also H Dreier, 'Art 19' in Dreier, *Grundgesetz Kommentar*, vol 1 (n 218) para 13.

before an order for interim relief was available, and/or in the case of an unsuccessful court action, ie if the administrative court rejects the injunction or holds FJ's action in the main proceedings unfounded. In the latter situation, the issue arises as to whether the civil court hearing the subsequent liability case is bound by the administrative judiciary's decisions (see case 5).

The key issue in terms of liability is whether the legislator is able to breach an official duty intended to protect specific individuals. For, according to the orthodox position, legislation implies rule-making for an indeterminate number of persons and situations and is thus widely understood as taking place not in the individual, but in the general interest.[437] This assumption extends to executive rule-making, particularly to executive regulations.[438] Other commentators draw attention to the fact that the breached norm—like fundamental rights—may confer individual rights which must be decisive.[439] At any rate, an exception is made in cases where an act/regulation concerns a limited number of addressees who, consequently, might be regarded as a sufficiently delimitable circle of persons with regard to whom the legislator has acted.[440]

Turning to our case, as discussed before, the regulation did not constitute a 'disguised' individual measure, since it cannot be ruled out that other importers of 'fruits of the forest'—for example not importing from the Blefuscu Island, which the block does not seem to be limited to—exist. Moreover,[441] even if one accepted liability for acts of the legislator, it might—as the example of EU law, requiring such a liability also in the national context, demonstrates—be difficult to establish fault (intention/negligence) on the part of the legislator.[442]

If one assumed a breach of duty, the rules shown in case 2 would apply with regard to lost profit and its determination.

If FJ is entitled to damages at all, these are likely to be limited to damage arising from the block, since at least the new testing rules are lawful and the enactment of the regulation did not breach an official duty intended to protect third parties. A final decision, however, would require more information.

E. Hungary

LB

In this case, the claim is likely to be unsuccessful. A preliminary remark must be made with regard to judicial review: the ordinary court has no jurisdiction on deciding whether a legal regulation is an individual or general measure: only the Constitutional Court (CCt) can decide that an act or regulation is in fact an individual

[437] BGH 10 December 1987—III ZR 220/86, BGHZ 102, 350 (367ff); 24 October 1996—III ZR 127/91, BGHZ 134, 30 (32). See also Maurer and Waldhoff (n 222) § 26 para 53.

[438] See the cases listed in n 437 and C Dörr, '§ 839' in Gsell and others (n 69) para 291; Papier and Shirvani (n 141) para 260 (differentiating). See also Ossenbühl and Cornils (n 145) 108.

[439] cf Maurer and Waldhoff (n 222) § 26 para 53.

[440] BGH 10 December 1987—III ZR 220/86, BGHZ 102, 350 (367f).

[441] In addition, it is discussed whether the (parliamentary) legislator exercises a public office within the meaning of Art 34 GG, disagreeing with Maurer and Waldhoff (n 222) § 26 para 53.

[442] Maurer and Waldhoff (n 222) § 26 para 53.

measure and can annul that act or regulation as unconstitutional. There are two ways to do this. First, the court can suspend its procedure and submit a petition to the CCt for a declaration that the legal regulation or a provision thereof is contrary to the Fundamental Law, and/or the exclusion of the application of the legal regulation contrary to the Fundamental Law. Second, the claimant may initiate the proceedings of the CCt if the infringement is due to the application of a legal provision contrary to the Fundamental Law, or when, in the event that a legal provision becomes effective, rights were violated directly without a judicial decision, and there is no procedure for a legal remedy to repair the violation of the rights, or the petitioner has already exhausted the possibilities for obtaining a remedy. If the CCt annuls the legal regulation, even if the annulment is not *ex tunc*, judicial practice considers that the regulation was *ab ovo* an individual decision, which was born as a result of dysfunctional operation, and this dysfunctional operation can be considered as a basis for awarding damages. A further question is whether the damage caused by the legislation can be investigated: the judicial practice before the new Act on the CC argued that there is no civil law relationship between the legislator and the aggrieved party. However, the import ban was based on the Regulation, so even if it were an individual decision, it is not an infringement, and there is no culpability: the safety concerns alone justify the restriction.

F. Italy

FC

First of all, it can be said that, in Italy, FJ could start by challenging the legitimacy of the administrative measure. The fact that the measure, although general in scope, essentially only damages FJ's position, allows FJ itself to turn to an administrative court to have it repealed.

It is not easy, however, to predict the outcome of this appeal, since the law grants the authority broad discretional powers on matters such as this, allowing it, in accordance with the precautionary principle, to act even when there is no consolidated scientific certainty regarding the real and present danger of the circulation and ingestion of certain food products.[443] It is also important to consider that the timeline of the block on imports is not particularly long, and might even be considered adequate and proportional to the (provisional) need for protection that the authority has put forward, and that the authority's discretion is very powerful even, generally speaking, with regard to providing for new operational rules, to be applied in all future cases.

The compensation is difficult to determine.

According to the most prevalent interpretation, if the block is lawful, no other damages would be acknowledged.

[443] It should be noted that in this case the private applicant could ask the court to adopt interim measures, eg the suspension of the block. But the court could also consider the protection of fundamental rights to prevail and dismiss the appeal for suspension.

It is also important to note that, in Italian law, there is no agreement on the hypothesis of damages 'due to a not wrongful act', resulting, as in the specific case, from the adoption of an action that is lawful but causes 'unjustified' financial loss to FJ.

On the other hand, if the (positive) case law of the CJEU could hypothetically be applied to these types of damages,[444] it would be easy to ascertain that they would be recoverable only as a consequence of 'abnormal risk'. And it is difficult to argue that the risk usually faced by an importer of food products from an area of the planet known to host a considerable number of nuclear power plants is such.

G. Poland

Katarzyna Chojecka

The case study concerns the Feed and Food Regulation issued by the so-called governmental administration FJ, incurring certain economic losses as its ability to conduct business activity was restricted, and it now wishes to seek damages. It can only do so in a civil law litigation, not in an administrative one.

For the reasons that will be indicated in detail, the following requirements must be fulfilled if the claim is to be successful. First, issuing the act must have contravened the Constitution, a ratified international treaty or a statute. A court will consider the act unlawful, but this unlawfulness will be considered normative or constitutional. Second, the existence of the damage must be ascertained. Third, a causal link between the unlawful act of the public authority and existing damage must exist.

As regards the legal basis, according to Article 417[1] section 1 CC, if damage was inflicted as a result of issuing a normative act, redress can be sought after that act is deemed to contravene the Constitution, a ratified international treaty, or a statute upon conclusion of relevant proceedings. The entities responsible would be the State Treasury, a local government, or a legal person wielding public authority under the law. In simple terms, this Article states that in order to seek damages from public authorities one must first obtain a ruling in a separate process to the effect that the incriminated act is contrary to the Constitution, a ratified international treaty, or a statute. Such ruling is referred to as *preiudicatio*. A *preiudicatio* is not required where damages are sought on the grounds of non-compliance with the EU law of a normative act. In this respect, the courts in their judicial practice[445] and legal commentaries[446] take consistent views. However, with respect to the case at hand, I would like to focus on the option of alleged inconsistency of the 'Feed and Food Regulation' with domestic law. Otherwise, in the case of inconsistency with EU law, the inconsistency would be examined and resolved by the court examining the lawsuit for damages, most probably after first enquiring about *preiudicatio*.

[444] Joined Cases C-120/06 P and C-121/06 P, *Fiamm and Fedon v Council and Commission* [2008] ECR I-6513, Grand Chamber 9 September 2008.

[445] Supreme Court, judgment of 19 June 2013.

[446] J Gudowski 'Komentarz do art 417[1]' in J Gudowski (ed), *Kodeks Cywilny* (Wolters Kluwer 2018).

With regard to the existence of the damage and the assessment of liability, the following questions must be addressed:

(1) Which court is competent to hand down a ruling that will serve as *preiudicatio*? Since the regulation is neither an act of domestic law nor an act issued by a local government, the competent court will be the Constitutional Tribunal.
(2) Did the Constitutional Tribunal in its ruling on unlawfulness specify a date as of which the challenged normative act would become ineffective and whether it ruled out the liability of the State Treasury? In a Resolution, the Supreme Court stated that an assertion of unlawfulness of a legal act does not itself constitute a basis for awarding damages.[447] The Constitutional Tribunal may, in its ruling, preclude such liability in advance.
(3) Is seeking damages even possible, notwithstanding the binding force of the questioned act/provision? A ruling of the Constitutional Tribunal has the effect of eliminating the unlawful norm from legal dealings. On the other hand, if the Constitutional Tribunal specifies a date from which the norm will cease to bind, then seeking damages will not be possible because the existing legal environment is (and also the future legal environment will be) deemed fully lawful.
(4) Have the other requirements concerning the damages been satisfied? If the Constitutional Tribunal indeed rules that the norm (the Feed and Food Regulation in the contemplated case) will contravene (for instance) the Constitution, a lawsuit initiated before an ordinary court will involve an assessment of such factors as the lawfulness of actions of the public authority, the existence of actual damage, and the existence of a causal link between the unlawfulness of the act and the damage. The point here is not to establish whether the economic interests of the entity seeking damages suffered as a result of the issuance of the act, but rather whether the damage was caused by some specific actions of the public authority.
(5) How will the amount of the damage be established? Under Polish law, damage means the difference between the injured party's present economic condition and the condition that would exist had the event which caused damage not occurred.[448] There are two forms of damage: *damnum emergens*—the actual diminishment of the injured party's property; and *lucrum* cessans—loss of benefits, a hypothetical one. It is the injured party's responsibility to prove the damage; therefore in the contemplated case, FJ will have to corroborate beyond reasonable doubt that it indeed incurred damage.

A twofold conclusion may be drawn from this. First, it will only be possible to seek damages before an ordinary court if the Constitutional Tribunal clearly rules that the challenged regulations will become ineffective as of a specific date in the future, the past environment will be deemed lawful, and it will not be possible to pursue damages

[447] Resolution of 7 December 2007 III CZP 125/2007.
[448] Supreme Court 11 July 1957 2 CR 304/57.

before ordinary courts. Second, the damages can only be adjudged under certain conditions: the damage must be defined, a causal link proved etc, as mentioned above. If these conditions are fulfilled, the damages will be determined in accordance with the general rules: it may include lost benefits, but proving such losses may be difficult. Such damage is of a hypothetical nature and does not include any potential damage (chances to obtain benefits), and the burden of proof will rest with the claimant.

H. Romania

RV

FJ's claim for damages would only be admissible if a prior action for annulment were successful before Romania's administrative courts. The action for damages is therefore not admissible independently of an annulment claim. FJ would first need to argue and prove before a national court that Terranova's measures are discriminatory and that they directly impede access to the internal market and therefore breach Article 34 of the TFEU/Article 7 of the EEA.[449]

Furthermore, for its claim for annulment to be admissible, Terranova would have to prove that the illegal measure breaches its personal interest. In Romanian law, claims for annulment brought for the protection of a general interest are inadmissible. FJ would therefore have to argue before a national administrative court that the block and the measures violate the Treaty/Agreement provisions and that the compensation due to FJ is damage stemming directly from the breach of the Treaty.

Therefore, an action for damages for breach of EU law is available, but it is limited by its dependency on the claim for annulment of the illegal act. If the measures are found to be illegal and the administrative act is annulled, FJ would be entitled to compensation for all the damage suffered, including the lost profit. The principle applicable is that of integral reparation of the prejudice, which is a civil law principle, but applicable nonetheless to administrative liability in the absence of more specific provisions in administrative law.

We have identified no instance in Romanian case law where an action for damages for breach of EU law was judged by applying the core conditions of State liability, determined by the CJEU in its *Francovich/Brasserie du Pécheur/Kobler* line of cases. This CJEU case law is often invoked by Romanian courts as an argument in favour of the need to grant and recognize access to effective judicial protection to those who have suffered loss because of a breach of EU law, but the conditions for liability that they apply are those stipulated under national law.[450] Romanian law guarantees full compensation for the loss incurred and does not impose specific restrictions such as misfeasance or proof of fraud, or the impossibility of recovering loss of profit.

[449] According to Art 7 of the EEA, 'Quantitative restrictions on imports and exports, and all measures having equivalent effect, shall be prohibited between the Member States.' The text of Art 35 TFEU is identical, and so are the texts on the exceptions to this prohibition: Art 36 TFEU.

[450] See eg Decision No 1639 of the Cluj Court of Appeal, and Decision 2149/R/2009 of the Cluj Court of Appeal, and Decision 2745/2012 issued by the Suceava Court of Appeal, all unpublished.

I. Spain

EMNG

Since the damage suffered by FJ is caused by the block and the new rules, a case for damages is admissible whether the court declares the contested measures void or no. FJ may therefore challenge the block and the new rules before a Terranova court (eg for lack of proportionality or because measures are producing a special sacrifice to FJ), and, at the same time, also claim compensation for damages caused by the contested administrative decision.

Although the court would declare the measures legal, FJ should claim a compensation, because those are a special sacrifice for FJ. Spanish Constitutional Court has recognised recently the special sacrifice as a base to claim compensation for administrative measures (Sentencia del Tribunal Constitucional 85/2019, de 19 de junio).

Damages will cover lost profit, which can be calculated by considering the average earnings that FJ obtains at that time of year.

J. Switzerland

TT

It should be stressed, concerning this case, that Switzerland is not a member of the EEA, whose rules will thus not apply. There are, however, several agreements between Switzerland and the EU pertaining to agricultural products that may have a bearing on the lawfulness of the litigated ban, provided that Terranova is a member not only of the EEA but also of the EU.

The kind of measure described in this case would be taken in Switzerland through a so-called 'decision of general scope' ('*decision de portée générale*'), which would be subject, firstly to an objection procedure and, second, to an appeal before the FAT.[451] Failure to object and eventually to appeal would preclude FJ to claim damages.

The liability of the Confederation would be governed by the GLA. As for all decisions, to be deemed unlawful within the meaning of the GLA, the decision to ban importation for a month and to impose testing for exposure to radiation should have been taken in breach of a fundamental duty. In view of the arguments made by FJ and the precautionary principle enshrined in Article 22 FSA, this criterion would probably not be met, even if, on appeal by FJ, the ban were quashed by the FAT. Therefore there is very little chance that, even if FJ were successful in an appeal against the measure, it would be awarded damages.

In the unlikely event that damages were awarded, their amount would be calculated so as to order to attain full compensation for the harm caused by the measures. Lost profit would not be excluded; it is related to natural and adequate causation with the measures.

[451] See Arts 67–71 of the Foodstuffs Act 2014 (FSA).

K. United Kingdom

GA

The principal questions that have been asked in this case appear to concern matters of procedural law, and might be answered in the following way:

(1) The premise of the scenario is that loss has been occasioned by the exercise of discretion under the Feed and Food Regulation. Plainly, in that instance, FJ would first wish to establish that the exercise of discretion was tainted by a public law illegality, and it would do so by bringing an application for judicial review to seek a quashing order (which would annul the decision as *void ab initio*). If successful on that point, FJ could also seek damages within the judicial review proceedings, where, as has been explained at comment (h) at the beginning of Chapter 13, it would be able to do so only where the facts would be actionable in private law. The most likely causes of action here would be for negligence and/or breach of statutory duty, though there might also be a claim for a breach of FJ's rights under the Human Rights Act 1998 (where it might be possible to raise a point under Art 1 of Protocol 1 ECHR). In the event that the judicial review judge considered that the matters relating to damages were self-evident, he or she could deal with the matter within the judicial review proceedings. In the event that he or she considered that the matters required further evidence, he or she might order that the case be transferred to the branch of the High Court that hears tort claims (see comment (j) at the beginning of Chapter 13).

(2) It is also possible that FJ might simply bring a private law action seeking damages (ie forego a judicial review challenge), though there may be procedural difficulties in doing so. An obvious difficulty might arise from the choice of procedure: the defendant ministry would argue that the private law claim ultimately concerns a matter of public law and that an application for judicial review should first have been brought to challenge the legality of the ministry's decision. If the court were to be attracted to that argument, a second procedural difficulty might concern time limits—while there is a three-year time limit for private law actions, applications for judicial review should normally be brought within three months of the impugned decision having been taken.

(3) Would a claim for damages succeed if one were brought in a procedurally acceptable manner? This is difficult to assess. On the one hand, a successful application for judicial review on the second of the grounds noted might point towards breach of a duty of care, whether that duty is found in the law of negligence and/or some statute on the law of undertakings. However, the fact that the impugned decisions were taken for reasons of public health might also be said to point away from liability. The point here is about the breach of a duty of care, where the courts ask whether the actions or inactions of a defendant have fallen beneath an objectively 'reasonable' standard. The government might here argue that its motivation in making the measures was entirely reasonable, and that it acted on limited information given the urgency of the situation. This is a point that would probably gain some traction in the context of a negligence

claim, while its strength in any claim for breach of statutory duty would depend on whether the statute was read as imposing strict liability on the defendant ministry.

(4) On the assumption that damages would be payable, the approach to quantum would depend on evidence of actual and projected loss that could presented to the court (there is no suggestion on the given facts that the ministry has acted arbitrarily, so exemplary damages would not be appropriate—see comment (m) at the beginning of Chapter 13). The applicable principles that would govern any award would start with the understanding that damages should seek to put the plaintiff back in the position that it would have been in it had it not suffered the wrong in question. In a case of this kind, the court would consider actual loss and projected loss, at least to the extent that the latter can be measured with reference to the suffered wrong. Claims for speculative damages or 'loss of chance' are typically more difficult to sustain, at least in negligence actions (on 'loss of chance' in contractual cases see case 4 above).

(5) One further comment concerns the possibility that the government might make an *ex gratia* payment of compensation to FJ (see the beginning of Chapter 13). As noted at point (3) above, the measures in question have been taken for reasons of protecting public health, where government schemes will often make provision for the voluntary payment of compensation to affected undertakings. While there is no indication that any such compensation has been contemplated here, the existence of such compensation can often remove the need for legal proceedings to claim damages. In the absence of such compensation, FJ would be left with only the options that are outlined above.

To recap: FJ would likely challenge the ministry's decisions by way of an application for judicial review and include within that a claim for damages. Whether a damages claim would succeed is unclear but, if it did, the court would approach quantum by trying to put FJ back in the position it would have been had it not been for the government wrong. Legal proceedings would probably be unnecessary were there to be a scheme for the *ex gratia* payment of compensation.

VIII. Case 7—a licence withdrawal *inaudita altera parte*

Ms Tramp has a licence to sell newspapers and maps in a kiosk. The licensing authority decides to withdraw her licence because it intends to renew the offer of such services, but gives her no opportunity to be heard. Ms Tramp challenges the withdrawal before a court, arguing that the decision was taken in breach of duties of fairness and rationality in decision-making, and asks for damages.

Would the national court endorse Ms Tramp's argument only if a specific requirement to hear affected parties has been laid down by legislation for this type of administrative procedure, or would it use general principles of law such as fairness or due process? And would the court be satisfied to ascertain the existence of a procedural wrong, or would it also consider whether the licensing authority was in breach of rationality? In either case, would Ms Tramp's action be successful? Is annulment a precondition for awarding damages? And would damages cover lost profit?

A. Austria

SS, KB, DB, and LM

It is necessary to register to sell newspapers and maps pursuant to the Austrian Commercial Code (GewO).[452] This is because this activity is conducted independently, regularly, and aims to generate income, regardless of how this income is intended to be used.[453] Once registered, the competent public authority may prohibit Ms Tramp's commercial activity only under the substantive circumstances laid down in the GewO.[454]

The procedural issue of whether Ms Tramp has the right to be heard in relation to the prohibition of her commercial activity is regulated in the AVG. The AVG is, in principle applicable, to all administrative procedures, including the prohibition of the respective commercial activity under the GewO.[455] The AVG guarantees, inter alia, the right of a person who has an interest of a legal nature in administrative proceedings—such as the prohibition of Ms Tramp's commercial activity—to be a party to them.[456]

As already pointed out in detail in section II.A, the right to be heard is of crucial importance in administrative proceedings. Since Ms Tramp was not granted the opportunity to inspect the files, to be heard, and to issue a statement concerning the prohibition of her commercial activity, her 'right to be heard' has been infringed.

The competent VwG will base its judgment regarding the infringement of Ms Tramp's 'right to be heard' primarily on existing legislation, and hence endorse

[452] Gewerbeordnung 1994—GewO 1994, Federal Law Gazette No I 314/1994 as amended.
[453] §1(1) GewO.
[454] The conditions for the prohibition of the commercial activity are laid down in §§ 87, 88, and 361(1) GewO.
[455] Pursuant to Art 1(1)(2) No 1 Introductory Act to the Administrative Procedure Acts 2008 (*Einführungsgesetz zu den Verwaltungsverfahrensgesetzen* 2008—EGVG), Federal Law Gazette No I 87/2008 as amended.
[456] § 8 AVG.

Ms Tramp's arguments without using general principles. However, the aforementioned existing legislation securing the 'right to be heard' is qualified as a fundamental principle of administrative proceedings.[457]

Due to the VfGH's restrictive interpretation of the notion of civil rights pursuant to Article 6 ECHR,[458] the prohibition of commercial activity pursuant to the GewO does not fall within the scope of Article 6 ECHR. Hence the prohibition procedure needs to adhere only to the general constitutional requirements for an administrative procedure governed by the rule of law.[459] Without the AVG, the constitutional principle of the rule of law would have been relevant. According to the established case law of the VfGH, the efficiency of legal protection—which encompasses safeguarding the 'right to be heard'—constitutes a core element of the principle of the rule of law,[460] which would be infringed if a party to administrative proceedings is denied the right to be heard.

A negligent infringement of the 'right to be heard' is classified as a procedural error that may be enforced via the appropriate legal remedy.[461] As already pointed out in section II.A, the competent VwG has two main options under the VwGVG: it may issue a judgment on the merits[462] or annul the decision of the public authority and refer it back to renew its decision.[463] Issuing a merits judgment—even if this requires carrying out further investigation on its own—is deemed to be the rule; annulling and referring back should be the exception.[464] Therefore, the competent VwG is obliged to grant Ms Tramp the 'right to be heard', summon her before the court for this purpose, and give her the opportunity to issue a statement. The procedural error may be restored by guaranteeing her the right to be heard during the proceedings before the VwG and through its judgment. Ms Tramp's action will thus be successful.

If the VwG does not uphold the claim regarding the procedural error and does not grant Ms Tramp the 'right to be heard', its judgment may be appealed against at the VwGH. The VwGH may not restore the infringement of the 'right to be heard' itself. If the VwG has failed to 'hear' Ms Tramp, the VwGH may only annul its judgment and refer the case back to the VwG to renew the judgment, adhering to the binding legal opinion of the VwGH.[465]

If the 'right to be heard' is deliberately and arbitrarily infringed, therefore in a qualified manner, this is not only considered to be a procedural error, but is also a breach of

[457] For the established case law of the VwGH, see only VwGH 18 October 2001, 2000/07/0003; 26 May 2008, 2005/06/0024; 8 April 2014, 2012/05/0004; 20 December 2017, Ra 2017/03/0069.

[458] VfGH 13 December 1988 B 1450/88 (Withdrawal of a pharmarcy licence); 16 June 1990 B 1225/89–B 1229/89 (Prohibition of a commercial activity pursuant to the Commercial Code); 2 July 1993 G 226/92 (Prohibition of the employment of foreigners).

[459] VfGH 15 October 2004 G 237/03.

[460] VfGH 13 March 1991 G 199/90; 16 June 1999 G 56/99; 15 October 2004 G 237/03.

[461] The respective legal remedy is the '*Bescheidbeschwerde*' under Art 130(1) No 1, 132(1) No 1 B-VG.

[462] Art 28(2) VwGVG.

[463] Art 28(3) VwGVG.

[464] This is the settled case law of the VwGH; see only VwGH 26 June 2014; Ro 2014/03/0063; 24 June 2015; Ra 2015/04/0019.

[465] § 42(2) Z 3 lit c Supreme Administrative Court Act (*Verwaltungsgerichtshofgesetz*—VwGG), Federal Law Gazette No 10/1985 as amended.

the constitutionally guaranteed right of equality before the law.[466] Against such a qualified infringement of 'the right to be heard' caused by a judgment of the VwG, a legal remedy may be lodged with the VfGH; this is not admissible for judgments handed down by the VwGH.[467]

The actual annulment of the decision prohibiting Ms Tramp's commercial activity does constitute a precondition for bringing an action claiming public authority liability. The district court may not independently accept the unlawfulness of the decision, finding, or order (§ 11(1) AHG).

Another decisive condition which needs to be met when bringing an action for public authority liability is that the legal remedies provided by the legal order must have been pursued unsuccessfully. Public authority liability under the AHG has a subsidiary character and is only permissible if the existing legal remedies were not able to prevent the occurrence of the damage.[468] Therefore Ms Tramp has to appeal against the prohibition before the VwG. If the procedural error is not remedied by the VwG, she will have to appeal against its decision—depending on the gravity of the infringement of the 'right to be heard'—before the VwGH or the VfGH. Only after filing those last-resort legal remedies unsuccessfully will she be eligible to bring an action for public authority liability before the competent civil court.[469]

As already pointed out in section II.A, the extent of public authority liability under the AHG is determined by the degree of fault pursuant to the provisions of Austrian civil law.[470] According to the ABGB, lost profit due to an unlawful action by a civil servant public authority may only be claimed if it has been conducted deliberately (with intent) or grossly negligent.[471] The notion of lost profit comprises the prevention of a hypothetical chance to generate income which, indeed, may be expected in the normal course of matters,[472] providing that its realization is not virtually certain.[473] However, the loss of a chance to generate income is classified as actual damage if the injured party's position has already been legally secured, for instance on the basis of a valid contract or a binding offer.[474]

[466] Pursuant to Art 7 B-VG. This view is shared also by the VfGH, see only VfGH 11 March 1998 B 2287/97.

[467] Pursuant to Art 144(1) B-VG.

[468] § 2(2) AHG; for the established case law of the OGH see, for instance, OGH 21 February 1990 = ecolex 1990, 607 (Kletečka); 30 January 1996 = ecolex 1996, 597 (Kletečka); see also W Schragel, *Kommentar zum Amtshaftungsgesetz* (3rd edn, Manz 2003) s 2 para 182; H Ziehensack, *Amtshaftungsgesetz—Praxiskommentar* (LexisNexis 2011) s 1 para 158ff.

[469] Pursuant to § 9(1) AHG.

[470] § 1(1) AHG; for the established case law of the OGH see, for instance, OGH 23 November 2004 1 Ob 298/03k; 10 August 2010 1 Ob 114/10m; 27 February 2014 1 Ob 222/13y.

[471] § 1324 CC; see also R Reischauer, '§ 1324' in P Rummel (ed), ABGB (3rd edn, Manz 2004) para 10ff; M Hinteregger, '§ 1324' in A Kletečka and M Schauer (eds), ABGB-ON$^{1.03}$ (version of 1 July, rdb.at) (Manz 2016) para 11.

[472] OGH 15 September 2005, 4 Ob 74/05v; 22 May 2007, 4 Ob 79/07g; Kodek (n 12) para 16.

[473] OGH 24 June 1992, 1 Ob 15/92; OGH 1 July 2004, 1 Ob 173/03b; Reischauer '§ 1293' in Rummel (n 471) para 8.

[474] OGH 28 April 2000, 2 Ob 82/00y; 30 August 2007, 2 Ob 268/06k; 27 July 2017, 2 Ob 142/17x; Reischauer '§ 1293' in Rummel (n 471) para 7.

B. European Union

BM

The right to be heard is one of the general principles affirmed in the Court of Justice case law[475] and laid down in Article 41 of the Charter of Fundamental Rights of the EU.[476] Its validity in EU law is undoubted even when no specific rule prescribes it in relation to a specific administrative action. In particular, it applies when the administration adopts an unfavourable decision towards a private party, which is what happens in this case, where the authority withdraws a decision that had previously conferred a right to the person concerned.

In the event of an action for annulment, the court will annul the decision for breach of essential procedural requirements or for infringement of a general principle of EU law (right to be heard).

In the case of an action for damages, assuming the limited degree of discretion of the authority and the infringement of principles intended to protect individuals,[477] the condition for a serious and manifest violation could be met, and Ms Tramp could be entitled to compensation for the earnings lost since the withdrawal of the licence.

C. France

TP

In France, 'private use of public spaces' that are public properties, such as kiosks, parts of streets, or of a port could be allowed by either a concession or an authorization. In the event of a withdrawal of the licence or termination of a contract, the actions and compensation vary, especially in the second case. As Ms Tramp has a licence, we will focus on this.

Her action would be successful regarding the procedural wrong (i); however, it could be better to claim for damages directly (ii) because the same decision will probably be made after a regular procedure, and there would thus be no causal link

[475] The leading case is Case 17/74 *Transocean Marine Paint Association v Commission* [1974] ECR 1063, judgment of the Court 23 October 1974; the Court referred to this fundamental principle in many other cases in the following decades. See Case 222/86 *Unectef v Heylens* [1987] ERC 4097, judgment of the Court 15 October 1987; Joined Cases 46/87 and 227/88 *Hoechst AG v Commission* [1989] ECR 2859, judgment of the Court 21 September 1989; Case C-27/04 *Commission v Council* [2004] ECR I-6649, judgment of the Court 13 July 2004; Case T-315/01 *Kadi v Council and Commission* [2005] ECR II-3649, judgment of the Court of First Instance 21 September 2005. On the EU general principle of due process, see Craig, *EU Administrative Law* (n 123) 321; G della Cananea, *Due Process of Law beyond the State. Requirements of Administrative Procedure* (OUP 2016).

[476] It is well known that Art 41 establishes, that:

> [e]very person has the right to have his or her affairs handled impartially, fairly and within a reasonable time by the Institutions and bodies of the Union. This right includes: the right of every person to be heard before any individual measure which would affect him or her adversely is taken; the right of every person to have access to his or her file, while respecting the legitimate interests of confidentiality and of professional and business secrecy; the obligation of the administration to give reasons for its decisions.

[477] Joined Cases T-481/93 and T-484/93 *Vereniging van Exporteurs v Commission* [1995] ECR 1995 II-02941, judgment of the Court of First Instance 13 December 1995.

between the procedural wrong and her losses. Instead, she can claim for the limited compensation established in the General Code of public ownership when a license is withdrawn before the expiration date.

Whether the withdrawal is a sanction or is made regarding the personal circumstances of Ms Tramp, the right of defence must undoubtedly be guaranteed. As observed in case 1, this right has been a principle of French administrative Law since 1944.[478] The *Conseil d'Etat* established it when a licence for selling newspapers in a kiosk was withdrawn without giving the licensee any opportunity to present her observations about the alleged misconduct.

According to the Code of relations between the public and the administration (CRPA), the right of defence must be guaranteed before any individual decision that would adversely affect a person.[479] As Ms Tramp was notified of the withdrawal decision without her having any possibility of commenting before it was made, there is a procedural flaw that denied her the exercise of the right to be heard, and this is a ground for the annulment of the decision.

Regarding the breach of rationality, it is important to consider that withdrawal is a discretionary prerogative of the public authority. Therefore, the court cannot evaluate the merits of the decision; it must control competence, procedure, whether the facts happened, and whether there was a manifest error of assessment or misuse of power (*détournement de pouvoir*). The administration has a wide power of appraisal because it is the owner, and Ms Tramp only has a licence. Thus, the authority may consider the public interest of the public space and other public interests related to its ownership. It is difficult to establish whether there is a gross breach of rationality that could be considered a manifest error of assessment, because we only know that the authority wants to 'renew the offer of such services'. This may mean creating a new type of kiosk, initiating a new opening procedure, or making a change before a new concession. In any case, we can assume that the decision is based on the public interest.

An argument to challenge the decision might be the procedural wrong regarding the right of defence. In a case of misconduct, Ms Tramp must establish the damage and the causal link to engage public liability. If the authority can show the public interest and that the same withdrawal decision would be made after a lawful procedure, there is no causal link between the misconduct and the harm, which would have existed in any case.[480] The court would then order the authority to pay only the compensation established by law in the event of withdrawal before the fixed term. Therefore, Ms Tramp would not be interested in annulment, and would prefer to claim for damages. This option is possible but limited, because of her precarious title, namely a licence.

The private use of spaces under public ownership is governed by the principle of 'precariousness' (*le principe de précarité*), which means that the public owner may decide any change at any time regarding its property; thus nobody, whether concessionaire or licence holder, has a 'right' to be in the public space, and its 'use' is always precarious. This principle is codified by Article L2122-3 of the General Code of Public

[478] *Dame Veuve Trompier-Gravier* (n 18) Rec 133.
[479] Articles L122-1 and L211-2.
[480] CE 16 April 1975 *Secrétaire d'État à la Culture cAssoc dite 'La Comédie de Bourges'* No 96289, Lebon 231.

Entities' Property in connection with unilateral authorizations: 'The permission of article L-2122-1 is precarious and revocable.'[481]

This principle constitutes an exception for awarding damages because the person was aware of being in a precarious situation, accepted it, and consequently must bear the consequences of public works without any right to compensation, such as the construction of a new side of the port if this is a port licence.[482] However, if the reason for the withdrawal was not related to the interest of the public space itself (the kiosk or the port) but to other public interests (ie public order), the *Conseil d'Etat* would grant compensation, for example if the authority had closed the port in view of a new land-use plan.[483]

This complex system has been simplified by the General Code of Public Property. In the event of a withdrawal before the authorization expires, the aggrieved person has a right to (i) the reimbursement of the royalty fee already paid for the remaining time; and (ii) compensation for the expenses regarding the equipment and facilities expressly authorized if these are still present at the date of the withdrawal, minus the depreciation calculated in accordance with the conditions of the authorization.[484] In conclusion, any withdrawal before the authorization expires would be compensated for, albeit in a limited way and not including lost profits, due to the principle of precariousness.

The situation seems more favourable in the case of concessions. The *Conseil d'Etat*, in the case of *Société Jonathan Loisirs* of 2008 established that the expiry of the concession before its due date, without any fault of the concessionaire, gives rise to the right to compensation,[485] including any investments not amortized, additional expenses, and loss of profits if they were directly and certainly caused by the authority's decision; however, it did not recognize any harm related to the loss of the *fonds de commerce*[486] because the concession is always revocable, and it impedes the formation of this *fonds*.[487] However, in 2014, Article L2124-32-1 was introduced in the General Code to open up to the possibility of having *fonds de commerce* in public spaces if they have their own clientele.

D. Germany

FW and JS

Ms Tramp is obliged to challenge the decision of the licensing authority in order to be eligible for damages (§ 839 para 3 BGB). Hence, she has to lodge an action for

[481] Article L2122-1, moreover, sets limits to individual use, in order to protect public use.

[482] CE 10 October 1986 *Port autonome de Marcheille c GDF*, Lebon 228; Rev adm 1986 571, note Terneyre.

[483] If the withdrawal purpose regards renewing kiosks, this concerns the interest of the particular domain and the person will not receive any compensation. However, if the purpose is public works in the street to improve traffic, this is another public interest, and the person could claim for damages. One example concerning a port is CE 29 March 1968 '*Ville de Bordeaux c Soc Menneret*' No 68946.

[484] See Art R2125-5.

[485] Unless a contract clause settled a different solution.

[486] In France, the *fonds de commerce* are composed of a set of elements contributing to an economic unit whose object is commercial; it includes tangible elements, such as goods and equipment, and intangible items, such as the clientele, the leasing contract, and the trade name.

[487] CE 31 July 2009 *Société Jonathan Loisirs* No 316534.

annulment (*Anfechtungsklage*, § 42 para 1 alternative 1 VwGO). Such an action has suspensive effect, ie the withdrawal is suspended (§ 80 para 1 VwGO), if the suspensive effect is not excluded by statute or an order of the administration (§ 80 para 1 VwGO) against which, in turn, interim relief may be sought (§ 80 para 5 VwGO).

As to the merits, the administrative court would determine whether the withdrawal, an administrative act, was unlawful and infringes Ms Tramp's individual rights (§ 113 para 1 sentence 1 VwGO).[488]

Regarding the formal error, § 28 VwVfG[489] or the corresponding *Länder* statute applies. These provisions contain a duty to hear the respective party prior to the issuing of an administrative act which adversely affects the party's rights. Being laid down in the general law on administrative procedure, this provision is universally applicable. Therefore, it is not necessary to incorporate the duty to hear the adversely affected party in the specific statutes on special areas of administrative law. There is, furthermore, no need to refer to general principles of law such as fairness, rationality, or due process, since these have been concretized in § 28 VwVfG and the corresponding *Länder* laws.[490] The failure to hear the adversely affected party does not automatically render an administrative act unlawful. § 28 paras 2 and 3 VwVfG and the relevant *Länder* statutes put forth situations where agencies can refrain from the hearing. This covers cases like the necessity of an immediate decision for exigent circumstances (para 2 No 1), the issuing of administrative acts which affect a large number of people (para 2 No 4), or the existence of an overriding public interest (para 3). Ms Tramp's case does not come under these exceptions. Thus, her right to be heard was violated.

Yet, § 45 para 1 No 3 and para 2 VwVfG and the respective *Länder* statutes allow for remedying this procedural error (see case 1). This would require a hearing and a reconsideration of the decision, which has not taken place so far. Moreover, in particular in view of the discretion to be exercised, the omitted hearing was evidently not without any influence on the substance of the decision; thus, the procedural error is not irrelevant according to § 46 VwVfG and the respective *Länder* statutes (see case 1).[491]

With regard to damages under the general rules on public authority liability, the situation of Ms Tramp corresponds to the situation of North Lake in case 5. In particular, in view of the exclusion contained in § 839 para 3 BGB, a claim to damages is only possible with regard to damages not avertable by a remedy, notably because they occurred before a remedy was effective, and/or in the case of an unsuccessful court action, ie if the administrative court rejects the injunction or holds Ms Tramp's action in the main proceedings as unfounded. However, the civil court hearing the matter

[488] The licensing authority might have based the withdrawal on s 49 VwVfG para 2 sentence 1 or the corresponding *Länder* law. These provisions allow the repeal of an administrative act which is lawful and beneficial for its recipient, but only under certain circumstances.

[489] See n 52.

[490] F Wollenschläger, 'Verfassung im Allgemeinen Verwaltungsrecht: Bedeutungsverlust durch Europäisierung und Emanzipation?' (2016) 75 VVDStRL 187 (199f, 244, 250f); F Wollenschläger, 'Constitutionalisation and Deconstitutionalisation of Administrative Law in View of Europeanisation and Emancipation' (2017) 10 Rev Eur Adm L 7, 65; cf U Ramsauer, '§ 28' in Kopp and Ramsauer (n 53) para 3, invoking the rule of law, human dignity, and the protection of fundamental rights as the underlying constitutional principles.

[491] Schwarz '§ 46' (n 53) para 29; Ramsauer, '§ 46' (n 53) para 25ff.

of liability would be bound by a final court decision. Thus, only very limited space remains for a claim for damages.

Additionally, it should be noted that in the event of a lawful repeal of the administrative act, § 49 para 6 VwVfG requires compensation if Ms Tramp's legitimate expectations were frustrated. This provision would not apply if the licensing authority can base the withdrawal on § 49 para 2 sentence 1 No 1 alternative 2 VwVfG or the corresponding *Länder* statute (reservation of a right to repeal), since Ms Tramp would have been aware of the possibility of a repeal then.[492] Anyway, this claim is limited to recovery of the actual loss, but does not comprise lost profits.[493]

Irrespective of whether property in the sense of Article 14 GG is affected by the repeal of the licence,[494] § 49 para 6 VwVfG provides sufficient compensation so that no further property issues arise.[495]

In summary, Ms Tramp may only claim damages for harm that could not have been averted by challenging the authority's withdrawal. In the event of a justifiable withdrawal, Ms Tramp may claim compensation for frustration of legitimate expectations.

E. Hungary

LB

An infringement of the right to be heard may give rise to government liability only if the infringement is serious, very clear, and culpable, which is rarely the case.

If a licence is required, in general, some legal conditions must be met for withdrawing it, for example a serious infringement that can be justified or refuted before the court. In the code of administrative procedures, the right of the individual to make a statement or comment at any time is part of the principles and—in theory—infringing a principle in itself leads to annulment. It is also considered a part of the due process of law (Article XXIV of the Constitution).

This interpretation is, however, weakened by the following elements emerging from judicial decisions. First, a hearing can be considered an important factor in determining the facts, because the authority must clarify the facts that are necessary for decision-making. Second, and consequently, omitting this can be a serious infringement. Third, to award damages, the infringement must be serious, very clear, and culpable. Fourth, if the statement is not necessary for determining the facts of the case, then the infringement was not serious or it is not an infringement at all. Fifth, the public authority may remedy the infringement afterwards, during the judicial procedure. Finally, it is a different matter if the person concerned is not a party to the procedure, so he or she does not even have a legal opportunity to make a statement or present evidence, etc before the decision is made about him or her, which is a serious and culpable infringement.

[492] cf the *ratio legis* stated in Bundestags-Drucksache 7/910 of 18 July 1973, 73.

[493] M Sachs, '§ 49' in Stelkens and others (n 55) para 130.

[494] cf BVerfG (3rd chamber) 10 June 2009—1 BvR 198/08, [2009] NVwZ 1426 (1428); H-J Papier, 'Art. 14' in T Maunz and G Dürig (eds), *Grundgesetz Kommentar* (83rd edn, CH Beck April 2018) para 770.

[495] Sachs, '§ 49' (n 493) para 126.

F. Italy

FC

In Italian law, the possibility of withdrawing Ms Tramp's licence could certainly arise. It is, in other words, possible for the authority to withdraw an act of this kind due to 'emerging reasons of public interest'.[496] This, however, must occur in respect of the principle of fair proceedings,[497] which can be applied without challenge to the exercise of all the powers over the authority's previous provisions. Therefore, from this point of view, Ms Tramp's grievance would be founded, without the court needing to assess the actual unreasonableness of the withdrawal.

If the withdrawal, therefore, were declared unlawful, then Ms Tramp could certainly also obtain, upon request, compensation for any damages that this provision might have caused her in the meantime, even in terms of lost profit.

Nevertheless, it is worth pointing out that the law[498] states that, even when a withdrawal can be carried out lawfully as in the case examined here, the licensing authority has to provide compensation to the owner of the withdrawn licence. This provision expresses the need to consider, case by case, the importance of the trust that may have been built up by the person affected by the withdrawn act.[499]

G. Poland

Łukasz Dziamski

A licence withdrawal *inaudita altera parte* is unlawful, as a party's right to actively participate in the proceedings has been infringed, a right directly defined in Articles 10 and 81 of the Polish Code of Administrative Procedure (CAP). This should be confirmed by the competent administrative authority or administrative court. Damages could be awarded to Ms Tramp in separate proceedings before a civil court, as this is bound by the decision confirming that the withdrawal of the licence was unlawful.

As noted in case 1, according to Article 77(1) of the Polish Constitution, everyone shall have the right to be awarded damages for any harm done by an action of an organ of public authority contrary to law. Article 417 CC supplements such provision, laying down a general principle of strict liability of the State Treasury for any illegal act.[500]

[496] See Art 21-*quinquies* L No 241/1990.

[497] See eg Council of State No 6539/2010; Council of State No 5863/2015.

[498] See Art 21-*quinquies* L No 241/1990.

[499] In such a case, it would be possible to ask the court for other forms of compensation, eg compensation of damages incurred from the violation of the general principle of fairness (Art 1337 CC; see theories illustrated above in n 176).

[500] See Art 417:

> § 1. The State Treasury or an entity of local government or some other legal person who by virtue of law exercises public authority shall be liable for the damage inflicted by an illegal act or omission committed while exercising public authority. § 2. Where the exercise of duties within the scope of public authority has been commissioned on the basis of an agreement to an entity of local government or to some other legal person, the executor of these duties and the entity of local government or the State Treasury commissioning it will be held jointly and severally liable for the damage incurred.

The damages granted under the provisions of Article 417 CC are calculated according to general principles pertaining to the estimate of damage, and include actual losses (*damnum emergens*) and loss of future profit (*lucrum cessans*),[501] in which the Constitutional Tribunal deemed it unconstitutional to limit the liability of the State for defective administrative decisions to *damnum emergens* (actual losses).

In the case discussed here, the law has been breached because a party's right to actively participate in an administrative procedure, as defined by Articles 10 and 81 CAP, has been infringed.

However, the procedure to seek damages must take into account the fact that it is the administrative courts who supervise the legality of administrative actions. However, general courts award damages pursuant to a separate procedure. One should also take into account the provisions of Article 417[1] § 2 CC, which reads that if the final decision gives rise to damage, such damage may only be redressed after a decision in question is deemed unlawful pursuant to appropriate proceedings, unless otherwise provided for by separate provisions of law. It means that a party needs to obtain *praeiudicium* during different proceedings before the redress proceedings as such may be instituted at all. In practice, bringing a claim for compensation for an administrative decision issued in conflict with the law requires two subsequent proceedings, which postpones real redress of damage.

In order to obtain *praeiudicium*, one must adhere to an appropriate legal standard, ie an extraordinary procedure to delete defective decisions set forth in the Code of Administrative Procedure, the procedure under which the annulment of a decision is sought, and the administrative proceedings ending with such illegal decision are re-instituted (the invalidity of a decision may only be determined through an administrative court judgment). When analysing how such procedures are applied, it becomes clear that defects of administrative decisions or proceedings that preceded issuance must be of material importance. Hence, not every defect of a final decision would lead to the *praeiudicium* necessary to seek damages. In the case in question, it seems that administrative courts have a tendency to lessen the importance of violation of Article 10 CAP, and limit it only to cases in which a party was unable to enjoy specific rights to which they were entitled (eg notification was not sent, so the defendant was unable to provide evidence, ie the effective remedy, '*środek zaskarżenia*'). Therefore, the way is still long for Ms Tramp to get compensation, which anyway will only be awarded after the whole administrative proceedings have been finalized. Her appeal would lead to a situation in which a competent authority of higher instance or an administrative court would challenge the decision subject to appeal, with the ultimate purpose of issuing a correct administrative decision (this in turn makes it impossible to seek damages under Article 417[1] § 2 CC).

A material problem arises here, ie the possibility of seeking damages for an illegal decision that is not final. As a rule, submission of the appeal will stay the enforcement of the decision (Article 130 § 2 CAP) unless the decision has been appended with an immediate enforceability clause (Article 130 § 3 CAP). Appending the decision with an immediate enforceability clause is subject to the provisions of Article 108 § 1 CAP.

[501] K 20/02 OTK-A 2003 No 7 item 76, Decision of the Constitutional Tribunal (TK) of 23 September 2003.

Said Code, however, does not contain a provision that would constitute an equivalent of Article 338 of the Code of Civil Procedure, confirming that an injured party has the right to seek damages on the basis of a decision made immediately enforceable by an authority of first instance.

Civil law practitioners are involved in a dispute between the following two concepts. First, Article 417[1] § 2 CC regulates, in a comprehensive manner, liability for damages for administrative decisions, excluding the possibility that liability for damages inflicted by decisions which are not final may be based on other provisions (Art 417 CC). Second, liability for defective decisions which are not final may be based directly on the provisions of Article 417 CC.

The first concept was supported by the Supreme Court.[502] It found that the Civil Code exhaustively regulates the liability of the State Treasury for any damages caused by administrative decisions, but also excludes the possibility of seeking damages for decisions that are not final under the provisions of Article 417 CC.[503] The Supreme Court allowed for granting damages for a non-final decision, but stated that 'the reasons for the liability of the State Treasury for a defective decision which is not final may only exist if such decision grossly violates the law'.[504]

The other concept was supported by a resolution of the Supreme Court (7)[505] as well as legal commentaries,[506] is of the opinion that seeking compensation for damage caused by a decision which is not final is not possible under Article 417[1] § 2 CC because of its literal wording, but is possible under the provisions of Article 417 CC). However, it should be pointed out here that the resolution in question concerned a period before Article 417[1] was introduced in the CC. The Supreme Court found in the said resolution that:

> the provisions of Article 417 § 1 of the Civil Code, in conjunction with the provisions of Article 77 Section 1 of the Constitution of the Republic of Poland applicable to events and legal circumstances prior to 1 September 2004, constitute a legal basis for the liability of the State Treasury for any damage caused by the issuance and execution of a non-final decision of a tax authority of the first instance, subsequently dismissed.

A similar position was previously expressed in the Supreme Court's case law, particularly in a judgment of 2002.[507]

The second solution is more favourable to a citizen, and many arguments can be voiced to support such view. First, hypothesis of Article 77 section 1 of the Polish Constitution is not limited to damages inflicted by final decision only. According to

502 V CK 250/04 OSP 2005 No 7–8 item 98, judgment of 19 November 2004.

503 Similar opinions are voiced by A Olejniczak, the legal commentator, in Kidyba, *Komentarz* ('*Legal Commentary*'), vol III, part 1 (Wolters Kluwer 2014) 442, Nb14, ie there were no grounds to seek damages for any damage caused by a defective administrative decision that was corrected by an appellate authority.

504 V CSK 176/05, judgment of 19 April 2006.

505 III CZP 125/05, OSNC 2006 No 12 item 194, Resolution of 26 April 2006.

506 R Szczepaniak, in M Gutowski, *Komentarz* ('*Legal Commentary*'), vol I (CH Beck 2016) 1669, Nb 31; Z Banaszczyk, in K Pietrzykowski, *Komentarz* ('*Legal Commentary*'), vol I, (CH Beck 2015) 1391 Nb 18; J Kremis in E Gniewek and P Machnikowski, *Komentarz* ('*Legal Commentary*') (CH Beck 2016) 828, Nb 112.

507 V CKN 1248/00, OSP 2002 No 10 item 128, judgment 6 February 2002; I CK 443/02, judgment 18 December 2003, as well as in IV CK 190/05 Bulletin SN 2006, judgment 18 November 2005 No 5, 10ff.

the said provision, the State Treasury shall be liable for the illegal action of public authorities. Issuing of a decision by an administrative authority of the first instance also constitutes such action. The interpretation of the provisions of the CC, which results in the lack of liability for damages caused by such decisions, would mean that such provisions are not in compliance with the Constitution of the Republic of Poland. Second, the provisions of Article 417^1 § 2 CC do not constitute *lex specialis* with respect to Article 417 CC as regards the liability for non-final decisions because it does not concern such decisions at all. Third, the award of damages for a decision issued by the authority of first instance does not necessarily mean that the courts will interfere with the authority of administrative bodies. Such verdict may be issued after the decision of the authority of the first instance has been repealed (it should be noted that pursuant to the provisions of Article 417 CC the award of compensation is not conditioned upon *praeiudicium*). Assuming that the State Treasury and local government units bear no responsibility for decisions of the authorities of first instance would mean that the risk related to the defectiveness of such decisions is shifted onto the citizens.[508]

The second solution—as more current and offering better protecting to citizens—should be upheld in court decisions.

Answers to the specific questions pertaining to this case are as follows:

(1) The domestic administrative court would share Ms Tramp's arguments, relying on general provisions of the Code of Administrative Procedure.
(2) The domestic court would overrule the decision due to the existence of a procedural flaw.
(3) Ascertaining that the decision is unlawful is a pre-condition for awarding compensation and takes place in separate proceedings.
(4) Compensation awarded under Article 417 of the Civil Code is calculated according to general rules for estimating damages under the Civil Code and includes losses and loss of profit, as evidenced by Ms Tramp.

H. Romania

RV

According to Law 554/2004, Romanian courts are competent to review acts of the administration that had been issued with an excess of discretionary power. Legal scholars usually agree that there is an excess of discretionary power whenever the administration has a power of discretion over a certain decision or course of action and goes beyond the limits of this discretion by breaching individual rights.

The power of discretion given to the administration is embedded in what Romanian law calls the 'opportuneness' of the administrative act. According to Romanian administrative law, an act issued by the administration has two main dimensions: (i) lawfulness; and (ii) opportuneness, the latter being intrinsically connected to the

[508] See P Sobolewski, in K Osajda (ed), *Kodeks cywilny. Komentarz* ('*Civil Code. Commentary*') (CH Beck 2017) 556ff.

administration's discretionary power.[509] The standard of judicial review in the Romanian legal system includes lawfulness and opportuneness (as this is also an indicator of their lawfulness). The opportuneness of the administrative act is a rather flexible concept and entails an assessment of the proportionality or reasonableness of the decision by reference to (i) the time chosen by the administration to issue the act; and (ii) the means used by the administration to reach its goal. However, Romanian administrative courts do not apply a consistent methodology or set of rules when assessing the opportuneness of administrative acts, and in fact, scholarly contributions of no more than a decade ago still questioned the court's power to review anything other than the 'lawfulness' of the act (referring to its compliance with the law and the question on whether it was issued ultra vires).[510]

The opportuneness of the act is included in the more modern court's standard of review. However, neither scholars nor case law draw sufficient parallels between opportuneness and the principles of reasonableness, fairness, and proportionality as shaped in comparative administrative law, as well as the CJEU or the ECHR's methodology when applying the principle of proportionality.[511]

Returning to the case in point and the questions that need to be addressed, I will analyse first *whether the national court would endorse Ms Tramp's argument only if a specific requirement to hear affected parties has been laid down by legislation for this type of administrative procedure or whether it would use general principles of law such as fairness or due process*. The answer is that procedural fairness or due process principles would apply.

Procedural fairness or due process are usually described as entailing: (i) an obligation of decisional transparency; (ii) a duty to give reasons; and (iii) access to judicial protection and remedies.[512] As shown above, in Romania access to judicial review of administrative acts is recognized both constitutionally (Art 52) and through the provisions established under the general law on judicial review, ie Law 554/2004.

Transparency and the duty to give reasons also find constitutional expression under Article 31 paragraph 2 of the Constitution, providing: 'Public bodies, in accordance with the competencies they are given, are under an obligation to make sure that citizens are informed of public matters as well as matters that are of personal interest to them.' The administration's duty to give reasons is acknowledged in both case law and scholarship as one of the criteria for establishing the legality of the act itself. An act issued in breach of the administration's obligation to provide reasons is deemed unlawful. In an often-quoted Supreme Court administrative ruling, the Court stated that:

> A detailed description of the reasons for issuing the administrative acts is necessary even when the administration has broad discretionary power because the reasons of

509 In Romanian, RN Petrescu, *Drept Administrativ* (Editura Hamangiu 2009) 336.

510 ibid.

511 See a contribution underlining the same shortcomings in O Podaru, *Actul administrative (I) Repere pentru o teorie altfel* (Hamangiu 2010) 252.

512 See, for instance, G della Cananea, 'Equivalent Standards under Domestic Administrative Law: A Comparative Perspective', in F Ortino et al. (eds), *Investment Treaty Law II. Fair and Equitable Treatment in Investment Treaty Law* (BIICL 2006) 159; G della Cananea, *Due Process of Law Beyond the State. Requirements of Administrative Procedure* (OUP 2016) 35 and 61.

> the administrative decision grant transparency to the administrative action and allow private individuals to verify whether the act is well founded as well as allowing the courts to judicially review them.
>
> The interested party's participation is therefore intrinsically connected to principles of EU law, including transparency, so interpreting the duty to give reasons as mandatory is the only way to make these principles effective.
>
> In fact, the Romanian Constitution too lays down under article 31(2) the public authority's obligation to correctly inform the citizens on public matters but also on matters of private and personal interests. This is all the more so in this case, where the administrative act concerns the citizen's right to work, which is a fundamental right and cannot therefore be breached through an act that was issued without reasons being given. As a consequence, the Supreme Court will consider that the acts are not reasoned and, as we have seen, the duty to give reasons is a general obligation of the administration, which has a double role: that of transparency in favour of the beneficiary of the act and the one that gives courts the possibility of verifying the factual and legal elements considered when the act was issued.[513]

The Romanian legal system also includes a general legislative act on transparency in the work of the administration, ie Law 52/2003 on decisional transparency in the administration.[514] However, this law only refers to normative administrative acts issued by the administration, and thus to acts of general application. There is no provision under this statutory instrument that the administration is under an obligation to inform the interested party before an individual act that might affect its rights and interests is issued. Law 554/2004 on judicial review of the administration does not establish such an obligation either, and neither do the special legislative instruments applicable to the facts of the matter, ie Law 215/2001 of local public administration[515] and Government Ordinance No 99/2000 on the selling of products and services.[516] However, the concept of excess of power established by Law 554/2004 would be applied in conjunction with Article 31 of the Constitution quoted above on the citizens' right to be informed by the administration in matters of personal interest.

The definition under Law 554/2004 of an excess of power is: 'an *ultra vires* manifestation of the administration's discretionary power or a manifestation of that power that breaches the rights or liberties of citizens'. Again, the concept of excess of power has been tackled quite vaguely and inconsistently in both the case law and the literature. However, one scholar draws much from principles like proportionality and reasonableness and mentions that the following criteria characterize the act of the administration as being issued with an excess of power (excess

[513] See Supreme Court Decision 1580/2008 in Romanian <https://legeaz.net/spete-contencios-inalta-curte-iccj-2008/decizia-1580-2008≥ accessed 22 June 2020.

[514] Republished in the Official Gazette No 749 of 3 December 2013.

[515] Published in the Official Gazette No 123 of 10 February 2007.

[516] Republished in the Official Gazette No 603 of 31 August 2007.

of power and excess of discretionary power are interchangeable in Romanian administrative law):

a) The measure has no legitimate purpose;
b) The decisions/acts are not proportional—they are not adequate or beyond what is needed to reach their purpose;
c) The decisions are unreasonable.[517]

But, in order for Ms Tramp to be granted damages, she would first have to prove that the withdrawal/act of revoking her licence was an unlawful act. To show this, Ms Tramp could argue that: (i) it was unfairly issued through a breach of her constitutional right to be consulted before the issuance of an act that is of interest to her and breaches her rights and interests; but also that (ii) it was unlawful due to its lack of opportuneness; and that (iii) it was unlawful, being issued through an excess of power (the two latter being grounds for unlawfulness specific to administrative acts), thus allowing Article 31 of the Constitution to be invoked and applied in conjunction with the provisions under Law 554/2004.

If the court annuls the withdrawal of Ms Tramp's license and decides the act is unlawful, only then damages can be awarded under Article 18 of Law 554/2004. The administrative court can order that lost profit be compensated according to the civil law general principle of integral reparation of damages. The principle's source is the civil law, which, in the lack of more specific provisions in the field of administrative liability, applies to liability due to illegal administrative action as well.

I. Spain

EMNG

The national court would uphold Ms Tramp's argument based on general principles of law that are also included in the Spanish Common Administrative Procedure Act (*Ley 39/2015, de 1 de octubre, de Procedimiento Administrativo Común*). This is a basic national regulation that must be followed by every public authority in any administrative procedure.

A Spanish court could refer to Article 105 of the Spanish Constitution (on the right of the citizen to participate),[518] but also, and more probably, the court would refer to Article 24.2 of the Spanish Constitution, which focuses on judicial procedural rights,

[517] See, in Romanian, DA Tofan, *Puterea discreționară și excesul de putere al autorităților publice* (All Beck 1999) 29; RA Lazar, *The Legality of Administrative Acts. Romanian and Comparative Law* (All Beck 2004) 165.

[518] Article 105 of the Spanish Constitution provides that:

> The law shall make provision for: a) The hearing of citizens, directly, or through the organizations and associations recognised by the law, in the process of drawing up the administrative provisions which affect them. b) The access of citizens to administrative files and records, except to the extent that they may concern the security and defence of the State, the investigation of crimes and the privacy of persons. c) The procedures for the taking of administrative action, with due safeguards for the hearing of interested parties when appropriate.

<www.boe.es/buscar/act.php?id=BOE-A-1978-31229#a105> accessed 22 June 2020.

such as the right to a defence that includes the right to be heard.[519] These are fundamental rights applicable in criminal and punitive administrative cases. Nonetheless, courts refer to rights regulated by Article 24.2 of the Spanish Constitution also in cases of non-criminal or administrative sanctions.

The court would declare void an administrative decision based on a breach of the rights of the individual within the common administrative procedure, or based on lack of rationality in the decision-making. Whether the licensing authority intends to renew the offer of such services, in spite of Ms Tramp still fulfil the requirements for having his licence, it should compensate damage caused to the former.

Annulment for breaching general law principles or the lack of rationality in the decision-making is precondition for awarding compensation for damages. The amount of which would also cover lost profit. The latter award would be assessed taking into account the benefits Ms Tramp normally earns at that time of year.

J. Switzerland

TT

For the case to be plausible in Switzerland, one has to assume that Ms Tramp's kiosk is located on public property (eg place, street, pavement, park), which justifies needing a licence (probably awarded by the municipality) to run it. Selling newspapers and maps in a kiosk located on private property is never subject to a licensing requirement in Switzerland.

Ms Tramp will have the opportunity to appeal the withdrawal of the licence before the cantonal administrative court. The appeal will normally have suspensive effect. If the appeal were successful, Ms Tramp would thus suffer no harm. If she failed to appeal or if the appeal was rejected, the lawfulness of the withdrawal cannot be challenged in liability proceedings.

As noted previously,[520] the right to be heard before an administrative decision is issued is a constitutional right in Switzerland. There is also a constitutional right to be treated in a non-arbitrary manner (Art 9 of the Federal Constitution): a decision taken in breach of rationality would be arbitrary. Thus the court's decision on Ms Tramp's appeal would entertain both her arguments.

The only hypothesis in which the question of damages could actually arise would be if the municipality, without hearing Ms Tramp and in breach of rationality, not only withdrew the license, but revoked the suspensive effect of an appeal against that decision (and the court did not reinstate it) and immediately took steps to forcibly evict

[519] Article 24(2) provides that:

> Likewise, all have the right to the ordinary judge predetermined by law; to defense and assistance by a lawyer; to be informed of the charges brought against them; to a public trial without undue delays and with full guarantees; to the use of evidence appropriate to their defense; not to make self-incriminating statements; not to plead themselves guilty; and to be presumed innocent. The law shall specify the cases in which, for reasons of family relationship or professional secrecy, it shall not be compulsory to make statements regarding allegedly criminal offences.

[520] Switzerland, case 1.

Ms Tramp from the kiosk. In this case, if Ms Tramp appeals successfully against all these measures, she could be awarded damages (which would essentially compensate for profit loss during the period in which she could not use the kiosk), provided that the municipality action is deemed in breach of a fundamental duty (which would certainly be the case with the facts as assumed here). However, such a hypothesis is highly unlikely.

K. United Kingdom

GA

This kind of scenario is very well known within the common law tradition, and it is often used to illustrate the interplay between the rules of common law fairness and procedural requirements that might be contained in statute (see further the beginning of Chapter 13). It is also factually close to a number of leading cases that are synonymous with common law principle, most famously *ex parte Hook* and *McIness v Onslow Fane*.[521]

The following points might be made in relation to Ms Tramp:

(1) The approach that the courts take towards questions of fairness always depends upon the context to a dispute. The context for these purposes can include considerations such as: (i) the nature of the decision-maker; (ii) the nature of the decision-maker's power (statutory or not); (iii) the implications that a decision may have for an individual; and (iv) the 'public interests' that may be engaged by a decision.[522]

(2) Where a dispute concerns a licence, the courts sometimes make a distinction between three scenarios: (i) those in which a person is applying for a licence for the first time; (ii) those in which a person who has held a licence is applying for it to be renewed; and (iii) those in which a person who is holding a licence has it withdrawn. In general terms, the common law rules of fairness will be at their most demanding in instance (iii)—the category that embraces Ms Tramp's case.

(3) If there is a legislative requirement to consult with persons in Ms Tramp's position, and that does not occur, it is likely that the courts would regard this a procedural irregularity and/or as an illegality (on the applicable principles see further case 2 above). It is also likely that the courts would quash the decision to withdraw the licence, where the illegality might also make it possible for Ms Tramp to sue for damages for breach of statutory duty. (It might safely be assumed that a statute that imposes a duty to consult a closed class of persons—licence holders—would give rise to a cause of action, unless the statute expressly excluded the possibility of a damages claim.)

(4) If there is no legislative requirement to consult, or if legislation is silent on the point, it could be expected that the common law would 'fill the gaps' to ensure

[521] *R v Barnsley MBC, ex parte Hook* [1976] 1 WLR 1052 and *McIness v Onslow Fane* [1978] 1 WLR 1520.

[522] See further Lord Bridge's comments in *Lloyd v McMahon* [1987] 1 AC 625, 702.

that Ms Tramp is treated fairly (the courts sometimes say that they will imply 'so much and no more . . . by way of additional procedural safeguards as will ensure the attainment of fairness'[523]). This is very much the realm of the common law 'right to a hearing', and it could be expected that the common law would offer its fullest protection to Ms Tramp, particularly as there does not appear to be any pressing matter of public interest that would justify the immediate withdrawal of her licence. At its most basic, this would mean that Ms Tramp should be given advance notification of the proposed withdrawal of her licence; that she should be given advance access to documentation relevant to the proposed withdrawal; that she should be allowed to make representations before any final decision about withdrawal was taken; and that she should be given reasons for any decision to withdraw her licence.

(5) If the court holds that there has been a breach of the requirements of fairness, it may, though not necessarily will, consider the question of rationality. All will depend here on the preference of the judge: one judge may say that it is not necessary for the court to do so, given its finding on fairness; another judge may well proceed to consider the point afresh.

(6) The issue of damages for breach of the common law right to a hearing is less straightforward. While a failure to observe a statutory requirement might give rise to an action for breach of statutory duty, it is less clear that a failure to observe the common law's right to a hearing would be actionable in, most obviously, negligence. This is because the licensing authority may not owe her a common law duty of care and, if it did not so, Ms Tramp would not (of course) be able to sue for loss. In order to safeguard her interests, she may therefore need to initiate judicial review proceedings immediately and either (i) ask the court to grant a mandatory interim injunction to compel the authority to reinstate her licence; or (ii) invite the authority to give an undertaking that it would allow her to continue to trade pending the outcome of her case.

(7) On the question of annulment as a precondition to a damages claim, much would depend on whether there was, or was not, a statutory requirement to receive representations from Ms Tramp before making a decision about whether to withdraw her licence. If there was such a requirement, she should first seek to establish that it has been breached in a public law sense, as that would also establish a breach of a statutory duty for the purposes of a private law damages action. The relationship between annulment and the common law would, again, be less straightforward: it is unclear whether the authority would owe any common law duty of care, so an action for annulment may be the only meaningful remedy open to Ms Tramp.

(8) If damages are to be awarded, they would be intended to put Ms Tramp back in the position she would have been in had she not suffered the harm in question. The approach to quantum would depend on evidence of actual and projected loss across the lifespan of the case. Loss of profit would be included, but only to

[523] ibid.

the extent that the court would be satisfied that any loss could be directly attributed to the impugned decision.

To recap: (i) It is very likely that Ms Tramp would win her case on public law/procedural grounds—in the event that statute law does not require an *ex ante* hearing before withdrawal of her licence, the common law would almost certainly require such a hearing; (ii) it is probable that a damages claim could be sustained if the failure to consult her amounted to a breach of a statutory requirement; (iii) a claim in negligence, viz where there had been a breach of the common law right to a hearing, may be more difficult to sustain; and (iv) if bringing an application for judicial review, Ms Tramp should seek formal interim relief in the form of a court order or an undertaking from the respondent authority.

IX. Case 8—a licensed fisherman

Santiago is a licensed fisherman. Licensing is the prerogative of a local authority, namely the Fisheries Commission ('the Commission'), which reviews existing licences and renews an unlimited number every four years. Under existing rules, the Commission may, at its discretion, refuse to renew any licence upon conviction within national territory of any person for breach of any of the commercial fishing laws or rules. When Santiago applies for renewal of the licence, the Commission refuses to grant it, claiming that he had loaned his licence to another person. Santiago challenges this decision before the competent court on two grounds. He argues, first, that no existing rule explicitly prohibited anyone to borrow from or loan to any other person any licence or permit issued by the Commission and, second, that no evidence was brought against him.

Is Santiago's argumentation likely to be endorsed by the court? If so, can he claim damages against the Commission and, that being the case, would damages, if any, be limited to actual loss or extend to cover lost profit?

A. Austria

SS, KB, DB, and LM

There are nine laws relating to fishing in Austria because regulations governing fishing fall within the regulatory competence of the provinces (Art 15(1) B-VG). Under national regulations, it is not possible to transfer a fishing licence, as stated above. So-called fishery cards are issued personally and apply to the issuing province. Issuing a guest fishing card is specific to certain fishing waters and is only valid for a certain period (eg § 9(2) Styrian Fishing Act, Stmk FischereiG).[524] If the holder of the fishery card is not authorized to fish (ie not the owner of a fishing right), he must obtain a written permit in his own name and identify himself (eg § 11 Stmk FischereiG). A fishing card (and guest fishing card) is subject to certain conditions, including a written test (eg § 9(3) Stmk FischereiG).

However, the answer to the case is based on the facts mentioned above (no existing rule explicitly prohibits anyone from borrowing or loaning any licence issued by the Commission to any other person).

If Santiago is denied the licence (for whatever reason), as a result of § 2(2) AHG, he must in any case first go through an administrative procedure before public liability claims can be considered. Santiago would either have to appeal the negative decision of the Commission, or, if he had not already done so, try to obtain an opposable negative decision ('*Feststellungsbescheid*') in order to fight it. In the administrative proceedings, the VwG of the Austrian province where the licence is to be obtained would examine whether the two arguments can be followed.

[524] *Gesetz vom 18 Mai 1999 über das Fischereirecht in Steiermark* (Steiermärkisches FischereiG 2000) LGBl 1999/85 as amended.

(1) Argument 1: If (as indicated) there is no legal basis prohibiting the loan of fishing cards to any other person, the VwG would make a divergent decision, and award Santiago the licence, as long as all other statutory requirements are fulfilled.
(2) Argument 2: If the VwG concludes that no proper administrative procedure has been carried out because no evidence of the alleged infringement has been obtained, the legal situation has to be assessed accordingly.

Depending on the decision of the VwG, a public liability claim against the province (as the legal entity for which the Commission implements fishing law) is possible. Granting licences is to be considered as 'implementing the law'.

Unlawfulness and fault always depend on the individual case. Unlawfully not granting the licence must be impeachable—in particular if on the basis of an unjustifiable legal view. This arguably seems to be the case here—assuming that there is no legal basis for not granting the licence on the ground that it had been transferred. In this case, both financial loss and (in the event of gross negligence) lost profits can be asserted. Procedural costs should also be reimbursed.

B. European Union

BM

1. *The loan of a licence to third parties is not considered a violation of fishing regulations*

If renewal can be denied only for violation of the rules on fishing, a non-renewal based on a different reason would be unlawful and would constitute a breach of EU law in terms of breach of legitimate expectations, misuse of powers, reasonableness, and the specific rules governing the fishing authority's powers.

The decision to deny renewal would also be unlawful because it was not based, in any case, on evidence of the loan of the fishing licence to third parties.

If Mr Santiago proves that the unlawful conduct prevented him from exercising an activity to which he was entitled, and provided that, in the absence of substantial discretion, a law designed to protect him was infringed, he should be able to obtain compensation for the loss of income produced from the time when the non-renewal was enacted until the moment when the new licence was adopted.

2. *The loan of the licence to third parties could constitute an infringement of the regulations on fishing, so that the authority can, in the light of its discretionary power, deny the licence renewal*

In this second hypothesis, the authority may, in the exercise of its discretion, refuse to renew the licence, but its decision has to be supported by adequate evidence that such a loan took place.

If the court ascertains that this circumstance has been proven by the administration, it will not annul the decision, and a claim for compensation will be denied.

C. France

TP

In this case, as an explicit prohibition is not necessary, only Santiago's argument relating to the lack of evidence could be endorsed. Although the rejection may be annulled, damages depend on whether or not the licence is ultimately awarded to him.

Santiago has two grounds to claim that the decision is unlawful: first, there is no rule explicitly prohibiting the loan of the fishing licence; second, there is no evidence against him.

The first ground relates to the principle of legality concerning crimes and punishments, which is recognized in criminal law and also, in an attenuated form, in relation to administrative sanctions. The question that arises is whether the licence may be refused if there is no explicit prohibition on loaning it.

The *Conseil d'Etat* held that in the case of regulated professions or activities the principle of legality principle is respected when the law provides sanctions for any breach of the obligations of the respective profession or activity.[525] Therefore, an exhaustive list of offences is not required, and it suffices to refer to a 'breach of professional obligations'. The *Conseil Constitutionnel* confirmed this solution in case No 2011-199 QPC. The petitioner alleged that the veterinarian's offences sanctioned by the '*chambre de discipline*' were not sufficiently established, because this entity punishes any breach of the '*duties of the profession*'. However, the *Conseil* established that the principle of legality is less strict in the case of regulated professions or activities than it is in criminal law; therefore, the reference to the respective obligations of the activity or the profession was adequate.[526]

Santiago's argument would probably not be upheld, because the fishing rules most likely include either some provisions regarding the 'personal' use of the licence or some duties of correct use (eg any transfer is probably subject to a prior authorization of the Commission). There is no need for exact wording regarding the prohibition to loan the licence. Indeed, verifying the identity and conditions of the fisherman is the very purpose of a licence, and the existence of a general obligation regarding its personal use will suffice to satisfy the principle of legality.

Even though loaning the licence infringes the fishermen's duties, the Commission's refusal may still be unlawful, first, if the facts were not established. The court cannot examine the merit of discretionary decisions, thus limiting the power of appraisal of the administrative authority; however, it has the power to ascertain the facts, ie whether the alleged facts really happened. Second, the rejection had to respect the right of defence. As this point is not contested by Santiago, the question that arises is whether the facts happened as alleged or not.

According to the *Camino* case, the court may annul an administrative decision if the facts are not established, fully established, or do not correspond to reality.[527] In

[525] CE 7 July 2004 *Assemblée* No 255136, Rec.

[526] Cons Const 25 November 2011 No 2011-199 QPC.

[527] CE 14 January 1916 *Camino* (Rec 15; RD publ 1917 463, concl Corneille, note Jèze; S 1922.3.10, concl GCJA vol 1 No 57, concl).

this case, the result of the action will depend on the facts proved.[528] If the facts are established, the administrative decision is lawful, and Santiago would have no right to compensation. If the facts are not proven, the court would declare the rejection void. We may now turn to the problem of compensation.

To establish whether Santiago has a right to redress, it is necessary to prove the three elements: the misconduct, the damage, and the casual link between them. Even if the rejection decision is annulled, and the Commission's misconduct is established, Santiago will not receive any compensation for damage if the court does not find a *direct and certain* loss caused by the rejection. In fact, the court is not able to know what the administration's decision might have been in the first case.[529]

If Santiago did not loan the licence and begins the procedure again, the Commission cannot refuse it on the basis of 'false' facts. However, it is not obliged to grant the licence, as it has a discretionary power. It is therefore very difficult to determine whether the unlawful decision causes 'certain and direct' damage to Santiago in relation to the lost profits. However, Santiago might receive a reimbursement of the expenses related to the first licence procedure, because he should not have gone through this procedure twice, and there is a casual link between the expenses for a second procedure and the unlawfulness of the first refusal.

Another option for Santiago is to claim damages after the renewal of his licence. The cause of the damage would be the unlawful refusal and the delay between the first unlawful decision and the licence finally awarded if the conditions between the first and the second procedure have not changed. This case is not very common, but the *Conseil d'Etat* awarded damages for the additional expenses and the loss of profits after four years between two unlawful rejections of a building permit and the final, favourable, decision.[530]

D. Germany

FW and JS

Santiago is obliged to lodge an enforcement action against the rejection of the licence (§ 42 para 1 variant 2 VwGO) in the main proceedings before the administrative courts. Moreover, in view of the time the main proceedings take, Santiago is also obliged to ask for an interim order (§ 123 para 1 VwGO). If Santiago failed to do so, a claim for damages would be excluded insofar as the damage could have been averted by asking for an interim order.

Santiago's enforcement action would be successful if the denial of the licence had been unlawful and his rights thereby infringed (§ 113 para 5 VwGO). This is the case if Santiago has a claim to be awarded the licence, which depends on whether a refusal to

[528] CE 4 February 1981 *Konaté* No 23491.
[529] CE *Société d'aménagement du Bois de Bouis* (n 365).
[530] CE 26 October 1989 *Ministre de l'Équipement c SCI 'Les Moulins d'Hyères'* RD publ 1990 1176.

renew the licence may be based on its transfer to a third person (i) and whether such a transfer—if it is considered unlawful—has been established (ii).

First, the legality of this criterion (loan of the licence) is questionable. For, also in view of transparency and the fundamental right to professional freedom, it is doubtful whether a sufficient legal basis exists when applying a criterion not explicitly laid down in legislation, but resulting in the exclusion of occupational activities.

Irrespective of this, as far as the transferability of licences in general is concerned, such a criterion may be established. In this respect, one has to distinguish between licences referring to a person or to an object, or to both combined.[531] With Santiago being described as a 'licensed fisherman', the licence appears to have been awarded with respect to the person of the licensee. This does not preclude a transfer of the licence.[532] However, there must be a legal provision allowing the transfer.[533] This is limited to exceptional cases[534] which apparently do not apply here.[535] Given that the loan of a personal licence contradicts its very purpose (ie guaranteeing reliability, a sufficient financial basis, and sufficient knowledge of the business),[536] a breach of the commercial fishing rules could be established if Santiago in fact loaned his licence.

Second, the administration is obliged to investigate the case *ex officio* (§ 24 para 1 sentence 1, para 2 VwVfG and the corresponding *Länder* laws). However, if no evidence was brought against Santiago, meaning that the breach of the obligation not to loan the licence to another person could not be proven, the refusal to renew the licence is unlawful.

The same outcome can be reached if the administrative court itself finds that a breach did not occur. It thus depends on whether the administrative court is capable of finding sufficient facts against Santiago. According to § 86 paragraph 1 sentence 1 VwGO, it 'shall investigate the facts *ex officio*; those concerned shall be consulted in doing so'. Hence, Santiago's case (ie whether or not he violated the commercial fishing laws or rules), would have to be examined, even if 'no evidence was brought against him'.

If it can be found that a breach of the commercial fishing laws or rules did not occur or cannot be proven, Santiago's enforcement action would be successful, since his occupational freedom (Art 12 para 1 GG) would thereby be infringed.

In summary, the enforcement action brought by Santiago would only be successful if the court, after its own assessment of the law and the facts, does not regard a breach of the commercial fishing laws as established.

With regard to damages under the general rules on public authority liability, the situation of Santiago corresponds to the situation of North Lake in case 5. In particular,

[531] See J Dietlein, *Nachfolge im Öffentlichen Recht* (1999), 365f.

[532] cf ibid 368ff, also 407f.

[533] ibid 377f, 407f; J Ziekow, *Öffentliches Wirtschaftsrecht* (4th edn, CH Beck 2016) § 5 para 14.

[534] For instance, the continuation of a business by a 'competent representative' on behalf of a spouse after the death of the licensee, see s 46 para 1 of the *Gewerbeordnung* (Trade Regulation Act), German version <www.gesetze-im-internet.de/gewo/BJNR002450869.html> accessed 22 June 2020.

[535] German law prohibits the loan of fishing licences, cf s 3 para 1 sentence 3 No 3 SeeFischG. See also VG Hamburg 25 June 2007—15 K 1994/06, juris para 25; T Markus, *Seefischereigesetz* (2nd online edn, Nomos 2016) s 3 para 6.

[536] Ziekow (n 533) para 14.

in view of the exclusion contained in § 839 paragraph 3 BGB, a claim for damages is only possible with regard to damages not avertable by a remedy, notably because they occurred before an order for interim relief was available, and/or in the case of an unsuccessful court action, ie if the administrative court rejects the injunction or holds Santiago's action in the main proceedings unfounded. In the latter situation, the issue arises whether the civil court hearing the subsequent liability case is bound by the administrative judiciary's decisions (see case 5).

Regarding the prerequisites of Article 34 sentence 1 GG, read in conjunction with § 839 paragraph 1 sentence 1 BGB, which have been described in case 2, it can be stated that the duty to use all necessary evidence (§ 24 paras 1f, § 26 para 1 sentences 1f VwGO) constitutes an official duty incumbent upon an official of the Commission in relation to a third party[537]. There has also been a breach of this duty, and this was at least negligent.

However, it is questionable whether this breach caused damage if it can be proven that Santiago loaned his licence. As established above, the loan of a licence that refers to a specific person is *per se* unlawful. One could then argue that the Commission would have had to deny the renewal anyway (*Einwand rechtmäßigen Alternativverhaltens*).[538] Hence, the failure to bring evidence would have been unlikely to influence the decision.[539] However, if the denial of the licence is in fact either founded on a deficient assessment of the legal situation (loan of licences in fact not prohibited) by the Commission, or if a breach cannot be proven, causation may be established.

In conclusion, it depends on whether there was an actual breach of a duty by Santiago and whether, as the case may be, this can be proven. The adjudication of damages would follow the rules put forth in case 2 (§§ 249 para 1, 252 BGB, § 287 para 1 sentence 1 ZPO).

Santiago may only claim damages for harm which could not have been averted by challenging the authority's denial to renew his licence. This includes damage incurred before a successful interim decision was handed down or incurred because of an unjustified rejection of an interim order. However, the civil court hearing the matter of liability would be bound by a final court decision. Thus, only very limited space remains for a claim for damages. In substance, the success of his remedies depends on whether he actually breached the commercial fishing laws/rules and whether this can be proven. The damages that can be obtained under the general rules on public authority liability also comprise lost profits.

E. Hungary

LB

Because issuing a licence is based on a public legal relationship and not a contractual one, the licence is only valid for the fisherman—the general rule is supposed to be that the licence is only valid for the person to whom it is issued, and

[537] cf D Kallerhoff and F Fellenberg, '§ 24' in Stelkens and others (n 55) para 1.
[538] See case 2 (section III with n 168); see also cases 4, 10 and 11.
[539] cf BGH 6 November 1961—III ZR 143/60, BGHZ 36, 144 (154).

an explicit regulation is needed to borrow or loan it. This should be the same in the case of transferral. The law should determine whether the right to fish can be transferred or given to another person, for example through a contract—or at least there is supposed to be some kind of obligation to inform the authority about the changes. There is a reason why fishing is subject to official licensing, for example to safeguard nature, which in itself can support the strict procedure. However, if there is no proof that Santiago committed an infringement, because he needs to exhaust the possible remedies before bringing a claim to the court, he must first turn to the administrative court, which can change or annul the decision if it is unfounded.

In the civil procedure for damages, the question remains as to how wide the discretion of the authority is: it can hardly be proven that renewal would have been granted automatically without the infringement. Also, in deciding how serious the infringement was, the establishment of the facts must be very clear—for example, there was no evidence at all. Coverage for lost profit can be awarded if the fisherman can prove the exact amount he lost during the time he had no right to fish due to a causal link with the infringement.

F. Italy

FC

In Italian law, Santiago's claim has a very good chance of being upheld.

The refusal to renew the licence appears to be unlawful, especially given the absence of any preliminary investigation geared to concretely proving that Santiago loaned his licence to another person (and so irrespective of whether or not loaning the licence is prohibited).

Once the refusal to renew has been rejected, however, it is not certain that Santiago will be awarded compensation for damages (even for the lost earnings, at least for the profits lost due to the suspension of fishing activities during the time in which the refused renewal was in effect).

From this point of view, the aggrieved party would need to prove (as in cases 2 and 5 that he had a concrete 'right' to renew his licence. But this is difficult because, as described in the case in question, the authority seems to have broad discretional power in renewing licences.[540]

The fact remains, however, that compensation can be requested later, if, when renewing the procedure after the annulment, the authority actually renews the licence.[541] In this way, the recoverable damages (to the same amount) would be considered 'prejudice due to delay', resulting from the fact that Santiago was not put in a condition that allowed him to enjoy the benefits to which he was legitimately entitled right from the start.

[540] In other words, this case involves an *interesse legittimo* ('legitimate interest'), not a *diritto soggettivo* ('individual right'). See Cortese, Chapter 8 in this volume (n 174), section I.

[541] See n 175.

G. Poland

Marek Wierzbowski

In this case, we may expect the decision refusing to renew the licence to be set aside by the administrative court on grounds of grave violation of the Administrative Procedure Code, namely the lack of evidentiary proceedings and the issue of a decision without evidence. The lack of proof that he had loaned his licence to another person would most likely result in rejection of the fact—the problem of a loan of the licence to another person.

The case would be decided again by the Fisheries Commission. Santiago may bring a case against the State Treasury (Fisheries Commission), seeking damages—both real loss and lost future profits. The case will be decided by an ordinary court like any other tort case. The claim will be based on Article 417 of the Civil Code. '§ 1. The State Treasury or a local government unit or another person legally exercising public authority is liable for any damage caused by an unlawful action or omission while exercising public authority.' The claimant has to prove the amount of the losses.

The regulation of commercial fishing is very complex and requires the possession of several documents; in addition, it is strongly policed by the government. Lending the licence to another non-authorized person may result not only in revocation of the licence, but in other penalties too.

H. Romania

RV

Under Romanian law, there are various types of administrative acts that grant the right to fish. These are (i) the fishing licence, which is issued for a specific ship and in consideration, inter alia, of its technical specifications; (ii) a fishing licence granting an individual the right to undergo a commercial fishing activity; and (iii) a recreational fishing permit.[542] Both the fishing licence granting an individual the right to carry out a commercial fishing activity and the recreational fishing permit are issued *intuit personae*. This aspect would therefore trigger an obligation for the grantee not to lend the permit, as such conduct would go against the objectives of the provisions of fishing licences. However, the fact that the Commission has no evidence of Santiago lending his permit would impact the legality of the Commission's decision. Lack of evidence for the Commission's allegations leading to refusal of renewal would lead a Romanian court to the following conclusions:

(1) the act was issued without sufficient reasons and in breach of the administration's obligation to give reasons;
(2) the act was issued with an excess of power.

[542] Regulated under Law No 192/2001 on fishing, published in the Official Gazette No 627 of 2 September 2003.

Both reasons could be sufficient to trigger the annulment of the act. If the act is annulled, Santiago can ask for damages, and they will be calculated as the amount of profit that Santiago lost from the date when the Commission should have issued his renewal until the date of the final decision.

Santiago should, however, bring evidence for the profit he had registered in the same periods of the year as a result of his licensed fishing activity. The administrative court would order that lost profit be compensated according to the general civil law principle of integral reparation for damages. As mentioned above, the principle's source is the civil law, which, given the lack of more specific provisions in the field of administrative liability, applies to liability due to illegal administrative action as well.

I. Spain

EMNG

The Spanish legal system envisages both subjective and objective licences. The former are granted by the public authorities when the applicant fulfils some legal requirements that can sometimes be met by passing an examination, such as the driving licence. It is prohibited to borrow or loan such licences (eg fishing or hunting licences, among others), because the applicant must personally fulfil certain legal requirements.

Objective licences, however, are granted by public authorities, taking into account whether the object of a particular activity fulfils some legal requirements, such as licences to build a building, to open a discotheque, and so on. These licences can be borrowed, sold, and so on.

A Spanish court would uphold Santiago's claim if no evidence was brought against him, but the court would not uphold his claim based on the absence of any rule that explicitly prohibited anyone borrowing or loaning a licence to another person. Subjective licences are granted when the applicant fulfils all the requirements established by the regulations, so they cannot be lent to another person.

If the court declares an administrative decision void, and the applicant has sought compensation for damages, compensation would be awarded to cover actual loss and lost profit.

J. Switzerland

TT

As for Santiago's arguments, the lack of evidence is obviously something that would be entertained by the court: any decision must be based on facts, and the burden of the proof is on the competent authority. It is more difficult to assess Santiago's other argument without being able to compare it to specific and precise statutory language. At first glance, the loan of a licence appears to be in breach of good faith (which applies not only to authorities, but also to individuals), even though there might not be a specific provision prohibiting it. But since Santiago has seemingly not been 'convicted' for the loan of his licence, the criterion set by the governing rules was not met.

Thus Santiago might succeed in having the refusal to renew his licence quashed. Since the appeal would normally have suspensive effect, if the Fish Commission decision is quashed, Santiago would suffer no harm; thus no compensation would be necessary.

Again, the question of damages would only arise if the Commission revoked the suspensive effect of Santiago's appeal, and the court refused to reinstate it but eventually found that the licence should have been renewed, which is rather unlikely. For damages to be awarded (obviously for lost profit during the period when Santiago would have been unlawfully deprived of his licence) the Commission's action would have to be deemed in breach of a fundamental duty. The facts as stated in the case do not allow for a definite answer to that question. If the Commission has grossly erred in establishing the facts (because it was obvious that Santiago had not loaned his licence and it would have been easy for the Commission to reach that conclusion on the basis of the record or on the basis of documents or testimonies readily available), there was probably a breach of a fundamental duty. But that would not be the case if the Commission had simply constructed the relevant statutory provisions in a way ultimately not followed by the court.

K. United Kingdom

GA

This is a relatively straightforward scenario, which can be addressed briefly:

(1) The Commission's discretion, which is presumably sourced in statute, must always be exercised in a manner that is consistent not just with the statutory scheme but also with common law principles. Those principles include, for present purposes, reasonableness, fairness (both procedural and substantive), the requirement to consider all relevant considerations, and 'abuse of power'.[543]

(2) If the statute that underpins the Commission's powers does not expressly state that licences can be refused where they have previously been assigned to a third party, it is unlikely that the Commission's decision could stand. While there might well be an argument about spirit of the scheme being frustrated and/or the existence of implied conditions within the licence, the exercise of a statutory power for a reason that does not have an express basis within the statute would almost inevitably be deemed unlawful. This is all the more so given the serious economic consequences for Santiago.

(3) The suggestion that the decision was taken without evidence would potentially offend each of the common law principles noted above. For instance, the decision could, at its height, be said to be tainted by an abuse of power and/or be one that is 'so unreasonable that no reasonable decision-maker' could have taken it (this is the classic *Wednesbury* formulation of unreasonableness[544]).

[543] Though for recent judicial reticence about the value of terms such as 'substantive unfairness' and 'abuse of power', see *Gallaher v Competition and Markets Authority* [2018] 2 WLR 1583 para 41, Lord Carnwath.

[544] *Associated Provincial Picture Houses v Wednesbury Corporation* [1948] 1 KB 223.

It is also the case that, by making a decision without supporting evidence, the Commission would have failed to have taken all relevant considerations into account (where the failure may exist as a subset of unreasonableness). The requirements of substantive and procedural unfairness would arguably also be breached: refusal of a licence for a reason that is unsupported by evidence would be substantively unfair; while Santiago's inability to test the evidence would amount to a procedural unfairness. (Santiago might also argue that the decision interferes with his Article 1 Protocol 1 rights—though he would here need to show that a time-limited licence constitutes a property right for the purposes of the ECHR.)

(4) The remedy which Santiago should seek is a quashing order that would render the Commission decision *void ab initio* and which would require it to reconsider his application for renewal. If his licence was subsequently renewed, and if the court was satisfied that the public law illegality amounted to breach of a statutory duty, he may also obtain damages for loss of profit to the moment that he was able to use his licence again.

(5) The position in relation to damages would be more complex if there were other grounds for refusing him a licence within the terms of the statutory scheme. If there were such grounds, and if the Commission subsequently refused to renew his licence for one or more of those reasons, this could lead to interesting arguments about whether his loss could be recognized in law. While Santiago would inevitably say that it could be recognized, the Commission would argue that he could have expected to make a profit only until the moment that he had to apply for renewal of his licence. A (belatedly) lawful refusal might therefore mean that he never had any entitlement to make profit from use of the licence (though it might be expected that a small amount of compensation would be paid on a voluntary basis to address the period of time between the unlawful and lawful decisions).

To recap: Santiago would have very strong public law grounds for challenging the decision, and he may well be granted a quashing order. The success of a damages claim would depend upon whether he was subsequently granted a licence by the Commission.

X. Case 9—suspending the sale of beauty creams

Beauty Box has been authorized by the National Health Authority (NHA) to produce and sell a new set of beauty creams. Following a press campaign sponsored by activists who claim that Beauty Box used certain undisclosed ingredients in its new creams, which might be hazardous for human health, the NHA decides to temporarily suspend the sale of Beauty Box's new set of creams. Beauty Box then challenges the NHA's suspension order before a national court and claims damages on the ground that the order was not preceded and justified by an adequate fact-finding scientific procedure.

Would Beauty Box's action be successful? If so, how would the amount of any damage be determined?

A. Austria

SS, KB, DB, and LM

Placing cosmetic products on the Austrian market is regulated in the LMSVG. The directly applicable legal acts of the EU in this field are listed in the annex of the LMSVG and implemented within its framework.[545] In general, cosmetic products need to adhere to certain legal standards in order to be eligible for market placement.[546] In particular, cosmetic products must not be hazardous to human health, which is the case if the respective product is capable of endangering or harming human health.[547]

In the event of perceived infringements of the LMSVG's safety standards for products like cosmetics, the competent authority has to adopt the necessary measures pursuant to § 39(1) LMSVG to correct faults and minimize risks. In doing so, the type of infringement needs to be taken into account, and the principle of proportionality has to be respected.[548] The temporary suspension of sales in order to scrutinize the cosmetic product with regard to the alleged hazardous ingredients is considered a measure pursuant to § 39(1) LMSVG, specifically mentioned in § 39 (1) paragraph 1 LMSVG. The suspension order has to be qualified as an administrative act.

The notion of perceived infringements has to be understood as a reasonable suspicion based on either the observations of a control organ or another qualified body mentioned in the LMSVG.[549] A press campaign sponsored by activists on its own is not suited to meet these standards.

Adopting measures pursuant to § 39(1) LMSVG merely on account of statements by the activists—without ascertaining the alleged infringements by means of control organs or other qualified bodies—constitutes an unlawful administrative act by the public authority. Even if sale of the alleged hazardous cosmetics has been temporarily suspended to carry out thorough tests and assess whether the allegations have merit or

[545] LMSVG s 4(1).
[546] ibid s 18(1)(2).
[547] ibid s 18(1) No 1 in conjunction with s 5(1) No 1.
[548] ibid s 39(1). According to this provision, the state governor (*Landeshautpmann*) is the competent authority.
[549] M Blass and others, *Lebensmittelrecht* (14th suppl, Manz 2018) s 39 para 3.

not, it would have been necessary to further investigate the allegations of the activists and analyse whether they are capable of raising a reasonable suspicion as to the infringement of the product standards established by the LMSVG.

If an infringement has been perceived, the public authority is obliged to perform a public administrative procedure under the AVG, encompassing the right of Beauty Box to be heard and the conduct of the necessary scientific investigation of the allegations.[550] Pursuant to § 39(3) LMSVG, in cases of real and present danger the control organ of the public authority may—after informing the business owner or the person in charge—adopt the immediate measures mentioned in § 39(1) without conducting an administrative procedure as established by the AVG. The adopted measure ceases to be in force if the public authority fails to produce a written administrative act repeating the adopted measures within one week.

Beauty Box is therefore eligible to challenge the administrative act before the competent VwG. In fact, the VwG will state the unlawfulness of the suspension order of the competent public authority, annul its decision, and refer the case back to the public authority with the order to conduct further investigations up to the point where the criterion of reasonable suspicion for an infringement of the LMSVG is fulfilled.[551] Furthermore, legal remedies against administrative acts generally have a suspensory effect, which means that the suspension of sales does not enter into force until the VwG has delivered its judgment.[552] The suspensory effect may—under certain circumstances—be excluded by an order of the public authority.[553]

As already pointed out in section I.A, the extent of public authority liability is determined by the degree of fault pursuant to the provisions of Austrian civil law. If there is an aggravated degree of fault, namely gross negligence or intent, the claimed damages would cover the chance to generate income through the placement of the cosmetic which was temporarily suspended due to its alleged hazard to human health on the market. However, to qualify the authority's temporary suspension merely based on the allegations of activists—without having investigated whether those allegations are capable of having potential merit insofar as they meet the criterion of reasonable suspicion for an infringement of the LMSVG—as a grossly negligent measure appears to be disproportionate. Although the public authority adopted the suspension of sales prematurely and without conducting the necessary preliminary investigation, it was only concerned with protecting human health from the allegedly hazardous cosmetics, suspending sales only for a limited period of time in order to assess whether the allegations have merit. As a result, a gross breach of diligence did not occur; it should be considered a minor form of negligence.

Either way, according to the general rules of civil law, the claimant bears the full burden of proof, especially regarding the circumstances regarding the damage incurred and the fault of the public authority.[554] The claimant is therefore obliged to

[550] ibid para 2.
[551] VwGVG s 28(3).
[552] ibid s 13(1).
[553] ibid s 13(2).
[554] OGH 15 September 1992, 1 Ob 28/92; 25 February 2016, 9 Ob 83/15v; Ziehensack (n 468) s 1 para 1070; Kodek (n 12) para 15.

quantify his own damages. Nevertheless, this burden of proof is reversed in the context of public authority liability with regard to establishing the public authority's fault. Since the organs of a public authority are strictly obliged to obey the law, the burden of proof to establish the absence of fault as the defendant in a public authority liability suit rests upon the public authority itself.[555] As a consequence, the public authority is obliged to prove minor negligence when basing its temporary suspension of sales only on the allegations put forward by the activists.

As pointed out in cases 1 and 7, a prerequisite to claim lost profit successfully is the establishment of gross negligence. Since the public authority's temporary suspension is not considered a gross breach of diligence, but merely a minor negligence, Beauty Box will not be eligible for damages against its lost profit due to the suspension of sales. In the hypothetical case that issuing the suspension order were to be classified as a gross breach of diligence, the lost profit would need to be calculated in a subjective-concrete fashion.[556] The detrimental effects of the suspension order on Beauty Box's assets would be analysed in such a way that a comparison would be conducted between the assets after the suspension order and the hypothetical assets if the suspension order had not been issued.[557] It is sufficient to identify the selective effects on the assets.[558]

B. European Union

BM

In the EU, any restriction based on a public health risk must be based on a rigorous, scientific, independent, and up-to-date risk assessment. A decision to suspend the marketing authorization of a cream must be based on an independent risk assessment and respect the principle of proportionality. A press campaign promoted by activists cannot be the basis for suspension by the authority.

Beauty Box is entitled to challenge the decision to suspend the marketing authorization of the product before the court, complaining about the lack of reasonableness and proportionality and the absence of adequate scientific evidence.

In a claim for damages, however, Beauty Box cannot simply prove the economic damage resulting from the suspension of the marketing authorization and the causal link between the suspension and the economic loss suffered. It must demonstrate that the rule breached was intended to protect individuals and that the breach is sufficiently qualified. Even if the last condition is not easy to prove when the decision involves objectively complex scientific assessments,[559] in this case a fact-finding

[555] Schragel (n 468) s 1 para 161; OGH 30 September 2008, 1 Ob 225/07ff; Ziehensack (n 468) s 1 para 1073.

[556] Kodek (n 12) para 25 with further evidence.

[557] OGH 24 June 2003, 3 Ob 304/02ff; 9 July 2008, 7 Ob 81/08z; 11 November 2010, 3 Ob 109/10s; Kodek (n 12) para 21.

[558] Reischauer '§ 1293' in Rummel (n 471) para 2a; Kodek (n 12) para 21.

[559] Case T-199/96 *Bergaderm and Goupil v Commission* [1998] ECR II-02805, judgment of the Court of First Instance 16 July 1998; Case C-352/98 P, *Bergaderm and Goupil v Commission* [2000] ECR I-05291, judgment of the Court 4 July 2000 paras 40 and 42– 44. In this ruling, the Court asserted that the

procedure was totally lacking and the court could conclude for a manifest error of assessment and a breach of the principle of proportionality, with the consequence that a serious breach of a higher-ranking rule of law for the protection of individuals can be declared.

C. France

TP

The success of Beauty Box's action depends on the existence of the urgency condition that determined whether or not the suspension order should have been preceded by a complete procedure. If the order is annulled, damages will vary according to the direct and certain losses caused by the unlawful suspension.

In France, a cosmetic product is regulated by Article L-5311-1 of the Code of Public Health, as well as by EU norms. It is not subject to a prior authorization procedure, but the producer is responsible for the safety and must ensure that Beauty Box undergoes an expert scientific safety assessment before it is put on the market. Moreover, every cosmetic product has a file with all the information about its ingredients and the safety evaluation, which must be updated and made available for the Health Authority. Therefore, undisclosed ingredients that may be hazardous for human health may be a serious breach of legal obligations by Beauty Box and can cause the suspension of the cream until full compliance with regulation. But Beauty Box has not hidden any ingredient or safety information, and this is the reason why it challenges the suspension order.

The suspension powers of the Health Authority (HA) in France regarding cosmetic products are regulated by Article L5312-1 of the Code of Public Health,[560] which explicitly sets out a procedure within which the company may present its observations and show evidence allowing a 'fact-finding' scientific procedure, before a decision is taken.

However, there is an exception in cases of emergency. If the HA considers that human health is in danger or that the cream can cause immediate serious damage, it is required to suspend Beauty Box's product before 'completing' a procedure and inform EU authorities immediately. This is important, because if the HA is aware that the cream can cause damage and does nothing about it in good time, it is liable for supervisory misconduct. The action brought by Beauty Box would only succeed if the court finds that there was no urgency. To respect the HA's prerogatives, the court should check whether there has been any manifest error of assessment of the emergency condition.

Commission made a correct evaluation of the facts and that there was nothing in the documents before the judge 'to support the conclusion that the Commission misunderstood the scientific arguments concerning the extent of the risk involved in the use of sun oil containing bergamot essence' (para 63). Furthermore, in the light of the precautionary principle, 'where there is uncertainty as to the existence or extent of risks to the health of consumers, the institutions may take protective measures without having to wait until the reality and the seriousness of those risks become fully apparent' (para 66).

[560] See Art L5312-1.

In *Menarini*, the *Conseil d'Etat* annulled the suspension order on the basis of these facts: the product's effects on human health, their seriousness (the secondary effects were temporary and caused by misuse), the number of cases, and the absence of any action of European countries and/or the European Commission after the suspension information by the French authority. All available information proved that there was no serious and convincing evidence of the risk to human health justifying the emergency; thus, there was a manifest error of assessment and the HA should have followed the ordinary procedure.[561]

Regarding Beauty Box, we do not know whether the suspension order is the consequence of the campaign or if there were serious consequences and effects on human health to justify an urgent decision. Therefore, it is not possible to conclude whether the claim will succeed or not.

If the court establishes that there was an emergency, Beauty Box would have no right to compensation and should make its observations during the procedure for the final decision.[562] If the order is annulled, Beauty Box could claim compensation for the profits lost during the suspension and any actual loss it suffered as a direct consequence of the suspension order, including the additional expenses to remove its products from the market. The lost profits may be established in accordance with the information available and the company's turnover.[563] The court may consider that the HA would not be liable for the loss caused by the campaign, and in determining the compensation, would verify whether there had been any previous reduction of profits after publicity, because this damage had been caused by third parties. The court may then compensate only the profits already reduced after the campaign. The damage to the company's reputation may also be awarded on a case-by-case basis considering the publicity surrounding suspension and its impact on the company, for example by a reduction in sales of other products on the market, and its conditions.[564]

Finally, if Beauty Box makes a claim about interests, the court would order this payment from the date of the compensation claim, even if this was after the annulment of the suspension decision.[565] The court must explicitly address the interest[566] and capitalization question when claimed by the company. The interest rate is legally[567] established every six months by an order of the Ministry of Economy, and interests can be capitalized after a delay of more than one year for payment according to Article 1343-2 CC. If the HA does not pay the compensation ordered within the next two months after notification, the interest rate increases by five points (*taux majoré*)[568] if the court does not decide otherwise.

[561] CE 7 July 2010 *Société Menarini France* No 335101.

[562] Directive 2001/83/CE of the Parlement Européen and Council of 6 November 2001, amended by Directive 2010/84/UE of 15 December 2010.

[563] CE *Ministre de la Santé publique et de la Sécurité sociale c Union des sociétés de secours mutualiste de la région de Dieppe* (n 363).

[564] Cour Administrative d'Appel de Paris 25 March 1993 Req No 90PA00839, Lebon T.

[565] Picard (n 197) No 256.

[566] CE *Société Pradeau et Morin* (n 198).

[567] According to Art L313-2 of the *Code monétaire et financier*, this rate is defined by financial and monetary conditions, and the methodology for its calculation is established in a Decree.

[568] L313-3 *Code monétaire et financier*.

D. Germany

FW and JS

Beauty Box is obliged to challenge the suspension in order to avoid the preclusion of damages. Hence, Beauty Box has to lodge an action for annulment (*Anfechtungsklage*, § 42 para 1 alternative 1 VwGO). In principle, such an action has suspensive effect. Yet, *in casu*, an exception applies; the suspensive effect is excluded by § 80 paragraph 2 sentence 1 No 3 VwGO in conjunction with § 39 paragraph 7 No 3 LFGB[569]. The latter provision stipulates that certain actions have no suspensive effect. This includes measures taken in order to enforce § 26 LFGB, which prohibits the handling of cosmetics that might pose a threat to health. Since this provision applies here, Beauty Box is required to lodge a request for ordering the suspensive effect of its action for annulment (§ 80 para 5 sentence 1 VwGO).

With regard to the merits of an action for annulment, § 113 paragraph 1 sentence 1 VwGO stipulates that '[i]nsofar as the administrative act is unlawful and the claimant's rights have been violated, the court shall rescind the administrative act and any ruling on an objection'. The administrative act—ie the suspension order—may lack a valid legal basis or be formally and/or substantively unlawful. As for a valid legal basis, § 39 paragraph 2 sentence 1 LFGB authorizes:

> the competent agencies to issue the necessary ordinances and adopt the necessary measures
> - to confirm or dispel a sufficient suspicion of a breach or
> - to remedy detected breaches or
> - to prevent future breaches, dangers to health, or deceit.[570]

§ 39 paragraph 2 sentence 2 LFGB lists examples of possible orders and measures: No 2, the right to temporarily prohibit the placing on the market of products subject to sampling measures whose results have not yet been presented, might be particularly relevant here, since it could serve as a valid legal basis for the suspension order. Number 3, authorizing bans of, or limitations on, the 'production, treatment or placing on the market', would require that the insufficiency of the product be proven.[571]

Provided that all formal requirements—ie the NHA's competence as well as the rules on procedure and form of the action—have been observed, the lawfulness of the suspension order depends on whether all the substantive prerequisites of § 39 paragraph 2 sentences 1 and 2 LFGB can be established.

If the NHA invokes § 39 paragraph 2 sentence 2 No 2, sentence 1 LFGB, the alleged lack of an 'adequate fact-finding procedure' might be overcome, since this provision does not require the procedure to have been completed, but authorizes temporary

[569] See n 428.
[570] Own translation of the *Lebensmittel-, Bedarfsgegenstände- und Futtermittelgesetzbuch* (see n 428).
[571] AH Meyer, '§ 39' in AH Meyer and R Streinz (eds), *LFGB-BasisVO-HCVO* (2nd edn, CH Beck 2012) para 22.

measures until the results of a sampling measure are available.[572] This means, however, that § 39 paragraph 2 No 2 LFGB only applies in cases where a fact-finding procedure has been started, but not yet concluded. Furthermore, No 3, authorizing bans of, or limitations on, the 'production, treatment or placing on the market', requires that there already be proof of the unsuitability of the product.[573] This is not the case here, since the NHA merely reacted to allegations by activists. Therefore, the administrative court would annul the suspension order. As an interim measure, it would order the suspensive effect of the remedy.

With regard to damages under the general rules on public authority liability, Beauty Box finds itself in the same situation as North Lake in case 5. In particular, in view of the exclusion contained in § 839 paragraph 3 BGB, a claim for damages is only possible with regard to damages not avertable by a remedy, notably because they occurred before a suspensive order was available, and/or in the case of an unsuccessful court action, ie if the administrative court rejects the suspensive order or holds Beauty Box's action in the main proceedings unfounded. In the latter situation, the issue arises whether the civil court hearing the subsequent liability case is bound by the administrative judiciary's decisions.

In casu, an official of the NHA acted at least negligently by breaching the duty to act according to the law (*gesetzmäßiges Verhalten*)[574] which exists in relation to a third party when NHA issued the suspension order. This caused Beauty Box damage, the amount of which is to be determined as explained in case 2: actual loss arising, for example, from the disposal of creams that reached their expiry date in the course of the suspension is to be compensated according to § 249 paragraph 1 BGB. According to § 252 BGB, Beauty Box can also claim lost profits. The burden of proof with regard to the actual amount of the damage is relaxed under § 287 paragraph 1 sentence 1 ZPO, as shown in case 2.

In summary, Beauty Box may only claim damages for harm that could not have been averted by challenging the authority's suspension order. Thus, only very limited space remains for a claim for damages. Damages under the general provisions on public authority liability also comprise lost profits.

E. Hungary

LB

In Hungary, the marketization of beauty creams can be suspended in the event of serious risk to human health. Both EU and national rules are relevant for these purposes. A claim for damages is unlikely to succeed.

First, EU Regulation No 1223/2009 applies. Under its rules, the competent public authority shall take all appropriate measures to prohibit or restrict making available on the market the cosmetic product or to withdraw the product from the market, or to

[572] It can therefore be regarded as a manifestation of the precautionary principle. For an overview of the application of the precautionary principle in food and feed law, see Rathke (n 429) paras 14f.

[573] Meyer (n 571) para 22.

[574] See n 143 and n 367.

recall it where an immediate action is necessary in the event of serious risk to human health. More specifically, according to Article 4(2) for each cosmetic product placed on the market, the responsible person shall ensure compliance with the relevant obligations set out in the Regulation. The 'responsible person' is the one primarily responsible for product safety; this person must intervene if there is a problem, but other authorities have an obligation to protect human life and health, too. The aim to be achieved (that human health should be exposed to no danger, or as little danger as possible) is consistent (to a large extent) with the possibility that the authority may intervene in the absence of any action by the responsible person, or even without waiting for the actions taken by the person responsible.

Second, in a claim for damages, the court would not hold the decision taken by the public authority to be an infringement of the law and would thus reject the claim.

F. Italy

FC

The claim filed by Beauty Box could plausibly be accepted by an Italian administrative court. And, similarly, a connected claim for compensation would be accepted, covering all damages, including lost revenue and damages to the image (ie the business reputation) of Beauty Box.

Indeed, the fact that the authority can invoke the general precautionary principle does not exclude the applicability to the case in question of the principle that requires the authority itself to perform an adequate preliminary investigation, initiating a procedure in which the party involved can intervene by producing the documentation that they consider actually relevant and that the authority itself is obliged to examine.

In practice, however, in debating the possible legitimacy of the act adopted by the NHA, it might be important to consider the duration of the suspension of the distribution of the product in question: if it were a very short period of time, it might be considered reasonable, and therefore lawful, to adopt an urgent provision, which could ultimately be replaced by a permanent provision, adopted as a result of a procedure to collect all possible scientific evidence.

G. Poland

Łukasz Dziamski

The solution that a court would be likely to give is as follows. First, the suspension order would be annulled by the competent public administration authority or administrative court as a party's right to adequate fact-finding proceedings has been infringed; this right is directly defined in Articles 7, 77, and 80 of the Polish Code of Administrative Procedure. Second, if Beauty Box obtains the above-mentioned annulment decision, this decision is a precondition for awarding damages. Third, in separate proceedings before the civil court, damages could be awarded to Beauty Box.

Damages are awarded provided that an act of a public authority is deemed unlawful. It does not matter whether there is a breach of substantive or procedural law. In the above case, if any investigation or research gives rise to reasonable suspicion that a given medicinal product does not comply with the quality requirements specified for such a product, the bodies of the State Pharmaceutical Inspection issue appropriate decisions: first, the Chief Pharmaceutical Inspector will issue a decision to suspend the distribution of specified batches of the medicinal product in the area of its activity; second, the Chief Pharmaceutical Inspector will issue a decision to suspend distribution of a product nationwide under the provisions of Article 121 section 2 of the Act of 6 September 2001—Pharmaceutical Law. Following such decisions, the distribution (sale) of specified batches of the medical product by wholesalers and pharmacies, is suspended until the results of laboratory analysis confirm or rule out a defect in the product.

An analogous solution occurs if the creams produced by Beauty Box are qualified as cosmetic products. In this case, the national authority competent to apply provisional measures under Article 27 of Regulation (EC) No 1223/2009 of the European Parliament and of the Council of 30 November 2009 on cosmetic products (recast) will be the Chief Sanitary Inspector (in accordance with Art 21 para 1 of the Polish Act of 4 October 2018 on cosmetic products).

Hence, Beauty Box must prove that the decision to suspend the distribution of the specified medicinal product was issued in violation of the law, and must subsequently institute a civil claim with a court of general jurisdiction. According to Articles 7, 77, and 80 of the Polish Code of Administrative Procedure (CAP), a party has a right to adequate fact-finding proceedings, and violation of this right is qualified as an authority's serious misconduct, leading to the annulment of a decision made without any fact-finding procedure.

Similarly to cases Nos 7 and 9, it is theoretically possible to be awarded damages; however, this would be preceded by a long procedural battle before various authorities.

As set forth in legal commentaries, in the event of loss of profit, and while determining its value, one of the most difficult issues is to differentiate between the loss as such and the lost opportunity (*utracona szansa*).[575] It is the obligation of the injured party to identify, to a high degree of probability, the circumstances regarding profit that might have been gained and which is sought; such circumstances are necessarily hypothetical. The courts assume that a loss occurred if the injured party is able to prove the probability of so great a financial advantage that one may reasonably assume that the injured party would have certainly gained financial advantage if the event preventing such gain had not occurred.[576]

In conclusion, the appeal and possible claim by Beauty Box may be effective based on the grounds that procedural rules have been violated. Moreover, compensation awarded under Article 417 CC is calculated according to general rules for

[575] See E Bagińska, *Przesłanki odpowiedzialności deliktowej za niezgodne z prawem wykonywanie władzy publicznej* in R Hauser, A Wróbel, Z Niewiadomski (ed), *System prawa administracyjnego* ('Administrative Law System'), vol 12 (CH Beck 2010) 421.

[576] II CR 304/79, OSN 1980 No 9 item 164, judgment of the Supreme Court 3 October 1979; III CZP 123/08, OSN 2009 No 11 item 45, Resolution of the Supreme Court 5 December 2008.

estimating damages under the Code and includes losses and loss of profit, evidenced by Beauty Box.

H. Romania

RV

In order for Beauty Box's claim for damages to be successful, it would first have to prove that the act of temporary suspension was illegal. Insufficient scientific fact-finding procedures would lead to the temporary suspension being considered in the judicial review proceedings as an excess of power by the NHA.

A successful line of defence for the NHA would be that the scientific *status quo* at the time when Beauty Box was authorized to market the products has changed and that scientific discoveries have led to a new factual situation that needs to be reflected in a new administrative act.

Pursuant to a possible successful annulment claim, Beauty Box can ask to be compensated for the damage, consisting of loss of the profit they would have registered through commercialization of the products for the entire duration of the suspension order.

I. Spain

EMNG

The success of Beauty Box's case would depend on the justification given by the NHA. The court would decide whether, on the basis of the data available, the NHA's decision was reasonable in terms of protecting public health. If the court declared the NHA decision void, either because there was no evidence that any undisclosed ingredient was used to produce the new creams or because the order was not preceded and justified by an adequate scientific fact-finding procedure (although such a procedure is imposed by a regulation), the court would grant compensation for the damage caused to Beauty Box.

The amount of damages would be determined by taking into account the damage to Beauty Box's reputation, how much it would cost to recover its market reputation, and current lost and loss profit. To assess the amount of compensation, the court would stick to a factual assessment, without considering whether the void decision was reasonable or not.

J. Switzerland

TT

In Switzerland, the marketization of a beauty cream does not require authorization, but the use of a new substance in the said beauty cream must be notified to the competent federal authority. If this authority has good reason to believe that substances or preparations represent a health hazard, it may, amongst other measures, prohibit placing them on the market, or make them subject to special conditions (Art 41 of the Federal Chemical Act 2000, ChemA).

The decision to suspend the marketization of the beauty cream pursuant to Article 41 ChemA can be appealed before the FAT. In the present case, it is very likely that the competent authority would have revoked the suspensive effect of the appeal. Beauty Box would therefore be prevented from marketing the product pending appeal.

Since Article 41 ChemA only requires the authority to have 'good reason to believe' that some new ingredients of the beauty cream represent a health hazard, the argument that its order was not preceded and justified by an adequate scientific fact-finding procedure has little chance of prevailing. Article 41 ChemA works as a 'safeguard clause' (as indicated in the heading of the Article). Thus, a full fact-finding procedure would normally follow, not precede, the safeguarding orders issued under this provision.

If Beauty Box nevertheless prevails, the award of damages would require the authority to have acted in breach of a fundamental duty. A mere misjudgement of the facts or an erroneous interpretation of the law would not suffice. Beauty Box's chances of obtaining damages are thus even slimmer than of having the order quashed. If, against those odds, damages are nevertheless awarded (following the procedure set out in Chapter 12, Section III), their amount would be assessed in order to fully compensate the loss that could be traced (natural and adequate causation) to the temporary deprivation of the right to market the beauty cream or to the harm to the commercial reputation of Beauty Box.

K. United Kingdom

GA

The issues arising here would essentially concern the use of statutory powers for reasons of protecting public health. Two assumptions are made for this purpose: (i) that the NHA is a body established by statute; and (ii) that its underlying legislation includes a 'catch-all' provision that gives it a general role in protecting public health.

Were Beauty Box to bring proceedings, the following points might arise:

(1) Whether it is possible for the NHA peremptorily to suspend a product and to conduct an *ex post facto* investigation into the issue of undisclosed ingredients. Broadly speaking, there is some legal authority that would suggest that such steps might be taken to protect public health,[577] though the courts would expect investigative steps to be taken immediately, given the impact on Beauty Box's commercial interests. Were the NHA able to demonstrate that it was actively examining the issue, this would potentially provide it with a defence to a challenge to the suspension order.

[577] See eg *R v Davey* [1899] 2 QB 301.

(2) If it would not be legally permissible for the NHA to act in a peremptory fashion, the NHA would need to have verifiable evidence of risk in advance of making the suspension order. This is perhaps where the word 'adequate' that is used in the scenario becomes important. For instance, if the NHA had relied solely upon the details of the press campaign, Beauty Box would have a strong argument about a lack of evidence to support a decision (the decision thereby being unreasonable, or based upon a failure to have regard for relevant considerations). However, if the NHA had conducted preliminary tests on samples of the product, or if the press reports referred to scientific studies that indicated that there was a risk to health (and the NHA acquired copies of those reports before acting), this may bring its actions within the term 'adequate'. (Of course, the greater the evidence, the greater the adequacy of the fact-finding process.)

(3) The next question would concern the intensity of review that the court might use when assessing the legality of the NHA's suspension decision. At one level, there would plainly be a link to the quality of the evidence that would be before the court, where the court could be expected to be more restrained in the face of greater amounts of scientific evidence. However, even if there is only a limited amount of evidence in support of the NHA's decision, the court might still adopt a restrained approach if the evidence is credible and can be objectively assessed as such. This is because the court would be keenly aware of the public health dimension to the case and may consider that it should defer in the face of expert evidence and the powers of the NHA.

(4) The issue of damages in a case of this kind is potentially very vexed. Certainly, it is highly unlikely that the courts would read the NHA's general statutory powers as giving rise to a statutory duty of care towards Beauty Box, as the powers in question would be owed to society as a whole, rather than sectors within it (here, a commercial interest). Moreover, the case law on investigative powers in the UK has historically been reluctant to impose a common law duty of care on decision-makers, for the reason that the imposition of liability would undermine the very purposes for which statutory powers have been granted. Beauty Box may therefore be able to obtain compensation only if it were to be paid to it on an *ex gratia* basis, or if a subsequent complaint to the ombudsman resulted in a recommendation that compensation should be paid (see comment (m) at the beginning of Chapter 13). An action for breach of statutory duty and/or negligence—not to mention misfeasance in public office—would face significant challenges.

To recap: Beauty Box's case would be at its strongest if the courts were of the view that the NHA would need objectively verified evidence before imposing a suspension order. However, if such evidence was in existence, a reviewing court may well exercise great restraint, given the public health and expert evidence dimensions to the challenged decisions. A formal private law cause of action would face significant difficulties: compensation may be payable only on an *ex gratia* basis of a recommendation of the ombudsman.

XI. Case 10—a negligent drug authority

Peter's young son, Luka, is harmed by a defective pharmaceutical product. The product entered the market with the approval of the national drug authority a month before Luka's accident. Subsequently, due to the high number of adverse drug reactions, the company producing the product withdraws it from the market and goes bankrupt. Peter, on behalf of his child and himself, sues the national drug authority for damages on two grounds: (i) the authority had received scientific evidence from an NGO contrary to issuing the authorization, but this evidence was not taken into account; (ii) under national legislation, when private parties provide different or contrary scientific evidence, the national drug authority is obliged to consult a technical body, but in this case it failed to do so.

Would the national drug authority be held liable, and if so, under what conditions?

A. Austria

SS, KB, DB, and LM

As already pointed out earlier in Chapter 3, a key feature of the Austrian law on public authority liability is that claims in this context may only be brought against legal entities under Article 23 B-VG in conjunction with § 1(1) AHG: namely the Federation, the Provinces, and the municipalities, in addition to any other bodies based on public law.[578] The Austrian drug authority (the *Bundesamt für Sicherheit im Gesundheitswesen*, BASG) is responsible for adopting public authority measures in the field of the control and sales of drugs on the Austrian market.[579] Despite exercising public authority, it is not categorized as another legal entity pursuant to § 1(1) AHG, because the BASG is a subordinate department of the Austrian Ministry of Health and Women.

The BASG is thus not a suitable defendant for a public authority liability claim, which would have led to the rejection of Peter's claim by the competent court. In the event that Peter sued the right legal entity, namely the Austrian Federation, which the Ministry of Health represents, the claim would have been admissible. As a result, the competent court would have been able to rule on the merits of Peter's allegations.

Based on the requirements for public authority liability, which are assessed on the basis of civil law,[580] Peter has to establish that the BASG failed to consider the received scientific evidence insofar as it did not consult the technical body provided for by law, to determine who was responsible for the occurred damages. Therefore Peter has to prove that the BASG was legally obliged to consult the technical body due to the presentation of the contrary scientific evidence by the NGO, that this omission amounts to an unlawful action, and that if the BASG had obeyed the law, Luka would have suffered no harm. As pointed out in Chapter 3, the burden of proof regarding the lack of fault rests with the public authority.

[578] Schragel (n 468) s 1 para 19ff; Ziehensack (n 468) s 1 para 500.

[579] Pursuant to the Austrian Law on Medicinal Products (*Arzneimittelgesetz*—AMG), Federal Law Gazette No 185/1983 as amended.

[580] The criteria have been set out in Storr and others, Chapter 3 in this volume (n 344), section I.

Luka's suffering is certainly qualified as actual damage, and needs to be quantified by Peter as the claimant. This injury was caused by the BSAG's omission to consult the technical body with the evidence presented by the NGO, since further assessment of the hazardous drug in the light of the new evidence would have resulted in it not entering the market[581] and could therefore not harm Luka's health. Not consulting the technical body amounts to a procedural error that constitutes the unlawfulness of the BASG's conduct. It will not be possible for the defendant to prove its lack of fault.

As a result, Peter's claim for public authority liability will be successful.

B. European Union

BM

The centralized procedure for the authorization and supervision of medical products (governed by Regulation EC No 726/2004) provides that the decision to authorize (and revoke) the sale of a drug is adopted by the Commission on the basis of an opinion issued by the Committee of Medicines of the European Medicines Agency (EMA).

According to European regulations, a company that intends to commercialize a drug must submit the application to the Commission, supporting its application with the required scientific documentation. During the procedure, the EMA Committee can provide, in turn, for consultation with NGOs, associations, and other interested parties. Once the opinion has been delivered, the EU Commission acknowledges it and publishes the proposed decision, giving the Member States an appropriate deadline (twenty-two days) to present observations.

A decision to authorize the marketization of a drug adopted without the opinion of the EMA Committee would be radically unlawful and voidable under Article 263 TFEU for infringement of an essential procedural requirement.

In an action for damages, however, it should first be established whether the rules providing for the opinion of the Medicines Committee are intended to ensure not only the institutional balance, but also the protection of the rights of individuals.

Furthermore, the court should determine whether the procedural unlawfulness is such as to integrate a sufficiently serious breach of the limits to the discretion of the Commission. Only if these conditions are fulfilled, can the Union's liability for damage suffered by Luka can be affirmed. Since the Commission's decision is entirely based on the opinion delivered by the Committee, an authorization issued without the EMA Committee's opinion (and lacking the scientific evaluation of the drug's harmfulness), could constitute a qualified breach leading to liability.

C. France

TP

Peter's action for damages would be successful because there is a procedural wrong that would have affected the authorization if the other elements of public liability are

[581] Under s 3(1) AMG, the sale of hazardous drugs is prohibited.

proved. In the last case, the recoverable losses for bodily injuries include damages for Luka and his parents.

According to both the *Danthony* case law and Article 70 of Law 2011-525, as explained in case 2 above, a procedural irregularity will lead to the annulment of the decision only if this defect (i) deprives the interested parties of a guarantee or a right; or (ii) it will have an influence in the outcome of the decision. In the second case, the court must analyse and consider the effects of the irregularity to determine whether the procedural argument is endorsed.[582]

Consultation with a technical body could have influenced the issuance or otherwise of the authorization. As the NGO had provided evidence against the drug, the technical body could have considered this material and more scientific information to provide an opinion. In fact, if there were several adverse reactions to the drug in a short period of time (one month), the technical body could probably have been able to foresee the negative effects and the HA should have refused to grant the drug's approval. The absence of consultation is a procedural weakness sufficient to annul the authorization decision, and misconduct is the first element of government liability. However, this would not automatically imply reparation for Luka and his family. The other two elements of liability, the damage and the causal link, must be proven to affirm that the drug caused the injuries suffered by Luka.

As the State is only liable for direct and certain damage,[583] Peter must demonstrate Luka's personal health condition, the quantity of the drug, and the effects, based on the scientific evidence and his personal circumstances, as well as the harm suffered. Nevertheless, the HA would be liable even if the authorization was lawful but the authority had failed in its pharmacovigilance duties. When a drug is authorized, the HA must monitor it. If it has new information regarding dangerous effects or a serious increase of adverse effects on human health, it has the power to suspend the product immediately when an emergency is recognized.

According to the *Conseil d'Etat*, 'simple misconduct' (*toute faute—faute simple*)[584] is sufficient to establish government liability in cases of pharmacovigilance, in view of the nature of the health authorities' powers. For other public activities, the State is only liable in cases of gross or voluntary misconduct (*faute lourde*). This is the case in some 'difficult' domains, such as financial supervision, in order to mitigate the administration's reluctance to act, because its inaction may be more harmful to the public interest, or when it is very difficult to foresee the consequences.[585]

In conclusion, 'simple' supervisory misconduct when the HA does not suspend or withdraw the authorization in the light of new evidence suggests that serious risk to

[582] CE *Danthony et autres* (n 125).

[583] CE 9 November 2016 *Affaire Mediator* No 393108.

[584] CE 9 November 2016 *Mme B et Ministre des affaires sociales, de la santé et des droits de la femme* Nos 393902, 39392.

[585] For instance, in the case of supervision of financial institutions, the *Conseil d'Etat* stated that the *faute lourde* is required to establish liability if the savers claim for compensation because of a surveillance fault. CE 22 June 1984 *Société 'Pierre et Cristal' et autres* No 18371 T and CE 30 November 2001 *Ministre de l'économie c K et autres* No 219562 Rec.

human health is enough to establish its liability, beginning from the moment the authority has enough evidence.[586]

In order to more clearly determine what damages are compensated in cases of bodily injury claims, in 2006 the Cour de Cassation organized an expert group headed by the president of the Second Chamber at that time, Jean-Pierre Dintilhac. This group proposed a classification of economic and non-economic losses ('*postes de prejudices*') before and after the definitive consequences for direct and indirect victims.[587] Although, this report was not binding, the Ministry of Justice recommended its use to the courts in 2007. However, the *Conseil d'Etat* proposed its own classification[588] up to 2013 and 2014, when it used Dintilhac's main categories for the first time.[589] Compensation must be proportionate to the damage suffered by Luka and his family. The award covers (i) material loss; and (ii) suffering.

Material losses cover past and future medical expenses (1),[590] including the extra costs associated with being disabled (2—*frais liés au handicap*),[591] for example adapting one's home or vehicle, or paying a nurse for assistance in daily-life activities. The loss of wages (3) by Luka's parents[592] and the loss of future earnings due to the temporal or permanent corporal damage suffered would be included (4): as Luka is a child, he would not normally receive wages at this stage, but if the damage is permanent, the compensation will include his future earnings. In the case of a permanent disability, the court may order an amount of money as an annuity if it is demonstrated that he will not be able to work and that the current amount will not ensure the variable future expenses.[593]

Courts would consider the victim's circumstances in assessing one or more recoverable losses: first, pain;[594] second, psychological suffering;[595] third, aesthetic loss[596] if, for example, Luka has lost a limb[597] or has a serious scar or a malformation;[598] fourth, damage to the sexual functions;[599] fifth, the loss of capacity for enjoyment[600] if he will not be able to enjoy activities such as his favourite sport; sixth, if Luka suffers damage

[586] CE *Mme B* (n 584).

[587] See the Justice webpage: <www.justice.gouv.fr/publication/dacs/consult/20141120-projetannexe.pdf> accessed 22 June 2020.

[588] CE *avis* 4 June 2007 *Lagier et Consorts Guignon* No 303422, 304214.

[589] CE 16 December 2013 *Mme Moraes* No 346575 and CE 28 May 2014 *Assistance publique–Hôpitaux de Paris* No 351237.

[590] Insurance companies may be part of the process of claiming reimbursement for the expenses paid by them. In the event of misconduct also by the aggrieved, special rules apply. See case 11. CE 25 June 1965 *Peyre* No 58465 60737, Lebon 388, is an insurance company's case.

[591] CE 10 December 2015 *Assistance publique–Hôpitaux de Paris (AP–HP)* No 374038, AJDA 2016 500.

[592] ibid.

[593] CE 12 June 1981 *Centre Hospitalier de Lisieux* No 02569.

[594] CE 6 June 1958 *Commune de Grigny*, Lebon 323. Before this decision, the *Conseil d'Etat* required that the pain be very serious and long term for compensation to be granted.

[595] CE 16 December 2013 *Mme Moraes* No 346575 (n 199).

[596] CE 23 March 1962 *Caisse régionale de sécurité sociale de Normandie et Souillié*, Lebon 211.

[597] CE 9 5 February 1954 *Sarotte* No 05082, Lebon 591.

[598] CE 27 September 1989 *Mme Karl c CPAM de la Marne* No 76105, Lebon 176.

[599] CE 28 May 2014 *Assistance publique–Hôpitaux de Paris* (n 589).

[600] CE *Mme Moraes* (n 199).

in relation to a 'future family project',[601] should he lose the possibility of having a family.

After the *Mediator* case,[602] the *Conseil d'Etat* also recognized a seventh type of damage: anxiety,[603] for example if the person did not suffer the adverse effects but was concerned about the negative consequences of the drug. In order to claim for this compensation, a person must prove his or her state, a serious risk, and anxiety at the prospect of having a worse illness or consequence.[604] Finally, there is a eighth category to compensate for any other damage to living conditions and expectations,[605] which the *Conseil d'Etat* defined before the Dintilhac classification and which compensates damage not only related to bodily injures. As a non-pecuniary loss, Luka's parents may claim for damages regarding changes to their living conditions because of their child's illness and/or damage.[606]

D. Germany

FW and JS

Since primary legal protection cannot prevent or limit the damage that has already been inflicted on Luka, § 839 paragraph 3 BGB does not preclude claiming damages.

A claim based on Article 34 sentence 1 GG read in conjunction with § 839 paragraph 1 sentence 1 BGB requires, as stated in case 1, that (1) an official (2) intentionally or negligently (3) breached the official duty incumbent upon him or her (4) in relation to a third party which (5) caused (6) the claimant harm. Finally, (7) the claim must not be excluded according to § 839 paragraph 1 sentence 2 BGB.

At the outset, it should be noted that the general provisions on public authority liability also apply alongside liability on the part of the drug company as stipulated in § 91 alternative 2 AMG[607]. This provision reads (with reference to the liability of the

[601] Dintilhac classification:

> Ce poste de préjudice cherche à indemniser la perte d'espoir, de chance ou de toute possibilité de réaliser un projet de vie familiale en raison de la gravité du handicap permanent, dont reste atteinte la victime après sa consolidation. Il s'agit de la perte d'une chance de fonder une famille, d'élever des enfants et, plus généralement, des bouleversements dans les projets de vie de la victime qui la contraignent à certains renoncements sur le plan familial.

[602] In the *Mediator* case, the Servier laboratory did not disclose (and hid) the effects of benfluorex: arterial hypertension and valve damage. This even caused the death of some patients. Some victims chose to bring criminal charges against the laboratory, and others also tried public liability for the supervisory negligence of the French Health Agency.

[603] This recoverable loss is not included in the Dintilhac classification and demonstrates that the *Conseil d'Etat* uses the categories, but it maintains its autonomy to recognize different losses.

[604] CE 9 November 2016 *Mme K et Ministre des affaires sociales, de la santé et des droits de la femme* No 393108. This prejudice is not recognized explicitly in Dintilhac, but it can be considered as part of suffering.

[605] CE 12 December 1975 *Guyader* No 95405; see also CE 2 November 2005 *Mme M* No 263059 and more recently, for a negative decision, 24 December 2019 *Societé Paris Clichy* No 425981.

[606] CE 28 May 2014 *Assistance publique–Hôpitaux de Paris* (n 589).

[607] *Arzneimittelgesetz* (Medicinal Products Act), English version <www.gesetze-im-internet.de/englisch_amg/englisch_amg.html> accessed 22 June 2020; A Spickhoff (ed), *Medizinrecht* (3nd edn, CH Beck 2018) s 91 para 3 AMG.

drug-producing company): 'This shall be without prejudice to legal provisions [...] according to which another party is responsible for the damage incurred.'

The fact that Peter would have acted also on behalf of Luka falls under § 51 paragraph 1 ZPO, which states that:

> [u]nless stipulated otherwise by the subsections hereinbelow, the ability of a party to appear before a court, the representation of parties having no capacity to sue or be sued by other persons (legal representatives), and the need for a special authorisation for the pursuit of court proceedings, are determined pursuant to the stipulations of civil law.

The respective civil law provisions allow Peter to represent Luka, either jointly with Luka's mother (§ 1629 para 1 sentence 2 BGB) or solely, if only he is entitled to custody (§ 1629 para 1 sentence 3 BGB).[608]

A breach of an official duty can be seen first in approving a drug despite the existence of (not further investigated) evidence contrary to issuing the authorization. Second, the officials of the national drug authority did not consult a technical body after they had received scientific evidence from an NGO and thereby acted contrary to national legislation. However, it remains questionable whether these duties exist in relation to a third party, which would only be the case if the duty aims to protect the third party's interests.[609] This cannot be determined without knowing more about the legal framework. Generally speaking, it is disputed whether the supervisory task of the German national drug authority aims to protect third parties.[610]

The court must then determine whether the wrongful decision was reached intentionally or negligently. In addition to the general obligation to adequately investigate the case (§ 24 paras 1f VwVfG and the corresponding *Länder* laws),[611] national law furthermore requires the national drug authority to consult a technical body upon the reception of 'different or contrary scientific evidence'. Since, generally speaking, officials are required to have or provide themselves with the legal and administrative knowledge which they need to carry out their profession,[612] the authority's officials can be assumed to know about this obligation. Therefore, officials from the national drug authority acted at least negligently in failing to consult the technical body after the presentation of evidence by an NGO.

There must also be a causal link between the breach of duty and the damage.[613] Luka's injury was caused 'by a defective drug product'. In the first place, the

[608] cf S Weth, '§ 51 ZPO' in Musielak and Voit (n 165) para 4.

[609] cf BGH 6 June 2013—III ZR 196/12, [2013] NJW 3370 (3371); Papier and Shirvani (n 141) para 227 with further references.

[610] Pro, W Kügel, '§ 25' in W Kügel, R-G Müller, and H-P Hofmann (eds), *Arzneimittelgesetz* (2nd edn, CH Beck 2016) para 230, pointing out BGH 16 February 1995—III ZR 135/93, BGHZ 129, 17, which dealt with official weather alerts. Contra, WA Rehmann, '§ 25' in WA Rehmann (ed), *Arzneimittelgesetz* (4th edn, CH Beck 2014) para 26 with further references.

[611] See case 8 for further details.

[612] cf BGH 11 December 1997—III ZR 52-97, [1998] NJW 1307 (1308); 10 February 2011—III ZR 37/10, BGHZ 188, 302 (307). See also Papier and Shirvani (n 141) para 289.

[613] H Oetker, '§ 249' in Säcker and others (n 171) paras 109ff; Papier and Shirvani (n 141) para 276.

company producing the product can be blamed. However, the product would not have reached Luka if officials had re-examined the product in view of the evidence contrary to issuing the authorization. The same is true of the second breach of duty, ie if the national drug authority had consulted a technical body after they had received scientific evidence from an NGO. The causation may also be attributed to the national drug authority, since there is neither any indication of an unusual or inappropriate action by Peter or Luka[614] nor any other unusual materialization of a hazard.[615] Of course, in both cases, affirming causation supposes that the authority would not have approved the drug if it had properly assessed its risks.

The national drug authority cannot argue that the damage would even have occurred had it not breached its duty (*Einwand rechtmäßigen Alternativverhaltens*)[616]. A different decision with regard to approving the drug cannot be excluded.

The obtainable damages generally include actual loss (§ 249 para 1 BGB), comprising medical expenses (§ 249 para 2 sentence 1 BGB) and damages for pain and suffering (§ 253 para 2 BGB). With regard to medical expenses/medical treatment, it has to be considered that they are initially covered by Luka's health insurance (§ 192 para 1 VVG[617] or §§ 1 sentence 1, 2 para 1 sentence 1 read in conjunction with §§ 11ff SGB V[618], depending on the kind of insurance). Subsequently, the insurer may claim reimbursement from the drug producer (§ 194 para 1 sentence 1 and § 86 para 1 sentence 1 VVG or § 116 para 1 sentence 1 SGB X, depending on the kind of insurance).[619] Peter might also claim costs for nursing[620]. Further claims might arise if Luka's injuries diminish his professional prospects.[621]

Finally, there is no indication here that Peter himself acted negligently, for example when applying the defective drug product to Luka, which might otherwise amount to contributory negligence and negatively affect Luka's claim (§ 254 paras 1 and 2 sentence 2 BGB).[622]

According to § 839 paragraph 1 sentence 2 BGB, liability may be excluded because of a third party's liability. This provision stipulates: 'If the official is only responsible because of negligence, then he may only be held liable if the injured person is not able to obtain compensation in another way.'

614 cf BGH 16 January 1992—III ZR 197/90, [1992] NJW 2086 (2087).

615 cf Papier and Shirvani (n 141) para 281.

616 See case 2 n 168; see also cases 4, 8, and 11.

617 *Versicherungsvertragsgesetz* (Insurance Contract Act), English version <www.gesetze-im-internet.de/englisch_vvg/englisch_vvg.html#p0675> accessed 22 June 2020.

618 *Sozialgesetzbuch, fünftes Buch* (Social Security Code, 5th vol), German version <www.gesetze-im-internet.de/sgb_5/BJNR024820988.html> accessed 22 June 2020.

619 Concerning problems arising from the insolvency of the drug-producing company, cf n 626.

620 J Eichelberger '§ 842' in Gsell and others (n 69) paras 350ff. Costs for intensified parental care can be claimed only under stringent prerequisites, namely when the care 'leaves the scope of "unfungible" affection which can only be granted by parents as the closest references and goes so far beyond the self-evident genuine task of the parents that support by third parties might become relevant not only in theory but as a practical alternative', own translation of BGH 8 June 1999—VI ZR 244-98, [1999] NJW 2819 (2819).

621 BGH 5 October 2010—VI ZR 186/98, [2011] NJW 1148 (1149), also pointing out s 287 ZPO to overcome difficulties in assessing the actual amount. Concerning s 287 ZPO, see case 2.

622 G Schiemann, '§ 254' in von Staudinger and others (n 65) para 104; H Oetker, '§ 254' in Säcker and others (n 171) para 134.

With regard to claims against the drug company, it should be noted, first of all, that § 25 paragraph 10 AMG[623] stipulates that the approval by the national drug authority is without prejudice to the criminal or civil law liability of the drug-producing company. However, this form of recourse, provided for by § 84 paragraph 1 sentence 1 AMG, is not available in Peter's case, since the drug company has gone bankrupt. § 839 paragraph 1 sentence 2 BGB thus does not exclude the liability of public authorities here, since 'the injured […] does not have to accept being referred to claims for reimbursement which he cannot enforce, at least not in the foreseeable or appropriate future'[624].

However, an insurer's liability might become relevant. § 94 paragraph 1 sentence 1 AMG contains an obligation to possess sufficient insurance coverage which, according to sentence 2 No 1,

> can only be made available by means of […] a third party insurance taken out with an independent insurance company authorised to conduct business within the purview of the present Act, for which, in the event of a reinsurance, a reinsurance contract exists only with a reinsurance company that [imposes further requirements regarding the reinsurance company].

Sentence 2 No 2 also allows for warranty obligations by credit institutions.

Under § 115 paragraph 1 sentence 1 No 2 VVG[625], which applies under § 94 paragraph 2 AMG,

> [t]he third party may also assert a claim for compensation against the insurer […] 2. where insolvency proceedings have been opened in respect of the assets of the policyholder or an application for such opening has been dismissed on account of a lack of insolvency estate or a provisional insolvency administrator has been appointed […][626].

Since the liability of the drug company was incurred before the opinion of the insolvency procedure was handed down, a claim against the insurer exists. Thus, the exclusion stipulated for by § 839 paragraph 1 sentence 2 BGB applies.[627]

If the exclusion did not apply, both the insurer and the public authority would be liable according to § 840 BGB.[628] The internal share of the damages to be paid is governed by §§ 421ff BGB; the division of liability depends on the respective degree of responsibility.

In summary, only if the licensing is qualified as taking place also in the individual interest may a claim for damages under the general provisions on public authority

[623] See n 607.

[624] BGH 26 March 1997—III ZR 295/96, [1997] NJW 2109; cf Papier and Shirvani (n 141) paras 317f.

[625] See n 617.

[626] The general provision on claims against insurers in cases of insolvency (s 110 VVG) is regarded as irrelevant in cases where s 115 VVG applies; see S Littbarski, '§ 110' in T Langheid and M Wandt (eds), *Münchener Kommentar zum VVG* (2nd edn, CH Beck 2017) para 11.

[627] It should be remarked, that s 839 para 1 sentence 2 BGB does not apply with regard to insurance policies that the injured party has taken out; see Papier and Shirvani (n 141) para 309.

[628] G Spindler, '§ 840' in Bamberger and others (n 63) para 2.

liability exist. In the event of direct liability on the part of the insurer, this claim would be excluded under § 839 paragraph 1 sentence 2 BGB. Otherwise, there would be joint liability of the public authority and the insurer.

E. Hungary

LB

Unlike previous cases, for which an answer could be found on the basis of both existing rules and the decisions taken by the courts, it is hard to find a solution for the issues raised by this case.

As a first step, the public authority can be held liable not for product liability but under the general rules concerning the liability of public authorities, including those of the CC, as well as those of the 2005 Act concerning medicinal products for human use.[629] This being the case, damages for infringement of personality rights can be awarded from the viewpoint of restitution, which is based on objective liability. Accordingly, only the gravity of the injury will determine the amount of restitution.

The general rules concerning government liability may be applied as follows. First, the infringement committed by the authority can be considered serious, because it had scientific evidence, but it did not take it into account and did not give any explanation concerning this evidence. The infringement, therefore, seems obvious. Second, and consequently, it engages government liability because, according to the preamble of the Medicine Act, the protection and restoration of human health is an activity of the State, and falls within its responsibility. Taking this into consideration, too, we can clearly state that the responsibility of the authority is high. Judicial practice rarely states that the infringement is serious, but in cases where it is quite obvious, it does not require much scrutiny and weighing: the courts tend to award damages. Finally, the difficult point would be to prove the causal link between the damage and the infringement, but with independent scientific evidence, it would probably be easier.

Regarding product liability, before the new Act on the Civil Code, the State had underlying liability when the manufacturer of the product was being exempt from liability and needed to award the damages according to the general rules, but with the new act this has changed, and there is no underlying liability. Also, third-party involvement does not exempt from liability, but the manufacturer can subsequently claim it for its damages. Without judicial practice concerning the liability of the public authorities, we cannot know if the negligence on the part of the authority can be considered as third-party involvement. If so (probably not), the manufacturer can bring a claim in court against the authority.

[629] Section 21 of this Act states that:

> (1) If, during the clinical trial of an investigational medicinal product, or as a consequence thereof, a natural person suffers health impairment, the injured person, or in the event of death, his/her family member provided for in the Civil Code' restitution shall be paid by either the sponsor of the trial or the authority which has authorized the clinical trials, if the death, disability or severe health impairment occurs in consequence of the specifications issued by such authority.

F. Italy

FC

The compensation claim filed by Peter could be accepted.

Indeed, in Italy there is an interpretation (and application) that considers authorities (even 'independent' ones[630]) whose lack of supervision contributed decisively to causing or aggravating damage potentially liable.

More specifically, it is necessary to prove the 'culpability' of the supervising authority. This means that the authority's failure to observe the general principles of public administration (Art 97 para 2, Const[631]) has to be proved; in other words the rules of impartiality, appropriateness, and good administration by which the exercise of its administrative functions must be inspired.[632]

In the specific case, what can be considered 'culpable' is the failure to observe a procedural obligation, which, if it had been followed, would have allowed the authority to substantiate the warnings received from the NGO and give notice of the real potential danger constituted by the product placed on the market.

G. Poland

Zbigniew Banaszczyk and Marek Wierzbowski

In this case, the State Treasury's liability could be based on Article 417(1) § 2 CC,[633] which makes public authorities liable for damages arising from final administrative decisions. However, when asserting claims for damages before an ordinary court, pursuant to the said provision, claimants should demonstrate the unlawfulness of the decision from which the damage resulted, established 'in relevant proceedings'; that is, they must produce a relevant administrative decision stating that the decision

[630] See Cour de Cassation No 3132/2001, in a case concerning the liability of the authority supervising financial markets. According to this ruling, a private applicant for damages could be considered a holder of a *diritto soggettivo*: so it is possible that compensation for this kind of damages falls to ordinary courts (Arts 24, 103 Const; Art 2 L No 2248/1865 Annex E; Art 7 CAT). On these types of controversies, see F Sclafani, 'La responsabilità civile delle autorità indipendenti nelle funzioni di regolazione e vigilanza dei mercati: molti interrogativi e poche certezze' (2017) 1 Rivista della Regolazione dei Mercati 8.

[631] 'Public administration offices shall be organised according to the provisions of law, so as to ensure the efficiency and impartiality of administration.'

[632] For this interpretation, see Cour de Cassation Joint Session No 500/1999, cited in F Cortese, Chapter 8 in this volume (n 174), section I. This interpretation is rather obscure, both because it makes it difficult for the claimant to prove this element (being a feature of the internal organization of the administration and not easily discernable to an outsider) and because it is very often the infringement of the rules on impartiality and correctness that makes the decision unlawful (such infringement therefore, would be implicit in itself in evaluating the unlawfulness of the act). For these reasons, for instance, the administrative court takes a different, objective approach: when the harmful decision is unlawful, misconduct on the part of the administration is assumed to subsist in itself (which works in effect like a presumption of the *res ipsa loquitor* type); however, the administration may successfully contend that the unlawfulness is not attributable in practical terms to fault on its part, pleading the existence of specific, reasonable justification (justifiable errors include interpretative complexity, due to differing case law guidelines, error occurring due to subsequent amending legislation or difficult-to-interpret legislative action, etc). On the topic of culpability, in general, see S Cimini, *La colpa nella responsabilità civile delle amministrazioni pubbliche* (Giappichelli 2008).

[633] See Arts 417, 417(1), 417(2), and 421 and M Wierzbowski, M Grzywacz, J Róg Dyrda, and K Ziółkowska, 'The Principles Governing Public Authority Liability in Poland', Chapter 9 in this volume, fn 2.

authorizing the medicine for trading is incompliant. This may be a decision that deems the medicine authorization invalid (Article 156 § 1 of the Code of Administrative Procedure—CAP), or even a decision limited to stating that the defective decision was issued in breach of the law (Art 158 § 2 of the Administrative Procedure Code). If there exist grounds for reinstating the administrative proceedings, a decision may be issued under Article 151 § 1 item 2 CAP, repealing the decision flawed with defects described in Article 145 § 1 or Articles 145a and 145b CAP. If the non-compliant administrative decision may not be repealed in administrative proceedings for reasons referred to in Article 146 of the Administrative Procedure Code, it may also be a decision limited to stating that the challenged decision was issued in violation of the law (Art 151 § 2 CAP).

In the circumstances of the case at hand, in which a public authority omitted the mandatory consultations with a 'technical authority' regarding the scientific evidence with which it was provided and contradicting the arguments presented by the manufacturer of the medicines, the decision could be challenged. However, the results of such challenges are not to be taken for granted, and the entire proceedings may be renewed.[634] Private opinion is not a conclusive proof in such proceedings.

As an alternative basis for the liability of public authorities for damages, if none of the above decisions can be obtained, Article 472 CC may be applied, which provides for the possibility of awarding equitable damages and cash compensation for an injury suffered, from a public where personal harm is inflicted as a result of the lawful exercise of its powers by a public authority and the circumstances of the case provide an additional proof of this, especially the injured party being unable to work or finding him- or herself in a poor financial condition.

Under the current law, authorization of a pharmaceutical production and distribution is a complex and multi-stage procedure. It does not, however, permit entities that are not parties to the administrative proceedings to submit evidence for use in the proceedings. The authority is required to assess the application filed by an entrepreneur, which consists of many elements that are designed to prove that the product satisfies rigorous safety requirements. Should any doubt arise, the authority may apply for an opinion by external experts.[635]

It therefore appears that the failure to consider a scientific opinion ('external' to the legal proceedings contemplated by law) referred to in the case at hand could not be deemed a sufficient ground for challenging the decision and hence for liability on the part of the State Treasury. With respect to the provisions regulating administrative proceedings themselves, it should be noted that proceedings are governed by the rule of the so-called freedom of assessment of evidence. According to this rule, a piece of evidence presented does not have to be taken into consideration by the relevant authority, although it should be objectively assessed in the context of the entire body of evidence gathered.

[634] Z Banaszczyk, *Odpowiedzialność za szkody wyrządzone przy wykonywaniu władzy publicznej* (CH Beck, 2015) 293ff.

[635] R Stankiewicz, *Instytucje rynku farmaceutycznego* (Wolters Kluwer 2016) 1.

H. Romania

RV

The national drug authority would be held liable if Peter can prove that the market approval of the product was illegal. The approval would be illegal under Romanian law if the national drug authority is obliged to consult a technical body, but in the particular circumstance, does not do so. There are two types of prior consultations in Romanian administrative law: the mandatory ones and the consultative ones. The mandatory ones finalize with a prior mandatory notice that is very similar to the French *avis conforme*. Whenever an administrative authority issues an act for which the *avis conforme* was necessary and was not obtained, said act is subject to annulment by the judicial review court.

The debate is more nuanced if the prior advice is not mandatory. The lack of such an advice could still lead to the annulment of the act if the court considers this element (in conjunction with other elements) as a proof of excess of power by the administration under Article 2 of Law 554/2004.

I. Spain

EMNG

The national drug authority will be held liable for having breached the administrative procedure to introduce a new drug product onto the market, because according to national legislation it should have consulted a technical body but failed to do so.

The national drug authority could also be held liable on the grounds of not having taken into account the scientific evidence provided by the NGO contrary to issuing the authorization (as national authorities must take into account opinions and recommendations, although they do not necessarily have to follow them), and because the national drug authority failed to consult a technical body.

According to the facts of this case, the national drug authority was legally obliged to consult a technical body. The national drug authority infringed this law, which could bring about the annulment of the administrative decision. Furthermore, if national drug authority had asked technical body's opinion, no following that opinion does not always lead to the annulment of the administrative decision, but if damage arises as a consequence of a decision, this may be a strong argument for a compensation claim.

As a precondition for awarding damages, there must be a link between Luka's injuries and the effects of the drug. To calculate the amount of compensation to be awarded, the court will take into account the duration of the illness, whether Luka has suffered permanent damage and, for instance, whether he will be able to work in the future. Peter will have to claim compensation for damages within one year in order for it to be possible to establish the compensation due to Luka.

J. Switzerland

TT

The drug authority in Switzerland is Swissmedic, an independent federal agency (Art 68 of the Therapeutic Products Act 2000, TPA). Its liability is governed by the

GLA (Art 80 TPA), without any special provision in the TPA. Since Swissmedic is an independent body with financial autonomy, it is directly liable, while the liability of the Swiss Confederation is only subsidiary (Art 19 I GLA). Peter and Luka should thus claim for damages directly before Swissmedic, which will issue a ruling on the claim. This ruling can be appealed before the FAT, and eventually, if the conditions of Article 85 I FTA are met as explained in Chapter 12, before the Federal Tribunal.

In that case, it could not be expected that Peter, or *a fortiori* Luka, would have appealed the approval of the drug at the time it was issued. Thus, Article 12 GLA does not apply, and Luka may challenge the lawfulness of the said approval during the liability proceedings.

For Swissmedic to be liable, its approval of the drug must have been issued in breach of a fundamental duty. If one assumes that Swiss law contains the provisions set out in the case, their clear violation by Swissmedic would certainly represent a breach of a fundamental duty. In addition, the TPA and Swissmedic aim to protect the public, of which Peter and Luka are a part. From the facts stated in the case, it can be assumed that the harm sustained by Luka is in a relation of natural and adequate causation with the drug and its approval for the Swiss market. Under these conditions, Swissmedic would be held liable, and Luka would be awarded damages.

K. United Kingdom

GA

This is a problem that would be litigated solely by way of a private law claim for damages, where the relevant causes of action would be breach of statutory duty and/or negligence (procedurally these would be brought by Luka acting through his father as his 'next friend'—Peter would not have any cause of action in his own name). On the face of it, it looks very much as if the national drug authority has acted in flagrant breach of its legal duties and, depending on the nature of the evidence that was overlooked, one might expect it to seek to settle this case without the need for a court hearing. However, it is also true that the authority might make arguments about why it should not be held liable, where there may be points of law and of fact that it could plead in its favour. The points of law are noted in more detail below, but the main point of fact might concern the nature of the evidence that was overlooked: if that evidence was not material to the injuries that were suffered by Luka, the authority might feasibly argue that its omission did not 'cause' Luka's injuries.

Taking first an action for a breach of statutory duty, the following points might be made:

(1) To succeed in a claim for breach of statutory duty, Luka (acting through his father) would have to show that three elements were satisfied: (i) that the authority owed him a duty under the statute; (ii) that the authority had acted or failed to act in breach of that duty; and (iii) that the breach of the duty had caused the harm that was suffered by Luka. (These are typically termed the 'duty', 'breach', and 'causation' elements.)

(2) The question whether the authority owed Luka a duty under the statute is a matter for statutory interpretation. Here, the courts will look at the statutory scheme in its full setting and decide whether a duty is owed to the public at large, or whether it can be read as imposing duties in relation to particular individuals. If the court is of the view that the duty is owed to the public at large, this should ordinarily lead it to the conclusion that Luka cannot sue, for the simple reason that the legislature did not intend to give him a private law cause of action. In the converse circumstance that the court reads the legislation as imposing duties in relation to private individuals such as Luka, this will mean that he will be able to bring an action. In either instance, 'The central question is whether from the provisions and structure of the statute an intention can be gathered to create a private law remedy.'[636]

(3) The court's approach to the issue of breach will depend on whether the legislation is interpreted as imposing strict liability or fault-based liability. If it is read as imposing strict liability, this will mean that the mere failure to consider evidence and/or to consult with the technical body would amount to a breach, at which stage the issue would become causation. However, if the legislation is taken to centre upon fault-based liability, the court would ask whether the authority had failed to do that which a reasonable authority could have been expected to do in the circumstances. On the given facts, it would seem that the authority would be in breach on either approach: it has manifestly failed to do that which was required by the statute so that, even if liability is fault-based, it is difficult to conceive how its actions could be regarded as consistent with those of a reasonable authority.

(4) The matter of causation has two limbs: factual and legal causation. Of course, this is where the nature of the evidence that was overlooked may potentially be relevant, as the authority may be able to demonstrate that the evidence in question did not relate to the injuries that were suffered by Luka. In the contrary event that the evidence was directly relevant, arguments about legal causation (and resultant liability) would centre upon whether the harm was reasonably foreseeable.

Turning next to negligence, the law here too centres upon duty, breach, and causation, albeit each of the elements have their source in the common law, rather than statute. The following points are to be emphasized:

(1) The common law duty of care: the law here is not immune to public policy arguments (see comment (g) at the beginning of Chapter 13), and the authority may argue that the imposition of a common law duty of care would complicate the discharge of its more general statutory functions. This is a point that would inevitably have some overlap with arguments about the interpretation of the relevant legislation, where the authority would already have argued that it acts in the public interest rather than with reference to individual interests. The

[636] *Gorringe v Calderdale MBC* [2004] 1 WLR 1057, 1059, Lord Steyn.

approach that the court will have earlier adopted to the question of statutory interpretation may well determine its approach to the existence of a common law duty of care.

(2) Breach: this element is always fault-based in the law of negligence, meaning that the authority will need to have fallen beneath the 'reasonable' standard of care by failing to consider the evidence and/or to consult with the technical body. For the reasons noted above, it is difficult to see how the authority could argue that it has not fallen beneath that standard.

(3) Causation: the points of fact and law noted above in relation to breach of statutory duty would apply equally here.

To recap: there are strong reasons for believing that the authority would be held liable in this case. While it is possible that the evidence that was overlooked may not have been directly linked to Luka's injuries, there is little doubt that the authority's actions fell beneath a reasonable standard of care. Subject to the evidence being linked to the injuries, the case would therefore centre on whether the courts considered that duties were owed either under statute and/or at common law.

XII. Case 11—a violent police officer

Two police officers stop a driver, Agatha, and ask her quite ruthlessly to get out of the vehicle and show her documents to the officers. Agatha vehemently protests and resists the officers' request, stating that she is being treated unfairly. One of the two officers, without warning Agatha as required by Police Department rules, moves towards her, grabs her left arm, and twists it into an armlock. The torsion causes Agatha's elbow to crack, and permanent injury ensues. She refuses any assistance from police officers and is brought to the hospital by some witnesses. Subsequently, Agatha sues the two police officers and the State for damages.

Under what conditions would her action be successful, and to what extent? Would it be relevant that the two policemen infringed the guidelines set out by the Police Department?

A. Austria

SS, KB, DB, and LM

A right to compensation may arise from § 1 AHG. As federal civil servants, the police officers are organs of the security administration (§ 5 s 2 No 1 Security Act (*Sicherheitspolizeigesetz*—SPG, original version: Federal Law Gazette No 566/1991). The police officers were executing the law when Agatha's rights were violated. Their actions led to actual harm (hospital treatment, permanent injury). Causality is obviously present. The action of the police officers was unlawful. In particular, an arrest was unlawful. In principle, a person may be arrested if he or she—inter alia—is suspected of having committed a criminal offence (§ 170—Code of Criminal Procedure, *Strafprozessordnung*—StPO, original version: Federal Law Gazette No 631/1975) or if he cannot identify himself to the police (§ 35 No 1 Administrative Penal Act (*Verwaltungsstrafgesetz*—VStG, original version: Federal Law Gazette No 52/1991). In any case, there was no prior announcement of the use of coercive measures. According to § 50, section 2 SPG, the organs of the public security service must announce the use of direct coercive force before affecting a person. Only in the case of self-defence or the cessation of dangerous attacks may this be waived. In addition, the arrest was made in a disproportionate manner because it led to physical injury. The fault of the police officers can be assumed. The police officers should have known that they should not have used excessive force.

The damage can only be compensated in money. As far as the amount of compensation is concerned, § 1325 ABGB states:

> whoever causes someone bodily harm must compensate for the injured person's medical expenses, as well as any loss of profit. If the injured person becomes incapable of earning, any earnings lost in the future must also be compensated. Furthermore, the injured person can claim reasonable compensation for pain.

It is irrelevant whether the two police officers breached the guidelines set by the police. Here, they breached a regulation of the SPG. Otherwise, according to AHG, liability is only accepted if the damage was caused 'when implementing the law', which means a breach of statutes and regulations, not guidelines.

As for the procedure, to claim compensation, it is not necessary to name a particular organ; the evidence that the damage may have resulted only from a violation of a law on the part of an organ of the legal entity sued is sufficient (§ 1 AHG).

The fact that Agatha did not want help from the police officers is irrelevant. Damages shall only not be due if the injured person would have been able to avoid the damage by any legal remedy or by a complaint to an administrative court (*Verwaltungsgericht*) and a final appeal (Revision) to the Supreme Administrative Court (*Verwaltungsgerichtshof*, § 2 s 2 AHG). However, Agatha was not able to avert the damage by having recourse to a remedy.

The injured party shall demand the legal entity against which the claim for damages is to be raised in writing to forward him or her a statement within one month indicating whether it accepts or partially (or totally) rejects the claim for damages (§ 8 s 1 AHG).

A lawsuit against the police officers is not feasible: damage caused by an organ of a legal entity in the course of implementation of the law cannot be claimed by the injured party in standard legal procedure (§ 9 s 5 AHG).

B. European Union

BM

The EU has no police forces conducting similar actions. Sometimes it carries out inspections, through its officials—for example, in the areas of competition, State aid, and banking and financial supervision—which could lead to the necessary use of force in the event of resistance by the companies or individuals concerned.

However, in this case it would still be the Member State, through its own officials, who would assist the EU agents with their police forces.

Therefore, in the event of harmful conduct by the officials of the Member States, it is primarily the Member State's conduct, and not the Union's that causes the damage, especially in cases such as the one considered here.

If, on the other hand, the unlawful action was carried out by national agents under instructions given by the EU officials, it would not be easy to identify the authority actually responsible for the harmful conduct.

Generally, in relations with members of the public, the duty to act diligently is inherent in the principle of sound administration and applies to all actions of the EU administration.[637] But a mere breach of the principle of diligence is not sufficient to render the EU liable, because only a sufficiently serious breach of a rule of law (protecting individuals) can lead to liability in tort.

[637] Case C-337/15 *European Ombudsman v Staelen* [2017] ECLI:EU:C:2017:256, judgment of the Court 4 April 2017.

C. France

TP

Agatha's action against the State before the administrative court would be successful considering that the infringement of the guidelines proves the authority's misconduct, although her behaviour implies her own responsibility, and compensation would be reduced proportionally.

Two preliminary remarks can be helpful. First, government liability concerning the police is different depending on whether it concerns the exercise of a 'judicial' function or an 'administrative' function.[638] If the claim relates to the judicial police, ordinary courts are competent; if it relates to an administrative function, administrative courts will consider it. As establishing the identity of a passenger in a vehicle is an 'administrative' function,[639] Agatha's claim will be heard by the administrative courts.

Second, police misconduct is related to clumsiness,[640] negligence,[641] abuse and brutality,[642] or excessive use of force.[643] In Agatha's case, the behaviour of the police is unlawful, and constitutes misconduct, because the officers did not warn Agatha, as the guideline establishes, and this warning could probably avoid the injury; moreover, they employed more force than was reasonably necessary, considering she was merely protesting and not resisting physically, using any weapon, or threatening the police.

Agatha sues both the two police officers and the State.[644] This raises the question whether her action concerns either misconduct by the officers, which would be judged by ordinary courts, or is a 'service fault', for which government would be liable before an administrative court.[645] If both faults exist, still other consequences would follow from this.

In the former case, personal misconduct is a serious or brutal action, for example gross negligence or a voluntary act, a criminal offence or a crime,[646] bearing no relation to 'police service', such as revenge,[647] or an action that is so serious that it can be considered as an act of the person,[648] rather than a public official. In these cases, only the person is liable, and ordinary courts are competent. In the latter case, the fault is 'committed' by an agent, but it is an act related to public office. The misconduct is thus

[638] The judicial police is in charge of criminal investigation and enforcement, and the 'administrative' police oversees general public order. Briefly, the first one is related to repression and the second to prevention. This distinction is more difficult in practice because one agent can be entrusted with both functions (but cannot exercise both at the same time) and because there is no material difference in the 'external acts'; the difference is in the objectives of the action.

[639] T confl 28 April 1980 *Waroquier* No 02155, Lebon T 643, AJDA 1980 541.

[640] CE 11 June 1947 *Dame Vergne*, Lebon T 69.

[641] CE 25 May 1928 *Dame Minereau*, Lebon 682.

[642] Cour Administrative d'Appel de Lyon 10 October 1990 *Hamoumou* Req No 89LY01690.

[643] CE 12 February 1971 *Rebatel*, No 72495.

[644] In France, police activities may have a State function or a municipal function. Therefore, the State is sometimes liable, while at others, liability is borne by the City. In this case, we will assume that liability lies with the State. See R Vandermeeren, 'Police', in *Répertoire de responsabilité de la puissance publique* (Dalloz April 2017, updated February 2018) s 3.

[645] T confl 30 July 1873 *Pelletier* Rec 1 suppl 117, concl David; D 1874.3.5, concl GAJA 2.

[646] T confl 30 July 1873 *Pelletier* Rec 1 suppl 117, concl David; D 1874.3.5,

[647] concl GAJA 2. 975 *Pothier*, Lebon 190.

[648] CE 17 December 1999 *Moine* Rec 425; JCP 2001.II.10508, note Piastra.

regarded as a 'wrongful act related to service', only government is liable, and the administrative courts judge about it.

However, the *Conseil d'Etat* took measures to protect the victims from an officer's insolvency. In cases of personal misconduct in connection with public service or when the wrongful acts coincide, the aggrieved party can bring a claim against government directly, and in turn government would bring its action against the agent (*action récursoire*). Personal misconduct is connected with service when (i) it actually coincides with a 'service fault';[649] (ii) the officer is carrying out a public function;[650] or (iii) even when a link can be found between the function and the fault, for example, if officers use confidential information from their office[651] or police guns,[652] or do so in the workplace.[653] In conclusion, almost every personal misconduct has a link with public service. Only acts for personal reasons (revenge or personal relationships) would not lead to public liability.

When personal and official wrongdoing co-exist, administrative courts assess the responsibility of both the officer and government so as to order reimbursement of their respective parts.[654] If government has paid, it can use '*l'action récursoire*' against the agent for the total or a part of the compensation before the administrative courts. If the officer has paid compensation after a claim before the ordinary courts, he or she can also bring an action before the administrative court to determine government liability and be reimbursed.[655]

If Agatha sues both the officers (for their personal misconduct) and government, she must bring a claim against the former before the ordinary court following the rules of private law and another action before the administrative court against the State. As she cannot receive compensation twice, if the ordinary courts award damages, and the police officers first pay the total damages, government will not pay any compensation. However, if the police officers are not solvent and the administrative judge holds government liable, it awards damages, and government pays first and can bring an action against the two police officers for the reimbursement of all or part of the compensation, in proportion to their responsibility. In Agatha's case, it would be better to choose one action and claim only government liability before the administrative jurisdiction, because the police officer's misconduct was committed in the exercise of a governmental function; that is, checking identity on the road.[656] In this way, she would neither run the risk of their insolvent, nor bear the cost of two law suits.

Once the misconduct, the causal link, and the damage are established, Agatha has a right to compensation. In this case, it is easy to determine the causal link (the police

[649] CE 28 July 1951 *Laruelle et Delville*, No 04032.

[650] CE 25 February 1949 *Dame Vve Augereau*, Lebon 97; Cour de Cassation crim 14 June 2005 No 04-83.574.

[651] CE 18 November 1988 *Ministre Défense c Épx Raszewski*, Lebon 416.

[652] CE 26 October 1973 *Sadoudi*, Lebon 603; D 1974.255, note J-M Auby.

[653] CE 12 May 1950 *Épx Giorgelli*, Lebon 287.

[654] In cases of personal misconduct, the State can claim reimbursement from police officers. CE *Laruelle et Delville* No 04032 (n 649).

[655] ibid.

[656] Recent case law includes buttock stroking and other abusive use of force among forms of personal misconduct by police officers: Cour de Cassation crim 16 November 2004 D 2005.17 and Cour de Cassation crim 16 November 2004 No 03-87.114.

grabbed her arm and her elbow cracked), and the damage has been established by a medical expert.

It is important to remember that Agatha must file a request for compensation to the respective administrative authority and wait two months for the answer (the absence of which means a rejection) prior to making a claim before the administrative courts.

As it is a bodily injury—all the recoverable loss is explained in case 10 above—the court may consider all the following: first, past and future medical expenses; second, extra costs associated with being disabled;[657] and third, past and future loss of wages caused by the permanent injury. It would be possible for Agatha to claim non-economic losses if she can prove them, including fourth, pain;[658] and fifth, suffering.[659] After these damages have been determined, it would be possible to claim for sixth, aesthetic damages;[660] and seventh, loss of capacity for enjoyment.[661] Depending on her health conditions, eighth, permanent injury may also cause additional damage to her living conditions and expectations.[662]

If Agatha claims interests, the court must determine whether the amount of compensation includes the interests before the judgment date and from the date of the administrative request.[663] However, it must also consider Agatha's behaviour[664] and her responsibility to decrease the amount of compensation, in relation to the evidence and the context.[665] Agatha refused to obey the police officer's request to establish her identity and show the vehicle's documents, and she refused immediate police assistance (which probably made her arm injury worse). This normally leads to government liability being retained for around three-quarters or four-fifths of the compensation, according to more detailed facts.

When the compensation is reduced, the Social Security Law of 2006 determines that the decrease is calculated on the basis of each of the recoverable losses to ensure that the injured party and the insurance companies receive their respective portion.[666] For example, if the past medical expenses' compensation was €600, the insurance company would pay €500 and the injured party €100; if the loss of past wages was €200, the loss of amenity was €3,000. In Agatha's case, the State is 75 per cent liable, so it would pay €450 for medical expenses, which would go to the insurance company and not to

[657] CE 10 December 2015 *AP–HP* (n 591) 500.

[658] CE *Commune de Grigny* (n 594) 323. Before this decision, the *Conseil d'Etat* required the suffering to be very serious and long lasting for compensation to be granted.

[659] CE *Mme Moraes* (n 199).

[660] CE *Caisse régionale de sécurité sociale de Normandie et Souillié* (n 596) 211.

[661] CE *Mme Moraes* (n 199).

[662] CE 12 December 1975 *Guyader* (n 605); CE 15 June 1988 *Grandmaison* (n 605), but this *chef de préjudice* has not been recently used in cases of bodily injuries; CE *Mme M* (n 605).

[663] F Sernes, 'Préjudice réparable' in *Répertoire de la responsabilité de la puissance publique* (Dalloz 2011, updated December 2017) 253.

[664] CE *Rebatel* (n 643).

[665] Cour Administrative d'Appel de Lyon 10 October 1990 No 89LY01690.

[666] 'Les recours subrogatoires des caisses contre les tiers s'exercent poste par poste sur les seules indemnités qui réparent des préjudices qu'elles ont pris en charge, à l'exclusion des préjudices à caractère personnel.' Loi No 2006-1640 de 21 December 2006 de financement de la sécurité sociale pour 2007.

the victim; €150 for the wages, which would be paid to the victim, and €2,250 for loss of amenities, that would go to Agatha as well.[667] The insurance company would not receive compensation for the remaining €50 (the difference between the amount the insurance company paid—€500—and the amount payed for medical expenses by the State—€450) because the other recoverable losses are to be paid to the victim directly.

D. Germany

FW and JS

At the outset, it has to be noted that the applicable rules depend on the aim of the police officers' measures.

If serving repressive purposes, ie aiming to prosecute criminal offences, the rules on criminal procedure would apply (cf § 23 para 1 sentence 1 of the Introductory Act to the Courts Constitution Act – EGGVG). Hence, § 161 paragraph 1 sentences 1 and 2 or § 163 paragraph 1 sentences 1 and 2 StPO[668] might serve as a legal basis[669], provided that Agatha was regarded as a suspect[670]. Compensation might then be awarded under §§ 2ff StrEG[671], namely § 2 para 2 No 2 StrEG read in conjunction with § 127 para 2 StPO, which provides for compensation in cases of unlawful[672] provisional arrest. The general provisions on public authority liability would also apply.[673] However, there is no clear indication that Agatha was stopped for such repressive purposes.

If the police officers acted to prevent a crime or a danger to public safety (including individual rights), the rules of general police law apply. In Germany, it is the competence of the *Länder* to legislate in this area, so, the applicable law depends on where the action took place.[674] The following considerations are based on Bavarian police law. At the outset, it will be noted that two levels of police action have to be distinguished, namely (i) the identity check; and (ii) its enforcement because of Agatha's non-compliance with the police officers' order.

Under (Bavarian) police law, Article 13 PAG[675] might serve as the legal basis for the identity check. This provision allows police officers to verify the identity of a

[667] This example is just to facilitate the explanation about security social system indemnity, but it does not fit Agatha's case, as we do not have enough information.

[668] *Strafprozessordnung* (German Code of Criminal Procedure), English version <www.gesetze-im-internet.de/englisch_stpo/englisch_stpo.html> accessed 22 June 2020.

[669] Depending on the nature of the criminal offence, police forces of the *Länder* (eg in Bavaria Art 2 para 4 PAG para 4, see n 675) or the *Bund* (s 12 *Bundespolizeigesetz* (Federal Police Act)] would be competent to investigate.

[670] Ossenbühl and Cornils (n 145) 489f.

[671] See n 208.

[672] Ossenbühl and Cornils (n 145) 488ff.

[673] ibid 490.

[674] cf ibid 487; W-R Schenke, *Polizei- und Ordnungsrecht* (10th edn, CF Müller 2018) para 23; F Wollenschläger, '§ 4' in PM Huber and F Wollenschläger (eds), *Landesrecht Bayern* (Nomos 2019) para 5.

[675] *Gesetz über die Aufgaben und Befugnisse der Bayerischen Staatlichen Polizei* (Bavarian Police Duties Act), German version <www.gesetze-bayern.de/Content/Document/BayPAG/true> accessed 16 August 2018.

person under certain conditions. The conditions which might be relevant in Agatha's case comprise a verification of identity in order to prevent a danger for public safety for which Agatha may be responsible, a verification of identity at a checkpoint set up to prevent certain crimes, or a verification of identity in the context of cross-border crime if Agatha was stopped within 30 kilometres of a border or on a transit road. In these cases, the police are authorized to take the measures necessary to identify a person: these include stopping, asking for personal data and identification papers, and asking to take off such clothes or items which prevent or complicate identification. Furthermore, the person may be detained if the identification is impossible or otherwise endangered, and the person as well as his or her personal belongings may be searched under these conditions. Whether these requirements are met cannot be assessed on the basis of the information provided in the questionnaire.

A further legal basis for the identity check may be § 6 paragraph 1 No 3 StVG[676] read in conjunction with § 36 para 5 StVO.[677] These provisions allow police officers to stop drivers in order to perform traffic checks, including the assessment of fitness to drive.[678] They also comprise checking documents, namely the driver's licence and vehicle registration certificate.[679]

Since Agatha refused to comply with the police officers' order, they used force. Under Bavarian police law, the use of force is lawful if the conditions stipulated in Article 70 paragraph 1, Article 71 paragraph 1 No 3 and paragraph 2, Article 76 and 81 PAG are met.

The first substantive prerequisite for the lawfulness of using force is the existence of a police measure, which does not need to be lawful (in order to guarantee an effective prevention of dangers),[680] but creates a duty for its addressee to perform, forbear, or refrain from an action and be enforceable (cf § 80 para 2 No 1 VwGO). These requirements are met. Moreover, the addressee of the order must have failed to comply,[681] which is also the case here.

Second, a means envisaged under police law must have been employed (*numerus clausus*), in our case the use of force (cf Art 78 para 1 PAG).

Third, and with regard to the specific requirements for the enforcement of a police order as stipulated by the 'police department rules', the police officers did not warn Agatha before using force. Since Article 81 paragraph 1 sentence 1 PAG lays down

[676] *Straßenverkehrsgesetz* (German Road Traffic Act), German version <www.gesetze-im-internet.de/stvg/BJNR004370909.html> accessed 22 June 2020.

[677] *Straßenverkehrsordnung* (German Road Traffic Rules), German version <www.gesetze-im-internet.de/stvo_2013/BJNR036710013.html> accessed 22 June 2020. The rules are based on s 6 para 1 No 3 StVG .

[678] cf No 2.5 point 9 of *Vollzug des Polizeiaufgabengesetzes, Bekanntmachung des Bayerischen Staatsministeriums des Innern vom 28 August 1978*, MABl 1978, 629.

[679] M Kniesel, 'Straßenverkehrsrecht' in H Lisken and E Denninger (eds), *Handbuch des Polizeirechts* (6th edn, CH Beck 2018), ch J.VIII para 40. Given the purpose of s 6 para 1 No 3 StVG (maintenance of security and order on public roads), checking identity cards is not included; cf the *Allgemeine Verwaltungsvorschrift zur Straßenverkehrs-Ordnung—VwV-StVO* (General Administrative Instructions on the Road Traffic Rules) of 26 January 2001, Bundesanzeiger 1419, 'Zu § 36 Zeichen und Weisungen von Polizeibeamten—Zu Absatz 5', No 1 which refers to the 'documents whose carriage is stipulated by the traffic laws'.

[680] BVerwG 13 April 1984—4 C 31/81, [1984] NJW 2591 (2592).

[681] W Schmidbauer, 'Art 70' in W Schmidbauer and U Steiner (eds), *Bayerisches Polizeiaufgabengesetz und Polizeiordnungsgesetz* (5th edn, CH Beck 2020) para 8; Wollenschläger, '§ 4' (n 674) para 286.

an express duty to warn the addressee of force prior to its use, and exceptions do not apply in view of the circumstances of the case, the additional assessment of a breach of 'police department rules' is hypothetical (and not relevant to the outcome of the case).[682] It would most likely constitute a violation of a *Verwaltungsvorschrift* (administrative regulation), ie a violation of an internal provision 'governing how and under what circumstances agencies must carry out their administrative tasks in relation to the citizens'[683]. Since the binding effect of *Verwaltungsvorschriften* is limited to the internal sphere of the administration, a breach can be challenged only on grounds of inequality. By failing to apply the *Verwaltungsvorschrift*, the officers might treat Agatha differently from other addressees of police action, thereby infringing her right to equality before the law (Art 3 para 1 GG).[684] In order to establish a breach, however, an administrative practice must actually exist, and it can be refuted by proving that Agatha's case was non-standard.[685] While the first requirement cannot be assessed from the information provided, it seems unlikely that Agatha's case was non-standard. If all the criteria are met, the police action would be unlawful. Even if there was no formal requirement to warn, and the violation of the 'police department rules' did not render the police action unlawful, the use of force without seeking to apply more lenient means (eg threatening) would be disproportionate.

Fourth, in view of the circumstances of the case, the use of force might also be disproportionate (Art 4 paras 1f PAG).

Thus, at least by not warning Agatha before using force, the police officers' measure was unlawful.

Under Bavarian law, Article 87ff PAG governs compensation for police action aiming to prevent crimes or a danger to public safety.[686] These provisions differ from the general provisions on public authority liability. On the one hand, they only require that a person not responsible for a police measure suffered damage, but no further unlawfulness surrounds the police action; moreover, culpable—ie at least negligent behaviour on the part of the police—is not required either. On the other hand, the provisions on public authority liability also apply to claims brought by persons responsible for police measures,[687] a group whose entitlement to bringing claims under Article 87 PAG by analogy is controversial.[688] Furthermore, unlike Article 87 PAG, the

[682] At any rate, a missing formal restriction of the use of force would most likely violate the primacy of law which 'requires the legislator [. . .] to make all relevant decisions in the basic normative fields, especially in the field of the exercise of fundamental rights as far as this is available for public regulation' [own translation of BVerfG 8 August 1978—2 BvL 8/77, BVerfGE 49, 89 (126f with further references)]; see also K-P Sommermann, 'Art 20' in H von Mangoldt and others (eds), *Grundgesetz*, vol 2 (7th edn, CH Beck 2018) paras 273f.

[683] Own translation of Maurer and Waldhoff (n 222) § 24 para 26.

[684] This indirect effect of *Verwaltungsvorschriften* is referred to as *Selbstbindung der Verwaltung* (administrative self-commitment), see Wollenschläger 'Art 3' (n 432) para 193. ; Wollenschläger, '§ 4' (n 674) para 253.

[685] Maurer and Waldhoff (n 222) § 24 para 29.

[686] Claims against the federal police (see n 669) can be brought under s 51 *Bundespolizeigesetz*. They would have merit only if the measures were found unlawful, which is assessed in the section on general provisions on public authority liability below, pp. 282–83.

[687] J Unterreitmeier, 'Art 87' in M Möstl and T Schwabenbauer, *BeckOK Polizei- und Sicherheitsrecht Bayern* (13th edn, CH Beck 1 May 2020) para 25.

[688] Wollenschläger, '§ 4' (n 674) para 358.

general provisions on public authority liability also allow for compensation for immaterial damages.[689]

Article 87 PAG is limited to claims by persons who are not responsible for a disturbance of public order and safety. According to Article 87 paragraph 2 sentence 1 PAG, a person who is not responsible for a danger, but has been subject to a police measure, may claim damages if he or she has been killed or injured or suffered any other unacceptable damage. In addition, the provision can be applied by analogy under certain circumstances.[690]

Agatha would be compensated for her material loss in money (Art 87 para 7 sentences 1 and 4 PAG). This would include medical expenses. However, in this regard, the same problems as in case 10 arise with regard to the fact that, in the first instance, the health insurance covers the expenses. In addition, Article 87 paragraph 7 sentence 3 PAG stipulates that contributory negligence must be considered when assessing the obtainable amount. It should be noted that Agatha did not obey the order 'to get out of the vehicle and show her documents to the officers', which led to the use of force. Even if the police officers disregarded the 'Police Department Rules', which could be regarded as safeguards against physical harm, it seems tenable to assume a certain contributory negligence on the part of Agatha.

Agatha may thus claim damages if she is not responsible for the police action, but her contributory negligence would reduce the compensation.

The general provisions on public authority liability apply alongside the specific compensation rules of police law[691]. The former are of practical relevance, since the latter do not cover damages for pain and suffering and do not apply if Agatha is responsible for the police measure, even if she suffered harm for some other reason.

Article 34 sentence 1 GG read in conjunction with § 839 paragraph 1 sentence 1 BGB stipulates the conditions of public authority liability as put forth in case 1, ie that (1) an official (2) intentionally or negligently (3) breached the official duty incumbent upon him (4) in relation to a third party which (5) caused (6) the claimant harm.

At the outset, it shall be noted that § 839 paragraph 3 BGB does not preclude a claim for damages, since primary legal protection would not have averted or limited the damage Agatha suffered.

The police officers are (1) officials within the meaning of § 839 paragraph 1 BGB.

The question whether the police officers (2) breached an official duty depends, first, on whether they carried out official tasks or merely acted while carrying out such a task. In the latter case, the general provisions on public authority liability do not apply.[692] Merely acting 'ruthlessly' or not respecting 'police department rules' does not suffice for such an assumption; rather, carrying out official tasks is to be construed broadly, thereby covering cases where an official position is exploited for 'selfish purposes,

[689] Unterreitmeier (n 687) para 25; Wollenschläger, '§ 4' (n 678) para 374.

[690] Wollenschläger, '§ 4' (n 678) para 362.

[691] H-U Gallwas and J F Lindner, 'Das sicherheitsrechtliche bzw. polizeirechtliche Rechtsverhältnis zwischen Aufgabenträger und Betroffenem – Rechtsschutz des Betroffenen' in H-U Gallwas, J F Lindner, and H A Wolff (eds), *Bayerisches Polizei- und Sicherheitsrecht* (4th edn, Boorberg 2015) para 807; Wollenschläger, '§ 4' (n 678) para 374.

[692] cf Ossenbühl and Cornils (n 145) 28. See also BGH 16 June 1977—III ZR 179/75, BGHZ 69, 128 (132).

chicanery or even indictable purposes, a breach of duty for egoistic or merely personal reasons'.[693] Even if the police officers acted beyond their authorization, they were carrying out official tasks within the meaning of § 839 paragraph 1 BGB.

Next, the duty to act in conformity to the law[694] was at least breached by not warning Agatha before using force as required by Article 81 paragraph 1 sentence 1 PAG. If this provision did not exist and the duty to warn was codified only as a 'police department rule' with internal effect, some would decline assuming a breach of duty within the meaning of the general provisions on public authority liability.[695] The prevailing opinion, however, assumes a breach of duty even in these cases,[696] a position which is shared by the judiciary[697]. Moreover, a disproportionate use of force, which also amounts to a breach of an official duty,[698] seems likely.

These breaches of duty (3) result from at least negligent behaviour on the part of the police officers. Moreover, (4) these duties aim to protect specific individuals.

With regard to (5) causation, assessed by considering 'the course of events if the official had acted according to the law and what the (financial) situation of the aggrieved party would look like in this case',[699] the police might argue that the course of events would not have changed if the officers had warned Agatha.[700] However, this must be proven by the authority;[701] the mere possibility is not sufficient[702]. *In casu*, it may be excluded that such a proof is possible. For, although Agatha had not obeyed the order 'to get out of the vehicle and show her documents to the officers', it cannot be excluded (and might even be considered likely) that she would have changed her mind if she had been warned of the imminent use of force. Moreover, in view of a likely disproportionate use of force, this objection to causation does not apply from the outset.

With regard to (6) the damage to be compensated, it extends to the actual loss (§ 249 para 1 BGB), including medical expenses (§ 249 para 2 sentence 1 BGB), and to damages for pain and suffering (§ 253 para 2 BGB). However, with regard to medical expenses, the same problems arise as in case 10 with regard to the fact that Agatha's health insurance initially covers the expenses.

At any rate, in view of the circumstances of the case, Agatha's claim will be reduced because of contributory negligence on her part (§ 254 BGB; see above).[703]

Agatha may thus claim damages, reduced by her contributory negligence.

[693] Own translation of BGH 1 August 2002—III ZR 277/01, [2002] NJW 3172 (3173).

[694] See n 143, 367. This duty is concretized in the 'Police Department Rules', cf n 368.

[695] Papier and Shirvani (n 141) para 192, who emphasize that both Art 34 GG and s 839 BGB extend solely to official duties 'in relation to a third party'.

[696] Baldus and others (n 214) para 123; Ossenbühl and Cornils (n 145) 47; Dörr '§ 839' (n 438) para 141. See also T von Danwitz, 'Art 34' in H von Mangoldt and others, *Grundgesetz*, vol 2 (n 682) para 76.

[697] BGH 13 July 1989—III ZR 52/88, [1990] NJW 505 (506); 21 June 2001—III ZR 313/99, [2001] NJW 3065 (3056 para 6).

[698] Ossenbühl and Cornils (n 145) 49.

[699] Own translation of BGH 6 April 1995—III ZR 183/94, BGHZ 129, 226 (232f). See case 2.

[700] See case 2 with n 168; see also cases 4, 8, and 10.

[701] BGH 11 December 1997—III ZR 52-97, [1998] NJW 1307 (1308); cf also BGH 25 November 1992—VIII ZR 170/91, BGHZ 120, 281 (287).

[702] BGH 9 March 2012—V ZR 156/11, [2012] NJW 2022 (2023).

[703] cf Dörr, '§ 839' (n 438) para 1203.

The ECHR[704] stipulates in Article 5 paragraph 5: 'Everyone who has been the victim of arrest or detention in contravention of the provisions of this Article shall have an enforceable right to compensation.' The German civil courts are competent to hear claims brought under this provision.[705] Article 5 paragraph 5 ECHR can be invoked as the legal basis of these claims.[706]

In casu, Article 5 paragraph 1 sentence 2 letter b alternative 2 ECHR might have been contravened. It states: 'No one shall be deprived of his liberty save in the following cases and in accordance with a procedure prescribed by law: […] (b) the lawful arrest or detention of a person […] in order to secure the fulfilment of any obligation prescribed by law.' It is questionable whether there was a deprivation of liberty within the meaning of Article 5 paragraph 1 ECHR, or rather a restriction on liberty of movement within the meaning of Article 2 of Protocol No 4 to the Convention in Agatha's case.[707] According to the European Court of Human Rights (ECtHR),

> [i]n order to determine whether someone has been 'deprived of his liberty' within the meaning of Article 5 (art. 5), the starting point must be his concrete situation and account must be taken of a whole range of criteria such as the type, duration, effects and manner of implementation of the measure in question[708].

In a later case, it was held:

> that although the length of time during which each applicant was stopped and search[ed] did not in either case exceed 30 minutes, during this period the applicants were entirely deprived of any freedom of movement. They were obliged to remain where they were and submit to the search, and if they had refused they would have been liable to arrest, detention at a police station and criminal charges. This element of coercion is indicative of a deprivation of liberty within the meaning of Article 5 § 1 […][709].

This construction of the term 'deprivation of liberty' can include the measures taken with respect to Agatha.

[704] See on its status in the German legal order (rank of a statute, but interpretation of fundamental rights in the light of the ECHR) BVerfG (3rd chamber) 4 May 2011—2 BvR 2333/08, 2 BvR 2365/09 and others, BVerfGE 128, 326 (367); F Wollenschläger, 'Art 25' in Dreier, *Grundgesetz Kommentar*, vol 2 (n 83) para 27; J Meyer-Ladewig and M Nettesheim, 'Einleitung' in J Meyer-Ladewig, M Nettesheim, and S von Raumer (eds), *Europäische Menschenrechtskonvention* (4th edn, Nomos 2017) para 18.

[705] O Dörr, 'Freiheit der Person' in O Dörr, R Grote, and T Marauhn (eds), *EMRK/GG Konkordanzkommentar*, vol 1 (2nd edn, Mohr Siebeck 2013), ch 13 paras 106ff; J Meyer-Ladewig, S Harrendorf and S König, 'Art 5' in Meyer-Ladewig and others, *Europäische Menschenrechtskonvention* (n 704) paras 107, 109. In contrast, compensation under Art 41 ECHR is adjudicated by the ECtHR; as to further differences between Art 5 para 5 and Art 41 ECHR, see O Dörr, 'Chapter 33' in O Dörr, R Grote, T Marauhn (eds), *EMRK/GG Konkordanzkommentar*, vol 2 (2nd edn, Mohr Siebeck 2013) paras 4 ff.

[706] BGH 19 September 2013—III ZR 405/12, [2014] NJW 67 (67 with further references).

[707] On this issue in general, cf *Guzzardi* App No 7367/76 ECtHR 6 November 1980 paras 90ff.

[708] ibid para 92.

[709] *Gillan and Quinton* App No 4158/05 ECtHR 12 January 2010 para 57. In contrast, *Gahramanov* App No 26291/06 ECtHR 15 October 2013 para 41, finding that in situations 'where a passenger has been stopped by border officials during border control in an airport in order to clarify his situation and where this detention has not exceeded the time strictly necessary to comply with relevant formalities, no issue arises under Article 5 of the Convention'; this result is based on the assumption that '[a]n air traveller may be seen in this regard as consenting to a series of security checks by choosing to travel by plane' (para 40).

With regard to the prerequisites of Article 5 paragraph 1 sentence 2 letter b alternative 2 ECHR, the obligation to verify one's identity upon request by the police as laid down in Article 13 PAG constitutes an obligation prescribed by law. Moreover, the measures taken by the police officers were unlawful under national law,[710] as seen before, and therefore not 'in accordance with a procedure prescribed by law'. A violation of Article 5 paragraph 1 ECHR may thus be established.

Article 5 paragraph 5 ECHR establishes strict liability.[711] It covers damages for both material loss and pain and suffering within the meaning of § 253 BGB.[712]

However, it is questionable whether Agatha's case falls under Article 5 paragraph 5 ECHR, since 'in proclaiming the 'right to liberty', Article 5 contemplates the physical liberty of the person; its aim is to ensure that no one should be deprived of that liberty in an arbitrary fashion.'[713] It does not, however, comprise the protection of physical integrity.[714] The latter is rather the object of Article 3 ECHR. This provision applies to checks by the police.[715] However, only the ECtHR can adjudicate damages for the impairment of this provision under Article 41 ECHR, and only if a Member State of the Convention does not provide for appropriate legal redress itself.[716] The latter does not seem to apply here, given the provisions illustrated before. Therefore, only damages caused by the deprivation of liberty can be adjudicated to Agatha under Article 5 paragraph 5 ECHR, but not her medical expenses.

Whether contributory negligence (§ 254 BGB) must be taken into account when assessing the amount of damages has been left open.[717] Even though the courts tend to apply the German rules on liability, it is questionable whether contributory negligence would reduce a claim, since Article 5 paragraph 5 ECHR does not require intent or negligence on part of the police.[718]

In summary, Agatha may claim damages for actual loss and for pain and suffering under the provisions on public authority liability, but compensation will be reduced in view of her contributory negligence. The specific police law rules on compensation would only apply if Agatha is not responsible and would, moreover, be limited to her material loss. Article 5 paragraph 5 ECHR does not cover medical expenses.

[710] Article 5 para 1 sentence 2 ECHR refers to the procedure prescribed by national law which itself must, true, be in accordance with the ECHR; see C Grabenwarter and K Pabel, *Europäische Menschenrechtskonvention* (6th edn, CH Beck, Helbing & Lichtenhahn and Manz 2016) § 21 para 12.

[711] Meyer-Ladewig and others, 'Art 5' (n 704) paras 108.

[712] Grabenwarter and Pabel (n 710) para 55; cf also *Wassink* App No 12535/86 ECtHR 27 September 1990 paras 37ff. Concerning the applicability of § 253 BGB see BGH 29 April 1993—III ZR 3/92, BGHZ 122, 268 (279f).

[713] Council of Europe and European Court of Human Rights (eds), *Guide on Article 5 of the Convention—Right to Liberty and Security* (2014, updated on 30 April 2020) para 1.

[714] cf BGH 29 April 1993—III ZR 3/92, BGHZ 122, 268 (270); 4 July 2013—III ZR 342/12, [2013] NJW 3176 (3179).

[715] cf *Dembele* App No 74010/11 ECtHR 24 September 2013; cf Grabenwarter and Pabel (n 710) § 20 para 59.

[716] cf S Gerhold, 'Art 3 EMRK' in J-P Graf (ed), *BeckOK Strafvollzugsrecht* (17th edn, CH Beck 1 February 2020) para 19; cf also n 705.

[717] BGH 4 July 2013—III ZR 342/12, BGHZ 198, 1 (13f), however, in the context of the duty to seek primary legal protection first.

[718] See B Elberling, 'Art 5' in U Karpenstein and FC Mayer (eds), *EMRK* (2nd edn, CH Beck 2015) para 136. At any rate, s 839 para 3 BGB is held applicable eg by OLG Naumburg 3 August 2004—4 W 20/04, [2005] NJW 514 (515).

E. Hungary

LB

This is a complex case. The disproportionate use of force by police officers is likely to give rise to government liability in tort, though Agatha's conduct should be considered, too. For a better understanding of the solution, two preliminary remarks must be made. First, in Hungary, it is not possible to sue the police officer directly, because police authorities are liable for the actions of their officers. Second, an individual can only resist a police measure if it is obviously unlawful. This is not the case here. If the person resists a measure taken by the police, police officers can use coercive measures, in accordance with the principles of necessity and proportionality. Coercion directed towards the body is the least serious coercion they can use. The rules are stated in the Police Act and in the Police Service Regulations. So in general, if someone resists, the action taken by the police officer cannot be considered an infringement. However, judicial practice makes a difference between verbal and false resistance. There have been some cases over the past ten years where the court has decided that using a coercive measure because of a verbal protest without physical resistance (eg attacking the police officer) cannot be necessary and proportional (these requirements are included in the Police Act) and found for the violation of personality rights. Also, the way or method they use as a coercive measure itself can be unlawful, too.

Though in this case police officers seem to have infringed the principles of necessity and proportionality, other issues must be considered. It is necessary to prove that the damage and disadvantage caused by the infringement can only be compensated with non-pecuniary damage. In determining the measure, the court must take into account all the circumstances of the case, in particular the material gravity of the infringement, the actual consequences, and the judicial practice with regard to the sum of the facts.

The claimant can bring an action for both the infringement of his or her personality rights, which is more common in these cases. Most police measures do not necessarily cause any damage to property, so asking for pecuniary damage is rare. Although there is no possibility of repairing the damage through the administrative remedies, with the new rules they most probably have to be exhausted. This is unclear for now, but the main cause for declaring that the civil court is bound by the final decision of the administrative court concerning the lawfulness was that the civil courts tended to misinterpret the administrative law, and legally unfounded decisions have therefore been made. Because of this, the remedies will probably need to be exhausted.

F. Italy

FC

In Italian law, Agatha's case is a specific instance of the potential civil liability of a public authority and its employees, similar to the situation described in section XII.A above.

It is important to point out that the two policemen, who did not observe the specific guidelines established by the authority, could be charged with serious misconduct: they might, therefore, be directly liable.

As far as the amount of damages is concerned, this might include both the strictly financial damage and the non-financial damage. Basically, Agatha would be awarded damages due to the fact that she was unable to go about her normal business while the injury she sustained was healing, and permanent damages due to the seriousness of the injury itself (to this end, Italian ordinary courts apply a number of factors, calculated on the basis of the age of the injured party and on the applicable percentage of invalidity actually identifiable for the same party based on the degree of severity of the injury).

It is perhaps debatable whether Agatha's refusal to receive assistance should be taken into account with the possible application of Article 1227 paragraph 2, CC, which lays down that 'Compensation is not due for damages that the creditor could have avoided by using ordinary diligence.'

G. Poland

Zofia Roguska

While it is relatively easy to affirm that, if either criminal or civil courts will find that the conduct of the policemen was unlawful, Agatha will be able to seek to obtain damages, it must be said at the outset that the courts will take account of a wide variety of factors in deciding on the content of the procedural constraints that are imposed on public authorities. These will include the nature of the sources that set out such constraints (whether they are limited to legislation or they include internal guidelines) and the circumstances of the case, such as Agatha's conduct. In particular, the possible contribution of the injured party to the occurrence or to increasing the loss will have to be considered.

As far as unlawfulness is concerned, a final criminal judgment stating professional misconduct by the policemen would make the issue of loss unequivocally clear for the civil court. If no such criminal judgment has been passed, the civil court is entitled to award damages for inflicted losses autonomously, since in the proceeding under consideration the issue is the damage suffered by Agatha, not the guilt of the public officials. A claim for damages will be successful only if the policemen's conduct is classified as unlawful. This, however, is not unequivocal due to existing divergences in the Polish civil law scholarship: some commentators think that unlawful behaviour is only conduct in breach of positive law (ie the breach of guidelines would be irrelevant in this case), while others favour a wider approach. Taking into account the relevant case law of the Supreme Court, examination of the exact wording of the applicable guidelines is needed. Nevertheless, the protest raised by Agatha during the incident does not, in itself, affect the decision of the court. If awarded, damages may cover both damage to property and health impairment, as well as compensation for the injury suffered.

As noted earlier, damages are primarily claimed in civil proceedings.[719] This means that unless an act has been deemed unlawful (either by a civil court during the

[719] It is noteworthy that damages can also be awarded in the criminal proceedings.

damages proceeding or earlier in a separate criminal proceeding), it will be impossible to effectively seek damages from police officers and/or the State Treasury.

Pursuant to civil law, a victim of an unlawful act committed by the police is entitled to damages. As stipulated in Article 417§ 1 CC,[720] the State Treasury, a local government unit, or another legal person exercising public authority can be held liable for damage suffered due to an unlawful act or omission in exercising its authority. In this case, civil law liability will include damage to property, bodily injury, and health impairment (Arts 444 and 445 CC). Furthermore, the CC provides for one more type of compensation: claims for the violation of personal rights (Art 448 CC). The Code defines personal rights as dignity, health, personal liberty, honour, freedom of conscience, personal image, etc. If these rights are infringed, a court may award an appropriate amount of cash compensation for the harm suffered.

As provided in Article 362 CC, if an injured party contributed to the occurrence or increase of the loss, the obligation to remedy the damage is reduced accordingly. The injured party's contribution to the occurrence or increase of the damage also takes place if the damage is incurred as a consequence of the injured party's conduct. As emphasized by the Supreme Court in its judgments, 'contributing' within the meaning of Article 362 means that there exists an adequate causal link between the injured party's conduct and the damage incurred. The fault, or an obvious misconduct (or the absence thereof), on the part of the injured party are taken into account when assessing if, and to what extent, such contribution justifies a reduction of the compensation.[721]

The general criteria for the liability for an inflicted loss, which must be met jointly, include: first, the existence of damage, understood as infringement of rights protected by law; second, an event triggering a statutory obligation to remedy the damage; third, the existence of a causal link between the occurrence of the damage and the relevant event.

The adjudicating court is bound by the findings of a final and non-appealable criminal judgment sentencing the perpetrators of an offence (Art 11 of the Code of Civil Procedure). This means that in civil proceedings, the court is not only bound by the very determination that the prohibited act was actually committed, but also by other findings as to the facts and circumstances of the offence. The purpose of the provision is to facilitate the civil proceedings by, inter alia, skipping an additional hearing of evidence. However, even if such a judgment by a criminal court has not been delivered (or the criminal court has stated that no offence was committed), a civil court is entitled to decide by itself whether compensation is due or not.[722]

[720] See Art 417 CC:

> 1. The State Treasury or a local government unit or another person exercising public authority by force of law is liable for any damage caused by an unlawful action or omission while exercising public authority. 2. If performance of public authority tasks is contracted under an agreement to a local government unit or another legal person, joint and several liability for any damage caused is borne by the contractor and the local government unit contracting the tasks or the State Treasury.

[721] Case No IV CSK 228/08, judgment of the Supreme Court 29 October 2008.

[722] Case No II CKN 1370/00, judgment of the Supreme Court 26 March 2003; Case No 15562/02 *Lewandowska and Lewandowski v Poland*, judgment of the ECHR 13 January 2009; Case No 10049/04 *Staszewska v Poland*, judgment of the ECHR 3 November 2009.

All services operating in Poland are subject to separate statutory legal regulations, referred to as professional conduct regulations (*pragmatyki służbowe*). The regulations govern non-employment-related professional legal and administrative relations. The employment of a police officer, a particular form of an employment is regulated in the Police Act (hereinafter the Police Act).

As set forth in the Police Act, a policeman is liable for a disciplinary offence consisting in either a breach of discipline at work or professional misconduct. An appeal against a disciplinary decision issued by a disciplinary superior may be filed with a disciplinary superior of a higher level. Subsequently, a decision of the appellate authority may be subject to a complaint filed with an administrative court, in which it will be subject to a two-instance review.

Article 132 of the Police Act stipulates that a perpetrator of an act that represents a disciplinary offence and simultaneously satisfies the criteria of an offence or misdemeanour, or a tax offence of tax misdemeanour, is subject to disciplinary liability as well as criminal liability.

A police officer bears criminal liability, including the special liability imposed on persons practising a profession of public trust. Article 231 § 1 of the Criminal Code ('the Criminal Code') provides that a public official who abuses his/her authority or commits acts of professional misconduct, thereby acting to the detriment of the public or a private interest, is liable to imprisonment for up to three years.

Pursuant to the Act on Direct Coercive Measures and Firearms, when performing statutory tasks of the police unit in which they serve, police officers are permitted to apply direct coercive measures. Article 6 of the said act stipulates that direct coercive measures are applied to the extent necessary to achieve the purpose of such application or use, in proportion to the seriousness of threat, choosing the least onerous measure of direct coercion available.

Professional misconduct may consist in complete omission or partial performance (negligent, improper performance of duties) and/or in acting in a situation that requires certain behaviour to be refrained from. Abuse of authority occurs when a public officer takes an action that comes under his/her authority, but no criteria for doing so have been satisfied, or the action was performed in breach of the appropriate procedures.[723]

In the case of police officers, given the nature of the perpetrator, prosecutors conduct an obligatory preparatory proceedings in the form of an investigation (Art 309 item 2 of the Code of Criminal Procedure, hereinafter the Code of Criminal Procedure). The proceedings are independent of the disciplinary proceedings pending on the police. A criminal court is not bound by the relevant disciplinary decision (Art 8 of the Code of Criminal Procedure).

It should be noted that in order to establish that a perpetrator committed an act set forth in Article 231 § 1 of the Criminal Code, the scope and type (content) of the authority abused by the public officer or the duties which he or she failed to fulfil need

[723] D Mocarska, *Przestępne nadużycie władzy przez funkcjonariuszy Policji w ujęciu prawnokarnym I kryminologicznym* (*'Offensive Abuse of Authority by Police Officers in the Criminal Law and Commentaries'*) (Wydawnictwo Wyższej Szkoły Policji, Szczytno 2013) 108–10.

to be determined. The source of the duty may be of a general, special, or individual nature. Sources of general duties most often include regulations applicable to all officers or to their individual categories. Sources of special duties generally represent regulations applicable to a certain category of public officers, and thus they apply to the activities of individual services and are more specific than the general regulations (eg the Police Act). Finally, sources of individual duties include applicable provisions of rules and procedures, and instructions, as well as official orders to take certain actions.

Furthermore, it is generally assumed that some of the duties of public officers may arise from the very fact of holding a public office.[724] In order to hold a policeman liable for professional misconduct, the content and source of the officer's duties should be established, and it should subsequently be assessed whether the alleged misconduct actually breached any of the duties. It should be borne in mind that the misconduct itself does not satisfy the criteria of a prohibited act as defined in Article 231 § 1 of the Criminal Code—it is also necessary to prove that the person acted to the detriment of the public or a private interest.

A person stopped by traffic police claims damages for health impairment caused by the police officer's misconduct. The woman refused to comply with an aggressively expressed order. In response, the policeman—acting in breach of the internal regulations of his police unit—used physical force to overpower the woman, which resulted in her suffering a permanent injury.

In the light of the general criteria for the liability for an inflicted loss, as mentioned above, it should be noted that in Polish civil law the criterion of unlawful behaviour (infringement of rights protected by law) is variously interpreted in the legal doctrine. Some scholars think that unlawful behaviour only consists in a breach of positive law (ie a breach of guidelines would be irrelevant in this case), while their opponents favour a wider approach (ie a duty of care of health and life might stem not only from positive law, but also from basic common sense supported by experience[725]).

As stated above, the rights and duties of policemen are primarily based in legislation, including, specifically, the Police Act. The Guidelines of the Police Department do not represent a source of generally applicable law, being internal recommendations or instructions addressed to police officers. However, according to the Supreme Court, the rights and duties of a police officer as set forth in legislation may also be defined in more detail based on acts of internally applicable law or relevant rules and procedures containing instructions or official orders.[726]

In the light of Article 231 § 1 of the Criminal Code, and considering the facts described above, there is no doubt as to the contents and the source of the police officer's duties, the fact that he violated applicable regulations, and did harm to a private interest. At the same time, the offender should also be examined in order to determine that an abuse of authority or professional misconduct occurred within the meaning of Article 231 § 1 of the Criminal Code, in addition to the object of the offence. As

[724] Compare: A. Zoll (ed), *Kodeks Karny. Część szczególna. Tom II. Komentarz, pod red. A. Zolla, Wyd. II, Zakamycze* (Wolters Kluwer 2006) 991; A. Wąsek and R. Zawłocki (eds), *Kodeks Karny. Część szczególna. Tom II. Komentarz* (*Criminal Code, Detailed Part, Title II. Commentaries*) (CH Beck 2010) 114–15.

[725] Case No I CR 126/68, judgment of the Supreme Court 9 May 1968.

[726] Case No V KK 388/15, judgment of the Supreme Court 4 May 2016.

indicated in the case law, an act defined in Article 231 § 1 of the Criminal Code referred to above may be committed only intentionally, both with a direct and possible intent. Therefore, the intent of a public official has to include both abuse of authority (or professional misconduct) and acting to the detriment of the public or a private interest.[727]

The facts presented above do not permit us to unequivocally determine whether the policeman committed the act intentionally, and in particular if he was aware of the contents of the relevant guidelines and the fact that the degree of physical force he used might cause a permanent bodily injury to the woman. Thus, prior to passing criminal judgment against the policemen, further investigation is needed, which would clearly determine the situation.

It should also be noted that the civil court can autonomously award damages for inflicted losses, as in this proceeding the issue under consideration is the harm suffered by Agatha, not the guilt of the public officials. In this case, the extent to which the victim herself contributed to the damage should also be examined. Depending on whether it was a routine traffic stop or, for example, a stop in connection with a car chase to detain an offender, the result of any examination may vary. If the victim did not comply with the police officer's orders issued under law, the policeman was permitted by law to apply certain direct coercive measures, including physical force, provided that they were proportionate to the circumstances (namely the direct coercive measures employed corresponded to the needs arising from the situation, and in that particular case were necessary in order make the person being stopped comply with the officer's orders). However, neither the circumstances of stopping the car, nor the details of the victim's conduct have been specified in detail in the description of the circumstances presented.

In conclusion, the answers given initially can be better clarified as follows. There are two conditions for a successful claim. First, the claim for damages will be unequivocally successful if, in the earlier proceeding, a criminal court determines that the offence consisting in an abuse of authority by a public officer (Art 231 § 1 of the Criminal Code) was actually committed. The key requirement in this respect will be to prove that the policeman committed the offence intentionally. It remains to be seen whether such a judgment is passed, and if it will form the basis for a civil court to establish that the State Treasury is liable for the damage incurred due to the unlawful exercise of public authority (Art 417 CC). Second, if no such criminal judgment has been passed, a civil court may award damages for inflicted losses independently of the result of the criminal proceedings. A civil claim will only be successful if the policemen's conduct is classified as unlawful. This, however, is not unequivocal due to existing divergences in Polish civil law scholarship: some commentators think that unlawful behaviour is an action in breach of positive law alone (so that a breach of guidelines would be irrelevant in this case), while others favour a wider approach.

Once unlawfulness has been determined, damages may cover both damage to property and health impairment, as well as compensation for the injury suffered (in relation to the violation of personal rights). The amount of damages awarded will depend

[727] Case No WK 3/03, Decision of the Supreme Court 25 February 2003.

on the extent to which the victim herself contributed to the fault, which the court would be able to establish based on all relevant circumstances. The significance of the violation of internal guidelines by police officers may be defined in the light of the case law of the Supreme Court. A breach of internal guidelines in the above situation is significant to the extent that their content represents a statutory obligation set forth in greater detail.[728] The solution will vary, depending on the different views concerning the nature of the provisions that may set out legal duties for public officers.

H. Romania

RV

In Romania, Agatha would have to go before the civil courts and request that the civil liability of the police officer be triggered. Law 554/2004 establishes that a claim for triggering administrative liability can only be dependent on, and subsequent to, a claim for annulment of an illegal administrative act. Agatha is not in this situation, so an independent claim for damages brought before the administrative court would either be considered inadmissible or the court could invoke *ex officio* its lack of jurisdiction and order that the claim be registered on the docket of the civil court. Law 188/1999 on the status of public servants does in fact clarify that the civil servant's liability can be disciplinary, civil (Art 84 of Law 188/1999), or arise from a contravention. Under Article 84 of Law 188/1999, the law establishes specific civil liability insofar as it is triggered pursuant to certain illegal conduct/facts (connected to the civil servant's duties in the public interest).

Therefore, the legal ground for Agatha's claim for damages in the Romanian legal system is general civil law, namely Article 1349 CC on the general conditions for extra-contractual liability. Agatha's claim could also be formulated against the Police Department, which would be held vicariously liable under Article 1373 CC. The latter provides that 'The employer is bound to repair the damage caused by his or her employees every time the damageable acts or conducts are related to the purpose of their functions.'

I. Spain

EMNG

Agatha's action would be successful whether or not she proves the police offers' action was disproportionate under the circumstances. Her resistance to the request by the authority is irrelevant.

To avoid government liability, it is very important to follow the guidelines or protocols set out by the relevant department. In principle, the normal discharge of public functions and powers is characterized by respect for existing guidelines and protocols. However, this does not mean that public authority liability cannot arise when damage

[728] Case No V KK 388/15, Supreme Court 4 May 2016.

is caused as a consequence of the normal discharge of public functions and powers. *A fortiori*, liability arises outside the normal performance of a public function or power, for instance, when a public authority does not follow the guidelines or code of conduct laid down by its department.

Agatha could thus seek compensation on the basis of the disproportionate conduct of the police officers. The amount of compensation due to her would be calculated on the basis of the days of sickness leave granted and any permanent consequences. These include psychological damage, such as depression, because one of the principles of the Spanish system is that of complete reparation for damages (see Chapter 11).

J. Switzerland

TT

First, it must be stressed that Agatha could only sue the State (in Switzerland, it would be the canton or the municipality), not the officers. If the State is held liable, it could then turn to the officers if their fault is not minor.

The central relevant question here is whether the officers' action was unlawful, ie whether there was a use of excessive force. To give a definite answer to that question, one would need a much more detailed description of the facts. However, the fact that the officers seemingly infringed the guidelines set out by the Police Department certainly points towards the unlawfulness of their conduct. If this is indeed the case, then the canton would be liable and Agatha would be awarded damages for all her medical costs, and, depending on the circumstances, loss of work capacity and even moral wrong, albeit to a very limited extent (see case 3),[729] but by no means would there be punitive damages, which are unknown in Switzerland.

K. United Kingdom

GA

This is a very straightforward problem from the perspective of UK law, where Agatha could initiate a private law action under the common law of trespass to the person and/or under the Human Rights Act 1998 for breach of her rights under Articles 3, 5, and 8 ECHR. Her case would be brought against both of the officers and their chief constable—though, in reality, the chief constable would be vicariously liable for the actions of his or her officers. The permanency of the damage to Agatha's arm means that the action may be heard by way of civil claim in the High Court, viz if the compensation that is to be paid to her is significant (there are qualifying thresholds of c €40,000 under the rules of court). In the alternative scenario, where the amount of compensation would be less significant, the action would be brought in the County Court (a lower court in the UK). (It might be added that one would expect that a case of this kind would settle out of court.)

[729] Switzerland, case 3.

The following points are to be noted:

(1) Trespass to the person is actionable where there is a direct and intentional interference with the body, or bodily integrity, of the individual (Agatha). In this instance, the focus of her claim would be assault and battery (there may also be a point about false imprisonment, see (3) below). Assault, for these purposes, may be defined as 'any act of the defendant that directly and intentionally ... causes the claimant reasonably to apprehend the imminent infliction' of harm; while a battery can be defined as 'any act of the defendant that directly and intentionally ... causes some physical contact with the person of the claimant without the claimant's consent'.[730]

(2) The police officers (chief constable) would have a defence if they could show that they had lawful authority for acting in the manner in which they did. On the facts, it would appear that the initial demand for Agatha to exit her car and produce documentation was lawful—the police officers were presumably exercising stop-and-search powers, or reacting to a driving offence. However, from the moment the officers failed to follow department rules, their claim to lawful interference with the person would encounter difficulties. The law on trespass to the person is applied strictly by the courts, and, unless the police officers could explain that there was some reason of necessity for the breach of the rules, they would be liable for their actions.

(3) The police officers' failure to follow protocol may also mean that Agatha could bring a claim for false imprisonment. That tort fastens upon the common law right to liberty, and can be defined as 'involving an act of the defendant which directly and intentionally causes the confinement of the claimant within an area delimited by the defendant'.[731] While such a claim may well be speculative on the given facts, it would seek to enforce the point that the police are expected to act lawfully at all times. By locking Agatha's arm behind her back, the police officers may therefore have interfered unlawfully with her common law right to liberty.

(4) The nature of Agatha's injury appears to be severe, and the police will be fully liable for whatever amount of compensation is deemed appropriate on the medical evidence. It would not matter whether Agatha had unusually brittle bones or such like—the common law operates an 'egg-shell skull' rule whereby a defendant must take his or her claimant as he or she finds them.

(5) The claim under the Human Rights Act 1998 could be brought either alongside, or instead of, the common law claim (there are shorter time limits under the Human Rights Act—one year, as opposed to three years for a claim in the law of tort). As indicated above, Agatha might claim for a breach of her rights under Article 3 ECHR (the prohibition of torture, inhuman, and degrading treatment), Article 5 ECHR (the right to liberty), and Article 8 ECHR (the right to respect for private life). In terms of Article 3 ECHR, much would depend on

[730] C Witting, *Street on Torts* (14th edn, OUP 2015) 250, 257.
[731] ibid 264.

what was seen by the witnesses and whether Agatha's treatment reached the minimum level of severity for the purposes of that Article (she would wish to focus upon the degrading treatment element of the right). Her corresponding claim under Article 5 ECHR would be for unlawful interference with liberty (see the analogous issues arising at common law, above), while that under Article 8 ECHR would emphasize the violation of her personal integrity.

(6) If a claim under the Human Rights Act 1998 was brought alongside a common law claim, damages would potentially be payable for each respective tort and breach of Agatha's rights (though the court may also make a finding about each tort and breach of rights, but award a composite amount). If a claim were brought solely under the Human Rights Act 1998, damages would be awarded in the light of the approach to compensation that is adopted by the ECtHR.[732]

To recap: there is no doubt that Agatha would be able to bring a successful damages action against the police on the given facts. The infringement of the police's own rules by the officers would be the key to her claim and its success.

[732] Human Rights Act 1998, s 8 and eg *R (Sturnham) v Parole Board* [2013] UKSC 23, [2013] 2 AC 254.

PART IV
COMPARATIVE ANALYSES

15
France, Italy, and Spain

Jean-Bernard Auby

I. Comparison of general features

A. Legal bases

1. Constitutions
Some provisions addressing explicitly governmental liability can be found in both the Italian and Spanish Constitutions (respectively Arts 28 and 106-2): in both cases, a principle of liability in tort is laid down.

The French Constitution does not contain any express provision on the matter. However, the Constitutional Court ruled that a converging principle was a side consequence of Article 4 of the 1789 Declaration on Human Rights, which is a component part of the Constitution.

2. Legislation
Below the constitutions, a certain role is played by legislation. In Italy, the Civil Code (CC), through its Article 2043, serves as a practical basis for the regulation of governmental liability, while in Spain some general rules on the latter can be found in 2015 legislation concerning the law applicable to the public sector.

In French law, there is no general legislation on administrative liability. Various pieces of parliamentary legislation have touched upon the matter, but they serve to cover it through specific rules concerning specific sectors.

B. Courts and procedures

1. Preliminary complaint before the administration or an ombudsman
Spanish law used to impose a preliminary complaint before the administration, but this rule has been abandoned: nevertheless, courts can retain the fact that the claimant delayed bringing an action as a factor of possible reduction of compensation.

In French administrative law, claimants bringing an action for government liability must submit a decision taken by the administration on their claim ('*décision préalable*' rule) to the court: in practice, this leads them (in most cases) to make a preliminary administrative appeal in order to obtain the decision they will then challenge in court.

Jean-Bernard Auby, *France, Italy, and Spain* In: *Tort Liability of Public Authorities in European Laws.*
Edited by: Giacinto della Cananea and Roberto Caranta, Oxford University Press (2020).
DOI: 10.1093/oso/9780198867555.003.0015.

2. Competent courts

In the Spanish system, the entire litigation concerning administrative liability is within the competence of administrative tribunals at the first level and then to the administrative sections of higher courts.

In the French system, administrative liability litigation is mostly brought before the administrative courts: ordinary courts are only competent in cases concerning situations where the administration is submitted to private law—essentially within the scope of 'industrial and commercial public services'.

In the Italian system, administrative courts have jurisdiction on cases where liability stems from administrative orders. Ordinary courts are competent on all other cases.

C. Other aspects

In the three systems, the liability of administrative institutions prevails over the personal liability of its agents: this means that claimants can ask the administrative entity to compensate them, provided that the latter can afterwards turn to its agents and have them share the burden of compensation where the damage is totally or partially due to their personal misconduct.

In Spanish administrative law, claims regarding government liability are enclosed in a time limit of one year. In Italian law, where such claims are based upon the unlawfulness of an administrative act, a time limit of 120 days applies. In French law, there is no direct procedural time limit for actions concerning administrative liability, but an indirect deadline intervenes: a traditional rule according to which the administration's debts lapse after four years.

II. Drawing from the case studies

A. Conduct likely to give rise to administrative liability

1. The existence of a general concept of fault

French law on administrative liability relies on a general concept of fault, as a general condition for administrative liability to be invoked. No precise definition of this concept exists, but standard case law applies it to various types of situations involving misadministration, such as delays, inertia, errors ... or unlawfulness, as we will see in section II.A.2. We will also see that governmental liability can sometimes arise without any misconduct having been committed.

Italian and Spanish law on public liability is not organized in the same way. In Spanish law, administrative liability is conceived as 'objective', insofar as the situations in which the administration can be held liable are posited on a continuum along which cases of obvious misfunctioning can be found, or cases where liability will derive from unlawfulness,or cases in which liability will be admitted with no culpable behaviour being observed.

In Italian law, the essential divide is between cases in which liability stems from unlawfulness—which means that a breach of '*interessi legittimi*' has occurred, and cases where administrative liability is predicated on negligence within the meaning of the CC.

2. Liability and unlawfulness
In all three administrative laws, it is accepted in principle that irregularities in administrative decisions can induce liability on the part of the issuing administration. However, this principle has been difficult to stabilize in the Italian system, due to the traditional separation between situations where citizens hold subjective rights and situations where they can only claim legitimate interests in their relationship with the public administration.

In all three systems, it is not to be excluded that liability would arise from a mere procedural irregularity, but they commonly restrict this assumption to cases where it is established that the irregularity has had some influence on the substance of the decision.

3. Liability without wrongdoing (strict liability)
French administrative law has long allowed that, in certain situations listed in case law, the liability of the administration could be upheld without any fault on its part: these are situations where an act of the administration produces a specific risk and situations where albeit lawful administrative decisions cause abnormal and special damage on one person or category of persons.

Spanish administrative law also envisages cases of government liability without wrongdoing in relation to administrative activities that create risks.

Italian administrative law seems to accept strict administrative liability only where it is provided for in legislation.

B. Some practical issues raised by the introduction of liability

1. Types of compensable damage
In all three administrative law systems, the most sensitive issue is that of hypothetical damage, such as the loss of a chance (eg the loss of the chance of being selected in a tendering procedure) and loss of profit (where the conduct of the administration constituted an obstacle to a business activity that could have been profitable). The claimants have to prove that they had a good chance of obtaining what they were applying for and/or that the activity they intended to carry on would probably have been profitable.

2. Nature of the remedy
In Spanish law, legislation has opened up to the possibility of the remedy of specific performance, and not only equivalent measures. French administrative law was traditionally opposed to this alternative, and only accepted pecuniary damages: the situation is evolving slightly thanks to the powers administrative courts now have to grant injunctions.

16
France and the United Kingdom

Carol Harlow

I. General context

This comparative study of government liability focuses very deliberately on outcomes. It posits a number of situations involving the present-day activities of present-day public authorities with a view to comparing the respective answers of the UK[1] and French administrative legal systems, and deliberately rejects the more usual comparative method of comparison at a highly abstract level of general principle. But although the focus is on outcomes rather than principle, some knowledge of context and structure is necessary for an understanding of outcome. Administrative liability needs to be understood against a background of two different systems of civil liability, which in turn sit within very different constitutional frameworks.

A. Is there any formal constitutional provision concerning public authority liability?

Thus the first introductory question is significant, but it is also misleading, especially in the UK, where the fact that there is no 'formal constitution' seems to dictate the simple answer 'No'. In both countries, the answer is more complex. In France, one can apparently suggest constitutional bases for state liability, notably Article 4 of the 1789 Declaration of the Rights of Man and the case law of the Conseil Constitutionnel. In the UK, by way of contrast, the legal doctrine of parliamentary sovereignty leaves the legislature with the last word, unless exceptionally EU law or the European Convention on Human Rights (ECHR) can be invoked, as, for example, in the *Marshall* case, where the court of Justice ruled that an award of damages in a discrimination cases could not be limited by a bar on paying interest or otherwise capped.[2] Whether the UK courts would go as far as the Conseil Constitutionnel in creating a constitutional right to compensation is extremely doubtful, though they might annul an attempted ouster

[1] It should not be forgotten that Scotland has a separate legal system with formal constitutional protection in the Act of Union 1707. In general, the principles of tortious liability in the two systems do not greatly differ, partly due to the joint appellate system at the level of the House of Lords, now the Supreme Court. The Scottish principle of culpa famously influenced the leading case of *Donoghue v Stevenson* [1932] AC 562, and the controversial case of *Burmah Oil v Lord Advocate* [1965] AC 75 was set down for hearing in Scotland in order to benefit from the principle of eminent domain. For our purposes, however, it is convenient to refer to UK law.

[2] See Case C-271/91 *Marshall v Southampton and South-West Hampshire Area Health Authority* [1993] ECR I-4367.l.

Carol Harlow, *France and the United Kingdom* In: *Tort Liability of Public Authorities in European Laws.*
Edited by: Giacinto della Cananea and Roberto Caranta, Oxford University Press (2020). © The Contributors.
DOI: 10.1093/oso/9780198867555.003.0016.

of their jurisdiction,[3] and would certainly interpret attempts to deprive claimants of compensation narrowly.[4]

B. Are there different courts or other public agencies for the annulment of unlawful administrative decisions and for the award of damages?

More pertinent to France, where separation of powers is deeply embedded in the constitution,[5] is the answer to the third introductory question. The well-known fact of the dual jurisdiction of French administrative law means that a jurisdictional line must be drawn between what is public and what is private (eg as between administrative and judicial police in case 11; see Chapter 14, section XII) and it is sometimes hard to work out on which side of the public/private line a function or authority falls (eg as in case 4; see Chapter 11, section V). In general, however, the answer to the third introductory question in France is affirmative: the same set of administrative tribunals, headed by the Conseil d'Etat, has jurisdiction in cases of annulment (*le recours pour excès de pouvoir*) and claims for damages (*le recours de pleine jurisdiction*). This creates a clear link between the concepts of legality and liability, which has facilitated the growth of a holistic system in which illegality can ultimately be encompassed within the concept of fault.

No such link exists in the UK, where liability and legality are sharply distinguished.[6] At least theoretically, there is no separate administrative jurisdiction in the UK, where the so-called 'private law model of public law' is in force. This means that in principle the state and its officials are answerable to the 'ordinary courts', supposedly in the same way as any private individual. The constitutional foundation for this doctrine is Professor AV Dicey's famous principle of equality, according to which not only is 'no man above the law, but (what is a different thing) ... every man, whatever be his rank or condition, is subject to the ordinary law of the realm and amenable to the jurisdiction of the ordinary tribunals'.[7]

In practice, however, at least in England and Wales, liability usually falls to be decided by the civil divisions of the High Court or for smaller claims, a district court (UK, vi, ix, x), whereas the key principles of judicial review have been built up in actions for judicial review in the administrative division (today called the Administrative Court). In consequence, there have been problems over differing interpretations of key terms such as 'duty', where a statutory duty in public law is interpreted as general in character

[3] See now *R (Privacy International) v Investigatory Powers Tribunal and others* [2019] UKSC 22.

[4] See eg, *R (Reilly) and another v Secretary of State for Work and Pensions* [2013] UKSC 68; *Reilly and another v Secretary of State for Work and Pensions* [2016] EWCA Civ 413 concerning deprival of compensation by retrospective legislation. And see *AXA General Insurance Limited and others v The Lord Advocate* [2011] UKSC 46.

[5] On which, see M Troper, *La séparation des pouvoirs et l'histoire constitutionnelle française* (LGDJ 1980).

[6] D Fairgrieve, *State Liability in Tort, A Comparative Analysis* (OUP 2003) ch 3. See for discussion, C Harlow, *Compensation and Government Torts* (Sweet & Maxwell 1982) 51–58. And see P Cane, 'Damages in Public Law' (1999) 9 Otago L R 489.

[7] AV Dicey, *Introduction to the Study of the Law of the Constitution* (10th edn, ECS Wade-MacMillan 1959) 193.

or owed to the public at large, as distinct from a common law duty of care on which tortious liability can be founded.[8] Again, 'reasonableness' is narrowly interpreted in public law,[9] but given a more generous meaning in tort law. The Supreme Court has recently made a brave attempt to clarify the general principles in a case concerning the duties of a local authority in administering public housing.[10] The link in French administrative law between illegality and liability, and the use of the flexible formula of 'fault of such a nature as to incur liability' allows such difficulties to be avoided.

Famously (though inaccurately), Dicey also asserted that 'every official, from the prime minister down to a constable or collector of taxes, is under the same responsibility for every act done without legal justification as any other citizen.'[11] At the time these words were written, Dicey's theory of personal liability was functional. No judge-made system of government liability would have been possible at a time when the doctrine of Crown immunity sheltered central government departments from liability and extended even to vicarious liability. Personal liability afforded a way round this problem. It was not until 1947 that Parliament intervened to end government immunity with the Crown Proceedings Act 1947. An expansive period followed, when the courts expanded vicarious liability into a 'guarantee'.[12] However, the Supreme Court has recently changed direction, restricting vicarious liability for third parties.[13] A cursory look at the questionnaire shows, however, just how unrealistic Dicey's model is for modern times.[14] Citizens are not in a position to sanction banks, prohibit imports, or block the sale of beauty creams. Officials, on the other hand, are endowed with a multiplicity of statutory powers and duties—to licence, control traffic, and regulate markets, amongst many other things.[15] This essential difference underlies the complex distinctions made in the case law between statutory powers and duties and common law duty of care.

It is important to bear in mind that the non-contractual civil law of liability (in brief, tort law) has never been codified in the UK. Unlike the flexible French fault principle, it is largely made up of a disparate series of nominate wrongs or torts, held together by the modern tort of negligence. Some of the nominate torts are as antiquated as they are ancient. When, for example, the House of Lords was asked to impose liability on the Bank of England for negligent use of its statutory regulatory powers, leading to the collapse of a bank, causing substantial financial losses, the claimants turned to the virtually moribund tort of misfeasance in public office, with a dubious seventeenth-century

[8] The differences are classified and discussed by Lord Browne-Wilkinson *in X (Minors) v Bedfordshire County Council, M v Newham London Borough Council* [1995] 2 AC 633.

[9] The so-called 'Wednesbury test': see *Associated Provincial Picture Houses Ltd v Wednesbury Corporation* [1948] 1 KB 223.

[10] *Poole Borough Council v GN* [2019] UKSC 25.

[11] Dicey (n 7).

[12] *The Catholic Child Welfare Society and others v Various Claimants and The Institute of the Brothers of the Christian Schools and others* [2012] UKSC 56; *Armes v Nottinghamshire CC* [2017] UKSC 60.

[13] *WM Morrison v Various Claimants* [2020] UKSC 12; *Barclays Bank v Various Claimants* [2020] UKSC 13.

[14] For a defence of the 'private law model', see C Harlow, '"Public" and "Private" Law: Definition without Distinction' (1980) 43 MLR 241 disputed by G Samuel, 'Public and Private Law: A Private Lawyer's Response' (1983) 46 MLR 558.

[15] Dicey's proposition has been heavily criticized: see eg Dicey (n 7) 'Introduction' to the 9th and 10th editions; WI Jennings, 'In Praise of Dicey' (1885–1935)' (1935) 13 Pub Admin 123.

precedent for support.[16] 'Misfeasance in public office' is applicable where loss or damage is suffered through an exercise of public power by a public official acting intentionally, maliciously, or recklessly. Clearly, it could have been brought into use—if the House of Lords had acted creatively, more particularly by interpreting intention widely as relevant to the act rather than the damage—as a general principle of government liability to cover situations like those in the hypothetical cases 2 (section III), 3 (section IV), 7 (section VIII), and 8 (section IX) in Chapter 14 in this volume. Instead, the Lords, no doubt conscious of the financial implications, chose to shut the tort down.[17] A similar disinclination to act marks the case law concerning breach of statutory duty, referred to in the UK questionnaire answers.

The case of the violent police officer illustrates this proposition nicely. As stated in the UK answer, this is readily soluble. The officer is liable for an assault and battery (UK answer to case 11, Chapter 14, section XII.K), one of number of trespass torts including false imprisonment, which are torts of strict liability (actionable *per se*) and where liability exists to vindicate a violated right. To defend himself, the official must show 'justification and lawful excuse'. Not only can Agatha succeed in an action for damages, but the case is one in which a power to award exemplary damages to express the court's disapproval of a public official who is abusing his powers has been expressly preserved by the House of Lords.[18] On these facts, the judge might very well decide to use it.

The trespass torts are not without their problems for public law. In *Lumba*,[19] the Home Secretary, exercising powers under the Immigration Act 1971 to detain and deport illegal immigrants, maintained a published policy on the application of the power to detain. Subsequently, she adopted a new and more rigorous policy, which was not published. When this hidden policy came to the surface and was tested in an action for damages, it was found to be unlawful. The government sought to avoid compensation, however, in reliance on the defence that the failure to disclose was a minor procedural irregularity, and that the claimants could have been lawfully detained. By a majority, the Supreme Court ruled in favour of strict liability for false imprisonment, disallowing the defence, but (perhaps illogically) allowing the defence to mitigate the quantum of damages. Nominal damages of £1 were awarded and exemplary damages were expressly disallowed.

A marked disinclination to expand the liability of public authorities, notable on the part of the British judiciary, is to a limited extent offset by a reliance on extra-legal compensation. In the case of the Crown, the gap left by the maxim that 'the Crown can do no wrong' was to a certain extent filled by a systematic practice of ex gratia payments. This tradition endures. Negotiated settlements are commonplace and it would, as stated, be extremely unlikely that a case as clear as that in hypothetical case

[16] *Three Rivers District Council v Bank of England* [2001] UKHL 16. Compare the brave Australian decision in *Beaudesert Shire Council v Smith* (1966) 120 CLR 145, though this was later doubted in *Northern Territory v Mengel* (1995) 185 CLR 307.

[17] See *Watkins v Home Office* [2006] UKHL 16. And see M Aronson, 'Misfeasance in Public Office: Some Unfinished Business' (2016) 132 LQR 426.

[18] *Rookes v Barnard* [1964] AC 1129 (Lord Devlin). And see J Varuhas, *Damages and Human Rights* (Hart Publishing 2016) 123–26.

[19] *Walumba Lumba (Congo) v Home Secretary* [2011] UKSC 12.

11 would ever reach a court. Departments are empowered to make ex gratia payments and publish online guidance on how to claim them, while the Treasury issues guidance on the calculation of compensation.[20] Local authorities have similar powers, subject to ministerial approval. As emphasized in the comments at the beginning of Chapter 13 (UK (a)), ombudsmen frequently make recommendations as to compensation for maladministration, which is often substantial and may be used by courts as a precedent for quantum of damages and, although the source of the power is not obvious, it has seldom been questioned.[21]

II. Hypotheticals

Several striking differences between the two systems emerge from the answers to the hypothetical cases. First, the French liability system is seen as comprehensive; the general administrative courts are seen as the right place to decide questions of compensation, and it is understood that administrative law will provide answers to all (or most) of them. The UK answers, on the other hand, treat litigation as a last resort and focus on alternative methods of dispute resolution, designed to keep potential litigants out of court. Maurice, the wrongfully dismissed civil servant (case 1), for example, can in principle go to court once he has exhausted his internal remedies, but the affair is far more likely to end in an internal appeal under the Civil Service Management Code[22] or by an employment tribunal.[23] (Whether this is also the case in France is not quite clear). Several of the hypotheticals suggest maladministration and point to redress through an ombudsman (UK comment (a) in Chapter 13). Thus case 5 (section VI; delay in an administrative process) might best be handled by the local government ombudsman, and the same is true of the two licensing cases (cases 7 and 8 in Chapter 14, sections VIII and IX, respectively) provided the agencies fall within an ombudsman's jurisdiction. The fact that Ms Tramp has already challenged the withdrawal before a court' indicates either that the agency is not listed, or a characteristic lack of knowledge of the ombudsman system or, if she has consulted a lawyer, a predilection for legal over extra-legal remedies. Hypothetical cases 9 and 10 (sections X and XII of Chapter 14, respectively) potentially involve maladministration, but the advantages of ombudsman procedure are less clear, first, because questions of legality are involved, which are best settled in court and might be contested by the agency if ruled on by an ombudsman, and second, because the agency must be listed in to the relevant legislation, here the schedule to the Parliamentary Commissioner Act, 1967 (as amended).

Second, the French fault principle emerges as more flexible and easily adapted to administrative liability than the common law tort of negligence.[24] In the common law,

[20] HM Treasury, *Managing Public Money* (2013, rev 2018).
[21] Though see *In the matter of an application by JR55 for Judicial Review (Northern Ireland)* [2016] UKSC 22 (Lord Sumption).
[22] See Part I of the Constitutional Reform and Governance Act 2010. The Code is available online in the 2016 version.
[23] See *Jobcentre Plus Department of Work and Pensions v Graham* [2011] UKEAT 0610_10_0306.
[24] Fairgrieve (n 6) ch 4.

the respondent must be shown to owe a duty of care on an individual basis to the claimant. Where a public authority is acting under a statutory duty or powers, this may be difficult; a statutory duty is not the same as a duty of care. The basic principle was explained by Lord Reid in the seminal case of *Home Office v Dorset Yacht Co*:

> Parliament deems it to be in the public interest that things otherwise unjustifiable should be done, and that those who do such things with due care should be immune from liability to persons who may suffer thereby. But Parliament cannot reasonably be supposed to have licensed those who do such things to act negligently in disregard of the interests of others so as to cause them needless damage.[25]

But the exercise of a discretionary power is not actionable unless it is highly unreasonable, perhaps unreasonable in the public law sense:

> But there must come a stage when the discretion is exercised so carelessly or unreasonably that there has been no real exercise of the discretion which Parliament has conferred. The person purporting to exercise his discretion has acted in abuse or excess of his power. Parliament cannot be supposed to have granted immunity to persons who do that.[26]

I have emphasized and reiterated this point because, since negligence is the general principle of civil liability, it follows that most of the hypothetical cases are likely to be affected by the extremely complex and tangled case law, which has accumulated over the years around this apparently simple principle.

As indicated earlier, the Supreme Court has just made a serious attempt to clarify the law in a case where a local authority had allocated public housing to a single mother and refitted it for the use of her disabled son. Unfortunately, they were consistently harassed by a neighbouring family and became seriously upset before they were moved. Mother and son sued for damages. It was held in a unanimous judgment that, in the circumstances, the authority was not liable; neither claimant was owed a duty of care and no responsibility lay on a public authority for the acts of third parties in these circumstances. The basic principle, as articulated by Lord Reed, clearly illustrates the framework of the 'private law model of public law' in which the case was decided:

> It follows (1) that public authorities may owe a duty of care in circumstances where the principles applicable to private individuals would impose such a duty, unless such a duty would be inconsistent with, and is therefore excluded by, the legislation from which their powers or duties are derived; (2) that public authorities do not owe a duty of care at common law merely because they have statutory powers or duties, even if, by exercising their statutory functions, they could prevent a person from suffering harm; and (3) that public authorities can come under a common law duty to protect from harm in circumstances where the principles applicable to private individuals

[25] [1970] AC 1004 [1030].
[26] ibid [1031].

> or bodies would impose such a duty, as for example where the authority has created the source of danger or has assumed a responsibility to protect the claimant from harm, unless the imposition of such a duty would be inconsistent with the relevant legislation.[27]

Third, a point of interest in the hypothetical cases generally is that so many involve claims for economic loss. Here, it is clear from the answers that French administrative law has a full and sophisticated case law. By way of contrast, courts in the UK have not shown themselves especially willing to expand tortious liability to cases of economic loss. Fairgrieve correctly notes the 'reluctance' of UK courts to allow recovery of financial loss that is unconnected with physical damage, and the 'prevailing judicial approach' of protection of public authorities from financial reparation. He notes also that courts 'have generally been very wary' of imposing liability on regulators, and lists specifically, economic regulation, safety inspection, and certification, planning, welfare benefits, and licensing as areas illustrative of this reluctance.[28] There is in principle liability for negligent misstatements or advice,[29] and local authorities have been held liable for loss caused through negligence in the execution of building inspection or planning powers[30] but these are exceptional cases. The mere fact that the withholding of a licence is unlawful or that there have been procedural irregularities is insufficient to found liability. In *Trent Strategic Health Authority v Jain*, for example, the authority had applied to a magistrate's court to close down the claimants' nursing home, acting under statute but in gross breach of the *audi alteram partem* principle. Yet the House of Lords, though expressing sympathy, refused to impose a common law duty of care, reasoning that 'the imposition of such a duty would or might inhibit the exercise of the statutory powers and be potentially adverse to the interests of the class of persons the powers were designed to benefit or protect, thereby putting at risk the achievement of their statutory purpose'.[31]

The only saving grace for this notably unjust case was that it took place before the Human Rights Act 1998 came into force, and that the House of Lords specifically stated in the judgments that a breach of ECHR Article 1, Protocol 1 had occurred, which might, they thought, have been actionable had the Human Rights Act been in force.

To summarize, French administrative law on liability is both more systematic and more flexible than the 'private law model of public law' in the UK. A tendency on the part of the judiciary to limit the financial obligations of public authorities can certainly be observed. It must be borne in mind, however, that the law of torts as applied to private individuals and corporate entities is itself often limited—sometimes perhaps too limited. The judges are disinclined to engage in a substantial exercise of law-making, while Parliament too often leaves law-making in the area of civil liability to the courts.

[27] *Poole Borough Council* (n 10) [65] (Lord Reed).
[28] Fairgrieve (n 6) 193–95. And see P Cane, *Tort Law and Economic Interests* (2nd edn, OUP 1996).
[29] Following *Hedley Byrne v Heller* [1964] AC 465.
[30] The case of *Anns v Merton LBC* [1978] AC 728 is now a doubtful precedent.
[31] *Trent Strategic Health Authority v Jain* [2009] UKHL 4 [28] (Lord Scott).

As an endnote, what Parliament expects of the courts in respect of government liability can be deduced from two different incidents. First, section 8 of the Human Rights Act 1998 provides that damages for a violation of listed Convention Rights can only be awarded by a court that has power to award damages or order the payment of compensation in civil proceedings, and only then where the court is satisfied that the award is necessary to afford just satisfaction to the person in whose favour it is made. The courts must take into account the notably ungenerous jurisprudence of the Strasbourg Court of Human Rights, something that they have done enthusiastically.[32] Second, when the Law Commission undertook a review of redress, including liability, in the public sector with a view to simplification and reform, the programme had to be whittled down at the request of government to a consideration of ombudsmen.[33] This hardly points to the likelihood in a time of austerity of a wholesale reform of damages as a remedy in public law cases.

[32] See notably *Anufrijeva v Southwark LBC* [2003] EWCA Civ 406; *R v Home Secretary ex p Greenfield* [2005] UKHL 14.

[33] See Law Commission, *Administrative Redress: Public Bodies and the Citizen*, Law Com no 322, HC 6 (2009-10).

17

EU Law and UK Law

Paul Craig

I. General issues

A. Is there any constitutional provision concerning public authority liability?

There are three dimensions to this inquiry that should be disaggregated for the purposes of analytical clarity: the existence of such a constitutional provision; the existence of a general principle of liability for public authorities, even if it does not have formal constitutional status; and the normative content of the rules concerning public authority liability that prevail in the respective legal systems. These issues shape the very nature of the damages liability of public authorities in any legal system, and they should therefore be addressed at the outset.

The brief answer to the question of whether there is any constitutional provision concerning public authority liability is 'No' for both the UK and the EU, insofar as the question signifies the existence of a formal constitution that is separate from the general body of law in that country.

The UK has no written constitution, and there is therefore by definition no written constitutional provision concerning public authority liability. The rules concerning damages liability have been developed by the courts, with the principal legal developments dating from the fifteenth century onwards.

The EU has no written constitution that is distinct from the generality of the Treaty provisions that deal with other aspects of EU law, such as the single market, the environment, the common commercial policy, and the like.

The answer to the question of whether there is a general principle of liability for public authorities, even if it does not have constitutional status reveals greater differences in this regard. The salient inquiry is whether the UK and the EU have anything that could be regarded as a general principle concerning damages liability, irrespective of whether this has canonical status as a formal constitutional provision. There are differences between the two systems and they reflect deeper distinctions as to how legal systems conceptualize damages liability in their respective systems.

The UK does not have what would be recognized by other legal systems as a general principle of damages liability, nor do we have any wholly separate body of law dealing with damages actions against public bodies. The basic premise is that an ultra vires or illegal act will not per se give rise to damages liability.[1] The claim must therefore

[1] *X (Minors) v Bedfordshire CC* [1995] 2 AC 633, 730.

Paul Craig, *EU Law and UK Law* In: *Tort Liability of Public Authorities in European Laws*. Edited by: Giacinto della Cananea and Roberto Caranta, Oxford University Press (2020). © The Contributors. DOI: 10.1093/oso/9780198867555.003.0017.

be fitted into a recognized private law cause of action.[2] It is for the plaintiff to fit the claim into one of the established causes of action in order to seek damages. There are a number of causes of action that might avail a plaintiff against a public body. These include: negligence; breach of statutory duty; misfeasance in a public office; nuisance; *Rylands v Fletcher*; false imprisonment; and damages under the Human Rights Act 1998. There is no cause of action based simply upon the careless performance of a statutory duty in the absence of any other common law right of action.

The EU does have a general principle of damages liability for losses caused by the EU institutions. Article 340 of the Treaty on the Functioning of the European Union (TFEU) provides that 'the Union shall, in accordance with the general principles common to the laws of the Member States, make good any damage caused by its institutions or its servants in the performance of their duties'. This does not contain any substantive liability rule in itself, but entrusts the Court of Justice of the European Union (CJEU) to develop and create these principles in the light of the principles common to the laws of the Member States. The CJEU has performed this task since the inception of the European Economic Community (EEC). It is now clear that there are three conditions for liability: there must be proof that the contested action was unlawful; there must be a manifest and serious illegality; and there has to be a causal link between the unlawful conduct and the damage, and the existence of damage that is certain and quantifiable.

The EU has also developed a general principle of damages liability for Member States that act in violation of EU law. The principle originated in *Francovich*,[3] and was developed in *Brasserie du Pecheur/Factortame*.[4] The CJEU has consciously drawn links between the liability rules under Article 340 and those developed pursuant to *Francovich*. Thus, the CJEU has reasoned that the rules concerning the damages liability of the EU under Article 340 should not be markedly different from those concerning Member State liability. This is reflected in the conditions pertaining to Member State damages liability: the rule of law infringed must have been intended to confer rights on individuals; the breach of the rule of law must have been sufficiently serious; and there must have been a direct causal link between the breach and the damage.

The third limb of the inquiry concerns the normative content of the rules concerning public authority liability in any legal system. This is perforce a complex issue that cannot be addressed in detail here. Nor, however, can it be ignored, since it reveals the values concerning damages liability that pertain in that legal system, and shapes the application thereof to particular fact situations. While detailed exegesis of the normative foundations of such liability is beyond the remit of the present inquiry, we can nonetheless discern some of the central features thereof. The key issue concerns the meaning of fault within the regime of damages liability.

This may be treated as equivalent to illegality, which is the approach in some civil law systems. Thus, in France, the starting assumption is that illegality connotes fault,

[2] ibid 633.

[3] Cases C-6 and 9/90 *Francovich and Bonifaci v Italian Republic* [1991] ECR I-5357.

[4] Cases C-46 and 48/93 *Brasserie du Pecheur SA v Germany, R v Secretary of State for Transport, ex p Factortame Ltd* [1996] ECR I-1029.

and hence responsibility in damages. This is also the case in EU law for acts where there is no real discretion. The only circumstance in which the common law approximates to this position is where there has been a finding that a breach of a statute gives rise, in and of itself, to liability in damages.

Fault may alternatively be seen as distinct from illegality, which is the general approach taken in common law jurisdictions. Proof of illegality, in the sense of an ultra vires act, is not treated as the equivalent of fault for the purposes of damages liability. The plaintiff has to prove the existence of a duty of care, a breach thereof, and recoverable damage.

There is yet another meaning of the term 'fault' in EU law. Where there is some significant measure of discretion, and/or where the meaning of the EU norm is imprecise, illegality per se will not suffice for liability. The applicant will have to prove that the breach was sufficiently serious. There is, however, no requirement of fault going beyond proof of the serious breach of EU law.

These different meanings of the term 'fault' reflect different underlying values. Thus, the civilian idea that illegality constitutes, in many cases, fault, is predicated on the normative assumption that an error that suffices for the annulment of an act, should prima facie suffice also for the award of damages. This in turn is based on the normative assumption that the State should bear the responsibility for the losses caused by such unlawful conduct, which should not be left to lie with the individual who has been harmed.

The UK regime is starkly different in this respect. It is based on the substantive disaggregation of illegality and liability. Proof of the former tells one nothing about proof of the latter. Illegality may be a necessary condition for liability, although this is not always so, but it is certainly not sufficient for liability. It is for the claimant to fit the case within one of the standard common law causes of action. These are derived from private law, with some modification when the claim is brought against a public body. If the claimant is unable to do so, then the loss lies with the claimant.

The EU regime is different yet again. The normative values that underpin this regime are distinct. Thus, for cases where the EU or the Member State possess discretion, illegality is a necessary, not a sufficient condition for liability. The rationale for the reluctance to ground liability on illegality per se in such instances resonates with the values underlying the UK regime. The administration commonly has to make complex discretionary choices, and there is the concern that while illegality should suffice to annul the contested measure, it should not suffice for damages liability, since this would be too onerous for the public purse and would render the administration too cautious in making its discretionary choices.[5] This is reflected in the EU test for liability under Article 340 and *Francovich*, which is different from that in the UK. The key element in the EU test is the need to show a manifest and serious breach. This constitutes the general principle of liability, and is different from the meaning of fault in the UK system

[5] See eg Case 5/71 *Aktien-Zuckerfabrik Schöppenstedt v Council* [1971] ECR 975; Case C–352/98 P *Laboratoires Pharmaceutiques Bergaderm SA and Goupil v Commission* [2000] ECR I–5291.

B. Is there any general requirement to carry an administrative appeal or to bring a complaint before an ombudsman or another public agency before bringing an action for damages against public authorities?

This question is interesting, since it reveals how a legal system conceptualizes the relationship between damages liability and other mechanisms for securing redress.

In the UK, there is no requirement to pursue an administrative appeal, or bring a complaint before the ombudsman, before claiming damages. The claimant may seek to do so, because it may be felt that this is a more expeditious and cheaper way of securing redress than through the ordinary courts. There is, however, no compulsion to do so. The position is different if the claimant is seeking judicial review. There is a complex body of case law in the UK, whereby the courts have increasingly insisted that claimants should exhaust administrative remedies before seeking judicial review to annul the contested act.[6]

In the EU, the position is similar, although not identical. The early approach of the European Court of Justice (ECJ) did not augur well for individuals: it held in *Plaumann*[7] that annulment of the norm was a necessary condition precedent to using Article 340 TFEU. If this requirement had been retained, then Article 340 would have been of little use, given the difficulty for an individual to prove *locus standi* for annulment. The necessity for annulment was, however, generally discarded in later cases, and the action for damages came to be regarded as an independent, autonomous cause of action.[8]

There may, however, be instances where the failure to proceed with an Article 263 TFEU action will have consequences for an Article 340(2) TFEU action where the individual was directly and individually concerned by the offending norm and could have successfully challenged it under Article 263 TFEU, but either failed to do so entirely or failed to do so within the period for challenge laid down in Article 263.[9] There are, in addition, difficult issues that can arise where there is joint liability in damages of the EU and the Member States.[10]

[6] P Craig, *Administrative Law* (8th edn, Sweet & Maxwell 2016) 27-044–27-055.

[7] Case 25/62 *Plaumann v Commission* [1963] ECR 95.

[8] *Aktien-Zuckerfabrik Schöppenstedt* (n 5); Cases 9 and 11/71 *Compagnie d'Approvisionnement de Transport et de Crédit SA et Grands Moulins de Paris SA v Commission* [1972] ECR 391; Case T–178/98 *Fresh Marine Company SA v Commission* [2000] ECR II–3331 [45]–[50]; Cases T–3/00 and 337/04 *Athanasios Pitsiorlas v Council and European Central Bank* [2007] ECR II–4779 [281]–[284].

[9] Cases C–199 and 200/94 *Pesqueria Vasco-Montanesa SA (Pevasa) and Compania Internacional de Pesca y Derivados SA (Inpesca) v Commission* [1995] ECR I–3709; Case T–93/95 *Laga v Commission* [1998] ECR II–195; Case C–310/97 P *Commission v AssiDomän Kraft Products AB* [1999] ECR I–5363 [59].

[10] A Durand, 'Restitution or Damages: National Court or European Court?' (1975–76) 1 ELRev 431; TC Hartley, 'Concurrent Liability in EEC Law: A Critical Review of the Cases' (1977) 2 ELRev 249; W Wils, 'Concurrent Liability of the Community and a Member State' (1992) 17 ELRev 191.

C. Are there different courts or other public agencies for the annulment of unlawful administrative decisions and for the award of damages?

The position in the UK is complex. The answer in essence is as follows. The default position is that, in institutional terms, the ordinary courts will decide an issue of annulment, and the damages action.

This does not, however, necessarily mean that both issues will be decided in the same legal action. Annulment is not a formal pre-condition for damages actions in the UK. It is therefore common for the damages claim to proceed, even though there has been no separate and prior action for judicial review to annul the contested measure. The court may, however, determine the legality of the contested act collaterally in the context of the claim for damages. An action for damages may, subject to certain conditions, also be appended to a judicial review claim.

There are two principal qualifications to the preceding picture. The first is that, as indicated in section I.B above, a claimant may have to exhaust administrative appeal procedures before seeking judicial review to annul the measure. The second qualification is in relation to tribunals. The initial route for challenging many administrative decisions in the UK is via a tribunal. The tribunals exercise an appellate role, and also, in certain circumstances, they have supervisory powers akin to those of the High Court, which they can use to annul the measure.

The position in relation to the EU depends on whether the action involves illegality and damages against an EU institution, or against a Member State which is acting in the sphere of EU law.

If the action is brought against an EU institution, then the operative institutions for annulment actions and damages claims will be the General Court and the CJEU. If the action is brought by an individual, then the annulment action, or action for failure to act, will proceed via Articles 263 and 265 TFEU, respectively, before the General Court, with onward appeal to the CJEU. This is also true for the damages action, as indicated by Article 268 TFEU.

The matter may be somewhat different if the operative illegality relates to action by an EU agency. The foundational agency regulation may specify that the action should initially be challenged via appeal to an agency board of appeal. Where this is so, the appeal will be brought before the board of appeal, and the damages action will be brought pursuant to Article 340. Moreover, the claimant can challenge the decision of the agency board of appeal in an annulment action before the General Court.

The answer to the question will be different where the individual is contesting the legality of Member State action and also seeking compensation for breach of EU law. In these circumstances, the individual will proceed via Article 267 TFEU. The claimant will argue that a Member State has violated EU law by, for example, not providing a hearing as required by EU law, and will claim damages for the resultant loss. It will be for the national court to determine the success of both actions.

The national court can make a reference to the CJEU if it is uncertain with respect to the principles of legality, or damages liability that pertain to the instant case. There is, however, no obligation to do so, unless the national court is a court of last resort and resolution of the EU issue is necessary for the disposition of the case. The CJEU encourages national courts to apply established EU law without the need for a preliminary reference, where the content of the relevant EU law is clear from established case law.

II. Hypotheticals

When undertaking comparative law, including comparative administrative law, there is always an inherent challenge. We need to understand which of the following best describes the facts.

First, does the comparison reveal similarity, such that although some detail differs, the principal contours are the same, as judged by the way in which the respective legal systems conceptualize the issues, and apply the law to the facts?

Second, does the comparison reveal that the outcome may be the same or very similar, but the way in which it is reached, the legal conceptualization of the issue, differs as between the legal systems?

Third, does the comparison reveal some deeper differences between the respective legal systems, which reflect different normative assumptions underlying the salient legal rules?

Academics may well disagree as to which of the previous categories best captures the comparison of an issue between the legal systems. Moreover, there may be instances where more than one of the preceding possibilities is applicable. Thus, it is logically possible for the second and third category both to be applicable to the same factual scenario. We should nonetheless be mindful of the preceding categories, if only as a rough guide that helps us to navigate through the comparative exercise. This is exemplified by the hypothetical cases, which raise both similarities and differences as between the two legal systems concerning the resolution of these fact patterns. The principal similarities and differences may be charted as follows.

A. The rules concerning procedural fairness and their application

A great many of the hypothetical cases raise issues concerning procedural fairness. The precise nature of the procedural error varies. In some instances, it is failure to be heard; in other instances, it is lack of evidence; in yet other instances, it is a failure to consult or breach of legitimate expectation.

In relation to such issues, the similarity outweighs the difference between UK law and EU law. We should clear the ground at the outset. The resolution of the same hypothetical case in two or more legal systems is never going to be exactly the same in all respects. To search for this is to seek a chimaera that is illusory. There will perforce always be some differences in detail.

The extent of those differences will be determined, in part at least, by the relative level of abstraction or specificity through which one perceives the respective systems. If you fly at 50,000 feet, then pretty much everything looks the same. If you fly at 50 feet, then pretty much everything looks very different. Neither is particularly helpful. The challenge is to find the optimal level of abstraction versus specificity, bearing in mind that the two systems will inevitably differ to some degree.

Viewed from this perspective, the UK and EU rules on procedural fairness have a good deal in common. They have both been fashioned by the courts. There is no general code of procedural fairness in either system. The key components of due process are very similar in both systems: there are rules requiring notice, provision of a hearing, reason-giving, provision of evidence, representation, and the like. The application of the rules in both the UK and the EU entails balancing, sometimes explicit, sometimes implicit, concerning, for example, what is required in terms of a fair hearing, or the degree of detail demanded in the provision of reasons.

In both systems, moreover, there is an overlap between the norms of procedural justice and those concerning substantive review. In the UK, this is manifest in, for example, doctrinal requirements to take all relevant considerations into account, which has both a procedural and a substantive dimension. In the EU, it is apparent in the contours of the duty to take care, which straddles the procedural/substantive divide.

There are some differences as between the systems, the most significant being that access to the file is conceptualized as an aspect of due process in the EU, and it has no counterpart in the UK. This is especially important given that the right of access to the file operates both at the stage when the initial administrative decision is made and thereafter, when it is challenged before the reviewing court.

There are also some institutional differences, in that in the UK a judicial review action before the High Court for failure to comply with natural justice is perceived as a last resort, to be used when the claimant has exhausted internal administrative remedies. Moreover, there is a likelihood that some of the claimants in the hypotheticals would seek to remedy their situation through recourse to the ombudsman at central or local level.

B. The rules concerning damages liability and their application

The overall picture in relation to the comparison of the rules relating to damages liability is rather different. This is so notwithstanding the fact that the outcome in a particular case may be the same or similar as between UK law and EU law.

The EU has a general principle of liability that applies when the EU has committed the wrong. The relevant rules are found in Article 340 TFEU and the case law decided pursuant thereto. The EU also has a general principle of liability that operates where it is the Member State that has committed the legal wrong and caused damage within the confines of EU law. The relevant rules are found in *Francovich* and the extensive case law developed thereafter.

There have been, and still are, live issues concerning the application of the legal criteria laid down in the jurisprudence under Article 340 TFEU and *Francovich*. However, the case law has 'settled down' as compared to the state of the jurisprudence in the 1990s. There are perforce still questions and uncertainties as to what will constitute a manifest and serious breach for the purposes of Article 340 TFEU and for *Francovich* liability. For example, the hypotheticals raise interesting issues as to whether all of the procedural errors would be regarded as manifest and serious breaches for the purposes of damages liability. The case law has nonetheless provided increased certainty in this respect, and this is so notwithstanding that there are, inevitably, issues as to whether the CJEU is being too restrictive in its application of the criteria.

UK law is different in this respect, and the difference is reflected in the way in which the hypothetical cases have to be approached from the perspective of UK law. It is necessary for the claimant in all the questions posed to search for a private law cause of action that might be used in the instant case. It is then necessary for the claimant to demonstrate that the criteria for the application of that cause of action are met.

This latter requirement demands that the claimant show, in addition to the ordinary requirements of the relevant tort, that any further conditions specific to the application of the particular tort to public bodies have also been met. Thus, to take but one example, many of the actions in the hypothetical cases involve pure economic loss. UK courts have been wary of imposing such liability in actions between private individuals, and this wariness is heightened when the defendant is a public body exercising regulatory responsibilities. To take a further example, the general law of negligence requires that the claimant show that the imposition of a duty of care was fair, just, and reasonable in all the circumstances of the case. However, the application of this condition becomes considerably more complex and difficult where the defendant is a public body, as attested to by the existing case law. Consider in this respect the following statement of principle by Lord Reed in a recent case before the Supreme Court.[11]

> It follows (1) that public authorities may owe a duty of care in circumstances where the principles applicable to private individuals would impose such a duty, unless such a duty would be inconsistent with, and is therefore excluded by, the legislation from which their powers or duties are derived; (2) that public authorities do not owe a duty of care at common law merely because they have statutory powers or duties, even if, by exercising their statutory functions, they could prevent a person from suffering harm; and (3) that public authorities can come under a common law duty to protect from harm in circumstances where the principles applicable to private individuals or bodies would impose such a duty, as for example where the authority has created the source of danger or has assumed a responsibility to protect the claimant from harm, unless the imposition of such a duty would be inconsistent with the relevant legislation.

The reality is that the modification of existing causes of action in cases where the defendant is a public body has led to the cause of action being more difficult to satisfy than where the same action is pursued between private individuals. This is true not

[11] *Poole Borough Council v GN* [2019] UKSC 2 [65].

only in relation to the tort of negligence, which is the most commonly used cause of action, but also for the tortious actions for breach of statutory duty, nuisance, and the action in *Rylands v Fletcher*. Moreover, the courts have construed damages liability under the Human Rights Act 1998 narrowly, and have given a narrow reading to the one tort that is specific to public bodies, the tort of misfeasance in public office.

18

Austria, Germany, and Switzerland

Angela Ferrari Zumbini and Otto Pfersmann[*]

I. Introduction

The three States selected for this comparative analysis show many commonalities and some distinctive features.

A. Background commonalities

First of all, from an institutional point of view, they are all Federal States. This implies that in all three countries there are many different regimes for public authority liability, one set at the Federal level regarding federal authorities, and many others at State, Land, and canton level, as far as local authorities are concerned. The Federal and local regimes are generally consistent (in Switzerland, every canton has either a constitutional or a statutory provision that renders cantonal government liability uniform with Article 146 of the Federal Constitution), but may well differ in some important aspects (in Switzerland itself, even though there is a single jurisdiction for annulment and damages at Federal level, in the Geneva canton there is dual jurisdiction, divided between administrative and ordinary courts).

Second, from the perspective of supranational influence, the three States are all signatories of the European Convention on Human Rights (ECHR) (Germany 1952, Austria 1956, Switzerland 1974). This common circumstance brought them all under the jurisdiction of the European Court of Human Rights (ECtHR) and obliges them to comply with the Convention, fostering the development of some common principles.

Third, from the doctrinal point of view, all three States have had members in the *Vereinigung der Deutschen Staatsrechtslehre* since its establishment in 1922. The founder of this association sought to bring together German-speaking public law scholars, hence Austria- and the German-speaking part of Switzerland were, and still are, included.[1]

Finally, as noted above, the three States share a common language, considering the German-speaking part of Switzerland, and it is well known that language is a fundamental element to be considered when comparing juridical concepts.[2]

[*] Paragraphs I.B, II, VI.B, and VI.C are co-authored. Angela Ferrari Zumbini is the author of the other paragraphs.

[1] M Stolleis, 'Die Vereinigung der Deutschen Staatsrechtslehrer. Bemerkungen zu ihrer Geschichte' (1997) 80 *Kritische Vierteljahresschrift für Gesetzgebung und Rechtswissenschaft* 339–58.

[2] Among the most recent works, see V Grosswald Curran, 'Comparative Law and Language' in M Reimann and R Zimmermann (eds), *The Oxford Handbook of Comparative Law* (2nd edn, OUP 2019).

Angela Ferrari Zumbini and Otto Pfersmann, *Austria, Germany, and Switzerland* In: *Tort Liability of Public Authorities in European Laws.* Edited by: Giacinto della Cananea and Roberto Caranta, Oxford University Press (2020). © The Contributors.
DOI: 10.1093/oso/9780198867555.003.0018.

B. Background distinctive traits

The possibility of considering the State capable of inflicting damage when acting unlawfully through its *competent* organs and thus liable to pay compensation to the aggrieved party has only been fully recognized relatively recently, and has led to different conceptions and frameworks in terms of practice. Whereas, for instance, the French system entrusts this task to the administrative courts, Austria and Germany opted—sometimes after hesitation—to have such cases brought before the *civil* courts. The civil courts apply the general Civil Code (CC) in relation to the nature and degree of the damage, even though the wrongful conduct was carried out in the form of administrative acts following the appropriate administrative procedure.

State liability in the three systems considered here is only one form of general liability, and appropriate constitutional provisions are needed to entrench the very principle that claims against the State (whether the Federation, or decentralized entities) are legally possible under a general—rather than a specific—regime. Procedures concerning damages and procedures internal to the administration ought thus to be strictly distinguished. As far as the former are concerned, only the basis of principle and competence is constitutional, and even the distinction of degrees of liability and the proceedings themselves pertain to the civil law of liability: any award of damages to the aggrieved person is contingent on culpability in general conditions, so 'intent or gross liability' implies legal recourse against the organ acting unlawfully, and simple illegality implies that the State will bring a claim against an organ causing harm to the State itself (paras 2 and 3 of Art 23 of the Austrian Federal Constitution). In all cases (Austria, Germany, Switzerland), the Constitution complements elements of the CC.

Of course, many differences emerge when comparing different legal systems, some of which may be of a more fundamental nature, while others are more superficial. The three States selected for this comparison show at least one fundamental distinctive trait, namely their relationship with the EU. While Germany was one of the founding States, Austria only joined in 1995, and Switzerland is not an EU Member State at all. This distinction is fundamental not only from a general point of view, but also from a very specific one, as public authority liability is an area of law that has been deeply influenced by EU legislation.

Article 340 of the Treaty on the Functioning of the European Union (TFEU) (as in its original version, former Art 288 of the Treaty Establishing the Economic Community, TEC) states that 'the Union shall, in accordance with the general principles common to the laws of the Member States, make good any damage caused by its institutions or its servants in the performance of their duties'. This provision fostered the evolution and the identification of 'general principles common to the laws of the Member States' regarding public authority liability. It is therefore of particular interest to focus on and compare public authority liability in three countries with many points in common, but with this fundamental difference regarding Union membership (founding Member, member joining in the Nineties, and non-Member).

Overall, with regard to the role of language in legal theory, the work of HLA Hart, *The Concept of Law* (Clarendon Press, OUP 1961) is still fundamental.

The very principle of EU membership with respect to State liability mainly concerns the breach of directly applicable EU law by organs of a Member State. Unlike the liability triggered by the infringement of internal law, a breach of EU law is not contingent on fault. The breach of EU norms is an objective fact, but it remains to be examined whether a Member State has significant discretion, and whether the wrongdoing in question actually caused the reported damage. In both Austria and Germany, again, the civil courts are competent to hear claims and follow the substantive rules regarding liability as laid down in the CC. Switzerland is, of course, exempt from these requirements, but the Swiss Federation is liable, according to Article 19a of its Liability Statute (*Verantwortungsgesetz*) 'for the damage suffered by a person arising from the unlawful application of the Schengen Information System by a person acting on behalf of the Federation or a Canton'.[3] Also here it is the objective unlawfulness of an act that triggers liability.

The common characteristics (constitutional basis, statutory concretization, civil courts having competence, and substantial civil liability law) are independent of any membership of the EU. All three States may amend the foundational principle of State liability, competence, and substantive law, regardless of their relation with the EU. What the two Member States in question cannot alter is their obligation to give full effect to Article 340(1) and (2) TFEU as directly applicable primary law, whereas Switzerland is only bound to respect specific treaty ties with the Union, such as those arising from adherence to the Schengen System. Whether a State is a founder member or joined later makes no difference (except if a new treaty would introduce a difference among members in the future, which is not very likely). If a European State outside the Union joins the Union, the principles of Article 340 TFEU apply without distinction—again, it seems highly unlikely that a new Member would obtain preferential treatment in this respect from the act of membership. If a State leaves the Union, these rules cease to apply according to the treaty establishing the terms of exit.

II. Constitutional provisions for public authority liability

Article 23 of the Austrian Federal Constitutional Law of 1920 provides that:

> [t]he Federation, the provinces, the municipalities and the other bodies and institutions established under public law are liable for the injury which persons acting on their behalf in execution of the laws have by illegal behaviour culpably inflicted on whomsoever.

Article 34 of the Basic Law for the Federal Republic of Germany of 1949 states that:

> [i]f any person, in the exercise of a public office entrusted to him, violates his official duty to a third party, liability shall rest principally with the state or public body that

[3] *Bundesgesetz über die Verantwortlichkeit des Bundes sowie seiner Behördemitglieder und Beamten* (*Verantwortlichkeitsgesetz*, VG) vom 14 März 1958 (Stand am 1 January 2020).

employs him. In the event of intentional wrongdoing or gross negligence, the right of recourse against the individual officer shall be preserved. The ordinary courts shall not be closed to claims for compensation or indemnity.

Article 146 of the Federal Constitution of the Swiss Confederation of 1999 states that '[t]he Confederation shall be liable for damage or loss unlawfully caused by its organs in the exercise of official activities'. The Constitution has constitutionalized the principles already expressed by the Government Liability Act of 1958. All cantons have either a constitutional or a statutory act providing for State liability compliant with Article 146.

In the case of Austria and Germany, State liability for breaches of EU law also has a constitutional basis (Art 23 of the Basic Law, Constitutional Statute on the Austrian Republic's Membership of the European Union BGBl 744/1994). As this basis is also the limit of direct applicability and primacy, the question may occasionally arise as to how far EU law has become concretely integrated within domestic law and under what circumstances the Member States may claim that an act of the Union was ultra vires and thus unable to trigger any liability.

The key concepts are similar: liability is connected to the 'unlawful' (Switzerland), the 'illegal' (Austria), and 'breach of duty' (Germany); damage must have been caused by the behaviour or acts of a public officer 'in the exercise of official activities' (Switzerland), 'in execution of the laws' (Austria), and 'in the exercise of a public office entrusted to him' (Germany).

There are, however, some important differences; for example, in the Austrian Constitution there is an explicit reference to 'culpably', while this concept is not normally required in Swiss law, and the degree of the fault in the German *Grundgesetz* is relevant only with regard to the right to recourse. The German Constitution is also the only one to contain a provision concerning jurisdiction for awarding damages. In the Austrian case, we can observe an interesting mixture of conceptions: wrongfulness is assessed in relation to the relevant administrative requirements; culpability is ascertained with regard to the categories of liability established by the CC. In Austria, 'culpability' is required in order to distinguish between the liability of persons acting in their official capacity causing injury to 'whomsoever'—which requires culpability—and actions causing harm to the State and its decentralized entities themselves—for which no culpability is required.

III. Dismissal without notice and hearing

The dismissal of a civil servant for improper conduct is a paradigmatic example for analysing public authority liability deriving from authoritative decisions, ie sanctions.

In Germany, the solution will derive from the application of both sector-specific rules (the statutes regulating disciplinary procedures regarding civil servants) and general administrative procedural law. The *Bundesdisziplinargesetz* provides two fundamental procedural requirements for dismissal, which have been disregarded by the public authority: the right to a prior hearing and an accurate investigation that must also include the acquisition of exonerating evidence. Even though both requirements were clearly overlooked in case 1 (Chapter 14, section II), the rules of general administrative law apply. This leads to two important consequences: first, the authority might remedy both the procedural errors before the end of the court proceeding, healing the administrative procedure and preventing the annulment. Second, the procedural errors by themselves are not sufficient to annul the act of dismissal if they did not influence the outcome, meaning that no different decision might have been taken, even if Maurice had been heard and the investigation had been accurate.

If Maurice is able to successfully challenge his dismissal, all his lost salary payments will be restored, albeit without interest (if he is not a civil servant but an employee on a contract in the public service, he will be paid interest too). It is unlikely that he will be awarded compensation for damage to his reputation, as a public counterstatement seems better suited to restoring his reputation, while monetary compensation is subsidiary. He will also be indemnified for actual loss, ie real expenses incurred while looking for a new job.

It should be noted that since there are explicit norms regulating the case, the German court would not refer to Article 6 ECHR.

Austria has a similar legal framework, though the solutions are different in some aspects. There are two national laws applicable here: the sector-specific Federal Civil Servants Employment Act and the general Administrative Procedure Act (APA). The sector-specific law has an explicit provision stating that the APA is 'subsidiary' in disciplinary proceedings. Both laws clearly establish that the interested party must have the right to be heard. Unlike the German solution, even if there are explicit rules regulating the case, disciplinary measures against civil servants fall within the scope of Article 6 ECHR, to which the court will refer, granting Maurice a public oral hearing before the court even if the procedural code does not require it.

The administrative court will not only quash the decision in the light of the breach of some fundamental provisions (the right to a hearing and the duty to carry out the necessary investigations), but it will also probably decide the case on the merits. In Austria, annulling the act and referring it back to the authority must be the exception, while the court generally decides the case on the merits if the relevant facts are clear (the court may also further investigate and determine the relevant facts for itself). If the further investigation reveals that the allegations against Maurice were unfounded, he will be successful.

A civil action for damages is likely to be successful, as the authority has disregarded a substantial provision, namely the defendant's right to a hearing. This right is clearly stated in the law, so the authority may be accused of an unlawful omission. In the event of intent or gross negligence, Maurice will be indemnified for both positive damages and lost profit (including lost salaries, expenses for repairing the damage, expenses accrued looking for a new job, and the loss of new earning opportunities). However, there will be no damages for his tarnished reputation.

The Swiss legal framework shows some more striking differences, which lead to partially divergent solutions. Starting from the legal framework, the right to a hearing is stated not only in the APA 1968, but also in Article 29 II of the Federal Constitution. The sector-specific law relevant to the case is not a law concerning civil servant disciplinary proceedings, but the Government Liability Act (thus regulating only the conditions for the award of damages, but not setting appropriate procedures for dismissal, for which general APA standards apply). The mere unlawfulness of the decision that caused harm is not sufficient for the award of damages. Even though the law does not require 'fault' as a condition for State liability, the courts with their ruling reintroduced it by asking the injured party to demonstrate that the officer 'infringed a fundamental duty of his office'.

Moving to the damages to be awarded, one main difference concerning salaries is that Maurice can ask for the dismissal to be suspended, and, if this is granted, he will receive his salary for the duration of the court proceedings. Therefore, if the dismissal is proven unlawful, he will be able to seek redress for actual harm suffered (such as the costs incurred in looking for a new job). He may also claim damages for his tarnished reputation if he can prove the fault of the wrongdoer. Another interesting difference arises if the dismissal is not suspended. In this case, if the dismissal is proven unlawful, the court will award damages generally amounting to between six months and one year of earnings. Moreover, in this case, the harm to his reputation and the expenses incurred in looking for a new job will be considered 'circumstances' relevant to determining the amount of damages to be awarded, and not as an individual item to be included in the compensation.

IV. A licence withdrawal *inaudita altera parte*

It may be interesting to analyse how public authority liability is construed when the same unlawful circumstance (the omission of the right to a hearing) occurs in the withdrawal of a former benefit (concession or licence) (Chapter 14, case 7, section VIII).

The legal framework and the outcome in Switzerland seem similar to case 1 (Chapter 14, section II). The right to a hearing is stated in both the APA and the Constitution, and the appeal to the court will normally have suspensive effects, thus preventing Ms Tramp from suffering any harm. She will continue to run her kiosk while the process in court takes place, and no other damages seem likely to occur.

In Austria too, the relevant regulation will be the APA, which considers the right to a hearing as a fundamental requirement for administrative proceedings. Ms Tramp is therefore likely to be successful, and the administrative court will decide the case on the merit, not simply annulling the act. In this case, the annulment of the act is a precondition for awarding damages in civil courts. Damages will again depend on the degree of fault. If the unlawful withdrawal was made with intent or gross negligence, Ms Tramp may ask not only *damnum emergens* but also *lucrum cessans* (including the lost chances to generate more income, based on a contract or an offer).

Also, the German APA requires the authority to hear the interested party before taking a measure that may adversely affect the party's rights. As in Switzerland, the affected party must file an action for annulment, which normally has suspensive effects, thus preventing the party from suffering any harm. If her claim is successful, in the subsequent civil case she may only seek compensation for the harm she suffered that could not have been averted by the remedy (eg the damage incurred before the action was available). Interestingly, Ms Tramp may claim some damages even if the administrative court finds the withdrawal justifiable: she may claim compensation for the frustration of her legitimate expectation.

V. Physical coercion: a violent police officer

It is useful to compare the liability deriving from a physical act rather than from a legal one (see Chapter 14, case 11, section XII).

In the case of the violent police officer, even though there is a common core of fundamental provisions, many important differences are evident.

The common core regards two aspects: one key element for liability and the amount of damages that will probably be awarded.

Regarding the key element for assessing liability, in all three countries the unlawfulness of the police action can be assumed without any further complicated investigations. The reasons why unlawfulness may be assumed differ, however: in Austria and Germany the absence of a warning before using force plays a relevant role, as well as the evident disproportionality of the measure used by the police officer; in Switzerland a central role is played by the infringement of guidelines set out by the Police Department.

Regarding the damages that will probably be awarded, in all three countries they will cover the actual loss (mostly medical expenses) and the pain Agatha suffered.

Moving to the distinctive features, one has already been mentioned regarding the reasons for presuming the unlawfulness of the officers' behaviour.

Moreover, there are different conditions regarding liability for the use of force in police actions compared with those of the general public authority liability, and these differences involve various aspects. For example, in Austria in this case the fault of the officer can be assumed, while in Germany culpability of the officer is not required at all.

Furthermore, Agatha's behaviour in resisting the officer's request is relevant in Germany, leading to reduced compensation, while it is irrelevant in Austria.

Finally, the amount of damages awarded may well be different in the three States. In Germany, there will be a reduction in relation to the common core, as stated above (medical expenses and pain) due to Agatha's behaviour. In Switzerland, the common core will be increased due to the loss of Agatha's ability to work. In Austria, damages will also include the loss of profit and any earnings lost in the future if Agatha becomes incapable of earning.

VI. Some cross-cut issues

A. The distribution of competence between ordinary judges and administrative courts

On the Federal level, in Switzerland, the administrative courts have competence to annul the unlawful administrative decision and to award damages. However, these two actions are handled in two different proceedings, so the claimant must file two different and subsequent cases, even if they will be heard by the same court (the injured party must challenge the act before the Administrative court, and if the act is annulled, he can file a claim for damages with the Federal Ministry of Finance, whose decision may be appealed at the administrative court). In some cantons (such as Geneva), the proceeding to ascertain unlawfulness and the one to seek damages are not only separate and subsequent, but they also take place in different courts (administrative courts for the unlawfulness and civil courts for damages, the latter being bound by the administrative court's decision on unlawfulness).

In Austria, the two cases (annulment and damages) are not only simply two different cases, they are also connected to two different jurisdictions. While the decision on the unlawfulness of an administrative decision is attributed exclusively to administrative courts, awarding damages is regarded as a civil matter and is exclusively within the remit of civil courts. However, there is not necessarily an administrative preliminary ruling on the unlawfulness of the decision.

In Germany, the situation is a combination of the two previous ones: there is both a distinct jurisdiction, as in Austria (administrative courts have jurisdiction for the annulment of unlawful administrative decisions, and civil courts have jurisdiction for awarding damages) and the necessity of a preliminary administrative ruling, as in Switzerland.

The distribution of jurisdiction is not homogenous between the three countries, as there is a split jurisdiction in Austria and Germany, and a single jurisdiction in Switzerland. However, even where the Administrative Courts do have jurisdiction for both actions (annulment and damages) the two actions must be filed in two separate and subsequent procedures, unlike in other States with single jurisdiction, where the two actions can be filed together (as in Italy).

B. Liability for procedural errors or faults? Do mere infringements of procedure always lead to government liability?

In Switzerland, the unlawfulness of the act is in principle sufficient to grant compensation for the damage caused by the unlawful act. This means that in general there is no need to prove the fault of the wrongdoer. Nevertheless, in some cases, the definition of unlawfulness as construed by the courts implies the existence of a fault. The Government Liability Act (GLA) does not require fault as a condition for State liability (it is explicitly required only to award moral damages for loss of reputation). However, in their ruling, courts require the injured person to demonstrate that an officer violated 'a fundamental duty of his office', interpreting this condition as intentional misconduct or negligence, hence reintroducing fault via judge-made law. In proceedings to award damages, the court is bound to the administrative court decision on the unlawfulness of the act, as clearly stated in Article 12 GLA: 'the legality of a ruling entered into force cannot be challenged in proceedings for liability'.

In Austria, on the contrary, liability requires 'culpability' in the meaning of the Austrian CC, in addition to unlawfulness (which is, however, a sufficient condition for the liability of a person acting in an official capacity in relation to the State itself).

In Germany, strong primacy is attached to primary legal protection, meaning that the most effective legal protection consists in the quashing of unlawful decisions. Moreover, the general rules of administrative procedure are applied. This means that mere procedural wrongs may be remedied by the authority before the conclusion of court proceedings. Furthermore, mere procedural wrongs, even if not remedied, do not lead to the annulment of the act if they did not influence the outcome of the decision.

C. Legal formants: constitution and legislation

All three countries have both a constitutional provision regarding public authority liability and some legislative norms regulating the topic in greater detail. However, the nature of legislative acts, and the relationship between the two levels of discipline are different.

In addition to the Constitutional provision of 1920, Austria also has a 'Federal Act on the Liability of Territorial Authorities and other Bodies and Institutions of Public Law for Damage Caused when Implementing the Law', enacted in 1949, which regulates the liability of public authorities in greater detail. In Switzerland, the temporal sequence between the constitutional provision and the legislation is the reverse: the GLA was enacted in 1958, and the constitutional norm regarding public authority liability was introduced only in 2000, thus consolidating the liability of the Confederation on the constitutional level. In Germany, as in Switzerland, the legislative provision came before the *Grundgesetz*, but the nature of the norm is different, as the legislative basis for public authority liability is paragraph 839 CC of 1900.

Hence, the German legislator wrote in the Constitution that jurisdiction for public authority liability is vested in the civil courts, and inserted the relevant legislative provision into the CC. The Austrian legislator too stated in Article 1 of the Federal Liability of Public Bodies Act that public entities 'are liable under the provisions of Civil Law'. This provision distinguishes between systems such as the Austrian one and systems of administrative justice like that of France, where questions of lawfulness and those regarding the liability of public bodies are both handled according to different procedural rules by the same (administrative) judge. The Austrian model considers problems of liability to pertain not only to substantial civil law, but also to the proper competence of the civil court as an organ entirely independent of the administrative authorities and thus deemed to decide with complete impartiality. It is also of note that both competence and substance are dealt with at the highest level of the legal hierarchy. This means that the rule concerning competence and substance pertains to public law, but its concrete application is tasked to private law (meaning in compliance with the CC and the civil courts).

Finally, all three countries have a general APA. Austria was the first Country to enact an APA in 1925; Switzerland followed suit in 1968, and Germany introduced one in 1976. All these APAs contain a specific requirement concerning the right to a hearing before an act is issued.

VII. Conclusion

Three general remarks need to be made in this concluding section.

First, administrative decisions breaching legal requirements do not always lead to governmental liability, as some other conditions need to be satisfied.

Another important feature is the relationship that exists with administrative remedies: is it always necessary to exhaust them prior to filing an action for governmental liability?

In Switzerland, if the damages are caused by a material act, the injured person may immediately claim damages with no preliminary proceedings. On the contrary, if damages are caused by a legal act (such as an administrative act), it is necessary to challenge its lawfulness within the appeal deadline before seeking damages. If the court upholds the act in question, it will not be possible to claim damages.

A preliminary ruling of this kind is not necessary in Austria, where the injured party may (generally) seek damages regardless of any prior annulment action or any other appeal to an administrative court. However, this independence between the claim for damages and the action to seek annulment has some important constraints: first of all, the injured party is obliged to minimize the damage she or he suffers, and this implies that damages will not be due if they could have been avoided by filing for an administrative remedy; second, before claiming damages in court, the party must inform the administrative authority that he or she intends to claim damages, asking whether the public authority is prepared to pay damages or not. If the party is satisfied with the authority's proposal, he or she may simply accept it; otherwise he or she may go to court. Interestingly, omission of this preliminary request does not make the claim for compensation inadmissible, but if the administration admits the damage in court, the latter may ask it to reimburse litigation costs.

In Germany, there is a strong principle of the primacy of primary legal protection, which means that quashing unlawful administrative decisions is the first and most effective legal protection.

Finally, in Switzerland and Austria, only the State is liable towards injured parties, who can sue the State and ask it for damages. State officials are not liable towards the injured party, but the State may subsequently bring a case against the official if his or her fault is not minor (Switzerland), or if he or she acted with intent or gross negligence (Austria).

19
Hungary, Poland, and Romania

Giacinto della Cananea

I. Introduction

Analysis of government liability in tort in Hungary, Poland, and Romania offers several interesting insights for our 'common core' research, because they changed their constitutions after 1989, which suggests a little digression, and later became members of the EU. We can thus appreciate the relationship between continuity and change.

II. Three post-1989 constitutions

It is fitting from the outset to look at national constitutions, because they 'constitute' and limit the powers of government, are higher law and are justiciable, and play a symbolic role.[1] That is not to say that written constitutions are the only source of first principles. Indeed, sometimes there is no actual written document self-qualifying as a constitution, and when one does exist, it is often complemented by custom. The constitution is nonetheless one of the best starting points. This is, *a fortiori*, the case of the three legal systems selected for comparison here, as their constitutions changed after 1989, and did so as 'symbolic markers of a great transition' in political life.[2] This can help us to understand the ideas and beliefs about public law that shape the framework for government liability. Socialist constitutions were based on the idea of sovereign immunity, though legislation and judicial doctrines attenuated it.[3] Quite the contrary, the new constitutions regulate government liability.

The new Hungarian Constitution (2011) is of importance in this respect. Its Article XXIV (1) practically reproduces the provision of the EU Charter of Fundamental Rights concerning the right to a good administration and specifies that this right shall include the requirement to give reasons 'as determined by law'. The second part of the same provision lays down a general standard concerning government liability: 'Every person shall have the right to statutory State compensation for any unlawful damage caused by the authorities while performing their duties.' There is, thus, a connection between transparency and liability.

Article 52 of the Romanian Constitution regulates this matter in a similar, though not identical, manner. It has a broad scope of application, both subjectively and objectively.

[1] B Constant, *Cours de politique constitutionnelle* (first published 1836, Sklatine 1982) 8–9.
[2] B Ackerman, *The Rise of World Constitutionalism* (1997) 83 Va L Rev 771, 778. See also J Elster, *Constitutionalism in Eastern Europe: An Introduction* (1991) 58 Univ Chicago L Rev 447.
[3] See R Wagner, *Recent Developments in State Liability in Poland* (1972) 20 AJCL 247.

Giacinto della Cananea, *Hungary, Poland, and Romania* In: *Tort Liability of Public Authorities in European Laws.*
Edited by: Giacinto della Cananea and Roberto Caranta, Oxford University Press (2020).
DOI: 10.1093/oso/9780198867555.003.0019.

Subjectively, it applies to 'any person aggrieved in his/her legitimate rights or interests by a public authority', a duality of legal situations that reflects the clauses of the Italian and Spanish Constitutions. Objectively, liability arises both as a consequence of an 'administrative act' and as a 'a failure of a public authority' to respond to the individual's claim within the lawful time limit. This being the case, the individual is entitled to the acknowledgement of the invoked right or legitimate interest, the annulment of the act, and reparation for the damage. However, the Constitution specifies that 'the conditions and limits on the exercise of this right shall be regulated by an organic law'.

The Polish Constitution goes one step further, because its Article 77 constructs the 'right to compensation' in a very broad manner. This right belongs to 'everyone' and for 'any harm done ... by any action of an organ of public authority contrary to law' in the broader sense. The Constitution lays down a further safeguard for individual rights by preventing Parliament from enacting statutes that 'bar the recourse by any person to the courts in pursuit of claims alleging infringement of freedoms or rights'. Accordingly, the contours of the right to compensation are not determined by the Constitution itself, but it is strengthened by a clause that prohibits any immunity on grounds of process.

Two brief comments follow on from this analysis. First, though not all systems have what could be conceptualized as a general principle of damage or tort liability, this is the case here, though it must be ascertained how the courts interpret and apply this principle. Second, all the three constitutions are clear about the relationship between liability and unlawfulness, insofar as the former presupposes the latter. But it remains to be seen whether unlawfulness, under the form of infringement of statutory purposes or misuse of powers, gives rise in itself to liability for damages, the type of damages that are admissible, and how compensation is assessed.

III. Same issues, same solutions?

Ambiguity arises when we speak of the State. Our administrative laws were built in an era when the main concern was governmental interference (the 'negative' State) with rights and freedoms, while the twentieth century saw the growth of functions related to welfare (the 'positive' State), and there is also a higher number of people working for the State in one way or another. All these aspects deserve attention and will be considered.

A. The State as employer

Case 1 (Chapter 14, section II) is concerned with deprivation of office within a process that lacks at least one essential procedural element: notice and a hearing prior to deprivation. It is interesting to see what happens in a group of legal systems that have experienced a specific version of the 'omnipotent State'.

Let us first consider the Romanian legal framework, where legislation concerning administrative disciplinary procedures, which entered into force in 1999, allows public employers to apply sanctions 'only . . . after a prior investigation of the misconduct and after the public servant is heard', which includes the right to legal assistance or representation. It also requires the affair to be handled by a commission. These requirements are reinforced in two ways: there is a duty to produce a written record of the hearing, and any transgression of this duty renders the procedure void. The courts are willing to enforce these requirements, insofar as infringement of process rights gives rise to the annulment of the contested measure. The courts would also consider the aspect of proportionality, though it remains to be seen whether liability arises and what damages the court will award. Whilst observing that the rules governing public employees did not expressly mention the possibility of awarding moral damages, the highest court interpreted those rules in the light of the 'generally applicable law', but with an important qualification: any such damages are not to be granted automatically as a consequence of annulment.

Polish administrative law, too, establishes both the organizational (it is for a disciplinary commission to investigate) and the procedural (prior notice and hearing) requirements. But there is both legislation setting out staff rules (the Civil Service Act of 2008) and a general code of administrative procedures. Moreover, legislative provisions are supplemented by generally applicable government ordinances. Finally, while moral damages are in principle admissible, they would not be granted in this case, due to Maurice's improper behaviour. Moreover, it is precisely because he holds a public office that the courts would not rule out that information regarding him be made public, without the restrictions that would generally apply to protect privacy.

The Hungarian legal framework differed from the previous two up to 2012. There was no general legislative provision imposing the requirement of prior notice and hearing on public employers, and the courts would be reluctant to ground their review directly on the Constitution. Still today, notwithstanding the changes that were made in the Civil Service Act of 2011 (like in the other two legal systems, a disciplinary board will be appointed, and there will be a hearing), it is not necessarily the case that, if a civil servant has infringed one or several rules of conduct, the lack of a hearing would make the final decision illegal. This would inevitably impinge on the recognition of liability for damages.

A twofold preliminary conclusion emerges from this. In all the three legal systems selected for our comparison, there is a general constitutionally established principle of tort liability, and there is a specific body of law dealing with disciplinary procedures against public employees. However, the scope of this body differs: it is broader and more long-standing in Poland and Romania than in Hungary. Moreover, unlike in the former, in the latter it appears that it is not uncontroversial that deprivation of office without prior notice and hearing is unlawful, and this impinges on liability.

B. The 'negative' State

The last nine hypothetical cases of Chapter 14 concern the 'negative State'. Let us first consider the case of sanctions against a bank (case 3, section IV). EU law sets out common goals and defines the role of national regulators. But it is for national legal systems to carry out checks and inspections and to impose sanctions on banks. In our case, a pecuniary sanction is issued, but the regulator's action appears to be based on an error of fact, because it did not consider all relevant elements. Even a cursory look at the three administrative systems shows various differences concerning their organization, depending on whether the competence lies with the central bank or with a sectorial regulator. However, in all cases, surveillance and inspections are carried out through administrative procedures, and the final measure is a binding decision, which can be appealed against through mechanisms internal to the regulator, but eventually it is subject to judicial review before ordinary or administrative courts. Moreover, in all three countries, the courts will include an error of fact within the grounds of reviewable administrative action, though it is clear that a claimant who relies on an error of fact will have to prove its existence. Eventually, if the error of fact is proven, the courts will either annul the sanction or reduce it. Thus far, there is some common ground, but as we move away from illegality, in order to consider liability, things become more complex. The Hungarian legal system would allow the bank to sue the public authority for damage to its reputation, including moral damage, before the administrative panel. Within the Polish legal system, on the other hand, the bank would initially have to contest the sanction before an administrative court, and would then be entitled to sue the authority before a civil court. This would decide in accordance with the criteria laid down by the Civil Code (CC), as interpreted by the courts. Similarly, in Romania, it would be for special courts to judge on the action. On the merits, the prejudice, as well as the causal link with the sanction, should be proven, and the court might be expected to be reluctant to grant moral damages to an undertaking. Even if they were willing to do so, and the claimant were to satisfy the burden of proof, the damages would have to be assessed after a consideration of the social values recognized and protected by the legal system.

Let us consider now case 6 (Chapter 14, section VII), the case of a public authority that prohibits, by way of a generalized block, the import of fruit from a country that is located outside the European Economic Area (EEA) after an alleged incident in a nuclear power plant, on the grounds that it might be radioactive. As in case 3 above, in all three countries the action would be carried out through an administrative procedure; it would be possible—in principle—for the affected importer to show that its interests fall within the class of interests that are protected by the legal order, and the normal standards of administrative conduct would apply, including the lack of accurate fact-finding, viewed either as an excess of discretion or as a deviation from the principles of reasonableness and proportionality. However, judicial review would be problematic, and the courts would be reluctant to subject public bodies to liability. Hungarian courts could both judge whether the ban, though generalized, in reality affects only the applicant, and refer the case to the Constitutional Court. Similarly, in Poland, it would be for the Constitutional Court to judge on the legality of the ban and, though it may annul it, the court may also preclude a suit for liability. Finally, in Romania, the applicant should initially ask an administrative court to annul the ban and then sue the public authority before a civil court. As far as liability is concerned, under Polish law the applicant would have to show 'beyond reasonable doubt' the existence of damage in the form of *damnum emergens* and *lucrum cessans*, which might be an impossible hurdle to overcome. In Romania, the action itself would be inadmissible, because what is at stake is a collective interest, unless the applicant shows that the ban infringes either EU law or an international treaty. Similarly, Hungarian courts would not uphold the tortious claim, on the grounds that the ban is intended for the benefit of society in general, including public health.

It may be interesting to briefly contrast these findings with those from case 4 (Chapter 14, section V), concerning the exclusion of a tenderer by the contracting authority. All three legal systems are subject to EU rules governing public procurement, under which liability should be made dependant on misconduct. There is, thus, a standard of strict liability. But national rules often give weight, directly or indirectly, to misconduct and, that being the case (eg in Romania), the courts could be expected to conceive EU rules as a *lex specialis*. Alternatively, the courts may deem that there is no reason in principle why they should not apply ordinary standards such as the violation of the duty of care and find for the claimant because of the inaccurate assessment carried out by a public body (eg in Poland and in Hungary).

Three comments are relevant in this context. The first is that government liability in tort is subject to a distinctive legal framework only as far as the exercise of powers is concerned, with the exclusion of the cases in which a public authority has entered into a transaction with private bodies. The second comment concerns the principle of legality. A literal interpretation of existing provisions may give a wrong impression; that is, that any breach of the principles and rules governing the exercise of those powers would give rise to liability. But it is readily apparent from national reports that the general duties of accuracy, propriety, and procedural fairness imply discretion as to how they should be carried out, and that even when specific duties are set out by legislation, they must be interpreted in the light of the interests that public authorities must protect and promote. Finally, the standard of liability will not necessarily be a strict one. It may be strict in some cases but in many, if not most, other cases it will require public authorities to take action when this is reasonably practicable, especially when they have to make complex discretionary determinations.

C. The 'positive' State

Another type of administrative action concerns the use of government largesse, particularly through concessions, licences, and the like. A distinction can be made between the procedures for issuing them and the procedures for withdrawing them.

Let us suppose, as in case 5 (Chapter 14, section VI), that a public authority causes significant delay in issuing a concession (or entering into a transaction)—for which there is only one applicant—to have exclusive use of the waterfront, close to the sea or a lake, at least as regards the use of sun umbrellas, deck chairs, and tables. It is evident from the nature of this activity that an unjustified delay preventing the applicant from obtaining the concession in time for the summer season will damage its interests. The applicant may prefer not to sue the competent authority, out of fear or strategic behaviour. But, if it chooses to do so, could it seek damages in a broad sense, including *damnum emergens* and *lucrum cessans*? Interestingly, in all the three legal systems, discretion matters. As a result, no award for damages will be made unless, bearing in mind all the circumstances of the case and, in particular, the length of the delay and the reasons, the court is satisfied that such an award is necessary to afford the claimant just satisfaction. Moreover, in Romania a particular provision states that there must be wrongdoing. There is no similar condition in Poland, but here the courts would bear in mind the 'rules of equity'.

Let us now suppose that a licence has been issued to someone to sell newspapers and maps, or any other product for which some kind of permit is required by law or customs, in a kiosk, for example tobacco in Hungary (case 7, Chapter 14, section VIII). Some years later, the licensing authority decides to withdraw the licence without giving the permit holder any opportunity to be heard, with the sibylline declaration that it intends to change its policy. This case is interesting because all legal systems have to decide whether a government authority may unilaterally withdraw or revoke its acts on the grounds of legality or convenience, as well as whether, if one or several procedural constraints are infringed, this is in itself relevant in terms of unlawfulness and tortious liability, without the need to consider any grounds of substantive unlawfulness.

In Poland, the lack of a hearing would be relevant under general rules (those of the Administrative Procedure Act, APA) and would be reviewed by an administrative court, with the power to quash the contested decision. This is the likely outcome in such an extreme case, while in others the courts would probably be more indulgent towards the administration. Only if the decision is annulled can the applicant ask for damages, which would be awarded by an ordinary court and would include both *damnum emergens* and *lucrum cessans*. In Hungary too, the APA would apply, also in the light of the constitutional requirement of fair and impartial administration, and in a case of this type it would give rise to the annulment of the contested decision if it can be demonstrated that hearing the other side was relevant in determining the facts. That being the case, the infringement would be regarded as being serious and would give rise to damages under the general rules. In Romania, on the other hand, there is no general requirement of notice and comment. However, the conduct of the administration would be regarded as unlawful due to misuse or excess of power, and the general principle of full reparation for damages would apply.

D. Physical coercion

It remains to consider whether government has the power 'to inflict injury on others, under prescribed circumstances, in established ways, and in carefully (and sometimes not so carefully) calibrated amounts',[4] in the context of police activities.

In case 11 (Chapter 14, section XII), we supposed that two police officials stop a driver, ask her quite ruthlessly to get out of the vehicle and show her documents, and, when she protests, one of the two officials, without warning her as required by Police Department rules, applies excessive physical force and breaks one of her arms. In a

[4] JL Mashaw 'Civil Liability of Government Officials: Property Rights and Official Accountability' (1978) 42 LCP 8.

civilized nation, where the exercise of force is not standardless and immune from review, there can be a variety of ways that an individual can obtain justice. There can be either direct or indirect State liability for the intentional wrongdoing of its officials. Government liability in tort may be subject to limitations or qualifications; for example, it may be based on the existence of some serious breach of the rules of conduct, or it may be excluded by particular norms. Otherwise, it can be excluded if there is wrongdoing on the part of the individual.

In all three countries, the exercise of police powers is subject to standards set out either by politically representative officials or by the head of police units; such powers must be exercised in conformity with the principle of proportionality, and there is an action against the State in the guise of vicarious liability. But there are important variations that cannot be neglected. In Hungary, the courts make a distinction between verbal and physical resistance to the exercise of administrative powers insofar as the former is less likely to justify the use of coercion, which must in any case remain within the limits of necessity and proportionality. Whether the courts would be more reluctant to apply this policy, due to the changing political and legal context, it remains to be seen. Also, the Polish courts would apply proportionality and would not hesitate to argue that disregard of existing standards and guidelines gives rise to misconduct if a specific condition is met. However, disregard for standards should previously have been deemed intentional by a criminal court, which would imply basing liability on intentional wrongdoing, which is a high threshold. Only if this condition is met would the Treasury be held liable for the damage caused by the unlawful exercise of public authority. There is still another situation in Romania, where administrative courts would be likely to decline jurisdiction on the grounds that there is no administrative act to be annulled, while civil courts would consider the infringement of internal guidelines under non-contractual liability.

IV. Assessing liability

The rules that govern the liability of government officials in tort seem to be influenced by several legal formants, including constitutions and statutes, governmental practices, judicial decisions, and the works of learned lawyers.[5] In the following paragraphs, these will be examined in greater detail.

A. Legal formants

The remarks made initially with regard to national constitutions can be integrated in two ways. First, though 1989 was a watershed event, constitutional change was not immediate. For example, the Constitution adopted by Romania in 1948, following the Soviet model, remained partly effective between 1989 and 1991, when the new one entered into force. Additionally, even though all these legal systems now have a

[5] R Sacco, 'Legal Formants: A Dynamic Approach to Comparative Law' (1991) 39 AJCL 21.

constitutional charter that recognizes and protects the rights that are generally shared by liberal democracies, and are members of the EU this does not necessarily imply that a sort of 'progressive' account would be justified.[6] History, does not exclude stops and turning back, and there are some signs that this may have happened within the legal systems under examination.

Second, there may be a lack of harmony between constitutional provisions and other sources of law. Interestingly, the civil codes enacted in all the three legal systems during the first half of the twentieth century remained effective from 1948 to 1989, though the meaning of their provisions governing the liability of State officials changed remarkably through time. For example, after a 1955 ruling of the Hungarian Supreme Court, government liability would arise only if the official was found guilty in a criminal or disciplinary proceeding, which was not easily the case. Quite the contrary, in Poland, the Constitutional Court has recently held that limiting government liability to *damnum emergens* (actual loss) is unconstitutional. While the former case confirms that political doctrines determined the interpretation of legislation, the latter shows the potential importance of constitutional provisions, which becomes actual when the courts are willing to do so. In Romania, though conditions and limits to government liability may apparently only derive from legislation, it is a governmental Ordinance that set out one important condition (the demonstration of fault) for the exercise of the right to compensation.

B. Doctrines of 'essential procedural infringements'

It is important, at this juncture, to reflect on the relationship between procedural fairness and liability. First, not all legal systems have what could be conceptualized as a general principle of damage or liability in tort. This is the case in most European legal systems, but not in all. Second, there is a relationship between unlawfulness and liability everywhere, but it differs from one system to another. Third, unlike in EU law, in many national systems a further condition must be fulfilled, namely, the existence of some serious breach, negligence, or even intentional wrongdoing. This section focuses on unlawfulness, while the ambit of liability will be considered in section IV.C.

The term 'unlawfulness' may be a very imperfect guide, because lawyers and judges look at both constitutional provisions and unwritten general principles of law, including reasonableness and proportionality. Moreover, the principles of administrative conduct are often either supplemented or specified by regulations and guidelines. It is with this further *caveat* in mind that we can now examine two questions that are closely related, but distinct. The first is whether a distinction between process and substance emerges. The second is whether, in the three legal systems under examination, there are not only differences but also some common and connecting elements. The distinction between process and substance does exist, but is variably substantiated by legal formants. It may be found in the provision of the Hungarian Constitution

[6] A Sajo, 'On Old and New Bottles: Obstacles to the Rule of Law in Eastern Europe' (1995) 22 JL & Soc'y 97.

that affirms the principles of fairness, impartiality, and the justification of administrative decisions, practically reproducing Article 41 of the EU Charter of Fundamental Rights. It can be found, too, in the rulings of the Polish Constitutional Court. It can also be found in legislation, more specifically in the APAs adopted by Hungary and Poland, as well as in the Romanian legislative provisions aimed at ensuring that transparency is respected.

However, government rules sometimes seek to limit the constraints imposed on public authorities. Moreover, if we look more closely at judicial decisions dealing with public bodies, it appears that they follow a twofold policy, insofar as they reiterate the importance of procedural fairness but qualify its consequences for liability. Not all infringements of procedural requirements, not even of those laid down by legislation, give rise to the annulment of the contested administrative acts or measures, but only those for which some serious breach emerges, with the consequence of depriving individuals of any meaningful possibility to protect and promote their interests as recognized by the legal order. What emerges is not a narrow conception of the procedural framework, but an 'essentialist' conception, in the sense in which this term was used by the Treaty of Rome (Treaty establishing the Economic Community, TEC) with regard to one of the grounds of action before the Court of Justice: the 'infringement of an essential procedural requirement'.[7] There are, of course, variants of this test, but it gives a sense of how the courts consider the relevant factors in their determination as to whether there has been a serious breach in a particular case.

C. A shift away from immunity?

There is another important element shared among the three legal systems examined here and that of the EU: there is no general clause or cloak of immunity. This is not only the case in the areas where national authorities implement EU law, for the simple reason that no Member State enjoys discretion as to whether a sufficiently serious breach of the relevant EU norm gives rise to liability, for which individuals have a right to compensation. It is the case also in the areas that are not subject to EU law but to national law, though the respect of the European Convention on Human Rights must be ensured, since this contains provision for awarding damages in certain circumstances.

However, if we look more closely at how liability is conceived within the three legal systems, the recognition of the existence of a general principle of compensation must be accompanied by some qualifying remarks. It is not so much the nature of the subject that is entrusted with the discharge of functions and powers, but the nature of the interests for which such functions and powers are attributed that justifies, in particular, the recognition of discretion, as was observed with regard to the issuance of a concession for the exclusive use of the waterfront in case 5 (Chapter 14, section VI), as well as for the adoption of a generalized block of imports. Moreover, the general position in domestic law is that some type of fault or intentional wrongdoing is required

[7] Article 173(1) TEC. See E Stein and P Hay, 'Legal Remedies of Enterprises in the European Economic Community' (1960) 9 AJCL 381, 383 (noting the analogy between this concept and the notions of due process and fair play in US law).

to establish that liability arises, for example, in the case of delays. Fault is perhaps to be viewed more as an element not to be ignored than as a precondition. Similarly, an intentional wrongdoing is not necessarily to be equated with the wilful intention to break the law. However, the general point to be made is that all these ways serve to qualify and limit government liability in tort.

Similarly, there appears to be a reluctance to award full compensation. This reluctance emerges not only when the courts refuse to award exemplary damages, but also when they argue that the loss should be real, and clearly caused by the illegal conduct, when they take for granted that the quantum of damages should be on the low side, when they indulge in generic considerations about 'equity'. Whether the underlying rationale is, as suggested in section III.B earlier, the weight given to collective interests or the persisting influence of the conception of the State characterizing the political regime before 1989, is another question, which requires further analysis, perhaps of an interdisciplinary nature.

There will be no attempt to summarize the observations made thus far. Rather, two general points will be made: government liability in tort is recognized and regulated by constitutional and legislative provisions; however, it can be limited. The existence of discretion assumes relevance in this respect in the three legal systems, which are also characterized by the acceptance of an 'essentialist' conception of procedural fairness.

20

Concluding Remarks: Towards Convergence?

The Road beyond Institutional and Doctrinal Path-Dependence

Roberto Caranta

I. Introduction

As Chapter 1 makes clear, government liability has been the stage for considerable convergence across Europe. Up to the middle of the twentieth century, and in some cases even later, government liability was largely excluded in a number of jurisdictions. Today, the right to damages is widely acknowledged, at least in theory, and, in some cases, it is even enshrined at constitutional level, as in many Eastern European countries.[1]

This fall from privilege is more marked in relation to material acts, including police operations (case 11, Chapter 14, section XII). As the Polish report highlights, State liability creates no doubts, for example, in the case of a car accident caused by a car belonging to the government.[2]

The picture becomes more nuanced when liability flows from unlawful decisions or omissions. Gordon Anthony claims that: 'The law on public authority liability is complex insofar as it straddles the public–private divide in UK law.'[3] This is not the case solely in the UK, but in Europe generally. The private law influence is clearly more direct and stronger in relation to government liability for material acts. These cases easily find analogies in private law, even when they have strong public law specificities, such as concerning the use of police power in case 11.[4] *Os fractum* and *membrum ruptum* (broken bones that in case 11 would not recover their full functionality) were two of the three types of torts already envisaged by the *Lex XII Tabularum* in the fifth century BCE.[5]

[1] G della Cananea, 'A "Common Core" Research on Government Liability in Tort: A Comparative Introduction', Chapter 1 in this volume, also discussing to what extent convergence was imposed and how much was spontaneous.

[2] M Wierzbowski, M Grzywacz, J Róg Dyrda, and K Ziółkowska, 'The Principles Governing Public Authority Liability in Poland', Chapter 9 in this volume, p. 67.

[3] G Anthony, 'Public Authority Liability in the United Kingdom: A Common Law Perspective', Chapter 13 in this volume, p. 81.

[4] ibid.

[5] A Watson, 'Personal Injuries in the XII Tables' in A Watson, *Studies in Roman Private Law* (Hambledon Press 1991) 253ff; R Zimmermann, *The Law of Obligations: Roman Foundations of the Civilian Tradition* (OUP 1996) 1050ff; M Talamanca, 'Delitti e pena privata nelle XII Tavole' in MF Cursi and L Capogrossi Colognesi (eds), *Forme di responsabilità in età decemvirale* (Jovene 2008) 80ff.

Roberto Caranta, *Concluding Remarks: Towards Convergence?* In: *Tort Liability of Public Authorities in European Laws.*
Edited by: Giacinto della Cananea and Roberto Caranta, Oxford University Press (2020). © The Contributors.
DOI: 10.1093/oso/9780198867555.003.0020.

Table 20.1 Relevant procedural rights/breaches in the different cases

	Right to be heard	Failure to ask for advice	Irregular inspection	Fact-finding inadequate/ erroneous information relied upon	Delayed decision/ inaction
Cases	1, 2, 7	2, 10	3	1, 3, 4, 6, 8, 9, 10	5

The public law aspects obviously become more significant once we focus on government liability for unlawful measures. This by itself might be a reason to rule out liability when the public law powers involved bear no relation to a cause for action under private law, which might be the case in the UK.[6]

The contributions in this book focus precisely on the non-contractual or tortious liability of the State and other public law institutions (government liability, essentially) for breaches of procedural rules. The possibly relevant procedural breaches in the different cases are listed in Table 20.1.

The focus on non-contractual or tortious liability for breaches of procedural rules generally excludes liability for breach of contract.[7] However, potential liability for breach of rules enacted for the awarding of State or public contracts in the form of procurements and work or service concessions is still relevant and may be considered pre-contractual (case 4, Chapter 14, section V). Such cases might be classed outside the area of non-contractual or tortious liability in some jurisdictions, but an aggrieved party often has grounds for action under both remedies. The reports sometimes reveal limited differences in the criteria for liability in relation to those two actions.[8]

Liability or the right to indemnity in cases of lawful administrative action are also excluded. Expropriation is the best-known example of liability or right to indemnity for lawful administrative decisions, but Germany, for instance, approaches these cases by means of a more general doctrine ('*enteignungsgleicher Eingriff*').[9] France too offers compensation in cases where legal measures create special and abnormal damage,[10] while in the UK ex gratia payments might be available.[11] Again, in Germany a lawful decision frustrating a legitimate expectation can lead to compensation for actual loss (but not lost profit).[12] It should be noted that, while cases of liability or the right to indemnity in the event of lawful administrative action are not covered in this volume, some of the respondents might have difficulty in finding the measures taken in some of the proposed cases unlawful.[13]

[6] See eg case 5 (Chapter 14, section VI). See critically C Harlow, 'France and the United Kingdom', Chapter 16 in this volume, p. 340.

[7] Contractual liability might still be relevant in bringing claims for damages in some of the jurisdictions covered: eg Germany, in case 1 (Chapter 14, pp. 107–8).

[8] See eg Germany in cases 1 (Chapter 14, p. 108) and 4 (Chapter 14, p. 176).

[9] F Wollenschlaeger and J Stapf, 'The System of Public Authority Liability in Germany', Chapter 6 in this volume, pp. 51–52; see also Wierzbowski and others (n 2), p. 66.

[10] T Perroud, 'Government Liability in France: A Special Regime under General Principles',Chapter 5 in this volume, p. 47; also case 6 (Chapter 14, p. 205).

[11] Case 6 (Chapter 14, p. 216).

[12] Germany, case 7 (Chapter 14, p. 224).

[13] See eg France, case 6 (Chapter 14, p. 204).

The reports and comparative chapters collected in this book are particularly dense, and a synthesis of all aspects is simply impossible. It has therefore been decided to focus on three aspects of relevance in assessing whether (and if so, to what extent) the jurisdictions analysed are converging beyond the widespread acceptance of government liability for unlawful decisions or omissions. The first aspect to be investigated will be whether annulment or other specific administrative law remedies must be sought before (or along with) damages (section I). The answer more often than not revolves around the institutional question of whether the same court has jurisdiction over both sets of remedies (section II). A second aspect will be whether additional requirements, besides illegality and—needless to say—causation and damages, are required for a successful claim for compensation. This might include a subjective element or a varyingly objectivized reference to the gravity of the breach (section III). Finally, as we are addressing procedural breaches here, their actual causal link to potential compensation might be questioned, with courts possibly resorting to different techniques to exclude or mitigate government liability (section IV). The conclusions will assess both the extent of convergence and anything hindering its increase (section V).

Again, the information provided by the reports collected in this book is much broader and more varied with regard to grounds for damages or mitigation, for instance. Compensation for lawful actions and non-judicial redress mechanisms also deserve specific attention.[14]

Much more comparative research than is possible here may take these reports as their point of departure.

II. Damages as a secondary remedy?

Primarily addressing issues of lawfulness, the first relevant question is whether the aggrieved have a duty to challenge the administrative measure or inaction before the competent court as a pre-condition for an action for damages. As the Swiss report clarifies very well,[15] this question is limited to cases where a challenge of this kind would be meaningful, which is not the case with regard to material issues (case 11, Chapter 14, section XII), but also arguably when the harm does not flow directly from an unlawful decision (case 10, Chapter 15, section XI).[16]

A duty to challenge an administrative measure or inaction as a pre-condition of a claim for compensation is recognized in Germany, in jurisdictions such as Austria, which share the same scholarly environment as Germany, or in those that have undergone the influence of Austro-German law, such as Hungary, Poland and, to a certain extent, Switzerland.[17] The basic idea in this intellectual framework is that what is called

[14] See Harlow (n 6) p. 306.

[15] T Tanquerel, 'Constitutional Principles and Judicial Remedies in Switzerland', Chapter 12 in this volume, p. 78.

[16] UK, case 10 (Chapter 14, p. 271), excluding judicial review and other administrative law remedies. In Poland, however, a declaratory judgment as to the question of unlawfulness might yet be a precondition for a claim for liability, even in case 10 (Chapter 14, section pp. 268–69).

[17] On the role of the *Vereinigung der Deutschen Staatsrechtslehre*, see O Pfersmann and A Ferrari Zumbini, 'Austria, Germany, and Switzerland', Chapter 18 in this volume, p. 319.

'primary legal protection' takes precedence over damages in the hierarchy of remedies.[18] This is often linked to the automatic suspensive effect of annulment actions.[19] In the event of an unlawful decision or inaction, the claimant must first challenge them *and*, in the absence of automatic suspension, seek an interim order. Otherwise, it will not be possible to make any claim for damages.[20] Poland is a very interesting case. Even though an arguably neo-liberal impulse brought lawsuits for damages under the jurisdiction of the ordinary (civil) courts, these have no say on the unlawfulness or otherwise of the measure from which the damage arises. On the contrary, it is necessary to obtain a judgment from the competent administrative court regarding the question of lawfulness.[21]

In France, on the other hand, there is no duty to challenge the legality of the relevant administrative decision or omission. Simply, the alleged tortfeasor must first be asked for damages, and in some cases the claimant must also bring an appeal, before applying to the courts.[22]

Overall, the duty to bring a case for judicial review of an unlawful decision or omission before (or at the same time, as in Romania) seeking compensation would seem typical of jurisdictions where the two actions come under the jurisdiction of different, or differently specialized, courts.[23] This is so especially where the civil courts competent to hear actions for damages do not have the power to declare the unlawfulness of an administrative decision, as in Poland and Romania.[24]

Instead, 'the heart of French public authorities' liability is defined by the *Conseil d'Etat*'.[25] One and the same (administrative) court hears both annulment and damages cases, so the previous annulment requirement does not respond to any reason pertaining to the judicial structure of the French legal order, as it does in Poland.[26] As Carol Harlow brilliantly put it, there is 'a clear link between the concepts of legality and liability, which has facilitated the growth of a holistic system'.[27]

The situation in the UK is unique. Damages are a private law issue, but may be litigated along with legality issues. Procedures are distinct, the courts are specialized, but the divisions are not rigid, and do not amount to a barrier to seeking action for damages.[28]

A sort of prohibition of abuse of process is used by EU courts to deny damages when a liability action aims to achieve the same effects as an annulment claim that has either become time-barred or failed.

Finally, in Italy, not having sought annulment, including foregoing the possibility of seeking interim relief such as the stay of the disputed decision, although not acting

[18] See eg Wollenschlaeger and Stapf (n 9) pp. 50 and 52.

[19] Germany, eg case 9 (Chapter 14, p. 252); Switzerland, eg case 2 (Chapter 14, p. 142) and case 7 (Chapter 14, p. 252); Poland, case 7 (Chapter 14, pp. 226–27); the latter is particularly instructive because of the in-depth discussion of the legal position when the automatic suspensive effect is lifted.

[20] Eg Austria cases 5 (Chapter 14, p. 187) and 8 (Chapter 14, p. 236).

[21] Wierzbowski (n 2) (Chapter 9, p. 68).

[22] Perroud (n 10) (Chapter 5, pp. 47–48).

[23] See Pfersmann and Ferrari Zumbini (n 17) p. 320.

[24] In Switzerland, the difference at federal level is not the court, but the procedure followed for the different kinds of actions: Tanquerel (n 15) p. 79.

[25] Perroud (n 10) p. 47.

[26] This chapter, section II.B.

[27] Harlow (n 6) p. 303.

[28] Anthony (n 3) p. 82.

Table 20.2 Review of legality taking precedence over actions for damages

Jurisdiction	Duty to bring judicial review action against an unlawful measure	Reduction of compensation if the measure is not challenged
Austria	X	—
France	—	—
Germany	X (except for procurement cases)	X (for procurement cases)
Hungary	X	—
Italy	—	X
Poland	X	—
Romania	X	—
Spain	—	—
Switzerland	X	—
UK	—	—
EU	—	—

as a preclusion to an action for damages per se will still be a reason for mitigating and possibly denying damages.[29]

The approach in the different jurisdictions analysed is summarized in Table 20.2.

III. More than illegality

Many of the jurisdictions analysed in this book require a further element in addition to illegality (and causation and damages) if a liability action is to be successful. In some jurisdictions, this includes a subjective element variously described as fault, negligence, or similar. In some of those jurisdictions, however, courts seem to tend to consider that the breach of the rules implied in the illegality requirement was at least negligent.[30]

The latter approach very much narrows the distance with regard to those systems which, basically following the French approach, simply equate illegality and fault (‘*toute illégalité est constitutive d'une faute*’).

In other jurisdictions, the ‘subjective’ requirement is to a more or less significant extent ‘objectivized’ into a serious or obvious breach,[31] sometimes related to a fundamental duty.[32] The same approach is followed in Italy. Culpability is not generally

[29] F Cortese, ‘The Liability of Public Administration: A Special Regime between Formal Requirements and Substantial Goals’, Chapter 8 in this volume, p. 64.

[30] See eg Germany, cases 3 (Chapter 14, p. 152) and 8 (Chapter 14, p. 241).

[31] See eg L Berkes, ‘Public Authority Liability in Hungary: Constitutional Principles and Judicial Remedies’, Chapter 7 in this volume, p. 58.

[32] See eg Switzerland, case 1 (Chapter 14, pp. 121–22); see also Pfersmann and Ferrari Zumbini (n 17) p. 320; see R Vornicu, ‘The Sufficiently Serious Breach Test in Action’ (2019) 25 EPL 587.

required, but the administration may exonerate itself, showing an excusable mistake (eg because of unclear legislative provisions).[33] It is well known that a serious or a manifest and serious breach is a requirement for the liability of EU institutions when they enjoy more than marginal discretion.[34]

The—possibly implicit—reasoning in requiring a serious and/or obvious and/or manifest breach is that an egregious breach cannot but be negligent. Still, this requirement shifts the focus away from negligence, fault, or even intent, all concepts that are more suited to individual than to institutional tortfeasors.

In some cases, discretion is considered to exclude the very possibility of finding a serious (or very serious) infringement, therefore precluding actions for damages.[35]

The common law approach is based on named torts having different requirements. Government liability too requires intention, negligence, or none, depending on the cause of action (specific tort on which the damages claim is based).[36]

The different approaches are summarized in Table 20.3 below.

Table 20.3 Approaches concerning the subjective and/or 'gravity' element of tortious liability

Jurisdiction	**A 'subjective' or 'gravity' condition**
Austria	Fault/culpability
France	NO (illegality equates to fault)[a]
Germany	Intent or fault/negligence
Hungary	Culpability(?)/Serious/obvious infringement
Italy	Administration may exonerate itself by showing an excusable mistake (this defence not allowed in procurement cases); higher threshold culpability required for liability of vigilance authority (case 10)
Poland	NO
Romania	NO (illegality equates to fault)[b]
Spain	NO
Switzerland	Fault/breach of a fundamental duty
UK	YES/NO (it is complicated, depending on the grounds for action)
EU	Manifest/serious breach

[a] See eg case 1 (Chapter 14, p. 98).

[b] However, specific rules requiring fault apply to the award of concessions: see case 5 (Chapter 14, p. 197).

[33] R Caranta, 'Les fondements de la responsabilité des pouvoirs publics en droit italien' in A Antoine and T Olson (eds), *La responsabilité de la puissance public en droit comparé* (Société de législation comparé 2016) 95ff.

[34] B Marchetti, 'The EU Institutions Liability between the Member States Principles and the Causality Standards of the EU Court of Justice', Chapter 4 in this volume, pp. 42–43.

[35] Berkes (n 31) p. 58; case 8 (Chapter 14, p. 242); this also appears to be the *ratio* for case 6 (Chapter 14, pp. 209–10).

[36] Anthony (n 3) p. 81; see also eg case 10 (Chapter 14, p. p. 271).

IV. Causation, discretion, and the role of courts

In terms of procedural breaches, a key issue is that, alone, they are not conducive to answering the question of whether a substantially lawful decision would have gone the way its addressee wished. As case 1 in Chapter 14, section II shows, for instance, Maurice could still be fired after being heard and having failed to exonerate himself. The same reasoning applies to case 2 in Chapter 14, section III. Since the number of applicants far exceeded the frequencies available, there is no reason to conclude that New Tv would have been awarded a frequency had the correct procedure been followed. Many of the cases discussed present the same pattern of uncertainty as to what the decision would have been if the decision-making process had been devoid of procedural mistakes.

In private law, tort liability generally, uncertainty is addressed under causation (section IV.A). In administrative law, discretion is often used to describe situations in which the applicable rules leave the decision-makers variably ample margins of choice as to the substance of the decision to be taken (section IV.B). The extent to which—if at all—courts are ready to second-guess or substitute the discretionary choices of decision-makers could theoretically affect the issue of liability (section IV.C). All three aspects will be examined in turn.

A. Causation

Different standards may be used to assess causation, having a more or less restrictive impact on liability: certainty, or a balance of probability (more probable than not), or a more or less serious chance may be required, the latter being the case in France.[37] As the UK report puts it, this is 'a notoriously complex area of the law of damages'.[38]

As to the question of how far an illegality might be equated to fault (see Table 20.2), the question of causation remains fully open, with major consequences on the burden of proof. In Hungary, for instance, the burden of proof on whether or not the illegality affected the substance of a final decision is on the appellant, rather than on government.[39]

Even in those jurisdictions more demanding in terms of causation, in procurement and other cases concerning limited rights some damages (costs) will be awarded to a claimant showing he or she had a 'real chance' to be awarded the contract, licence, or other right. This approach is for instance followed in Germany[40] and Romania,.[41] This similarity is easily explained as it flows from Article 2(7) of Directive 92/13/EEC coordinating the laws, regulations, and administrative provisions relating to the application of Community rules on the procurement procedures of entities operating in the water, energy, transport, and telecommunications sectors. However,

[37] Case 2 (Chapter 14, p. 129).
[38] Case 4 (Chapter 14, p. 185).
[39] Hungary, case 3 (Chapter 14, p. 154).
[40] Germany, cases 2 (Chapter 14, pp. 133–34) and 4 (Chapter 14, p. 165).
[41] Case 4 (Chapter 14, p. 183).

this rule on damages is often applied widely to all procurements, and not just to those regarding utilities.[42] Nevertheless, it is worth noting that the EU law provision is not even mentioned in most of the reports, and the question is answered on a basis of domestic law.[43]

Causation in particular may work differently depending on the different nature of the damage, such as actual loss or lost profit, or non-pecuniary damages (such as damage to reputation).[44] For instance, courts in Romania may be somewhat relaxed when awarding compensation for damage to reputation and require a criterion of certainty to grant damages for lost profit,[45] while in France and Spain courts will be more willing to award costs than lost profit.[46]

B. Discretion

Discretion is used here in its somewhat generic sense, covering government choices that the courts leave undisturbed. The term 'merits' is often used to cover the same semantic area.[47]

In some jurisdictions, the specifically administrative law concept of 'discretion' is relevant when analysing causation. As the German report puts it, 'causation is difficult to prove if the administration enjoys discretion'.[48] Indeed, the French approach to case 7 (Chapter 14, section VIII) shows that the discretion enjoyed by the administration may provide a reason to exclude fairly strong chances of being awarded damages.[49] On the other hand, EU discretion triggers a further requirement vis-à-vis liability, ie that breach of applicable rules must be manifest and serious.[50]

Discretion includes the power of appraisal, as discussed by the French report in connection with case 5 (Chapter 14, section VI). The power to decide—in the public interest—not to grant a concession, even if there was only one applicant and it met the stipulated conditions, is seen as a manifestation of such power.[51] This shows that cases of omission are especially difficult when it comes to suing for damages. In a number of jurisdictions, a claimant would be successful in case 5 only if the concession were ultimately granted.[52]

[42] R Caranta, 'Damages for Breaches of EU Public Procurement Law: Issues of Causation and Recoverable Losses' in D Fairgrieve and F Lichère (eds), *Public Procurement Law. Damages as an Effective Remedy* (Hart 2011) 167.

[43] See eg Italy, case 4 (Chapter 14, p. 178).

[44] See eg Switzerland, case 3 (Chapter 14, p. 161), case 4 (Chapter 14, pp. 184–85), and case 6 (Chapter 14, p. 214); Poland, case 9 (Chapter 14, p. 255).

[45] Contrast cases 1 and 2 (Chapter 14, pp. 120 and 140, respectively).

[46] France, case 2 (Chapter 14, p. 101); Spain, case 4 (Chapter 14, p. 184).

[47] R Caranta, 'On Discretion' in S Prechal and B van Roermund (eds), *The Coherence of EU Law. The Search for Unity in Divergent Concepts* (OUP 2008) 185.

[48] Case 2 (Chapter 14, p. 132); see also Cortese (n 29) p. 63.

[49] See also cases 5 (Chapter 14, p. 191) and 8 (Chapter 14, p. 239).

[50] Marchetti (n 34) pp. 42–43.

[51] Case 5 (Chapter 14, p. 191).

[52] See eg the EU and Spain.

Discretion is normally wider in normative acts and in health measures. This goes some way to explaining why case 6 (Chapter 14, section VII) is particularly problematic in many jurisdictions, leading to low success rates (see Table 20.5).

C. The role of courts

Finding a procedural breach is still at a far remove from concluding that Maurice should have not been fired in case 1 or that New Tv should have been granted the authorization sought in case 2, all the more so when the authority has discretion as to the merits of the decision to be taken. In terms of damages, this is reflected with regard to causation. However, much depends on the role courts are acknowledged—or acknowledge for themselves—to play in the review of unlawful decisions or omissions.

According to a basic nineteenth-century approach, the courts will content themselves with annulling the unlawful decision—or declaring that an omission was unlawful—and then send the file back to the competent authority for reconsideration. In most cases, an action for damages would have to wait for the renewed (or new) decision. The UK is unique in that annulment does not necessarily flow from a finding of illegality.[53]

In Poland, for instance, annulment or another judicial remedy declaring the illegality of the decision taken (or inaction) is not sufficient to give rise to a right to damages. Instead, the issue is sent back to the competent authority to re-evaluate the merits of the administrative case. If the new decision is this time legal but still detrimental to the interests of the harmed party, the latter will have no redress in damages.[54] The same holds for Italy and Spain: damages will be awarded (for delay) only if a favourable decision is handed down.[55]

This kind of approach gives the decision-maker enjoying discretion perverse incentives, as he or she can end up having to face damages claims when issuing a positive decision. This clearly circuitous approach is to some extent mitigated in jurisdictions like Germany, Hungary, and in some cases France, where an administrative appeal must be brought before applying to the court, including for a claim for damages.[56]

There is, however, no guarantee that the procedural defect will be remedied on appeal, so hands-off courts will still have to quash the decision and send the file back for reconsideration.

The situation is rather different in jurisdictions that allow some procedural breaches to be remedied as part of the judicial procedure or an extension to litigation.

[53] See eg case 2 (Chapter 14, pp. 145–46).

[54] So procedural breaches might not be enough to warrant annulment: case 7 (Chapter 14, p. 226).

[55] Cases 8 (Chapter 14, p. 242) and 2 (Chapter 14, p. 142), respectively.

[56] Germany, eg case 1 (Chapter 14, p. 104); see also Hungary, case 4 (Chapter 14, p. 177); this appeal for reconsideration is mandatory in France: Perroud (n 10) pp. 47–48 in some instances only. See also the pre-action protocol in the UK, Anthony (n 3) p. 84.

Germany provides a role model insofar as the provision in § 46 VwVfG rules out annulment, and therefore damages, if it is proven that the procedural error did not influence the outcome of the decision.[57] Analysis of case 1 in Chapter 14, section II opens an interesting window as to what courts can do in Germany to remedy wrongdoing: they can provide a fair hearing, but they cannot conduct an investigation regarding the facts of the alleged disciplinary wrongdoing.[58] In Romania, courts can modify the sanction inflicted, possibly based on a *de novo* review of the decision taken by the administration.[59]

When applicable, this approach leads to a decision on the merits of the case, and therefore either establishes both breach and causation or rules out both and precludes a claim for damages.

France has a unique approach. While the procedural breach will, in principle, lead to the annulment of the decision,[60] when hearing the damages claim the administrative courts enjoy *plein contentieux* and can therefore assess the case possibly ruling out liability if the measure was well grounded in terms of the substance.[61] This power is not without limits, and a French court could evaluate the appropriacy/convenience of all possibilities.[62]

An evolving pattern widespread in the jurisdictions chosen is the progressive de-quotation of procedural breaches. While the topic exceeds the remit of this book and will be addressed repeatedly in other parts of the 'The Common Core of European Administrative Laws' (CoCEAL), it is worth noting that rules similar to § 46 VwVfG were adopted in Italy in 2005 and in France in 2011.[63]

Table 20.4 lists cases where national courts are either ready to remedy procedural errors, thus ruling out annulment, or to check whether the decision was correct on its merits in order to adjudicate a liability claim. As a consequence, damages may ultimately be denied in both cases. The first is the archetypal German approach excluding annulment. The second is the traditional French one weakened by the 2011 reform mentioned above.

While this point is not always immediately apparent from all the cases discussed in the national reports, and some assumptions have been made, it is already clear that jurisdictions where procedural breaches are de-quoted are very much those where damages are a subsidiary remedy. France is shifting towards this position, while still not making annulment a precondition for compensation proceedings.

[57] Germany, eg cases 1 (Chapter 14, pp. 103–4) and 2 (Chapter 14, pp. 130–31).

[58] Germany, case 1 (Chapter 14, p. 104): '§ 46 VwVfG [German Administrative Procedures Act] would neither apply here, since the investigation of facts in favour of Maurice could at least influence the decision'; see also case 7 (Chapter 14, p. 223).

[59] Case 1 (Chapter 14, pp. 116–17).

[60] But see case 2 (Chapter 14, p. 128), with reference to the 2011 reform.

[61] Case 1 (Chapter 14, p. 102); see also J-B Auby, 'France, Italy, and Spain', Chapter 14 in this volume, p. 301.

[62] Case 7 (Chapter 14, p. 211).

[63] Case 2 (Chapter 14, p. 128).

Table 20.4 Remedying procedural breaches with reference to specific cases

	Right to be heard	Failure to ask for advice	Irregular inspection	Fact-finding inadequate/erroneous information relied upon	Delayed decision
Austria	1,2, [7]	2	3	3 [8]	[5]
France	1,7	2	—	—	—
Germany	1,7	2	3	6, 8, 9	5
Hungary	7	2	3	4	—
Italy	—	—	—	—	—
Poland	1,7	?	—	8	—
Romania	—	—	—	—	—
Spain	—	—	—	—	—
Switzerland	—	—	—	3	—
UK	—	—	—	—	—
EU	—	—	—	—	—

Note: Brackets are used when this was not explicitly indicated in the report but may still be assumed from the answer given. Bold jurisdictions regard courts that do not enter into the merits of a case, but the file is sent back to the administrative authority for assessment, which in turn forms the basis for a possible action for damages.

V. Conclusions

In some jurisdictions, (lack of) fundamental breach, causation (and related proof) or simply a lack of rules providing for liability are used to exclude or extensively limit damages.[64] Also, whether or not the rule aims to protect the rights of the injured party might be relevant. How arbitrary and capricious the application of the latter requirement may be is shown by how case 10 (Chapter 14, section XI) is treated differently in Germany and Switzerland, with courts in the two countries reading what are arguably identical rules in opposite ways.[65] The French have no hesitation in allowing damages in this case, considering 'the nature of the health authorities' powers'.[66]

Table 20.5 sums up the findings from this research. The jurisdictions covered in this book have been re-arranged. The jurisdictions appear in order from left to right reflecting their degree of strictness in awarding damages.

[64] This is the case of Switzerland, eg cases 3–6 (Chapter 14, pp. 161, 184–85, 198 and 214 respectively).

[65] Contortions are required in the UK as well: CaseS 9 and 10 (Chapter 14, pp. 258 and 272 respectively).

[66] Case 10 (Chapter 14, p. 261).

Table 20.5 Overall comparative results

Case	G	A	H	P	Switz	R	I	F	Sp	EU	UK
1	W	W	Y	Z	X	X	X	X Y	X	X	X
2	Y	S	Z	X	Y	X	Y	Y	Y	Y	Z
3	Z	S	Y	Y	W	Y	X	X	X	X Y	Y
4	Y	S	Z	Y	Y[a]	W	X	X	X	X Y[b]	X
5	W Y	Y	Y	Y	Y	Y	X	X Z[c]	Z	S	Z
6[d]	W Y	Y	W	Y	Z	Y	Y, Z	Z	X	Z	Y
7	W Y	W	W	W Y	Y	W	X	Y	X	X	W
8	W	X	W	W	Y	X	Y S	S	X Y	X	W
9[e]	W	X	Z	X	Y	Y	X Y	X Y	X	X	Z
10	Y Z	X	X	W	X	Y	X	X	X	X	X
11	X	X	Y	X Y[f]	X	X	X	X	X	NA	X

Note: X: at least some damages; Y: unclear/not easy, depends on a number of conditions (beyond breach affecting the substance of the decision/omission); Z: no liability; W: liability only in the event of breaches affecting the substance of the decision/omission; S: liability only for damages not redressed by annulment.

[a] Depending on differences in rules among the cantons.

[b] Depending on whether costs or lost profit are considered.

[c] Depending on whether a positive decision was ultimately handed down or not.

[d] The variations in answers to this question are often due to the fact that (i) the measure was considered lawful in many reports; and (ii) damages for lawful administrative measures are not available.

[e] Here too a number of reports tended to consider the measure lawful.

[f] Conviction of the police officers in criminal proceedings would make it easier to win a claim for damages.

It is clear that some jurisdictions are more restive in allowing successful actions for compensation. The hardest place to win damages is Germany. Making compensation a merely subsidiary remedy for annulment and other actions, together with the wide-ranging powers of the courts in reassessing the facts and the merits of the case for themselves go a long way in this direction, which is also true of Austria. A very restrictive approach to whether a duty is owed to a third party sets Germany apart from all other jurisdictions however, as demonstrated by the case of the negligent drug authority.[67]

Clearly, Germany and Austria are leading a number of physically neighbouring countries close in terms of legal culture to de-quote damages as a remedy for unlawful administrative actions and omissions.[68] The 'Latin' countries go the other way, and the EU falls within the latter fold. Switzerland falls somewhere in between.

This divergence is deeply ingrained in the different jurisdictions, so much so that we could talk of cultural path-dependency, which, as such, is not easy to overcome.

[67] Case 10 (Chapter 14, p. 264); see also case 11 (Chapter 14, pp. 280–81), concerning lack of relevance of internal police rules.

[68] See, in a more nuanced approach, Pfersmann and Ferrari Zumbini (n 17).

Michel Fromont has suggested that three main models emerge in the field of administrative law in Europe: (i) France, Italy, Portugal, Greece, and in some respects Spain; (ii) England, with Ireland and Norway; and (iii) Germany, Austria, Switzerland, and in some respects Poland.[69] This research very much corroborates this classification, adding Romania to group 1 and Hungary to group 3. On a limb, Switzerland is contended by the two groups now mentioned.[70]

The results in Table 20.5 are consistent with the picture provided by Tables 20.2 and 20.4. The jurisdictions in the first group have different courts—or specialized courts—for annulment and other purely administrative remedies on the one hand, and for damages on the other hand. The latter come under the jurisdiction of 'ordinary' or 'common' or 'civil' courts, which are not ready—nor most probably have the expertise needed—to second-guess what the outcome of a lawful administrative procedure should be. We are faced with institutional choices by EU countries enjoying residual organizational autonomy. As such, the differences in the liability regime for unlawful procedural breaches that these institutional preferences entail are bound to stay.

Above and beyond this major cleavage, a number of points in common nonetheless emerge. Liability is not only more easily invoked for material acts, but also for insufficient vigilance when the health of the population is affected.[71] Reciprocally, discretion is an issue almost everywhere, and taking a decision—or forecasting one for the purpose of assessing liability—is not an option in most jurisdictions.

Apart from the above, a cross-cutting and possibly widening divide exists between courts ready to take a hard look at the measure taken by authorities (Germany and Austria, but also France, Italy, and—if current trends become established—Romania) and those maintaining a hands-off approach. Courts in the former group are increasingly going further into the merits of the decision taken by the administration, looking for the 'right' decision. As such, procedural breaches are more and more de-quoted. It does not seem from the reports that even the right to be heard, with its roots in the European Convention on Human Rights, escapes this development.

When a hands-off approach to judicial review is combined with stinginess in awarding damages—as seems to be the case in both Hungary and Poland—citizens and companies both risk being very much left to the mercy of the State.[72]

[69] See M Fromont, *Droit administratif des Etats membres de l'Union européenne* (PUF 2006) 15.
[70] della Cananea (n 1) pp. 14–15.
[71] Conversely, concerns over health protection might militate against providing damage in case 9: see UK (Chapter 14, p. 258).
[72] G della Cananea 'Hungary, Poland, and Romania', Chapter 19 in this volume, writes of 'reluctance to award full compensation' (p. 338).

Select Bibliography

Aalto P, *Public Liability in EU Law* (Hart Publishing 2011).

Albors-Llorens A, 'Remedies against the EU Institutions after Lisbon: An Era of Opportunity?' (2012) 71 CLJ 507.

Allison JWF, *A Continental Distinction in the Common Law: A Historical and Comparative Perspective on English Public Law* (OUP 2000).

Antoine A and Olson T (eds), *La responsabilité de la puissance public en droit comparé* (Société de législation comparé 2016).

Barry H, 'The King Can Do No Wrong' (1925) 11 Va L Rev 349.

Bell J, 'La responsabilité de l'administration en droit anglais: caractéristiques générales, torts et compensation' (2013) 147 Rev fr adm publ 691.

Bermann GA, 'Integrating Government and Officer Tort Liability' (1977) 77 Colum L Rev 1175.

Bonnard R, 'Civil Responsibility towards Private Persons in French Administrative Law' (1932) 36 Economica 141.

Bradley AW and Bell J, 'Governmental Liability: A Preliminary Assessment' in Bradley AW and Bell J (eds), *Governmental Liability: A Comparative Study* (BIICL 1991).

Cane P, *Tort Law and Economic Interests* (2nd edn, OUP 1996).

Caranta R, *La responsabilità extracontrattuale della pubblica amministrazione* (Giuffrè 1992).

—— 'Governmental Liability after Francovich' (1993) 52 CLJ 272.

Colombi Ciacchi A and others (eds), *Haftungsrecht im dritten Millennium—Liability in the Third Millennium* (Nomos 2009).

Cornford T, *Towards a Public Law of Tort* (Routledge 2008).

Cortese F, *La questione della pregiudizialità amministrativa. Il risarcimento del danno da provvedimento illegittimo tra diritto sostanziale e diritto processuale* (Cedam 2000).

Craig P, 'Legality, Standing and Substantial Review in Community Law' [1994] OJLS 507.

—— *EU Administrative Law* (OUP 2012).

—— *Administrative Law* (8th edn, Sweet and Maxwell 2016).

Davies A, 'State Liability for Judicial Decisions in European Union and International Law' (2012) 61 ICLQ 585.

Davis KC, 'Administrative Officers' Tort Liability' (1956) 55 Mich L Rev 201.

—— 'Tort Liability of Governmental Units' (1956) 40 Minn L Rev 751.

della Cananea G, *Due Process of Law beyond the State. Requirements of Administrative Procedure* (OUP 2016).

della Cananea G and Mannoni S, *Administrative Justice Fin-de-Siècle. Early Judicial Standards of Administrative Conduct in Europe (1890–1910)* (OUP forthcoming).

—— and Bussani M, 'The Common Core of European Administrative Laws: A Framework for Analysis' (2019) 26 Maastricht J Eur & Comp L 217.

Dicey AV, *Introduction to the Study of the Law of the Constitution* (10th edn, MacMillan 1959).

Diez-Picazo LM, 'La générosité de la responsabilité "objective" de l'administration en droit espagnol' (2013) 147 Rev fr adm publ 654.

Fairgrieve D, *State Liability in Tort. A Comparative Analysis* (OUP 2003).

—— and Lichère F (eds), *Public Procurement Law. Damages as an Effective Remedy* (Hart 2011).

—— and D Squires, *The Negligence Liability of Public Authorities* (2nd edn, Oxford University Press 2019).

——, Andenas M, and Bell J (eds), *Tort Liability of Public Authorities in Comparative Perspective* (BIICL 2002).
Falcon G and Cortese F, 'Civil Liability of the Public Administration: Jurisdiction and Process' [2011] *Ius Publicum Network* 3.
Favre AC, Martenet V, and Poltier E (eds), *La responsabilité de l'Etat* (Schulthess 2012).
Fenyes A, Karner E, and Koziol H (eds), *Tort Law in the Jurisprudence of the European Court of Human Rights* (De Gruyter 2012).
Garcia De Enterria E, *La responsabilidad patrimonial del Estado legislador en el Derecho español* (Civitas 2007).
Giliker P (ed), *Research Handbook on EU Tort Law* (Edward Elgar 2017).
Gonod P, 'Les tendances contemporaines de la responsabilité administrative en France et à l'étranger: quelle convergences?' (2013) 147 Rev fr adm publ 720.
Gross J, *Schweizerisches Staatshaftungsrecht: Stand und Entwicklungstendenzen* (2nd edn, Stämpfli 2001).
Harlow C, 'Francovich and the Problem of the Disobedient State' (1996) 2 Eur L J 199.
—— *State Liability. Tort Law and Beyond* (OUP 2004).
—— *Understanding Tort Law* (3rd edn, Sweet and Maxwell 2005).
——, Leino-Sandberg P, and della Cananea G (eds), *Research Handbook on European Union Administrative Law* (Edward Elgar 2017).
Hauriou M, 'La consécration de la responsabilité de l'administration dans les services de la police. Note sous Conseil d'Etat, Section, 10 février 1905, Tomaso Greco, et Conseil d'Etat, 17 février 1905, Auxerre (1905)' [2013] Revue générale du droit, <www.revuegeneraledudroit.eu/?p=11579>.
HWR Wade and CF Forsyth, *Administrative Law* (11th edn, Oxford University Press 2014).
Kijowski D and Suwaj K (eds), *Patologie w administracji publicznej* (Wolters Kluwer 2009).
Mashaw JL, 'Civil Liability of Government Officers: Property Rights and Official Accountability' (1978) 42 LCP 25.
Maurer H and Waldhoff C, *Allgemeines Verwaltungsrecht* (19th edn, CH Beck 2017).
Minet A, *La perte de chance en droit administratif* (LGDJ 2014).
Moreau J, 'La responsabilité administrative' in Gonod P, Melleray F, and Yolka PP (eds), *Traité de droit administratif*, vol 2 (Dalloz 2011) 636.
Mosler V (ed), *Liability of the State for Illegal Conduct of Its Organs* (Heymanns Verlag 1965).
Muscat H, *Le droit français de la responsabilité publique face au droit européen* (L'Harmattan 2001).
Oliphant K (ed), *The Liability of Public Authorities in Comparative Perspective* (Intersentia 2016).
Oliver D, *Common Values and the Public–Private Divide* (Butterworths 1999).
Picard E (ed), *Répertoire de responsabilité de la puissance publique* (Dalloz 2015).
Priel D, 'The Indirect Influence of Politics on Tort Liability of Public Authorities in English Law' (2013) 47 Law & Soc'y Rev 169.
Sorace D (ed), *La responsabilità pubblica nell'esperienza giuridica europea* (Il Mulino 1994).
Street H, *Government Liability: A Comparative Study* (CUP 1953).
Tanquerel T, 'La responsabilité des autorités indépendantes' in Bellanger F and Tanquerel T (eds), *Les autorités administratives indépendantes* (Schulthess 2011) 153.
Tobias J, 'Staats- und Beamtenhaftung' in Schindler B and others (eds), *Schweizerisches Bundesverwaltungsrecht*, Band I, Organisationsrecht, Teil 3 (3rd edn, Helbing & Lichtenhahn 2017).
Toth A, 'The Concepts of Damage and Causality as Elements of Non-Contractual Liability' in Heukels T and McDonnell AM (eds), *The Action for Damages in Community Law* (Kluwer Law International 1997) 192.
Travi A, 'L'extension de la responsabilité publique en Italie' (2013) Rev fr adm publ 685.

Türk A, *Judicial Review in EU Law* (Edward Elgar 2009).
Uhlmann F, *Schweizerisches Staatshaftungsrecht* (Dike 2017).
Van Gerwen W, 'Bridging the Unbridgeable: Community and National Tort Laws after Francovich and Brasserie' (1996) 45 ICLQ 597.
Varuhas J, *Damages and Human Rights* (Hart Publishing 2016).
Wagner WJ, 'Recent Developments in State Tort Liability in Poland' (1972) 20 AJCL 248.
Wieland J, 'Art 34' in H Dreier (ed), *Grundgesetz Kommentar*, vol 2 (3rd edn, Mohr Siebeck 2015).

Index

For the benefit of digital users, indexed terms that span two pages (e.g., 52–53) may, on occasion, appear on only one of those pages.

Tables are indicated by an italic *t* following the page number.